RACE FOR THE IRON THRONE

Political and Historical Analysis of
A Game of Thrones

Steven Attewell, PhD

Copyright © 2014-2018 Steven Attewell
All rights reserved.
Cover Deisgn by Joanna Lannister
ISBN: 9781980635932
Blue Buddha Press
1st Edition

OTHER BOOKS PUBLISHED BY BLUE BUDDHA PRESS

The Last Awakening:
Insight into and Analysis of *Star Wars: The Last Jedi*

It Is Known: An Analysis of Thrones, Vol. I
(*Game of Thrones*, season one)

It Is Known: An Analysis of Thrones, Vol. II
(*Game of Thrones*, season two)

It Is Known: Season 3 Deconstructed
(*Game of Thrones*, season three)

It Is Known: Seasons 1-5 Deconstructed
(*Game of Thrones*, seasons one through five)

Race for the Iron Throne:
Political and Historical Analysis of *A Game of Thrones*
(*A Song of Ice and Fire*, book one)

Waiting for Winter: Re-Reading *A Clash of Kings*, Part I
(*A Song of Ice and Fire*, book two)

Tower of the Hand: A Flight of Sorrows
(*A Song of Ice and Fire*, books one through five)

Tower of the Hand: A Hymn for Spring
(*A Song of Ice and Fire*, books one through five)

The Supreme Court of Westeros, Vol. I
(*A Song of Ice and Fire*, books one through five)

Kings, Hands, & City-States:
Analyzing a World of Ice and Fire
(*A Song of Ice and Fire*, books one through five)

Green Switch Palace:
A Year in the Life of Nintendo Fandom

CONTENTS

Introduction
1

Prologue
5

Bran I
11

Catelyn I
17

Daenerys I
25

Eddard I
33

Jon I
41

Catelyn II
45

Arya I
51

Bran II
57

Tyrion I
63

Jon II
67

Daenerys II
71

Eddard II
75

Tyrion II
83

Catelyn III
89

Sansa I
95

Eddard III
101

Bran III
107

Catelyn IV
111

Jon III
117

Eddard IV
125

Tyrion III
131

Arya II
137

Daenerys III
141

Bran IV
149

Eddard V
155

Jon IV
159

Eddard VI
169

Catelyn V
177

Sansa II
183

Eddard VII
191

Tyrion IV
203

Arya III
209

Eddard VIII
217

Catelyn VI
227

Eddard IX
235

Daenerys IV
239

Bran V
245

Tyrion V
251

Eddard X
259

Catelyn VII
265

Jon V
273

Tyrion VI
279

Eddard XI
285

Sansa III
293

Eddard XII
299

Daenerys V
309

Eddard XIII
315

Jon VI
327

Eddard XIV
333

Arya IV
341

Sansa IV
345

Jon VII
353

Bran VI
361

Daenerys VI
369

Catelyn VIII
377

Tyrion VII
387

Sansa V
397

Eddard XV
403

Catelyn IX
413

Jon VIII
423

Daenerys VII
429

Tyrion VIII
435

Catelyn X
445

Daenerys VIII
455

Arya V
459

Bran VII
469

Sansa VI
473

Daenerys IX
479

Tyrion IX
487

Jon IX
497

Catelyn XI
503

Daenerys X
515

About the Author
522

SPOILER WARNING

These chapter analyses contain spoilers for all *Song of Ice and Fire* novels and *Game of Thrones* episodes.

Caveat lector.

INTRODUCTION

A Song of Ice and Fire is an extremely long – and, more importantly, an extremely multi-faceted – series of novels, and one of the major reasons I started this project of writing essays that do a close reading of each chapter is that there's unseen depths and richness to the series that can be quite easy to miss on the first reading (it's taken me at least five read-throughs to get to where I am now, and I'm still finding new layers that I'd missed before). My hope is that *Race for the Iron Throne: History and Politics of "A Clash of Kings"* will serve as a useful companion to the series, so that you can enjoy finding all of the hidden gems that George R.R. Martin has scattered throughout his work.

First, a word on how this book is structured. Each chapter in *A Clash of Kings* is discussed in order, with one essay per chapter, so that you can follow along as you read. Each essay has the same structure for ease of reading, which begins with an opening section with one of my favorite quotes from the chapter and a brief synopsis of the important events in the chapter to jog your memory.

Second, there's a section of *Political Analysis*, where I focus on how Westeros (and Essos) works as political systems and how the different individuals, factions, and conspiracies are working within or without those systems to achieve their ends, with a specific emphasis on how political institutions function. As the War of the Five Kings continues to rage, I spend a lot of time focusing on how the military strategy influences the political position of the various contenders, and vice versa.

Third, there's a section of *Historical Analysis*. As a PhD historian, one of the things that drew me to the *Song of Ice and Fire* series was the way in which Martin infused his work with a sense of realism, drawn from a close study of medieval history and the warts-and-all lives of rulers, rebels, and common folk who lived lives far removed from the black-and-white morality of most fantasy series. In this section, I write about the historical parallels between his characters and historical figures and between events in Westeros's history and events in our own, as well as places or institutions that Martin has drawn on to help make his world come to life. I set out both what actually happened in history and also what Martin either changed or kept the same in order to make a better story.

Fourth, I have a section on hypothetical scenarios titled What If? As a historian, one of the first things you learn is the power of contingency and chance to change the course of events, suddenly and violently upending ancient institutions and seemingly unstoppable social forces. This is especially true in *A Song of Ice and Fire*, where George Martin bombards the reader with missed opportunities and crucial choices, and where the timing of character movements and events are of the utmost importance. In this section, I show how choices made by characters have unforeseen consequences that ripple and cascade throughout the series, so that a slightly different decision at a given point could have led to a totally different ending to the book.

Fifth and finally, I have a section titled *Book vs. Show*. In this section, I'll point out the places in which HBO's *Game of Thrones* diverges from the book series. However, this isn't a section to list mistakes or complain about the purity of vision slowly draining away – I actually think the series has made certain critical improvements over the books in particular areas – but rather to talk about the necessity of narrative and story, and how mediums change the story without us realizing it.

Finally, a word on what I've taken away from this project, after two years of writing. George R.R. Martin's work has become a global phenomenon, with his books topping the *New York Times* Best Seller lists and selling more than 24 million copies, and the HBO *Game of Thrones* show has become a global phenomenon – and I think I have a few ideas about why his work has become so compelling to so many. Many reviewers and commentators have praised the gritty realism of Westeros, but to me, realism goes beyond the inclusion of sex or violence. Rather, I think readers and show watchers respond to a world which is both far removed from their own (ice zombies, dragons, shadow assassins, and the like not being a part of most people's lives) and also familiar. Namely, Westeros is a world in which inequality and class conflict is always bubbling under the surface, only to erupt violently, explaining why some children become lords and others end up in the Night's Watch; a world in which sexism and patriarchal social structures constrain the lives of all of the female characters, who both struggle against and critique these forces. It is a world in which hunger and disease and injustice are as big a threat as the White Walkers.

Moreover, I think people also respond to the ways in which Martin's focus on social structures and institutions resonate with their own lives. Often in epic fantasies, our heroic protagonists are Chosen Ones, detached from the societies they live in, who act as lone individuals to reshape their worlds with an act of will – that's fine for escapism, but it's not how we experience the world or try to change it. Martin's characters are deeply embedded in social structures and institutions that they have to work within, be it Jon Snow trying to navigate the Night's Watch, or Eddard struggling with the duties of the Hand of the King and the complicated world of King's Landing politics, or Daenerys Targaryen trying to assimilate into a brand-new culture.

There's a level of familiarity, a sense of recognition that just doesn't exist in most other fantasy novels.

Indeed, I think a lot of the power in George R.R. Martin's writing, especially his ability to shock and surprise people grown just a tad jaded with the traditional Hero's Journey they've seen done over and over again in Hollywood movies, fantasy novels, and videogames, comes from his project of deconstructing the romantic clichés and tropes of the fantasy genre. In Martin's world, the handsome princes, brave knights, and beautiful queens turn out to be the real monsters, while it's the outcasts and oddballs who take center stage as the protagonists of *A Song of Ice and Fire*.

PROLOGUE

Ser Waymar had been a Sworn Brother of the Night's Watch for less than half a year... it is hard to take orders from a man you laughed at in your cups.

He lifted his sword high over his head, defiant. Yet in that moment, Will thought, he was a boy no longer, but a man of the Night's Watch.

Synopsis

Three Night's Watchmen – Gared (a scarred veteran), Will (a former poacher), and Ser Waymar Royce (newly-fledged officer, third son of Lord "Bronze" Yohn Royce of the Vale) – conduct a ranging nine days beyond the Wall in search of wildling raiders. Will finds the wildling camp, with eight men and women seemingly dead from the cold. Ser Waymar orders an inspection, but when the watchmen arrive at the campsite, the bodies have vanished. Will climbs a tree and, thus, is unseen as Ser Waymar is surrounded by White Walkers; Gared runs away sometime around when they appear. Ser Waymar duels vainly against one of the White Walkers, but his sword breaks, blinding him, and he is butchered. Will climbs down to retrieve Royce's sword as proof but is captured or killed by the wight of Ser Waymar before he can make his escape.

Political Analysis

More focused on horror, suspense, action, and setting and mood than plot or world-building, the "Prologue" nevertheless gives several clues as to the social and political customs and institutions of Westeros. George R.R. Martin sets up a dramatic throughline of class conflict between the grizzled, experienced commoner and the inexperienced young nobleman that builds and builds before suddenly and terrifyingly being interrupted by a far more explicit form of conflict. Gared and Waymar clash repeatedly, over whether to press on to fulfill a pointless mission (who cares about finding dead wildlings?), over their respective equipment (Gared's insufficient clothing, Waymar's inappropriate mount and weaponry), whether to set a fire, and, most importantly, about fear.

And what we see here is that even in the supposedly meritocratic Night's Watch, where "even a bastard may rise high," in Ned's words, the class system of feudalism and serfdom is perpetuated. Ser Waymar is patently unfit to lead this expedition, and yet he is in command because he is a knight and the son of a lord, and Will and, likely, Gared are criminals and peasants, doubly chained. It is likely from the text that Ser Waymar knows that he has no idea what he's doing, but he's terrified of "going back to Castle Black a failure on [his] first ranging," terrified of failing to live up to his role as a knight and officer, and, thus, resentful of Gared's superior expertise. To restore the correct order, Waymar projects his fears – the dead, the dark, the wind, the cold, the strange sounds – onto the veteran and remind him who's boss by countermanding Gared's suggestions in ways that get them killed. Throughout the history of war, there have been thousands of Waymars, ignorant young officers who resented and feared the expertise of their subordinates, who acted to preserve their egos and save face rather than from good military sense, and who got their men killed as a result. Waymars ordered men over the top in the trenches of WWI, Waymars ordered men to charge tanks with cavalry in WWII, and Waymars were fragged in Vietnam.

Gared, by contrast, knows the north-beyond-the-Wall, knows the business of ranging better than his better, but he must obey Ser Waymar. Unlike those citizen-soldiers of a democracy in Vietnam, Gared does not and cannot truly think himself the equal of a knight. Every time he clashes with Ser Waymar with those 40 years of experience (40 years in an age in which a man of 21 would live, on average, to only 64) behind him, Gared backs down. He can mock Waymar behind his back, but when the final clash comes over whether they should build a potentially life-saving fire (given what we learn later about White Walkers and fire), and Will thinks Gared might go for his sword and butcher the green knight, he acquiesces. His capacity for rebellion is summed up by his decision to quietly go AWOL so that he might die a few weeks later at Lord Stark's own hand.

A few more points: we learn that the nobility claim exclusive rights to particular woods and punish poaching, and inherit by primogeniture. Historically, the claiming of exclusive hunting and foresting rights was a chronic source of conflict and controversy between local peasantry and their feudal lords – there's a reason why the rebel Robin Hood was an archer. Likewise, the practice of primogeniture in the nobility caused problems as thousands of heavily armed, trained men without regular income took to brigandry and warfare. Europe turned to the Crusades as a solution to too many knights for too little land; Westeros seems to have turned to the Wall instead. For both lords and peasants, then, the Wall is a social safety valve. We also learn that the Night's Watch acts more like a sieve than a wall as regards to what lies beyond the Wall; they ensure that wildlings can only creep past the wall in small groups, at high potential costs of death.

Finally, a thought about bravery and cowardice. While Ser Waymar spends most of the chapter trying to stave off failure (although he does catch that it's been too warm for people to freeze to death), he does something that few men could actually do – surrounded by five beings of nightmarish legend, he fights on to the death in defense of king and country – something he holds in common with all the other doomed Waymars of history. Will stays silent up in his tree, not even giving Ser Waymar the warning that might have prompted him to flee. Does this make Will a coward? For all his experience, in the moment of crisis, Gared abandons his mission, his oath, and runs away to die an oathbreaker's death; Will doesn't run, although his position up the tree didn't give him the opportunity. Left alone, he makes the choice to pick up the sword, to continue the mission and warn the Night's Watch about a deadly and unseen threat. There's bravery there.

Historical Analysis

George Martin has said in interviews that his inspiration for the Wall and the Night's Watch came from a visit to Hadrian's Wall on what was once the Scottish border, imagining himself a legionary sent to guard a wall at the end of the known world, waiting for barbarians to come howling out of the forests to ravage the civilized world and thinking, "What if the legionaries were facing something worse than barbarians?" Hadrian's Wall was constructed roughly between AD 118-128 as part of the Emperor Hadrian's larger defensive policy of retreating from Trajan's expansionist policy in Dacia, Armenia, and Mesopotamia to more defensible lines across the Roman Empire. The historical Wall is about a fourth as long and a *seventieth* as tall as Martin's Wall, but, then again, it didn't need to hold out White Walkers.

The ironic thing is that recent historians have substantially overturned that old image of Hadrian's Wall as a grim holdfast against barbarian invaders. Historians now think that the Wall was more of a political and economic instrument, a way to impress Rome's power on the Pictish tribes, to cut down on cattle rustling and smuggling, and to serve as a trade entrepôt where customs duties could be imposed more easily on cattle and hides. Hadrian's Wall was never attacked by the Picts and was superseded by a further Antonine Wall, built about 20 years later as the line of pacification advanced further north. Letters home from the garrison depict a less grim life than that of the Night's Watch - official requests for more beer and only occasional reports of skirmishes beyond the wall, letters from soldiers asking for more shipments of socks and underwear and starting lucrative sidelines as merchants trading cloth, pottery, jewelry, and the like for livestock, religious festivals, and invitations to birthday parties. The Roman emperors encouraged their soldiers, recruited from all over the Empire (to discourage separatist rebellions), to marry and have children, and offered them land near their old postings upon their retirement; the idea was to settle the frontier with trained military men who would produce sons to follow them in their profession. Aside from the weather, it sounds like a fairly decent life.

Martin's Wall has very different purposes and, thus, a totally different feel. The unnatural nature of the Wall mirrors the unnatural nature of what the Wall is supposed to keep out; the brutish life of Night's Watchmen calls into question how different they really are from the wildings on the other side of the Wall, as Tyrion notes. And unlike Scotland, the north-beyond-the-Wall cannot be pacified. Only until the wildings come south can the people, not the land, begin the process of "civilizing."

What If?

For all that people say that the "Prologue" of *Game of Thrones* is something of a tease, and as a supernatural bit of horror, unconnected to the larger plot of political maneuverings, murder investigations, jousting, and war that makes up the rest of the book, there is one important connection to the rest of the plot that had the potential to really change events: Ser Waymar Royce's shattered sword. If Will had been less paralyzed by the sight of the wight-Royce and made his way back to Castle Black, what would have happened?

Firstly, the Night's Watch is instantly alerted to the threat of the White Walkers at a time when the Warden of the North and the king are present in the north, as opposed to when the two "corpses" are discovered at Castle Black, at which point Lord Eddard Stark is imprisoned in the Red Keep, the Lannisters and Starks are at war, and King Robert is dead. While it's far from certain that King Robert would have listened to Benjen Stark's warnings, a broken sword, and a poacher, Eddard Stark would have. In that situation, it's hard to see Eddard Stark leaving the north as the Hand of the King. For the want of a sword...

Secondly, Benjen Stark isn't sent out to find what happened to Ser Waymar Royce. By itself, this has the potential to change the plot up at the Wall. With Benjen Stark present, Jon Snow doesn't become commander of the Night's Watch after the death of Jeor Mormont, since Stark is the obvious candidate – which possibly means that Snow isn't assigned to serve as Mormont's squire and becomes a ranger instead. And, possibly, if the theory that Benjen Stark took the black shortly after the Rebellion because he was complicit in Lyanna's elopement with Rhaegar is accurate, Jon Snow finds out the truth of his parentage.

But that's not what happened. Martin needed Eddard Stark to go south so that the War of the Five Kings could happen and the Night's Watch warning lost a second time, and Jon Snow's heritage has to be postponed until after he's earned the right to be called a hero.

Book vs. Show

For the most part, the opening scene in episode one of *Game of Thrones* plays out more or less like the book. We see the three Night's Watchmen passing under the Wall and out the other side, and there's less of a sense how far out they are from the Wall, but the conflict between Gared and Ser Waymar is still there. The first big difference is in the appearance of the dead, who look to be dismembered and laid out in an occult circle of some kind.

This is immediately more shocking than George R.R. Martin's more sedate image of the dead, and I think it's a good example of why fidelity to the spirit, rather than the letter, of the work is better for adaptations. Martin has hundreds of words to build up the tension of what's happening, bringing in the cold, the wind, the noises, and, thus, it's not as crucial that we only hear second-hand what the camp-site looked like initially. In a visual medium, there's only a few minutes to accomplish the same effect, so first impressions matter – the sudden visual of these mutilated bodies and the unnatural positioning hits the viewer *with the same disoriented shock that Will experienced*, bringing them almost bodily into the haunted woods of the far north.

What does change rather dramatically is that Ser Waymar Royce is decapitated without a fight, which is a dramatic choice that I respect, although I feel it wrongs the doomed noble idiot. Instead of bringing up questions of courage and honor right away (since that's going to be brought up in the very next scene at Winterfell), the writers and director opt instead for maximum shock – Royce dies, the two remaining Watchmen run, and we get a chase sequence through the woods which ends with the sudden death of Gared. This amps up the White Walkers considerably, which may be necessary, given that we don't see even wights until episode seven.

All the same, something is lost here of the lives of three ordinary men beset by the extraordinary. It might not matter for the show that Waymar goes down without a chance to fight back, that Will runs immediately, or that Gared dies in the forest from a very different icy blade, or that there's a slight plot hole as to how Will gets away from the wights (maybe the White Walkers are sending a message, but that dramatically changes their nature). But it matters to the Waymars, Gareds, and Wills of Westeros; the story is all they have, after all.

Finally – people have argued that there's a plot hole in that Will is last seen north of the Wall kneeling in shock and horror as Gared's head is tossed to him amidst the unearthly laughter of the White Walkers; how did Will survive to desert? I actually don't think this is a plot hole but, rather, a rather unusual dramatic choice – the White Walker tosses Will Gared's head as a warning and lets him live to bear witness to the horror that awaits the realms. This is a bold choice; on the one hand, it makes the White Walkers definitively intelligent, whereas Martin avoided tying himself down on this question, which might have the effect of anthropomorphizing them and making them less inhuman. On the other, and this is where I come down, it really gives us a moment of Fridge Horror when we realize the White Walkers are so powerful that *they don't care if the Night's Watch knows they're coming.*

BRAN I

"In the name of Robert of the House Baratheon, the First of his Name, King of the Andals and the Rhoynar and the First Men, Lord of the Seven Kingdoms and Protector of the Realm, by the word of Eddard of the House Stark, Lord of Winterfell and Warden of the North, I do sentence you to die."

"Yet our way is the older way... we hold to the belief that the man who passes the sentence should swing the sword. If you would take a man's life, you owe it to him to look into his eyes and hear his final words. And if you cannot bear to do that, then perhaps the man does not deserve to die."

Synopsis

Bran Stark is brought along by his brothers Robb Stark and Jon Snow, as well as the hostage-ward Theon Greyjoy, to witness his father, Lord Eddard Stark of Winterfell, execute Gared the deserter. Bran and his father discuss the nature of capital punishment, bravery, and courage; Robb and Jon do the same. Robb and Jon discover a dead female direwolf and five direwolf pups; Robb and Bran claim the pups, and Jon convinces his father to allow the legitimate children of House Stark to keep the symbols of their house alive. As they prepare to return to Winterfell, Jon discovers a sixth direwolf.

Political Analysis

As the first chapter of *A Song of Ice and Fire* written by George R.R. Martin, we can see a key theme being developed in "Bran I" – the nature of political power as embodied in Lord Eddard Stark and the present-in-name-only King Robert Baratheon and its relation to capital punishment.

First, a note on wildlings. At this point in the series, we know little of the wildlings, and what we do know of them is from those who fear and hate them, and the theme of how different perceptions are based on one's viewpoint is baked into the very structure of the novel from the beginning. From the "Prologue," we know only that wildlings live north of the Wall and raid south, and that the Night's Watch tries to stop them. Here, we see something more of how the north views those who live beyond the Wall. As far as Bran knows, "the wildlings were cruel men... slavers and slayers and thieves. They consorted with giants and ghouls, stole girl children in the dead of night, and drank blood from polished horns. And their women lay with the Others in the Long Night to sire terrible half-human children." On first glance, this is a perfect example of how propaganda is used to dehumanize the "other" and justify a permanent state of war against them – when we meet actual wildlings in *A Clash of Kings*, we see that the wildlings are ordinary people who live ordinary lives, who see themselves as the only free people in Westeros. And there's something to that.

However, Martin is even more complex here; rather than portray the wildlings as "noble savages" done wrong by evil Westerosi, we learn that the wildlings live up to part of the legends. Wildlings historically have raided and warred the south both in armies and smaller groups, and although Mance Rayder romanticizes this with a certain Robin Hood-esque charm, it's unlikely that the reality of abductions of women are as consensual as he claims. The vaunted freeness of the Free Folk is brought into question by the fact that the wildlings do raise up kings, and have done so long before Rayder's time. There is even an element of truth in the more fantastical elements of Nan's stories – wildlings do actually mate with giants, although we haven't met any ghouls, and we know that at least one wildling does have some kind of pact with the Others. And yet for all that, they are still human beings trying to survive in an environment hostile to all life, not the subhuman, purposeless evil of Tolkien imitators; even slavers and slayers have motivations.

But largely this is a sideshow. Gared isn't a wildling but an oathbreaker and a deserter, and the task at hand is that he must be executed under someone's law, and someone's hand – the law is King Robert's and the hand is Lord Stark's. There's an interesting moment where Bran shows his awareness that the position of the ruler is not the same thing as the personality of the man when he sees that "he had taken off father's face... and donned the face of Lord Stark of Winterfell."

And in the sentence that the de-personified Lord Stark gives out, we see a theory of politics in miniature. The nature of kingship is never simple, and titles tell you a lot; Robert Baratheon claims the throne as the head of a noble household with royal blood, but the nature of his kingship is multifaceted. He is king of three races of men who all surrendered at different times and on different terms: the Andals who populate the realm between the Neck and the Dornish Marches submitted at the Field of Fire, with their kings dead around them, and saw their swords melted into the Iron Throne; the Rhoynar who maintained their independence in Dorne for a century-and-a-half and who joined the Seven Kingdoms in marriage; and the First Men, the oldest human inhabitants of Westeros who held off Andal invasions and Andal culture, and whose lands were never invaded by the Targaryens. He is also the feudal overlord of Seven Kingdoms who swear personal fealty to the king, and who pointedly swear fealty through their overlords – a sign of weakness in the monarchy to counterbalance the seeming total conquest of Aegon and Dareon. Finally, he is – as were the kings of England in the time of the Plantagenets – Protector of the Realm (that oft-repeated, ambiguous, and all-important object of Martin's analysis). This last title is significant, as well, because it suggests that there is a unified nation beyond the personal loyalties of vassals to their lord and a nation that a king has responsibilities to; there is a sense of a nascent social contract there.

Ned Stark acts both in his own right as the hereditary lord of Winterfell, a man with a lineage that outstrips his king's by a factor of 26, but also a royal, military appointee – the Warden of the North. Lord Wardens of the Northern Marches and the Cinque Ports, the Wardens are military commanders, charged with defending a cardinal direction from foreign invasion, and automatically outranking all other lords in any war in that region – a sign that the Targaryen kings did not solely rely on their dragons to hold down trouble areas from threats foreign and domestic.

The space between these roles is as thin as Ice's edge. Eddard Stark is a man who believes in a public and personal exercise of the ultimate power of the state and makes a choice to implement the "older ways" instead of the ways of the Baratheons and Targaryens of King's Landing. There should be no division between the ruler as an entity of power, a "majesty" that exists like godhood, and the man. The north cares whether a man has the physical strength to wield the sword – there's no idolizing of heritage here, no Joffreys or Viserys tolerated, and every Stark has to prove himself in the face of the Umber's challenge, in the eyes of the hill clans at their feasts, and against the Boltons in battle, and the fact that the Starks have ruled for 8,000 years, questioned every step of the way, is testament to how strong a lineage Ned has. However, the north also cares about the moral strength of their rulers, whether they can look a man in the eyes, hear his final words, and do the deed without taking pleasure in it.

Ned Stark, for all his detractors who think him a fool or too gentle to be a good Hand or king, is a man who will swing the sword even when it comes to a man who swears he's seen the White Walkers; his son is a man who will swing the axe on his own lords if he must. The question throughout *Game of Thrones* isn't whether Ned is so pure that he'll walk himself into slaughter, but where and when and on whom he can bear to swing the sword and what that means to him.

Historical Analysis

As far as I can tell, the "older ways" are without historical precedent in Medieval Europe. Kings did not swing the sword or axe themselves for a reason. As Michel Foucault writes in *Discipline and Punish*, the medieval execution was a "spectacle of torture," a kind of carnival of the obliteration of the body meant to instill in every witness a sense of awe at the superhuman power of the king. The punishment was supposed to be as savage, if not more so, than the crime – proof that the king was more powerful than any treason, and a symbol of what happened to those who cared to damage the sacred body of a monarch. This was before there was such a thing as a state or a nation, only a physical link between humanity and God; a crime was not against a statute but against the person of the monarch, either through robbing him off his property (even his human property, in the case of murder) or "compassing and imagining" an attack on his kingliness itself.

The act of execution was to invert this crime, to reveal the utter frailty of the human creature who had rebelled against the will of God. To have the king swing the sword, or extract the bowel or burn the human heart before the horrified eyes of a still-living victim, would be to reduce him in the eyes of his people from a holy object to a mere man tainted with mortal sin. There's a reason executioners wore masks and received ritual forgiveness and payment from the victim – the sin of murder had to be hidden, de-personalized until only the Majesty and the Condemned stood upon the stage, as if majesty was a kind of shadow cast by the flames.

That Eddard Stark swings the sword himself has to be a critique of this system of justice, to re-insert the human element and remove the divine. Ned Stark doesn't torture people and he claims no majesty; rather, he listens to a man's last words and gives him a "single, sure stroke" in a square in a nameless holdfast, and then, recognizing that, in killing a man, he has himself committed a crime against nature, however necessary, goes to cleanse himself and his blade before the faces of his gods.

What If?

There's only one major what-if in this chapter, and it's a doozy: **what if Eddard had refused to allow his children to adopt the direwolves?** On the face of it, it's a rather pointless hypothetical. The direwolves are a quite obvious deus ex machina, and they're meant to be so. Their appearance stirs up a sense of omens, fate, and luck, whether ill or good, in the heart of everyone who sees or hears of the event. The implication is strong that the mother and children were sent by the old gods themselves, acting as they do through nature, as a most ambiguous sign - are the wolves a symbol of protection or death? Magic or corruption? As protectors, they are most inconsistent - Bran's wolf saved his life twice, once mystically and once physically; Arya saved hers from Joffrey's blade. So there we have one answer to our question - with no wolves, Bran, Catelyn, and Arya are all likely dead. But on the other hand, Sansa has lost her protection but seems to have survived as well as any of the Starks, as has Arya, who drove away her guardian. And what protection could Grey Wind give his master, in the end?

Book vs. Show

Most of the differences between these two scenes are rather cosmetic. The condemned man is switched, the execution takes place in a standing stone circle (which, if anything, is more evocative of the older ways of the north), and so forth.

The two major changes are that the condemned man's final words are spoken openly - that the children know he saw the White Walkers - and denied openly, which is a major difference from the book. Would BookNed have denied such a claim from a man who, unlike in the book, died without question, a courageous man ready to pay for his crime?

The second is more subtle: in the book, Robb and Jon discover the direwolf first, before Ned does, as they are racing. Throughout this chapter, the two are set up as rivals and complementing mirror images - Jon is slender, dark, graceful, and quick; Robb is muscular, fair, strong, and fast. Robb thinks the deserter dies bravely; Jon is more cynical. Robb is first to see the cause of the direwolf's death, while Jon picks out an albino in the snow. And to my mind, the two are set up throughout the series as contrasting takes on heroism and leadership - and yet here, Robb is backgrounded while Jon is emphasized, something that may be reversed as we head towards season two.

CATELYN I

In his youth, Ned had fostered at the Eyrie, and the childless Lord Arryn had become a second father to him and his fellow ward, Robert Baratheon. When the Mad King Aerys II Targaryen had demanded their heads, the Lord of the Eyrie had raised his moon-and-falcon banners in revolt rather than give up those he had pledged to protect.

Synopsis

Catelyn Stark goes to the godswood in Winterfell to speak with her husband, Lord Eddard Stark. The two discuss the children and the potential threat of Mance Rayder before Catelyn breaks the news that Jon Arryn, Hand of the King and Lord of the Eyrie, has died. Catelyn and Ned discuss Jon's widow, Lysa Arryn, and Catelyn informs her husband that King Robert Baratheon and his court are coming to Winterfell.

Political Analysis

This chapter is a short one, very much a literary message to the reader that an event – the king coming to Winterfell – will happen, but there are some interesting political themes: the threat of Mance Rayder, the nature of fosterage in the feudal system of Westeros, the issue of Jon Arryn (who we know so little about, given his importance in the overall plot) as the Hand, and the question of why Ned hates the Lannisters.

Ned brings up Mance Rayder almost immediately after discussing the execution of the deserter, who we learn was the fourth in the current year, an ominous sign of the weakness of the spirit as well as the body of the Night's Watch. In Eddard's eyes, the loss of rangers is the work of Mance Rayder, who is well-known as the King beyond the Wall, which suggests that he's very well-established as wildling kings go – although he presumably heard from the deserter about the fate of Ser Waymar Royce's party, Eddard Stark is responding to the familiar threat. Wildling kings coming around or over the Wall have happened many times before: Raymun Redbeard scaled the Wall 150 years ago, threw down rope ladders behind him, and brought over an army that took King William Stark by surprise at the Long Lake and killed the king, only to be killed in turn by the King's brother, Artos the Implacable. Three hundred years ago, Bael the Bard seduced and impregnated the only daughter of Brandon Stark the Daughterless, only to be slain and defeated by his own son – showing that the Starks have both northern and wildling blood in them, and which is the wolf blood? Before that, it was Gorne and Gendel, the Horned King, and Joramun.

Which, I think, tells us a lot about the character of Eddard Stark – as his wife says, he's not a man to "put faith in signs." He's a practical man, one who believes in what he can see with his own eyes, yet, unlike in the show, he's actually fairly attuned to the threat to the north. He believes that he will have to call his banners and march north. It's a choice he'll never have the opportunity to make.

The news of Jon Arryn's death completely derails this line of thought for reasons personal and political. Jon Arryn raised Ned Stark, and that's more important than people realize; Eddard's sense of honor, his intense idealism, his willingness to suffer for the sake of principle comes as much from the Vale as it does from the north. And while we don't really get a chance to see the positive of the Vale in the novels rather than the xenophobic arrogance and elitism displayed by Lysa's court, Lord Arryn must have had a huge impact on Ned's development. We get the sense that Eddard's "second father" was closer to him than Lord Rickard Stark, and the TV show at least suggests that Ned was the star pupil and Robert Baratheon the rebel. And the lessons learned at the Eyrie were all about principle – Jon Arryn went to war alone, before Eddard could raise the north or Robert conquer the stormlands, rather than be forsworn even by royal command.

At the same time, there is always political advantage at stake. As will be discussed more in the historical section, the oath to foster was absolutely sacred and a critical part of the feudal order. What Jon Arryn was being asked to do was to destroy his own reputation in a world in which all political ties ran on reputation, and not only would his rulership over the Vale be forever thrown in doubt in the eyes of his vassals, but it would also mean blood feud with two of the seven Kingdoms. To be given the heir of the Baratheons and the second son of the Starks was an enormous honor, but it was also a political advantage, tying three great houses into an abiding sense of loyalty and kinship. This may very well have been part of what the learned Stefan Sasse calls the "Southron ambitions" of Lord Rickard Stark. In Stefan's telling, the lords of Stark, Tully, Baratheon, and Arryn had been comrades-in-arms in the War of the Ninepenny Kings, a war in which an unlikely king died suddenly and was replaced by a weak king, and had made some sort of pact to bind enough great houses together into a power bloc that could fill the power vacuum left by a weakened monarchy. Starks were engaged to Tullys, Baratheons were engaged to Starks, and childless Arryn was given two foster children. Given Robert's position as heir to the stormlands, Ned

Stark might well have become Arryn's heir had Jon chosen the son of his heart rather than his nephew by blood.

This, in turn, brings up a question we will continue to examine throughout the series – was Jon Arryn a good Hand? Most people in the *Song of Ice and Fire* fandom assume not, but I think the case is more difficult than people think. After all, Jon Arryn pulled off something that no one had ever pulled off in 300 years: a successful rebellion against the Targaryen monarchy. Despite losing Rickard and Brandon Stark, which potentially eliminated the Tully alliance, and despite having to wage a war on three fronts and against their own vassals, Arryn held together an alliance that conquered the loyalist areas of the stormlands, saw off the armies of four separate Hands, re-forged an alliance with House Tully, and then took the Throne. Once the war was over, Arryn successfully reintegrated the Lannisters and Dorne into the Seven Kingdoms and served as Hand for 14 years, longer than any Hand in living memory other than Tywin Lannister. For all but one of those years, the Seven Kingdoms were at peace and generally prosperous, thanks to the weather. Arryn uncovered Cersei Lannister's infidelity and was preparing to act against the Targaryens when he was struck down by a force he could not have seen coming. In the end, I think we have to say that Jon Arryn, while certainly imperfect in terms of fiscal policy and dealing with the Lannisters, was certainly one of the better Hands we've seen in the series.

Finally, a point on Eddard Stark's dislike of the Lannisters. Part of this comes from when the "Lannisters of Casterly Rock had come late to Robert's cause, when victory was all but certain"; part of this certainly comes from Eddard's furious row over the murder of Elia and her children and finding the Kingslayer sitting on the Iron Throne, which, for a man who'd fought the war for murdered relatives and whose putative leader was badly injured at the Trident, must have seemed like a coup in the making. However, if we accept the R+L=J thesis, there may be another reason for Stark's fear and hatred – the Lannisters killed Targaryen children, and now they have a Lannister heir to the throne to kill for. While Jon Snow faces a certain amount of threat from Robert Baratheon – although it's uncertain if Robert could actually murder Lyanna's only child – the greatest threat to Jon's life certainly comes from the Lannisters.

Historical Analysis

Trying to figure out the feudal system of Westeros is rather complicated; on the one hand, we're talking about formerly independent kingdoms, and certainly a system in which local vassals swear loyalty to a lord paramount, who, in turn, pledges loyalty to the king. However, as we see from the Freys, the local lords also swear loyalty to the king himself, an adaptation of the feudal order notably put in place by the Norman kings of England following the Conquest in 1066, which is a good parallel for the Targaryens. The reason I bring this up is that as Stark's proposal to call his bannermen and march north of the Wall suggests, as befits his title of Warden of the North, my previous description of Lord Eddard Stark as a Lord Warden of the Marches is quite accurate, but I'm beginning to think there's an element of Welsh as well as Scottish Marches.

Like the Scottish Wardens, the Anglo-Norman marcher lords were military men sent to hold down rebellious and disputed territories. However, the Marcher lords "ruled their lands by their own law - *sicut regale* ('like unto a king')," as Gilbert, Earl of Gloucester, stated (Nelson 1966), whereas in England, fief-holders were directly accountable to the king. Marcher lords administered laws, waged war, established markets in towns, and maintained their own chanceries that kept their records, which have been completely lost. They had their own deputies, or sheriffs. Sitting in their own courts, they had jurisdiction over all cases at law, save high treason. "They could establish forests and forest laws, declare and wage war, establish boroughs, and grant extensive charters of liberties. They could confiscate the estates of traitors and felons and re-grant these at will. They could establish and preside over their own petty parliaments and county courts." This seems quite similar to Eddard Stark's powers - he administers the law, he declared Jorah Mormont traitor, and he's proposing to start a war against the wildling king on his own initiative. Which, if true, makes Eddard Stark virtually a king in his own country - virtually.

Historically, fostering was an absolutely vital part of the feudal system, on the same level as dynastic marriages and the oath of homage between lord and vassal, one that many historians have spent a great deal of time studying. As with marriages and oaths, the point was to build relationships that were both political and personal at a time when the abstract entity of the state didn't exist. Scholars believe that fostering was intended to spread the idea of "familial sense," that at a time in which bonds of loyalty were incredibly fragile and the pursuit of the family's interest was everything, having people identify a second family as part of their own was a way to build trust between families, especially at a time when most people didn't travel that much and so didn't have many opportunities to get to know their neighbors as more than that bastard who stole my cattle because I sacked his abbey. The major departure in the case of Ned and Robert Baratheon is that it tended to happen between lords and their vassals, to cement those vertical relationships - here we have Lords Paramount exchanging children. This, I think, is a point in favor of Stefan's thesis - this seems like more than just building a dynastic alliance, but rather the medieval equivalent of a merger.

Finally, a point about Robert's procession to the north. Many have tended to see Robert's huge entourage, with all the ostentatious carriage houses and the extremely slow movement, as a sign of the decadence of the court, and that's not completely wrong. However, this kind of traveling court was absolutely standard in the early Middle Ages. Traveling courts were enormous affairs, as the king was essentially hauling around his justice system and his treasury from place to place. They were a way for the king to see and be seen by the different parts of his kingdom, a vital task for securing the monarchy at a time when royal infrastructure linking the capital to the provinces was non-existent. On procession, the king would assess taxes on the spot, settle court cases, grant charters for fairs and towns, and generally make himself known as the ruler.

They were also a way to cut down on the costs of administration by foisting them on local lords, and one weapon that a king had to deal with an unruly vassal was to give him an extended visit and eat and drink him into near-bankruptcy. There is something of an anachronism here - King's Landing has a permanent infrastructure more associated with the Late Middle Ages: a permanent court, office buildings (the Tower of the Hand), and a permanent sitting small council with well-defined ministries (the Hand, the Justicar, the Lord Treasurer, the Grand Admiral, the Spymaster, the Grand Maester, the Lord Commander of the Kingsguard, and the Wardens Cardinal). So perhaps it does speak to Robert's decadence, after all.

What If?

There's three interesting what-if moments in this chapter:

What if Lord Stark called his banners and went north? Let's say that Will actually got that shattered sword to the Wall or to Eddard himself, and he acted (even if he had thought simply that Rayder was on the move) - a lot of things change. To begin with, it's highly unlikely that he accepts the position of Hand of the King, since he's busy as Warden of the North. That more or less short-circuits much of the plot right there. However, it also might change some other things - 18,000 men rather than 300 go on the Great Ranging, which means a disciplined force survives the Fist of the First Men. It's also likely that Mance Rayder is confronted, not by 600 men at the Wall, but by an entire army - and perhaps a deal gets worked, or the old enmity between Starks and wildling kings continues. It also guarantees that credible warning of the White Walkers makes it out before the War of Five Kings, which might drastically change Robert Baratheon's final months as king. Targaryen children seem less consequential when there's a war at hand up north.

What if Catelyn took the younger children to the Vale? This is a subtler, but equally important, change. Catelyn in the Vale perhaps means that Bran never witnesses the queen's incest, which avoids an immediate catalyst for Stark/Lannister conflict; regardless, it means that Catelyn is twigged to her sister's incapacity much earlier – would Catelyn in that position, with her children at stake, depose her sister as regent if, perhaps, war were to break out between the Starks and Lannisters? It also means that Tyrion likely never gets arrested/kidnapped, which means that Stark is likely in good health when the clash comes and doesn't lose that vital week out of his mind on opium, and that Tyrion is there to witness what happens at court. Does Tyrion go with his sister's plans? Without a Hand's chain around his neck, does he even have the power to stop her?

What if Ned was adopted by Jon Arryn? Let's say that Jon Arryn decides to go with a carefully-groomed heir over a distant relative. This means that when Brandon Stark dies, Eddard Stark falls heir to two kingdoms. This has, as far as I'm aware, never happened before in Westerosi history and would likely have increased tensions enormously. No way Tywin feels that easy about a man who either controls or is married into three contiguous northerly kingdoms, or Renly and the Tyrells, for that matter. It's questionable whether even the strong friendship between Ned and Robert could have survived the tensions between a king and a vassal strong enough to overthrow the king.

Book vs. Show

This scene is fairly faithful to the book, except for the narrative economy that limits Eddard and Catelyn's discussion to the news of Arryn's death and what that means for the Starks. However, for a rare change, ShowNed is smarter than BookNed – he realizes right away that Robert's visit means he's going to be asked to be the Hand of the King. For all those viewers and reviewers who complained about how Eddard Stark looked like an idiot in the show (a topic I'll be addressing later), here's a case of the reverse – Eddard Stark is canny enough to read an entire political situation into a sentence on paper.

Secondly, and I'll also get into this later, Catelyn Stark's position is reversed; in the book, she convinces Eddard that he cannot refuse the king. Here, she speaks solely as a mother. I understand, to an extent, the desire on the part of showrunners David Benioff and Dan Weiss to drive for narrative economy, to present Catelyn from the outset as a mother first, and then reveal her more political side, but at the same time, I think they did miss a chance to show the particularly medieval strong female character of the highborn lady. Medieval ladies did not always spend their time sewing; they were expected to manage households and estates, and, if necessary, to conduct a siege defense if their castle was attacked while their lord was away. This was Catelyn Stark's political training, and it would have been nice to see it.

DAENERYS I

And perhaps the dragon did remember, but Dany could not. She had never seen this land her brother talked of, Casterly Rock and the Eyrie, Highgarden and the Vale of Arryn, Dorne and the Isle of Faces – they were just words to her.

"They are your people and they love you well," Magister Illyrio said amiably. "In holdfasts all across the realm, men lift secret toasts to your health while women sew dragon banners and hide them against the day of your return from across the water..." Dany had no agents, no way of knowing what anyone was doing or thinking across the narrow sea, but she mistrusted Illyrio's sweet words.

Synopsis

Daenerys Targaryen receives a gift from Magister Illyrio at the hands of her brother, Viserys Targaryen, who advises and warns her on her presentation before Khal Drogo of the Dothraki. As Daenerys, Viserys, and Illyrio go to meet her bridegroom-to-be, they discuss the loyalties of Westerosi folk both great and small. In the wedding party, they encounter Ser Jorah Mormont, the exiled lord of Bear Island. The bride and groom meet for the first time.

Political Analysis

Many observers talk about Daenerys undergoing a hero's journey in *A Game of Thrones*, from a terrified, abused little girl into a khaleesi and the Mother of Dragons, and they're right. But politically, we see some very early signs of Daenerys being something much more – especially in comparison to her brother.

In this chapter, Viserys Targaryen is very much introduced as a romantic, monarchist exile, weaving "his web of dream," obsessed with the day when "we will have it back... the jewels and the silks, Dragonstone and King's Landing, the Iron Throne and the Seven Kingdoms, all they have taken from us." (And how typical that when Viserys speaks of Westeros, he always speaks of things, not people.) As a result, he believes all of the lies that Illyrio Mopatis pours into his ear –

because he wants to believe them, because they fit into the drama he's constructed in his head about the way his life is going to happen. By contrast, Daenerys Targaryen is essentially a second-generation immigrant – and a political realist. Her home is "the big house with the red door" where she had "a lemon tree outside her window," and that is the restitution she initially wants – to have her childhood back. Because she knows she doesn't know anything about the Seven Kingdoms, because these places are just names to her, she has a more calculating approach. She doesn't trust Illyrio's descriptions of Westeros on the grounds of her experience of Essos, because Illyrio reminds her of the faithful servants who stole their money and left them destitute, because she listens to "talk in the streets" that Illyrio sells his friends like commodities, and because, in her world, no gift is given without a price.

It's in this decision, to trust one's own experience over one's dreams, that we begin to see why Daenerys and not her brother is the true dragon, that it is the traumatized 13-year-old who can see the mocking smiles that her manic-depressive brother cannot. And as we learn later, one of the horrifying ironies is that the world Viserys has constructed of the noble exiles in flight from the hired daggers of the evil usurper is a paranoid illusion – Jon Arryn had called off the assassins long ago, and Robert Baratheon had spent decades interested in other matters. Had Viserys not schemed to make himself a military threat to King Robert, he might well have lived a long and peaceful life in Essos or seen the fruition of Illyrio and Varys's great scheme. It was only when he made himself into a threat that the dream he had lived was summoned into reality.

Another political theme that's set up in this chapter is how conflicting perspectives shape our understanding – in this case, our understanding of Robert's Rebellion. After being introduced to Lord Eddard Stark as a noble and honorable man, and to the rebellion as the act of a courageous man defending the lives of the wards he had sworn to protect, we see Stark as "the Usurper's dog" and party to the murder of children in the Sack of King's Landing. We will later see how Robert interprets the actions of Rhaegar, but here they are seen as the romantic efforts of a man "dying for the sake of the woman he loved." What we believe, who we believe depends on who we trust, which side we're on. For all that Viserys is a romantic fool who, for some strange reason, thinks that the Greyjoys might welcome his return, he's not totally wrong – the Martells really do "burn to avenge Elia and her children" and, as we learn so much later, are genuine Targaryen loyalists. The Darrys lost much when they went down fighting to the last for the Targaryens and might well welcome a chance for revenge; the Redwynes are unlikely to move with both heirs in King's Landing, but Viserys has no way of knowing that. The Tyrells are more mercenary and have their own plans in the works, but they are the most powerful house that's on the outside looking into the halls of power.

What Martin is showing us here – even through Viserys's rose-tinted glasses – is that no civil war is ever over, no civil war is ever won.

A third theme we can explore here is the Targaryen practice of marrying brother to sister, to keep the line pure. This (supposed) Valyrian custom was imported by the Targaryens upon their arrival in Westeros, although apparently no one not of the Targaryens outside of Cersei Lannister actually has ever adopted it. Why the Valyrians actually practiced incestuous marriage, let alone polygamous incestuous marriage, is unexplained and fairly inexplicable; the Valyrian Freehold was a republic, not a monarchy, so there was no dynastic purpose, no royal blood to keep pure. The only explanation is that it might have something to do with the sorcery of dragons, since the Valyrian Freehold's empire and the Targaryen dynasty both rested on the ability to control dragons reliably.

However, as a method of avoiding political conflict by keeping legitimacy in the family, as it were, it was a miserable failure. No less than four political crises – the revolt of the Faith Militant, the Dance of the Dragons, the possible murder of Baelor I, and the Blackfyre Rebellion – can be linked to incest. Directly following the death of Aegon the Conqueror, the Faith Militant rose against Aenys I, as the practice of incest is a sin in the eyes of the Seven. This revolt lasted 10 years, brought down Aenys I, outlasted Maegor the Cruel, and nearly ended the Targaryen dynasty in its first generation. While the Dance of the Dragons wasn't directly prompted as much by incest as by conflict between egalitarian primogeniture and male succession, the fallout from the war, where Aegon III married his cousin, which resulted in two sons and three daughters, had huge long-term consequences.

When Baelor I refused to consummate his incestuous marriage, it created a political crisis of succession, where the children of his sister Elaena (who had married her cousin), the child of Daena (supposedly by Aegon IV), and his uncle Viserys all had claims to power – and may well have led to his death as a way of resolving the crisis. The Blackfyre Rebellion was doubly the result of incest. Daemon Blackfyre, despite having been born a bastard, could claim legitimacy, not merely from his natural father, Aegon IV, but also from his mother, Daena Targaryen, and, through her, from Aegon III. Moreover, Daemon's claim could be bolstered by the rumor that his rival, Daeron II, was actually the child of Queen Naerys and Aemon the Dragonknight. At the same time, Daemon's motives for claiming the throne supposedly include his love for his half-sister, Daenerys.

It's quite likely that even had Viserys not married Daenerys to Khal Drogo, the custom would have failed – Viserys ultimately was trapped between his feelings of fraternal love, incestuous love (hinted at in *A Game of Thrones* and confirmed in *A Dance with Dragons*), and his hatred for his sister: "Her mother had died birthing her, and for that, her brother Viserys had never forgiven her." In this way, Viserys actually mirrors Cersei Lannister, that great admirer of Targaryen traditions – like her, Viserys hates a sibling for having caused the death of their mother and desires a sibling carnally, but in his case they're the same person.

A final political theme is the question of what exactly Illyrio is doing with the marriage to Khal Drogo, and how it fits in with his and Varys's overarching conspiracy. Clearly, he's the originating force of the marriage, and he gets his finder's fee for making it happen; he seems to be acting as Viserys's handler, although he doesn't try very hard to keep Viserys close at hand in Pentos after the wedding (this is perhaps due to Viserys's superfluity, given that they have a personally-trained Targaryen male in hand). When we see him later in "Arya III," he seems to be preparing a Dothraki invasion that he wants to time with the birth of Daenerys's son, although it's probably not the case (as Robert Baratheon thinks) that he's waiting for the next generation to act. Given his gifts to Dany of the dragon eggs and bed slaves, he seems to want the marriage to work. At the same time, however, we learn from *Dance of Dragons* that "I did not think Daenerys would survive for long amongst the horselords" – so what was the purpose? Was it merely an attempt to bolster the military forces open to Illyrio and Varys, adding the horde of Khal Drogo to the Golden Company, so that Aegon VI would have an additional 40,000 men behind him? If so, why did Varys deliberately botch her murder, since we know he can assassinate with precision? Why complicate matters by adding Rhaego to the line of succession, or was Rhaego supposed to be a backup if Aegon VI died in the process of conquering Westeros?

A few things seem probable. To begin with, Varys and Illyrio made no effort to hide Viserys and Daenerys from Robert Baratheon in comparison to their intense efforts to keep Aegon's identity a secret; indeed, they didn't offer even financial support between the death of Willem Darry and the arrival of the siblings at Illyrio's doorstep, although that might have been deliberate neglect in order to make Viserys desperate enough to wed his intended bride to win an army. Although they knew through Varys that Jon Arryn had forestalled any assassination attempts, it's probable that they intended Viserys and Daenerys to act as decoys – why look for the supposedly deceased Aegon when there are two Targaryen pretenders right in front of you? It's also clear from *Dance of Dragons* that an enormous amount of effort went into Aegon's training and that Varys intended him to be the main Targaryen claimant. In the end, I think we're going to have to wait for *The Winds of Winter* to fully map out a conspiracy that, by this point, has collapsed into so many contingency plans and adaptations to unforeseen events, that its original shape is very hard to understand.

Historical Analysis

Despite the seemingly obvious drawbacks of hemophilia, porphyria, and flipper babies, royal incest was a historical phenomenon in many cultures. The pharaohs of Egypt most closely resemble the Targaryen pattern, although they tended to stick to half-brother/half-sister marriages until the Ptolmys, who went in for direct brother-to-sister marriages. The Incas and the royal house of Hawaii also went in for brother-sister marriages. In medieval Europe, direct incest was both illegal and condemned by the Church, with the bizarre case of Jean V of Armagnac the only case I could find of a brother-sister marriage.

The danger of this practice can be seen in the case of the House of Hapsburg; in both its Austrian and Spanish lines, it was well-known for "consanguineous marriage," including one marriage of an uncle to a niece. Even avoiding direct incest of brothers and sisters or fathers and daughters, they still succeeded in increasing the inbreeding coefficient tenfold, to the point of parent-child and brother-sister levels. This lead to recurrent problems with deformity, infertility/importance, mental disorders and retardation, and other genetic abnormalities.

Given these problems, it's surprising the Targaryens lasted as long as they did with so few obviously deformed offspring, given how brother-sister marriage increases the risks of genetic disorders beyond the levels associated with marrying first cousins. It's possible that, like some royal houses engaged in direct incest, they practiced infanticide to weed out obvious cases of maladaptive traits. This might explain how so many Targaryens are described as having been beautiful (although part of that may be the association between Targaryen traits like silver hair and purple eyes with power and, therefore, beauty) - although they clearly missed a spot when it came to Maelys the Monstrous. Their track record when it comes to weeding out less obvious conditions that might have affected the mind is less good (although it's hard to separate nature versus nurture in these circumstances): Maegor the Cruel, Aerion Brightflame, Rhaegel Targaryen, Mad King Aerys II - the list is hardly inspiring.

The marriage between Daenerys and Khal Drogo brings up an interesting historical point - it's probable that the Dothraki are patterned not off the Mongols, but rather the Huns, and Khal Drogo himself on that most famous Hun, Attila, and Daenerys off of the Roman Princess Honoria. In AD 450, the willful and infamous lady Honoria, sister to the weak Emperor Valentinian III, sent a plea for help to Attila in overcoming her brother, and offered in exchange her hand in marriage - and half of Gaul. At the time, Attila was one of the greatest warlords in the known world, extracting tribune from Constantinople, laying waste to the Balkans, and smashing Roman armies. To win Honoria's hand and secure her position, Attila invaded Gaul, capturing Metz, Rheims, and Paris - before being defeated at the Battle of Châlons. When Valentinian III denied him his bride, Attila invaded Italy and practically burnt it to the ground – the city of Venice was founded out in the lagoon by refugees trying to get away from his horsemen. So like Khal Drogo, Attila would lay kingdoms to waste for the sake of his bride – and like Drogo, Attila would die no warriors death, but from a most minor injury; he suffered a massive nosebleed while intoxicated, and choked to death on his own blood.

What If?

I see three possible what-ifs emerging out of this chapter:

What if Viserys had succeeded in his effort to deflower his sister the night before her marriage? Besides the likelihood that Drogo would have called the wedding off, it's quite possible that Rhaego might have been born even more deformed than he was – interestingly, the only example I can find of an obviously deformed Targaryen baby. However, Illyrio had foreseen this possibility and put guards outside her door that night – lest "Viserys might have undone years of planning." This last phrase is tantalizing; clearly Daenerys was an integral part of their planning, yet Illyrio was expecting her to die on the Dothraki plain, and her son seems far less crucial, given the existence of Aegon VI. Indeed, had Daenerys been groomed as a perfect Targaryen queen, why not save her for Aegon?

What if Khal Drogo had turned Daenerys down? Here we have a hypothetical that only brings up further questions about this conspiracy – why did Varys and Illyrio want a Dothraki khal and his *khalassar*, given how unlikely it would be that the khal would have taken orders from Jon Connington or Aegon? Did they want cannon fodder for a failed invasion meant to draw away attention from the real threat, like one of Varys's mummer tricks?

What if Viserys and Daenerys were assassinated before they arrived at Pentos? This, I think, is actually one of the least consequential hypotheticals for Varys and Illyrio – they would have lost their decoys, but the core of their plan would have been intact. However, just as with the second hypothetical, we have some enormous consequences for the larger plot – with no Drogo, no Rhaego, and, thus, no dragons. Robert Baratheon's desire to extirpate the Targaryen line might have brought about the downfall of the world, depending on how crucial those dragons are to stopping the Others. Even leaving aside the larger metaphysics, it's possible that Eddard Stark becomes so disillusioned with Robert, coming hard on the heels of the murder of Elia and her children, that he flat-out refuses the Handship.

Book vs. Show

The show plays this chapter fairly straight, although they shift the meeting of Drogo and Daenerys to have Drogo on his horse - which I think is an improvement, actually. One interesting little change is that the phrase "a man should be able to do what he likes with his chattel" is shifted from Illyrio the slave-trader to Viserys, which emphasizes Viserys's lack of empathy for anyone but himself, and also his unfamiliarity with Westeros. Westerosi peasants are not chattel, insofar as much as they have the right to appeal for the king's justice - which suggests they have a legal status above that of property.

EDDARD I

Fifteen years past, when they had ridden forth to win a throne, the Lord of Storm's End had been clean-shaven, clear-eyed, and muscled like a maiden's fantasy… in those days, the smell of leather and blood had clung to him like perfume. Now it was perfume that clung to him like perfume, and he had a girth to match his height… a beard as coarse and black as iron wire covered his jaw to hide his double chin and the sag of the royal jowls, but nothing could hide his stomach or the dark circles under his eyes.

"I swear to you, sitting a throne is a thousand times harder than winning one. Laws are a tedious business, and counting coppers is worse… the lies they tell… and my lords and ladies are no better. I am surrounded by flatterers and fools… there are nights I wish we had lost at the Trident… Lord Eddard Stark, I would name you the Hand of the King."

Synopsis

King Robert Baratheon arrives at Winterfell, and Eddard Stark takes him down into the castle's crypts to see the tomb of Lyanna Stark. The two discuss the death of Jon Arryn, the disposal of the Wardenship of the East, and other political matters. The king offers Eddard the Handship and marriage between their two houses. And winter is coming.

Political Analysis

This chapter introduces us personally to King Robert Baratheon, whose name has run through the proceeding chapters, and it's here that we get our first sense of his character and our most intimate glimpse into the relationship he has with Eddard Stark, and the origins of the rebellion that placed him on the Iron Throne. I'm going to address three key themes: Robert Baratheon as Henry VIII and the nature of royal decadence, the nature of the Hand and other royal appointments in the geopolitics of the Seven Kingdoms, and the subtle-yet-vital importance of the mystery of Robert/Robin Arryn's fosterage.

When Robert Baratheon hooves into our view like an aging battleship, the comparisons to Henry VIII are really quite stunning (especially when we find out later that Renly and Loras are scheming to put Margaery into Robert's bed and supplant the queen). Like Robert, Henry was a jock in his youth, "the most handsomest potentate I have ever set eyes on," according to one ambassador, who went to seed when inactivity stopped him from burning off his excess consumption of food and alcohol – a keen tennis player, hunter, and jouster. In history, Henry suffered the fate that Robert avoided in the melee, having his horse fall on his leg, which left him permanently injured and unable to exercise as he had been accustomed to. Here, the Elvis-like change is unexplained. Despite the opinions of many fans who see only the drunken, absentee king, Robert is seen as having been active and dynamic until recently – when Eddard saw him "nine years before, during Balon Greyjoy's rebellion, when the stag and direwolf had joined to end the pretensions of the self-proclaimed King of the Iron Islands," Robert was still fit and engaged in his reign (although how much of that has to do with a rebellion being more in his wheelhouse than peacetime government is hard to say). At the very least, we know Robert had eight good years before his decline – but we never quite find out what caused this change, why he stopped participating in his jousts and other exercises (although he's clearly hale enough to hunt boar when sober), why all of the sudden his "pleasures were taking a toll on the king."

One thing is very clear: Robert isn't a micro-managing king. "Laws are a tedious business, and counting coppers is worse," he declares, and we learn that he basically devolves his government to his councilors – much as Henry VIII did with Thomas Wolsey and Thomas Cromwell – when it comes to "coins, crops, and justice," which are the chief peacetime functions of the government (although it's clear that Robert is very much in charge when it comes to military and national security, more generally). This isn't necessarily a bad way to govern a kingdom when you have a monarch without a talent for monetary, agricultural, and judicial policy, as long as you have good advisors. And there's the problem for Robert – he's at the mercy of his talent pool. Part of this problem is an inherited one: as part of the post-rebellion reconciliation urged by Jon Arryn, his Hand, Robert kept on Grand Maester Pycelle (a Lannister spy who betrayed the last king) and Varys (whose competence and devotion to the realm is genuine, although his loyalty is less so), who he can't trust. He did, however, bring in his brothers, who he could count on being loyal to the family. Stannis was a good Master of Ships, and Renly is at least a good courtier, although we don't get the sense that he's paying much attention to his job as master of laws. As we discussed previously, Jon Arryn seems to have been a fairly competent Hand, and while Littlefinger is a devious and untrustworthy man, no one's ever said that he was bad at his job as master of coin.

Overall, what personnel mistakes there seem to have been look more like Jon Arryn's doing than Robert's, and Robert recognizes that "I am surrounded by flatterers and fools... half of them don't dare tell me the truth, and the other half can't find it." If nothing else, he's not a deluded king. His major failures seem two-fold: finances and his over-reliance on the Lannisters. The first is indisputable; plunging a kingdom with ample reserves into six million dragons in debt is a massive failing, one that Robert shares with his historical counterpart. Although I imagine that paying for two major rebellions had something to do with it, his penchant for tourneys is a good sign of the costs Robert was incurring – 90,000 dragons for the Hand's Tourney represents the yearly income of almost 50 nobles, going by *Game of Thrones*'s pen-and-paper RPG. It's a situation that Baelish seems to have dealt with largely through borrowing, simony (selling of offices), bribery, and kickbacks, which probably meant that the kingdom's economy did rather well through the stimulus of royal spending (historically, Henry balanced the books with high taxes and the confiscation of the monasteries).

Keynesianism in action aside, the more dangerous mistake was to plant so many Lannisters around him – Lancel and Willem are harmless as squires, but keeping Jaime Lannister in the Kingsguard was a huge mistake (indeed, sending him home to Tywin would probably have won him support from the Lord of Casterly Rock), and so was allowing the Lannisters to keep 500 men in King's Landing.

This brings us to the second theme – the role of the Hand of the King and the other royal appointments, specifically the royal Wardens Cardinal, as I call them. Eddard describes the Hand as "the second-most powerful man in the Seven Kingdoms. He spoke with the king's voice, commanded the king's armies, drafted the king's laws. At times, he even sat upon the Iron Throne to dispense justice." This makes the Hand far more powerful than the historical Lord Chancellor, Lord President of the Council, Marshall, or Lord High Constable – essentially a deputy king, capable of doing a lot more than "building" or "wiping." As I will argue later on, I think Eddard's major failing as Hand later on isn't as much his honor as his lack of understanding about how his office could be used – for example, Eddard Stark did not compel Hugh of the Vale or the other members of Jon Arryn's household to give testimony, which he could have done under royal warrant; neither did he raise any royal troops to supplement the gold cloaks or counterbalance the Lannister forces, which was likewise in his power to do.

The situation of the Wardens shows something of the costs of Robert's dependency on the Lannisters. While it's true that Tywin is a capable military man and organizer, putting Jaime in as Warden of the East (since he stands to inherit the Wardenship of the West) threatens to destabilize the balance of power between the great houses, as well as alienating the lords of the Vale. As we've discussed before, the Wardenships are incredibly powerful positions, essentially mini-Hands with large military forces in each of the Cardinal Directions – the Warden of the North guards against wildlings; the Warden of the East is responsible for pacifying the hill tribes, maintaining the Vale as the ultimate stronghold, and dealing with pirates and potential invasions from across the narrow sea; the Warden of the West deals with the Ironmen; and the Warden of the South holds the Dornish Marches against rebellion or invasion from over the mountains. A man with the West and East essentially has the combined powers of the westerlands and the Vale at his disposal, a true kingmaker (as no doubt was Cersei's plan). To his credit, Ned Stark realizes this instantly and tries to persuade Robert to at least name Stannis or Renly, which suggests that he actually does have some political savvy.

One additional fact about the Wardens that didn't make the shift from outline to published post is that the Wardens have a seat on the small council, which gives an additional importance to Robert's move, as it gives the Lannisters two seats on a small council of only 11 members, even if they didn't have any other posts. It also suggests something more of Eddard Stark's distaste for politics, since he doesn't seem to have ever used that right.

Historical Analysis

In comparison to Henry VIII, who created enormous political time bombs in the form of his multiple marriages and his climactic break with the Catholic Church, Robert Baratheon actually seems to have ruled fairly well for 17 years, all things considered. In general, he seems to have avoided many of Henry VIII's major flaws – he didn't engage in a series of wasteful and pointless foreign wars, he didn't create massive religious conflict for selfish reasons, and he didn't use his royal favorites (who both Henry and Robert clearly accumulate) as scapegoats when things went wrong (after all, he keeps Lord Arryn and Lord Stark on for a long time despite heated disagreements with both), although Robert's mention of heads on spikes when Eddard crosses him on the matter of Daenerys's assassination suggests that he certainly has the tendency.

Historically, to be a royal favorite was very much a double-edged sword; it was a way to rise very quickly (as we can see with how Cersei maneuvers Lannister men into key positions at court), but it also made you a target for other nobles and popular dissent. In a monarchy where the king is seen as being anointed by God, you can't call for the king to be replaced or overthrown directly, so you direct your anger and frustration against the "evil ministers" who are deceiving the king, even when everyone knows that it's the king who's really behind whatever unpopular policy is being pursued. Clever kings used this tradition as a safety valve, using their ministers and favorites as buffers between themselves and public opinion, throwing them to the wolves when necessary to rebuild public support. The Peasants Revolt of 1381, the Pilgrimage of Grace in 1536, the political crisis that lead to the English Civil War in the 1630s and 1640s, the Glorious Revolution of 1688, and the American Revolution all started as rebellions against "evil ministers" and "cabals."

In this chapter, we get the first real descriptions of the Battle of the Trident, where Prince Rhaegar Targaryen and an army of Dornishmen, crownlanders, and Targaryen loyalists from the stormlands and the Vale attempted to block the crossing of Robert Baratheon, Eddard Stark, Jon Arryn, Hoster Tully, and the rebel forces of the stormlands, the north, the Vale, and the riverlands into the crownlands. We also learn more about the rebellion that brought it about – not only had the Mad King called for the heads of the heirs of the north and the stormlands, but he had murdered Brandon and Rickard Stark (we also learn that Jon Arryn's heir was also murdered), and Rhaegar had seemingly abducted Lyanna Stark. In the midst of this closely-fought battle between one larger army and one more seasoned army, Robert and Rhaegar came to a climactic duel in the middle of the ford, a dramatic throw of the dice that decided the fate of the Rebellion.

Robert won the duel, although he was injured so badly that it was Eddard Stark who carried the victorious army into King's Landing.

The Battle of the Trident very much resembles some of the great battles of the War of the Roses, from which Martin drew much of his inspiration for the novels, especially the Battles of Towton and Tewksbury. The Battle of Towton, the "largest and bloodiest battle ever fought on English soil," featured scarcely 10,000 men less than its fictional counterpart. Here, the young rebel prince Edward of York, son of a murdered father, marched on his enemies after winning a number of victories, and led his men straight into a numerically superior force. Despite having the better position and a favoring wind that allowed their archers to outshoot the enemy, the Yorkists were pushed back under weight of numbers and might have broken had not Edward personally seized command of the left wing and held it in pitched combat until the duke of Norfolk's men crested the ridge overlooking the Lancastrian left flank and attacked – routing the exhausted enemy. As the Lancastrians fled, the Rivers Cock Beck and Wharfe turned into deadly obstacles – with thousands drowning in the water, Yorkist archers firing into the swimmers, and bridges collapsing under the weight of the enemy. After Towton, the Lancastrians fled into exile, and Edward was crowned King of England.

By contrast, the Battle of Tewksbury was a much smaller affair, with only 10,000 men in attendance, but equally dramatic. Outnumbered two to one, the once-and-future Edward IV routed the Lancastrian army – with the Lancastrian Prince Edward and his father, King Henry VI, executed that day. To create the Battle of the Trident, then, Martin placed Towton's rivers right in the middle of the event rather than at the end and gave the battle Tewksbury's end.

What If?

This chapter gives us a whole bunch of juicy counterfactuals to play with:

The Trident – as the turning point of the entire Rebellion, the duel between Robert and Rhaegar is incredibly consequential. Had Rhaegar won the duel, it's unclear as to whether he would have won the battle; his right flank, the Dornishmen, had been broken by the forces of the Vale, and the rebels had motives beyond Robert's kidnapped bride. Had it led to Targaryen victory, Rhaegar still would have had to deal with four rebellious kingdoms. We know from Jaime that Rhaegar might have called a Great Council to try to settle the rebellion – which would have necessitated overthrowing his mad father. After the murder of Rickard Stark, Brandon Stark, and Elbert Arryn, it's unlikely that even the reveal of his marriage to Lyanna Stark would have been enough to bring peace, even had he brought the Lannisters on-side. Certainly, a second Great Council might have had tremendous political implications, leading to greater constitutionalism in the Westerosi monarchy. Had Rhaegar won the duel and lost the battle, or had both combatants died, we might have had a situation in which Eddard Stark rides into King's Landing, rousts Jaime Lannister from the Iron Throne, and sits down himself as the only other logical rebel leader. With the power of the north, the riverlands, the Vale, and the stormlands behind him, a King Eddard might have been Westeros's own Cromwell.

Lyanna's kidnapping/the murder of the Starks – for a supposedly intelligent man, Rhaegar Targaryen's actions in "abducting" Lyanna Stark are remarkably short-sighted. Regardless of how Lyanna herself might have felt, the act was an open insult, making Robert Baratheon out to be a cuckold, and showing Rickard Stark to be so weak that he can neither uphold his marriage promises nor protect his own family from outsiders; had the Targaryens gone no further, it's still likely that the event would have led to a civil war, and one in which Rickard and Brandon call the Stark banners rather than go to their deaths in King's Landing. We really have to ask why Rhaegar Targaryen didn't make an offer of marriage to Rickard Stark, perhaps offering Rhaenys or Daenerys to compensate Robert Baratheon – or leave any instruction for anyone in King's Landing about what to do if the Starks showed up angry. At the very least, it would have staunched the spread of the Rebellion, kept the north loyal, and perhaps isolated the Baratheons, and at least given the Targaryens a better public rationale for the civil war. Even more so, the "execution" of Rickard and Brandon Stark was an act of such folly that you really have to wonder why no one in the capital could at least delay matters so that Rhaegar could do something about this. Because what I don't think many fans of the series quite get is how threatening to the entire political order Aerys II's actions were - to begin with, to arrest the heir to a great house immediately raises the possibility that the crown might arrest the heirs of the other great houses while maintaining the troubling position that the Crown can kidnap the children of the great houses with impunity. But to then summon Rickard Stark and murder him rather than grant him a fair trial not only discredits royal justice, but brings into question the physical safety of the Lords Paramount of the Seven Kingdoms - if one law-abiding Lord Paramount can be executed on a whim, any of them can. In retrospect, it's rather amazing that any house took the Targaryens' side in the Rebellion.

The importance of Robert Arryn's fosterage - Robert Arryn has to be one of the least visible pawns in the great chess game between the conspiracies in *Game of Thrones*. As we learn much later, Jon Arryn had learned the secret of Cersei and Jaime Lannister's incestuous treason - although we never quite find out how Cersei planned to deal with this - and his attempt to foster his son at Dragonstone with Stannis Baratheon, safe from the hands of the Lannisters, shows that he was preparing to fight it out with them when he was blindsided by Petyr Baelish's treachery. It's equally clear that Cersei's attempt to have him foster with Tywin was a move to keep the truth of her children's parentage from being leaked (although how Cersei planned to sell this to her father is less than clear). Had Jon Arryn moved just a bit faster (or if he had made common cause with Renly and the Tyrells), Cersei might have been exposed and the Lannisters forced into a sudden reprise of the Greyjoy Rebellion against the Baratheons, Starks, and Arryns. Interestingly, had Cersei succeeded, it's possible that Baelish's plot (more on this later) to have Lysa Arryn stoke the flames of a Stark/Lannister feud might have been forestalled completely (no way Lysa sends that letter with her son in danger) - in which case, Ned Stark might have served out his time as Hand, the Starks and the Lannisters/Baratheons might have merged houses, and a very strange power bloc might have formed. Finally, Eddard Stark offers somewhat belatedly to foster the boy at Winterfell - which might have prompted the very paranoid Cersei to some action even rasher than her urging an attempt on the life of Bran Stark. (Incidentally, Cersei and Jaime were incredibly idiotic to fornicate in Winterfell, so soon after dodging the Jon Arryn bullet.)

What If the marriage pact had been Robb and Myrcella? - the fanfictionados are somewhat fond of this pairing, I think because Myrcella seems both non-sadistic and reasonably intelligent for a Lannister incest-baby. I must say that I find it unlikely - unlike the

Sansa/Joffrey match, it doesn't put Stark blood in the royal succession – although it's possible that it could have been combined with that wedding. In the larger scheme of things, Robb Stark's military gifts probably wouldn't have changed events much in King's Landing had the couple accompanied them south – although had Myrcella stayed in the north, it's less likely that Cersei allows Eddard Stark's death, given the risk to her child. Instead, we might have seen a very complicated Stark/Lannister conflict, with both sides trying to capture enough hostages to make the exchange favorable – or perhaps in that situation, Tywin forces a peace and deals with the Baratheons first.

Book vs. Show

There's a few interesting changes between the show and the book. A minor alteration is to have Robert call Ned fat rather than say he hasn't changed, which I rather like as a comedic beat in what can be a very bleak series. The exchange between Robert and Ned is pretty much straight from the books (omitting the Warden of the East plot as unnecessary), although I liked the addition of Robert saying "it's not [Jon Arryn's] fault I never listened" when he was being fostered, which nicely mirrors their relationship as Hand and king. The major change is more of a character moment – instead of Ned saying in the show, "this is where she belongs," in the book Ned says, "I was with her when she died... she wanted to come home." Not only does this give Lyanna more of an active presence, but it also brings up that Ned was present when Lyanna died.

As it is, I have no idea how the showrunners plan to bring this thread back into the plot. Although a flashback sequence to bring back Sean Bean would be nice...

JON I

Robb would someday inherit Winterfell, would command great armies as the Warden of the North. Bran and Rickon would be Robb's bannermen and rule holdfasts in his name. His sisters Arya and Sansa would marry the heirs of other great houses and go south as mistresses of castles of their own. But what place could a bastard hope to earn?

"Let me give you some counsel, bastard... never forget what you are, for surely the world will not. Make it your strength. Then it can never be your weakness. Armor yourself in it, and it will never be used to hurt you."

Synopsis

Jon Snow gets drunk for the first time at the feast, where he observes the principals of two great houses from his obscure position. He discusses going to the Night's Watch and fathering children with Benjen Stark before he gets ferklempt and has to leave. Outside, he meets Tyrion Lannister, who displays improbable acrobatics skills, and the two have a further discussion about bastardy and social conventions. Tyrion returns to the feast.

Political Analysis

Not much in the way of political *events* per se happen in this episode; instead, we are given more of an insight into some of our characters as political thinkers. Jon Snow is presented (or presents himself) as a highly observant person, since "a bastard had to learn to notice things, to read the truth that people hid behind their eyes," and claims to notice how the king, queen, and his father really feel under their courtesies. However, this seems like one of those character details that George R.R. Martin started out with, then dropped, a bit like Tyrion's acrobatics between the rest of book one and the end of book four. Snow's gift for observing human emotions seems to desert him thereafter, especially during *Dance with Dragons*; as a developing leader of the Night's Watch, Snow seems to rely more on a close circle of allies and his own heroic example as opposed to any ability to empathize with other brothers of the Night's Watch.

We do see a little bit more of the parallels beginning to be drawn between Theon, Robb, and Jon as different kinds of future leaders. Robb is the rightful heir and hereditary leader, someone who "would inherit Winterfell [and] command great armies as the Warden of the North. Bran and Rickon would be Robb's bannermen and rule holdfasts in his name." He's later shown as a natural military strategist, and someone who's quite good at impressing in his feudal vassals, but who lacks Bran's gifts at conciliating competing claims among them and in compromising, more generally. Jon is later shown as an elected leader, a dark-horse candidate who emerges only because two more established candidates split the vote, and yet not someone who's naturally good at working with subordinates outside of a small group of friends that he has to be reminded to create. Rather, he tends to lead by example, using his Valyrian sword, his direwolf, and personal prowess and mystique. Nevertheless, we do see that he's actually quite good at compromising when it comes to the wildlings, although less adept at gauging the effect this has on his men (so much for Jon the observant). Theon is neither fish nor fowl; a rightful heir to a nation that has a nasty tendency to elect their kings, but without any gifts of rulership, who inspires no loyalty in his subordinates nor can set any great example in himself. Theon, who has an extremely complicated relationship with Robb Stark, is set up as an instant antagonist to Jon Snow – in part, I think, because Jon is a dark mirror to Theon. Both are half-way exiles who have no true native home, but whereas Theon masks a sense of frustrated entitlement behind aloof mockery, Jon turns inwards. We'll see more later about how their respective leadership styles work out.

The second political theme we have is Tyrion's advice about the nature of public face and image versus truth, a theme that will follow Tyrion throughout the series. His recommendation is sound – "know thyself" was Socrates's guiding rule, the foundation of his search for truth; Sun Tzu saw it as the first step to victory, as "if you know the enemy and know yourself, you need not fear the result of a hundred battles. If you know yourself but not the enemy, for every victory gained, you will also suffer a defeat. If you know neither the enemy nor yourself, you will succumb in every battle." Certainly, by learning not to treat his bastardy as a scarlet letter, Jon does much better than, say, Ramsey Snow, who can be provoked into berserk fury by the mere word. Ultimately, he is but the mere student to Tyrion's master – as Tyrion's triumphant nickname of "Halfman" proves, he can use his stature to beguile his enemies into underestimating him, and goad his followers into acts of suicidal bravery. And yet... we'll see later that there is a limit to how far Tyrion's strategy can go.

Historical Analysis

George R.R. Martin's decision to make bastardy an absolute barrier to social advancement in Westeros is actually something of a departure from history, which was often more complicated. William the Conqueror was widely known as "William the Bastard" before his invasion of England in 1066, and yet he inherited the duchy of Normandy and laid claim to the throne of England. Beginning with the Normans, royal and noble bastards often were granted quite extensive lands and titles – Robert Fitzroy, the son of Henry I, became the First Earl of Gloucester and a powerful enough noble to lead the armies of the Empress Matilda against Stephen I in the civil war known as "the Anarchy" (and, indeed, was mentioned as a rival candidate to Stephen I as the successor to Henry I); Henry I's daughters became duchesses of Brittany, countesses of Perche, and abbesses of Montvilliers. Royal and noble bastards played the same role that legitimate siblings did in the feudal system: they were ways to play the feudal game of distributing lands and titles while still keeping land in the family, just as Bran and Rickon would be as rulers of holdfasts for Robb.

Why Jon can't do the same is a bit unclear, although it's possible that the fallout from Aegon IV's legitimization of the Great Bastards – Daemon Blackfyre, Aegor "Bittersteel" Rivers, Brynden "Bloodraven" Rivers, and Shiera Seastar – has created a general taboo against legitimization. We do see it being used – Stannis offers it to Jon Snow, Bran proposes it to deal with the Hornwood crisis, Robb turns to it to guarantee a succession – but we get the sense that it's only used in crises. Nevertheless, the fact that Eddard Stark doesn't even consider asking Robert Baratheon to issue a proclamation, however discretely, is significant.

Tyrion's in a more difficult position; there isn't a decree that can make him appear differently to those who would judge him based on his appearance. Another, more specific strike against him is perhaps the tradition of court dwarfs (which we see in action in Essos, if not in Westeros). Historically, they "were such an integral part of imperial activities — serving, entertaining, and present at royal celebrations — they are almost never depicted as autonomous beings; rather, they are shown as decorative elements situated at the fringes of the lives of others more important than themselves." This combination of being able to observe the most intimate secrets of royalty but still being treated as an object, a possession of the king or queen, gives us a sense of where George R.R. Martin was drawing on in constructing Tyrion's character. But as we'll see later in *Clash of Kings*, Tyrion's inconspicuousness becomes a double-edged sword once he becomes a more public figure.

What If?

Unfortunately, there isn't much in the way of hypotheticals for this chapter - but check back in "Catelyn II," where there are some really interesting what-ifs to talk about.

Book vs. Show

This is one scene where I think it's actually better in the show than in the book, distilled down to its essence. Jon Snow's teenage angst is pared down to tolerable levels (I think showing Kit Harrington crying his way out of a feast would have gone too far), Tyrion's inconsistent athleticism is removed - as it will be by the second Tyrion chapter, anyway - and we get straight into the heart of the matter: Jon Snow's decision to join the Night's Watch and his conversation with Tyrion.

CATELYN II

"He will not understand that. He is a king now, and kings are not like other men. If you refuse to serve him, he will wonder why, and sooner or later he will begin to suspect that you oppose him. Can't you see the danger that would put us in?"

"You must be Robert's Hand. You must go south with him and learn the truth… the Hand of the King has power, my lord. Power to find the truth of Lord Arryn's death, to bring his killers to the king's justice."

Synopsis

Eddard and Catelyn Stark enjoy the afterglow, and discuss Robert's political and marital offers. Maester Luwin arrives with a message from Lysa Arryn informing them that Jon Arryn was murdered by Cersei Lannister. All three discuss whether Ned should now take up the Handship - and decide that he will go south, as well as which children will go with him. Jon Snow's offer to take the black is discussed and agreed to.

Political Analysis

One of my favorite things about this chapter is that we get to see Catelyn Stark as a political analyst. For all that she seems to have a vocal hatedom, she's actually quite astute in this scene. In warning Ned that refusing an offer of friendship and patronage from the king would risk alienating King Robert (which is historically accurate), Catelyn anticipates Robert Baratheon's later reaction when Eddard Stark refuses to go along with the assassination of Daenerys and shows a keen judge of character when it comes to seeing that the king is motivated by his ego. She shows a good understanding of dynastic politics, as we'd expect a highborn lady to do - making a marriage alliance with the royal household, such that the next heir to the throne might be half a Stark, makes sense if you want to strengthen the Stark family's political position. It's something of a pity that so many fans overlook her acumen here.

The major political question in this chapter is whether Eddard should stay in Winterfell or accept Robert's offer to become the Hand of the King. As I've suggested before, I think there's a choice that Ned doesn't take: the choice to not merely be the Hand, but to use the powers of the Hand to accomplish his goals - namely, to uncover the truth of Jon Arryn's death and shore up Robert's government. The Hand has a broad portfolio of powers that we don't really see Eddard Stark using that much:

Lawmaking - if Eddard Stark is unhappy that the capital is so mired in corruption, he has the power to introduce reforms through royal decrees in the king's name. For example, given his frustration with the king's finances, he certainly could have introduced new taxes to balance the budget, he could have established a Westerosi reserve bank to provide the king with an alternative to borrowing from the Lannisters, or he could have cut Robert's spending in areas where the king wasn't looking. For all that Robert dislikes "counting coppers" and likes throwing tourneys, one does get the sense that Eddard could have pushed the king to clean up his act (I get the sense that Robert would do better with a minder telling him what he can't do than someone trying to offer him good advice) - after all, he succeeds in getting Robert to forgo the melee even when the king wanted to fight. He could have pursued legal reforms to bolster the crown's ability to see justice done (which would have helped him with his investigations), given that Westeros seems to lack the royal courts that were so crucial to the success of the Plantagenet dynasty.

Appointments - I think this may be Eddard's first and most consequential mistake. As essentially a new prime minister, he makes the decision to retain the cabinet of the previous incumbent (always a mistake), even though there's no one on the small council that is loyal to Eddard Stark. Replacing some combination of Littlefinger, Pycelle, and Varys with Stark loyalists would have greatly strengthened his hand - Wyman Manderly, for example, has some financial savvy that could substitute for Littlefinger's dubious loyalty, and Pycelle could have been quietly retired. Bringing the Tyrells onto the council as Wardens of the South would have at least created a more even balance of power. Given Eddard Stark's pre-existing dislike of Lannister appointees surrounding the king, there's no reason why Eddard couldn't have given him some northern squires. He certainly could have appointed someone better than Janos Slynt to be the commander of the City Watch. A relatively small number of appointees could have greatly improved Eddard Stark's position - instead, he tends to disperse his loyalists to the City Watch or to hunt for Gregor Clegane, which further weakens him.

Judicial powers - this is one of the few areas where Ned actually does make use of his power, by attainting Gregor Clegane (and, in the show, by summoning Tywin Lannister to court – more of which later). I'll discuss the wisdom of his actions later, but it's frustrating how Eddard Stark makes no use of his powers when he's investigating Jon Arryn's murder. He had the power to summon Hugh of the Vale to his presence (indeed, Littlefinger's suggestion to not do so may have been in order to delay his giving testimony – more on which later), to arrest him if necessary. Similarly, he could have issued a public arrest warrant for Tyrion Lannister – which would have made the actions of Jaime and Tyrion Lannister open treason.

Military powers – finally, there was nothing stopping the Hand from recruiting more troops than the 50 he brought to King's Landing so that he wasn't outnumbered 10-to-one by the Lannisters, so that he didn't have to rely on the gold cloaks for his final move. Given the disorder in the riverlands and the threat of a Dothraki invasion, he had every pretext for doing so.

The strange thing about Stark's choices is how vulnerable the various conspiracies were to an active Hand – for whatever reason, Ser Hugh of the Vale had been left in place in King's Landing. It's possible that he knew nothing of Jon Arryn's investigations or had no part in his murder, but it's extremely unlikely; he was Jon's squire and would have been in constant contact with him during his time as Hand. While Pycelle's suspicions aren't really worth much, given his... lack of skill at intrigue, Varys's suspicions are more credible – and he didn't have a motive to lie about that particular conspiracy. Similarly, Petyr's lie that he had lost the knife to Tyrion Lannister was easily verifiable – more on why he did so later on. Finally, most of Arryn's loose ends were still floating around – the book was easily available, as are all the royal bastards he visited.

Indeed, as I'll discuss when I get to *Clash of Kings*, Tyrion's reign as Hand shows how effective a Hand can be in uncovering conspiracies and in dealing with conspirators, and it's highly significant how his choices differ from those of his predecessor.

Lysa's message that Queen Cersei murdered Jon Arryn is one of the first truly significant political events in *Game of Thrones*, the first move in Littlefinger's conspiracy to turn the Starks against the Lannisters. It shows Baelish's characteristic style, always working at a step or two removed, through easily deniable and disposable cats-paws, and making use of personal feelings and attachments. Think about how this phase of his plan works and how long it must have been in the planning – he had been cultivating Jon Arryn's trust for years, ever since he became Controller of Customs at Gulltown and began to move up the ranks under his patronage. That trust, in turn, was built on his skillful manipulation of Lysa Tully's obsessive love, ever since he deflowered her and impregnated her – the event that likely caused her emotional and mental breakdown.

It's quite astonishing, the degree of control he has over Lysa – think about what she's doing in this letter. She's intentionally putting her sister and her entire family in mortal danger, driven by her own displaced guilt over the murder of her husband, which in turn was prompted by her built-up hatred and resentment over the abortion she was forced to have to marry an old man who gave her repeated miscarriages and one sickly child.

Two small points:

1. Using Bran as a bridge between Robb and Joffrey was doomed from the start, given Joffrey's sociopathic tendencies.

2. Ned's use of the phrase "he is of my blood" is one of the stronger pieces of evidence of the R+L=J theory, given that he doesn't ever call Jon his son. At the same time, it does make you wonder why Ned Stark doesn't encourage the Ashara Dayne story. Emotional trauma might explain it, but, at the same time, it would give a credible explanation for Jon Snow's birth, obscuring the truth under a widely believed and believable story. Unless there's something about the Tower of Joy he wanted to obscure.

Historical Analysis

Ned Stark had good reasons to fear royal favor. Jon Arryn had been murdered, the four Hands before him ended badly, and even Tywin Lannister saw his son and heir stolen from him. Historically, royal favors could very much be a double-edged sword. Henry VIII made Thomas Wolsey the king's almoner, Archbishop of York, and Lord Chancellor – as well as one of the richest men in England, but, just as quickly, he stripped him of his offices and properties and had him accused of treason; Thomas Cromwell started as a commoner, became Chancellor of the Exchequer and the king's principle secretary, and rose as high as to become Earl of Essex, but was attainted by the House of Lords for treason, heresy, corruption, and other sins, and lost his head.

Equally, conspiracy was very much a part of court life in the Middle Ages and beyond. In just the Tudor dynasty, we can find the supposed treason of Anne Boleyn, who was accused of adultery and incest with five men, including her brother (which Cersei's accusations towards Margaery Tyrell are based on), prompted by Thomas Cromwell; Thomas Cranmer's successful plot to bring down Catherine Howard; the Regent Edward Seymour (Duke of Somerset)'s successful domination of Edward VI's Council, and his brother's plot to secretly marry the future Elizabeth I; Wyatt's rebellion against Mary I; the possible murder of

Robert Dudley's wife by Dudley to free himself up for the queen; multiple assassination attempts; the Ridolfi and Babington plots to depose Elizabeth and replace her with Mary, Queen of Scots; as well as other assorted conspiracies that brought down Raleigh, the Duke of Essex, and so many other court favorites.

In my eyes, this puts Eddard Stark in better context. In the end, he lost the game of thrones and ended up with his head on a spike. But he's hardly the only one, and many great lords who were far better politicians and courtiers than he was ended up dead. Which I think is something that people fail to comprehend about George R.R. Martin's work – he's not an advocate of Machiavellian statecraft. Ned Stark does the honorable thing and loses, but master schemers like Tywin or Tyrion wind up betrayed and either murdered or attempted-murdered and exiled, and Cersei's more second-string efforts result in the realm being misgoverned by loyal incompetents and herself arrested for adultery, treason, and conspiracy.

If anything, what George R.R. Martin is saying is that there are no winners in the game of thrones. The good die unluckily, the bad die deservedly, and honest efforts and clever schemes all end in disarray.

What If?

I see two interesting hypothetical possibilities in this chapter:

What if Ned had refused the king? As discussed before, a lot of the plot hinges on Ned's decision to go south with the king. However, it's quite interesting to ask what might happen if he had said no – because Robert Baratheon is going to die, Stannis Baratheon already knows about Joffrey's bastardy, and Renly is going to make a move on the throne no matter what happens. In that situation, it's all but certain that Ned Stark would be one of the few men honorable enough to respond to Stannis Baratheon's letter and declare for the least popular candidate, which means that Stannis starts with an entirely different strategic picture. Instead of having only 5,000 men and a fleet, Stannis would have the north marching on King's Landing and, potentially, the riverlands (this time not having been burnt and invaded by the Lannisters prior to the war), as well. It's still a tricky situation; Stannis's two armies are separated by the Lannisters, after all. However, he now has the option to race Renly directly to King's Landing – perhaps arriving before Tyrion can get the boom chain and wildfire completed. On a side note, when Eddard Stark gets Jeor Mormont's letter that the White Walkers are coming, the Night's Watch is getting substantial reinforcements from the north.

What if Jon stayed in the north? I find it strange that Ned can think of so few options for Jon Snow; you certainly don't get the feeling that any of the other northern houses would really care about his bastard status. Why not send Snow to foster with the Umbers, or the Karstarks, or the Manderlys? I think Jon would really have shined in a context in which he was outside of Catelyn Stark's eyes, and once the war started, he certainly would have been an excellent bannerman for Robb. On the other hand, this does likely mean that Jeor Mormont gets murdered by a wight, which leaves the Night's Watch in a difficult situation (although they do avoid losing a third of their manpower in the Great Ranging) in terms of leadership.

Book vs. Show

The major difference between the book and the TV show is that Catelyn's position is completely reversed, with her arguing for Ned to stay in the north and refuse the king. While I understand the dramatic choice, in that it emphasizes her identity as a mother (which is something that book readers tend to be harshly critical of), I think, in the end, it serves to diminish her character, because we lose an opportunity to see right at the beginning that Catelyn Stark understands the game of thrones better than her husband.

ARYA I

It wasn't fair. Sansa had everything... worse, she was beautiful. Sansa had gotten their mother's fine high cheekbones and the thick auburn hair of the Tullys. Arya took after their lord father. Her hair was a lusterless brown, and her face was long and solemn.

"If a girl can't fight, why should she have a coat of arms? [...] Girls get the arms, but not the swords. Bastards get the swords, but not the arms. I did not make the rules, little sister."

Synopsis

Arya Stark shows her gender non-conformity and some strained relations with her sister, Sansa. She runs away from Septa Mordane to join Jon Snow as they watch the Stark and Lannister boys duel in the practice yard. The practice bouts don't end well, as Joffrey displays an interest in bloodsports and a natural talent for pissing people off. Arya gets caught by her mother and Septa Mordane and has 'splaining to do.

Political Analysis

Not a lot that's directly political happens in "Arya I," given that it's a chapter from the point of view of a child who's in a domestic setting, as opposed to later, when much of the book's narrative shifts to the more explicitly political King's Landing. However, there are some small details that have real significance to the longer plot.

To begin with, the issue of heredity and the "look of the north" or the "wolf blood" that Arya and Jon Snow share more than the other Stark children. What's a bit confusing is that the "north" or the "wolf blood" seems unrelated to the First Men heritage from which the ability to warg or become a greenseer comes from. After all, Bran has the "Tully look" and has the strongest warging ability of the children. Rather, the "wolf blood" seems to refer more to whether a Stark comes out "cold" and brooding like Eddard or "hot"-tempered like his older brother, Brandon. Certainly, the "wolf blood" seems to relate to poor impulse control and strong emotions – both Jon and Arya begin the book unable to restrain their feelings of embarrassment and have a tendency to lash out violently when they are angered (by their feelings of injustice), just as Brandon did when he challenged Rhaegar to a duel to the death or Lyanna when she donned the armor of the Knight of the Laughing Tree.

However, this brings us to a larger point – fans of the books and the show are judging Eddard Stark unfairly when they say the length of time it took him to grasp the truth of Joffrey's parentage shows he's stupid or unintelligent and, in fact, are betraying their own ignorance of genetics. Consider the following facts: Robert Baratheon has three children who all look like their mother... and so does Eddard Stark. Should we then presume that Catelyn Stark has been schtupping Edmure? No.

Below, you can see a hypothetical Punnett square looking at Eddard Stark, Catelyn Stark, and their first four children together. For the sake of argument, I'm assuming that Eddard Stark has one recessive red hair gene and one dominant brown hair gene (genotype Rr), while we know that Catelyn's red hair mean she's a double recessive (rr). So what are the odds that Catelyn Stark bore three children with the "Tully look" and only one with the "look of the north," given that there's a 50/50 shot that any one child will get a recessive r from Eddard?

It's still 50/50, no matter how many times Catelyn has a child; each child is an independent event with the same genetic odds. So while Catelyn finds the coloration of her sons in comparison to Ned's alleged bastard an aggravation, she really has no reason to complain.

The same situation should apply to Ned's thought process about Cersei's children – he has no reason to suspect that Cersei is cuckolding the king, and his own experience teaches him that multiple children can favor their mothers. Here, fans are committing the arch-sin of historians – presentism. Because we know that Cersei is sleeping with her brother, we assume that it should be obvious to everyone else, but we have access to information and viewpoints that no one else, especially Ned, has access to.

This is why Eddard's gradual process of tracking down all of Robert Baratheon's heirs is actually a necessary investigative step – if Robert Baratheon has the genotype (Bb) with a recessive blond gene, than it's not statistically improbable for him to have three blond children. And the fact that say Gendry looks like his father but had a mother with blond hair isn't statistically determinative on its own – just another 50/50 shot. It's only when Ned has tracked down multiple bastards with mothers with varying genotypes who all resemble their father, and when he confirms in the book that the Baratheon lineage has no examples of recessives (which is genetically improbable, but that's a topic for a different book), that he has circumstantial evidence that Cersei has been unfaithful – and even then, he has no proof that Cersei was sleeping with her brother as opposed to any other blond man in Westeros.

Given that his accusation would be not merely one of gross treason on Cersei's part, but also of an abomination in the eyes of the gods, and that Ned Stark will have to prove his accusations at trial, the methodical nature of his investigation is actually a point in his favor.

One interesting point that comes up in this chapter is the question of whether Joffrey knows or suspects about his parentage. In the books, Joffrey reacts with real anger when Eddard proclaims his bastardy; in the show, he's now been confronted with the rumor, and his actions seem to suggest he believes that it might be true. And yet... Joffrey's coat of arms have "on one side... the crowned stage of the royal House; on the other, the lion of Lannister... He makes his mother's house equal in honor to the king's." The sword he wants to fight with is called *Lion's Tooth*, not *Stag's Horn*. Given that Cersei certainly knows the truth, it's exceedingly stupid of her to allow her son to so over-emphasize his Lannister heritage when the truth of her son's heritage is possibly known to Lysa Arryn and Stannis Baratheon. Then again, given her son's... questionable sanity, it's possible that Joffrey would have done so, anyway.

Historical Analysis

In "Arya I," we're given an interesting scene where Joffrey antagonizes Robb Stark over the question of blunt versus bladed swords, provoking Robb to a profane outburst. It's interesting partly because it foreshadows Joffrey's taste for sadism and his twisted and insecure ideas about maturity and how Robb's temper is going to be a problem later on in the series. However, I think it also makes an interesting parallel to the obscure origins of the York and Lancaster feud that began the Wars of the Roses.

While the York and Lancaster feud was grounded in Henry Bolingbroke's (son of Jon of Gaunt, the brother of Edward the Black Prince) coup against Richard II and the violation of the feudal order of succession, and the conflict between Margaret of Anjou and the Duke of Somerset's francophile peace party and York's pro-war and pro-reform party, there were also personal conflicts that underlay the larger political division. The Beauforts had always hated the Yorks, and the Percys (the House of Northumberland) and the Nevilles (the house of Salisbury and Warwick) fought each other privately before the civil war properly broke out. In Shakespeare's *Henry VI* (Act II, Scene IV), there is a famous scene in which Richard Plantagent, the Earl of Cambridge (later, Duke of York), and the Duke of Somerset, the Lancaster champion, quarrel in a temple garden and call upon the lords of the land to choose one side or the other by plucking a rose off of a brier.

The initial conflict is a selfish one – which of them has the better claim to the Dukedom of York – but the arguments towards the two sides escalate to the point where Richard taunts his opponent, "Now, Somerset, where is your argument?" and Somerset replies, "Here in my scabbard, meditating that/Shall dye your white rose in a bloody red." By the end, the earl of Warwick prophecies that "this brawl to-day/Grown to this faction in the Temple-garden/Shall send between the red rose and the white/A thousand souls to death and deadly night." Here we see one of the great dangers of the feudal system – because political power is so intertwined in the persons of the nobility, their personal rivalries and injuries become casus belli between the regions they represent, are named for, and, in the feudal mindset in some mystical way, were.

Westeros's equivalent to the Wars of the Roses could have easily begun in such a trivial fashion (here's my <u>What If?</u> for the chapter). Had Robb Stark and Joffrey Baratheon dueled with live blades instead of wooden swords, it's highly likely that Joffrey would have attempted real injury and that Robb would have won the bout and injured Joffrey. While King Robert would have considered dueling scars in the practice yard to be an ordinary part of growing up for young noblemen, from what we see later, in the "duel" between Joffrey and Arya, the Lannister reaction to any injury is violent and immediate.

Similarly, there are interesting parallels between Prince Joffrey and another royal accused of bastardy, Edward of Lancaster, Prince of Wales – the only child of King Henry VI and his French queen, Margaret d'Anjou. Because of Henry's extreme piety (which especially manifested itself as a horror of public lewdness) and his recurrent bouts of insanity, which Yorkists argued overlapped with the conception of Prince Edward, it was widely rumored that Edward was the son of Edmund Beaufort, the Second Duke of Somerset, who was a leading Lancastrian (in part because his father had been the man who lost the Dukedom of York to Richard Plantagenet) and who was himself a grandson of Jon of Gaunt and, thus, a cousin to King Henry VI. Edward's parentage was the central conflict between York and Lancaster, as York argued that Edward was a bastard and, thus, he himself was the rightful heir to the throne, which convinced Queen Margaret that York was not merely a dynastic threat, but an active traitor.

The Prince of Wales, a handsome blond youth, was known for his fondness for blood; as one chronicler writes, "this boy, though only thirteen years of age, already talks of nothing but of cutting off heads or making war, as if he had everything in his hands or was the god of battle." At the battle of Wakefield, Richard of York (the closest equivalent to Eddard Stark dying) and his son, Edmund of Rutland, were murdered, and their heads were placed on spikes on the walls of York with a paper crown on Richard's head so that York could overlook the town of York – all before the approving eyes of the Prince. And, like Joffrey, the Prince of Wales came to a bad end – more on which later.

To prevent this chapter from growing overly long, I want to save the discussion of medieval gender roles and war for a later chapter, but

Arya's desire for a sword is definitely noteworthy.

Book vs. Show

This chapter is both condensed and moved around in the show – Arya runs away from her sewing to shoot a bow rather than swing a sword (ironically in the books, Arya's skill with a sword is not matched with any dexterity with a bow), and the parental reaction is rather more indulgent; the sword-fighting between the Stark and Lannister boys is omitted altogether.

While it might have been nice to see that, I think this is an example of the need for narrative economy in television and the importance of adapting in adaptations – while we can have an image of Robb and Joffrey fighting in our minds without a problem, a fight between Richard Madden and Jack Gleeson would look very different, given their respective ages and sizes.

BRAN II

"Stannis and Renly are one thing, and Eddard Stark is quite another... my husband grows more restless every day. Having Stark beside him will only make him worse... how long till he decides to put me aside for some new Lyanna?"

"We ought to count ourselves fortunate... give me honorable enemies rather than ambitious ones, and I'll sleep more easily by night."

Synopsis

King Robert, Prince Joffrey, Lord Eddard Stark, Robb Stark, Benjen Stark, Ser Rodrik and Jory Cassel, Theon Greyjoy, and, for some reason, Tyrion Lannister go out on their last hunt before leaving for King's Landing. A knight-crazy Bran is left in the castle but feels somewhat ambivalent about leaving his home or naming his direwolf. Bran goes climbing around some very significant Winterfell landmarks, until he overhears a very significant conversation between Queen Cersei and Jaime Lannister until he is discovered, and the best swordsman in the Seven Kingdoms decides to attempt murder on a seven-year-old.

Political Analysis

For my purposes, this chapter is one of the most invaluable in the entire novel, because it's one of the few times in which we see participants in a political conspiracy talking openly about what they are doing and how they perceive the other political actors in Westeros as opposed to trying to convince someone with their acting, because they think they're totally unobserved (which is a bit of an obvious literary ploy, but given that the two people in the conversation are reacting to new developments, it's certainly plausible) – which happens really only once again in the novel.

And we learn a lot in this conversation. We learn that the Lannisters are contemplating the death of the king, that they attempted to take Robert Arryn hostage in order to buy Lysa Arryn's silence, that they consider Renly, Stannis, and Littlefinger to be their enemies, and that they see Stark as dangerous because Robert trusts him, because Stark has no loyalty to Joffrey, and because Stark may reinvigorate the king to the point where he replaces the queen with a Lyanna look-alike (and we find out later that Renly and Loras are trying to inveigle Margaery Tyrell into the king's bed).

This gives us a fairly good overview of what I'll be referring to as the *Lannister Conspiracy*. The purpose of the conspiracy is quite simple – to place a Lannister on the Iron Throne as quickly as possible, before the truth of Joffrey's birth can be exposed, and then thereafter to make the Lannister bloc hegemonic by appointing Tywin as Hand and Jaime Lannister as lord commander of the Kingsguard. I think the element to have the king killed is a recent addition – after all, Cersei had a lot of opportunity to poison Robert, but she knew that it would have to happen at a time when she could deal with the Hand, who would be the most likely candidate to stand in as regent, rather than Cersei. It's also likely that Cersei would have preferred to wait for Joffrey to come of age before killing the king to avoid the danger of a non-Lannister regent.

This conspiracy shows clear signs of being put together rapidly once it became clear that Jon Arryn was investigating Joffrey's paternity – there doesn't seem to have been a plan on how to deal with Jon Arryn until after his death (unless the Lannisters contracted his assassination with Petyr Baelish, which seems unlikely, as I'll discuss in a second) or how to deal with the Renly/Tyrell threat, they let Lysa Arryn and Stannis Baratheon slip out of the capital, and there's very poor information control within the conspiracy (in part because Cersei can't risk Daddy finding out about her and Jaime's little indiscretions), which leaves Maester Pycelle dangerously out of the loop, given how much incriminating information he has on hand. Cersei's limited skills in covert conspiracy show in her incredibly risky decision to continue her affair in Winterfell and then to throw Bran from the Tower – while the two chose an unused tower and most of the men were absent at the hunt, the entire female population of the castle, as well as various guards and servants, were still present and could have discovered them instead of Bran, and Cersei and Jaime were conspicuously nowhere to be seen at the time of the "accident."

We also learn a lot about what the Lannister Conspiracy knows about the other political actors. They know that Jon Arryn and Stannis Baratheon were investigating Joffrey's birth, but they don't know whether either of them have any proof or what to do about it – and this point is very important. At the end of the day, we're not dealing with a constitutional monarchy; if Robert wants to violate custom and have Cersei killed for adultery, incest, and treason, no one can stop him, and Cersei knows it (this is something that the audience and even Ned Stark seem to forget). They know that Renly is trying to oust the Lannisters by planting a Tyrell in Robert's bed, which is a major threat, because their main hold on power comes through Cersei's ability to nag Robert into appointing Lannisters. Given that Cersei doesn't really have a hold on Robert's emotions or appetites, which is really a weakness on Cersei's part in terms of their control over the monarchy, their passivity here seems to be a signature of the Conspiracy – Cersei tends to react rather than act, which is something of a double-edged sword. It's extremely interesting that they consider Littlefinger to be an enemy or rival of some sort, although, unfortunately, we don't learn anything about why they may think that; whatever it may have been, it wasn't enough to prevent them from working with Littlefinger to capture the gold cloaks before Ned's abortive coup. Critically, they don't seem to know anything about what Varys is up to – and it's this intelligence failure which is the most dangerous.

Finally, we get to the issue of how the Lannisters view Eddard Stark as Hand. There's three things that worry them: first, Eddard is someone who's loyal to Robert personally, not the Iron Throne, and has been known to overthrow kings he believes to be beyond the pale of acceptability. The Lannisters are basically right about this; while Ned's rebellion against King Aerys II was prompted by the Targaryens' attack on his family and himself, when push came to shove, he made the choice to oust Joffrey and replace him with Stannis. Second, they fear Robert will listen to Eddard Stark. This turns out to be more ambiguous; Eddard is unable to get Robert to cancel the Hand's Tourney or to shift him on the Wardenship of the East, although he ultimately does get Robert to listen to him about Daenerys's assassination, albeit too late. The tricky thing here is that it's extremely unlikely that these three things are the only issues that Eddard Stark dealt with as Hand, but they're the only plot-essential issues that we get to see in our few scenes of his interaction with the small council or the king. Third, they fear that Robert will get restless and invigorated by the presence of his childhood companion, which might prompt him to welcome Margaery Tyrell into his bed. This may well have been a genuine longer-term fear, but there just wasn't enough time for us to see this play out.

Historical Analysis

The Renly/Tyrell plot to inveigle Margaery Tyrell into the bed of Robert Baratheon, along with her later trial for adultery, is the main reason I think the best historical parallel for Margaery Tyrell is Anne Boleyn. Both were dark-haired beauties who had been schooled in courtly arts and manners in the very heart of chivalry (in Anne's case, in France; in Margaery's, the Reach, which closely resembles late Medieval France), both were used as political pawns by ambitious relatives (Renly, Loras, and Mace standing in for Thomas Cranmer, George Boleyn, Viscount Rochford, and Thomas Boleyn, the Earl of Whiltshire), and both showed an aptitude for influencing monarchs quietly to their political ends (although Margaery had the easier task in Tommen than Anne did in Henry). Both were accused of adultery in virtually identical indictments – Anne was accused of adultery with a Flemish musician, Mark Smeaton, a number of courtiers, and her brother, George Boleyn; Margaery was accused of adultery with the Blue Bard, a number of knights, and Cersei considers naming Loras and Garlan first of all before she realizes that bringing up incest is perhaps not a wise course of action for a woman living in an extremely fragile glass house.

Like episode two, season two of *Game of Thrones*, Anne Boleyn's historical example points to the extremely gendered nature of political power in the Medieval world; not only was the patriarchy explicitly held out as the ideal of government, religion, society, and family, but queens' political power was ultimately dependent on their sexuality (not merely their physical beauty, but also their skill with the rhetoric and movements of courtly love, especially their facility with witty repartee) and their fertility (the paramount importance of a male heir, but also the reality that queens could best exercise political power through their children). As a result, a queen's position was never safe if she was seen to fall short on either of those qualities. While the divorce that Anne Boleyn prompted was unique, annulments, the legitimization of royal bastards, even bigamy was known throughout the courts of Europe (the position of royal mistress was formalized at several), a constant sword of Damocles over the heads of many a queen. At the same time, a mistress's life offered equal risk – as the case of Anne Boleyn shows, becoming the king's mistress offered landed wealth and titles to one's entire family despite the hint of scandal (and even then, it was not uncommon for a king to find a wealthy and compliant husband for his mistress), but at the same time, it also put a major target on one's back. A mistress only held power as long as she held the king's interest (although, in the case of royal mistresses like Diane de Poitiers, this could be for a long time and with more than one king), and kings are notoriously fickle when it comes to women.

A final point that I think sometimes escapes fans of the series: while we inhabitants of the 21st century are used to thinking of adultery as a personal transgression, in the Medieval era, it was very much still a criminal offense punishable by whipping, mutilation (often of the nose or ears, symbolically attacking the source of vanity and lust), and death. This went doubly for royal adulterers; in law, crimes were not acts committed in violation of a statute as much as they were an attack on the sacred body of the king, whose "majesty" from which laws derived their force was deemed to be a physical quality. To commit adultery was to attack the king's person in the most egregious form possible, given the implications for the line of succession – the fear was that someone would do what Cersei did deliberately, to change the succession by cuckolding the king and denying him legitimate heirs. Cersei's plot certainly did not lack for ambition – in one generation, she was trying to bring a purely Lannister dynasty to the Iron Throne, and, so far, she's succeeded.

What If?

There are two main counterfactuals that "Bran II" suggests.

What if Bran isn't thrown from the tower? This is perhaps the most obvious divergence from the major consequence of the chapter, and it has some interesting longer-term consequences. Firstly, it means that Bran doesn't get crippled, and likely obviates Joffrey's assassination attempt – this makes the Stark-Lannister feud much more long-term, since it means that Catelyn Stark has no reason to go to King's Landing, which means that, in all likelihood, Tyrion never gets captured, and it means that Bran likely goes to King's Landing with dreams of knighthood in his eyes (I like to think that Eddard might have arranged for Bran to squire with Ser Barristan, which would possibly have led to a Stark in Daenerys's retinue). It may also mean that Bran's greenseer abilities lay dormant, although it's unclear how important the trauma of his injury was in the awakening process, or whether Brynden Bloodraven would have been able to open Bran's third eye regardless. It also means that Eddard starts his investigation knowing much earlier what's going on with Cersei and Jaime (since Bran's inability to keep promises is foreshadowed in this chapter, and I don't see a seven-year-old boy being able to keep this under wraps) and is thus less likely to be led down blind alleys by Littlefinger – instead of pursuing a mystery, he's collecting evidence for a formal charge of treason. I think this last issue lays to rest Cersei's protestations of innocence in his maiming; at the end of the day, she and Jaime are too exposed to leave it up to chance that knowledge of her incestuous adultery can further spread, which means it probably was never going to happen that Bran actually makes it down unharmed.

What if Renly's plan paid off? Had Renly managed to place Margaery Tyrell in Robert's bed, this would have been a quite potent threat to the Lannisters' position in King's Landing. Margaery is very skilled at the arts of courtly love, and Robert is known to be rather lavish with those he loves – it's likely that several Tyrells make their way onto the small council, and the Tyrells replace the Lannisters as the king's "bank." This political power would have been quite tenuous given the presence of Joffrey – had Robert installed Margaery as the king's mistress/second-wife-to-be, it's likely that Cersei would have accelerated her assassination attempts in order to get Joffrey on the Iron Throne as soon as possible. In this situation, it's absolutely in the interest of the Tyrells to displace Cersei's children in place of a Baratheon/Tyrell heir, which brings in the question as to whether Renly actually knows about Cersei's adultery (given his constant sarcasm in *Clash of Kings*, it's a bit hard to say). While Eddard would have likely viewed Renly's plot with a very cool eye, especially if Renly had brought up the memory of Lyanna, he would ultimately back a legitimate heir over Joffrey, and with Tyrell military assistance, his coup might well have succeeded.

Book vs. Show

Ultimately, Benioff and Weiss decided against explicit exposition, which is understandable in an episode heavy with the same, although I do think something is lost when we don't see the Lannisters not just an inexplicably unnatural force of malice but as political actors in a political environment with real enemies around them.

Another thing we lose is some key foreshadowing moments – Bran is frightened of the heart tree, since "trees ought not have eyes... or leaves that looked like hands," which calls to mind his eventual use of that very tree in *Dance with Dragons*; he prefers to go barefoot when climbing because "it made him feel as if he had four hands instead of two," which is reminiscent of his warging into Summer beginning in *Clash of Kings*; and he describes the secret tunnels of Winterfell in great detail, which makes me think that a key part of the "Battle of Ice" in *Winds of Winter* will involve Bran giving Stannis a way past Winterfell's walls when Stannis comes to the godswood to execute Theon.

TYRION I

During all the terrible long years of his childhood, only Jaime had ever shown him the smallest measure of affection or respect, and for that, Tyrion was willing to forgive him most everything.

Synopsis

Tyrion spends a long night reading, slaps Joffrey around a bit to work up an appetite for breakfast – where he spends time verbally fencing with his brother, Jaime, and sister, Cersei – and chows down on good northern fare and some food for thought.

Political Analysis

It's an interesting bit of foreshadowing that the first we actually see of Tyrion from his own eyes is him reading Armydion's *Engines of War*, an early sign of Tyrion's application of his formidable intellect to military subjects. He might even have read something about the uses of boom chains in that book. Between that, his book on changing seasons, and his later book on the properties, we have the portrait of a polymath autodidact – which brings up the question of why Tywin never dealt with his hated son by sending him off to the Citadel to become a maester, which might have suited the both of them. Most likely, Aerys II making Jaime a member of the Kingsguard forced Tywin to keep his only heir close to hand rather than losing him to the maester's oath of celibacy.

While there's not much official politics in this chapter, we do get a very clear insight into Tyrion as a political observer, and the internal politics of the Lannister family. Our immediate impression is that Tyrion is very observant, capable of forming conclusions about the character of his contemporaries that others cannot: unlike the rest of his family, he can tell that his nephew, Joffrey, is not merely stupid, petulant, and vain, but also sadistic, cowardly, and totally unsuited to his future estate, a tyrant waiting to happen. Similarly, he sees behind Myrcella's fair features to see that she's basically a good person, unlike her mother's spiteful character. In regards to his older siblings, Tyrion can tell from a momentary glance that they had something to do with Bran's fall – and despite the abuse he's endured from his family, Tyrion understands his own interests well enough to say nothing and support the house of Lannister (while still maintaining an interest in what actually happened). Ironically, Tyrion is most like Tywin in that he stands for House Lannister rather than its individual members; while he's closest to Jaime, he's not blind to the man's flaws, and he's willing to forgive him "most anything," but not everything.

We also see from this chapter how dangerous Cersei and Jaime's actions were - if Bran woke up and remembered what he saw (which I'm a bit tired of waiting to happen, to be honest), they're stranded in Winterfell, far from the heart of Lannister power, and they've committed a gross breach of the sacred rule of guest right (whether this actually results in punishment from the gods is a good question for debate).

Historical Analysis

Finding a good historical parallel for Tyrion is a bit difficult in that George R.R. Martin has infused his favorite character with such a unique personality, and that he's brought in several influences from different historical periods. The best I can come up with is that Tyrion resembles a mix of Claudius and Richard III. Like Tyrion, Claudius was born with disabilities (a limp, stutter, and slight deafness) that led to his family ostracizing him yet who turned out to be a talented administrator, especially when it came to expanding the empire (he conquered Britain, Thrace, and Judea, among other nations), public works (two major aquaducts and the port of Ostia being some of the most prominent), and judicial matters. Similarly, Richard III was depicted by Tudor propagandists as having a hunchback and withered arm and leg as outward signs of his inward corruption, whereas, in reality, he was a quite conscientious monarch, who promoted economic development in the North of England and who created legal reforms on behalf of the poor, including the first courts where the destitute could be heard and the practice of bail. In both men, we see how disability, either genuine or invented, could be used to either protect oneself, in the case of Claudius, who survived all of his murderous family by pretending to be dimwitted, or to injure someone's reputation, as in the case of Richard III.

Disability studies is a huge subfield within Medieval history, and a very contentious one, at that, but one thing we can say about the period that George R.R. Martin drew most of his influences from is that they tended (although it wasn't universal, by any means, and there are many complexities) to view disabilities as a sign of sin, a judgment of God on the body. Hence the move by Tudor propagandists to turn Richard III's having broken his shoulder as a young man into a hunchback with withered limbs. We can see the same thing with Tyrion - part of Tywin's hatred stems from the circumstances of Tyrion's birth and the death of Joanna Lannister, but it equally stems from Tywin seeing Tyrion as a mark of dishonor on Tywin's house and Tywin personally. And as we'll see later, this unfortunately limits Tyrion's political effectiveness, since it becomes very easy to propagandize Tyrion into a murdering imp rather than the man who saved King's Landing.

The other thing we see from this chapter and from history is that the combination of family and power that you find in monarchy has a profound and often harmful effect on people. Tyrion's upbringing is quite traumatic, but his historical counterparts could boast equally horrific experiences: Claudius's father was possibly murdered at the behest of his Uncle Tiberius, his mother called him a monster and plainly hated him, he witnessed the paranoid Tiberius conduct wave after wave of executions, he barely survived the incestuous murderous insanity of his nephew, Caligula, who used him as the Roman equivalent of a Medieval fool, and on and on (really, read Robert Graves – it's quite impressive). Richard III's father and eldest brother died in the Wars of the Roses; his foster father, the earl of Warwick, betrayed his brother, Edward IV; and his middle brother, George of Clarence, betrayed Edward and Richard repeatedly and was executed for treason (although not in a but of wine, as the legend goes).

What If?

I see only one major hypothetical here – **what if Bran had died as a result of his fall?** As I've said, it's a bit hard to know what would have happened, given how incomplete Bran's mystical storyline is. What we do know is that it would have forestalled Joffrey's assassination attempt, which would have meant that Catelyn would not have left for King's Landing, which means that Tyrion doesn't get arrested at the Inn of the Crossroads. This likely delays the outbreak of Stark-Lannister hostilities, since there's no longer a pretext for Tywin to begin raiding the riverlands or for Eddard Stark to be attacked by Jaime Lannister.

As I'll discuss later, this last event not happening might have had huge consequences for the plot.

Book vs. Show

There's really only two major changes here. The first, interestingly, is that Tyrion's more rakish side is emphasized by having us first encounter him through his eyes in a brothel and then again waking up in the kennels, while his intellectual side is shunted to his later scene with Jon Snow – I suppose it's a change that makes sense, given Peter Dinklage's wonderful comedic talents, and that it avoids a repetition in that later scene, but I would have liked a bit of foreshadowing of what he's going to do with his knowledge of engines of war (maybe this could happen in the second season?). The other is that the role of the direwolves keeping Bran alive is made more subliminal and suggestive in the later scene in which Robb opens the windows so that Bran can hear the howling of the wolves. I don't really have much to say about that other than the obvious fact that it's better to show, not tell, especially in visual mediums.

JON II

Robb was in the middle of it, shouting commands with the best of them. He seemed to have grown of late, as if Bran's fall and his mother's collapse had somehow made him stronger.

"I wish you were coming with us."

"Different roads sometimes lead to the same castle."

Synopsis

Jon Snow makes his goodbyes before leaving for the Night's Watch – first to Bran, where he deals awkwardly with Catelyn Stark, next more amicably parting with Robb – then brings Arya a going-away present.

Political Analysis

Similar to the previous chapter, "Jon II" gives us more of a glimpse into family politics as Jon Snow visits the Stark siblings (all except Rickon, naturally). We see a bit of his relationship with Bran, whom he shares a certain romantic idealism and love of adventure with; to Bran, the brotherhood of the Night's Watch is a dark parallel to the Kingsguard, "almost as good as going south with the king." The Wall is an exotic location he very much wanted to visit, something that the show actually brings up here that the book doesn't.

Jon's relationship with Robb is more complicated, as we might expect between the heir and the bastard. As we saw in "Bran I" and "Jon I," the two are often matched against each other as rivals in the arts of war, and there's a strong undercurrent of competition between the two; for all their camaraderie, one will always be Stark and the other Snow. At the same time, the competition exists alongside a strong rapport – Robb seems to pick up on Jon's emotions regarding Bran and Catelyn, and Jon, in turn, notices the beginning of his brother's transformation into leadership, which, like Jon's, begins unexpectedly, amidst a crisis. Given that Robb's last command as King of the North was to legitimize his brother and name him as heir should he have no offspring, the relationship must have been quite strong, indeed.

By contrast, Jon's relationship with Arya, as many have said, stems from their mutual position as half-way outsiders. Given how much ink has been spilled analyzing this particular facet of their relationship, I think I'll let it pass and focus instead on what might be an interesting bit of foreshadowing near the end of the chapter where Arya vocalizes her desire to have Jon together with herself and Sansa, and Jon responds by saying, "Different roads sometimes lead to the same castle." While part of the complaints from fans about *A Feast for Crows* and *A Dance with Dragons* was that the plot seems to be atomizing the characters into a thousand different unconnected places, I actually think we're starting to see movement back towards the same castle - namely, Winterfell. Consider that Littlefinger is planning to marry Sansa to Harry the Heir once Robert Arryn dies and use the forces of the Vale to stake her claims to the north (which might get difficult, given that Sansa lacks the direwolf that northmen take as a seal of approval); that Davos Seaworth is sailing to Skagos to retrieve Rickon Stark so that the Manderlys have a Stark in Winterfell once again; and that Arya Stark has advanced in her training such that she now is entrusted with the face-changing arts of the Faceless Men, while her wolf waits for her at the Gods Eye (a place with many heart trees, and much potential for Bran Stark to act). It may well be that the surviving Starks are at long last on their way home, as they were always meant to be.

Historical Analysis

I did want to say one thing about Arya Stark getting her Needle and the larger question of medieval gender roles. While it's true that the prevailing role for medieval high-born women was closer to Sansa's ideal of ladyship than Arya's desire to be a swordswoman, it's not a totally hegemonic prohibition. Arya isn't an absolutely unprecedented misfit, but rather part of a distinct minority group of medieval warrior women who managed to break through the "glass ceiling" of their time. While they were generally not supposed to personally take part in battle, highborn ladies were expected to defend their lord's castles against siege if their husbands were away, and if they were feudal heiresses, they could call upon their vassals to serve them in the field - as the Empress Matilda, Eleanor of Acquitaine, and Margaret d'Anjou all did. Nor was Joan of Arc a statistical aberration - Sichelgaita of Salerno, Isabel of Conches, and a number of other women donned armor and fought in battle.

The point here isn't to diminish Arya's struggle against gender restrictions that are quite real, but rather to note that George R.R. Martin's realism is a literary technique, not a camera. What is achieved is not absolute fidelity to the world as-is, but a kind of hyper-realism that rubs our nose in the dirt and the grime, the poverty and bigotry, as a way of deconstructing Romantic conceptions about what the Middle Ages were like that have been foundational to the fantasy genre from the beginning. What Martin is doing is reminding us that there is no such thing as a rightful king, that peasants weren't happy and humble, that knights are only noble if they want to be, that beauty is not a reflection of character – and he's doing it by showing us a heightened, slightly exaggerated sense of frustration and aggravation from Arya's perspective. She's not completely wrong – very few people in A Song of Ice and Fire are – but the bear women of the Mormonts are real, as are Myra Reed and Mya Stone, Brienne of Tarth, and the relative egalitarianism of Dorne. It's just that, like most of the POVs in the book, she's reacting most strongly to what she sees and experiences.

What If?

I don't really see any good hypotheticals in this chapter, so I'll just say there are some really good ones in "Eddard II" that I'm working on.

Book vs. Show

There's actually a lot that's different in this scene between the book and the TV show, and some of it shows improvement in adaptation, while other choices are a bit more questionable. For example, the order of Jon's goodbyes – in the book, Jon says goodbye to Bran, then Robb, then Arya, which means that we get through the very abrasive interaction with Catelyn first and see that he actually has a fairly good relationship with most of his family that he's about to lose; in the show, Jon meets with Arya first, then Bran, then Robb, which is a bit more muddled in terms of showing an arc of different interactions.

I do think that the change to his scene with Catelyn was probably a necessary change from the book, given how so many of the fans base their extreme dislike of Catelyn on the emotional damage she inflicts on a fan-favorite character. I think this misses the point of what Martin was trying to get across in their encounter, which is that this kind of reaction is absolutely a normal reaction to grief and loss. Part of the audience reaction, I think, therefore is a kind of denial that they'd ever act the same and projecting their guilt that they probably would onto Catelyn. In reality, the second stage of the Kübler-Ross model is anger for a reason – we look for someone to blame, we demand "why me?" and "why not you?" when we experience a sudden, wrenching loss in our lives. The obverse is also true – when we escape loss, there is a sense of guilt that arises from our non-vocalized thought "thank god that's not me." So, in the end, given how strongly emotional visual mediums are compared to the written word, this shift was probably for the good if Catelyn Stark is to remain at all sympathetic as a character.

Another thing I like about the adaptation is that we have a more sustained transformation in Robb Stark as compared to the book, where Robb tends to switch back and forth between being a rather cartoonish boy, prone to waving his sword around at the slightest provocation, and a more mature figure. It may be more realistic for a 15-year-old boy to act this way, but it doesn't lend itself to a good narrative arc. In the show, Robb is seen as becoming more mature almost immediately and continuing to shift in this direction as he leads men onto the field, which I think works better and gives us a more interesting character.

Finally, we have the addition of Jon's farewell scene with Eddard, which I think is a major improvement, both in terms of highlighting the R+L=J theory, which is necessary given the excision of Eddard's interior monologue and flashbacks, and in giving Jon and Eddard some interaction together, which is something missing from the books. It's not really believable that Eddard would let his "son" leave for the Watch without even saying goodbye, and yet we don't get this scene in the book.

DAENERYS II

Daenerys Targaryen wed Khal Drogo with fear and barbaric splendor in a field beyond the walls of Pentos, for the Dothraki believed that all things of importance in a man's life must be done beneath the open sky.

The horselords might put on rich fabrics and sweet perfumes when they visited the Free Cities, but out under the open sky, they kept the old ways.

Synopsis

Daenerys Targaryen has a lively wedding to Khal Drogo, receives some rather significant wedding gifts from Viserys, Jorah, and Illyrio, and consummates her marriage.

Political Analysis

The second Daenerys chapter gives us another short glimpse into the *Varys/Illyrio Conspiracy*, especially regarding the timing, which allows us to refine our model from before. While trying to unruffle Viserys's feathers (scales?) over the Dothraki tradition of waiting for the crones of Vaes Dothrak to do their divination (although we learn later on that Drogo's stalling has a lot more do to with wanting Daenerys's child to be born before he goes on the campaign, which adds a layer of wiliness to the khal that's easy to miss), Illyrio argues that the prince should be willing to wait "another few months" or, even, "another few years."

Given what we learn during his later conversation with Varys, Illyrio's preferred timeline for the outbreak of war is at least nine months after Ned Stark's installation as Hand. He wants that child to be born so that the Dothraki can be brought into play, but it's not clear why he wouldn't want the Starks and Lannisters to wear each other out before the Targaryen forces arrive (possibly he was afraid that one side would win too quickly and have a chance to consolidate its grasp on power).

It may well be that Illyrio wanted to give himself time to get Aegon and the Golden Company the time to unite with the Dothraki, or that part of the illusionists' plan was to win bloodlessly by dividing the country between the Starks and Lannisters and Baratheon, delegitimize the sitting monarch by revealing the truth of Joffrey's birth and then confronting a disunited Westeros with an overwhelming army. This stick would be counterbalanced by a picture-perfect Targaryen king, queen, and heir (possibly Drogo "dies gloriously in battle" and Rhaego is passed off as Aegon's and Daenerys's child?).

A second theme we have here is the complication of our view of the Dothraki – presented here as a sophisticated, culturally flexible people who can put on "rich fabrics and sweet perfumes" when they visit their second homes among the palaces of Pentos, yet who still hold to their own culture where everything is done under the open sky. This is also a wealthy culture – Drogo personally owns a thousand horses, an opulent palace, and many slaves – and this wealth comes not merely from conquest but, rather, from their integrated role in the Essos economy. The Dothraki act as a kind of outsourced mercenary force, paid tributes by rival city states to go sack a different city; they are the chief producers of slaves for Astapor, Yunkai, and Mereen, who, in turn, export mercenaries, gladiators, and pleasure slaves for a vast continental marketplace in unfree labor, as well as using their labor to produce wine, olive oil, and other staple crops.

Ironically, both Daenerys and some of the audience miss some of this complexity – in part because George R.R. Martin chose to give us our initial glimpse into Dothraki culture through the eyes of a sheltered young woman in the midst of severe culture shock. Despite the fact that Daenerys knows all of these facts, the heightened impression she has is exactly the Orientalized image that critics of the HBO show criticized: "She was afraid of the Dothraki, whose ways seemed alien and monstrous, as if they were beasts in human skin and not true men at all." As Daenerys begins to acculturate to her new culture, both she and the audience begin to discover the diversity and depth of the Dothraki.

And one thing that Daenerys begins to learn is how the surprising nature of becoming a khaleesi literally elevates her above her brother. While khaleesi do not carry arakh, whip, or bow, she does have her own guards and command over the *khalasar* through her husband – as the Dothraki say, "her place [is] by the side of the khal," not behind. (And, eventually, as one of the dosh khaleen, she might have wielded enormous spiritual and political power.) And it's appropriate that this is the last chapter where Daenerys is truly afraid of her brother, and yet that fear only comes in dreams and sudden flashbacks where "the fear came back to her then, with her brother's words. She felt like a child once more, only 13 and all alone," because after this day, Daenerys is no longer alone but part of a great *khalasar*.

Historical Analysis

One of George R.R. Martin's innovations that sadly didn't make it onto the screen is the way in which he both displays and subverts the traditional fantasy tropes about barbarians and barbarism. These tropes are one of fantasy's troubling inheritances from our predecessors – J.R.R. Tolkien's depiction of the Easterlings and Haradrim are at least an unconscious reflection of racial ideas within the British Empire he grew up in; R.E. Howard combined his Texas border heritage of animus towards African-Americans and Native Americans with an idiosyncratic form of "noble savage" thinking to create his Hyborian Age.

At the same time, the historical reality is that the Medieval Europe which the fantasy genre was built on was profoundly shaped by invasions of Arabs (who conquered much of Spain and large parts of southern Italy), Ottoman Turks (who conquered much of southeastern Europe, all the way up to the gates of Vienna), the Vikings (who terrorized Europe and conquered Normandy, the "Danelaw" in England, coastal Ireland, Sicily, and Naples), Mongols, and other peoples. The cultural implications of these invasions were tremendous – the Frankish victory of Charles Martel over the Moors at Tours was critical in limiting the penetration of Islamic culture into Europe and creating a Frankish (and, later, French) identity as the defenders of a new thing called "Christendom" against outside forces; the Viking invasions spurred apocalyptic and millennial thinking within the Catholic Church; the national myths of the Hungarians, Transylvanians, Romanians, Serbs, Poles, Russians, and more were all built around narratives of resistance to foreign conquerors.

Any fantasy work with a foot in the Middle Ages has to reflect this history. And yet, the line between "Christendom" and "barbarism" was never simple – Medieval Europe was built out of the invasions of Goths, Franks, and Vandals into the Roman Empire, just as Westeros was built out of the invasions of the First Men, Andals, Rhoynar, and Valyrians.

Rather than a climactic fall into a Dark Age that historians from the Renaissance era pictured it as (in part, reacting to contemporary invasions of Italy by the French, Spanish, and the Holy Roman Emperor), there was an enormous amount of acculturation both before and after the fall of Rome – and many Goths, Franks, and Vandals spent quite some time living in the Roman Empire before they took it over. Alaric the Goth, who sacked Rome in AD 410, had served in the imperial auxiliaries and sought the position of commander-in-chief of the Roman army as part of his demands during the second siege of Rome. When the Ostragoths under their king, Flavius Odoacer, completed the conquest of Rome in 476, they kept the Senate in place, formally acknowledged the suzerainty of the Eastern Roman Empire, and took on Latin names and Roman dress.

And it went on and on – Spanish and Italian cultures were deeply influenced by Moorish and Arabian art, architecture, agriculture, and language, as were their peers to the east. Despite our rather schematic view of European relations with other cultures summed up in the image of the Crusades, the reality was that there was just as much commerce and cultural exchange as there was conquest. It's that complexity of experience, the blurring of the lines between two civilizations, the ambiguity between "invasion" and "internal political coup," that Martin hinted at in his depiction of the Dothraki, and that Benioff and Weiss didn't manage to get across in their depiction of the Dothraki arriving in Pentos.

What If?

Unfortunately, I don't really see any hypotheticals here that I didn't cover in "Daenerys I." Perhaps some readers could suggest some?

Book vs. Show

As I've already suggested, the wedding and the bedding are one of the biggest divergences between the book and the TV show. However, unlike certain podcasts that I normally quite like, I think the outcome is more complex than a flat failure. It's true that they've excised much of the complexity of the Dothraki culture; however, I don't think it's the multiculturalism that's the problem. The Dothraki are a slave-owning culture, and any slave culture is going to have a large, multi-ethnic population of slaves. The problem is that we don't get to see the Dothraki in Pentos as sophisticated, wealthy, acculturated people – and then the reveal of their maintenance of their original culture, with all of its violent, rapey, and slave-owning rough edges.

However, I do think (and I'm aware that this is going to be controversial, so bear with me) that the change to the consummation between Daenerys and Drogo makes sense dramatically. I've always found it a bit odd that the two of them have this rather tender, albeit awkward, first night, then Drogo relentlessly rapes her, then she learns how to "tame" him into accepting a more consensual relationship. The HBO version, by contrast, has a more realistic and consistent arc, and actually gives Daenerys more agency than in the book.

EDDARD II

"I've half a mind to leave them all behind and just keep going."

A smile touched Ned's lips. "I do believe you mean it."

"I do, I do," the king said. "What do you say, Ned? Just you and me, two vagabond knights on the kingsroad, our swords at our sides and the gods know what in front of us, and maybe a farmer's daughter or a tavern wench to warm our beds tonight."

"Would that we could," Ned said. "But we have duties now, my liege..."

Synopsis

Eddard Stark and Robert Baratheon go for a ride to the barrows of the First Men and discuss matters of state, including the marriage of Daenerys Targaryen, the moral and ethical question of assassination, the threat of the Dothraki, the Wardenship of the East, and the Sack of King's Landing.

Political Analysis

"Eddard II" is another short chapter that nevertheless packs in an enormous amount of political information about "matters of state" in Westeros. The subject of conversation: Daenerys's marriage to Khal Drogo as revealed by Lord Varys, the Talleyrand of Westeros, through his spy, Jorah Mormont. Like his Francophone spiritual counterpart, Varys shows the complicated nature of post-revolutionary consolidation. We often think of revolutions as events that sharply delineate the boundaries between eras, with the *ancien regime* thrown out completely. The reality is always more complicated; Charles Maurice de Talleyrand-Périgord survived the fall of Louis XVI, supported the French Revolution in its Girondist, Jacobin, and Thermidorean phases, served the Directorate, the Consulate, and Napoleon's Empire, and survived to serve the restored Louis XVIII. Likewise, important elements of the old

Targaryen regime (in the persons of Varys and Pycelle) survived the Rebellion through Jon Arryn's clemency.

Varys's mention in this chapter does show us something more about the *Illyrio/Varys Conspiracy* - clearly, the two of them intended for the Drogo/Daenerys marriage to be a visible threat to get King Robert to react to, since Varys could have very easily kept this information tucked up his sleeves. Instead, like the stage magician that he is, Varys is holding up one hand for the realm to focus on, while keeping the hand with Aegon and the Gold Company out of sight. And given that he also is in charge of assassinations, Varys can also modulate how effective Robert's response will be, which allows the Conspiracy to avoid taking an early loss (given what we learn from the Dunk and Egg stories, three dragon eggs are not merely a staggeringly large investment, but a huge symbolic statement of Targaryen heritage) while still keeping Aegon unseen. As we'll learn later, this use of misdirection is an absolute hallmark of the Illyrio/Varys Conspiracy, ever since Illyrio and Varys would "steal" and "return" sensitive information to their owners back during their youths in Pentos.

The news also brings up the major split between two men who are otherwise brothers in all but name – the murder of children, specifically the assassination of Daenerys. However, I think Ned's position here is more nuanced than just the honor-above-all that he often gets tagged with. Keep in mind that, unlike Robert, who rode to avenge a personal insult to his manhood, Ned rose up against a king because the king murdered children and, in doing so, violated the unwritten customs (which also include the guest-right, the right to trial, prohibitions on kin-slaying, the upholding of oaths, and other maxims) that pass for human-rights laws in Westeros. During the Rebellion, this was enough to cause Ned to break with Robert, which might have been a permanent division had not Lyanna's death and the Greyjoy Rebellion brought them back together. For Eddard, then, his support for Robert's regime is conditioned on a certain standard of government that goes above and beyond personal standards of behavior.

Eddard's position on this issue has often been held up as evidence that he's simply not suited to the Machiavellian power politics of King's Landing. However, I think we also have to consider the question of whether Ned, who was about Robb's age when the Rebellion happened, has some form of post-traumatic stress disorder that triggers specifically off of the death of children. Eddard begins to hear Lyanna's voice in the middle of this conversation, as he did back in the crypts of Winterfell and as he does in other moments of high stress throughout the book – and while his fever dream might be chalked off to delirium and the effects of opiates, I think his monologue while in the dungeons of the Red Keep is something closer to a nervous breakdown. Perhaps, as he mused to himself, "some old wounds never truly heal, and bleed again at the slightest word." To my mind, this should inform our judgment as to

Eddard Stark's skills as a politician; an Eddard Stark who never experienced the traumas of Robert's Rebellion might have acted very differently.

Certainly, in his own territory, Eddard has little qualms against executing traitors and oathbreakers, making war on the Greyjoys if they were to threaten him, and taking hostages to insure his safety. Given his posthumous reputation throughout the north, he was clearly adept enough at the rough-and-tumble politics of dealing with some rather touchy northern clans that they are willing to go to war for the Starks even after the virtual extinction of the house. As we see from Robb's and Bran's experiences as lords in Winterfell, the north isn't just a place of bluff, honest warriors, but just as much a place where power politics rule – the Umbers don't get along with the Glovers; the Manderlys (who like to build public works at Stark expense), Tallharts, Flints, Karstarks, and Boltons are interested in expanding their territories at the expense of the Hornwoods; the Boltons have only been relatively recently brought under Stark control, and clearly require a strong hand to keep in check, which Eddard did for 17 years.

Ned Stark's political savvy is further shown in his conversation with Robert about the Wardenship of the East (which I have discussed repeatedly, but I think there's more to say). He clearly can see the broader geopolitical issues that arise from making Lannisters the Wardens of East and West. "No one man should hold both East and West" because "the appointment would put half the armies of the realm into the hands of Lannisters." This phrase – echoed in "Jon I" – that the Wardens command great armies in the king's name shows two things.

First, it shows the danger that Robert's Cersei-inspired favoritism has created; this goes beyond the Starks' distrust of the Lannisters by antagonizing the Arryns and by destabilizing the balance of power between the great houses. In the past, there was always an element of balance – the Starks might have been Wardens of the North, but they still had the Greyjoys to their west (who we know have warred with the Starks at least three times) and the Arryns to their southeast (despite the recent good relations, the Starks and Arryns warred over the Sisters for a thousand years) to balance them; the Lannisters as Wardens of the West had to contend with Greyjoys, Tullys, and Tyrells; the Tyrells as Wardens of the South were, in turn, checked by Lannisters, Baratheons, and, especially, the Dornish. This move puts the Lannisters in the position of cutting the Seven Kingdoms virtually in half and beginning to encircle the crownlands. It also antagonizes the rest of the great houses by putting the Lannisters a level of power above them.

Second, it raises the rather perplexing question of how far along the line between early feudal monarchy (which has little direct power apart from the loyalty of its vassals) and Renaissance nation-state (with its large standing army and developed bureaucracy) the Seven Kingdoms are. On the one hand, the crownlands are rather small in comparison to the rest of Westeros, and in descriptions of previous wars fought by the kings, their armies are always described as being composed of various nations (Dornish, the Vale, etc.), which suggests a feudal model with a weak king. On the other hand, we have multiple references to the Wardens commanding "armies of the realm," which are described as unusually large, and these armies are repeatedly distinguished from the levies they command as feudal overlords. My best guess is that the Wardens are something in between – they are royal officials who can command all of the vassals of their cardinal direction, including those of neighboring regions, against a threat to the realm. Thus, a Stark Warden of the North would likely be able to call upon the Iron Islands, the Sisters, and the northern riverlands in the event of a Wildling assault on the Wall, while an Arryn Warden of the East could command the lords of the crownlands and the stormlands in the event of invasion from Essos. This raises a second danger: not only could an ambitious Warden raise large numbers of troops, but he can also disrupt the feudal relationships of his rivals.

Finally, we learn more about the source of Eddard Stark's antipathy to the Lannisters, which has previously been only intimated. I've already discussed how the murder of Elia, Aegon, and Rhaenys could, in addition to being driven by Eddard's own trauma, be a reflection of his fear for Jon Snow's life at the hands of the Lannisters who "helped taint the throne you sit on." We now learn that Eddard believed that the Lannisters' treachery against King Aerys and his encounter with Jaime Lannister in the throne room of the Red Keep meant that the Lannisters were making a move to take the Iron Throne for their own house. Ironically, although Robert discounts this threat, Eddard is one of the few in the kingdom who actually believes what is true – that the Lannisters are planning a coup d'état.

Historical Analysis

Eddard's conversation with Robert about the potential dangers of the Targaryen heirs invading from Essos brings up another similarity between Westeros and the England of the Wars of the Roses – both are island nations, which can be either an advantage (it spared Westeros from the wars between Valyria, Ghis, and the Rhoynar, the Doom of Valyria, and the wars between Essos city-states over the disputed lands), or a disadvantage, if Essos becomes a springboard for invasion by royal pretenders.

Arguably since the Norman Conquest in 1066, England had always been in danger of invasions from the European continent, especially when said invasions were tied to disputed successions over the English throne. The so-called Anarchy between King Stephen and the Empress Maude saw repeated landings from Normandy as the Empress Maude sought to establish her claim to the throne; Henry Bolingbroke returned from exile overseas to overthrow Richard II and install himself as Henry IV; the Wars of the Roses were especially known for this, with Margaret D'Anjou of Lancaster and Edward IV of York both repeatedly fleeing to the Continent following major defeats, only to return when the tide had shifted. This phenomena of royal pretenders using mainland Europe as a base had real geopolitical implications – at various times, the French (especially following the English Civil War and the Jacobite Wars) and Spaniards (during the time of Elizabeth, for example) sought to place a friendly monarch on the throne of England in order to tip the balance of power in Europe towards themselves and away from their rivals.

We see the same phenomenon in Westeros – even after the Targaryen invasion seems to have put an end to large-scale invasions from the east, the first Blackfyre Rebellion ended not with the complete extinction of the rival Targaryen claimants, but rather with Bittersteel Rivers taking the remnants of the Blackfyre loyalists across the narrow sea to Essos, where he founded the Golden Company. For 60 years, the Blackfyre loyalists threatened invasion, with the great danger being the confluence of a Blackfyre heir bearing Daemon's sword arriving from across the sea with an army at his back. This never came to pass, but not without great effort and much luck – the Second Blackfyre Rebellion featured a credible and charismatic heir, but no sword; the War of Ninepenny Kings saw Maelys Blackfyre and the Golden Company consolidate Tyrosh, the Disputed Lands, and the Stepstones into a dagger aimed at the Targaryen throne.

This tradition, I think, should give us a different impression of Robert's obsession with wiping out the Targaryen threat; this is not simply the act of an irrationally vengeful man afraid of ghosts, but, rather, a practical statesmen dealing with a familiar danger to the realm. It also explains the importance of the Wardenship of the East and the Master of Ships to the defense of the realm – between these two offices, control of the narrow sea, Westeros's watery walls, lies. Given the close relationship between Jon Arryn and Stannis (another bit of backstory we unfortunately haven't seen), the realm was likely in good hands – until Jon Arryn died.

What If?

"Eddard II" gives us a whole host of interesting alternate histories to consider, thanks to the further explanation of Eddard and Robert's past:

King Eddard? A number of fanfiction writers have taken the moment when Eddard Stark rides his horse into the Red Keep and forces Jaime Lannister to relinquish his seat on the Iron Throne as their moment of departure. There are two problems that tend to crop up here: first, the Stark/Tully/Arryn/Baratheon alliance had already agreed on Robert as the best claimant to the Throne, and Eddard was personally loyal to Robert. The only situation that conceivably could have led to a Stark king on the Iron Throne is if Robert had died of his wounds at the Trident, leaving Eddard as the man on the spot. The second error they make is to railroad Eddard into marrying Cersei, when the reality is that the Lannister marriage was driven by very specific circumstances. In Robert's case, he was unattached and able to bring the Lannisters into the fold (although they could have just as easily married him to one of Mace Tyrell's sisters for much the same purpose of bringing a wealthy great house with uncertain loyalty into the new regime). By contrast, King Eddard's Tully marriage would have been the lynchpin tying the Starks, Arryns, and Tullys together as the chief supports of the new regime. Marrying Cersei Lannister would have been a strategic mistake for the new king, weakening his base of support; the most likely outcome there is a marriage to Stannis or Edmure to broaden the alliance.

Eddard kills Jaime in the throne room - the more likely divergence is that Eddard was so enraged by the Lannisters' treachery and murder that he takes it into his head that the Lannisters are making a play for the Iron Throne and attacks the Lannister forces head-on. This would change the course of future events greatly. Instead of being one of the chief supporters of the new regime, the Lannisters are instead bitter enemies even in defeat, probably combining with the Greyjoys to broaden the later rebellion. The new regime would likely need to reach out to the Tyrells and the Martells (hardly an easy business), but given both houses' hatred for the Lannisters, I imagine a modus vivendi could have been worked out, with Robert likely marrying a Tyrell sister. However, the politics would be extremely tricky – the Tyrells are pure opportunists, but the Martells are both Targaryen loyalists (although it's not like none of those were found in original-timeline [OTL] Robert's government) and would likely work to build alliances against the Tyrells.

King Stannis - if Robert had made the decision after the Battle of the Trident not to take up the crown and had instead left to become a mercenary lord in Essos (where, honestly, I think he would have done quite well and been a lot happier) or had died of his wounds without Eddard feeling the need to take the Iron Throne, it's quite possible that the rebel alliance would have turned to Stannis Baratheon as their claimant, given his bloodline. A King Stannis would have made some interesting changes – for one thing, we know that Stannis opposed Jon Arryn's policy of clemency and would likely have had Varys and Pycelle executed as Targaryen loyalists. Gregor Clegane and Amory Lorch would probably have been executed as child-murderers and rapists, since the good doesn't wash out the bad in Stannis's eyes. The question of his marriage alliance is a tricky one – Stannis would likely be extremely wary of the Lannisters as murderous Johnny-come-latelys (although that might not have precluded a marriage out of duty), while hating the Tyrells as the men who nearly starved him to death. Relations with Dorne would probably improve as a result of Stannis's unflinching justice. And a certain half-handed Onion Knight might have become master of ships...

Ned and Robert permanently split - in OTL, Ned and Robert's split at King's Landing likely ended through a combination of their shared grief at Lyanna's death and the chance to fight together against the Greyjoy Rebellion? But it's certainly possible for them to have split; if Eddard had let slip that Lyanna had gone willingly with Rhaegar (while still maintaining the fiction of Jon's birth), if Robert had been more aggressively bloodthirsty regarding the surviving Targaryens, the two might have ended their friendship there. In that case, Eddard Stark never leaves for King's Landing, and sometime in 299 AL gets the news that Mance Rayder is mustering and the dead are walking – in which case, the banners are called and the north marches to defend the Wall as they have done so many times before. When Jon Arryn dies, Tywin Lannister replaces him as Hand, and the need for Robert to be executed so quickly fades. As Hand for a second time, Tywin probably would do a lot to reform the crown's finances and probably coughs up enough cash to hire a couple of Faceless Men to put an end to Daenerys and Viserys at the wedding.

Stannis becomes Warden of the East – if Eddard had actually persuaded Robert to make Stannis Warden of the East, some really interesting things happen. Firstly, given his immediate access to Lysa Arryn and Jon Arryn's household staff, it's quite possible that Stannis teases out the truth of Jon Arryn's murder, especially once Catelyn Stark shows up with Tyrion in tow. While Stannis is a hard man, I doubt he allows the farce of Tyrion's trial to go on as OTL, and then you have the interesting possibility of the Lannisters, Starks, and Baratheons uniting to quash the perfidious *Littlefinger Conspiracy*. Regardless, the military situation changes greatly in the War of the Five Kings - with Dragonstone and Gulltown at his command, and the might of the Knights of the Vale, as well, Stannis likely takes King's Landing well before Renly can get there. This raises some rather strange possibilities: a three-or-four-way siege of King's Landing, with Lannisters, Baratheon/Tyrells, and Starks all outside the walls. On the other hand, Renly might think again about trying for the monarchy if Stannis actually got onto the Iron Throne ahead of him, with three hostile armies in the field – in that circumstance, becoming Stannis's heir is a good move.

Book vs. Show

I thought this scene in the show did capture Eddard and Robert's friendship and their disagreement over the Targaryens, but I thought the loss of Ned's political savvy unfortunately contributes to the idea that Eddard Stark is honorable to the point of stupidity. On the other hand, given that neither the Wardenship of the East nor Stannis had been mentioned by this point, it likely would have undermined the scene's overall thrust.

TYRION II

"The Night's Watch is a midden heap for all the misfits of the realm. I've seen you looking at Yoren and his boys. These are your new brothers, Jon Snow - how do you like them? Sullen peasants, debtors, poachers, rapers, thieves, and bastards like you all wind up on the Wall, watching for grumkins and snarks and all the other monsters your wet nurse warned you about."

Synopsis

Jon Snow, Tyrion, and Benjen Stark travel towards the Wall, where they encounter Yoren and two imprisoned "recruits" for the Nights Watch. Snow and Tyrion have a heart-to-heart about literacy, disability, and the true nature of the Night's Watch, although Tyrion gets knocked down by Ghost when he angers the nascent warg.

Political Analysis

"Tyrion II" is another short chapter where we learn a lot about the politics of Westeros, here through one conversation between the outcasts of two great houses. Interestingly, despite the parallels made between bastards and dwarfs in "Jon I," here it's made clear that Jon has a clear advantage over Tyrion in his physical ableness (in part because Tyrion's unlikely tumbling skills abruptly vanish), and what makes them equals is that they share a common envy of their older siblings (although we don't get confirmation on Jon's side until *A Storm of Swords*). Another interesting aspect of their conversation is that we get a much richer view of how the Lannisters view themselves - more so than virtually any Westerosi great house, the Lannisters see themselves as a common enterprise where Tywin the Hand, Jaime the Kingslayer, Cersei the queen, Joffrey the prince, and Tyrion all do their "part for the honor of [their] house."

Tyrion both understands and embodies the endless grasping ambition of his house - as he puts it, "the Lannisters never declined, graciously or otherwise. The Lannisters took what is offered," even as he takes Benjen's cloak to spite the Stark's anti-Lannister prejudice. This ambition springs, I think, from the fact that the Lannisters remember not only that they were kings before the Targaryens, but also that King Loren Lannister of the Rock came inches away from carrying the day at the Field of Fire, whereas the Starks knelt and were largely left alone.

However, the real topic of Jon and Tyrion's conversation is the virtue of realism – whether Jon Snow will become a man who "sees the hard truth" – through their conversation on the Night's Watch. In previous chapters, we've seen the typical northern view through the eyes of the Starks that the Night's Watch is an honorable vocation, a necessary defense of their realm from the wildlings (if not from the White Walkers), and now we get a rather harsher view from Tyrion. The "Prologue" shows us something in between: the Watch may be "a midden heap for all the misfits of the realm," but in the face of supernatural evil, Ser Waymar Royce fights to the death and even the former poacher Will risks his life to bring proof of the Others back to the Wall.

While it takes Jon Snow a good deal of time to get there (and, personally, I find Jon Snow a much more interesting character when he jettisons the hero's journey and settles down to work), I think a good bit of Jon's successes as lord commander of the Night's Watch stem from his taking this advice to see the Night's Watch as it really is. His decision to focus the Night's Watch on archery rather than swordplay is a good innovation, given the reality of a relatively small force defending a 700-foot-tall wall; likewise, his decision to settle the wildlings on the Wall and the Gift comes from his experience that the men of the Watch and the wildlings are basically the same, despite their cultural differences. And yet, at the same time, I think Jon Snow ends up seeing even further than Tyrion – he is perhaps one of the only men in the world to understand that the Night's Watch was never meant to fight wildlings.

And what is Tyrion's scabrous view of the black brothers of the Wall? Chiefly, and not without reason, he sees the Night's Watch as basically a gigantic penal colony, with two rapers standing as evidence. Not only that, but the first three categories of criminals Tyrion names – sullen (i.e., uppity) peasants, debtors, and poachers – paint the Night's Watch as complicit in an unequal and unjust legal system meant to oppress the vast majority of the population into submission. As I discussed way back in the "Prologue," poaching was a heavily politicized crime as peasants sought to defend customary privileges to game, firewood, and grazing land in the face of the encroachments of their overlords. Likewise, the practice of debtor's prison was a constant catalyst for class conflict between the rich and the poor going back to classical Athens and the Roman Republic. Finally, the label "sullen" was historically applied to a particular form of resistance among the peasantry, a kind of silent work-to-rule where peasants simply ignored their feudal obligations without making any affirmative steps towards rebellion. The Night's Watch therefore protects the landowner against the landless rural laborer, the moneylender against the debtor, and the lord against the unruly vassal.

However, we can learn two important things from this list: first, it's unlikely that the peasants of Westeros are fully serfs (which is also indicated by the prohibition against slavery and the fact that peasants tend to move about quite often throughout Martin's oeuvre). We also learn that the Night's Watch is a place for bastards (and, later, for second and third sons of the nobility). While incompletely egalitarian, at best, the Night's Watch does at least offer a hope for social mobility in that virtually everyone there is an outcast, and most of them are low birth.

Historical Analysis

This irony – that a place meant to keep down the lowly becomes a place where the lowly can rise, however difficult it may be – parallels nicely with the historical policy pursued by the British Empire in the 18th and 19th centuries of using penal colonies, chiefly to deal with a rise in property crimes brought on by the completion of the enclosure of the commons and the first true recessions under a wage-based labor market. For those looking for a good popular account of this period, Robert Hughes's *The Fatal Shore* lays out in some really inspired writing how the British turned to Australia both out of fear of the discontented lower classes and a fear of the larger state required to imprison them on British soil. And yet, despite their initial enslavement and use as unfree agricultural laborers, the former convicts rose unstoppably – thanks in large part to the availability of virtually free land – to claim equal status to the so-called "Bunyip aristocracy" of soldiers and officials.

The Night's Watch is quite different in two respects: instead of enslaving the Night's Watch, the government of Westeros arms and feeds them as a military force (granted, much of the British military of this period was also forcibly recruited from the jails, so there's a parallel there), and, at the same time, it limits their potential rise by forbidding them the right to hold land or start families. Why this doesn't lead to rebellion or desertion isn't entirely clear – in part, it may be that the Gift allows the members of the Night's Watch to enjoy the benefits of land-holding without the work, and it may be that the enmity of the Wildlings and the privations of life beyond the Wall are sufficient to prevent most from escaping into the north (historically, convicts in Australia managed some pretty dramatic escapes despite equally foreboding surroundings).

And yet in Jon Snow's tenure, this distinction is beginning to blur. The marriage of the Magnar of Thenn to Alys Karstark, the tentative relationships forming between brothers of the Night's Watch and wildling spearwives, the transplantation of Stannis Baratheon's Stormlander lords, the building of beacon towers along the Wall, the settling of new peoples along the Gift – change is coming to the Night's Watch, sooner or later.

Finally, this chapter gives us a good glimpse into the Field of Fire, the climactic battle at which the Targaryen ascendancy over Westeros can truly said to have begun. At this battle, the foot soldiers of the Targaryens broke and ran before the charge of a force 10 times their size, as two Andal kings sought to drive out this invader. Unfortunately for the Andals, three dragons are worth more than 45,000 soldiers, as the sheer shock of losing 4,000 men and the last Gardener King brought the heart of the Seven Kingdoms under Targaryen rule. I'm not the first to have said this, but there is an eerie similarity between the Field of Fire and the Battle of Hastings in 1066, where the death of Harold Godwinson brought about the end of Saxon Britain and the beginning of Norman rule, with all of the political, economic, social, and cultural consequences this entailed. In both cases, a relatively small force (William the Conqueror's army numbered only 20,000) won the battle despite an initial rout due to the sudden death of a king on the field of battle.

What's a little frustrating about Martin's work is that for all the thought he's put into the series, we don't get as clear of a sense about the consequences of the Targaryen invasion beyond the political. We know that seven kingdoms were united, we can see the creation of a royal bureaucracy, and so forth, but there isn't much of a sense of cultural change. Unlike the Normans, who brought their own language, legal system, and culture to England, and who imposed it by force on the country for hundreds of years until they finally assimilated as English, the Valyrian heritage seems to be much thinner on the ground than that of the Andals. Surely, when Aegon conquered a continent with 1,500 men, more than just Orys Baratheon must have gained from it. And yet, most of the great houses – Starks, Tullys, Lannisters, Arryns, and Martells – are either First Men, Andals, or Rhoynish in origin. There seems to be relatively little in the way of Valyrian names to distinguish the new arrivals from their Andal subjects, the legal system seems to have remained largely Andal in origin, written records seem to have remained largely in the Andal tongue, and so forth.

It may well have been that the smaller invasion force was too outnumbered compared to the conquered population, and the lack of a Valyria to drive immigration to the new lands, blunted this cultural effect, but it would be nice to see some exploration of how the conquest of Westeros shaped more than the Targaryens themselves.

What If?

Sadly, because this chapter is more about a conversation that reveals the characters' personalities rather than decisions being made or actions being taken, I don't really see much scope for hypotheticals in "Tyrion II."

Book vs. Show

This scene in the TV show is actually almost identical to that in the books, although we don't quite get the political side of Tyrion's perspective on the Night's Watch, though I understand that that's an incredibly minor detail. The main loss is unfortunately driven by the change in format – without Tyrion's interior dialogue, we can't learn about his fascination with dragons or get any of the info-dump on dragonbone and the like.

On the other hand, as much as I like reading about that, I can only imagine how dull it would be to watch on the television screen.

CATELYN III

Catelyn had always thought Robb looked like her; like Bran and Rickon and Sansa, he had the Tully coloring, the auburn hair, the blue eyes. Yet now for the first time she saw something of Eddard Stark in his face, something as stern and hard as the north.

"He came for Bran," Catelyn said. "He kept muttering how I wasn't supposed to be there. He set the library fire thinking I would rush to put it out... if you are to rule in the north, you must think these things through, Robb. Answer your own question. Why would anyone want to kill a sleeping child?"

Synopsis

Catelyn Stark has an unproductive meeting about appointments with Maester Luwin, talks with Robb about the beginning of Rickon Stark's inevitable descent into feral madness, fends off an assassination attempt on Bran with the timely assistance of Summer, although not without injury, and discusses the Lannister conspiracy with Robb, Luwin, Theon, and Ser Rodrick Cassel, deciding to go to King's Landing herself.

Political Analysis

One of the major themes in a rather packed chapter is the interplay between Catelyn Stark's initial failure to uphold her role as the lady of the manor in the absence of her lord and the halting emergence of Robb Stark as "the master of Winterfell" (more on this later). Her nervous breakdown is critical to the plot in more ways than one; had she not been mentally out of commission after Bran's injury, it's quite possible that earlier attention to the Stark household (the hiring of a new stable master, for example) could have uncovered the assassin before the attack.

This is complicated by the almost completely ahistorical idea that "there must always be a Stark in Winterfell." The often fractured nature of feudal landholding, where lords often held non-contiguous fiefs that were quite widespread and frequently traveled between them, many manors were primarily managed by stewards or vassals and rarely, if ever, experienced the presence of their liege lord, and highborn ladies were expected to manage households and castles for quite some time if the liege lord was absent. During the Crusades or extended wars, this could be for several years. Having a (male) member of the family in residence at a single castle at all times would be highly unusual.

However, this anachronism might be explained by the relatively unique nature of Winterfell as both a castle, the north's capital, and a natural hot-spring area. Ordinarily, a lord of the Stark's status would directly own many castles and generally move between them; the Starks have opted instead for concentrating their power into a single indomitable fortress. This has several advantages. Winterfell is centrally located in the north and both equidistant from all sub-regions and well removed from outside threats from any direction, so it allows the Starks to operate efficiently without a network of smaller castles. More importantly, as one of the few (possibly the only) holdfasts built on top of a natural heat source, it's the major sanctuary from winter, capable of sheltering and (with its greenhouses) feeding thousands and thousands of people through the long winters. Given these two factors, Winterfell is a strategic resource without exact historical parallel, and it would make sense that the Starks would draw political and symbolic power from being the lords of Winterfell and vice versa.

The other major political theme is the attempted assassination of Bran Stark. The plot itself is an odd mix of accomplished and amateurish – the assassin is relatively skilled, enough to hide undetected for a week, to set a fire and sneak past the guards to get into Bran's room and yet, at the same time, takes an enormous risk both in gambling that he would remain undetected in the stable for eight days and the choice of weapon is quite conspicuous (why send a dagger to kill a comatose child when a pillow over the face would have been equally effective and far less identifiable?). While we learn in *Game of Thrones* that Tyrion isn't involved in the assassination attempt from his POV chapters, it's not until *Storm of Swords* that Cersei is eliminated as a suspect. Interestingly, we never quite get confirmation that it was Joffrey's doing – Tyrion deduces that it is most likely the case, given Joffrey's means and opportunity; Cersei offers a potential motive. However, like many political assassinations throughout the year, the truth is never fully known, but rather vanishes into the mists of history.

Catelyn Stark's political skills are a matter of some dispute within the fandom, both of *A Song of Ice and Fire* and HBO's *Game of Thrones*. We see both sides in this chapter. On the one hand, Catelyn immediately and correctly concludes that Jaime Lannister threw Bran from the tower in order to conceal evidence of some wrongdoing, simply by recalling that Jaime Lannister unusually did not join the king's hunt (despite being one of only two Kingsguard with the royal party) and without any *CSI: Winterfell* stunts with long blond hairs. Interestingly, she doesn't make anything of the fact that Cersei and Jaime were the two Lannisters remaining in Winterfell during the hunt. On the other hand, her decision to go to King's Landing herself is rather lacking in forethought, given the evident danger that the Lannisters pose to members of the Stark family. Given that Eddard Stark is known for his trust in and even-handed dealings with his staff (as we see from Arya's chapters), the idea that Eddard wouldn't trust Ser Cassel, Maester Luwin, or his ward if they came bearing news of the attack rather strains the belief.

Rather, her decision seems to stem more from a personal need to be proactive in dealing with the Lannister Conspiracy.

Historical Analysis

While there isn't really a historical equivalent to Winterfell, I do think that there's a mythological or folkloric equivalent – Corbenic, or Caer Bran, as it's written in Cornish. In the Arthurian saga, Corbenic is the domain of the Fisher King, whose legs and/or groin are eternally wounded (the so-called Dolorous Stroke), so that the king cannot move and is reduced to fishing in the river near his home. The wounding of the king becomes the wounding of the land, such that the land surrounding Corbenic becomes the Wasteland, until a true knight, who has the purity necessary to touch the Holy Grail, can cure him. In the earlier Celtic myth, Bran the Blessed is the prophetic King of the Island of the Mighty, who possesses a cauldron that can bring the dead back to life, who is similarly wounded in the leg and healed by the magic of the cauldron.

The similarity of the name and the parallels between Bran Stark's wounding and the Fisher King's is hardly accidental. Dramatically, there is a parallel between the health of the Starks in Winterfell, Winterfell itself, and the north. When all of the Starks are present in Winterfell, the castle is an unconquerable citadel that offers shelter and survival from winter when all around it is dead and buried in snow, a warm, beating heart that keeps the people of the north alive, and the realm is at peace. When the Starks begin to leave and the Stark in residence is a crippled child, Winterfell is threatened by besiegers and the north is invaded and the people scattered by the Ironborn; when the family is symbolically slain, the castle is destroyed and the north faces existential destruction from within and without at the hands of the Ironborn, the Boltons and Freys, the wildlings, and the Others.

Perhaps this crippled Bran will yet be healed, so that spring can come again, the land restored, and the castle rebuilt. We shall see.

What If?

While I've already covered several possible counterfactuals in previous chapters that relate to the basic situation – Bran in a coma, what could happen to him – there are several new ones that are suggested by events in "Catelyn III":

What if Hodor or someone else found the assassin before the attack? The discovery of the assassin hidden in the stables could potentially change much or little. If the assassin doesn't know the identity or the appearance of his employer (assuming for a moment that Joffrey was intelligent enough to keep himself hooded during his discussion with the assassin), not much changes – the Starks at Winterfell already know from the dagger and payment that this is a political assassination, as opposed to the typical motiveless lone madman. However, if the assassin did know who paid him, or even remembered enough about his employer's appearance (there aren't that many blond young lords of Joffrey's age in the area at the time), this potentially changes everything.

While the word of a common assassin is nowhere near enough evidence for an accusation against the prince, the knowledge that Prince Joffrey is responsible would certainly change the behavior of Eddard and Catelyn Stark while complicating the politics – Eddard's investigation would probably focus more quickly on royal heritage and finding an alternative successor knowing how un-Robertlike the prince is, and it's highly likely that Eddard breaks off the engagement at a much earlier point in such a way that Sansa is highly unlikely to inform to the queen (even Sansa would find the attempted assassination of her brother too much to forgive). Similarly, Catelyn would probably not capture Tyrion if she wasn't operating in such a vacuum of information, where the only intel she's sure of (thanks to Lysa's letter) is that the Lannisters are involved as a group in nefarious doings; this likely delays war mobilizations (on the Lannister side especially) by several months.

What if Catelyn doesn't go? One of the reasons why I love counterfactuals is that they allow us to see the pivot points in historical narratives. In this case, if Catelyn had chosen someone else to go in her place to King's Landing, it's much more likely that the message would have gotten directly to Eddard Stark (since a message from Winterfell would be much less conspicuous than the Lady of Winterfell herself), eliminating Littlefinger's opportunity to throw suspicion onto Tyrion and preventing Eddard from going down a blind alley on that particular investigation.

At the same time, this change would also prevent the capture of Tyrion, as a subordinate would lack the authority to call upon Tully bannermen to put a Lannister under arrest. This shows us something of

George R.R. Martin's literary choices – he clearly needed a catalyst for Tywin to mobilize the Lannister forces, for Tyrion to become personally involved in the overall plot as opposed to observing from the outside, for Littlefinger to insinuate himself into the investigation, and for Catelyn Stark to not return to Winterfell.

Consider the cascading consequences of Catelyn remaining in Winterfell. To begin with, the defense of the north when the Ironborn attack will not be resting in the hands of a seven-year-old boy; Catelyn would likely be more cautious as a leader, which would likely prevent the fall of Winterfell to Theon (and possibly result in Theon's earlier capture). Continuing on, with Catelyn in the north, Jaime Lannister isn't released from Robb's custody, which prevents Robb from losing the Karstark forces. With more men and without the necessity of returning to the north, and quite possibly with Roose Bolton having less motive to betray a much more successful cause than in OTL, the Red Wedding might be obviated, even had Robb screwed up by marrying Jeyne Westerling.

What if both die? One possibility I haven't considered at all is what would happen if both Bran and Catelyn die. In addition to the obvious changes (no Tyrion kidnapping, no Jaime being released), this would probably massively ramp up the nastiness of the resulting War of the Five Kings. A Robb Stark who blames the murder of his father, mother, and younger brother on the Lannisters is a Robb Stark who does not take prisoners; Jaime Lannister probably is executed after the Battle of the Whispering Woods, which might result in retaliation against Sansa, and so on, with Roose Bolton possibly becoming Robb Stark's right-hand man urging him on to further revenge. Truly a darker timeline.

Book vs. Show

One of the ongoing controversies about the adaptation from novel to TV show is the way in which Robb and Catelyn Stark's characters have altered, with Robb gaining some of Catelyn's political nous and becoming more of a conventional heroic figure, while Catelyn is shaped into more of a conventional "mother first" character who primarily wants to get back to Winterfell to be with her family. There is some merit to this argument; the Catelyn of the books is substantially more politically involved than the Catelyn in the show.

However, I think maintaining BookRobb would have been a huge mistake. While Catelyn sees "something of Eddard Stark in his face" when Robb steps up to take charge of the Winterfell estate, he immediately reverts to immaturity. In part this is due to his youth compared to the TV show; Robb's admission that "I can't do it all by myself" would be credible coming from a 14-year-old boy but wouldn't have worked for a 17-year-old. However, other parts of his behavior in this chapter really make him out to be a complete idiot – Catelyn pointing out the obvious motive for attempting to kill Bran would be bad enough, but waving his sword around (something that Robb repeats when Tyrion and Yoren show up at Winterfell) is not merely idiotic and childish by our standards, but also by the standards of everyone around him. And unlike child characters like Arya, Robb's growth as a character is incredibly halting and inconsistent (although this is probably due to the fact that we only see him through his mother's eyes), which is dramatically unsatisfying.

Given how close parts of the audience have come to dismissing Eddard Stark for his holding of the idiot ball, I don't think BookRobb would be a character that the audience would sympathize with and want to succeed – which has to happen for the "Scarlet Reception" to have the necessary dramatic heft.

So the question becomes: does it have to be all or nothing? Is it necessary for Robb Stark to be dim in order for Catelyn to be politically savvy? Edward IV, who Robb Stark is largely based on (more on this later), made political mistakes despite being a rather clever politician as well as a strategic genius. His mother, Cecily Neville, was a formidable political actor who acted as ambassador to kings and parliaments in the interests of her family, who kept the Yorkist cause going when her husband and oldest son were executed after the Battle of Wakefield, and who carried the banner of the Yorkist king in triumph into London. Her skills did not diminish her son's, and vice versa.

SANSA I

Sansa already looked her best. She had brushed out her long auburn hair until it shone and picked her nicest blue silks. She had been looking forward to today for more than a week. It was a great honor to ride with the queen, and, besides, Prince Joffrey might be there. Her betrothed. Just thinking it made her feel a strange fluttering inside... Sansa did not really know Joffrey yet, but she was already in love with him. He was all she ever dreamt her prince should be.

Sansa could not take her eyes off the third man... a terror as overwhelming as anything Sansa Stark had ever felt filled her suddenly... the queen had descended from the wheelhouse. The spectators parted to make way for her. "If the wicked do not fear the King's Justice, you have put the wrong man in the office."

Synopsis

"Once upon a time," Sansa Stark readies herself for a special day with Queen Cersei and Princess Myrcella and fails to come to an understanding with her sister, Arya, over the relative merits of the countryside, riding, lemon cakes, and the royal prerogative. On her way to the royal wheelhouse, she meets Ser Barristan Selmy and Renly Baratheon, but Ilyn Payne and Sandor Clegane make more of an impression. To recover from this shock, her **fiancé** takes her out for a ride, and nothing bad or fateful happens at all.

Political Analysis

I wasn't sure at first how to approach this chapter, since virtually nothing political actually happens, and I wanted to think through the historical questions thoroughly. It also doesn't help that Sansa Stark is one of the more controversial protagonists in the series, with a significant hatedom. There's a reason why Sansa Stark is so controversial (besides her fateful decision to prize her loyalty to her prince over her loyalty to her father): she is a deconstruction of the romantic tendency within fantasy genre as a fundamentally reactionary force. By this point, it's not a very original thought, I know. A lot of people have pointed out that we're supposed to find Sansa annoying because Sansa has been raised to be what a Disney Princess would be in real life – naive to the point of obliviousness, ignorant and incurious, superficial both in the sense of being obsessed about her own appearance and judging others largely on theirs, and (to us) unbelievably passive – and that George R.R. Martin is criticizing how gender is presented in fantasy. While it's absolutely true that the romantic tendency has particular poisonous heritages when it comes to gender and race (and, as I'll discuss later, class, as well), I think George R.R. Martin is also critiquing the central concepts of the romantic tradition. Consider some of the things that Sansa believes because she has learned them through stories:

Kings and queens (and princes) are inherently good and therefore deserve to be in power, and they shouldn't be questioned. We can see this most clearly in Sansa's hero-worship of Queen Cersei, where she finds it difficult to conceive of refusing the queen or even disliking her personally. This diverges quite a bit from her father's more paternalistic conception of rulership, in which there's a sense of an implicit social contract where the ruler should know his people and look out for their interest, which Arya is shown as having championed (more on this later).

Beauty = goodness. Sansa thoroughly believes that appearance and inner nature are one and the same – the good are beautiful and graceful; immorality is seen in the unsightly face of the wicked. Throughout this chapter, we see Sansa using this precept as her guide: it's a huge part of her problems with her sister (Arya isn't just plain-faced, but she's messy and, most importantly, disorderly, and therefore slightly dangerous), it greatly influences her belief that Sandor Clegane is a "baddie" (just like the dastardly Ser Morgil) and Joffrey must be a gallant knight because he's handsome, and it's part of the reason why she reacts to Queen Cersei differently than from King Robert (who no longer looks like a king ought).

Good things happen to good people. This comes up most often in Sansa's fantasies of romantic tableaux of what should happen (a lovely day in the queen's wheelhouse, a romantic ride with her prince) and her anger and confusion when outside forces conspire to ruin things for her. Beyond the obvious naiveté of this belief, there's a subtle conservatism here – unlike Arya, Sansa never really reacts to the fact that Mycah is mutilated at the hand of her prince and, later, executed by the Hound; rather, her anger comes out when punishment is meted out on the "good dog." In other words, the consequence of this kind of thinking is that it makes people accepting of suffering and injustice (bad things are happening to Mycah, therefore he must be bad – you can tell because he's a dirty commoner) as well as passive.

These are ideas that go beyond the problematic. To begin with, they lead to bad consequences, not just by the end of *Game of Thrones*, where her father is murdered and Sansa becomes an abused captive, but almost immediately. Beyond that, I think George R.R. Martin is arguing that they convince people to not just accept injustice as inevitable, but to see the same act as just, and that they have done so in the past – because they are many of the same romantic ideals that legitimated the feudal order.

Historically, the ideal of chivalry was concocted to paper over a crisis in Western society that had emerged in the early Middle Ages: the Carolingian system, where a strong monarch would grant fiefdoms for loyal service, had the power to retract them for disloyalty, and received them back when the current titleholder died (thus allowing the central authority to enforce loyalty by keeping titleholders anxious about keeping their grants and non-titleholders believing that loyal service might get them lands), had broken down in favor of inherited lands that now left thousands of trained heavy cavalrymen destitute, with no central government to restrain them. The promulgation of the Catholic Church's doctrine of Just War and Just Peace was intended to protect the lands and persons of the Church itself, with women and children tacked on very much as an afterthought. Critically, the prohibition on violence towards women and children largely applied to the nobility, who, being "gently born," should be treated gently; the killing or robbery of the peasantry continued apace.

Likewise, the ideal of courtly love was designed to reconcile Marianism (the veneration of the Virgin Mary as a symbol of female divinity) within the Church, the problematic role of landed – and, thus, powerful – women in a society that treated women as chattel, and the tension between the medieval Church's impossible ideas about sex and marriage, on the one hand, and on the other, the reality of human sexuality. The whole thing, which, in some ways, continues through to the logic behind of "rom coms," is actually a weird parable about adultery rather than a stable relationship. Courtly love treats a breach in the social order as an acceptable inversion of power relations by filtering the whole thing through the lens of feudalism. The woman, who ensnares a man via attraction and then worship from afar, is declared the man's liege lord, which is then followed by a ritual rejection. The knight, being rejected, falls literally love-sick to the point of death (a symbolic punishment for his destabilizing, excessive lust), and must then do heroic deeds in order to prove himself to his lady (again, echoing a knight's service to his liege lord) before he is finally allowed consummation. And once consummation occurs, it must be followed by subterfuge, discovery, and death, so the natural order is restored. In other words, stories of courtly love allowed vicarious enjoyment of adultery while repeatedly reinforcing that breaking the rules = death;

romance requires tragedy to elevate it above sin. And, again, lest we forget, none of this applies to 90% of women who don't count as ladies.

Finally, the idea that there are such things as good and "rightful" kings and "true" knights is an endorsement, however subtle, that the social order of feudalism is good and righteous and, in some way, ordained by God (when you consider that kings and knights both undergo ceremonies where they are specially anointed and denoted as agents of the divine), and that any attempt to change this would violate the Great Chain of Being. And this idea, which is so often accepted at face value within traditional "high" fantasy (you can see equally cursory thinking about this when it comes to such disparate phenomena as the *Star Wars* movies, the Disney Princess franchise, or *The Return of the King*), is one that condemns 90+% of the population as property, virtual property, or lesser kinds of men than those of "noble blood." If you're of European origin or nationality, chances are that would have meant you. And sure enough, the one peasant who appears in this chapter receives the full brunt of medieval justice from "good" King Robert in the form of the Hound.

And at the end of the day, what happens in the very first chapter? The handsome prince turns into a date-rapey, sadistic psychopath and coward; the Good Queen turns into a vindictive, manipulative would-be tyrant; the Good King accepts an injustice in his name; and the knights either stand around or run down the only named peasant we meet this chapter, who dies in the name of royal injustice.

Historical Analysis

Finding historical parallels for young women in medieval societies isn't the easiest thing to do. However, in Sansa's case, I think the best historical parallel is Anne Neville. The daughter of a powerful northern lord, himself Edward IV's Hand of the King in all but name and renowned as a man who took it upon himself to decide who would become king of England, Anne Neville was engaged at various times both to Prince Edward of Lancaster and Richard (later the III), Duke of York.

Like Sansa torn between her captivity and marriage into the House of Lannister, Anne Neville found herself split between the House of Lancaster and the House of York; and just as Sansa found herself married to a skilled administrator with bad publicity and a rumored deformity, Anne Neville found herself married to Richard III, that much-maligned and recently-disinterred monarch. If anything, this should make us even more sympathetic to Sansa's situation. Both in literature and history, noblewomen were used both as marriage tokens and hostages (although the difference between the two is hard to spot). Far more worldly, willful, and experienced women than Sansa found their agency and free will curtailed at the hands of their enemies and their families.

What If?

Oddly enough, the decision of Sansa to skive off with Joffrey and eventually go walking down by the riverbank is actually one of the more important turning points in *Game of Thrones*. The intersection of Arya, Sansa, Joffrey, Mycah, and Nymeria have huge consequences that ripple outwards through the rest of the series. And, like many events revolving around violence and children, there are many potential outcomes, none of them good.

What if Joffrey had connected with his sword? Either killing or seriously wounding Arya had the potential to massively shift the plot. Had this happened, the Stark-Baratheon marriage is off, and probably Eddard Stark's Handship, as well. This changes the political calculus dramatically – Robert's out a Hand, and the Starks are out of pocket (which makes life difficult for Renly, but also for the Lannisters, since the Starks start out less exposed, and Varys and Littlefinger no longer have a Hand to steer).

What if Joffrey dies? Cersei goes on a rampage, which could start a hot war right on the spot, but the long-term picture is problematic. She could get away with rushing the coronation of Joffrey to forestall Eddard Stark, but no one is going to buy Tommen in charge, which means she can't get rid of Robert anytime soon. On the other hand, without a sneering psychopath on the throne, the people of King's Landing might be less rebellious – or might direct their hatred entirely towards the "evil councilors," allowing Cersei more leverage to dump Hands and/or small councils.

What if Lady is there, or survives? If Lady is on the spot and acts protectively when Joffrey loses his temper, it's possible that Joffrey gets backed off without serious harm. This probably defuses the immediate crisis, as no one's going to kill butcher's boys or wolves because of a stick to the back. At the same time, Lady surviving and/or Nymeria not being driven off has some interesting possibilities down the line: if Nymeria is on the scene when Syrio and Arya's last lesson gets interrupted, there's a shot that Syrio's death gets butterflied and Arya gets out of King's Landing at least a couple days earlier than OTL. Likewise, the survival of Lady could mean that Sansa now has the wolf equivalent of a one-shot pistol in dealing with the many threats of violence she's faced with immediately after Cersei's coup.

Book vs. Show

The differences between the book and the show for this chapter aren't that many: Arya and Sansa's conversation about looking for Rhaegar's rubies was filmed for auditions but never used (perhaps for time reasons?), which means we get less of the sisters' interactions. Joffrey's violence is toned down significantly; in the book, he goes for Arya in a sustained and deliberate attempt on her life, backing her all the way up to the tree-line.

The biggest difference, I'd say, is how we're introduced to Renly. To begin with, in the book, Renly appears in this very different context and is immediately set up as a character the audience identifies with (he's funny, he's mocking the Lannisters at their most hateful), and he's set up as an opponent to Cersei and Joffrey. In my opinion, this makes his offer to Eddard seem more promising, and would have heightened the reaction when he's killed by Melisandre. Even more than his introduction, the change in his personality and appearance is quite dramatic. In the first book, Renly is portrayed as a young Robert, butch and warrior-like, perhaps a bit dandyish in his love of fine clothes and snarky putdowns, but much more conventionally masculine. At least in my eyes, this is actually a much more subversive portrayal – George R.R. Martin sets up the very image of a "Good King," literally Robert stripped of his flaws and his realism, and then, in book two, gives him a massive army ready to save the day, a beautiful queen, a band of heroic knights, everything short of a Round Table, and then upends conventional expectations completely. The (mostly) macho warrior turns out to be gay and masculine at the same time, the "good king" turns out to be just as underhanded and scheming as anyone else, his marriage is a quasi-incestuous fraud, and everything is going to fall apart.

EDDARD III

"If it must be done, I will do it." Cersei Lannister regarded him suspiciously. "You, Stark? Is this some trick? Why would you do of such a thing?" They were all staring at him... "She is of the north. She deserves better than a butcher."

Synopsis

Eddard Stark arrives back at Castle Darry to find his daughter has been taken by Queen Cersei's guards before the king. The new Hand clashes with Cersei over the disciplining of his children and the execution of their pets; Sansa and Arya have a breakdown in their normally stable sisterly relations; and Renly finds everything rather amusing.

Political Analysis

In this chapter, we see Cersei Lannister for the first time as a political actor (as opposed to a political observer in "Bran II"). So what should we make of the woman often considered the worst politician in Westeros? Well, I think we can see in this really brief encounter some of Cersei's strengths and weaknesses become readily apparent, and she does have both (although that doesn't prevent her from being a deeply flawed and ultimately doomed ruler).

To begin with, the queen is actually quite good at using Lannister numbers and an understanding of strategic choke-points to her advantage – here, she uses the placement of Lannister gate guards (rather than Baratheon guards, a sign of how successfully she's insinuated her independent military power into the royal court) to bring Arya before the king before Eddard could get hold of her, put himself as a parent in between his children and the court, or negotiate with King Robert in a private context. It's a smart political move, and she makes the most of it, just as she will later when she uses her control over the throne room and the person of her son to preempt Eddard's installation as regent.

Cersei also has something of a gift for revisionist history, creating propaganda that puts herself on the moral high ground and demonizes her opponents, but it's a limited one. Her story, that "this girl of yours attacked my son. Her and her butcher's boy. That animal of hers tried to tear his arm off," is clearly not believable. Arya's story is clearly believed over the queen of Westeros, and Cersei and her son are exposed to public mockery at the hands of Lord Renly, a major political rival. Likewise, when it comes later in the series to developing propaganda to smear Lord Stannis and, later, Margaery, her instant go-to suggestion of sibling incest is laughably bad. On the other hand, her initial story about the supposed treachery of Eddard Stark does succeed, at least initially – in part because, for once, she goes with the simplest story.

I think the reason that her first foray into revisionist history fails is one of Cersei's major weaknesses: she's not good at understanding other's motivations or figuring out their levers. She can rather crudely manipulate Robert – she succeeds in publicly shaming him into executing the wolf, she can use reverse psychology on him to try to get him into the melee at the Hand's Tourney, and she can wheedle him into making Lannister appointments. However, Robert clearly sides against her in favor of Eddard when it comes to the punishment of Arya, and will do the same when it comes to taking Eddard back as Hand. Likewise, she shows no understanding of Eddard's motivations at all in this chapter, or any understanding that people might be motivated by impulses other than self-interest, and she has no way of dealing with Renly at all.

Secondly, Cersei displays a strangely vindictive, scorched-earth approach without thinking deeply about how her actions are syncing with her long-term motivations. It is simply not worth it to spark a vendetta against the Starks, who Cersei already has reason to fear the enmity of (due to her role in the attempted murder of Bran), over a bitten arm and a pet wolf. In the end, she succeeds in having Lady executed, but gains nothing by it – indeed, Cersei potentially undid her endgame by alienating her son's fiancée (and this is a point where I think George R.R. Martin's normally solid characterization breaks down; I find it odd that Sansa would go running to the woman who had her pet executed).

Finally, I'd say Cersei's biggest problem as a politician is that, because of the fact that her political gifts and education were completely neglected by her father (who, curiously, seems to have never really taught any of his children his own political skills), and the way that her own gender constraints have created this curdled resentment inside, she's really only suited to destroy rather than to build. As a usurper, Cersei is remarkably successful – she manages to thoroughly cuckold her husband, eliminate a formally more powerful enemy in the Hand of the King, and install herself as queen regent of Westeros. However, once she finally gets to the position she's been working for her entire life, she has no idea what to do. She immediately loses control over her son's actions, turning the relative cold war in the riverlands into an immediate war with the Starks, and has no plans for dealing with either Baratheon beyond trying to command her father to abandon the war effort against the Starks and allow them to pin his army against the walls of King's Landing.

The most instructive moment comes when the immediate threat to the Iron Throne is crushed; once Tywin actually establishes an alliance with the Tyrells and Martells (a diplomatic coup of the ages), her immediate instinct is to destroy this coalition, because she has no understanding of allies on an equal footing, again because she can only conceive of others as either servants or enemies. This quality follows through to her choice of subordinates, where Cersei instinctively avoids competence for fear of competing agendas, and instead somewhat subconsciously appoints incompetents and traitors who she feel won't question her decisions.

In the end, though, I think the real question is what Cersei would have looked like as a politician if she had grown up in a context where her gender and her political interests weren't in conflict. Because, for all that the medieval society of Westeros is truly oppressive to women, there are survival strategies for women with Cersei's interests and qualities that she never had access to at the decidedly woman-free Casterly Rock. Margaery and Olenna Tyrell make the cultural proscriptions of gender work in their favor, Arianne Martell and the Sand Snakes show that there are alternative cultural spaces in Westeros, and even Catelyn Tully doesn't let the frustrations she feels with gender-imposed limitations poison her life.

Historical Analysis

Robert Baratheon was, in his lifetime, a flawed king, although I have argued that not every flaw of his should be blown out of proportion; most medieval monarchs were perpetually in debt, if not chronic bankrupts. However, this chapter does show one of his more egregious shortcomings – Robert has no interest or ability in his role as the chief judicial power in Westeros. To be fair, it's not the easiest situation to sit in judgment of one's own son and heir over a domestic matter, but Robert Baratheon completely dithers, swayed first by Eddard and then by Cersei, motivated more by his desire to have the thing over and done with than any interest in truth or justice.

This negligence is quite bizarre when you consider how absolutely central the position of king-as-judge was to the centralization of power in the monarchy from the Middle Ages onward. The best example of this is the case of England: Henry I was known as "Beauclerc" and the "Lion of Justice" for his creation of the Charter of Liberties; Henry II standardized judicial decisions into English Common Law, established itinerant royal justices to tour the country, and popularized the use of juries and the creation of legal handbooks; Edward III created Justices of the Peace to keep the peace; Henry VII spread them to every county, and created the Star Chamber; and so on and so on down the centuries.

They did not do so just out of the goodness of their hearts, but because exercising judicial power allowed the kings to intercede between the great lords of their lands and their vassals and create direct connections between king and subject that could be the source of a base of popular support for the monarchy; it allowed the king to interject himself into conflicts between lords, and, thus, make the lords need to curry favor with the monarch; and, finally, it allowed the king to act through the courts against his enemies, and, thus, use the machinery of the law to force them into outlawry, seize their lands and properties, mobilize other lords against them under the guise of law enforcement, and so forth.

Robert's consistent neglect of this, avoiding conflicts here at Castle Darry and also when Eddard and Jaime come to blows and when Tywin Lannister moves against House Tully, is perhaps the worst thing he does as king. By refusing to take action to keep the peace outside of a military situation, he created the environment in which a War of Five Kings could break out.

What If?

Overall, I can really only see one major "what if" coming out of this chapter: **what if the judgment had gone differently?** Now, I find it unlikely that Robert would have ordered any punishment for Arya or that Eddard would have allowed him to do so, but it's not impossible – and the result would be an early breach of trust between the king and his Hand, which might have made Eddard more likely to reach out to allies if he thought he couldn't rely on Robert's judgment at all (as opposed to his rather mixed feelings in OTL).

It's more likely that Robert reflexively sides with his old comrade and lets the wolf alone. The results of this are rather subtle – namely, that the relationships between Eddard and his daughters (and between Sansa and Arya) aren't damaged as they are in OTL. Eddard's failure to prevent the execution of Lady causes a breach between himself and Sansa; removing that may mean that Sansa doesn't run to inform Cersei. This potentially could butterfly away Cersei's successful coup against the Stark regent, or, at the very least, allow Eddard to successfully smuggle his daughters out of King's Landing. This, in turn, has huge effects – Catelyn Stark has no reason to release Jaime from captivity and probably heads to Winterfell with her children, the Sack of Winterfell is probably butterflied away, and it's possible that Jaqen H'ghar dies in the riverlands.

Book vs. Show

There are a couple of big changes between the book and the series. In the show, Arya is found first by the Lannisters, as opposed to by Jory and then brought before the king, and likewise in the show, Sansa is brought to the king by Cersei behind Eddard's back. Both of these changes give a sense of the Lannisters' ubiquitous power and makes the Starks seem even more hapless or in danger; my own sense is that it over-eggs the pudding a bit, but, then again, it's perhaps necessary for first-time viewers.

A big change is the removal of Renly's presence – in the books, Renly provides the reader with a third perspective outside of the Stark-Lannister conflict, and gives a sense of how ridiculous Cersei's story is. It also changes how Robert plays out – in the show, Robert is openly contemptuous of his son (which adds another layer of complexity into Joffrey's abnormal psychology), but in the book, it's more that he's embarrassed by his son's obvious failure, especially in the presence of "the young, slim Robert," Renly Baratheon.

BRAN III

A face swam up at him out of the grey mist, shining with light, golden. "The things I do for love," it said.

Bran screamed.

The crow took to the air, cawing. Not that, *it shrieked at him. Forget that, you do not need it now, put it aside, put it away.*

Synopsis

Bran Stark dreams of the three-eyed crow, discusses the merits of flying versus falling, wakes up, and names his wolf.

Political Analysis

There isn't a lot of political content in this rather short chapter, given that it largely consists of Bran experiencing his first prophetic dream. Indeed, due to his age and metaphysical connections, Bran spends much of *A Song of Ice and Fire* aloof from the world of politics. (Which will make some of his chapter analyses a bit problematic, but I'll roll with it.)

But to avoid giving short shrift to this chapter, there is one thread that's relevant to the political saga of *A Song of Ice and Fire* - the question of Bran's amnesia.

Why does George R.R. Martin have Bran be the sole witness to Cersei and Jaime's conversation, and then have him repress this memory for four more books? As a result of this choice, not only does the secret of their incest go unrevealed for most of the rest of the novel, but so does their conversation from "Bran II" regarding what Jon Arryn was up to, their attempt to quasi-legally kidnap Robert Arryn, and hastening King Robert's death. On one level, it allows George R.R. Martin to insert an important conversation that otherwise the POV model would prevent while preventing Eddard from learning the truth too soon. If this is the only reason, it's kind of a clumsy kludge that we might need to chalk up to a writer still coming to grips with his material.

However, I think there's something else, largely due to that crucial "now" and the recurrence of the "things I do for love" line later in the series. What it is going to be, I'm not sure. To be honest, I don't have the best grasp on what's going to happen with Bran's storyline in the series. I do have some ideas – we know from "Bran II" that he knows all about the secret tunnels in Winterfell that I think are going to be a bit of a Chekov's Gun for the "Battle of Ice," and we know from the *Winds of Winter* Theon chapter that Stannis is going to execute Theon in a godswood, giving Bran access to him. However, I don't think there's a lot of narrative time for Martin to pull the trigger on Bran's realization – Jaime's heading into an ambush, Cersei's heading for an epic train crash of her own making, and I just don't think the Lannister incest plot is going to be that relevant for much longer.

On the other hand, there's also the question of what Bloodraven is up to. One of the few figures in the series who has been a major actor in both the sorcerous and political worlds of Westeros, he seems in this chapter to be trying to push Bran away from involvement in the plot going on down south or over in Essos and towards beyond the Wall and the coming of the heart of winter. The "bones of a thousand other dreamers impaled on their points" (which has always bothered me; if thousands of potential greenseers have died when their untrained dreams lured them too close to the Others, why haven't we seen any sign of this anywhere?) and his nebulous involvement with Euron suggests that Bloodraven is, in the rather callous manner of the former intelligence officer he is, trying to gather in as many potential resources as he can to fight the Others. Whether that comes through Euron Greyjoy's control over Targaryen dragons or Bran's greenseer powers, I don't think he really cares.

Historical Analysis

I don't have a lot to say here. The only thing I'd note, following from the discussion of the Fisher King in "Catelyn III," is the continuing theme of the wounded mystic. The potential references that follow from the idea of undergoing a sacrifice or injury in order to gain spiritual knowledge are encyclopedic: the association with ravens and the loss of an eye brings in the myth of Odin, who sacrificed his eye, pierced himself in the side with his own spear, and hung himself from Yggdrasil in order to gain wisdom (and the whole Tarot thing); there's the various traditions of mysticism and martyrdom within Christian traditions; the symbolic sacrificial death and resurrection also found in Dionysian, Osirian, and Mesopotamian traditions; and the third eye borrowed from Hindu traditions.

So if George R.R. Martin is borrowing from the idea that a shaman undergoes a physical injury/sacrifice in return for spiritual power, then it's possible that Bloodraven has been encouraging, causing, or looking out for potentially useful traumas, and it's no accident that he chose Euron Crows-Eye as his pawn.

Whether Martin has a plan here, or is just throwing as much imagery as he can at the reader so that she doesn't forget that this is all important as he parcels out the more high-fantasy elements drop by drop over the course of four more books, I don't know. If I'm being completely honest, this is the one part of the plot where I don't know where things are going.

What If?

There's really only one hypothetical that makes sense in this chapter – **what if Bran remembered everything?** On the one hand, this seems incredibly consequential; if Bran can transform Catelyn and Eddard's suspicions into proof well ahead of time, Eddard can potentially find out well ahead of arriving in King's Landing that Cersei is actively opposing him, that Jon Arryn was investigating the queen, that Cersei attempted to legally kidnap Robert Arryn, and that they're contemplating hastening the king's death. This would greatly speed up his investigations and probably dissuade him from just talking it over with Cersei. It might also put in Eddard's mind to reach out to Robert's brothers as potential allies.

On the other hand, as Arya will demonstrate later, it's not entirely clear how much of this information will actually be accurately recalled and believed – but as long as the key issue of who tried to kill his son and why gets across, Eddard's hand is potentially freed up for decisive action against the Lannisters.

Book vs. Show

This scene was entirely removed from the show in favor of a more subtle connection with the three-eyed crow, although it's quite possible that the showrunners will simply transpose much of this into the third season, when the Reeds show up.

Instead, they chose to merge the killing of Lady with Bran waking up, which added a nice mystical wolf-to-wolf-to-human connection. Overall, it's probably an improvement, given how poorly the dream would likely have transitioned from page to screen.

CATELYN IV

Varys giggled like a little girl... "I wonder if we might trouble you to show us the dagger?"

Catelyn Stark stared at the eunuch in stunned disbelief...

Littlefinger was lost. "I feel rather like the knight who arrives at the battle without his lance. What dagger are we talking about?"

Synopsis

Catelyn arrives at King's Landing. While Ser Rodrick goes to talk daggers with Aron Santagar, Catelyn is summoned to the Red Keep to meet with her old "friend," Petyr Baelish and Varys "the Spider," and is told that the dagger used in the assassination attempt against her son belongs to Tyrion Lannister.

Political Analysis

I have been looking forward to this chapter for a long time, because it's so damn rich in political intrigue and different conspiracies coming together. It's also the moment at which a lot of the key political players that hitherto have only been mentioned in the third person show up in the flesh, so that the reader can begin to make his own assessments independent of the point-of-view narrator.

There's a lot to talk about, but I'm going to concentrate on Petyr Baelish and the *Littlefinger Conspiracy*, and Varys and the *Varys/Illyrio Conspiracy*, because I really see the two of them as contrapuntal figures, who would be far less interesting or meaningful without someone to compare themselves to, compete against, and manipulate.

The Baelish Conspiracy - I've written a bit earlier about what Littlefinger is up to, but it's a good idea to go over the basics: Littlefinger, using his control over Lysa Tully's emotions and Arryn's reliance on his evident gift for finances (more on this later), has worked his way up from a hedge lord to customs collector at Gulltown to the master of coin, through which office he has created a vast network of influence. Recently, he convinced Lysa Tully to murder her husband and send her sister a letter placing the blame on Cersei Lannister once it became clear that Eddard Stark would be the next Hand of the King, with the intent to set House Stark and House Lannister against each other.

And now Catelyn Stark arrives in King's Landing. Baelish is informed of this by Varys, and understanding – as a good covert operative must – the importance of information, he tries to pump Catelyn Tully for information by playing on their shared history and his understanding of the Tully mindset (this understanding and calculated use of personal relationships and pasts is a signature of the Baelish conspiracy). When Varys arrives, Baelish is informed of the attack on Bran's life (probably for the first time) and sees the knife in question. It is at this moment that Baelish makes a critical decision: knowing the dagger for his own, he concocts the story of losing it to Tyrion Lannister at Joffrey's name day tourney.

It is hard to state how much of a gamble this decision was. Baelish, improvising in reaction to a potentially transformative unforeseen event, departs from his previous narrative – that Cersei Lannister is the threat to the realm – in a flagrant and easily disprovable lie. Had Catelyn or Eddard or any of their staff asked any of the hundreds of people who were nearby during the joust, he would have been instantly exposed. It has been argued that Baelish somehow could judge Catelyn's and Eddard's (*who he had never met*) temperaments to such an extent that he knew they would trust his word rather than verify. However, we have to consider that Littlefinger couldn't have known whether they might have simply picked up the fact due to an unknowing exchange (Ser Rodrick Cassel was talking about the dagger with the master-of-arms of the Red Keep at the time!), and that *he was saying this in front of Varys*.

While Littlefinger claims to Catelyn that he holds Varys's "balls in the palm of my hand... if he were a man, or had any balls," it's not clear whether he believes this when he says it. If he doesn't, then Littlefinger at the moment he spoke Tyrion's name knowingly handed Varys a knife to put into his back if the spymaster wanted to shiv him. If he believes or believed it, that's an astonishing failure of judgment in a man who clearly prides himself in his ability to understand and manipulate others.

Given that he could have just as easily said, "I lost it to King Robert; the queen must have stolen/borrowed it from her husband to sow distrust between your husband and the king," I think this choice shows a lot about Littlefinger as the mastermind of the Baelish Conspiracy: he's clearly talented at manipulating people whose character he's familiar with, he is very decisive in seizing his chances, but he's also reckless and impulsive. His spiriting away of Catelyn, the dramatic way he revealed his ownership of the dagger, and the way he will later needle Eddard all speak to a deep-seated need to prove his superior intelligence to those around him and insert himself into the foreground.

Like a classic pulp villain, he can't stop himself from monologuing (even when bragging about the maidenheads of other men's wives). And the targets of his monologues are universally either Starks or Tullys, because I think another part of the signature of the Baelish Conspiracy is his emotional obsession with his own past: he fell in love with Catelyn Tully, was seduced by Lysa Tully, was nearly killed by Brandon Stark when he tried to win the Tully he wanted, had his child aborted at Hoster Tully's command, and is exiled back to his despised birthplace. In his conspiracy, he murders the liege lord who raised him up from obscurity (an ultimate victory of the underdog) by seducing the Tully who loves him, then turns Lysa against Catelyn in order to betray the man she married instead of him, then seeks the position of Lord Paramount of the Riverlands that had belonged to Hoster Tully, then kidnaps the daughter who most resembles Catelyn, then murders Lysa and slowly poisons the last Arryn in order to seize the regency of the Vale. My suspicion is that this idée fixe will be the cause of his downfall.

At the same time, there are a number of questions that are up in the air:

1. **Why did Littlefinger murder Jon Arryn when he did, and did he do it only on his own behest?** The murder of Jon Arryn follows Littlefinger's overall strategy of turning Stark against Lannister, but the precise timing interests me – Littlefinger clearly knew that Queen Cersei had cuckolded King Robert, and that his own plans would require House Lannister to remain powerful enough to keep the war going (which they wouldn't have, had Cersei been exposed and the house politically isolated prior to Robert's death). Given what we know about the fostering of Robert Arryn, it's possible that Littlefinger saw that Arryn was getting ready to make his move and then used the move to leverage Lysa to act as his poisoner. It's also possible that Littlefinger accomplished this by spying on Jon Arryn through bribing Ser Hugh of the Vale (hence the sudden inheritance and his equally sudden death). However, Cersei's seeming passivity in the face of an existential threat from Jon Arryn makes me wonder whether Cersei sought to use Littlefinger as her catspaw, in turn (which might further explain how it is that Gregor Clegane came to end Ser Hugh's life).

2. **What was Littlefinger up to as master of coin?** I raise this mostly as a placeholder, to make sure that people are paying attention to this question, which I will address in detail in "Eddard IV."

3. **What did Littlefinger think Varys was up to?** While Littlefinger later displays a fairly good grasp of Cersei's motivations and actions, we don't get any sign that he had any grasp on Varys's plans.

Perhaps he thought Varys was simply a gun-for-hire with no motivation of his own, but it would be interesting to know what the hypothetical balls Littlefinger thought he had.

The Varys/Illyrio Conspiracy – comparing Varys to Baelish, we might as well be comparing a classical composer to a jazz soloist, or perhaps comparing the relative virtues of wisdom versus cunning. Recapping the Varys/Illyrio conspiracy is far more complicated: for all that Varys seems to be a Targaryen loyalist, his history of running cons with Illyrio where he steals objects for Illyrio to sell back to their original owner suggests a more complicated long con is in the works.

As spymaster for King Aerys II, Varys cemented his own power by encouraging the king's paranoia, building an enormous network of spies, and mastering the system of tunnels under the Red Keep. While Varys argued against opening the gates to Tywin, which would suggest Targaryen loyalty, the fact that he deliberately encouraged a split between the reformist Rhaegar and his father (see "Barristan III" in *Dance with Dragons*) and switched the baby Aegon rather than hide or smuggle mother and children out of the capital (which he demonstrably has the ability to do) suggests that his long-term goal was to destabilize the monarchy, provoke a rebellion (while notably keeping his hands clean enough of the lawless executions and tortures to avoid execution by the new regime), and use the chaos to steal the rightful heir to the throne so that Varys could have him trained to his precise specification.

Figuring out Varys's true loyalties is truly ambiguous – on the one hand, his commitment to serving the realm is belied by his repeatedly successful efforts to destabilize the kingdom during the reign of King Aerys II and then again by executing the remaining competent members of King Tommen's small council, and his placement to gain personally from installing his "mummer's dragon" on the Iron Throne. On the other hand, one could argue that Varys's ultimate objective of placing the perfect king in charge of Westeros suggests a genuine, if extremely utilitarian, approach to long-term reform, and he does at least try to mitigate the brutality he instigates (as we see through his efforts to save the lives of Eddard Stark, Gendry Waters, Tyrion Lannister, et al.).

In this scene, the Spider executes a quietly understated piece of intrigue - through his massive network of spies, he knows about Catelyn's trip to King's Landing (by paying off either the captain or through an agent he undoubtedly has in White Harbor), and he knows about the attack on Bran (probably through a "little bird" overhearing Ser Rodrick at a tavern, although that requires some very quick footwork). He alerts Littlefinger with the irresistible bait of Catelyn's presence, thus allowing him to observe his rival closely. When he's handed the dagger, he undoubtedly recognizes the blade as Littlefinger's, but says nothing about the blade's owner even after Baelish lies about who ended up with the knife. This reticence and self-control is the signature of Varys's conspiracy, as we will see later when he carefully conceals what he knows when he deals with Eddard Stark and Tyrion Lannister.

To me, it is this quality that puts Varys ahead of his rival – unlike Baelish, Varys knows to keep to his shadowy web, only ever revealing himself in a supposedly deserted storeroom with his co-conspirator or while explaining himself to a man who's murdered. Varys, at least, knows that dead men tell no tales.

Historical Analysis

Sometimes it's hard to find an exact historical parallel for a historical figure. There are dozens of palace eunuchs who wielded enormous power through their bureaucratic skills, court intrigue, and espionage who could serve as models for Varys: the *Dar al-Saada Ağası* (Chief Eunuchs) of the Ottoman emperors who operated eunuch spy rings in the imperial palaces, oversaw the education of princes, and ruled from the shadows behind the thrones for centuries; the palace eunuchs who served the emperors of China in much the same capacity; and so on. In Peter Baelish's case, the historical parallel is blindingly obvious.

Thomas Cromwell, First Earl of Essex, began his life as the ruffian child of a Putney blacksmith. Running away from home in his teenage years, Cromwell served as a mercenary in Italy before entering business as a banker, merchant, and spy in Italy, France, and the Low Countries. Returning home a wealthy, cosmopolitan, and multilingual expert, Thomas became a London barrister and member of Parliament before the age of 40. Entering into the service of Cardinal Thomas Wolsey, Cromwell orchestrated the dissolution of the monasteries but managed to survive his master's downfall and, within a year, was appointed by King Henry VIII to the Privy Council.

Within a year, Cromwell was the chief legal and parliamentary adviser to the king, and, over the next few years successfully, he orchestrated King Henry's divorce, his installation as spiritual head of the now-independent Church of England, his marriage to Anne Boleyn, and the conviction and execution of his spiritual and political rival, Sir Thomas More (Cromwell was a reformist Protestant, More a staunch Catholic). Handily dispatching his new rival, Anne Boleyn, by 1536, Cromwell was Master of Jewels, Chancellor of the Exchequer, Principle Secretary, and Chief Minister to the King, Vicar-General of the Church of England, Lord Privy Seal, and Baron Cromwell. His downfall – due to his selection of the over-hyped Anne of Cleves as Henry's next bride – came in 1540, mere months after being appointed Lord Great Chancellor and Earl of Essex.

This combination of lowly birth, immense talents and ambition, and a precipitous rise to power in periods of social change and disorder makes him a perfect model for the undersized son of a lord of sheep shit and rocks. If the gods are just (and if Martin has any gift for dramatic character arcs), his fall from grace will be as precipitous as his ascent.

What If?

This chapter contains yet another critical turning-point moment revolving around Catelyn Stark, who seems to be Martin's chief vehicle for advancing the plot in the most tragic fashion possible (incidentally, a thousand gold dragons to whoever writes an adaptation of *A Song of Ice and Fire* as a classic Greek tragedy). This meeting influences the rest of the plot enormously, as we'll see:

What if Catelyn hadn't been intercepted? If Catelyn had come to King's Landing under the radar, or had Varys decided to observe rather than pull in Littlefinger, a lot changes. To begin with, Eddard gets the news about the assassination attempt on his son without interference, which probably leads him to make independent inquiries about who the knife belongs to. While Eddard probably would never suspect Robert of such a thing, the dagger points to someone in the king's immediate household, confirming Eddard's suspicions about the Lannisters. It also probably keeps Littlefinger outside of Eddard's investigations, which would make it far more difficult for Littlefinger to manipulate him. Quite possibly, Eddard avoids the ambush outside the brothel, leaves the city with his family, and then declares for Stannis when the two of them meet at Dragonstone on Eddard's way home.

What if Baelish had told the truth/a better lie? Certainly, Littlefinger could have avoided potentially exposing himself to discovery had he just said the dagger was in Robert's possession and, therefore, easily obtainable by Cersei or any Lannister agent in the king's household. It keeps the Starks at odds with the Lannisters without confusing the plot and accomplishes his interests. Unbeknownst to him, it also means that Catelyn Stark wouldn't have arrested Tyrion Lannister, which, in turn, would mean no attack by Jaime on Eddard, delaying his departure from King's Landing, and no raiding of the riverlands by Gregor Clegane. This means that when the War of the Five Kings breaks out, it does so with House Stark under Eddard's command and with no children in harm's way, and with House Tully aimed to mobilize its forces before it's invaded. This greatly changes the strategic picture - Eddard Stark is at least the equal of his son when it comes to military tactics, would have been much better placed to make alliances (since he doesn't have to worry about his own marital status but has five children to work with), and had a stronger reputation with the other lords of Westeros.

What if Varys had betrayed Baelish to Catelyn and/or Eddard? On one level, I can see why Varys would want to avoid the Starks taking out the Lannisters before the succession can be screwed up, bringing about the war he needs when he needs it (i.e., he needs multiple claimants to be at war, but no one having won before his Targaryen claimant can land with his army). Delaying Eddard's realization of what's going on therefore makes sense, especially since he hasn't yet made a judgment about his character. On the other hand, Varys missed out on an opportunity to discredit his chief rival when it comes to intrigue, potentially turning Eddard against Littlefinger, and supplanting him as the puppet-master leading the Hand along. If this is the case, Eddard could have avoided the ambush outside the brothel. Likewise, Varys might have led Stark to the truth via different means and via different timing, with huge implications about what happens when Eddard moves against Cersei.

What if Catelyn had landed on Dragonstone? In the chapter, Catelyn notes that the stormy seas almost required their ship to seek shelter on Dragonstone. This could have changed things enormously if she had come to Stannis with her suspicions (or, less likely, if Stannis had learned of what happened to the Starks and reached out): by combining the separate sets of information being held by Eddard and Stannis, Catelyn could have allowed the Starks to make a giant leap forward in their investigations when it comes to Cersei's adultery, Jon Arryn's murder, and the attempt to legally kidnap his son. With Stannis's help, Eddard might have become the Cicero of Westeros's own Catiline Conspiracy.

What I think this all points to is that, however much the fans like to dislike Catelyn, it's not really her fault. In order for the plot to work, George R.R. Martin needs Catelyn to fail. I don't think we should judge her too harshly, any more than we should blame Oedipus or Cassandra or Orestes for their plights. In the Song of Ice and Fire, the god Martin uses Catelyn for his sport as flies to wanton boys, and all that.

<u>Book vs. Show</u>

Not a huge change here, with the most important alteration being the movement of Catelyn from the Red Keep to Littlefinger's brothel, which I like, because it underscores his messed-up relationship with Catelyn Stark and her conception of Littlefinger as an annoying, handsy, but nevertheless beloved little brother.

JON III

"Words won't make your mother a whore. She was what she was, and nothing Toad says can change that. You know, we have men on the Wall whose mothers were whores."

Synopsis

Now a novice of the Night's Watch, Jon Snow goes through a series of training bouts with Grenn, Pyp, Dareon, Jeren, and Halden under the watchful gaze of Ser Alliser Thorne. Donal Noye interrupts an attempt at revenge from the other initiates and lays down some sober truths about class politics, privilege, and leadership. After talking with Tyrion, Jon receives news from Winterfell and improves his mood and his relations with his peers.

Political Analysis

In this chapter, we get a much more expansive view of the Night's Watch as an institution, whereas before we got mostly hints emerging from individuals. The interactions between Jon Snow and Ser Alliser Thorne, between Jon and the other recruits, and between Tyrion and Ser Jeor Mormont suggest a deep and disturbing degree of institutional dysfunction and a tension between the ideals of the Night's Watch and its reality.

Not only is Ser Alliser Thorne an instant antagonist in the grand tradition of martinets like Gunnery Sergeant Hartman from *Full Metal Jacket* or Obadiah Hakeswill from the *Sharpe* series, but he's also an indicator of something seriously wrong with the Night's Watch. He's a sadist and a bully and a coward and a schemer, and, what's worse, he's bad at his job – as we can see between the contrast of his efforts and Jon's in teaching the finer points of swordplay. This would be a bad sign in itself (the Night's Watch doing a bad job when it comes to promoting people to positions of responsibility), but the reason for it, which we learn in "Tyrion III," is even worse: Mormont has put Ser Alliser in charge solely because Ser Alliser is an anointed knight.*

* Interestingly, the backstory behind Alliser's pathological hatred of Lord Snow hasn't been revealed in the show – Ser Alliser was a Targaryen loyalist and a veteran on the losing side of Robert's Rebellion. A native of the Crownlands around King's Landing, he saw Tywin Lannister sack the city from the battlements he was defending when Eddard Stark broke through the defenses – and Stark was probably the man who made him choose between death and the Wall. And here comes a boy with the face of the man who destroyed his life. No wonder Ser Alliser develops a pathological hatred of Jon Snow.

This runs contrary to the ethos that Jon Snow receives from Benjen Stark and Donal Noye (more on them in a second), but it's absolutely part and parcel with the reality of a Night's Watch where an order guarding an impossibly-tall wall emphasizes training with swords (the knight's weapon) over missile weapons, only occupies three out of 19 forts along the Wall, and when "a good many rangers have vanished of late," better men are sent out to the wilds to look for the likes of Ser Waymar Royce.* From the outset, we're seeing an institution that's falling to pieces very slowly, and part of what's killing it is the mistaken belief that knights are better kinds of people than commoners.

* On a complete side note, the price of a sword is something that Donal Noye points to as to the influence of class on the novices at the Wall. While it's true that the bow was the peasant's go-to weapon compared to the nobleman's sword, the exact cost of a sword is a bit more complicated. The price varied – at the time of Charlemagne, a sword is reported to have cost six cows, which would be an enormous cost for a peasant; however, by the 14th century, war swords are recorded to cost roughly 45% of a thatcher's monthly wages, which isn't nearly as costly.

What makes this all the more troubling is that the Night's Watch is supposed to be better than this. Benjen Stark represents the idea of the Night's Watch as the renunciation of privilege along with family: "on the Wall, a man gets only what he earns... we put aside our old families when we swear our vows." And although Jon Snow doesn't really verbalize it that much, I think this is what attracted him to the Watch – a chance to set aside the family he's so torn over and to prove his worth independently of them . And it's not an empty ideal – for all that high officers are often officers of high birth, there are also the Cotter Pykes of the Night's Watch, who have risen from the lowest of births to the command of Eastwatch-by-the-Sea. Even in decline, there is still the lingering remnants of what it used to be.

If Benjen Stark represents what might be called the literally vanishing past of a Night's Watch that once was a place where younger sons of the wealthy freely chose to serve, that was once the first line of defense of the north from the outside threat, Donal Noye represents the hardcore of value that keeps the Night's Watch going. Far more so than Alliser, Donal Noye, the uncommon commoner, the one-armed master smith who had crafted Robert Baratheon's warhammer, destined for greatness in a way that only a Night's Watchman could be, is the true teacher. Noye has two lessons to offer: one is for Jon Snow to recognize the ways in which he is privileged (grew up in a castle, is literate, trained in combat), and that he needs to stop wallowing in his personal issues (because, otherwise, Jon Snow will turn into another Alliser Thorne), but the other is about leadership.

"Robert was the true steel. Stannis is pure iron, black and hard and strong, yes, but brittle, the way iron gets. He'll break before he bends. And Renly, that one, he's copper, bright and shiny, pretty to look at but not worth all that much at the end of the day."

First, a word on Donal Noye's political theory. I don't have any good figures on this, but my feeling is that the pro-Renly crowd in the *Song of Ice and Fire* fandom is a lot larger than the pro-Stannis fandom, and it's interesting to see such a critical view expressed by a character who is generally positively regarded. Noye hits on a weak point – Renly is fixated on appearances of power, relies upon the Tyrells even more than Robert was dependent on the Lannisters, and, tactically speaking, misses an enormous opportunity to seize the throne when he chooses to turn around and relieve the siege on Storm's End rather than press on to King's Landing. There's an extent to which his image as the king-who-might-have-been is just an image. On the other hand, Donal Noye's perception might not be the most accurate: Robert, despite being the "true steel," turned out to be a less than effective king, whereas Stannis has proven himself to be willing to adapt repeatedly to new situations (converting to a new religion, holding back his desire for revenge when it comes to his turncoat vassals, making the call to go to the Wall's aid, negotiating with Jon Snow and the Iron Bank of Braavos, adapting his war aims to the politics of the north, etc.). So who knows how accurate the smith is?

Second, I don't think there's much of a chance that Jon Snow was going to turn into a Renly – from the beginning, he lacks the absolute self-confidence that comes from having both high birth and all of the qualities that high birth is supposed to come with (good looks, military bearing, charisma, and ease of command). But it's quite possible that Jon Snow could have ended up a Stannis, so brittle and damaged that he couldn't bend rather than break. And Jon Snow learns to bend almost immediately, taking up the role of the natural leader of his peers, and later bending sufficiently to rise within the wildling community. How consistently Jon learns is another question, and one we'll revisit later.

Historical Analysis

I keep looking for good historical parallels to the Night's Watch, and it's not easy. Especially with the Wall, there's a strong temptation to point to the Roman legions, especially the *limitanei*, the frontier legions who served as the first line of defense, especially in the late Roman army; however, the Roman emperors deliberately encouraged them to marry and settle along the frontier through the granting of farmland in border areas in order to create a pool of future military recruits, so that doesn't quite work.

Another comparison I'd like to try out here is with the militant orders who grew out of the Crusades, such as the Knights Hospitaller (also known as the Knights of Rhodes and Malta) or, even, the Teutonic Knights, especially given their stark heraldry. While the religious nature of these orders doesn't quite parallel, the strictness of the lifelong vows of the Night's Watch, especially in relation to chastity and inheritance, does have at least the flavor of monasticism that came with the militant Christian orders.

It's not just the monochromatic costumes that suggest a parallel; there's also the theme of institutions adapting to changing missions. The Knights Hospitaller actually predated the Crusades as an organization that built and operated a hospital on the site of the monastery of John the Baptist in Jerusalem for sick and injured pilgrims, but then started to act as armed escorts, and then as an independent military force in the Holy Land during the Crusades, culminating in holding seven castles and 140 estates in the 12th century. When the Crusaders were forced out of the Levant, the Knights Hospitallers shifted missions again and again to the island of Rhodes, the peninsula of Helicarnarssus, the port of Tripoli, and the island of Malta; as the Knights of Malta, they became famous as a defensive force against the Ottoman Empire and the Barbary Pirates, and masters of siege-craft. The Teutonic Knights started as a German-language breakaway from the Hospitallers, then switched missions to fighting Mongols in Hungary and then launching a Crusade to Christianize pagans in Prussia and the Baltics. Similarly, the Night's Watch, which began as a military force aimed at defending against the Others, has in its history variously been warring military camps or a would-be kingdom at the edge of the north, but, most of all, has reoriented itself as a force occupied with reconnaissance, interdiction, and static defense against wildlings.

The similarities don't stop there. Like the Night's Watch, the Knights Hospitaller were a multinational organization who managed to incorporate knights from eight different "tongues" in one institution; both the Knights Hospitaller and Teutonic primarily functioned financially through donations of land offered by rulers in exchange for guarding the frontiers from a cultural "other"; and both orders had an elected leadership, which offered some semblance of democracy (although, unlike the Night's Watch, which incorporates commoners and nobility into the same organization, both orders had affiliated non-knightly military forces of common soldiers they relied on).

So what does this suggest? One thing that comes to mind is that the eventual fates of both orders might point to the future of the Night's Watch: both orders eventually fell into decline when they repeatedly wore themselves out defending one chosen frontier after another, as the boundaries of what fell inside the borders of "Christendom" were continually reinvented. Without a self-directed change, as Jon will later offer, the Night's Watch might go the same way.

What If?

There aren't any really big and obvious hypotheticals here. Jon Snow might have not taken Donal Noye's advice for a while, but one gets the feeling that, eventually, the arrival of Samwell Tarly and his more balanced emotional state (compared to the show, more on that in a second) probably would have tipped him in the direction of warming up to his fellow recruits in the Watch.

Book vs. Show

If Robb Stark gets a better shake from the show than he did in the books, Jon Snow unfortunately comes out a bit worse (although I don't blame Kit Harrington for that, although he might not have been my choice for Jon Snow), and this chapter kind of shows why. To begin with, we see a different post-training fight in which both Jon Snow and the other boys engage in less of an attempted shanking and more of an understandable ass-kicking (albeit one in which Snow is giving just as good as he's getting); likewise, the fight is resolved within the Night's Watch, as opposed to Tyrion's intervention. Jon Snow overall seems less mopey than he does in the show, as we see from his change of attitude at the end of the chapter, where he's even making jokes.

The change in Tyrion's role is quite interesting. In the show, he steals Donal Noye's role, as well as playing the role of Jon's teacher and intimate. Here, Tyrion is more of the intellectual, focusing less on Jon's conflict with the Night's Watch as introducing him to more existential ideas about the Wall as a barrier that Jon Snow should be interested in finding out "what's on the other side" of, raising the question about whether the grumkins and the snarks exist in a more open-minded way than on the show, and continuing his advice on the theory of taking names used against you and turning them into armor.

It's a slightly more focused, if less impressive, performance, and I would be perfectly happy to enjoy the larger-than-life presence of

Peter Dinklage's Tyrion, if it wasn't for my nagging worry about whether Donal Noye's triumph in the tunnel (which we'll probably see in season four) is going to have the same impact as it would if we'd gotten to know him earlier.

We'll see.

EDDARD IV

"All justice flows from the king."

Synopsis

Eddard Stark, Hand of the King, arrives in King's Landing and meets with the small council. He is informed of the state of royal finances and then is led by Littlefinger to his wife, who informs him of a Lannister conspiracy. Eddard makes his plans for the future.

Political Analysis

This is where things really get interesting. Like a rollercoaster with a really long, slow climb to the first drop, "Eddard IV" is where the long transition of the Lord of House Stark from his seat of power in Winterfell ends and his trial by fire in the politics of King's Landing begins. And, appropriately, this is where our assessment of Eddard Stark as a political actor should begin.

The first thing that should be said is that Eddard actually has quite a bit of self-awareness and not bad political instincts when it comes to his new environment; indeed, people who started from the HBO show and then migrated to the books are often surprised when they find out how perceptive Eddard is, and how disciplined he is in keeping his own counsel rather than saying what pops into his head. His initial reactions are quite interesting: Eddard is "cool and yet polite" to Varys, the "councilor Ned liked least," who is, in reality, a traitor to House Baratheon; he finds Renly engaging and yet maintains a slight distance; and he deeply dislikes Littlefinger (who is the most active force trying to destroy him) and is happy to return the man's jabs and insinuations with verbal sallies of his own.

More importantly, he recognizes that "he did not belong here, in this room, with these men... Ned looked down at the council table and wondered which were the flatterers and which the fools. He thought he knew already." Whatever his faults, Eddard is not one of those romantics who believes that honesty is all that's needed to triumph; he knows from the outset that he is outmatched and attempts to compensate by "running silent," as it were. If nothing else, the revelation of Robert's profligacy (more on this in a bit) and inattention to the business of government is revelation enough; when he thinks back to Robert's behavior on the kingsroad, Eddard is hardly idealistic when it comes to his old friend.

Rather, I would argue that Eddard's critical weakness as a political actor comes from his tendency to think about politics in terms of people and personalities, rather than in terms of institutions and sources of power. This begins with how Eddard thinks of himself: "He would have to remember that he was no longer in Winterfell, where only the king stood higher; here, he was but first among equals." Eddard sees the role of the Hand to be one of *personal* adviser to the King. His objection when he learns that the crown is six million crowns in debt is that "I will not believe that Jon Arryn allowed Robert to beggar the realm," because he knew Jon Arryn as a man of honor. When he learns of the extent of corruption in the court, his first instinct is to "go to Robert... and pray that he is the man I think he is... and not the man I fear he has become."

We know from the history of Westeros that this is completely wrong; the Hand of the King is second to none but the king, clothed in immense power – as I have said before, Eddard has the authority to raise troops, to replace the leadership of the gold cloaks and the small council itself, to levy taxes and reduce spending, to throw men he believes to be corrupt into jail, and to summon men he wants to interview with warrants and armed officers of the state. Past Hands of the King have been able to dominate, even overthrow, kings if they understood how to make use of the machinery of government. What Eddard does not understand until too late is that the corruption of institutions is separate from the corruption of individuals, and that individuals can make use of institutions – even the very corruption of those institutions - in order to work reform. When he becomes Hand of the King, Tyrion Lannister will understand this at a bone-deep level.

This understanding of sovereignty as overwhelmingly personal is unfortunately just as bone-deep in Eddard Stark. He believes that "all justice flows from the king" because he was raised to believe in the old ways that say that a monarch should execute the sentence himself, that crimes established by law and punishments enacted by the state have to be mediated through the individual conscience of the man holding the sword. For him to accept that there is power outside of that is to reject what it means to be a Stark. And yet... it's fascinating how much Eddard understands his potential powers when he stands on the familiar ground of the north. When he is confronted with the threat of a Lannister conspiracy, Eddard acts with decisive, pragmatic action: he orders Houses Tallhart and Glover to reinforce and fortify Moat Cailin, he instructs Lord Manderly to increase the naval strength of White Harbor, and he prepares to threaten Theon Greyjoy's life to blackmail Balon Greyjoy for his fleet. These are not the actions of a naïf. Nor is Eddard mistaken when he says that "the Lannisters are merciless in the face of weakness... but they would not dare attack the north without all the power of the realm behind them, and that they shall not have. I must play out this fool's masquerade." On a crucial point of realpolitik, Eddard Stark understands at least somewhat that the monarchy itself is the high ground that will allow the possessor to marshal the forces of legitimacy and tradition against his foe.

The other major political thread here is our second direct glimpse into the Littlefinger Conspiracy at work. As I pointed out last time, Baelish has a major weakness in his ego and his need to continually show everyone around him how much smarter he is than them: consider that Baelish spends most of the chapter making veiled comments about his wife, Eddard's death, Littlefinger's plans to "[lead] you to the dungeons to slit your throat," that Eddard is an idiot, that he's old and slow, that Littlefinger hates his family, and so forth. Given that he's never met Eddard Stark before, this is incredibly risky behavior (he's all but telling Eddard what he plans to do and giving him a dozen reasons to consider him an enemy), and it winds up with Eddard shoving a dagger up against his chin, at the very edge of death.

Similarly, as I have discussed, his belief that he holds Varys's "balls in the palm of my hand... or would, if he were a man, or had any balls" is a dangerously and potentially deadly stupid belief, especially since, in lying directly to Eddard about the dagger, he's given the Spider a perfect opportunity to out Littlefinger's duplicity. At the same time, Littlefinger is successful in convincing Eddard to make use of him (if not to trust him) – although, notably, Eddard is clever enough to question why Tyrion Lannister would want Bran dead – and convinces Catelyn that, in him, she has "found a brother I'd thought lost."

Overall, it points to a conspirator with the soul of a high-stakes gambler.

Speaking of gambling, "Eddard IV" also brings us to the question of the six million coins in debt and to what extent Littlefinger engages in embezzlement and other financial misconduct, and what part this played in his overall conspiracy. Personally, I'm of the belief that, while Robert Baratheon did run up significant debts through high living and dealing with the Greyjoy Rebellion, Littlefinger probably did engage in corrupt practices in order to further his agenda. Here's how I think it worked:

1. Littlefinger got his start as the Master of Customs at Gulltown, by trading on Lysa Tully's unrequited love for him. He gains Jon Arryn's respect and patronage when he increases income ten-fold (*A Storm of Swords*, chapter 68) – although Tyrion says that it was only three-fold (*A Clash of Kings*, chapter 17). Increases of tax revenue of that extent (without any mention of increase in tax rates or increased enforcement, etc.) are unlikely to have come through strictly legal means. My guess is that what Littlefinger did was something like this: instead of passing on the legitimate revenue, Littlefinger instead diverted the funds to his own

accounts, along with bribes and kickbacks he takes from allowing selected merchants to avoid customs duties, and takes that money and lends it at high-interest rates and buying and selling high-value mercantile goods (again, favoring the merchants who owe him for the pass on customs duties, and probably getting preferable rates), and then using that money as collateral for loans that he would then represent as increased revenue.

2. After three years of minor positions within the bureaucracy of King's Landing, he is named master of coin, at which post he remains for seven years. Yet again, income is increased ten-fold (*A Clash of Kings*, chapter 17). And we know that a big part of the way that Littlefinger accomplishes this is by massively borrowing from House Lannister, House Tyrell, the Iron Bank of Braavos, Tyroshi trading cartels, and the Faith of the Seven, *and then not paying back either interest or principle on the loans*, instead using the money to speculate in real estate, shipping, commodities, and become a moneylender. He also engages in the sale of tax licenses and offices, receiving kickbacks from "the Keepers of the Keys... the King's Counter... the King's Scales... the officers in charge of all three mints. Harbormasters, tax farmers, customs sergeants, toll collectors, pursers, wine factors – nine out of every 10 belonged to Littlefinger." We know, moreover, that Littlefinger prevents exposure by convincing the king to excuse Janos Slynt's corruption, and by adding troublesome debtors to the crown to the death list of Antler Men.

3. This tells us several things. First, the only way that kind of scheme draws a profit is if tax farmers take in more than they pass on to the king, and moreover more than they paid for the license and the kickbacks. Hence, total royal taxation and total royal revenues can't have been matching up. Second, in addition to the sale of offices and kickbacks (which represents public corruption), the mention of wine factors (private citizens and businessmen, not royal officials), and the purchase of "wagons, shops, ships, and houses" at the same time that he's personally purchasing a number of brothels, suggests that there's a strong element of personal corruption here, as well. As a hedge lord and royal official, Littlefinger shouldn't have the personal capital to make these kinds of purchases, so he must be getting the money somewhere, and the most logical explanation is that he's using the royal treasury as his personal bank.

So how does this answer the question of tenfold increases in revenue and debt? What's going on here, I think, is that Littlefinger came upon a situation where the riotous living of the king could be used to hide his own actions: thus, by using the same divert-and-speculate model that he used in Gulltown (along with falsifying the books), Littlefinger is able to represent a vast increase in the king's revenues (even though much of that increase is being taken by Littlefinger and his army of corrupt officials) as collateral for massive loans from House Lannister, Tyrell, the Iron Bank, Tyroshi traders, and the Faith, which he uses to increase his own financial standing. In this fashion, Littlefinger kills several birds with one stone: he enriches himself at the expense of some of the most powerful houses and institutions in Westeros; he creates a political and economic powerbase in the merchant and bureaucratic classes of King's Landing; and he destabilizes the monarchy while creating the conditions for conflict between major powers when the whole house of cards comes tumbling down. Most importantly, Littlefinger makes himself indispensable - a prosperous monarch could easily replace him, but an indebted monarch needs a wizard to manage his shaky finances.

Historical Analysis

I'm not going to add much here, since I've already given my thoughts about Littlefinger's historical doppelganger. However, I would like to extend my previous comments about royal indebtedness. Medieval and royal monarchs were perennially in debt because they had a limited tax base (thanks to the tax-free status of the nobility and the clergy), a weak bureaucracy for the collection of said taxes, and because of the extreme expense of war and the high living monarchs were expected to maintain.

To give some examples: Robert Baratheon's spiritual counterpart, Henry VIII, was £3 million in debt (or £1.2 billion in today's money), and that was after he pillaged the monasteries of England and halted tithes to the Catholic Church. Other early modern monarchs fared even worse: Henry II of France (ruled 1547-1559) owed 40 million livres compared to an income of 12 million livres and went bankrupt in 1557. The French monarchy didn't recover its finances until around 1600 thanks to Henry IV's appointment of Sully as his chief minister. His contemporary, Phillip II of Spain, despite all the wealth of Mexico and Peru, went bankrupt three times (1557, 1560, and 1576), and historians suggest that his personal debts were equal to 60% of Spain's GDP at the time.

At the same time, these monarchs were constantly at war. Robert Baratheon experienced only two brief wars - his own rebellion and the even shorter Greyjoy Rebellion - and had the benefit of 10 years of warm and clement weather. That's a big part of the reason why I'm skeptical that even Robert could have spent that much money. The kings on the Iron Throne don't have a standing army to drain their finances, they don't have an early modern bureaucracy (even relatively decentralized early modern England had 1,000 royal officials) in anywhere near the size - the "usual suspects" just aren't there.

What If?

I only see one major hypothetical here: **what if Eddard had killed Littlefinger then and there?** We're talking an enraged Stark with a knife under Littlefinger's chin. Naturally, there's a short-term problem of having murdered a small councilor, but Littlefinger is roundly loathed, and Eddard could easily claim provocation. Littlefinger could be replaced by Wyman Manderly or even a Mace Tyrell, and an audit of his books, followed by the expropriation of his estate for corruption, would no doubt put some dent into the crown's debts.

Long-term, Eddard Stark avoids being double-crossed by Janos Slynt, arrests Cersei and Joffrey, Stannis is proclaimed king of Westeros, and Eddard Stark can go home in peace, securing his reputation as a reformist Hand on the Cincinnatus model.

Book vs. Show

There's a couple of minor-but-telling differences between the book and the show's depiction of Eddard's arrival in King's Landing. To begin with, in the book, Eddard as an educated nobleman asks for a change of clothes, whereas in the show, Benoiff and Weiss decided to reinforce the contrast between the gruff, no-nonsense northerners and the effete, cultured southerners. A minor detail, but one that points to a slightly more complex Eddard. Secondly, Eddard in the book actually draws steel on Littlefinger, whereas in the show, he just chokes him out, which I'm rather indifferent to.

Rather, the more important difference is that we lack Eddard's internal voice. I think Sean Bean's a great actor – don't get me wrong – but the disjuncture between Eddard's outward appearance, speech, and actions and his internal monologue is so stark that I don't think any actor could have expressed such complex inner life without resorting to the dreaded voiceover.

TYRION III

"Chip the ice off your eyes, my good lords. Ser Alliser Thorne should be mucking out your stables, not drilling your young warriors."

Synopsis

Tyrion has dinner with Lord Commander Mormont, Maester Aemon, Ser Alliser Thorne, and the other leadership of the Night's Watch. During a healthy exchange of views, Tyrion engages in a bit of harmless horsing around with Ser Alliser in a way that will have no repercussions whatsoever. Mormont and Tyrion discuss the sorry state of the Night's Watch. Tyrion bids Jon Snow goodbye and agrees to help out Bran.

Political Analysis

Tyrion Lannister has a keen eye for the inner workings of institutions and seeing how the pieces connect – whether as Hand of the King or master of Casterly Rock's sewers and cisterns – so it's appropriate that in "Tyrion III," we get a second glimpse into the dysfunctions of the Night's Watch.

And as we learn from the Old Bear himself, the statistical evidence of dysfunction is quite grim: in guarding a Wall four times as long as Hadrian's Wall and *27 times* taller than the Great Wall of China, the Night's Watch has less than 1,000 men (or three-and-a-third men per mile). Shortages of manpower affect the Night's Watch's ability to conduct reconnaissance and interdiction missions north of the Wall, to repair (let alone build) the Wall, to man more than a few castles, but, most critically, make the Night's Watch vulnerable to any loss in the field (as we will see in *Storm of Swords*). In this, the Night's Watch shares the vulnerability of the classical Spartans (who limited citizenship to those who could trace their ancestry back to the first Spartan ancestors and who excluded their helot slaves, the vast majority of the population, from military service) who could muster only a few thousand Spartiates (Spartan citizens fully educated as soldiers). While the Spartan army was supreme on the battlefield for 150 years, their low numbers and the difficulty of recruiting new Spartiates meant that any defeat could be crippling, if not fatal.

That defeat came at the hands of the Sacred Band of Thebes at the Battle of Leuctra in 371 BC. While the Spartan army only lost between 1,000-4,000 of their 10,000 hoplites, they couldn't replace the 700 Spartiate hoplites who served as the core of that army without waiting for a new generation of Spartiates to be born and raised, and this lead to the decline and fall of Spartan hegemony in Greece. Jeor Mormont faces a similar fate – with the 300 men he can bring to bear against Mance Rayder, he potentially could defeat a wildling host of a hundred thousand using his superior arms, cavalry, and discipline, but if he loses those 300 men, the Night's Watch cannot recover in the same way that the wildlings can.

All of this makes the problems of leadership in the Night's Watch even worse. As Jeor Mormont notes, "apart from the men at my table, I have perhaps 20 who can read, and even fewer who can think, or plan, or *lead*." A smaller military force isn't always the underdog – following from my analogy in "Jon III," I could point to the Siege of Malta in 1565, when 500 Knights of Malta along with 5,600 allies fought off an Ottoman army of 28,000-48,000. But in order for a smaller military force to succeed, they need a superior officer corps to ensure that what limited force they have can be brought to bear in the most effective manner possible and so that discipline is maintained. The fact that the Night's Watch's roster of competent officers is so low is an existential crisis for this organization.

Given these dismal facts, what can we say about the Old Bear, Jeor Mormont, as a leader? To be fair, Lord Commander Mormont is dealing with the legacy of centuries of royal neglect. And he does, at every opportunity, try to rectify the Night's Watch's shortcomings by lobbying Tyrion, by sending Ser Alliser Thorne to King's Landing with the wight's hand, and by sending out a letter to all five of the feuding kings of Westeros requesting assistance.

On the other hand, his comment that "the Watch has no shortage of stableboys... Ser Alliser is an anointed knight, one of the few to take the black" as his reason for employing someone eminently unsuitable to be an instructor suggests that Jeor Mormont is also something of a traditionalist who aspires to little more than maintaining the status quo. A more forward-thinking man might have looked for more than just one commoner to bulk up the officer corps, let alone something as revolutionary as having Maester Aemon teach some adult literacy courses. Mormont's blind spot when it comes to knights and nobles versus more qualified commoners (Cotter Pyke aside) trickles down throughout the Night's Watch, as we saw back in the "Prologue."

On the other hand, Jeor's use of Craster as an informant and resource base for Night's Watch rangers may argue instead that Lord Commander Mormont is really a pragmatist working with poor tools. Ser

Alliser is a lousy teacher, but he may not have many men with the formal military training that a knight receives who could teach, so he makes use of the man as long as he is necessary. One might question whether this strategy is good for the long term, but one also has to respect the choices of a man stuck between a rock and a hard place.

Two other actions point to Jeor as more than a traditionalist: his decision to lead a 300-man ranging to confront the twin threats of Mance Rayder and the appearance of the wights, and his decision to begin grooming Jon Snow as his successor rather than to promote from the current officer corps. Capacity for growth is one of the highest virtues we prize in our historical leaders, and when Jeor is forced to change, he does. Unfortunately, Mormont makes his move too late, without sufficiently preparing the groundwork for change.

More's the pity.

Historical Analysis

I've discussed previously any number of historical parallels for the Night's Watch, from the Hadrian-era Roman Legion to the Knights of Malta. However, there's an additional wrinkle to the Night's Watch: the way a long-standing institution in decline shifts its purpose. Once an army of 10,000 men tasked with defending the Wall from the threat of the Others, the Watch has become a barely-viable force for keeping out wildling invasions; the fact that Jeor Mormont admits that "the mountain people are moving south, slipping past the Shadow Tower in numbers greater than ever before" points to the reality that the Wall isn't really designed to prevent human beings from coming south.

I discussed the *limitanei* briefly in "Jon III," but they share this quality of mission creep with the Night's Watch and, thus, deserve to be discussed in greater detail. While the Roman army changed repeatedly during the Republic (from an organization of self-financing well-off farmers to a professional organization of working class Romans and so on) and early Empire, one of the ongoing principles of the Roman army was to prevent the emergence of a warrior caste that might spark regional rebellions: hence, limited tenures for propraetors and proconsuls as generals, time-limits for tours of duty, assignment of soldiers to places outside their homeland for their tours of duty, retirement packages in the form of land in places in the Empire in locations other than their homeland, and so on and so forth. Despite these efforts, this policy gradually broke down – leading to a series of destabilizing rebellions and civil wars.

The Emperor Constantine's military reforms in AD 300 were the logical extension of this process: Constantine divided the army into *comitatenses* (mobile cavalry and heavily-armed and well-armored professional soldiers stationed deep in the interior, who would intercept major invasion forces) and *limitanei*. The latter were frontier militias given land around *burgi* (fort-towns and resupply stations) in exchange for their hereditary service, and served under *comites* (counts) and *dux* (dukes). Normally, the *limitanei* acted as border guards and were only supposed to delay major invasions until the better-equipped mobile army could respond; in times of crisis, they would be drafted into service with the *comitatenses*. Many historians have argued that we can see the outlines of proto-feudalism in these social structures, especially once the victorious Goths, Franks, etc. took up Roman titles and ideology and sought to adapt Roman models of logistics and military organization for the new order.

As I've pointed out earlier, the fall of the Roman Empire was really less of a catastrophic break with the past and more of a gradual transition where institutions adapted and were adapted to changing political and social needs; we see the same process in Westeros. Just as the *limitanei* started as Roman legionaries and ended as feudal warriors, the Night's Watch has undergone a major shift in purpose in reaction to changing institutional imperatives. Without Others to fight, new enemies have to be identified so that the Wall and the men who guard it retain some purpose.

What If?

This isn't a chapter that necessarily brims with major hypotheticals, but there are two things that jump out at me:

What if Tyrion doesn't stop at Winterfell? If Tyrion doesn't speak with Jon Snow and agree to help out Bran, then he might well have avoided the castle on his way back. This has some rather subtle but important consequences – Bran doesn't get his new saddle, therefor he's not out in the woods when the wildlings attack, which means Osha probably doesn't get taken captive, which may well mean that Bran and Rickon Stark don't make it out from Winterfell when the Greyjoys take the castle. On the other hand, if Tyrion's isn't made suspicious by Catelyn Stark's absence, he doesn't make an issue of it when he gets to the Inn at the Crossroads and avoids being taken captive.

What if Tyrion refrains from antagonizing Ser Alliser Thorne? Now, I tend to avoid character moments as opposed to plot moments for this section, but I wonder if the two of them hadn't hit it off so badly at this meal, whether Tyrion wouldn't have Ser Alliser thrown into a dungeon cell for weeks, if not months, so that the wight's hand rots. I don't know how much this would have changed things in the short-term; Tyrion isn't about to dispatch thousands or even hundreds of men when the capital is under immediate threat. However, I think the long-run picture would change dramatically if people in the south other than Davos and Stannis actually considered events up at the Wall to be a legitimate threat to the safety of the realm.

Book vs. Show

The show kind of leaves out the Tyrion/Ser Alliser plot for the most point, since Ser Alliser doesn't even show up in the second season (which is going to be an issue when we get to the fourth season). Beyond that, the major difference between the book and the show is that Jon Snow explicitly asks Tyrion for assistance with Bran in the book, whereas in the show, he simply asks Tyrion to tell Bran he misses him.

ARYA II

"Stick them with the pointy end."

Synopsis

Arya sits through most of a rather uncomfortable dinner with her family before running off to her room and refusing to come out. Her father comes in to discuss swords, Lyanna, who is to blame for the death of Mycah, and the nature of wolf packs. Three days later, Arya is late to her first dancing lesson, where she meets the First Sword of Braavos.

Political Analysis

Recapping chapters that have child POVs is rather difficult for a blog like this, but Arya's storyline is something of an exception. The eponymous "Underfoot" Stark frequently acts as an unseen witness to political events in King's Landing, giving us further information filtered through an unreliable narrator, because nothing is ever easy. Here, we see that Lord Eddard Stark is fighting with the small council, although we don't learn why or the result of their conflict. We can sift out from this anecdote that Eddard hasn't made much in the way of allies on the council (although you'd think with Barristan and Renly, he could at least muster three out of six votes) and still hasn't realized that the Hand has power outside of the small council.

We get a clearer picture, however, of Eddard Stark's political theory of lordship as enlightened paternalism: "Her father used to say that a lord needed to eat with his men, if he hoped to keep them. 'Know the men who follow you... and let them know you. Don't ask your men to die for a stranger.'" It's not entirely clear where Eddard got his hands on a copy of Richard Neudstadt's *Presidential Power*, which recommends that political executives should cultivate multiple sources of information, especially at lower levels of their bureaucracy, so that they can get a more accurate grasp of the inner workings of their own government without the biases of their closest advisors, but it's a rare sign that the lord of Winterfell actually knows what he's doing. Far more so than most lords, Eddard is well-informed about accounting, blacksmithing, horse-breeding, literature, and current events from a variety of class perspectives, which helps to explain why men would be willing to fight and die in his name long after his family is thrown from power.

At the same time, it's important to recognize how this thinking is a hindrance when Eddard comes to King's Landing. Far too often, commentators focus on his honor as his Achilles's Heel, but, as I have argued, it's Eddard's conception of power as entirely relational as opposed to institutional that's the real problem. At the end of the day, Eddard doesn't have to fight the small council – he has the authority to command or to replace them. If he dislikes the tourney's drain on public funds, he could easily decree that competitors and audience members have to pay a per capita tax to defray the costs of the event. But as we will see again and again, to Eddard his role is to be Robert's friend and adviser.

An interesting second topic introduced in this chapter is Arya's resemblance to Lyanna Stark and what that tells us about the internal dynamics of House Stark. Not only does Arya share the same "Stark look" (perhaps another reason why Ned shows a particular interest in his youngest daughter) as the "beautiful and willful" Lyanna, but she also has the "wildness… the wolf's blood" that brought Lyanna and Brandon to an early death. Certainly, given Arya's disdain for gender roles and her aggressive temper, this is particularly accurate, although I think there's a strong argument to be made that the succeeding books have harshly tempered this tendency, focusing her aggression into sudden acts of violence through intense self-repression. I also think this resemblance explains why Eddard acts like a modern, "enlightened" parent in this chapter, then pulls back in "Eddard V": Eddard allows Arya to run wild because of his love for his wayward sister, yet, at the same time, fears that Arya will share her fate.

At the same time, Eddard's advice to his daughter that the Starks have to act as a wolf-pack in winter shows how the symbols and credos of the great houses shape their thinking. The Starks genuinely do form a united front against their enemies, while the Lannisters actively undermine and then murder each other, and the Greyjoys' dysfunction is riddled with abuse, assassination, and conflicting agendas. And while in the short run it hasn't stopped the Starks from falling from power, the growing likelihood is that the Lannisters will be brought down by their own actions and that the Greyjoys may well begin warring against each other.

Historical Analysis

One point before I get to the history: "Arya II" marks the entrance of fan-favorite Syrio Forel into the narrative, but it also marks the first really strong signifier that Arya Stark is beginning to walk down the path of the hero's journey. If Sansa's narrative throughout the *Song of Ice and Fire* series is a deconstruction of the Disney Princess myth, arguably Arya's narrative throughout the series is a deconstruction of the traditional fantasy protagonist. Consider the following: Arya is born into a noble household that is betrayed and overthrown, forcing her to assume a false identity as a **commoner** and often as a **boy**; gets not just one, but two mentors who train her and hand on moral lessons before disappearing from the narrative; has a list of people to revenge herself against in rising order of importance; and is currently hanging out with a bunch of mystic assassins in their secret temple. And, yet, the result isn't so much an upward slope of competence and empowerment and self-understanding, but a conga line of psychological trauma, identity loss, and an inability to deal with problems outside of violence (even as many of her revenge targets die unrelated deaths).

Now back to the history. In learning to become a "water dancer," Arya Stark joins the ranks of some pretty formidable historical women duelists who hacked their way through traditional gender roles centuries ahead of schedule. Julie d'Aubigny (aka "La Maupin") was trained in fencing by her father, became the mistress of the Comte d'Armagnac (Louis XIV's Master of Horse), dumped her husband to run off with a swordmaster and began dressing as a man, dueled three men at once and, later, seduced one of them when he turned out to be the son of a duke, kicked off her bisexuality by seducing a novice nun, stealing a nun's corpse and swapping it for her lover, and then burning down the novice's room to hide her abduction (for which she received a royal pardon from the Sun King), became an opera contralto superstar (where she busied herself chasing around sopranos and fighting duels), and became the subject of a best-selling novel.

Another duelist, Doña Catalina de Erauso, also known as the "Nun Lieutenant," escaped her nunnery by dressing as a boy, stowed away to Peru, where she became a duelist after a series of affairs with various married women and mistresses, rose to the rank of captain in the Spanish army, was discovered and shipped off to Rome, then arrested as a spy in France, and finally managed to get to Rome, where she received a Papal dispensation allowing her to cross-dress. The countess Madame de St Belmont, whose husband was imprisoned for rising up against Louis XIV, responded to a cavalry officer who had billeted himself on her estate by dressing as a man and challenging him to a duel as "le Chevalier de St. Belmont," which she then won, then dressed down the officer, saying, "You thought... that you were fighting with the Chevalier de St. Belmont; it is, however, Madame de St. Belmont, who returns you your sword, and begs you in future to pay more regard to the requests of ladies."

It's a pretty impressive track record for any young woman to live up to, but as we'll see, Arya is well on her way to historic levels of awesomeness. I'm still amazed that there aren't more movies about any of these women. Screenwriters, get on it!

What If?

I don't really see much in the way of potential turning points in this chapter. One could argue, I suppose, that it was possible that Eddard Stark could have not hired Syrio Forel, but in order for that to happen, I think you'd need to go back and rewrite most of Ned's childhood and personality.

This is one of those character-heavy, plot-light chapters that don't particularly lend themselves to hypotheticals, but "Daenerys III" should provide more material to work with.

Book vs. Show

The HBO show actually did this chapter fairly straightforwardly, with the only change being the addition of Sansa's doll (which I like, especially when we have the callback to it in season two), and leaving out Eddard storming off from the table due to being angry about the tourney, which isn't a particularly significant detail.

DAENERYS III

"The common people pray for rain, healthy children, and a summer that never ends... it is no matter to them if the high lords play their game of thrones, so long as they are left in peace... they never are."

Synopsis

Daenerys learns how to adapt both to the rigors of riding across the Dothraki sea and life as a khaleesi; after being attacked by her brother, Viserys, she rebels for the first time and orders that he be made to walk, shaming him in front of the *khalasar*. She discusses political theory with Jorah, and magic and dragons with her handmaidens. After introducing Khal Drogo to the cowgirl position, Dany celebrates her 14th birthday with a pregnancy.

Political Analysis

If some chapters are rich with political allusions or subtle advancements of the plot, "Daenerys III" is positively stuffed with characters openly debating political theory and its implications for their lives and the lives of millions of people in Essos and Westeros alike who have no idea how their futures might revolve around the fortunes of an exiled princess riding off into the trackless east. Just a warning: this may be a long one.

First off, we get an intriguing detail that raises some interesting questions about the Varys/Illyrio Conspiracy - that "Maester Illyrio had urged [Viserys] to wait in Pentos, had offered him the hospitality of his manse, but Viserys would have none of it." Illyrio's motives in trying to keep Viserys from following Drogo's *khalasar* to Vaes Dothrak are worth speculating on:

1. It's possible that Illyrio's understanding of the exiled prince's character and psychology led him to believe that the young man would not bond with the Dothraki and would possibly quarrel with Khal Drogo (whose psychology Illyrio understands quite well), and, thus, the offer is meant to keep Viserys safe. On the other hand, it's quite clear from *A*

Dance with Dragons that Illyrio considers Viserys "a vain young man, and greedy... Mad Aerys's son," and his overall solicitude for the siblings is further undercut by his comment that he did not expect Daenerys to survive.

2. It's possible, therefore, that Illyrio wanted to keep Viserys in his manse in Pentos in order to keep Viserys under his thumb. The question then becomes why Illyrio wanted the young man handy. It's possible that this was in order to follow through on Doran Martell's offer of marriage to Arianne Martell, as we found out in *A Feast for Crows*. However, the existence of Aegon VI under Varys and Illyrio's protection suggests a darker motive: perhaps Illyrio wanted Viserys safely under lock and key so that a consummated and fruitful union between Drogo and Daenerys could return to lead their army to Westeros in his name rather than her brother's (especially since, as Rhaegar's son, Aegon's claim, if genuine, would trump Viserys's, making the unstable young man extremely dangerous), with Viserys having quietly died offstage, as it were.

3. This suggests an alternate explanation for Illyrio's remarkable passivity in the face of Viserys's refusal ("Illyrio had blinked at that and wished him good fortune"): rather than an uncharacteristic moment of weakness, Illyrio's mildness might have been cover for a cool-headed decision that, with Aegon hidden, Viserys was simply disposable.

The second major political event in this chapter is the first major step in Daenerys's transformation from an outwardly-traumatized-yet-inwardly-perceptive child bride to a real political actor on the world stage. When Daenerys commands the *khalasar* to stop, in her own words she begins to speak "not [like] a queen" but, rather, "a khaleesi," a person who commands rather than gives commands. A khaleesi doesn't put up with even her brother manhandling her and shoves him back - her first act of rebellion in her life. A key theme underpinning this transformation is the importance of seeing: when Viserys screams at her to look at herself, she sees not "some horselord's slut," but someone who "looks as though she belonged here"; likewise, her rebellion is prompted not simply by pique, but by a sudden realization that Viserys "was a pitiful thing... had always been a pitiful thing." And, ultimately, a khaleesi is one who is one who makes things seen - her order to take Viserys's horse is less a punishment, since Viserys is incapable of understanding that he might be in the wrong, but rather a lesson directed at the Dothraki.

Throughout this chapter, assimilation is shown as a source of strength - it is Daenerys who dresses sensibly, who is beginning to learn their language, who understands their customs and cultural values, who, most importantly of all, learns to ride like them (there's a not particularly subtle theme of Daenerys learning to overcome the pains of riding her horse and becoming a true Dothraki rider with her overcoming her marital rape and learning how to ride her husband), who belongs out on the Dothraki sea. Viserys's failure to assimilate is a sign of his unworthiness – his impractical silks are rotting off his body, he struggles with new saddles and stirrups, and whose disrespect for Dothraki customs leads him to end up a disgraced figure (the "Cart King") who cannot possibly lead a *khalasar* across the narrow sea.

Jorah Mormont offers a third model for expatriates- like Daenerys and unlike Viserys, he understands the culture and language of the Dothraki and easily creates for himself a role as interpreter and guide for the new khaleesi; unlike Daenerys, Jorah is still "Jorah the Andal," still wears his Westerosi garb, and, while lacking the bitterness of Viserys's refusal to adapt, still prays for home. And just as Dany learns from Irri on how to adapt to the *khalasar*, she's also learning from Jorah how to adapt without leaving everything behind. Dany's vision of King's Landing and Dragonstone, where "all the doors were red," shows how Daenerys keeps a part of herself back from the *khalasar*, that she is extending her conception of "home" across two continents.

A third theme in this chapter is the khalasar as a social institution. While I've already discussed how the Dothraki's cosmopolitanism is a critical and under-appreciated aspect of their culture, there is a difference between the Dothraki in their tribute-mansions and in the "city on the march." Chiefly, the *khalasar* is a community whose members are seeing and being seen, in the same way that John Winthrop's "city on a hill" was supposed to be both an example to the world of a righteous community but also constantly observed by the world and its own inhabitants for how closely it hewed to its own examples. In a place where everyone lives in such close proximity without true walls to divide themselves, where the presence of slaves and servants and bloodriders and kos mean that people are always living in the presence of other people, "there are no secrets in a *khalasar*… no privacy in the heart of a *khalasar*."

The purpose of this surveillance is not, as we 21st century people might think, so much a matter of control and dominance, but more a mechanism for producing truths through acts of collective judgment in a society structured by honor. And the Dothraki need to know that because their society functions on the basis of honor relationships – a man is honored as khal because his strength and cunning are witnessed by the *khalasar*, and his reign lasts as long as his reputation does in the eyes of his people; a khal can rely on his kos and his bloodriders and honor them with his possessions because their oaths have been witnessed by the *khalasar*, so that violating that oath makes one a pariah; and so on down the social order to the lowest slave. Witnessing acts of honor and dishonor gives the collective a sense of character and the capacity to sanction through reputation. The Dothraki see Viserys for a walker so that they know the truth about his character; the Dothraki see Daenerys becoming a khaleesi so that they know the truth about hers.

A fourth theme is our introduction to Jorah Mormont's theory of politics. Following his decision to switch his loyalty from king to khaleesi, Jorah implicitly argues for what we might call a *meritocratic monarchism*, albeit a version that is extremely realistic or cynical about the peasant masses who are both ignorant of and continual victims of high politics. Rather than purely following the line of succession, Mormont seems to be arguing (and Daenerys accepts) that a true monarch has to live up to certain minimal standards – the monarch must have sufficient force of personality and strength of character that he or she inspires respect and loyalty both from the lords and knights who swear direct fealty and from the armies the monarchs seek to lead – without that, the monarch may lose her mandate to another. More on this as later chapters explore Jorah's relationship to his new monarch.

A final theme is the relationship between magic and dragons that had been hinted at vaguely before. In this chapter, we learn that it is common belief among the Targaryens that "magic had died in the west when the Doom fell on Valyria… and neither spell-forged steel nor stormsingers nor dragons could hold it back, but Dany had already heard that the east was different." This suggests that the standard narrative held by fans of the series – that magic returns to the world because Daenerys gives birth to three dragons – is not quite accurate; magic can die even in the presence of dragons, although the presence of dragons, like the appearance of the red comet, is both a sign of the rebirth of dragons and in some way a vector for the strengthening of magic. It also adds more weight to the idea that there is some localizing effect going on – the Long Night seems to have happened only in Westeros, just as the Doom has settled on Valyria rather than all of Essos, and Asshai seems to be an opposite pole to the "heart of true winter," a place where dragons and magic are still strong. (Incidentally, Daenerys points to blood magic and shadowbinding as arts that exist in Asshai, which suggests that much of what Melisandre is doing is using secular magic in service of religion, although pure R'hllorism does seem to have supernatural force in the form of resurrection, laying on hands, remote combustion, clairvoyance, and the capacity to do without sleep or food.)

Historical Analysis

The *khalasar* very much resembles many different nomadic peoples, from the Mongols to the Huns, but given the theme of assimilation in "Dany III," I wanted to bring in the historical parallel of the Comanche. As Professor Hamalainen describes in *Comanche Empire*, the Comanche were a horse-based nomadic society that maintained a vast empire in the American Southwest from the beginning of the 18th through to the late 19th century, managing to hold back the Spanish, Mexican, and American governments and to conquer and assimilate other southwestern Indian tribes, and building a vast economic trade network across the region. All of this – horse-based nomads who build cavalry-based military machines that raid at will and trade the resources gained through raiding and the tributes gained from refraining from raiding – very much resembles the Dothraki.

A further similarity is suggested by James F. Brook's *Captives and Cousins*, which points out that the raiding and trading of slaves (especially women and children) was a crucial aspect of this borderlands empire, in no small part because the ethnic and linguistic mixing were one of the few ways that interpreters and negotiators could be acquired. This is probably the case with the Dothraki – given that Drogo's marriage to a non-Dothraki is expected to give birth to a Dothraki child, the Dothraki do not require both parents of a Dothraki child to be of Dothraki blood; hence, the children of slaves sired by Dothraki are likely to be treated as part of the *khalasar*, suggesting a certain degree of cultural and ethnic diversity that would help to explain how the Dothraki are able to manage such a complex continent-spanning commercial empire of tribute and exchange with so many different cultures.

A second historical topic that comes up in this chapter is the character of Viserys. Judging simply from his personality – weak and bullying, paranoid and driven to fits of rage, prone to delusions about his political future and his own worth, his Oedipal obsession with his sister "killing" their mother – he seems a soul-mate for the Emperor Nero, the music and theater aficionado who cheerfully poisoned his adopted brother, assassinated his mother (after many unsuccessful and overly-theatrical attempts), who was accused of "fiddling while Rome burned," and who was easily dethroned. On the other hand, his rather gruesome passing is more clearly modeled on that of Marcus Licinius Crassus (who, in all other respects, doesn't resemble the young Targaryen at all).

At the same time, we can also view Viserys as part of a general historical trend of exiled royal pretenders whose exile shaped them to the point where they were no longer truly viable candidates for their nation's throne. James II's exile in France following the English Civil War meant that he spent the formative years of his life fighting for the absolutist monarchy of Louis XIV; thus, when he became king, he sought a large standing army, the proroguing of Parliament (too much like the Parlements that had led to the Fronde), and the relaxation of prohibitions on Catholicism, prompting his overthrow in 1688. Likewise, his son, James III, was ultimately hamstrung in his efforts to regain the throne by his refusal to recant his Catholic faith, which might have swayed otherwise pro-Stuart Tories who were staunch Anglicans. Like these figures, Viserys's experience of exile changed him – much of his paranoia can ultimately be traced back to his fear of (non-existent) Baratheon assassins, with his vanity, delusions, and bullying towards the one person he could dominate being something of a response to the repeated humiliations of a "Beggar Prince."

One could argue that it was Daenerys's own exile experience – her longing for the "red door" of home more than the Throne itself, her oppression at the hands of a would-be tyrant, her experience of slavery (however genteel it might be) – that inverted the usual trend of the royal exile.

What If?

Ironically for a chapter that focuses intently on Daenerys's growth as a character, most of the hypotheticals that arise have more to do with Viserys, given his increasingly erratic behavior.

What if Viserys had stayed in Pentos? As already discussed above, there are a couple different things that would have happened: Viserys might have gotten married off, he could have been quietly killed and replaced by Aegon, etc. However, the interesting question is what would have happened to Daenerys. Without Viserys attacking her in this scene and providing the catalyst for a personal revelation, it's quite possible that, however much she comes to see herself as a khaleesi, that she never comes to see herself as also the rightful queen of Westeros.

What if Viserys had (accidentally?) killed Daenerys (at this point in time)? I'll come back to this more when we get to Viserys's death, but the interesting thing is to see how close Viserys comes to destroying his chances (and Varys and Illyrio's plans) for a Dothraki alliance, again and again on the journey to Vaes Dothrak. The consequences would be quite interesting – while Varys and Illyrio would still have Aegon VI as backup (Viserys would definitely die a hideous death in this scenario), their potential invasion force would be reduced by several tens of thousands. One of the things we see is how contingent Dany's awakening of the dragons was – she had to avoid death but still be threatened with death (thus raising Drogo's attachment to the point where he's willing to invade Westeros), Drogo has to raid the Lhazareen and enslave Mirri Maz Duur, and so on and so forth. If Viserys had cut off that thread of the timeline ahead of schedule, then the dragons aren't reborn. Whatever that does to magic, the history of Essos is greatly changed: the House of the Undying goes unburnt, Astapor, Yunkai, and Meereen are not attacked, which means that the tigers don't seize power in Volantis, and so on and so forth.

What if Viserys had been killed then and there? This is a more subtle one. In OTL, Viserys dies at the hands of Khal Drogo after threatening Dany's life and the life of her unborn son, which gives Dany a way to process this otherwise traumatic event. But if Viserys were to die by Daenerys's orders, this changes things dramatically; while Dany arguably had been physically threatened, she's still a kinslayer. That's bound to have a psychological (if not a metaphysical) impact on Daenerys, possibly prompting her more towards the "mad" side of the family.

Book vs. Show

This is played fairly straight on the show, with one rather consequential change: in the book, taking Viserys's horse is Dany's idea, whereas, in the show, it's Rakharo's decision. On the one hand, I understand that, unlike in the book, where George R.R. Martin has to re-emphasize certain themes because it's been a while since you've read a Dany chapter, the TV show can focus more on a consistent character arc – from the Dany who still protects her brother to the Dany who hits him in the face with a belt. On the other hand, we lose the connection between Daenerys's assimilation and her rebellion against her brother – and a more realistic transition.

BRAN IV

"Oh, my sweet summer child... what do you know of fear? Fear is for the winter, my little lord, when the snows fall a hundred feet deep and the ice wind comes howling out of the north. Fear is for the long night..."

Synopsis

A depressed (and repressing) Bran listens to Old Nan tell some ghost stories, and then is summoned to the Great Hall, where Robb pointedly does not welcome Tyrion to Winterfell. Tyrion offers Bran a specially designed saddle, then is randomly assaulted by direwolves. Over dinner, Yoren shares the unwelcome news of Benjen Stark's disappearance, and Robb and Bran spend their first night talking in some time.

Political Analysis

Unfortunately, this is going to be a rather short chapter, since Bran's storyline doesn't really pick up on the political side of things until *Clash of Kings*, but let's make the most of it. While most of the chapter concerns itself with Bran grappling with his paralysis, there are a few political themes worth investigating.

First of all, we have Old Nan's (rather unreliable) histories that point to the extreme (and historically implausible) longevity of the Stark line. If Nan was brought into the castle as a wet nurse when Bran's grandfather's older brother was a baby, then given that Rickard was at least in his 40s at the time of Robert's Rebellion (17 years prior to the beginning of the narrative), than Nan is at least in her 70s. If, on the other hand, she was brought into the castle when Bran's great-grandfather's older brother was a baby, she may be pushing a hundred. Given Bran's vision in *A Dance with Dragons* and the title of the next Dunk and Egg novella (tentatively *The She-Wolves of Winterfell*), it's quite possible that Nan is the daughter of Dunk, or even Dunk's lover (which would put her at 120 years old, but you'd have to assume that she's mixed up some of the generations of her descendants, since her sons couldn't have fought in Robert's Rebellion if that were the case).

We also learn something of the Long Night and the Last Hero who saved Westeros from the Others - who, given the earlier discussion of recursive Brandons, may well have been Brandon the Builder and the source for the legend of Azor Ahai (given the similarities of both the Last Hero and Azor Ahai as heroes who successively lose everything they love in pursuit of a sword that will not break, and that Bran the Builder built the Wall during the Battle for the Dawn, stopping the threat of the Others). This also raises the interesting question: given the seemingly apocalyptic nature of the Long Night, with humanity pushed south and everyone left behind exterminated, how did we get wildlings? One possibility is that the wildlings were collateral damage caused by the construction of the Wall, or that they were later exiled beyond the Wall as part of some scheme of land clearances (as Ygritte will later suggest). A darker possibility suggested by the seductive quality of the Others in the Night's King story and Nan's stories of wildings sacrificing children to the Others, and one that the wildlings themselves would surely deny, is that the wildlings are the descendants of those who, during the Long Night, purchased safety from the White Walkers by sacrificing human beings to them as a sign of submission and who were banished for their crimes. Something to keep an eye on.

A second theme lightly touched on in "Bran IV" is the theme of Robb becoming "Robb the Lord," learning to put on "the stern face" and undescribed "voice" of this character. This process echoes earlier descriptions of Eddard "donning the face of Lord Stark of Winterfell" when he has to execute Gared for deserting the Night's Watch. What it entails is a bit more mysterious - we can see Robb finishing up his military training, both in terms of personal combat and leading other men, learning estate management with Maester Luwin, visiting surrounding holdfasts, and so forth. On the other hand, Martin almost immediately undercuts this by having Robb act impulsively with Tyrion, greeting him with an open blade (which symbolically denies Tyrion guest right at Winterfell), pointing his sword in Tyrion's face and failing the duties of courtesy and hospitality, and acting the idiot in front of Yoren later on that evening.

What this is trying to show, I'm not entirely sure, although my own guess is that this is part of Martin's early work that he might like to go back and revise a bit in the same way that Tyrion's tumbling didn't immediately make sense (likewise, the theme of Tyrion being repeatedly assaulted by direwolves is something that never really goes anywhere). After all, I think Robb's inexperience can be shown without the need for what reads like completely superfluous swordplay - but more on this in a bit.

Speaking of the duties of hospitality, or the "law of guest right" as it is commonly known, this is a running theme in the series that I want to highlight for a second for people to keep their eyes on - and keep track of what happens to people who violate them. Under guest right, once a guest has taken bread and salt (in other words, basic staple carbohydrates and an absolutely necessary mineral), they and their host are not to be harmed until the exchange of guest gifts ends the relationship. I'll talk more about this later, but it's interesting that guest right in Westeros dates back to the Age of Heroes (along with the northern custom that judges must also act as their own executioners) and that it is one of the few customs to have made the transition from First Men to Andal civilization in Westeros. Notably, those who violate guest right are deemed to have brought down the wrath of the old gods and the new.

Historical Analysis

The custom of guest-right seems to have been ubiquitous across the ancient world – it appears in Norse myth, in classical Greece, among the Celtic peoples, and in the Upanishads of Hinduism, which teach that "Atithi Devo Bhava" ("the guest is god"). This reference to the divine is not accidental – guest right is often explained through parables in which gods, usually the chief gods, appear as impoverished travelers, punish those who violate the custom, and reward those who uphold it.

By the laws of guest-right, hosts are bound to be hospitable (providing them with food, drink, and shelter generously), guests are bound to be courteous and respectful (which means keeping one's hands off the host's property and leaving after an appropriate period), gifts should be given upon parting to show respect for the honor of both parties, and violence is to be abhorred. Violations of guest right are shown to have cataclysmic consequences: the Trojan War begins when Paris abducts Helen while a guest under Menelaus's roof, angering Zeus (who, in addition to the god of the heavens, is also the god of travelers and hospitality); the suitors of Penelope earn their violent deaths by being bad guests who refuse to leave after ten years and abuse Odysseus when he arrives disguised as a beggar.

It's not surprising that Westeros, which we often forget spent almost 8,000 years as a mass of warring kingdoms (and the classical seven of the Kings of the North, the Iron Kings, Kings of the Reach, Storm Kings, Kings of the Rock, Kings of Mountain and Vale, and the Princes of Dorne were after a period of consolidation from hundreds of petty kingships), would so emphasize the custom of guest-right. In a situation where inter-kingdom raiding is ubiquitous and there's no central monarchy to prevent warfare, where the next village over might be part of an entirely different nation with its own legal jurisdiction, making any law enforcement impossible, travel becomes incredibly dangerous. Without a religious prohibition on killing guests, trade between regions, religious pilgrimages, and other vital exchanges would be impossible.

Finally, a quick note on prosthetics. While we often associate prosthetics with modern medicine, they're actually one of the oldest forms of medical technology we have records for. The Vedas of ancient India, dating back to 3500 BC, describe the Warrior Queen Vishpala losing a leg in battle and having an iron leg made so that she could continue fighting; the oldest surviving prosthesis is a wooden prosthetic big toe from Ancient Egypt dating back to 1000 BC. Götz von Berlichingen, a German knight who fought for the common people in the German Peasant's War and became known in folklore as the German Robin Hood, had an iron hand with springs and leather straps that could grip a variety of objects and move on command. Thus it's not particularly surprising that Tyrion would be able to divine a prosthetic saddle for Bran, given the level of scholarship that exists in Westeros - although it is surprising that Maester Luwin doesn't think of it, given his background in medical studies.

What If?

I've already discussed what would have happened if Tyrion had simply bypassed Winterfell on his way back, and there really aren't that many hypotheticals I could imagine that are consonant with the characters of the characters in this chapter: there's no way that Robb is going to be outwardly polite to a Lannister when he's just been told the Lannisters tried to murder his brother twice; it's unlike Tyrion to take out his anger with Robb on Bran by not giving Bran the saddle design (which actually would be significant, in that it would have meant Bran didn't go out riding that day, which probably means that either Osha dies at the hands of Robb Stark and Theon Greyjoy or simply slips past Winterfell on her route south, which, in turn, means that there's no competent adult to help Bran when the Greyjoys take Winterfell).

The only real hypothetical I can think of in this chapter is: **what if the direwolves had killed Tyrion?** It's not a very good one in that it ends a critically important character for no reason (indeed, I really doubt that the direwolves' hatred for Tyrion is ever going to be explained by Martin, given that they don't seem to react that way to other Lannisters who will actually do direct harm to their masters), but it would probably have started the war really quickly without the detour to the Vale and without Ned sidelined due to his injury.

Book vs. Show

This is one scene that I think the show actually does better than the book by toning down what I'll call "StupidRobb." Robb is certainly rude to Tyrion in this chapter, but the writers have wisely toned down his ridiculous pointing and drawing of swords (which is a rather odd relapse, given that he supposedly learned his lesson about that back when Catelyn revealed who was behind the assassination attempts on Bran) and taken out his rather childish display in front of Yoren. Now, granted, this kind of behavior is much more understandable coming from the book's 14-year-old Rob than the show's 17-year-old, but it's still problematic, given the need for the readers to care when the "Scarlet Rehearsal Dinner" happens.

    A little bit of teenage impulsiveness goes a long way, after all.

EDDARD V

"I have heard it said that poison is a woman's weapon... women, craven, and eunuchs."

Synopsis

Eddard Stark, Hand of the King, meets with Grand Maester Pycelle (the world's greatest conspirator and secret-keeper) to discuss the death of Jon Arryn and put in a library request for a certain book. On his way back to the office, he runs across Arya, and the two of them discuss the intersectionality of gender and disability in terms of social barriers to future careers. Finally, Eddard meets with Littlefinger and makes a huge mistake.

Political Analysis

With "Eddard V," we dive right back into the investigation of Jon Arryn's death and get a good look into the Lannister Conspiracy and the Littlefinger Conspiracy - which I'll take in chronological order.

First off, the *Lannister Conspiracy*, or, more specifically, Grand Maester Pycelle's role in the conspiracy. For all the crap that Eddard takes for being bad at King's Landing politics, I feel confident in saying that Pycelle is the *most inept political actor in the entirety of the* Song of Ice and Fire *series*. Consider what he lets slip in one conversation with Eddard: he lets slip that Jon Arryn was acting strangely before his death, that he asked for a particular book, that his symptoms are incredibly poison-like ("came to me one day... as hale and healthy as ever... the next morning, he was twisted over in pain, too sick to rise from bed"), that he sent away Jon Arryn's maester, and Jon Arryn's last words.

Had Pycelle kept any of that information back just by keeping his mouth shut (or had he came up with a plausible natural cause of Arryn's death, which would have further muddied the water), Eddard's investigation would have been virtually stillborn and the chance that he would have uncovered the secret of the father of Cersei's children, virtually non-existent. Even had Littlefinger or Varys put the Hand back on the track of Robert's bastard, there just wasn't enough evidence out there for them to lead him to the correct conclusion without revealing themselves. Now, to be fair, a big part of this has to do with the Lannister Conspiracy's failure to manage information well – Pycelle doesn't know exactly what Cersei's up to, didn't even get an order to kill Arryn, and I still think there's a possibility that his comments in "Tyrion VI" about knowing what Arryn was up to were made with 20-20 hindsight (given Eddard's statement in the throne room and Stannis's letter). However, given Pycelle's loyalty to the Lannister cause and the knowledge he definitely had that Cersei needed Arryn dead, that he himself helped him die, and a high likelihood that he knows why Arryn had to go, it is beyond idiotic for him to transmit any of this information to the Starks.

Then again, it's clear that tradecraft is not one of Pycelle's skills, as we then see with his laughably clumsy attempt to finger Varys, which Eddard Stark doesn't really buy, despite really disliking Varys. So unsuccessful is Pycelle that the Hand leaves the meeting believing that Pycelle has been lying to him and is a spy for some faction. (Note: for those of you who still believe that Eddard Stark is an idiot, let's acknowledge that Eddard doesn't trust either Pycelle, Varys, or Littlefinger initially, which puts him on par with Tyrion's Handship.)

On the other hand, as I've said, this also points to Cersei's weakness as a conspirator. Firstly, given the extreme danger of deliberately cuckolding the king and trying to place incestuous Lannister-spawn on the Iron Throne, the list of people who uncovered this deadly secret includes Stannis, Jon Arryn, Varys, Littlefinger, and Pycelle – doesn't speak very well to her ability to keep things secret. Secondly, despite the fact that she desperately needed Jon Arryn to die when he began investigating her, she seems to have taken no action to make that happen – despite his doctor being in her service, she doesn't give an order to have him poisoned or even to let him die when he was poisoned by a third party. That's suicidally passive unless... more on this later. Thirdly, after doing this, she seems to have given no instructions to Pycelle about what to say to the new Hand of the King she's made a mortal enemy of just recently.

One little detail I like in this scene is that George R.R. Martin gives a tiny hint that Lysa Arryn was responsible for the Hand's murder and why when Pycelle says "grief can derange even the strongest and most disciplined of minds, and the Lady Lysa was never that. Since her last stillbirth, she has seen enemies in every shadow." Depression, paranoia, and stillbirth – all the details are there, and I have to admit that I completely missed the significance of this until I began this project (which is approximately my fourth or fifth trip through the series).

A second quick theme we get here is the question of what Bran can be and what Arya can be in the society of Westeros. Both Stark children are at an interesting position; without his legs, Bran's ambition to achieve prominence through traditional masculine roles of warriorhood is over just at the time that Arya has begun her first steps in learning to become a warrior. And yet, Bran's future possibilities are far greater than Arya's – he can still be a lord, a councilor, a builder (I don't for a second think that it's an accident that Eddard mentions Bran building castles like the Bran who built Winterfell), an explorer, or a septon. (On a side-note, it's interesting that Eddard doesn't mention Bran becoming a maester. Outside of Lazy Leo and Aemon Targaryen, I can't think of a single maester from a major noble house.) By contrast, Arya's future path is that of a wife and a mother – gender discrimination in a nutshell. On the other hand, as I suggested in "Arya II," I think that part of Eddard's backsliding here has to do with his ambivalence about his daughter's similarity to his doomed, wayward sister. It may well be that Eddard's rather thoughtless reply is more of an expression of parental fear than patriarchy.

A third political theme in this chapter is a major step forward for the *Littlefinger Conspiracy*, in which the master of coin succeeds in getting Eddard Stark, who previously "could not find it in him to trust Lord Petyr Baelish, who struck him as too clever by half," to trust him by delivering the locations of the remaining members of Lord Arryn's staff, including Ser Hugh of the Vale. What Littlefinger is doing here is quite interesting. Given his closeness to Lysa, it's quite probable that Littlefinger was responsible for removing Arryn's maester, steward, captain of the guard, knights, and retainers from King's Landing, those who would have the highest chance of having pertinent information about Arryn's murder and his investigation. In this way, Littlefinger is able to gain Eddard's trust while dribbling out low-value information, thus gaining the ability to modulate the pace of Eddard's investigation; crucially, he steers Eddard Stark astray by dissuading him from using his power as Hand to summon witnesses directly, thus ensuring that he can track the Hand's investigations and slowing it down overall. Most likely, like Varys, Littlefinger wants to make sure that Lord Stark only finds out the truth at a time when the truth will bring about a civil war that Littlefinger has adequately prepared for.

More on this tactic when we get to the death of Ser Hugh of the Vale.

Historical Analysis

While I first brought up the topic of the genetic detective story back in "Arya I," I wanted to return to the topic as we begin Eddard's investigations in King's Landing. While it seems obvious to us that Cersei's children are the products of incest, as readers we have the advantage of having witnessed Cersei and Jaime having sex and having gone to school after the widespread acceptance of Mendelian genetics (and, keep in mind, it wasn't really until 1918, when

Mendelian inheritance theory [first developed in 1865] was synthesized together with Darwinian evolutionary theory, that it became widely accepted). Given that Eddard is working with the intellectual tools available to the fantasy equivalent of a 15th century English nobleman (and given the extreme length of Westerosi history compared to our own, it's quite possible that Westeros has been intellectually and technologically stagnant for quite some time), I think we have to be very clear about what Eddard knows and when he knows.

At the moment, all Eddard knows is that his crazy sister-in-law thinks the Lannisters murdered Jon Arryn, that Jon Arryn might well have been poisoned, that he asked to look at a book regarding lineages, and that he said "the seed is strong." He doesn't yet know that Arryn was investigating King Robert's bastards (which could be explained as having been asked by Robert to see to his children), that all of Robert's bastards have black hair no matter what the hair color is of the mothers, and so on. Given this limited information, Eddard's limited intuition – that Arryn's investigation is the reason he was murdered – is a logical conclusion. Going further at this point would be bad practice.

Indeed, there are good historical reasons for Eddard Stark to be suspicious that there was a plot against Jon Arryn at all. In the early modern era, a variety of factors (a lack of internal plumbing and other public hygiene measures, a tendency to avoid bathing, etc.) combined to cause a number of deaths that were widely believed to have been due to poisoning that were actually due to a sudden illness. Lucrezia Cosimo de'Medici, the wife of Alfonso II d'Este, the Duke of Ferrara, was widely believed to have been poisoned (possibly by her husband, who promptly remarried a daughter of the Holy Roman Empire), although historians now believe that it's much more likely that she died of tuberculosis. When Barbara Radizwell, the Queen of Poland and Grand Duchess of Livonia, died just five months after her coronation, it was likewise believed that she had been murdered by the Queen Mother Bona Sforza (the ultimate case of an evil mother-in-law), despite the lack of any evidence. Modern historians now believe that it's quite likely that the infamous Lucrezia Borgia, who was rumored to carry a hollow ring filled with poison which she would use to poison her lovers or her family's enemies over dinner, in fact never killed anyone and was simply tarred with the brush of her father and brother's cheerfully homicidal politics.

What If?

In general, "Eddard V" is a relatively slowly-paced start to what will become a breakneck rollercoaster ride, but there are two really important turning points in what will become Eddard's eventual doom:

What if Pycelle keeps his mouth shut? As I've already said, Pycelle has in his possession a huge amount of information that simply by holding back, he could greatly shape Eddard's interactions. Simply put, without this information, Eddard lacks the keystone information that links his information about Jon Arryn's death with Arryn's activities before his death. This requires either or both Varys or Littlefinger to take more direct action to force a civil war into happening, which, in turn, would require them to provide much more solid evidence than they did in OTL. However, given their extreme reluctance to do that (showing good tradecraft there), and the extreme difficulty in any situation of threading the needle such that Eddard's discovery ends up with a civil war rather than the decisive elimination of either the Starks (if Joffrey's control of the Throne is decisive) or the Lannisters (if Eddard is able to move against Cersei before Robert's death or more decisively than OTL after), it's possible that they might have to give Eddard a pass and find some other method.

What if Eddard decides not to trust Littlefinger? To give him credit, Eddard at least goes into the chapter not trusting Littlefinger and only changes his mind once Littlefinger "proves" himself by providing him with genuine information. If he had maintained that position despite Littlefinger's feigned helpfulness, the plot changes dramatically. If Eddard uses his powers as Hand to summon Ser Hugh or any of the other members of Jon Arryn's household (let alone summon Stannis), or if he sends investigators to the Eyrie or Dragonstone, his investigation would have sped up in comparison to OTL, which, in turn, means that it's quite likely that he finds out the truth when he's in a position to unmask Cersei, possibly before Robert dies, thus saving the Baratheon dynasty. At the very least, had Eddard directly assumed control over the gold cloaks (not trusting Littlefinger to do so for him), he could have either succeeded in deposing Joffrey or installing Stannis as king. Which might have warded off a civil war (given that Stannis would have the north, the riverlands, and the crownlands to muster against the Lannisters and that it's even money that Renly and the Tyrells might decide to bide their time as the direct heir to the monarchy), or, even if it hadn't, would have placed the north in a far superior position to win said war (with the legitimacy of the Iron Throne denied to the Lannisters).

<u>Book vs. Show</u>

There's not much difference between the HBO show and the book in these few scenes, at least on the level of dialogue or visuals. However, as I've said before, what we lose somewhat is Eddard's interior voice. While I won't say a bad word about Sean Bean's performance as Ned, without a seriously clumsy voiceover or dramatic monologuing, we can't really tell that Eddard believes that Pycelle is an obvious pawn, or that he wisely distrusts Varys and Littlefinger both.

JON IV

"We're not friends... we're brothers."

Synopsis

During training, Jon meets Samwell Tarly. Ser Alliser pits the unfortunate Tarly into combat with Halder, where he's beaten badly as Thorne orders Halder to beat him until he stands up. Jon puts a stop to the abuse, infuriating the instructor. Sam confesses his cowardice, but after a conversation about his abusive relationship with his father, Randyll, Jon decides to befriend Tarly and organizes the novices into protecting him, even if it means disobeying Ser Alliser or threatening Rast.

Political Analysis

"Jon IV" is a relatively brief chapter that nonetheless packs in a lot of detail about the Watch as an institution and Jon's role within it. In this analysis, I'm going to focus on three topics: the development of Jon Snow's leadership style, the day-to-day functions of the Night's Watch, and Samwell Tarly's problems with primogeniture.

The chapter begins with a scene that illustrates how Jon has embraced his new role as a teacher of his peers, turning his privilege from a source of conflict to something that binds his common-born brothers to them through their respect and trust in him as well as the concrete advantage they're gaining through his instruction. (At the same time, we see later that Jon Snow's teaching also helps him learn their weaknesses, allowing him to protect Sam even in uneven combats.) This trust and familiarity is crucial in allowing Jon Snow to mobilize the men of the Night's Watch: "he told them how it was going to be. Pyp backed him, as he'd known he would, but when Halder spoke up, it was a pleasant surprise. Grenn was anxious at the first, but Jon knew the words to move him. One by one, the rest fell in line. Jon persuaded some, cajoled some, shamed the others, made threats where threats were needed."

What we see here is that the bastard Snow's transition from a privileged-but-isolated-highborn-bastard to a budding leader is centered around a change in his identity – "Robb and Bran and Rickon were his father's sons, and he loved them still, yet Jon knew that he had never truly been one of them" – making the transition from Stark to Nightswatchman. Jon creates a pseudo-family of young men who have mutual trust in each other, even to the point of quietly defying a direct order from their superior officer – and it's this family that will protect him when he is accused of betraying the Night's Watch during his sojourn with the wildlings, that will form an ad hoc officer corps when Jon Snow commands the defense of the Wall against Mance Rayder, and that will engineer his election as lord commander. Sadly, it's also the family that Jon Snow distances himself from when attempting to reform the Night's Watch, rendering himself vulnerable to assassination.

Ironically, Jon's new endeavor, prompted by Donal Noye's populist class analysis, is seen by Ser Alliser as the reconstruction of class privilege, as when "Lord Snow" speaks, "the peasants tremble" and obey his orders despite being putative equals. Ser Alliser might have something of a point if it wasn't for the fact that his position as master-of-arms is dependent entirely on his own social class as a belted knight, given his manifest failures as a teacher. The reason Snow has gained power over his peers by acting as a teacher is precisely because Ser Alliser isn't actually teaching his men how to fight. The lessons that Jon is teaching them – maintain your balance, put your weight behind the blade, and so forth – are absolute beginner's material, and yet Ser Alliser hasn't covered any of it.

Ser Alliser's treatment of Samwell shows quite clearly his shortcomings as a drill instructor. Rather than have a newcomer use equipment that's fitted to him, he wastes hours putting Sam in unsuitable equipment, and then orders Halder to beat the youth despite Sam being on the ground bleeding from the head. What Thorne's up to here isn't training in arms, but a crude Darwinian hazing process that's supposed to weed out the weak from the body of recruits. This might make some sense in a more functional institution, but in an army that's down to less than a thousand men, they can't afford the human wastage, especially when new enrollees seem to number a few dozen.

Which brings us to our second theme, the functioning and malfunctioning of the Night's Watch – and what we see in this chapter is very much a mixed bag. On the one hand, the Night's Watch uses work as a form of career development in order to track soldiers into the stewards, builders, and rangers (which arguably points to rangers as being simultaneously the men most valorized but least useful outside of combat). This on-the-job training is good policy, because, like the modern US military with its ratio of seven soldiers in support to everyone in the field, the Night's Watch relies on support staff to function. Without the stewards, the Night's Watch would starve, their winter clothing would rot, their weapons would rust, and there would be no communication between the different castles of the Night's Watch.

Without the builders, the Wall that the Night's Watch relies on to provide a defensive multiplier against a foe that is hundreds of times its size would slowly break down, the castles that the Night's Watch needs to survive the harsh climate would collapse into disrepair, and the Night's Watch would have neither arms nor armor.

On the other hand, chronic manpower shortages have meant that the support staff are reduced to trying to maintain an undesirable status quo (Samwell immediately remarks on how many buildings have fallen down in the largest castle the Night's Watch has in operation), rather than attempting any net improvement. Likewise, Ser Alliser Thorne's teaching suggests that the training mechanisms are also beginning to break down – when the Night's Watch has only 20 literate brothers, someone like Samwell Tarly should have been fast-tracked to the stewards from day one, rather than nearly beat to death. And while one could plausibly argue that hazing has its functions in a military force which has to maintain a certain standard of combat ability, it's also the case that Ser Alliser's conception of fitness is limited to the needs of rangers, rather than to the needs of two-thirds of the Night's Watch. For example, Ser Alliser focuses entirely on sword drill, which only rangers would ever make any use of, when the defense of a 700-foot high wall would make archery and artillery training an absolute necessity and hand-to-hand combat a secondary priority. Moreover, even the most sadistic drill sergeants are usually trying to work to a purpose – they foster group cohesion by getting raw recruits to unite in their hatred of a single antagonist, to work together to meet the drill sergeant's standards, etc. In *Full Metal Jacket*, Sergeant Hartmann's verbal abuse is meant to get the unit to unite in bringing Gomer Pyle up to performance standard.

By contrast, Ser Alliser actively discourages the development of group cohesion and works to create rivalries and hatreds between novices rather than acting as the necessary "heel." This lack of cohesion becomes startlingly evident during the ranging to the Fist of the First Men, where the antagonistic, suspicious, and hostile attitude fostered by the master-at-arms results in a complete breakdown in military discipline and a mutiny. To the extent that Jon's class becomes an effective fighting force during the Siege of Castle Black, it's in spite of Ser Alliser and through the informal networks of friendship and trust that he discouraged.

On to our third topic: Westerosi inheritance law! Before everyone falls asleep or clicks away, let me just say that this is actually more significant than most people realize. Samwell Tarly's story of familial abuse isn't just a sob story meant to engender sympathy in the reader for a character who (to be fair) spends a lot of time whining and doubting himself; it's also revealing about some of the fundamental flaws in Westerosi society. House Tarly is a leading family, one of the most powerful lesser houses of the Reach; it has "rich lands, a strong keep, and a Valyrian greatsword" that symbolizes the connection between martial prowess and position. Samwell Tarly is unlucky enough to be born into a place he is absolutely not suited to, but as the first-born son, he's going to inherit everything, which potentially puts the house in danger.

TLDR? Primogeniture is problematic.

Historical Analysis

Historically, inheritance of land was one of the most significant customs that organized societies, especially agricultural societies where access to and distribution of land determined wealth, status, and, potentially, survival itself. Legal systems that required equal inheritances limited conflict between siblings and were intended to prevent younger siblings from becoming destitute; however, this had the long-term effect of reducing the size of inheritances to below the level of viability for a farm. The Popery Laws enacted in 1707 by the English government required Catholic estates to be equally divided between all sons (even bastard sons), unless the owner in question converted to Protestantism. These laws, intended to encourage conversion and to reduce the political influence of the large Catholic landowners who had led revolts against English rule, resulted in the constant sub-division of Catholic land holdings to the point where, in the 1840s, large numbers of holdings had dropped below the point where they could support a family on anything other than potatoes. Hence, the Great Famine of 1845 to 1852.

By contrast, primogeniture creates a problem of landless sons and sibling conflict (which becomes especially dangerous when we're talking about disinherited sons whose only skills are martial combat), but it also tends to increase the size of estates over time. Adam Smith argued that primogeniture was absolutely essential for safety in medieval societies:

> "[W]hen land was considered as the means, not of subsistence merely, but of power and protection, it was thought better that it should descend undivided to one. In those disorderly times, every great landlord was a sort of petty prince. His tenants were his subjects. He was their judge, and in some respects their legislator in peace and their leader in war. He made war according to his own discretion, frequently against his neighbours, and sometimes against his sovereign. The security of a landed estate, therefore, the protection which its owner could afford to those who dwelt on it, depended upon its greatness. To divide it was to ruin it, and to expose every part of it to be oppressed and swallowed up by the incursions of its

> neighbours. The law of primogeniture, therefore, came to take place, not immediately indeed, but in process of time, in the succession of landed estates, for the same reason that it has generally taken place in that of monarchies, though not always at their first institution."
>
> *Wealth of Nations*

While from a humanistic perspective, we have to condemn Randyll Tarly's abuse of his son, it's not entirely motivated out of sadism (or Randyll Tarly's seriously troubled gender issues). House Tarly's ability to maintain their rich lands and their strong keep depends on their ability to credibly use their Valyrian greatsword against any rival lord who would want to take it from them; and as we see from the case of Lady Hornwood and the Boltons, this is an omnipresent threat. Likewise, their ability to extract taxes from the peasants in exchange for physical safety and justice is similarly dependent on an ability to deal out physical harm to those who break the law, as we see in *A Feast for Crows*. If nothing else, Lord Tytos Lannister's disastrous tenure as lord of Casterly Rock shows that an unworthy heir can mean ruin for even the greatest of houses.

And here we see the shortcomings of primogeniture – order of birth is not a guarantee of fitness to govern. Aenys I was not a fit candidate for the crown at a time when the monarchy's grasp on the Seven Kingdoms was so weak, when someone like Maegor would have been a better candidate, but he got the throne. Likewise, had Baelor been made king before Daeron I, the highly costly invasion of Dorne might have been averted, saving 60,000 lives on the Targaryen side alone. Potentially, the Blackfyre Rebellion would have been averted had Aemon Dragonknight been older than Aegon the Unworthy (although the latter wouldn't have fared well with the Kingsguard's vows of chastity).

However, disinheriting an unworthy heir is a difficult process. In medieval law, disinheritance usually required either the heir to commit a criminal act that merited being disinherited as part of the sentence (for example, being declared an "outlaw," or literally no longer a person under the law), or "civil death" – joining a religious order whose vows of poverty forbade inheritance. For Randyll, the Night's Watch serves this purpose, but one wonders why he chose this institution, given the options available to him. Randyll's horror at the thought of Samwell becoming a maester is one of the more inexplicable moments in Sam's backstory.

Historically, sending a son off to church schools (later to university) was a common and useful practice for wealthy families; it got younger sons off the house's books and gave them a livelihood, but it also extended family influence into other arenas. An educated son could join the priesthood, where he could rise to control valuable church properties, have influence in clerical politics, and attend the family's spiritual needs; he could become a lawyer or doctor and provide legal or medical services, and in the former case, potentially gain a position in local government or in the royal court. Given the rich variety of skills that are the monopoly of the maesters, Randyll's opposition is deeply counter-productive. Moreover, Randyll had other options open to him – Sam could have become a septon and had his own sept, or joined a septonry of the monastic Contemplative Brothers, or become an itinerant "begging brother," any of which would have removed him from the line of succession.

Indeed, while we don't have a lot of evidence as to how common it is, a number of noble households have sent sons to the Citadel as a solution to their inheritance: the Tyrells have "Lazy Leo," the Martells sent Oberyn and Sarella went on her own (although Oberyn didn't join the order), and the Freys have their Maester Willamen.

So, at least for now, Randyll's thinking is going to have to remain a mystery.

What If?

Given how short this chapter is, and that it really involves only one major change to the status quo, there's really only one big question here: **what happens if something bad had happened to Sam?** If Sam had died accidentally at the hands of Halder, or if Jon hadn't decided to protect him (which would probably have led to same), then a lot changes – while much of what Sam does in *Game of Thrones* could probably have happened anyway, just with only Grenn and Pyp, it's starting with the second book that things really begin to change: with no Sam, Gilly doesn't get rescued from Craster's keep, which means that there's no baby to swap for Mance Rayder's child, and Sam doesn't slay an Other with an obsidian dagger, so the Night's Watch doesn't learn that dragonglass can kill Others. Critically, there's no Night's Watchman there at the Nightfort to let Bran, Hodor, Jojen, and Meera through the Black Gate, which means they don't get to Bloodraven, which has consequences we just don't know about yet.

Also critically, Sam doesn't rig the elections for Jon Snow to become lord commander, which means that the wildlings aren't allowed through the Wall, and that Jon Snow avoids being assassinated for his rapid reforms.

Likewise, with no Sam, Maester Aemon doesn't go on his fatal journey, and Dareon avoids being murdered by Arya, and Maester Marwyn doesn't learn Aemon's last words and depart for Essos in search of Daenerys, which has consequences we just don't know about yet.

All of which adds up to show that, as much as Sam can be a somewhat annoying character at times, he's actually incredibly consequential for much of the plot.

Book vs. Show

The show plays this one pretty straight, with some significant changes. Halder is replaced by Rast in the initial beating, which I think dilutes Thorne's sadism somewhat. John Bradley, who's a fantastic actor (also quite good in *Borgia: Faith and Fear*, BTW), really inhabits the Samwell Tarly role in a way that really does change how one sees the character. He plays Sam as just a touch more confident (also more self-aware, and willing to laugh at himself and others) than he is in the books, where the character really goes overboard on the self-loathing. It's a choice that really works well.

EDDARD VI

What had Jon Arryn wanted with a king's bastard, and why was it worth his life?

Synopsis

In a small council meeting, Eddard Stark deals with increasing disorder in King's Landing due to the Hand's Tourney by ordering the hiring of 50 new gold cloaks rather than firing Janos Slynt. When the meeting is over, Eddard goes back to his investigations (the book yields little answers), receives a dispiriting update from Jory Cassel, but has better luck when he travels to the Street of Steel and discovers Gendry Waters, a royal bastard (although actually a nice guy).

Political Analysis

"Eddard VI" is yet another juicy chapter, full of politics and intrigue. The roller coaster is heading downhill and beginning to pick up some real speed, which means we need to talk about such varied topics as public order, the economy of King's Landing, Eddard's investigations, Renly's conspiracy, and the mystery that is Gendry Waters.

We begin, unusually, in a meeting of the small council, discussing an issue of public policy. The city's population has swollen with the arrival of knights, freeriders, craftsmen, men-at-arms, merchants, whores, and thieves getting ready to fight, steal, and profit from the Hand's Tourney. The result is a decline in law and order: "last night, we had a drowning, a tavern riot, three knife fights, a rape, two fires, robberies beyond count... a drunken horse race... the night before, a woman's head was found in the Great Sept." The categories of crime described here – violence, disorder, drunkenness, robbery, disrespect to religion, and fire – sum up very much the medieval fear of disorder and riot. Violence is dangerous because it means that people's persons aren't safe, but also because violence gives rise to vendettas and, depending on how highborn the murderers and murdered are, local wars. Disorder is dangerous, not just because it results in damage to taverns, but also because it suggests that the king can't maintain his own peace, and part of the king's oath to his people (his constitutional quid-pro-quo for sovereignty) is that he's powerful enough to prevent disorder. Drunkenness is bad not so much in itself (confined to its proper place within taverns), but because people's excessive desires are causing disorder to spill over into the religious districts, culminating in the specter of death contaminating the holiest of holies. And standing as sign and signifier of all of these – the existential threat of fire in a city of wooden buildings, thatched roofs, no public water system, and no fire company.

All of this points to the very timely question posed by Renly Baratheon, who's supposedly the master of laws (but who shows little evidence of actually doing his job outside of court politics): why not replace Janos Slynt? As I have suggested before, Eddard has it within his power to replace Janos Slynt with Jory Cassel or any other loyal man, putting the gold cloaks under Stark control. Now, to be fair, he doesn't know that Slynt is a corrupt murderer and Littlefinger's henchman from early in Robert's reign, but the fact that Eddard doesn't reach out to Renly to find out more is a bad sign. And here's where Eddard makes a major political mistake: he disempowers himself by taking 20 men out of his own guard (incidentally, I don't think we ever find out what happened to these men when Eddard is deposed, but they're probably dead). His sense of duty leads him to take the right actions for the realm – his addition of 70 men to the City Watch increases their ranks by 3.5%, which is a good idea when you need more crowd control – but in ways that disempowers himself.

Now on to the tourney and the economy of King's Landing. The easy political joke – *ha ha, Eddard Stark is a conservative who's not down with Keynesian stimulus* – I think misses what's going on here. Robert Baratheon isn't spending 90,000 gold dragons on public works, or relief for the poor, or anything that would benefit the smallfolk of Westeros; rather, the money's going to less than ten noblemen who'll fight and win in the tourney. In other words, *Eddard Stark is opposed to trickle-down economics*. Pycelle outright admits that the tourney is mere "bread and circuses": "they bring the great the chance of glory, and the respite from their woes." To the extent that non-nobility in the city benefits, it's largely the hospitality, brewing, and prostitution industries, which means to people like Littlefinger himself (notably, these are industries that are capital-, rather than labor-, intensive, and in the case of prostitution, use essentially unfree labor). Notably, far less in the way of benefits goes to the residents of Fishmonger's and Cobbler's Squares, or the Street of Looms or Copper-smiths, or the Streets of Steel or Flour, let alone the destitute of Flea Bottom.

Which points to a split in the city's economy between those industries that cater to the appetites of the wealthy, those industries that produce goods, and a vast underclass. In an excellent essay on the economics of Westeros, Ken Mondschein reminds us that Dunk remarks in the reign of Dareon II that a man can live well on three dragons a year (or one stag and 43 copper a day) – adjusting for inflation, we're talking about five dragons a year (or a shade under three stags a day) by 298 AL. In other words, Robert Baratheon is giving away the equivalent of a comfortable yearly income for *18,000 people (or 4.5% of the population of King's Landing)*. Team Smallfolk is living in the land of the 1%.

But enough of the suffering masses – let's get back to the real story: Eddard Stark's investigations. The first thing that's worthy of note is how quickly Eddard hits on Stannis as a critical angle of investigation – even during the small council meeting, Ned "wonder[s] when he intends to end his visit to Dragonstone and resume his seat on this council," immediately realizes that Stannis and Jon Arryn going to a brothel is a sign of something else going on, and questions the meaning of Stannis's departure:

> *Why did Stannis leave? Had he played some part in Jon Arryn's murder? Or was he afraid? Ned found it hard to imagine what could frighten Stannis Baratheon, who had once held Storm's End through a year of siege, surviving on rats and boot leather...*

On the one hand, Martin is clearly foreshadowing Stannis's future importance and character by having Eddard focus on the topic for most of the chapter, but it's also interesting to see Eddard's admiration of Stannis's stoicism. This is especially so in comparison to Renly, who "Ned was not sure what to make of... with all his friendly ways and his easy smiles." There is a great irony, that of the two Baratheon brothers, it is the least likely conspirator and the closest to Eddard's own personality who hits at the heart of the conspiracy and then flees the capital, whereas the brother who stays, who could perhaps have lent much-needed skills and knowledge to Eddard's cause, fails to do so because of Eddard's distrust.

The second thing that pops up in Eddard's investigation is the ambiguity of the available evidence. Lord Stark now has a copy of Malleon's *Lineages and Histories*, but it's not clear how one is to interpret the "lists of weddings, births, and deaths" inside. Eddard not unreasonably decides to research House Lannister (given that he thinks they're the arch-conspirators at the heart of everything) instead of House Baratheon; Martin throws in a telling factoid that Lann the Clever "stole gold from the sun to brighten his curly hair," but it would be implausible in the extreme for Eddard to recognize the significance of blond Lannisters. (Indeed, if blond hair genes operate in Westeros anything like they do in our world, Eddard would have read a list of Lannisters that includes quite a few non-blond Lannisters, since quite a few Lannisters didn't follow Tywin's practice of cousin marriage.)

Likewise, the testimony Eddard gets is vague and rather unhelpful, because it's mostly coming from low-level Arryn householders:

the stableboy only knows that the Hand preferred to give apples to his horse, the serving girl knows only that Jon was unhappy, and the potboy knows mostly kitchen gossip. It's my belief that this is a deliberate part of Petyr Baelish's strategy as the mastermind of the Littlefinger Conspiracy: Ned notes that "Lady Lysa, Maester Colemon," and most of the household were "carried off to the Vale" on Lysa's instructions, and we know that Lysa is taking orders from Littlefinger. In this fashion, Littlefinger is able to steer Eddard's investigation and modulate the speed at which the Hand acquires significant information – Colemon could confirm poisoning and was probably consulted by Lord Arryn on questions of the inheritance of physical traits; the household guards could have led Eddard to the brothel where Robert's bastard is living (giving him another data point); and Lysa potentially could have cracked under interrogation, spilling the truth of Littlefinger's murderous plot. Finally, by advising Eddard to send Jory rather than summon Ser Hugh directly, he ensures that that testimony is delayed just long enough for another part of his plan that I'll discuss in a future post to come into fruition.

A quick side note: while I've talked in the past about how evil Lysa is being when she sends her letter to Catelyn, roping the Starks into Littlefinger's conspiracy to destroy their house, let's pause for a second to note the immorality of Petyr Baelish. Here is a man who murdered the man who was responsible for raising him up from nothing, who stole and then murdered his wife (and who may have cuckolded him, as well – it's not particularly clear), who is en route to murdering his son, and for whom gross fraud and embezzlement, the sale of offices in exchange for kickbacks, and the assassination of anyone who complained is probably the least of his sins. All of this done for the pettiest of motives: he wanted to marry Catelyn Tully and challenged the wrong man to a fight. While he may lack Joffrey's sadism or lack of impulse control, Littlefinger certainly displays the "Machiavellian egocentricity," "coldheartedness," and "blame externalization" of the classic psychopath.

Despite Littlefinger's hindrance, Eddard does pick up a good amount of information: he learns about both the brothel and the armorer's shop, both vital clues, and that Arryn and Stannis were clearly cooperating in some investigation. While he doesn't realize the import of two minor details of gossip – that Jon was sending his son to be fostered on Dragonstone (because he was planning to move against Cersei), and that he was studying the breeding of hunting hounds (a sign of some pre-Mendelian genetic studies) – he actually does a fairly good job of detective work in this chapter.

A third theme that's developed in this chapter is the Renly/Tyrell Conspiracy. I've talked about this briefly in the past, to note that Cersei and Jaime are aware of this conspiracy (although they seem to have taken no action against it), but it's interesting to note that Renly subtly is reaching out to Eddard to enlist him in the effort to replace Cersei with Margaery (whether that signifies that Renly knows or suspects Cersei's infidelity is something I've never been able to make my mind up on). In a moment of humor in hindsight, Ned completely misunderstands Renly's overture, doesn't understand why Renly's disappointed (although Robert probably would have been more than happy to bed Margaery regardless), and thinks that Renly's in love with the girl (despite being a "passing queer"). But, again, it's a sign that Renly, for all his political gifts, doesn't really know how to reach out to Eddard in a way the man is likely to respond to – and while we're used to condemning Eddard for his failure to agree to Renly's coup proposal, it's also true that Renly contributed to his own death by making a distasteful (to Ned) approach without considering the personality of his potential ally.

Finally, we get the discovery of Gendry, a young man who looks the spitting image of Robert Baratheon, and who has inherited no small amount of Baratheon stubbornness, despite having a mother with "yellow hair." Eddard sees his parentage immediately and realizes that the reason Jon Arryn was murdered was that he was looking into royal bastards – not half bad for an amateur detective (and for those of you keeping track, this is three correct conclusions to two political mistakes).

The question I have is what exactly Varys was doing in regards to Gendry: now, it's certainly to Varys's interests to have potential proof of Joffrey's illegitimacy on hand, and it's quite possible that Robert had asked Varys to discretely see to his bastard children, but Varys takes a lot of effort here. Indeed, his acting to smuggle Gendry out of the capital is one of the best pieces of evidence we have that argues that Aegon VI really is a Targaryen. However, if Varys is scheming to restore a "Targaryen" to the Iron Throne, why go to the effort of saving his life? Potentially, this speaks to Varys's relatively humanistic nature; if he can afford to (Ned, Gendry, Tyrion, etc.), he'll save someone's life, even if there's no immediate political gain to himself. On the other hand, it may be that Gendry is a Plan C: if the Targaryen invasion falls through, Varys could potentially have Robert's oldest natural son under his thumb; even if it doesn't, if Varys had planned for Khal Drogo to die, marrying Daenerys to the last remaining Baratheon is a good way of reconciling the former rebels to the Targaryen restoration (hey, it worked for Henry VII).

Historical Analysis

I'll try to keep this section short, because that was a lot of political analysis, but I'd like to highlight three themes: the medieval urban economy, pre-modern law and order, and royal bastards. On the first topic, it's curious to me that George R.R. Martin doesn't really feature the guilds as political actors in their own right, especially when there becomes a tug of war between Tyrion and Cersei over the Guild of Alchemists and the Guild of Smiths during *Clash of Kings*. Instead, the rebels against authority in King's Landing tend to be either the underclass (as in the case of the riots) or the merchant class (in the case of the potentially-invented Antler Men). This doesn't track well with history: the guilds of medieval Europe were quite powerful, often becoming the organs of city government (as in the case with the City of London).

By the 14th century, the guilds controlled access to skilled trades, prices and wages, maintained early welfare funds, and determined market shares. Trade guilds were heavily involved in the popular uprisings of the middle ages: the guilds of London were some of the fiercest partisans of Simon de Montfort in his attempt to establish Parliamentary government in the 13th century (de Monfort's Parliament was the first time that commoners were admitted to Parliament, or that any member of Parliament had been elected); the Great Peasant's Revolt of 1381 in England reached its peak of influence thanks in no small part to the artisans of London, who opened the gates to Wat Tyler and John Ball. The Franco-Flemish War, which was very much a revolt of commoners against French noble rule, saw one of the rare victories of commonfolk over knights at the Battle of Golden Spurs in 1302, where town militias organized by the guilds of Bruges, Ghent, and Ypres smashed the French cavalry with well-disciplined infantry wielding the fearsome goedendag.

Regarding pre-modern law and order, it should be noted that the gold cloaks would be highly anachronistic if they were to have appeared in England during the Wars of the Roses. After the fall of the Roman Empire, formal police forces didn't really exist in most of Europe (Spain being an odd exception), even in the more urbanized areas, throughout the medieval period. It wasn't until 1667, when Louis XIV established a police force to keep the unruly mob of Paris in check, that we get the first semblance of a modern police force, and for a long while thereafter, they were rather rare.

Indeed, England was a notorious laggard on this front, relying on a local force of constables appointed by local lords and justices to act on behalf of the sheriffs, and more often than not defaulting to the services of private thief-takers. It wasn't until the Bow Street Runners of 1749 and then the Metropolitan Police of 1829 that a true, professional, public police force was established in Britain. As a result, cities could be incredibly dangerous places to live in the medieval, Renaissance, and early modern periods – hence the genuine concern if a force of 2,000 armed men can't keep order in King's Landing.

Finally, the topic of royal bastards. I've discussed this before a bit, but it is highly unusual for a royal bastard to be raised as a mere artisan, even for a king with a legitimate heir. Much more commonly, kings gave out rich lands and titles to their bastard children in order to keep power and wealth within the family (and to keep them on hand as potential "backup heirs" should the trueborn heir die). For example, when Henry VIII, Robert Baratheon's spiritual and corporeal counterpart in our world, had the good fortune to get Lady Elizabeth Blount (his wife Catherine's Maid of Honour) pregnant, he made Cardinal Wolsey the boy's godfather, exhibited his son to the court with celebratory banquets, had him made the duke of Richmond and Somerset (and one of the wealthiest young men in England), and married him to the daughter of Thomas Howard, the Duke of Norfolk.

What If?

There are three interesting and plot-critical hypothetical situations that emerge out of "Eddard VI":

What if Eddard had used his office? As I have suggested before, had Lord Stark used his authority as Hand of the King to summon witnesses to him rather than acting through Jory Cassel, he certainly could have gotten most of Jon Arryn's retinue to testify as to what they knew, greatly speeding up his investigation. He would have known far earlier that Jon Arryn was definitely poisoned, that he was looking at all of Robert's bastards, that he was investigating questions of heredity, and so on and so forth. The interesting question is what he would have learned from Ser Hugh – my suspicion, which I'll expand on later, is that Ser Hugh at the very least knew the whole of Lord Arryn's investigation (since, as his squire, he would have accompanied him to most places), and may even have been privy to Lysa and Littlefinger's assassination. The larger point is that a faster investigation is absolutely critical for the plot: if Eddard finds out the truth before he is wounded and before Catelyn's abduction of Tyrion happens, then he's in a position to act before the Lannisters have mobilized for war, and doesn't get delayed by his injury (which would also mean that Arya and Sansa don't become hostages); quite possibly, this means that he finds out before Robert's death and averts Robert's assisted hunting accident. Robert not dying means that the Renly/Tyrell Conspiracy probably happens, and now we're talking about a united Stark-Tully-Baratheon-Tyrell-(maybe)-Arryn force against just Casterly Rock. Long live King Robert, and congratulations on his new bride.

What if Eddard had summoned Stannis to King's Landing? Now, it's possible that a pragmatist like Stannis would have kept his head down rather than to risk assassination, but given Stannis's dedication to the law, I doubt he would have ignored a summons from the Hand of the King. This would have meant that Eddard would have known that Stannis and Arryn were investigating the possibility that Robert's children with Cersei were not legitimate far ahead of when he found out in OTL, giving him the chance to act against Cersei well before Robert's death. Indeed, even if Robert had died anyway, Stannis's swords could have made the difference in Eddard's potential coup, bringing down Cersei and Joffrey. In that scenario, Renly would likely have married Margaery and become prince of Dragonstone, and the Lannisters would have had to face a united Stark-Tully-Baratheon-Tyrell-(maybe)-Arryn force against just the forces of Casterly Rock – and long live King Stannis.

What if Eddard had taken Gendry with him? In OTL, Eddard extends an offer of service to Gendry, but he could have easily just ordered his master to render over the young man. This could have some potentially interesting consequences: firstly, Gendry might have learned of his parentage (which he still hasn't, despite the news about Joffrey's bastardy); secondly, Gendry could have been legitimized as a potential heir should Stannis and Renly fall; thirdly, Gendry could have met Arya Stark earlier, which would have been interesting to see.

Book vs. Show

Nothing significant to report. Check back next time.

CATELYN V

Did she dare take the risk? There was no time to think it through, only the moment and the sound of her own voice ringing in her ears.

Synopsis

Catelyn Stark arrives at the Inn at the Crossroads and arrests Tyrion Lannister for the attempted murder of her son. *Dun-dun-dun!*

Political Analysis

Here we go – "Catelyn V," the kidnapping of Tyrion, and the moment at which open war between the Starks and the Lannisters becomes inevitable. It's also, next to Catelyn freeing Jaime at the end of *A Clash of Kings*, one of the major pieces of evidence used by those in the fandom who hate Catelyn as to why she should be held responsible for most of the things that go wrong in the entire series. I've talked before about the problem of presentism (i.e., judging people on the basis of future events that they had no knowledge of, also known as hindsight bias), and we get that in spades in discussions of this chapter, although one also finds a good deal of people judging Lady Stark on the basis of knowledge they have gained from other POVs – in other words, blaming her for her lack of omniscience. One example will suffice: Catelyn has no way of knowing, at the time that she arrests Tyrion, that when the news of this hits King's Landing, Ned will have resigned the Handship, leaving himself vulnerable to Jaime's assault.

If we're going to judge her fairly, we need to pay close attention to Catelyn's intent and thought process when she orders Tyrion's arrest, and, luckily, George R.R. Martin has given us an entire chapter of her thoughts. The first thing we see is that Catelyn is thinking very clearly about the larger strategic picture even before she meets Tyrion:

> "The crossroads gave her pause. If they turned west from here, it was an easy ride down to Riverrun… if Winterfell needed to brace for war, how much more so Riverrun, so much closer to

> King's Landing, with the power of Casterly Rock looming to the west... above the Vale, the Eyrie stood high and impregnable... there she would find her sister, and, perhaps, some of the answers Ned sought. Surely Lysa knew more than she had dared to put in her letter. She might have the very proof that Ned needed to bring the Lannisters to ruin, and if it came to war, they would need the Arryns and the eastern lords who owed them service."

It's not that Catelyn doesn't see that her actions will lead to war; rather, given Ned's instructions to her during their last meeting, she fully expects a war to come and shows a rather good strategic understanding of the Starks' need to bring the Tullys and Arryns into alliance. She also is thinking about helping her husband uncover an imminent threat to the king and their own house (which puts a rather different light on Eddard's resignation) by gathering evidence to bolster their case. Finally, it should be noted that Catelyn tries to avoid being recognized or having to confront Tyrion.

At the moment she is revealed, Catelyn makes a major decision on the spot, but she's fully aware that she's taking a major risk. She attempts to mitigate this risk in two ways: first, rather than simply kidnapping Tyrion by force of arms, she calls upon the crowd to "seize him and help me return him to Winterfell to await the king's justice... in the name of King Robert," making it a citizen's arrest. As a lady of rank in a world without a formal police force or public prosecutors, she has every right to make this arrest – indeed, private prosecutions is how criminal justice works in Westeros. Secondly, she shows her strong grasp on feudal politics by summoning the bannermen of House Whent (so the might of Harrenhal is involved), House Bracken, and House Frey to her aid (which she needs if she's going to actually effect arrest and transport her prisoner to the Eyrie); this follows a rather interesting passage where Catelyn ruminates that the loyalty of many of her father's bannermen (both those who fought for House Targaryen and the Late Lord Frey) are so uncertain.

These are not the actions of a stupid woman, and, self-evidently from the text, not the actions of a woman who's ignorant or uncaring of the risks she's taking.

Historical Analysis

The warp and weft of historical thought is the interplay between *historical forces*, those subterranean pressures of economics, society, culture, thought, and environment that build up over centuries and, unseen and unawares, guide the actions of entire civilizations, and *historical contingency*, the stubborn resistance of individual agency and human free will to the concept of "inevitability" or "destiny." The rebuke of "for the want of a nail" reminds us that the smallest of actions, the humblest of people, can shape the course of events.

And this is one of those moments of contingency. There simply was no way to predict that Catelyn Stark would arrive at the Inn of the Crossroads in time to run across Tyrion Lannister, nor was it at all likely that Littlefinger accused him with this in mind. Likewise, Catelyn has no way to know that her husband has resigned the Handship just long enough that Jaime Lannister can cripple him with legal impunity, which, in turn, will delay Eddard Stark's investigation long enough that, rather than the Lannisters being exposed as incestuous traitors and brought down by an alliance of Houses Stark, Tully, Baratheon, Tyrell, and, possibly, Arryn, Lord Stark will be executed at the command of King Joffrey.

Indeed, as people have noted, Martin has to do some rather fancy footwork to make their intersection work: Catelyn Stark arrives in King's Landing roughly at the same time that Tyrion leaves the Wall, and both of them are riding horses that can travel about 50 to 60 miles a day, maximum. *Tyrion then travels roughly 2,000 miles from the Wall to the inn, whereas Catelyn travels 400 miles from King's Landing to the inn, and yet arrives there at the same time.* You'd expect Tyrion to be four days from Winterfell when Catelyn hits the Inn of the Crossroads. *Realistically, they should have intersected somewhere around Moat Cailin* – but Martin clearly needed them to meet at a place on neutral territory so that word can get out and so that Catelyn makes for the Eyrie, since, at Moat Cailin, Catelyn could have thrown him into the Stark dungeons then and there, with no way for word to get out.

This gets us to not a historical but a literary principle – the demands of classical Greek tragedy. Developing out of the ceremonies of Dionysian worship in ancient Attic Greece, and given the key elements of the form (multiple actors so that dramatic conflict can occur, a chorus to both act as minor characters but also to provide the commentary that reinforces the key themes of the drama, and attention paid to psychology as well as circumstance), one absolute necessity is an act of tragic hubris that brings on the nemesis or destruction of the hero. Think Oedipus murdering a stranger in a fit of rage, unaware that his rash action will bring about the prophecy he's fled his home to avoid; Agamemnon stepping across royal purple to return to his home, where his murder is committed; or Orestes, who is commanded by the gods to murder his mother, despite the torment that must result; or Jason, whose desire for a new family destroys his own. Critical to the act of hubris is the ignorance of what will come:

> *There may be many shapes of mystery,*
> *And many things God makes to be,*
> *Past hope or fear.*

And the end men looked for cometh not,
And a path is there where no man thought.
So hath it fallen here.

Euripedes, *The Bacchae*

As I have argued before, Catelyn Stark is a Greek tragic heroine, a woman dedicated to family by her house and her character, who, in her second chapter, hopes for another child, but who nonetheless helps to bring about the downfall of her family. George R.R. Martin literally bends space and time in order to make her fateful meeting with Tyrion happen, just recently plants in her mind, from a trusted childhood friend, that Tyrion is responsible for the attempted assassination of her son. If you want to condemn Catelyn Stark for "starting the war," you might as well blame Oedipus for murdering his father and marrying his mother, or George R.R. Martin for writing her tragedy.

Note: this is not to say Catelyn is blameless. She can – and does – make some rather enormous mistakes with tragic consequences that she should have known better, but this isn't one of them. What is an act of omission that Catelyn can be blamed for is that she doesn't immediately send word to Riverrun and to Winterfell, if not to her husband in King's Landing, that she's captured Tyrion and that they need to prepare for war with the Lannisters. Her failure to communicate is that contingent "wanted nail."

What If?

As I've been re-reading *A Game of Thrones*, I've been thinking about what the crucial turning points are, those moments of maximum contingency where the course of events could have changed so drastically as to re-orient the entire future of Westeros. Eddard Stark becoming Hand of the King is definitely one of them, Bran's fall and, especially, the second assassination attempt against him, and Eddard's fateful cluster of choices once he learns the truth of the parentage of Cersei's children. Whatever the final list is, Catelyn and Tyrion meeting at the Inn at the Crossroads will be on the list of the most contingent moments:

What if Tyrion and Catelyn never meet each other? This hypothetical shows in reverse how vital this meeting is for Martin's plot: if the two ships pass in the night on their way north and south, the rest of the plot careens wildly off its tracks. First of all, war between the Starks and Lannisters is delayed – which means that the riverlands aren't burnt before the start of the war, which means Eddard doesn't send out Beric Dondarrion and Thoros of Myr, and Tywin doesn't start the war right in the middle between the west, Riverrun, and King's Landing. Second, and this is where you see the cost of Catelyn's actions, Eddard Stark's orders to fortify Moat Cailin and White Harbor and keep Theon Greyjoy under close watch are carried out. In other words, the north mobilizes for war before the Lannisters do – now, instead of a hastily-assembled scratch force being sent out to fight two Lannister hosts who have already reduced much of the riverlands, the Starks potentially have as many as 45,000 men of the north mobilized for war and, potentially, the capacity for a naval strike on King's Landing. Third, as I have already written, Eddard isn't wounded by Jaime, therefore Jaime's not on hand to lead an army against Riverrun, Eddard isn't delayed in his investigations, and it's quite likely that Cersei and Jaime are arrested as traitors by order of King Robert, which, obviously, changes everything.

What if they'd met at Moat Cailin? Had the two travelers moved at a realistic pace on their intersecting journeys, as I have said, they would have met at Moat Cailin. This would likely have meant Tyrion's arrest under circumstances in which Catelyn has no need to head to the Eyrie, can control the movement of news south, and where Catelyn has immediate access to ravens. This means that Eddard knows ahead of his resignation (and before the Lannisters) that Tyrion is under arrest and, thus, the Lannisters will act against him. It also means that Catelyn is also in a position to find out that Littlefinger has lied to them about the dagger used in the assassination attempt (as she will on the mountain roads to the Eyrie) and can inform Eddard of that, as well. Since Eddard can easily confirm this fact with anyone who attended that tourney, he now knows that Littlefinger is lying to him and trying to falsely implicate the Lannisters on the attack on his son. Potentially, this brings about the discovery of the entire Littlefinger Conspiracy if Littlefinger breaks under torture, and certainly means that Eddard won't rely on the master of coin when it comes to securing the gold cloaks, which, in turn, potentially means that the regent queen and Prince Joffrey are successfully arrested – hail King Stannis!

What if Catelyn hadn't arrested Tyrion at the inn? This is a bit similar to the first case, but it means that Tyrion's going to arrive in King's Landing knowing that something really weird is going on with House Stark, which potentially means that Tyrion will be arrested or, at the very least, contacted first by Eddard instead of his wife – which again means that Eddard finds out the truth of Littlefinger's treachery, that the north is mobilized ahead of schedule, and also that one of the sharpest political minds in Westeros is now present to witness what's about to go down in the capital. While it probably wouldn't have happened, an *Eddard/Tyrion odd-couple buddy-cop scenario* would have been amazing!

What if Catelyn had headed north? This is essentially similar to the Moat Cailin case, with the added wrinkle of a really fast chase as Catelyn tries to make it to safety before any ambitious sellsword decides to "rescue" Tyrion in exchange for lots of Lannister gold. It also means that Catelyn finds out Littlefinger's lies well before she gets to the dungeons, but without Lysa's interference. Which holds out the possibility that once they get to Moat Cailin, Catelyn sends a raven to King's Landing informing Ned what's going on, and Tyrion sends a raven to Casterly Rock telling his father that it was all a misunderstanding and that the real enemy is Littlefinger, who tried to set up a civil war.

What if Catelyn had headed west? The major difference here is that, with Tyrion behind Riverrun's walls, Jaime (and, to a lesser extent, Tywin) might act more cautiously in attacking the Tullys if they knew that the potential cost of an assault on Riverrun might mean Tyrion's death.

<u>Book vs. Show</u>

Unfortunately, this scene was pretty much lifted, word-for-word, from the book. Nothing to report here.

SANSA II

The young knight in the blue cloak was nothing to her, some stranger from the Vale of Arryn whose name she had forgotten as soon as she heard it. And now the world would forget his name, too, Sansa realized; there would be no songs sung for him. That was sad.

Synopsis

Sansa is giddy over all the knights at the tourney, especially that hunky Knight of Flowers. During the jousting, Ser Gregor Clegane "accidentally" kills Ser Hugh of the Vale, and she has a momentary sad. But no time to dwell on the fleeting mortality of human life, because Sansa then gets a red rose from Ser Loras (OMG!) and creeped on by Littlefinger (ewww). At the feast, King Robert gets reverse-psychologized by Queen Cersei. While escorting her back home, the Hound tells Sansa a not-so-nice story about the realities of knighthood. Totes emosh.

Political Analysis

If anyone didn't get that Sansa's POV chapters are a deconstruction of romanticism after this chapter, there really is no hope for him. Honestly, I kept laughing during this re-read at all the little digs that George R.R. Martin throws in to show you that Sansa is completely off her head in this chapter, drunk on the glamour and glory of tourneys: she spends the entire day in a typical teenage torrent of emotions, from giggling over all the handsome knights and thinking that "they were looking at her and smiling," to showing how totally grown-up she is by not flinching at the sight of men in pain, to being weirdly fascinated by the sight of Ser Hugh dying, to getting all ferklempt when the 100% heterosexual Loras Tyrell picks her out to receive a red rose, to getting depressed because Joffrey won't talk to her, to being scared by the Hound.

In other words, Sansa's own immaturity parallels the immaturity of people who believe that knights and tournaments are glamorous and, by extension, anyone who buys into the myth that war is glorious and romantic. Most people are familiar with George R.R. Martin's critical attitude to war from the later books in *A Song of Ice and Fire*, where the horrors of war are viscerally detailed, but I think Martin has a more nuanced approach than just "war is bad," as he's discussed in various interviews. What Martin gets at is that you have to show both the cost of war and the visual splendor and appeal of war to understand both why people like war and why they shouldn't. And the Hand's Tourney is the perfect depiction of his argument: the chapter begins with "the splendor of it all" taking "Sansa's breath away; the shining armor, the great chargers caparisoned in silver and gold, the shouts of the crowd, the banners snapping in the wind... and the knights, most of all." Sansa is directly experiencing the attraction of a spectator sport that is designed to legitimate both war and the warrior caste's superiority. Even as the crowd cheers on men who are both engaged in a prettified cage match and gambling for stakes that should infuriate any right-thinking member of the 99%, Sansa is virtually transported into the stories she so loves. And there's a core of truth there: Ser Jaime in his prime, Ser Barristan the Bold, Lord Yohn Royce with his magic runed armor, Lord Jason Mallister – these are genuinely the best fighters in Westeros showing off what is, in the end, a martial *art* at the best of their craft. Keen-eyed readers of *A Song of Ice and Fire* will also note how George Martin picks out yet-unsung heroes like Thoros of Myr and Beric Dondarrion as if shining a spotlight on them to suggest that they, too, might be heroes of stories someday.

And then Martin strips away each illusion, one after the other. We start with the drab Jory Cassel, whose true courage in a meaningless street fight will outstrip the hollow bravado of the better-ornamented knights; we see the handsome Lord Renly, the crowd's favorite, a man who knows exactly how useful tournaments can be as a way of building popular support, unhorsed by the Hound; the almost ludicrously Disney-like attentions of Ser Loras transform into Littlefinger's deeply disturbing harassment (more on this in a second); a handsome young man dies hideously on the field as his armor shines in the sunlight; and then Sandor Clegane, the man who refuses to be a knight, explodes the whole thing:

> "You think Ser Gregor's lance rode up by chance, did you? Pretty little talking girl, you believe that – you're empty-headed as a bird, for true... Gregor never said a word, just picked me up under his arm and shoved the side of my face down in the burning coals and held me there... our maester gave me ointments... Gregor got his ointments, too. Seven years later, they anointed him with the seven oils, and he recited his knightly vows, and Rhaegar Targaryen tapped him on the shoulder."

Underneath the veneer of oaths and ceremonies lies the truth of knighthood: knights may be gallant if they choose to be, if they want to woo the crowd, but what they actually *are* are people "no one could withstand." A monster like Gregor Clegane rides among the glory of Westeros's knighthood, but because he stood the vigil and was anointed and said words I doubt he understood the meaning of, even the prophetic romantic hero Rhaegar cannot see him for what he is. And when we look at what knights actually got up to in the epic chanson of Raoul de Cambrai (who, in the course of a petty conflict over a fief, burns a church full of nuns seeking sanctuary), Gregor Clegane, who never wins an honest fight in the entire series but whose legend is built on the butchery of unarmed men, women, and children, is perhaps the truest knight of them all.

Which brings us to the second major political theme in this chapter: *the assassination of Ser Hugh of the Vale*. I say assassination because Sandor's monologue is a pretty strong argument that Ser Gregor didn't accidentally kill Ser Hugh. Now, it's possible that Clegane acted out of simple sadistic bloodlust, which isn't exactly out of character, but the circumstances are rather suspicious: Ser Hugh had just been pointed out to the Hand by Littlefinger as someone to investigate (but, critically, not to be compelled to give testimony), and Jory Cassel had just contacted the newly-minted knight (and was rebuffed). Given that Ser Gregor is a Lannister bannerman, one might conclude that the Lannisters have been spying on Eddard and his staff and decided to clear up an inconvenient witness. I think this unlikely for several reasons:

1. As we saw in "Bran II," Cersei isn't very well informed as to Jon Arryn's investigation (she knows he was investigating her but doesn't know if he had evidence that Lysa might have access to), so it's unlikely that she would know the importance of his squire.

2. Likewise, Cersei seems to have taken no action to stop Jon Arryn when he was alive (instead, acting to silence Lysa via her son after the fact), which would make decisive action in the case of a minor potential witness uncharacteristic for her.

3. If Cersei wasn't behind it, the list of Lannister suspects is alarmingly short. Jaime Lannister wouldn't have hired a catspaw, Pycelle is too out of the loop, and Tywin was definitely kept out of the loop on the whole incest/adultery thing.

My hypothesis, and I'm not the only one who shares it, is that *Littlefinger arranged to have Ser Hugh killed*. Consider the following: Littlefinger is one of only two people who know of his importance (the other being Varys), and he was almost certainly the source of Ser Hugh's sudden windfall that allowed him to fight in the tourney in the first place. He also had the means and the opportunity to either rig the lists to place Ser Gregor up against Ser Hugh (knowing that his psychotic nature would make him take the obvious kill-shot) or to simply approach him in a tavern and pay Ser Gregor to kill the inconvenient knight. But the most significant factors that lead me towards this being part of the Littlefinger Conspiracy is motive. As part of his larger project of steering Ned's investigation, Littlefinger piques his interest in Ser Hugh and then arranges his assassination in front of the Hand, which (as we'll see in "Eddard VII") further convinces Eddard's belief in the Lannisters as the main conspirators and denies Eddard a source of information (while making it look like Littlefinger is his ally).

Even more important than this direct ploy is what Ser Hugh's position (and the fact of his sudden enrichment) suggests:

1. Firstly, as I've said before, at the very least, Ser Hugh as Jon Arryn's squire would have known his movements and been privy to his conversations, which means Ned talking to Ser Hugh would get Eddard to the truth too quickly, which means Littlefinger has a motive to keep Eddard from talking.

2. Secondly, given his access to Jon Arryn, it's possible that Ser Hugh might have either had a hand in (who knows if Lysa needed help poisoning her husband or procuring the poison) or been a witness to his poisoning – or knew the truth of what Jon Arryn had figured out – had been bought off by Littlefinger, and now needs to be shut up.

3. Thirdly, and I think this is the most likely explanation, Ser Hugh might have been Littlefinger's spy, keeping Littlefinger informed as to the course of Lord Arryn's investigations, and therefore needs to be shut up. Ser Hugh fits the model of a Littlefinger agent to a T: like the Kettleblacks, Ser Lothar Brune, Ser Shadrick, and Ser Dontos, Hugh is a poor knight who needs Littlefinger's money, he's someone Littlefinger has had occasion to come to know well in either the Vale or King's Landing, and he's a non-entity who's easily deniable.

4. The fourth possibility, which I don't particularly place much faith in, is that it's possible that there's a link between the Lannister Conspiracy and the Littlefinger Conspiracy. As I've suggested before, the strangest aspect of the Lannister Conspiracy is the nigh-suicidal passivity of Cersei in dealing with Jon Arryn, given the stakes involved for the queen. One rather remote possibility is that Littlefinger offered his services to Cersei to remove the Hand of the King and hush it up, probably without making any reference to knowing the truth about Cersei's incest-adultery-treason trifecta, and Cersei accepted so as to keep the whole thing at arm's length. It would at least explain why a Lannister asset like Ser Gregor suddenly acts to remove witnesses in a way that has not happened before.

Regardless of which motive you think is most likely, it's rather impressive work from Lord Baelish. However, it's really interesting that right after Ser Hugh dies, Littlefinger shows up and immediately begins obsessing over Sansa: staring, comparing Sansa to a young Catelyn, mentioning that "your mother was my queen of beauty once," and touching her inappropriately. Given what will transpire between Littlefinger and Sansa in *A Storm of Swords* and *A Feast for Crows*, I think Martin is deliberately foreshadowing that Littlefinger's romantic obsession with the Catelyn of his youth – and his really creepy desire to turn Sansa into both the daughter he might have had and a replacement for his lady love – will be the ultimate source of his downfall. Just as he can't keep himself from telling anyone who will listen that he took Catelyn's maidenhead, he can't stop himself from telling Sansa all of his crimes and his plans. My guess and my hope is that Sansa will use this against him at her upcoming nuptials, when she will have the entirety of the nobility of the Vale as a captive audience when she accuses him of the murder of Jon, Lysa, and Robert Arryn.

Finally, "Sansa II" shows Cersei setting up Robert to be assassinated in the melee. I'll cover that in-depth in "Eddard VII," but I just wanted to note that both Cersei and Renly are manipulating Robert in this scene, showing how Renly (unlike the queen) can do both the inside and outside game of politics.

Historical Analysis

Speaking of romanticism, let's talk about the Victorian rediscovery of jousting in the 19th century. I'll get into medieval jousting and why jousting was abandoned later, but take it for now that European noblemen decided to stop charging at high speed at each other with pointy sticks starting in the late 16th and early 17th century in favor of pastimes that were less likely to result in maiming or death. Then the French Revolution, the Napoleonic Wars, and the Industrial Revolution happened, and Europe was really busy for a while. There were these bourgeois people running around, and they had a lot more money than the aristocrats, and they kept coming up with new ideas and new values that were not merely alien but hostile to the values of the aristocracy.

And then in a completely unrelated development, the Romantics embraced medievalism, the Gothic Revival became really popular, and Sir Walter Scott published *Ivanhoe*. And a whole bunch of Europeans who should have known better went totally crazy for jousting. One example will suffice: the Eglinton Tourney of 1839. Sponsored by the Earl of Eglinton, Archibald Montgomerie (whose family had collected the pennon spear of Harry Hotspur of Shakespearean fame), the tourney was an extravaganza of nostalgia run amuck: the duchess of Sumerset was the Queen of Love and Beauty, the future Napoleon III took part, as did 40-

odd "knights," and 100,000 people visited (or .6% of the population of Great Britain).

The whole damn thing got rained out, in a sudden deluge of reality. And 100,000 people who now couldn't get back via their carriages, which were now stuck in the mud, tromped home in soggy finery. Despite the torrent of ridicule from the more progressive-minded of the era, the thing was a runaway success. Jousting became a sudden craze (someone even had the bad idea to import it to the United States, where it was briefly popular in the antebellum South, prompting Mark Twain to partly blame Walter Scott for the Civil War), and along with it came a torrent of popular interest in the Romantic conception of medieval society.

And if you're wondering why fantasy novels have rightful kings, brave knights, and humble peasants, and why the orcs are always ugly and the elves always pretty, well, you can blame the Victorians. Yeah, J.R.R. Tolkien loved him some *Ivanhoe*.

What If?

Duels are a tricky business; each one presents at least two possible outcomes (who wins, who loses?) and even more dire possibilities (does someone get injured, does someone die?). Here are some things to note:

What if Gregor didn't fight Ser Hugh? Well, I've already gone into the practical consequences of this before, but it's key that Gregor fights Ser Hugh really early on in the tourney, only his second joust of the day. Had the match been delayed somewhat, it's quite possible that Ser Hugh would have gotten knocked out of the tourney by someone not out to kill him.

What if Ser Balon Swann beats Gregor? If the Kingsguard had managed to win this joust, then Gregor doesn't pass through into the semi-finals, which means he doesn't fight the Knight of Flowers and try to kill him, Sandor doesn't win the tourney by default and maybe doesn't have any gold to be re-appropriated in the name of the people by the brotherhood without banners. Which, in turn, means that Sandor might not return to kidnap Arya Stark, which may mean she's re-united with her mother, right before the Red Wedding.

What if Renly had died in his fall? Renly is unhorsed by the Hound and lands on his head; had his helm been less well-made or had the fall been angled slightly differently, he could have died then and there. Result: with Renly dead, no one's left standing in between Stannis and the stormlands when he declares for the Iron Throne.

Without having to attack Storm's End, Stannis is free to assault King's Landing with 20,000 men long before any preparations can be made to stop him. All hail King Stannis!

Book vs. Show

I'm not the first person to say that HBO's *Game of Thrones* in its first season didn't really capture the scope and breadth of the Hand's Tourney. On the other hand, in the cold light of dawn, given the sheer expense of shooting any scene with horses (which turned out to greatly increase the shooting time required to do jousting scenes), I'm kind of glad that the showrunners decided not to blow their budget in episode four. Instead, we get a tight focus on Ser Hugh's death, which keeps the story moving along nicely.

However, and I'm also not the first to say it, Benioff and Weiss made an enormous mistake in shifting Sandor Clegane's monologue to Sansa about his brother to Littlefinger - and unlike the horses, this was something they could have done right within the budget. They really wasted the chance to cement, early on, Sandor and Sansa's relationship and to give Rory McCann one of the best monologues the Hound gets. Especially since it was the audition that won him the role.

EDDARD VII

"You are the King's Hand, and the king is a fool... your friend, I know, but a fool nonetheless... and doomed, unless you save him."

Synopsis

Eddard views the body of Ser Hugh of the Vale, succeeds in preventing (along with Ser Barristan Selmy) the assassination of King Robert completely by accident, watches the Knight of Flowers defeat the Mountain and get saved by the Hound, and goes through the looking glass with Varys.

Political Analysis

"Eddard VII" is almost overflowing with political content as Eddard deals with the fallout from the assassination of Ser Hugh of the Vale, inadvertently thwarts an assassination attempt against the king, considers the evidence he's gathered and begins to formulate a plan of action, and makes his first big breakthrough in his investigations when Varys decides to illuminate him.
Brace yourself, folks – this one's a doozy!

The assassination of Ser Hugh – first of all, the fallout from the assassination of Ser Hugh of the Vale. Regardless of whether Ser Gregor killed Ser Hugh on his own behalf or on orders from some third party, Eddard Stark's first reaction is to wonder "if it had been for his sake that the boy had died. Slain by a Lannister bannerman before Ned could speak to him." This belated paranoia has some interesting consequences: Eddard starts to really see the scope of "the Lannister appetite for officers and honors," noticing that "Robert [is] surrounded by the queen's kin, waking and sleeping." I would argue that it's hardly a coincidence that Eddard foils Cersei's attempt to kill Robert Baratheon by forbidding "him to fight, in front of his brother, his knights, and half his court," right after he begins seeing Lannisters around every corner; as he gains information, Eddard becomes more of a threat.
Varys arrives and provides further information about Ser Hugh in ways that are more revealing than at first glance. On the surface, Varys

confirms that Arryn was poisoned by the tears of Lys, a "rare and expensive poison," and speculates that Ser Hugh of the Vale ("one boy... all he was he owed Jon Arryn, but when the widow fled to the Eyrie with her household, he stayed in King's Landing and prospered") was responsible. However, we also learn something else that's not clear at first read: Varys is capable of making mistakes. As we will learn later, it was Lysa and Littlefinger who killed Jon Arryn (although it's still possible that Ser Hugh was a conspirator or a witness to that murder), but Varys doesn't know that, in no small part because Littlefinger has been very good at keeping the information to a few parties and then getting those parties far away from Varys's spies.

However, we also get further suggestion that Ser Hugh's murder was carried out to prevent him from talking to Lord Stark, and that the reason he died "so untimely" was that he had been bribed with enough money to purchase the "bright new armor" that was going to jumpstart the jousting career of an otherwise penniless knight. To me, this suggests that my theory about Littlefinger having arranged his death to clean up any loose ends in regards to Jon Arryn's investigations is on the right track. Moreover, the talk of expensive armor makes Varys's comment about the tears of Lys being expensive into, I think, a quiet hint (similar to Pycelle's mention of Lysa's mental state) that it would have taken someone with Petyr Baelish's wealth to acquire the tears of Lys.

The interesting question is how much Varys really knew about Jon Arryn and Ser Hugh. Varys definitely knew the secret that Jon Arryn was looking for, and also knew much, if not all, of what Jon Arryn had uncovered (given how he kept tabs on Gendry), but it's not clear whether Varys knew who had killed Jon Arryn (since Varys definitely benefits from the Starks blaming the murder on the Lannisters, provided he can time their conflict correctly) and is simply lying through misdirection, or whether Varys really did think Ser Hugh was responsible. In a sense, Littlefinger's assassination, meant to convince Eddard of the reality of the Lannister threat and that his investigation is on the right track, might also have been intended to act as a distraction.

Creating Ser Hugh as the very image of a patsy (a nobody hedge knight who was close to Lord Arryn, who then suddenly comes into a lot of money and a knighthood the moment Arryn dies, who then dies in a suspicious manner at the exact right time) is just the kind of twice-removed intrigue that is the signature of the Littlefinger Conspiracy. And insofar as we can tell, it seems to work, convincing Varys that he's found the hand who wielded the tears of Lys, leading him away from further investigation. After all, it's absolutely to Varys's interests – if he knew that Littlefinger were responsible – to uncover his rival and take him out of the game of thrones, and yet he misses a perfect opportunity. On the other hand, it's equally in Varys's interests to keep Stark focused on the Lannisters, hanging back to see what happens with Arryn's murder, and biding his time in dealing with Littlefinger (given his need to keep Littlefinger's eyes focused on Westeros, not Essos).

Ned and Rob, and why we should care about the bros – and to understand why Eddard Stark is genuinely a threat to Cersei and the other conspirators, why we shouldn't dismiss him as doomed by his honor, I think we have to understand the bond between Eddard and Robert in all its complexity. It's not as simple as Robert being willing to listen to Ned – as we have seen and will see, Robert is perfectly willing to overrule his Hand when he doesn't care about the issue at hand (the killing of the direwolf) or when Eddard is urging against a course of action Robert views as necessary to the security of the state (the killing of Daenerys). Rather, Eddard knows Robert, not perfectly (he doesn't yet know about the marital abuse, although he does know about the adulterous tendencies), but he knows his virtues and his vices. He knows that Robert is contrary when publicly told not to do something, he knows that, for all his drunkenness, Robert retains his memory (something that Eddard and Cersei share), but he also knows that Robert still has the qualities of the military leader that he displays later when Ser Gregor goes on a would-be psychotic killing spree in the tourney.

Secondly, he's willing and able to tell his friend, the king, some hard truths and get the king to accept them – while telling Robert he's grown too fat for his armor is a rather comic moment, telling a lifelong warrior that he can't participate in a melee because everyone will let him win, and telling Robert that he didn't know Lyanna as well as he thought, is far more serious. And Robert does, in fact, listen to Eddard at this point, and, in so doing, Eddard foils an assassination attempt without knowing. Certainly, Varus considers Eddard's closeness to the king to be a major asset, arguing that "you, Lord Stark, I think… no, I know, he would not kill you even for his queen, and there may lay our salvation."

It's Varys's opinion that made me re-think Eddard's plan to lay everything in front of the king, "prove that the Lannisters were behind the attack on Bran, prove that they had murdered Jon Arryn," gambling that Robert would act and "Cersei would fall," isn't such a bad plan, after all. Now, we know, in retrospect, that Joffrey is the likeliest candidate for the attack on Bran (although, as is often the case in Martin's work, we don't get any conclusive proof), and that Lysa Arryn and Littlefinger murdered Jon Arryn, but Eddard does ultimately succeed in gathering evidence of treason sufficient to bring down Cersei, and probably would have succeeded in getting Robert to move had he not been delayed just long enough by his injuries. After all, for Robert, Ned is the man in his life who is "always right," and even in the moment that most people hold up as evidence that Ned can't count on Robert (the decision to assassinate Daenerys), we should remember that Robert does ultimately accept the truth that Eddard was trying to tell him.

Granted, I still think Eddard makes a mistake in relying *solely* on Robert's good character, as opposed to uniting the powers of his office with the favor of his king, but I think much of the fandom also judges his proposal with the hindsight knowledge that Robert is going to die before Eddard can let him know. When a plan requires that kind of deus ex machina to be derailed, I think reassessment is due.

Eddard's investigation makes a breakthrough – by "Eddard VII," the lord of Winterfell has now proceeded far enough into his investigation that major players like Varys are beginning to come to him with significant pieces of information, and he's getting close to putting those pieces together into an overall picture of a conspiracy:

> *Littlefinger's dagger, won by Tyrion Lannister in a tourney wager, sent to slay Bran is his sleep. Why? Why would the dwarf want Bran dead? Why would anyone want Bran dead?*
>
> *The dagger, Bran's fall – all of it was linked somehow to the murder of Jon Arryn, he could feel it in his gut, but the truth of Jon's death remained as clouded to him as when he had started. Lord Stannis had not returned to King's Landing for the tourney. Lysa Arryn held her silence behind the high walls of the Eyrie. The squire was dead, and Jory was still searching the whorehouses. What did he have but Robert's bastard?*
>
> *That the armorer's sullen apprentice was the king's son, Ned had no doubt; the Baratheon look was stamped on his face, in his jaw, his eyes, that black hair... yet knowing all that, what had he learned? The king had other baseborn children scattered throughout the Seven Kingdoms... yet, in the end, it mattered little whether the king had one bastard or a hundred... none of them could threaten Robert's trueborn children.*

This summation is a pretty good barometer of the progress of Eddard's investigation: he's been misinformed about the dagger, but he is correct that Bran's fall was linked to Jon Arryn's murder, although the connection was somewhat tenuous; Littlefinger had been spying on Jon Arryn (who discovered, after months of searching, what Bran learned in an instant) and knew that if he had the Hand murdered, then it would be easy to direct suspicion towards the Lannisters, who would have had the strongest motive, and while the selection of the dagger was a complete accident, Littlefinger's decision to lie points the finger to him as someone who's trying to turn the Starks and Lannisters against each other. Likewise, although he doesn't realize it, the fact that he has proof in the form of Gendry and the other bastards that all of Robert's bastards bear the "Baratheon look" and that Cersei's children don't is threatening to the "trueborn" children and their mother. So there we have it – a man on the verge of breakthrough who doesn't realize what he has.

Ironically, Eddard comes incredibly close in this chapter to nearly busting open the Littlefinger Conspiracy, and finding out who was responsible for the attack on Bran. Had he inquired as to how Robert "know[s] [Joffrey] as I do," or had he inquired either with Robert about who won the dagger that was wagered when "the King of Flowers... dumped the Kingslayer on his golden rump," or had he thought to ask Renly the moment that Renly says, "A pity the Imp is not here with us... I should have won twice as much," who had won Littlefinger's dagger the last time Littlefinger had bet on the Kingslayer, he would have known that Joffrey is a psychopath, that only someone with access to the king would have had access to the would-be murder weapon, and that Littlefinger had lied to him. Unfortunately, Eddard is distracted by his thoughts on the Lannister Conspiracy and then by Ser Gregor's attack on Loras Tyrell, and the moment is lost.

Varys choosing this moment to come forward represents both a potential opportunity and a potential danger to Stark's investigation. On the one hand, he learns several important things from Varys – that Cersei attempted to kill her husband in the melee (more on that in a bit), that Robert is surrounded by Lannister loyalists who include two of the Kingsguard other than Jaime, that Jon Arryn had been murdered by the tears of Lys because he was asking questions, and that Ser Hugh was possibly involved. Outside of, perhaps, Stannis and the actual guilty parties, Varys is maybe the most valuable source of information in Westeros. On the other hand, Varys is clearly not telling Eddard everything he knows (he clearly knows that Cersei's children are not by Robert and that Littlefinger is deceiving Eddard about the dagger, for one), and is probably getting involved for the same reason that Littlefinger did: to guide Eddard's investigation and modulate its tempo (although Varys probably also got involved to prevent Littlefinger from having a free hand with the king).

However, Varys's motives for guiding the investigation are different from Littlefinger's; he has no interest in getting Eddard to trust him, because he has no intent to betray him. Instead, I think we have to look ahead to "Arya II," where he urges Illyrio to ready an invasion before the civil war is won; in order for the Varys/Illyrio Conspiracy to succeed, they can't have any side in the civil war win and consolidate power before a Targaryen army lands in Westeros. At this moment in time, Varys wants to help Eddard protect King Robert's life (note that he doesn't offer to help with the investigation) because he doesn't want the king to die and Joffrey to accede to the Iron Throne before Eddard can gather the necessary proof needed to discredit Joffrey and prevent a consolidation of the realm under the Lannisters.

Return to the Lannister Conspiracy – next, we need to discuss the Lannister Conspiracy. I put off discussing this in "Sansa II" so that I could put it all in the same post, because it's a critically important topic. In "Sansa II," we see the queen set up her husband for an assassination attempt in the melee, and here we get confirmation from Varys that her reverse-psychology was a deliberate attempt to maneuver him into a place where a "tragic accident could take place." This is very useful information, because it adds to our understanding of how the Lannister Conspiracy operates, and what its signature is – namely, the use of arranged "accidents" as a cover for murder, a tendency to passivity, and an overall sloppiness (Cersei couldn't really count on her assassination actually killing Robert, given his skill in battle and the general chaos of the melee, and we see this again with Cersei arranging for Lancel to slip Robert fortified wine on his boar hunt, which doesn't actually guarantee a kill).

This signature is important, because it allows us to rule out the Lannister Conspiracy for the attack on Bran (which, had it succeeded, would have been an obvious assassination) and the murder of Jon Arryn (which used poison), which bear no elements of this signature. The murder of Ser Hugh is an ambiguous case, since it relies on an accident (Ser Hugh's gorget being loose), but it also involves the blatant use of a Lannister bannerman (which isn't a part of the signature at all) – hence my conclusion that Littlefinger is to blame.

However, the incident itself raises other questions: what prompted this particular attack at this particular time? Given that this is only one of two times when the Lannister Conspiracy has actually acted, and that they didn't act against Jon Arryn when he posed an existential threat to the Lannister cause, it must have been something significant. My guess is that, following Varys's comment that "the queen is watching you closely," Cersei is worried that Eddard is coming too close to the truth and wants to kill Robert and have Joffrey crowned, with Eddard swearing an oath of fealty to the new king, in order to foreclose the possibility that Robert could be informed of the truth or that Eddard Stark might declare for Stannis.

The interesting question is why (as far as we know) Cersei hasn't tried to assassinate her husband before, especially given her thinking in *A Feast for Crows* about her desire to make Tommen's minority last as long as possible. My guess is that the problem was timing: if Joffrey was too young at Robert's death, her plan to install him on the Iron Throne immediately (which was a vital element of her coup d'etat) wouldn't be credible, and there would have to be a genuine regent the realm would accept, either Jon Arryn or Eddard Stark. As is, her presence as queen regent was politically dicey enough to bolster Renly and Stannis's support and, even, to create opposition within her own house.

Robert's political awareness and Renly's plan – another interesting moment in "Eddard VII" is that we finally get a sense of what Robert Baratheon thinks about the politics of the kingdom he supposedly is the monarch of. The first thing we learn is that Robert understands exactly how bad he is as king – "I was never so alive as when I was winning this throne, or so dead as now that I've won it" – and the only reason he stays on the Iron Throne is that he realizes that Joffrey on the throne and Cersei standing beside it would be so much worse than his benign neglect, given that his son is a sadistic maniac who shows many of the classic symptoms of psychopathy.

And Robert is also interested in doing something about it, when he has a Hand he can trust. "We'll make this a reign to sing of, and damn the Lannisters to seven hells," he declaims and then, in the same speech, brings up Renly's offer of Margaery Tyrell, which creates the potential for genuine change. If Robert is genuinely open to the Renly/Tyrell Conspiracy, this suggests an openness to dissolving his marriage to Cersei and disinheriting his children, bringing in the Tyrells to deal with the crown's finances, and diplomatically isolating the Lannisters with a Stark/Tully/Baratheon/Tyrell bloc far too powerful to successfully rebel against even with the Arryns MIA.

The love of the crowd – finally, one thing I wanted to bring up that was important in "Sansa II" but which I didn't have time to get to – the importance of tourneys as a place for the manipulation of public opinion. We see in that chapter how Renly has used his showings in tourneys to garner public support among the commons to become "a great favorite," which he definitely will trade on in his eventual bid for the throne. Loras Tyrell is also a skillful player in this particular political game, using his beauty, his wealth, and the tropes of romantic fiction to garner public support.

Jaime Lannister, no political aficionado, tries to win the public's support, and certainly is attractive to the female half, but finds that it's just as easy to become a figure of public mockery. Loras's display of wealth is far more effective, as the commons go mad for the display of sapphires and roses, but in a chapter filled with upsets, it's ironic that it's the Hound who wins "for perhaps the first time in his life, the love of the commons."

Historical Analysis

So, last time I talked about the Victorian reinvention of jousting, but why did jousting get abandoned in the first place? A big part of it was that the introduction of the more powerful musket that replaced the arquebus in the 1690s made knightly charges non-viable, but another part of it was that jousting was insanely dangerous and fell out of fashion as a result.

Henry VIII has passed into legend either for his divorce and remarriage to Anne Boleyn or as an obese wife-murderer, but the young Henry Tudor was considered a handsome, if somewhat bull-like, athletic young man and a keen enthusiast of jousting. However, in 1536, Henry VIII was badly wounded in a joust at Greenwich Palace when he was struck in the leg with his opponent's lance in such a way that his horse then fell on top of him. The injury to his leg, which never completely healed, made maintaining mobility much more difficult, and so the formerly svelte monarch went from 180-200 pounds (on a 6'1" frame) to 392 pounds at his death. Even more significant may have been the undiagnosed brain injury associated with the fall, which caused the young king to fall unconscious for two hours, after which the king's personality began to shift to the paranoid, vindictive man of legend.

Even worse is the case of Henry II of France, Henry VIII's contemporary, and sometime friend and rival. In 1559, at a tourney to celebrate a peace treaty with Austria and the marriage of his daughter to the king of Spain, Henry II jousted against Gabriel Montgomery, the captain of his Scottish Guard, and received a blow to the head when Montgomery's lance splintered. The resulting wound turned septic and led quickly to his death at the age of 40. After his death, his decidedly unhealthy son, Francis II, ruled only for 18 months before dying of a disease of the ear and, in turn, was replaced by the infant Charles IX. The result was four years of regency under Catherine de Medici, who oversaw the loss of virtually all of France's territories in Italy, the collapse of the "Auld Alliance" with Scotland, and the beginning of the French Wars of Religion, which would paralyze the country for 30 years.

It's not surprising, then, that the monarchs of Europe gave up a sport that could potentially wreck entire dynasties if the wrong monarch took a lance to the face. The interesting thing is that the same didn't happen in Westeros, despite the death of Baelor Breakspear in a "Trial of Seven" in AL 209, and that for some reason Robert Baratheon managed to gain Henry VIII's weight without suffering Henry's debilitating injury.

<u>What If?</u>

"Eddard VII" gives us a wide variety of hypotheticals to consider, from both past and present:

What if Ned became king? Let's say the rebel alliance had decided not to link back to the past, either because Robert Baratheon thought twice about becoming king or had died of his wounds after the Battle of the Trident; it's not unreasonable that Eddard Stark would have become king. The story of the Mad King's vendetta against the innocent

Starks would certainly work as dynastic propaganda, and the Stark/Tully/Arryn political bloc would be united by marriage along with the support of House Baratheon. Interesting things follow: Eddard Stark probably would have had great difficulty in the beginning, given the remoteness of his northern base, so he probably would have relied heavily on the Tullys to project his power in middle Westeros, but with three trueborn sons, his dynasty would have been well-founded. Policies would have been somewhat different – the crown would probably not have gone into debt, the Greyjoy Rebellion would have been handled swiftly, and I can't see corrupt members of the royal bureaucracy lasting long, but Eddard would have had to deal with discontent from the Lannisters, Tyrells, and possibly also the Martells (although, depending on how he handled Tywin's sack of King's Landing, that could have fallen out very differently), but he would have had Jon Arryn's support as Hand to help him. Jon Snow's presence would have proven exceedingly difficult, given his potential parentage, possibly leading to a Daemon Blackfyre situation, especially if Varys ever found out about his parentage.

What if Jon Arryn became king? Jon Arryn had political weight and the respect of most of the Great Houses and would have also had the Stark/Tully/Arryn power bloc and the support of House Baratheon. He probably would have had an easier time than Eddard, given his political experience and the closer proximity of the Vale to the crownlands, but he would also have had a different set of problems as king – namely, a wife of questionable fertility and mental capacity, and a sickly solitary heir. I could easily imagine King Jon's court becoming a den of intrigue, as the eligible daughters of the Great Houses are put forward to replace the barren queen, and the constant fear that if the "mature" king and his sickly son both die, the realm is potentially without a rightful heir to the throne. Littlefinger's rise to power would be all the more precipitous, given the allure of the Handship and the potential to become regent to the young King Robert Arryn. On the other hand, the crown would not be heavily indebted, and openly corrupt men like Janos Slynt would have been purged from government.

What if there is no Lannister marriage? Given that Robert had no great interest in marrying Cersei Lannister, it's possible that a different dynastic match could have been made. Who, precisely, that would have been is trickier: Margaery was born the year of the rebellion, so House Tyrell – the logical alternative to House Lannister as a rich and powerful House that needs to be brought into the fold – would probably have had to offer either Janna or Minna Tyrell (Lord Mace's sisters). House Martell was out of the question, both because of the murder of Elia and Arianne being six; House Tully's women were already married; House Greyjoy had no women of marriageable age; and House Stark's only daughter was dead. A Tyrell match would have probably resulted in the same scramble for royal appointments and favors, but the marriage would probably have been much more peaceful, and Robert would have had trueborn children. Hence, no need for Jon Arryn's investigation and assassination, and Eddard Stark would never have gone south.

What if Renly's plan worked? Margaery becoming the new queen is something I've brought up before, but it happening at this time would have been quite interesting. Certainly, I think a Henry VIII/Anne Boleyn-style match would probably have gone off like gangbusters, and Renly and the Tyrells would have certainly helped Eddard to root out the Lannister Conspiracy and install a new regime in King's Landing. What happens next is harder to say. Potentially, a civil war in the vein of the Blackfyre Rebellion could have broken out between those who favor the Lannister claimants and those who favor the Tyrells – Tywin would have a much harder time of it, but I could see him buying off Balon and using the Martell's historic hatred and fear of the Tyrells to counter-balance their hatred for his own person (although he'd probably have to trade them Gregor and Amory Lorch). That, plus a hefty investment in mercenaries, might have worked, but it would be a really heavy lift. Certainly, I think we would have seen an interesting situation emerge where, once Margaery gives birth to an heir, "Uncle Renly" begins working to isolate Eddard and get himself named as regent when his brother dies.

What if Cersei's plan had succeeded? If Robert Baratheon dies at this point, things become very interesting, indeed. Without firm proof of Joffrey's genetic bastardy, Eddard probably would have sworn an oath of fealty to the new king – but unless Robert dies instantly, Eddard's the new regent. With no cause to remove him, Cersei now has to work to unseat an Eddard Stark who now has the powers of the king of Westeros, and who will be quickly lobbied by Stannis and Renly (if not also by Littlefinger and Varys) with proofs that Joffrey is king. This could potentially kick off a Dance of the Dragons-style coup d'etat, with Eddard standing in for Ser Criston the Kingmaker. Alternatively, had Eddard ceased his investigations and truly believed Joffrey was the rightful king, I could see him unhappily leading the royal armies against Stannis and Renly before being dismissed from service or resigning when Joffrey's madness becomes evident.

What if the jousts go differently? If Jaime beats the Hound, then it's possible the Hound is injured or not on hand when his brother goes berserk, which might lead to a dead Ser Loras and the Tyrells and Renly joining Eddard in an anti-Lannister coalition. Moreover, without the tourney winnings, the Hound has no reason to return to the Brotherhood without Banners following his trial, which might have significant consequences for Arya. Alternatively, it could mean that Jaime and Loras have a re-match following Loras's defeat of the Mountain, and nothing more comes of it. And if the Mountain beats the Knight of Flowers without trying to murder him, maybe it's a total non-event.

Book vs. Show

This is one area where I feel the show diverges from the book in ways that diminish the narrative. Not showing the Hound versus Jaime I can understand, since it's not critical to the plot at all (although the idea of Jaime stumbling around unable to see is a funny sight), but what really gets me is the deletion of Cersei's assassination plot against Robert. This could easily have been added to the scene between Eddard and Varys without any increase in budget, and it would have accomplished several things: firstly, it would have meant that Eddard actually accomplishes something significant in the first half of the season; secondly, it would have ratcheted up the tension, as now viewers realize that the king could get whacked at any moment (it also makes Varys's reaching out to Eddard more significant); thirdly, it would have made Cersei more of a villain and an active presence in the plot, whereas she kind of disappears from the narrative between the death of Lady and Eddard's injury.

The only explanation I can think of is that the showrunners wanted to stick to the Jon Arryn assassination throughline to avoid confusion, which isn't a very satisfying answer.

TYRION IV

A Lannister always paid his debts. Kurleket would learn that someday, as would his friends, Lharys and Mohor, and the good Ser Willis, and the sellswords Bronn and Chiggen. He planned an especially sharp lesson for Marillon...

Synopsis

After being arrested/abducted at the Inn at the Crossroads, Tyrion Lannister learns that he is being taken to the Eyrie rather than to Winterfell. He's not particularly thrilled about being outsmarted by Catelyn Stark, or about being accused of attempting to assassinate Bran. After the revelation of Littlefinger's lies and Tyrion saving Catelyn's life during an attack by the men of the Mountains of the Moon, Tyrion and Catelyn end up on an ambivalent note.

Political Analysis

"Tyrion IV" is a relatively short and straightforward chapter: Tyrion and Catelyn talk on the road to the Eyrie, they are attacked by mountain men, in that fight Tyrion saves Catelyn's life for reasons unknown to even himself, and they finish their conversation about Tyrion's putative responsibility for the (second) attempt on Bran's life. However, a few political events of note do take place in this chapter.

The first event is the formation of a vendetta between Houses Stark and Lannister. From the first sentence, Tyrion "chalk[s] up one more debt owed to the Starks," and we know how Lannisters feel about paying their debts (indeed, even as he's put under arrest, Tyrion is marking people out for "rewards" and meting out his own brand of repayment to the singer who he partly blames for his arrest). Throughout the chapter, Tyrion is filled with "a bitter rage" that spirals beyond his immediate antagonist, damning "her and all the Starks." The vendetta is both familial and personal; while Tyrion knows that his father will avenge the insult to the family name, what truly inspires such intensity of emotion is the damage done to his self-image: "All his life, Tyrion had prided himself on his cunning, the only gift the gods had seen fit to give him, and yet this seven-times-damned she-wolf, Catelyn Stark, had outwitted him at every turn."

For her part, Catelyn Stark sneers at the very thought of "Lannister honor," despite the very real price that Tywin and, in his own way, Tyrion place on the honor of their house, and draws a bright line between the honor of the Starks, who don't murder people by the side of the road, and the Lannisters, who dispatch men with knives to slit the throats of children. "Tyrion IV" is right at the tipping point where this vendetta could be undone – in crisis, Catelyn is willing to accept the word of an honorable Lannister and arm her captive against the mountain men, and Tyrion is willing to save the life of his erstwhile kidnapper – but after this, there is no going back.

For those who scorn Catelyn Stark as a political actor, and there are many, this chapter should stand as counter-evidence and rebuke. Tyrion, himself one of the nimblest politicians in *A Song of Ice and Fire*, admits that Catelyn Stark completely bests him without lifting a finger, and repeatedly. I've already discussed how presentism is largely responsible for the fandom's selection of Catelyn arresting Tyrion as the one event that kicked off the War of the Five Kings, but it's also important for us to consider what Catelyn gains from Tyrion's arrest: first, she has a potentially quite valuable hostage to use against the Lannisters.

Secondly (and this is the second political event in the chapter), she advances her investigation enormously. In one stroke, she learns that it was not Tyrion's dagger, that "there is a serious flaw in Littlefinger's fable... I never bet against my family," and that Littlefinger has been lying in the royal court about taking her virginity. Tyrion ironically benefits from the kidnapping by learning that Littlefinger set him up and is working to poison the Starks against the Lannisters. (One of the most frustrating elements about *A Clash of Kings* for me is how little George R.R. Martin does with Tyrion's interactions with Littlefinger in that book, and in future books.)

While I think Catelyn doesn't get sufficient credit for her savvy, I don't think she is perfect, either, although she is being criticized for the wrong things. Kidnapping Tyrion and taking him to the Eyrie wasn't where Catelyn screwed up; rather, it's her actions after this point that are worthy of criticism. Potentially, Catelyn has everything she needs to unravel the entire Littlefinger Conspiracy: she knows that Littlefinger is clearly obsessed about her, to the point of spreading gossip about her virtue (which, if Eddard ever heard about it, would have absolutely provoked a duel to the death), which gives her motive; she knows that Littlefinger has lied to her about the Lannisters acting against her family, which is strongly suggestive of the fact that the Lannister Conspiracy against the Starks (as opposed to against the Baratheons) is being made up; and she knows that Littlefinger cannot be trusted. She doesn't put the pieces together, in part because of her past history with the man (and an underlying feeling of guilt about his near-death, probably), but what I find worthy of reproach is that *she doesn't inform Eddard about any of this the moment she gets to the Eyrie.* Or her father or Edmure, for that matter.

The third event of political significance is the attack by the mountain men, and what it tells us about the military situation in the Vale. Quite different from most of Westeros, where the major threat to law and order comes either from inter-noble warfare or from outside (wildling raiders, invasion from Essos, ironborn pirates), the Vale's enemies are internal – the mountain clans who "bowed to no law but the sword." From the description in "Catelyn IV," where she describes them "descending from the heights to rob and kill and melting away like snow whenever the knights rode out from the Vale in search of them," the Mountains of the Moon seem locked in a permanent cycle of guerilla warfare, where, at their best, the lords of Arryn can keep things sufficiently under control that well-armed bands can travel the high road in safety. What we don't know yet is that Lysa's madness has begun to destabilize the Vale, since by pulling her military forces back to the Eyrie, she's essentially encouraged the mountain clans to increase their raids on travelers – hence three assaults on a party of some 15 armed men.

Even before they arrive at the Eyrie, it's clear that something is rotten in the state of the Vale.

Historical Analysis

The Italian word "vendetta" takes its origins from the Latin word "vindicta," and that's not an accident. The essence of a vendetta is a blood feud between two families, where a crime (often, but not necessarily, a murder; the famous Hatfield and McCoy feud began from the theft of livestock) against an individual must be avenged by their blood relatives, and there's nothing more vindictive than when murder and family are combined. It's especially vindictive because vendettas have no terminus: the avenging of a crime against one family becomes a crime that needs to be avenged by the other, and so on for all time.

An inability to find resolution, save in the total destruction of one side or the other, is only one of the problems with vendetta. As the historian Marc Bloch once wrote:

> *The Middle Ages, from beginning to end, and particularly the feudal era, lived under the sign of private vengeance. The onus, of course, lay above all on the wronged individual; vengeance was imposed on him as the most sacred of duties... the solitary individual, however, could do but little. Moreover, it was most commonly a death that had to be avenged... no moral*

> *obligation seemed more sacred than this... the whole kindred, therefore, placed as a rule under the command of a chieftain, took up arms to punish the murder of one of its members or merely a wrong that he had suffered.*
>
> Marc Bloch, trans. L.A. Manyon
> *Feudal Society*, Vol. I, 1965, p. 125-126

Not only does vendetta privilege the strong over the weak, and essentially turn justice into the prerogative of those with sufficient military force, but it also results in not merely a continuation of violence, but an expansion of it. A crime of one individual against another turns into a conflict between anyone in two extended clans, and their friends and relatives, which means associated families get dragged in. It's not surprising, therefore, that one of the chief duties of kingship classically was to act as a judge who could forestall vendettas, by accumulating enough military force to cow both parties, but also by serving as an impartial mediator that both parties agreed would have the final say. Thus was begun the long transformation of crimes from offenses between private individuals that could only be settled through private means, than an act forbidden by the sovereign, who would then bear the responsibility for acting against those who challenged the king's law.

Whether the king could make it stick with the barons, or the barons with their knights, was always a crucial indicator of the health of the state, and by this metric the Westerosi state seems relatively weak at all levels. In virtually every corner of the Seven Kingdoms, we can find evidence of ancient blood feuds that feudal overlords and kings are more often than not incapable of stopping: the Brackens and Blackwoods have been feuding for eight thousand years, and it took a monarch of the caliber of Jaeherys the Wise to stop them for even a period of time, let alone the Tullys or most Targaryens or the Baratheons; in the north, the Boltons warred against the Starks for seven thousand years, and killed quite a few of their putative kings before bending the knee to the Winter Kings; the westerlands is only recently free of feuding due to Tywin Lannister's total war against the Reynes and Tarbecks; in the Reach, we have a number of houses, with the Florents in the lead, who challenge the right to rule of the Tyrells and the Red versus Green Fossaways; and in Dorne, Oberyn Martell seems to have started feuds as a form of entertainment.

What If?

As in any chapter where violence suddenly breaks out, the potential for sudden changes in history abound:

What if Tyrion doesn't save Catelyn? In "Tyrion IV," our eponymous protagonist makes a surprising decision to save the life of the woman who kidnapped him and accused him of attempted murder. To some extent, Tyrion doesn't have a whole lot of choice in the matter - if Catelyn dies, her fighting men have absolutely nothing stopping them from leaving him behind as they hightail it out of the Mountains of the Moon. However, if she dies, a lot changes: the Starks' deal with the Freys might be very different or not happen at all (which would possibly force Robb into a head-on fight with Tywin's army) - and if Robb's hand doesn't end up pledged to a Frey, it's possible the Red Wedding is butterflied away entirely; if the Starks get across the Trident, Jaime is not released from imprisonment, which gives the Starks something to negotiate with when things start to go bad for them and they need to pull back to the north; and a whole bunch of Freys live longer lives.

What if Tyrion dies? It's quite possible that Tyrion, for all his unexpected battle-rage, could have died in the fight with the Mountain Men, and then a lot changes. Firstly, the Lannisters will now fight to the death against the Starks with no peace possible. Secondly, Tyrion never becomes Hand of the King, which means that Stannis's ships will sail into a hail of wildfire but without the destructive impact of the fire-ships in the river and the boom chain across the Blackwater Rush. This means that Stannis's army will make it across the Blackwater largely unharmed, and the walls of the city are breached. What happens next is tricky - Tywin will still probably make his bargain with the Tyrells and move against Stannis, but will probably arrive too late, allowing Stannis to lock the doors against him. Tywin and the Tyrells greatly outnumber Stannis but now have to face an assault on the walls against an enemy ten times the size of Tyrion's forces. Moreover, if Stannis can breach the Red Keep, the political situation changes dramatically: the Lannister-Tyrell alliance requires a royal marriage, and either Stannis holds the putative king and the queen mother hostage or he executes them both and, now, the Lannisters and Tyrells don't have the basis for an alliance and are technically rebels against a sitting king, with Robb Stark still in the field with no love for either of them.

What if Catelyn does something with Tyrion's information? Timing is now starting to get very tricky - it's possible that Catelyn could get the news that Littlefinger lied about the second attempt on Bran's life before Eddard resigns the Handship and then gets disabled in the street fight with Jaime Lannister, but it's not likely. On the other hand, even if Catelyn is too late, giving Eddard forewarning that Littlefinger is acting against him could still be crucial in the final hours. Cutting Littlefinger out of the loop, and especially making sure that it's Stark coins that buy the loyalty of the gold cloaks, could have made the difference between overthrow and execution, and a successful dethroning of the false king and queen and mother and hail King Stannis!

Book vs. Show

One thing that the HBO show does differently from the books is to modulate Tyrion's "battle fury," still having him be active in combat (he saves Catelyn's life and kills a man), but pulling back slightly from the unstoppable killing machine that he becomes at the Battle of the Green Fork and the siege of King's Landing. I think it's a good change, for the same reason that eliminating Tyrion's inconsistent tumbling skills was a good change, in that it accommodates the greater realism that comes from the transition from a written to a visual medium.

ARYA III

"Delay, you say. Make haste, I reply. Even the finest juggler cannot keep a hundred balls in the air forever."

"You are more than a juggler, old friend. You are a true sorcerer. All I ask is that you work your magic awhile longer."

Synopsis

Chasing cats through the palace, Arya literally runs into Tommen and, in escaping from his guards, finds herself in the cellars of the Red Keep, where the dragon skulls of House Targaryen are stored. Hidden inside one of the skulls, she overhears Varys and Illyrio conferring about the status of their conspiracy. She manages to escape undetected and report back to her father, but her warning is garbled and Eddard dismisses it as the rehearsing of mummers (ironically, not that far off from the truth). Yoren arrives with bad news.

Political Analysis

"Arya III" is one of my favorite chapters in *A Game of Thrones* because, along with "Bran II," it's one of the rare times when we see the major political actors of Westeros speaking completely freely about their intentions, interests, and plans. Illyrio Mopatis and Lord Varys, the Master of Whisperers are some of the most secretive individuals in a series with more than its fair share of shadowy conspirators, to the extent that their true objective has remained an almost total mystery up until early drafts of *A Dance with Dragons* (and even then, we can't be totally sure). Feeling securely guarded by Varys's nigh-exclusive knowledge of the secret tunnels of the Red Keep, they meet and speak frankly about their conspiracy. Indeed, the fact that Illyrio meets with his old friend (and possible lover) the one and only time in five books in this scene suggests something of how confident they feel.

And yet they are overheard. (Incidentally, there's some fascinating stuff in this chapter about how Arya's gender presentation interacts with people's knowledge of her - she's able to "disappear" in the Red Keep, to step out of the role of the Hand's daughter, long before she becomes Arry – that I probably won't have space to get into in this recap, but I did want to highlight it.)

So, what do we learn about the Varys/Illyrio Conspiracy in this chapter?

Eddard is a few weeks away, at most, from finding out the truth that Jon Arryn had uncovered – this points to the critical importance of timing in *A Game of Thrones*: first of all, we can see how the short schedule influences the various conspiracies – Varys and Illyrio are wrong-footed, because they need more time to unite the Dothraki horde with the Golden Company; Renly and the Tyrells have a sudden opportunity to bring forward their plan, but they have to adapt quickly when Robert suddenly dies; Cersei has to accelerate her plan to assassinate Robert; and Littlefinger has to make some quick calculations about who to back and who to betray. Secondly, we can see how intricate George R.R. Martin's plotting is – the news of Daenerys's pregnancy arrives just in time to prompt Eddard to resign (since he likely would not have done so knowing the truth), and Eddard's injury has to happen in order to throw off his schedule long enough for Robert to die before Eddard can prevent Joffrey's coronation.

Varys and Illyrio (correctly) think a civil war is about to break out and feel differently about it – Varys knows before everyone else about Tyrion's abduction and instantly understands the consequences thereof: "Tywin will take that for an outrage... if the Lannisters move north, that will bring the Tullys in, as well," and once that happens, a vendetta between two families begins to spiral out of control as their relatives and vassals are called in to aid them. However, there's an interesting element of disunity in their reaction to this news: Illyrio wants to delay the civil war by killing Eddard Stark, saying "If one Hand can die, why not a second... you have danced the dance before." Our evidence for Lysa and Littlefinger's direct responsibility for Arryn's murder is too strong, but given Varys's knowledge about the tears of Lys (quite possibly, Varys has spies watching the city's poison-makers for this very purpose), it's quite possible that he stood back and allowed Arryn to die. Alternatively, Illyrio may be referring to Varys's previous influence over Aerys II and suggesting that it was Varys who suggested the appointment of the ineffectual Owen Merryweather and the sacking of **Jon Connington** as part of his larger scheme to destabilize the Targaryen dynasty.

Varys, by contrast, wants to accelerate the plan and thinks assassinating Eddard won't work (I'm not sure why he thinks that). Correctly, he understands that the Stark/Lannister feud is accelerating too quickly, and that even if Eddard dies (especially if he dies, as we'll see), it's not going to stop. Now, the more interesting question is why Varys thinks Drogo might be too late if he waits for his son to be born.

Part of the reason has to do with the overall strategic picture, as discussed above, but I think part of it has to do with the fact that Varys doesn't want the civil war to be over before they can get there, and if Eddard discovers the truth (and Varys has no way of knowing that he's about to get sidelined by his injury), it's possible that he could gather enough allies to make the Lannister coup impossible. This certainly fits his actions in *A Clash of Kings* in aiding Tyrion (he doesn't want Stannis to take the city and knock the Lannisters out of the war), or in *A Storm of Swords* of engineering Tywin's assassination, and in *A Dance of Dragons* of assassinating Kevan and Pycelle to prevent the Lannisters from consolidating power; he's keeping the civil war going so that Aegon/Daenerys can arrive as a savior/compromise monarchy. However, it's equally dangerous to get there too early, since it raises the possibility that the Seven Kingdoms unite against the foreign army... unless Varys was planning to use the army as a giant bluff/bargaining chip to force the succession by making an alliance that's impossible to stand against, or throwing the whole thing to a Great Council he could manipulate.

Interesting hypothesis: if Varys knows about R+L=J, it's possible that he's thinking that the Starks might accept a Targaryen monarch because of Jon Snow's heritage, because at the outset of the War of the Five Kings, most observers would guess that the Stark/Tullys would resist a Targaryen because of the Mad King, the Lannisters out of fear of retaliation for the Sack of King's Landing, the Baratheons because of Robert, and the Tyrells because they're committed to Renly, which isn't a good strategic picture.

Varys and Illyrio know that the game has spread beyond a "game for two players" – who the other player was that Varys/Illyrio thought they were playing against is hard to say – certainly Littlefinger makes the most logical sense, but Varys's statement that "the gods only know what game Littlefinger is playing" suggests otherwise. What's interesting is that their perspective on the overall strategic situation is an odd mixture of perspicacious and obscured: they know that Stannis and Lysa are gathering soldiers (but they don't seem to realize that Lysa is Littlefinger's puppet); they know all about the Renly/Tyrell plot, but they don't seem to know what Littlefinger is up to precisely (although Varys knows he's manipulating the situation to bring the Starks and Lannisters into conflict).

Typically for the Varys/Illyrio Conspiracy, they don't directly intervene against Renly/Tyrell, Stannis and Lysa, and the rest, preferring to sit back and watch the situation unfold. Part of this has to do with their larger strategic interest; the more sides in the civil war, the less chance there is of a conclusion, and the more the various parties will be worn down when the experienced-yet-fresh forces of Khal Drogo and the Golden Company arrive. But another part of it has to do with Varys's signature strategic caution – he hangs back to see what Eddard is about, and then interjects with his assistance when it suits Varys, but no so much that Varys falls when the Hand does; he'll do the same thing when Tyrion arrives to become the new Hand of the King; he completely disappears for the whole of *A Feast for Crows*, using his knowledge of the secret tunnels and his disguises, only to reappear with devastating effect in *Dance with Dragons*.

As a method goes, it has to be admired. While Littlefinger's manipulations in *Clash of Kings* and *Storm of Swords* in forging a Lannister/Tyrell alliance, abducting Sansa, and eliminating Lysa are quite impressive, leaving him in control of Harrenhal and the Vale (and, potentially, the north, as well), it's also the case that his assassination of Joffrey (meant mostly as a smokescreen but also to put Tyrion back in the dock) doesn't accomplish that much strategically – Tywin is the real power behind the Lannisters, and, arguably, Joffrey's death improved matters by replacing a potential Aerys with a pliable and good-natured child. Through his assassination of Tywin and then Kevan and Pycelle, Varys neatly undoes the Lannister/Tyrell power bloc even as he puts the Golden Company and Dorne into play. So far, I think the score between the eunuch and the whoremonger stands at a draw.

Varys and Illyrio consider the Stark-versus-Lannister fight an even match – I bring this up largely because the fandom, I think, tends to lapse into presentism when considering Robb's rebellion and assumes that the north can't possibly have ever succeeded, and that the King in the North was doomed from the start (you also find this in Catelyn apologias that seek to shift blame to Robb rather than to reject it altogether). However, two of the smartest political analysts on two continents think that the Starks have a good chance against the Lannisters.

The *Song of Ice and Fire* RPG (endorsed by George Martin) is one of the few estimates that's ever been done of the total military capacity of Westeros, and it puts the total strength of House Lannister at 50,000 men (which fits, given that the War of the Five Kings starts with Tywin in the field with 20,000 men and Jaime with 15,000, and the Lannisters are able to hastily raise another 10,000 at Oxcross while keeping 5,000 at the Golden Tooth). The total strength of the Starks is... 45,000, with the riverlands able to mount another 40,000 (this latter estimate makes sense, given that the incompletely-mustered Tullys had 4,000 men at the Golden Tooth and 16,000 at the Battle of Riverrun, and then have 20,000 men of arms immediately after the Battle of the Camps).

What people forget is that when Robb marched with 18,000 men to rescue his father, he did so at short notice in a desperate attempt to rescue his father. *Because Catelyn Stark was sidetracked before Eddard's instructions to mobilize the north were delivered* to Houses Tallheart, Glover, and Manderly, the north doesn't fully mobilize when it goes to war. My guess is that as many as 27,000 men were left behind or simply not mobilized – when you consider that the Boltons, Manderlys, and Tallhearts have significant forces left in the north in *A Clash of Kings* (and the first two never fight the ironborn), that the 3,000 men of the mountain clans were never mobilized, and that the Karstarks and Umbers still have men to aid Stannis with in *A Dance with Dragons*.

Again, note the intricacies of the plotting here: Catelyn Stark has to kidnap Tyrion, because otherwise Robb Stark doesn't march south with not-enough men to be the exciting underdog that inspires so much affection from the fandom (especially post-*Storm of Swords*), so that Robb has to settle for capturing Jaime rather than going for the lord of Casterly Rock, so that Tywin's 20,000 men remain in the field to relieve the siege of King's Landing, so that the defection of the Freys and the Karstarks are such a crippling blow to his hopes, so that Balon and Theon and Asha don't run headlong into 27,000 mobilized Stark soldiers (which, in turn, means that Winterfell can fall and Theon be captured). To quote Detective Freamon, "all the pieces matter."

Historical Analysis

I've already mentioned my pick for Varys's historical counterpart(s), so in this section, I'd like to talk about the nature of espionage in the Middle Ages and Early Modern period. Spying is one of the world's oldest professions, dating back to the 13th century BC, where we have evidence of spies being used in the wars between the pharaohs of ancient Egypt and the Hittite kings to undertake missions of misinformation about the locations of armies. The Arthashastra, 4th-century India's manual on government compiled for Chandragupta Maurya, advises the use of spies to gather information on the loyalty of one's people, guard the king from assassination, and carry out assassinations of high-ranking officials who might threaten the king.

Indeed, the main difference between historical spy networks and our modern intelligence services is the lack of formalized institutions. Spies tended to be recruited on an ad-hoc basis, often for particular military campaigns or to deal with particular political rivals: spies were used frequently in the Hundred Years' War, for example, to provide intelligence on which towns held valuable supplies for English armies to sack, or to provide notice when the English navy left port to give the French armies time to mobilize. As the Middle Ages passed on to the Early Modern period, we can see a slow movement to a more organized practice; the close link between spy networks and official embassies began to be forged as ambassadors were used as the "man on the spot" to acquire information, recruit agents, and carry out subversive missions, usually by the paying out of secret bribes. Francis Walsingham's was one of the most sophisticated of Renaissance spy networks, employing moles and double-agents through bribery, blackmail, and threats, intercepting communications without detection by developing new techniques for breaking and repairing wax seals, and employing dedicated cryptographers to break codes used by foreign monarchs. The results were quite impressive: the Throckmorton Plot was broken up, the Babington Plot was infiltrated and turned into the legal pretext for the execution of Mary, Queen of Scots, and plans for the Spanish Armada were uncovered long before the ships left Cadiz, giving England time to prepare for invasion.

By contrast, the state of espionage is rather underdeveloped in Westeros – other than Catelyn and Lysa, few of the great lords seem to encode their communications (which lends credence to the Maester Conspiracy theory), double-agents and moles are incompletely used (Littlefinger, Varys, and, to a lesser extent, Tyrion use them, but none of the other Lannisters, Starks, Baratheons, Greyjoys, Martells, Tyrells, etc. seem to), and Varys seems to have the only bi-continental spy network in existence.

One of the odd little details we learn in "Arya III" is that Varys's particular spy network is comprised of what must be hundreds of children (since he places an order with his friend, Illyrio, the occasional slaver, for fifty new "little birds"), who must be young and literate (highly unusual for this time and place) and then have their tongues removed – presumably because they're less likely to accidentally spill some of Varys's secrets. Partly, his decision to use children makes sense – one of his chief methods of gathering intelligence is by using the secret tunnels that honeycomb the Red Keep to spy on people, and children would have an easier time making their way through narrow, cramped passages to overhear conversations. On the other hand, there's something deeply creepy about the way Varys is essentially recapitulating his own mutilation every time he has an intelligent, literate child maimed, suggesting an unending cycle of abuse and exploitation in the pursuit of secrets (Martin is fond of characters recreating their own trauma – witness Cersei basically recreating her marriage to Robert but turned up to 11 with Joffrey and Sansa).

What If?

To me, there are three big hypotheticals in this chapter:

What if Arya is discovered? Well, this is something of a quandary. Murdering the youngest daughter of the Hand of the King is an incredibly risky step, but Varys and Illyrio can't afford to let the Hand know about their plot to bring the Targaryens back to Westeros. So it's possible that Arya might have died down in the darkness of some "accident." Alternatively, Varys is good enough at spinning that he might have been able to recover the situation short of murder by convincing Arya that he's working to save her father.

What if Arya gives a more coherent warning? To me, this is the most interesting possibility. If Arya doesn't get her message jumbled, it's possible Eddard Stark would have believed that his daughter had overheard two conspirators in the cellars of the Keep. What, precisely, he would have learned is unclear - Arya naturally focused on the threat to her father's life, and if Eddard took that threat more seriously, he might have brought more guardsman with him to the brothel and, thus, prevented his injury. He could have learned about Stannis and Lysa gathering troops (but that doesn't particularly help), and he could have learned about the Renly/Tyrell plot (but he basically knows about it, anyway). Most critically, he would know that Tyrion Lannister has been abducted because of Littlefinger, and at least been able to see the blowback coming instead of being suddenly confronted with it (which, in turn, might have influenced his decision to resign the Handship).

What if Arya sends her letter to Jon Snow, and it gets to the Wall? This one is a bit tricky, since it assumes that Yoren isn't intercepted and the information gets there before Jon Snow goes off ranging with Jeor Mormont, at which point the information will not be of any use. How Jon Snow would react to this information is unclear - it might give him more impetus to leave the Wall earlier, which, in turn, could well mean he doesn't go on the journey north, which, in turn, might mean Castle Black falls to the Thenns, and the wildlings pour into a north torn by war, with no one left behind them to guard the Wall. Alternatively, he might pass on the warning to Winterfell - which means that Robb and the rest of the Starks will possibly mobilize earlier than they do in OTL, potentially changing the course of the War of the Five Kings.

<u>Book vs. Show</u>

The only major change from the books is that they leave out Arya bumping into Tommen as the reason she runs down to the depths of the Red Keep where the dragon skulls are kept, which is relatively minor and probably done to save a bit of money and the fact that Tommen is pretty much a glorified extra at this point.

EDDARD VIII

"Do it yourself, Robert. The man who passes the sentence should swing the sword... you owe her that much, at least."

Synopsis

Eddard Stark quarrels with King Robert over the assassination of Daenerys Targaryen; only he and Ser Barristan Selmy vote against it, while the rest of the small council votes for it. Stark resigns over the issue and is preparing to leave King's Landing at once when Littlefinger distracts him with one last clue from Jon Arryn's investigation.

Political Analysis

There's a tipping point in every tragedy where inevitability locks the exit doors on free will and you know that, after this, there is no turning back. "Eddard VIII" is that moment; from the point where Eddard decides to follow one last lead instead of getting on the boat right that moment, he has only one way forward, and bloodshed is the only destination. Whether he had succeeded in his quest or not, Eddard was going to be right on the front lines of a Stark/Lannister war with no way to escape. George R.R. Martin will even go so far as to literally hobble our putative protagonist so he can't flee.

But before that, we get an incredibly momentous political moment: the decision before the small council whether or not to assassinate Daenerys Targaryen, and Eddard's decision to resign over the issue. This has often been portrayed as the second-biggest example of why Eddard was completely incapable of playing the game of thrones, a patsy who put honor above reason. However, I think this overlooks the complicated factors going into Eddard's decision, because it's more than a question of morality - arguably, there are four different reasons apart from that:

1. Doctrine of Necessity - next to the concept of truces, treaties, the white flag, and the idea that you don't touch envoys, the concept of "just war" is probably the oldest in international relations. It appears in the Sanskrit epic the *Mahabharata* (where it includes provisions like proportionality of violence, just means [no poison, you guys!], just cause, and fair treatment of wounded soldiers and prisoners), and Cicero wrote about it, as did the two intellectual heavyweights of Christian theology, St. Augustine and St. Thomas Aquinas. One of the chief elements of a just war is the doctrine of military necessity – violence has to be intended to have a military effect on the enemy, it has to be directed at a military target, and the harm caused to civilians has to be proportional to the military effect the attack is supposed to have. There's also the concept of a necessary war (i.e., defense of oneself or others) versus a war of choice.

As Ned Stark has made repeatedly clear, he sees no threat from the Targaryens that necessitates assassination: "there is no axe," he argues with his king, "only the shadow of a shadow." He doesn't see the Targaryens as a threat that rises to the level of military necessity, given Daenerys's age and the relative naval dominance of Westeros versus the Dothraki. Ironically, Eddard is unknowingly right about this – until such time as Westeros threatens his wife, Drogo makes no move to cross the narrow sea. From the perspective of military necessity, the assassination attempt on Daenerys Targaryen was completely counter-productive.

2. Different motives for rebellion, different causes for revolution – it's a short exchange, but this back-and-forth between Eddard and Robert is quite telling:

> "Robert, I ask you, what did we rise against Aerys Targaryen for, if not to put an end to the murder of children?"
>
> "To put an end to Targaryens!"

Something the two old comrades-in-arms have forgotten is that, from the very beginning of Robert's Rebellion, the two men had very different motives: Eddard's sister had been kidnapped, but compounding that was the fact that King Aerys murdered his father and brother without a fair trial, violating the common law of Westeros; Robert was acting purely from an insult to his honor and a direct threat to his life, and continues to hold personal grudges. Ned is something of a Kantian when it comes to situations of honor, and drew from the deaths of Rickard and Brandon the precept that monarchs who summarily execute unarmed people without due process lose their right to govern. For him to acknowledge that Robert has the right to assassinate Dany would be to accept that Aerys had the right to slay his family. By contrast, Robert is a man who ascended to the Iron Throne in part thanks to Tywin's murder of most of the Targaryen family and drew a very different lesson from that experience – as we shall see later.

3. **Eddard's theory of politics** – as I've discussed a few times before, Eddard Stark has a very idiosyncratic theory of politics. He believes that the person of the rules and the office should be one, as the old ways dictate, such that the ruler's conscience is sovereign; he thinks of his subjects and his peers not through the lens of powers and duties, but personal relationships, and, at the end of the day, he sees his role as Hand to be the king's friend and, ultimately, his conscience. These aren't bad ideas, necessarily; indeed, one could argue that the power of his name after his death to move the north into rebellion against the Boltons (who, at the time, are Lords Paramount and Wardens of the North) at a time when very few people in the rest of the Seven Kingdoms cares who Tywin or Hoster or Balon or Renly was is evidence of the advantages of this theory.

However, it's also a theory that makes this impasse with Robert inevitable – notably, Eddard doesn't use his office to act as a gatekeeper between the king and the rest of the small council, like any good chief of staff does, to decide what the king will hear and see. This prevents him from heading off the news of Dany's pregnancy until he's got his political ducks in a row. He doesn't meet with the small council individually to use the office to secure their support on the council. This prevents him from potentially winning Renly's vote by persuading him or making a deal with him ahead of time, or to try to persuade Varys to wait on sending the assassination order. It also means that he doesn't try to massage his disagreement with Robert – rather than making a reasoned argument that an assassination attempt might spark retaliation, or an appeal to Robert's vanity and self-image, he calls him out as a coward and a tyrant, when Eddard knows exactly how Robert reacts to being told he can't do something. Finally, it means that Eddard doesn't think of himself as a policymaker – hence, he doesn't try to preempt the assassination debate by proposing expansion of the navy to dominate the narrow sea or to negotiate with the Free Cities to deny Dany their ships.

4. **The other, other, other Targaryen** - we also have to keep in mind that Eddard Stark is a man who, for 15 years, has (most likely) been hiding a Targaryen from Robert's furious vengeance. Given how much his promise to Lyanna has cost him in terms of honor, reputation, and the happiness of his marriage, watching Robert salivate over the thought of butchering Targaryen children has to be the closest thing to a living nightmare. I'm absolutely convinced that, on a subconscious level, Eddard is thinking about Jon Snow during the entire meeting, imagining what might happen if the truth of his nephew's birth got out and he had to stand in between Robert and the child of Rhaegar and Lyanna.

Just as the memory of his dead kin means that Eddard cannot accept the legitimacy of Dany's assassination without retroactively absolving Aerys Targaryen, the knowledge of his living kin means that for

Eddard Stark to endorse the death of his "good-sister" is also to accept as legitimate the idea that the child he has been protecting for all of his life could be murdered by royal command, in secret, and without the color of law. That is not something Eddard Stark is going to accept.

Political Thought in King Robert's Council

Thanks to Martin's choice of point-of-view characters, we can see into Eddard's head and judge his actions based on both his thoughts and words at the time as well as what we've learned about him from earlier chapters. However, Eddard isn't the only political thinker in the room, and there's a lot we can learn by examining the rationalizations offered by King Robert and the small council.

Robert – there's a tendency among the fandom to reduce Robert Baratheon to a caricature, to stop at the drinking and the wenching (and the wifebeating...) and dismiss him as a mindless jock, the very reason why warriors don't make good kings. But as Martin has stated again and again, he doesn't believe in black-and-white characters, and Robert shows a moment of surprising depth here. Yes, there is an unrelenting hatred of all things Targaryen, but Robert also says "let be in on my head, so long as it is done. I am not so blind that I cannot see the shadow of the axe when it is hanging over my own neck." Robert understands that what he's doing here is dishonorable and immoral, but he is also an intelligent enough monarch to know that heirs to an overthrown bloodline are a danger to a new dynasty (witness the Blackfyres). As a realpolitikian, Robert's more on the money than he realizes: there are Targaryen loyalists in Westeros working against him, both in his small council and in Dorne, they are gathering military and political power against him and his heir, and a successful assassination of the Targaryens would short-circuit much of their planning.

Varys – Varys's motives here are quite interesting, given that he's the guiding force behind this decision (having informed the king about Dany's pregnancy). My working hypothesis is that, subsequent to his discussion with Illyrio, Varys is using this assassination attempt he can control to accelerate the Varys/Illyrio Conspiracy by provoking Drogo into action; he may also be trying to remove Eddard Stark from the Handship short of murder. The interesting question is whether he's acting with Illyrio here or separately; how much unity is there in this conspiracy?
Two other things of note:

1. "We who presume to rule must do vile things for the good of the realm, howevermuch it pains us." Leaving aside the possibility that Varys is always lying and has no motive other than to place a puppet

monarch on the Iron Throne, which I think flies in the face of the evidence about Varys's nature and rather underserves one of the best schemers in *A Song of Ice and Fire*, I think this quote sums up Varys's pragmatic political philosophy. He may have ventured to Westeros as part of a scheme to take his and Illyrio's steal-and-replace act on the road, but I think he was genuinely disgusted by a monarch as fundamentally unworthy as Aerys II and resolved to put the perfect monarch on the throne no matter the cost. If Littlefinger is prepared to start a civil war for his own personal benefit, Varys is far more dangerous because he will keep one going for as long as it takes to reform Westeros. And there is no creature on Earth half so terrifying as a pragmatist with an idealist's heart.

2. The other interesting thing Varys does here is to bring up the tears of Lys, the same poison that ended Jon Arryn's life. I think he does this in order to provoke a reaction and draw out Jon Arryn's assassin – ironically, he succeeds in drawing out Maester Pycelle, who recognized the poison and prevented effective counter-measures from being taken against it, but who didn't administer the poison himself. Littlefinger remains circumspect.

Pycelle – the false counselor naturally offers false counsel in this scenario, claiming "once I counseled King Aerys as loyally as I counsel King Robert now," given that he has always been Tywin Lannister's man in King's Landing, and far from being concerned about the "wiser, even kinder" nature of assassination over war being the mentality directly responsible for the death of soldiers, the burning of towns, and the murder of children when he persuaded the king to let Tywin's army into the city they promptly sacked (interesting that Varys was on the other side of that debate, possibly fearing a Lannister dynasty?). Ironically, he suspects Varys of the murder of Jon Arryn (as he did when he met with Eddard and as he will later when interrogated by Tyrion), in part out of his guilty conscience over what is essentially a life devoted to the forswearing of his maester's oath.

Littlefinger – Littlefinger likewise urges death for Daenerys Targaryen, although he claims later that his complaints about the price tag were designed to ensure the assassination attempt would fail (likely as a way to keep himself just enough on Eddard's side); however, he has no idea that the money he's handing over is going to a man who has no intention in successfully killing a Targaryen. However, it's worth noting for those Littlefinger fanboys who railed against the "Middlefinger" of season two the crude sexual metaphor he's using. Littlefinger is many things, but a perfectly controlled man he's not. This kind of uncouth sexual banter is something the hedge lord can't really stop himself from doing (hence his constant talk about bedding the Tully sisters prior to *A*

Game of Thrones and his dick jokes in *A Clash of Kings*), even when it clearly alienates the rest of the small council. It's part of the reason why as high as Littlefinger climbs, he's never going to be truly accepted as one of the nobility.

Renly – Renly also urges death, which would fit with his plans to uproot the Lannisters and install a Baratheon/Tyrell dynasty on the Iron Throne, and his general habit of sucking up to Robert by playing to his brother's worse angels, both alcohol and murder. Just wanted to point this out to the Renly fans – Renly is charming and charismatic, but he's not a nice person.

Selmy – moved by Eddard's mention of the fact that he owes his own life to royal mercy, Selmy reacts to the suggestion like the warrior he is, drawing a strict procedural line between "facing an enemy on the battlefield" versus "killing him in his mother's womb." This is important for two reasons: first, this is probably the moment where the impetus for joining Daenerys as opposed to either Stannis or Renly is generated. If Robert shows himself to be no true king by ordering the murder of children, then it doesn't matter who his heirs are. Second, it means Eddard isn't alone on the vote – more on this in a bit.

Eddard's Resignation

I've argued that Eddard's decision to oppose Daenerys Targaryen's murder isn't reason enough to count him out as a political actor. He's not a perfect strategist, either, and he makes a huge mistake (arguably one of the top five he makes in *Game of Thrones*) by resigning from the Handship over the issue. Given that he knows "the business with Catelyn and the dwarf... would come to light soon" and poses him a direct danger from Robert and Cersei both, he needs the office to protect him and his family – as Hand of the King, he could put the kidnapping of Tyrion under color of royal authority and make any move to stop him an attack against the crown; as Eddard Stark, he's a lord engaged in a blood feud and vulnerable to assault.

A big part of this decision is a feeling of frustration that:

> ...the truth of Jon Arryn's death still eluded him. Oh, he had found a few pieces, enough to convince him that Jon had indeed been murdered... Stannis shared the secret Jon Arryn had died for – he was certain of it... the Imp's knife. Why would the dwarf want Bran dead? To silence him, surely. Another secret, or only a different strand of the same web? Could Robert be part of it?

Ironically, Eddard is much closer to the truth (he knows about Jon's investigation, he's got the book and Jon's final words, he's seen that Robert's bastards bear the Baratheon look) than he thinks and just needs a good mental jog to help him put the pieces together. However, as I've said, he could know a lot more about what's going on if he knew that the knife didn't belong to Littlefinger, and that Littlefinger is lying to him. Moreover, Eddard's thought to sail to Dragonstone and directly confront Stannis is a good one.

However, if Eddard truly wants to, leaving right then and getting himself and his family clear of King's Landing is a smart move, as it brings them out of immediate harm's way and back to the north, where Eddard comprehends the direct authority he has and can muster the north's military strength against the coming threat. Hence why Littlefinger comes in right at that moment to delay Ned Stark's departure and get him into a place where he can be attacked by Jaime Lannister and further increase hostilities.

Historical Analysis

This chapter analysis is running long, and I don't have anything that particularly concrete in the way of historical analysis that I wanted to talk about beyond some thoughts about assassinations, which I'll save for a future chapter.

Moving on...

What If?

As you might expect from my initial discussion of the theme of fate and free will, "Eddard VIII" is absolutely rife with hypotheticals that could have dramatically changed the course of history:

What if Eddard had left rather than talk to Littlefinger? Thanks to the kidnapping of Tyrion, hostilities are going to commence whether or not Eddard hangs around King's Landing long enough to order royal retaliation against Gregor Clegane. However, if Eddard had left right then and there, the War of the Five Kings would change dramatically. First and foremost, the north begins the war with Eddard Stark, an experienced military campaigner who would have mobilized the north immediately and fully; Robb Stark's tactical and strategic genius would still make themselves known, but in a context where his father was around to keep his eye on logistics, manpower, and political maneuvering (Eddard Stark is canny enough to know that Theon has to be kept close to keep Balon out of the war). Second, the Lannisters have no Stark hostages to use; this means that the Starks aren't distracted by a clearly disingenuous peace process and have a larger strategic flexibility to enter and leave the war when it suits them. Third, being a more experienced hand at rebellions, Eddard is unlikely to declare independence for the north, especially when a letter arrives confirming what he's suspected all along about Prince Joffrey.

What if Eddard had visited Dragonstone? If Eddard visits Stannis on the way to King's Landing, there's a very good choice he learns the truth about Joffrey's parentage and Jon Arryn's murder, which he will no doubt tie to the assassination attempt on his son. At this point, one of two things happens: either Eddard's loyalty to Robert takes precedence, and he returns to King's Landing with Stannis and his army behind him, either to confront Robert directly if he's in time or to launch a coup against Cersei and Joffrey (which Renly would probably join, given that he's Stannis's heir by the laws of succession). And Stannis would temper Eddard's idealism – no telling Cersei ahead of time what they're going to do, no trusting Littlefinger with the gold cloaks (which raises an interesting point: as master of laws, the gold cloaks technically would report to Renly; why didn't he try to take over this force?). The alternative is that Eddard pulls a Stannis and keeps going north, preps the north to war, and Stannis starts the War of the Five Kings with the north and the riverlands on his side, which probably means all hail King Stannis.

What if Eddard had won the vote? If there's no assassination attempt against Daenerys, things start to change very quickly for that storyline. With no assassination attempt, Drogo doesn't make an oath to win his son the Iron Throne then and there – and will probably wait until Rhaego has grown a bit so he's viable as an heir to the Iron Throne. This means the Lhazarene aren't raided for slaves to buy boats, Drogo doesn't take his wound and isn't poisoned by Mirri Maz Dur, and Dany doesn't go in for the blood magic that will kill her son and lead her down the path to becoming the Mother of Dragons. Which might have doomed the world once the Others came... so mercy really would have been a killer there.

What if Eddard didn't resign? This one's a bit tricky, given that Eddard did get the Handship back really quickly after he was attacked by Jaime, but if he was Hand of the King, Jaime's attack would play very differently – rather than a brawl in the street that can be swept under the rug, this is an act of open outlawry and lèse-majesté. Jaime would flee the capital as before, but now does so as a condemned man, which could very well have put House Lannister under legal sanction at the outset of the war. This would complicate Tywin's mobilization and stiffen resistance against him; the Greyjoys and Tyrells would certainly have enjoyed the freedom to attack Lannister holdings at will.

Book vs. Show

The big change from book to show here is that Benioff and Weiss leave out Ser Barristan Selmy, making Eddard the lone dissenting voice within the small council. I'm not sure how I feel about this change – on the one hand, I can see how it intensifies the drama by isolating Eddard and sharpening the distinctions between the corrupt south and the noble north. On the other hand, it also contributes to the "Ned is dumb" meme by making him completely isolated from the political world whereas, in the book, he was able to persuade at least one member of the small council to see things his way. In addition, I think it removes a certain complexity from Ser Barristan's character arc – he wasn't just a man who tore off his armor because of the evil King Joffrey; he came to a moral decision gradually through a considered evaluation of the world around him.

CATELYN VI

"...the Eyrie is impregnable. You saw for yourself. No enemy could ever reach us up here..."

"No castle is impregnable."

Synopsis

Catelyn Stark makes her way from the Bloody Gate up to the Eyrie, where she meets a very different Lysa from the girl she remembers, and Jon Arryn's heir, God help them all.

Political Analysis

"Catelyn VI" is a nice little chapter that shows how a lot of political nuance can still be found in a segment that concerns itself mostly with someone climbing a mountain.

First, I mentioned back in "Tyrion IV" one of the side-effects of Lysa's paranoid call for all of the knights of the Vale to be "kept close at home, to defend the Vale... against what, no one is certain" has been to destabilize the military-political status quo in the Vale, freeing up the clansmen from the threat of reprisal, hence attacking a band of armed men repeatedly. Given Ser Donnel's comment that he could take "a hundred men into the mountains, root them out of their fastnesses, and teach them some sharp lessons," the disruption to the Vale seems truly needless* and a sign, like ghosts walking on the battlements of Dulsinore or the eternal wound on the thigh of the Fisher King, that there is something rotten in the House of Arryn.

> * Incidentally, one potential explanation might be that Littlefinger wants the Vale mobilized for an invasion of the north down the road, but that's a bit tinfoil-hatted for me.

Second, we get a good picture of the military defenses of the Vale and why it's considered so difficult to attack: the Arryns clearly believe in the virtues of defense in depth. To conquer the Eyrie, an invader would have to beat their way through no less than six castles, each of which is well-constructed and uses the native terrain of the Vale in its own way and to its best advantage:

1. **The Bloody Gate** – defended by the Knight of the Gate, the Bloody Gate is a massive wall "built into the very stone of the mountains... where the pass shrank to a narrow defile scare wide enough for four men," with "twin watchtowers... joined by a covered bridge of weathered grey stone." It's a defensive dream and an attacker's nightmare – the defile itself prevents armies from using their size to overpower the defenders; the high slopes on either side make knocking out either tower incredibly difficult (since the covered bridge allows mutual support and reinforcement); and attacking head-on means that you're taking fire from the front (the battlements), both flanks (the towers), and directly above (the bridge overhead). No wonder it has been the death of so many armies.

2. **The Gates of the Moon** – if an army could get through the Bloody Gate, it then stands at the mouth of the Vale and all its agricultural wealth, except that you're standing at the point where "the Vale was narrow here, no more than a half day's ride across," with the Giant's Lance right in front of you. Militarily speaking, if you try to bypass the Giant's Lance, you're going to be cut off from the rear and get attacked from the front and rear simultaneously, and bottling up the defenders and starving them out would require an enormous amount of manpower to encircle the entire mountain (because the natives don't have to get off the mountain via just the gates) and interdict resupply while giving the Vale time to mobilize and crush you against the mountain. So you have to confront the threat right on, which means you have to get through the Gates of the Moon. The Gates of the Moon are formidable: a "stout castle" with a moat, drawbridge, portcullis, and defensive towers can hold several thousand defenders – and it can be reinforced from Stone, Snow, Sky, and the Eyrie above.

3. **Stone** – after having to assault two major defensive fortifications in a row, you now have to climb up the mountain and get past the first of three way-castles. After several hours of climbing, you get to a keep with "a massive ironbound gate" with "iron spikes set along the tops of formidable stone walls and two fat round towers." The narrow path means once again you can't bring numbers to bear – or siege engines – and, once again, the defenders can be reinforced and resupplied from above.

4. **Snow** – the ascent gets even steeper and narrower at this point. Snow may be "smaller than Stone, a single fortified tower and a timber keep... hidden behind a low wall of unmortared rock," but it can't be bypassed, and the engineers who built it used the landscape to give

Snow the ability to fire on any army getting past Stone for the entire distance, and Snow can still be reinforced and resupplied from above.

5. **Sky** – at this point, the path is less than three feet wide, which means that even though "the waycastle called Sky was no more than a high, crescent-shaped wall of unmortared stone raised against the side of a mountain," you can't avoid anything being thrown your way, and if anything connects and you fall, you're dead. Even if you get past the wall, the defenders can retreat to a cave inside the mountains and force yet another head-on assault, and, once again, your opponent can be reinforced and resupplied from above.

6. **The Eyrie** – if Sky is breached, the basket can be reeled up, meaning that you have to climb "more like a stone ladder than proper steps" for six hundred feet straight up. The Eyrie itself might be small, but seven towers means you're absorbing a lot of punishment from five-hundred well-supplied men with their backs to the proverbial wall, who can furthermore use the winch in the cellars to cut you off from behind by recapturing Sky, or to slip out the back way and imprison you in the empty keep.

However, what this list doesn't really explain is the iterative nature of all of this – at each step, if an invader was able to overwhelm each line of defenses, they would take huge casualties while the defenders can easily retreat to a new set of defenses and augment the garrison there, so that the attacker is continually decreasing in numbers while the defender keeps losing manpower; the castles further down the line can send forward supplies and reinforcements easily, while the attacker has to haul everything up three vertical miles under conditions of punishing exposure; several of the castles offer vantage points where they can provide supporting fire from above. Between the casualties, the repetition of perilous frontal assaults, and extreme conditions, any army short of the Unsullied would likely break under the strain. In essence, the whole of the Giant's Lance is one big castle.

As long as Gulltown can protect the Vale from the sea, the only major threat facing the Val is internal – and the Arryns seem to have dealt with this problem in classic feudal fashion, by creating a series of positions of honor that it can dole out to buy the support of powerful houses of the Vale. The positions of Knight of the Gate, Keeper of the Gates of the Moon, High Steward of the Vale, and the likely-but-unconfirmed positions of Knight of the Stone, Knight of the Snow, and Knight of the Sky are influential and prestigious positions, not exactly rich in lands but offering proximity to the Lord Paramount of the Vale, and in politics, the closer to power you can get, the more of it you have.

Third, we get to meet Ser Brynden Tully, fan-favorite, guerilla warrior, and all-around badass. What we see in this chapter, however, is that Brynden is also a perceptive political observer where his brother is not concerned.* Being a good listener is key to picking up political information, and his strategic mind is clearly seen from the fact that he immediately tells Catelyn to tell her father about what she's done, since "if the Lannisters should march, Winterfell is remote and the Vale walled up behind its mountains, but Riverrun lies right in their path." More than most of the other men of the Vale Catelyn encounters, Brynden can sense the political tensions building in the Vale – pointing to the unspoken belief that Jon Arryn was murdered, the resentment towards the Lannisters, and the reality that the last remaining Arryn is "six-years-old, sickly, and prone to weep if you take his dolls away... too weak to sit his father's seat."

> * Incidentally, I do like how Brynden's backstory points out how dynastic arranged marriages can constrain both men and women's lives (patriarchy damages everyone, just not in the same way or degree). I don't know if the Blackfish is gay; I kind of want them to portray that in the show a bit, because they missed the chance with Loras and Renly to subvert traditional depictions of gay characters.

Likewise, it's telling that Brynden can parse that while "a woman can rule as wisely as a man," it takes the "right woman... [and] Lysa is not you." (Catelyn-haters should note that the Blackfish thinks of Catelyn as a woman who can rule.) Whether it's because of his sexuality or totally unrelated, Brynden can see past his culture's ideology of gender and see how Lysa has been fundamentally damaged by Westerosi gender roles: a "marriage... made from politics, not passion... two babes stillborn, twice as many miscarriages," and (although he doesn't know this) a forced abortion on top of it. For all that Lysa is a truly despicable character (murdered her husband, sent her sister and her brother-in-law into harm's way, attempts to execute an innocent man without trial, attempts to murder her niece), I think there's an argument to be made that she, more than any other woman in the series – including Cersei – has been a victim of the patriarchy.

Indeed, her obvious mental trauma causes her to almost give away the plot (the Littlefinger Conspiracy, that is) by acting in a way that belies her initial story – referring to "your quarrels with the Lannisters," and later changing her story about who assassinated Jon Arryn. Indeed, given how she snaps later on when Sansa arrives, either Littlefinger can't or didn't prep Lysa to keep her story straight, which is a major weakness in his conspiracy (his equivalent of Pycelle?).

Fourth, Catelyn makes two consequential decisions: she chooses to ignore her doubts about Tyrion's guilt (in part motivated by her guilt over the deaths of the men who rose to her call at the inn), and she decides to send letters to Riverrun and the north to pass on critical information about preparations for war... which she never does.

Historical Analysis

One potential historical counterpart to the Vale in our history is Wales during the process of English conquest; then as in the Vale, the population was divided between its "original" inhabitants (considered semi-barbarous by the new overlords), who used guerrilla warfare to stage hit-and-run attacks from mountain strongholds, and more recent migrants, who used a network of castles garrisoned by mounted knights to dominate the region. These castles, constructed during the reign of Edward I, acted as military protection for new colonies of English settlers and proved to be the rocks against which the rebellions of Madog ap Llywelyn, Llywelyn Bren, and Owain Glyndŵr would ultimately break.

The Eyrie is something of an exaggerated fantasy castle, but the question remains: could the Eyrie be taken by storm? History offers some examples of mountain-top castles that were taken by storm: during the Great Jewish Revolt in the 1st century AD, the Romans took a number of mountain-top fortresses, most notably at Masada, where they built a 375-foot earth and stone ramp up the side of the mountain to allow them to assault the walls. This tactic would be incredibly difficult with the Eyrie, given its three-and-a-half-mile height and the narrow width of the mountain path.

Another siege during Alexander's conquest of Bactria (modern Tajikistan and northern Afghanistan), the capture of the Sogdian rock, offers a better model. The Rock of Sogdia was the last fortress of the king of Bactria, a mountain stronghold "sheer on every side against attack," and well provisioned and garrisoned. When Alexander sent an envoy to demand surrender, the defenders refused flatly, taunting the Macedonian king that he would need "men with wings" to defeat them.

Alexander offered gold to any volunteer willing to brave the heights and got 300 men experienced in climbing sheer fortress walls in previous sieges. While it's not known exactly how high the Rock of Sogdia was, since the precise location was lost to history, a very similar Sogdian fortress on Mount Mugh stands some 1500 meters (or .93 miles) above sea level. These 300 men made a night climb up an almost completely vertical slope, picking out a route with iron tent-pegs, woven flax ropes, and linen route markers, losing 30 men on the way. When the defenders saw that Alexander had found "men with wings," they surrendered on the spot.

In the TV show, Bronn was probably exaggerating that a dozen men with climbing spikes could take the Eyrie – but enough determined and skilled men, willing to absorb casualties, could do it.

What If?

There's not much in the way of hypotheticals in this chapter, but I'll mention a couple for completeness's sake:

What if Catelyn falls? I don't really give this one credence, because one of the major reasons George R.R. Martin has sent Catelyn on this wild-goose chase is to have her meet her transformed sister. However, if it happened at this point, some interesting things happen: Catelyn wouldn't make the pact with the Freys, so Robb would have had to bargain a pact himself, or to attack Tywin Lannister directly; if Jaime Lannister is captured, he's not released and possibly is used by Robb to bargain a truce once the war starts to go sour in *A Storm of Swords*. And a lot of Freys live.

What if Bronn and/or Morrillon doesn't come up the mountain? In the chapter, Catelyn immediately regrets allowing the minstrel Morrillon to come with her to the Eyrie, which means she has to extend an invitation to Bronn, as well. Had she chosen not to bring them with her, some interesting things happen: without an introduction to Lysa, Morrillon isn't on hand to sexually harass Sansa or to take the fall for Littlefinger when Lysa goes completely mad and tries to kill Sansa in *Storm of Swords*. While Littlefinger could probably have finessed the immediate crisis by claiming she had lost her mind and thrown herself from the Moon Door over her son's declining health, certainly his prospects for dealing with the Lords Declarant really begin to narrow.

What if Catelyn sends either or both of her letters? This is the one that really kills me, as I've expressed before. Catelyn is reminded that she needs to pass urgent messages to mobilize for war to her father and brother in Riverrun and to the lords of the north (and really should be passing on what she learned from Tyrion to Ned) and then promptly forgets. According to the Global Timeline, she had seven days between her arrival at the Eyrie and Ned's resignation to get her messages out - personally, I think the alternation of chapters suggests more of a simultaneous or near-simultaneous timing. So it's possible Ned is forewarned about Littlefinger's treachery before he's led to the brothel where he will be injured, but, regardless, knowledge that Littlefinger is actively lying to him might have changed Ned's critical decision to leave the gold cloaks to the master of coin. Regardless, the impact on the War of the Five Kings is immense: the GT suggests that it takes eight days for news of Catelyn's capture of Tyrion to reach Robb, who, in turn, sends out riders for a mustering; eight more days could have meant thousands more soldiers mobilized to march south or to defend the north from the ironborn. Given that two weeks lapse between her arrival to the Eyrie and Gregor's predations in the riverlands, prompt warning could have meant the riverlands were better mobilized to meet the first Lannister attack, possibly preventing the complete collapse of their defenses.

Book vs. Show

There's a couple major changes between the book and the show in this chapter. First, we don't get multiple mountain men attacks (which would have been repetitive and expensive), or have it explained to us that Lysa is deliberately damaging peace and order in the Vale. Second, we don't get the Blackfish – which they did to save on actor budgets, by shunting the entire Tully family into season three, and also to avoid having to explain the dynastic links of Westeros (a common strategy used by the showrunners – hence Cleos Frey becoming Alton Lannister, which I see the merits of). At the time, I disliked this change, but if it means we didn't get an extra and instead got Clive Russell, I'm okay with it.

Third, we get a very different image of the Eyrie, and this I found to be an unnecessary mistake (since it doesn't cost more money to do a different matte painting instead of the one they went with). The show version is a rather unbelievable hollow mountain that the castle sits on top of, with a long bridge you ride right up; this lacks something of the size and scope of the sky-scraping Rock of Gibraltar-essence of the book's castle, and you don't get the sense of these iterative defenses that are so amazing on the page. I will say that a Moon Door in the floor is actually a substantial improvement, and I can't wait for it to be used again in season four.

Fourth, we get a quite different Lysa Arryn, where they went gaunt instead of corpulent. I like this change, which emphasizes more Lysa's madness than the fact that she's let herself go. I quite like Kate Dickie's performance of a woman who's clearly living on her very last nerve, and I'm glad to see she's returning in season three, although I don't think the scenes of Littlefinger wooing her are going to be easy on the stomach.

EDDARD IX

Ned Stark kept his vows. He thought of the promises he'd made Lyanna as she lay dying, and the price he'd paid to keep them.

Synopsis

After finding the last of Robert Baratheon's bastards, Eddard Stark and his men are attacked by Jaime Lannister and a group of Lannister soldiers. The Stark men are murdered, and Eddard's leg is broken when his horse falls on top of him.

Political Analysis

"Eddard IX" has the feeling of a noir action piece rather than much in the way of politics – Detective Eddard Stark finds one more clue, but it doesn't get him to the answers he's looking for, and then he gets jumped by a bunch of gangsters in the rain and his partner ends up dead. Swords and horses aside, it's not hard to imagine Mickey Spillane or Dashiell Hammett writing something like this. So… probably a short recap.

What we do get is further confirmation that the Baratheon look is absolutely de-rigeur in Robert's bastards, and a strong sense that Robert and Lyanna's marriage might not have been the happiest (although Lyanna doesn't seem to be that offended by Robert's straying, certainly not to the extent Cersei will be). We also see Ned rethinking his perceptions of his old friend, Robert, recognizing that he and his old friend share fundamentally different views on honor.

An interesting moment comes when Lord Stark finally just straight-up asks Littlefinger about what he knows about Robert's bastards – interesting both because Ned had never asked before (or anyone else, for that matter), and because it shows that Littlefinger is clearly trying to hide what he knows about Jon Arryn's investigation, mentioning Edric Storm to derail the conversation. At this point, I'm pretty convinced that Littlefinger has known this whole time about Cersei's bastards, enjoying the "lovely, tight little shiver inside" that he knew something Ned didn't know. At the same time, we learn something truly horrific about Cersei, something I feel a lot of her defenders don't contend with: *she had two babies murdered and a woman sold into slavery* for an "affront to Lannister pride." I think one can empathize with Cersei's plight but still note that this is deeply evil.

When the Starks are stopped by the Lannisters, who suddenly find them in a massive city, two interesting things happen. First is that, despite Littlefinger's rather transparent ruse to call the City Watch, the Lannister men let him through their lines unchallenged, which I take as further evidence that Littlefinger set up this ambush. What that betokens is unclear: it's possible that Littlefinger offered to spy on Ned for the Lannisters when Ned first arrived, which would explain how he had access to Ser Gregor, and why he kept his place on the small council despite Cersei considering him an enemy, or that this was an overture of Littlefinger's as he began thinking about which side he was going to back when Robert died.

Second, we see Eddard thinking rather strategically and pragmatically when he threatens Tyrion's life if he's harmed, which shows that, at least in settings he's familiar with, like battle, Eddard is more than simply an honorable man. And Jaime oddly begs off fighting to let the others do his dirty work for him – possibly a sign of George R.R. Martin still in the process of developing this character, or that Jaime's vaunted courage doesn't extend to fights where he wouldn't get any glory.

And just like that, Eddard's men are dead and he's got a broken leg. This is absolutely crucial, as we'll see later.

Historical Analysis

There's not much to discuss this week, except maybe the history of prostitution, but the upcoming "Daenerys IV" will be absolutely chockablock with historical parallels.

What If?

If there aren't a lot of historical parallels to discuss, this chapter – like any fight – opens up some really important hypotheticals for what might have happened had the violent clash of men with swords on horses in the driving rain gone slightly different:

What if Eddard died? Either due to the wound going septic or the femoral artery getting nicked or landing wrong, Eddard Stark could easily have died in this alley brawl. This changes the future dramatically: a grieving and remorseful Robert Baratheon would brand Jaime Lannister an outlaw, and would respond to Ser Gregor's attack on the riverlands as a challenge to his royal authority; Robb Stark might not rush down to save his father's life and instead musters the whole strength of the north to crush House Lannister, and, in all likelihood, Jaime Lannister loses his head to Robb Stark after the Battle of the Whispering Woods. So, potentially the War of the Five Kings starts with House Baratheon and House Stark united against House Lannister, and public opinion in King's Landing changed, with Eddard Stark as the murdered loyalist and the Lannisters as murderous traitors.

What if Jaime stays for the fight? I always thought it was a bit out-of-character for Jaime Lannister to let anyone else do his fighting for him, possibly a sign of Martin's "gardener" method of writing, where Jaime's character hadn't fully grown yet as it would once he started writing from Jaime's POV. A lot could hang on the outcome: Jaime could easily end up like Eddard, given the treacherous nature of trying to ride a horse on rain-slicked cobbles, which means that he can't flee from King's Landing and wouldn't be able to lead an army in the field – which means Tywin's left flank comes under the command of the more cautious Kevan Lannister, which might mean that Edmure Tully has more time to rally his banners and drill his men, and doesn't get ambushed and captured, which, in turn, would make Robb's shift over the Twins unnecessary – setting up an even fight between Robb and Tywin's armies, which could virtually end the war for either side. Jaime would definitely still be on the scene when the gold cloaks arrive, which possibly means he gets put on trial for murder and violating the King's Peace, but in any case definitely means that he's not able to lead an army in the riverlands, and so on and so forth.

What if Eddard doesn't break his leg? This is the chief consequence of the fight. Eddard's leg getting broken is absolutely crucial for Martin for both character reasons (it allows a way for him to bring in the Tower of Joy vision) and for plot reasons: Ned having a broken leg means he can't lead the king's armies into the riverlands, means that his realization about Jon Arryn's investigation is delayed until Robert Baratheon leaves for his fatal hunting trip, and means that he can't get his children out of King's Landing before his disastrous coup attempt. As I said before with Catelyn Stark, there's an element of Greek tragedy here: Eddard is hobbled, brought low by a complete accident, so that when the final clash comes, he's helpless before his enemies. Without this, it's much more likely that Robert Baratheon learns the truth, which sets off the Cersei/Jaime execution (exile, at best); the Tyrell plan comes into effect as Robert now needs a new queen, a new heir, and a new bank; and the Stark/Tully/Baratheon/probably-Arryn alliance comes together to smack down the Lannisters... in other words, the War of the Five Kings is completely unrecognizable.

Book vs. Show

Right up there with Eddard shouting "*Baelor!*" to Yoren, or Arya becoming Tywin's cupbearer, this is my favorite innovation of the HBO show. In the books, we never get to see Eddard fight, and, save for a few jousts and his duel with Brienne, we never get to see Jaime fight before he loses his hand. This fight gives Eddard Stark a properly heroic moment, where he goes toe-to-toe with the best swordsman in the Seven Kingdoms and holds his own, something that really builds up respect for the protagonist right before his downfall. Arguably, it's a better depiction of Jaime's character, from his ruthless predatory handling of Jory Cassel's attack to his honest enjoyment of a true challenge to his anger and frustration about having his artistic moment ruined by a thoughtless underling.

DAENERYS IV

"Your brother should have bided his time in Pentos. There is no place for him in a khalasar... *the Dothraki look on these things differently than we do in the west."*

Synopsis

Dany arrives in Vaes Dothrak, chats with Jorah about comparative cultural studies and warfare, and takes a belt to Viserys.

Political Analysis

It's quite refreshing to get back to Daenerys, since we haven't been to Essos for 13 chapters, and it's a nice break from the almost unrelenting focus on Eddard's investigation. And as with previous Dany chapters, there's a lot to work with here: the political economy of Vaes Dothrak, a further examination of how cultural ignorance and bigotry versus assimilation underpins the transforming relationship between Viserys and Daenerys, and the different worlds of war of Westeros and Essos.

Vaes Dothrak is a fascinating location sketched out in just a few words. To begin with, it's a city without walls on a continent of walled city-states, reminiscent of the famous Spartan boast that their hoplites were the walls of Sparta; in this case, the vastness of the Dothraki sea and the fierceness of their *khalasars* are their defenses. However, it's also a cultural statement: the Dothraki who value physical openness as truth and proof of courage divide the world into those who live their lives under the open sky and the "milk men in their stone tents" who practice deceit and concealment out of cowardice. It's impressive how George R.R. Martin is able to imbue every detail of the Dothraki world with not just material but cultural significance, showing how the Dothraki beliefs structure their world. All of this comes before we even get into the religious significance of Vaes Dothrak as the spiritual capital of the Dothraki world, the place where the *dosh khaleen* dwell to serve as the link between the mundane world and the supernatural, where the "warring *khalasars* put aside their feuds and shared meat and mead together... in this place, all Dothraki were one blood, one *khalasar*, one herd." Vaes Dothrak is a place of peace, and a place of prophecy, where the Dothraki will someday unite as one.

At the same time, the Dothraki are not "noble savages" distinguished from Westerosi decadence by superior moral virtue. Viserys's sneering dismissal, that "all these savages know how to do is steal the things better men have built... and kill," is based on his belief in racial and cultural superiority, but as Jorah points out, "[y]our brother had part of the truth... the Dothraki do not build... the buildings you see were made by slaves brought here from lands they've plundered, and they built each after the fashion of their peoples." Vaes Dothrak is an imperial statement – the Dothraki are warriors who are a higher order of person than people who build and work the land and craft with their hands, who are fit only to be slaves; by forcing their slaves to carry the remnants of their destroyed homes, their destroyed gods, across thousands of miles of grasslands to be heaped as tribute before the Mother of Mountains, the Dothraki are proclaiming their right to rule the world.

Yet again, Vaes Dothrak has another purpose, as we can see from "the Eastern Market, where the caravans from Yi Ti and Asshai and the Shadow lands came to trade." For all that the Dothraki disdain city-dwellers and peaceful occupations, they are also a structural link in the economy of Essos. Only a nomadic warrior people of the Dothraki's size could raid and conquer the thousands and thousands of slaves that serve as raw materials for the cities of Yunkai, Astapor, and Meereen, who "refine" the raw materials, training up the Unsullied and sorting out the skilled and the beautiful from the merely disposable, and then sold on to Volantis, Lys, Myr, and Tyrosh (although Braavos remains an anti-slave power, and has imposed its views on Pentos [and probably Lyrath, as well]). At the same time, the tributes the Dothraki receive from the Free Cities of western Essos are easily transported across the Dothraki sea to be exchanged for rare goods from far eastern lands, making Vaes Dothrak the land-bound equivalent of the great port cities of Volantis and Qarth.

Next, we return to the theme of cultural ignorance and bigotry. Viserys's "stubborn ignorance," and his refusal to assimilate to this new place and its culture, is at the heart of this chapter: to begin with, it's causing him to lose the respect of people he plans to lead into battle, who see him as the Sorefoot King and the Cart King, insults that he can't even perceive. Next, we see the physical costs of his refusal to change: his "tunic was filthy. All the silk and heavy wools that Viserys had worn out of Pentos were stained by hard travel and rotted by sweat," and yet he refuses the Dothraki tunic, leggings, sandals, and belt that are better-suited to the climate and the culture he has to work in. Even worse, he has fundamentally misunderstood the exchange he's made – the Dothraki are not a commercial culture where bargains are made and prices are defined in formal contracts; they are a gift culture, and Khal Drogo "will give Viserys a gift in return... in his own time. You do not demand a gift, not of a *khal*."

Finally – and most significantly – Viserys's ignorance causes a fatal break with his sister, who has so committed to assimilation that she sees the Dothraki as her people. Despite all of the abuse she's taken from him, Dany tries one last time to share the lessons she's learned so that her brother might succeed at the head of a Dothraki army (even though Jorah Mormont is always on hand to remind her that "Viserys could not sweep a stable with ten thousand brooms" and to subtly suggest that someone else, "someone stronger" could take the Seven Kingdoms). When Viserys refuses her and insults both her and the culture she's adopted, Dany finds the strength to strike back, and strike back as only a *khaleesi* can, threatening to "summon my *kos* to drag you out. And pray Khal Drogo does not hear of this, or he will cut open your belly and feed you your own entrails."

A third theme introduced in this chapter is the different worlds of war. Here, Jorah Mormont is our cultural interpreter, someone who's seen past his initial culture shock to recognize that the Dothraki are "better riders than any knight, utterly fearless, and their bows outrange ours... charging or retreating, it makes no matter." While the armor and momentum of the knight offers a certain balancing factor if the Westerosi knight can get into melee range and avoid being drawn out and surrounded, the major problem is actually the lack of disciplined infantry who lack the discipline needed to withstand the psychological shock of "forty thousand screamers howling for blood and the armor needed to protect themselves from Dothraki archers." As we'll see, the Dothraki are not invincible against disciplined infantry like the Unsullied, which is probably why the Varys/Illyrio Conspiracy includes the use of the combined-arms Golden Company, with its Essos-trained infantry combined with Westerosi knights and war elephant, as a backstop against the Dothraki deciding to stay in Westeros.

A side note: it's interesting to see the contrast between the bloodriders whose loyalty is so strong that they will unquestioningly follow their *khal* "into the grave" and the tarnished honor of the Kingsguard, filled with political appointees, Kingslayers, and would-be assassins. On the other hand, we'll see later that the vaunted honor of the bloodriders isn't exactly as strong as it would seem.

Historical Analysis

So, given this question about the Westerosi versus the Dothraki, we have to ask: how would medieval knights fare against the equivalent of Dothraki? On the one hand, at the Battle of Châlons, a mixed force of Roman, Visigoth, and Frankish soldiers, mostly cavalry, fought Attila's Hunnic army to a standstill, using their heavier armor and superior discipline to break Attila's cavalry charges with their own counter-charges.

On the other hand, when the Mongols came into contact with European knights in 1231, they achieved total victory at Legnica, where Subutai, Genghis Khan's chief general, used the classic Mongol tactics of feigned retreat and feigned attack to completely disrupt the formations of German, Czech, and Polish knights, force them to charge, cut them off from behind, and slaughter them, thereby winning a crushing victory. Henry II of Silesia, Boleslav of Moravia, and virtually the entire army of 40,000 men died on the field. Likewise, at Mohi, the forces of Hungary, the Teutonic Knights, and the Knights Templar were surprised, driven back into their camp, and then attacked from their rear flank as they sallied forth, and finally hacked down in flight as the Mongols allowed a deliberate escape route to more easily slay fleeing enemies. Tens of thousands fell, leaving Hungary basically defenseless as King Bela IV and the nobility of Hungary fled. In the ensuing invasion, 15-25% of the population of Hungary died, exposed on the broad plains, but the castles of the nobility held.

In the end, it was the castle, not the knight, that prevented total Mongol victory. Bela IV embarked on a policy of fortification, encouraging his nobles to build castles and cities to build walls to keep out the Mongols. When the Mongols were forced to besiege his castles, they began to take enormous casualties as they could no longer use their traditional tactics, which relied on open spaces. That, plus the death of Ogedei Khan, ended the Mongol invasions of Europe.

So, in the end, Jorah's right.

As for Vaes Dothrak, it resembles nothing so much as Genghis Khan's capital of Karakorum. Initially, it was a mobile yurt city, but walls were eventually built, with four gates facing the four cardinal directions from which the capital received tribute and visitors from their vast empire. Like Vaes Dothrak, Karakorum contained a section for visiting merchants from Arabia and China, many different temples of every conceivable religion (Christian, Muslim, pagan, etc.), and massive statues that came to symbolize the city.

What If?

Nothing really stands out as a potential hypothetical in this chapter. However, there should be some in the next chapter.

Book vs. Show

The Dothraki don't fare that well in the HBO version – while the great stallion statues are quite impressive, I didn't really feel a connection between Drogo's great hall and the merchant districts that Dany visits that you need to express the strange mix of cosmopolitanism and imperialism that makes Vaes Dothrak so interesting.

On the other hand, Dany's line that "the next time you raise your hand to me will be the last time you have hands" is a much more impressive line than "pray Khal Drogo does not hear of this." At this part in the books, Dany's made her transition from being a Westerosi expat to being a convert to Dothraki culture, but she still thinks of her child as the "true dragon," rather than herself. In the show, Dany's defiance of Viserys is tied more to her changing self-image, and the link between seeing herself as a bad ass who'll take matters into her own hands works better.

A rare moment where HBO is more feminist than the source material?

BRAN V

"Only a Stark would be fool enough to threaten where other men might beg."

Synopsis

Bran, Robb, Theon, and Maester Luwin go out riding in the Wolfswood. On the way, they discuss recent news about their mother and father. When Bran is momentarily left alone, he's mugged by a group of wildling and deserter raiders. Robb returns and, with the help of the direwolves, leaves four of them dead in the blink of an eye. Theon's indifference to the principle of the Dornish standoff ends the conflict, and Osha is brought back to Winterfell as a captive.

Political Analysis

"Bran V" is a nice change from previous Bran chapters, as we get a nice burst of action and something for me to sink my teeth into when it comes to the politics of Westeros. In this recap, I'll discuss primarily winter town and what it tells us about the political economy of the north, make a brief correction regarding Catelyn and talk about Robb's path to becoming a lord, and then get into the meeting with the wildlings.

Winter town - as Bran and the hunting party pass through the outer walls of Winterfell, they ride through the winter town, one of the stranger urban environments of Westeros. Unlike most castle towns, winter town (as one might guess from the name) is a seasonal settlement: despite the "rows of small, neat houses of log and undressed stone... less than one and five were occupied." Unlike the south, where we see more of the classical blurred lines between rural farmstead, village, market town, suburban estates, and cities, the north is rural until winter comes. Then, the political economy of the north shifts, and the rural becomes urban again, as "farmers left their frozen fields and distant holdfasts, loaded up their wagons, and then the winter town came alive." This means that, despite their low population density, the north is actually very sensible about their human capital, maximizing agricultural production during the spring, summer, and autumn, and then turning their population towards manufacturing in the long winters.

Winter town is the most profound explanation for why Winterfell is the heart of the north more so than any other regional capital in relation to their own territory: because of its warm springs, its greenhouses, and its vast storehouses, Winterfell is the one place in the north where complete safety from the winter can be found, and in winter, warmth means life and cold, death. This goes a long way to explaining why House Stark is the longest dynasty in Westeros (and is two to three times longer than any historical dynasty, the longest of which stretch to a mere *three* thousand years): as long as there is a Stark in Winterfell and Winter can last for years, the north will need to bow the need to the Starks eventually or die.

A brief correction - in this chapter, we see that "a message had arrived from the Eyrie, from Mother. She did not say when she meant to return, only that she had taken the Imp as prisoner." I had previously argued that Catelyn didn't send word of her actions and had thereby damaged the war effort, and this was incorrect, at least in part. Granted, the letter doesn't definitely contain the orders Eddard Stark gave for his bannermen, but Robb Stark's reaction points to something of the kind being included. At the same time, it's clear that there was a significant delay in terms of information getting to Riverrun (Edmure only mobilizes once word comes of Tywin's mobilizations) and Winterfell, and it's also clear that no information about what Tyrion said about the dragonbone dagger made it to Eddard at King's Landing.

All the same, my previous comments were unfair to Catelyn Stark, so I'll eat my words for the sake of accuracy.

The other thing that we learn from mention of the letter is that we see a further step in Robb's transition into becoming lord of Winterfell and leader of the northern war effort - he's graduated to taking preliminary steps toward calling the bannermen and reinforcing Moat Cailin. Moreover, Robb seems to have learned some of Ned's theory of lordship in establishing a policy of listening to all of his advisers to help him sort through the difficult problem of how to react to violent provocations, although his indecision in the face of what to do with Osha shows it's very much a work in progress. At the same time, as we'll see when the wildings pop up, he shows no such hesitation when it comes to battle - a trait he'll carry forward through the rest of his life.

Meeting the raiders - the meeting with the raiders is an interesting moment where two groups of very different cultural and class backgrounds suddenly and violently intersect. Bran begins the conversation thinking that they are the same as the "foresters [and] farmers" who "bent the knee when they saw the boys" and were "greeted... with a lordly nod." Suddenly, he realizes his mistake and his peculiar mix of privilege and vulnerability: "suddenly conscious of how richly he was dressed," Bran tries and fails to ward off these deserters with a declaration of his rank and a threat of death, but the reality is that his disability undercuts his class position. When Bran is cut down from his horse, the truth is made clear – he's completely exposed and likely to die.

From the raiders' point of view, they are confronted with a rare opportunity and danger all rolled up into one. The silver pin on Bran's shoulder, a mere bagatelle to the young man, represents a year's income easily; the horse means the possibility of getting out of the north, where they will be hunted down by a population vigilant against wildling raiders and Night's Watch deserters. The boy's person itself means much more: "Think what Mance would give to have Benjen Stark's own blood to hostage?" On the other hand, when Rob appears, the discrepancy in strength is notable; even outnumbered and a mere boy, Robb's castle-forged sword and his horse and his wolves allow him to cut through four opponents in the blink of an eye. Even threatening a child's life can't save them from a disastrous conclusion.

George R.R. Martin leaves this incident somewhat ambivalent. On one level, this is the story of a group of rich people who respond to an attempted mugging by murdering a bunch of poor people, who are driven by the most human of motives: the desire for life. Osha's comrades just want to get the hell out of the north ("as far south as south goes") before the White Walkers show up, and they probably desperately need the resources that Bran's silver and horse represent, and everyone in the north wants them dead because one of them is an escapee from a penal legion and the rest are foreigners.

At the same time, though, Martin doesn't truck with simplistic notions of wholly evil aristocrats and an innocent proletariat. The sad and illiberal truth is that suffering does not necessarily ennoble; sometimes, it just grinds down consciences. As Ned Stark says of deserters, "no man is more dangerous… the deserter knows his life is forfeit if he is taken, so he will not flinch from any crime, no matter how vile or cruel." These raiders attempt to rob and kidnap a child, they threaten to sexually mutilate said child, and wind up threatening his life; when Robb cuts them down, they've got weapons in their hands and are just as eager to end his life as he is to save his brother.

Historical Analysis

In an agricultural society based on fixed tenancies, and extremely localized communities wary of strangers, vagrants and "able-bodied beggars" posed an almost existential threat to the medieval social order, and it's not an accident that the concept of outlawry has such a close association to the vagrant, from the "Merry Men" of Sherwood Forest on down.

The first vagrancy laws emerged in the wake of the Black Death, where the vast loss of life (modern estimates suggest that 45-50% of Europe's population died in the 1348-1350 pandemic) had disrupted the system of serfdom by which peasants were bound to the land as quasi-property of their feudal overlords. With so many lords dead and unable to keep them on the land, and with the plague having greatly increased demand for labor and, thus, wages, millions of peasants fled their masters in search of a better deal – and thus created the figure of the "sturdy beggar," who was seen as a thief, a con-man, and a potential murderer, unrestrained by the normal relationships of serfdom and feudalism. The response was the Ordinance of Laborers of 1349 (which capped wages at pre-plague levels, banned employers from "enticing" other men's servants to leave their jobs, and made it illegal to be unemployed), and the Statute of Cambridge of 1388 (which made it illegal for any laborer to leave his home without papers of leave granted by local magistrates). By this method, the danger of peasants becoming free men who demanded wage increases was supposedly restrained.

It didn't work, of course. Laws designed to prevent workers from leaving their manors in search of employment instead sparked rebellions – the Great Revolt of 1381 in England, the Jacquerie in France, revolts in Hungary and Estonia, etc. Moreover, the feudal state simply lacked the capacity to prevent peasants from slipping away from their farms and making their way to the city, which meant that the "sturdy beggar" remained an object of fear for hundreds of years. Little separated the "vagabond" from bandits, and as late as the 18th century, bands of roving beggars (who were just as often rural laborers migrating from one seasonal crop to the next) were seen as violent drunks who had to be fobbed off with alms lest they begin stealing, damaging property, or beating people.

Which I think gets us closer to understanding the mindset of the people of the north in how they see wildlings and deserters. Life in the north is hard enough, with the constant, pressing need to harvest enough food to make it through a winter that might last a decade. But however romantic the wildlings' belief in freedom might sound to our 21st century ears, what the people of the north are most concerned with is that the wildlings' belief in freedom extends to the idea that the wildlings are free to rob them, and to kill anyone who tries to stop them.

<u>What If?</u>

Any clash of arms, no matter how small, brings with it the risk of death and, therefore, major changes in the plot. Some hypotheticals that are suggested by the encounter with the wildlings are:

What if Osha dies? Either in the fight, when she's in serious danger of being torn apart by a direwolf, or after, when Theon recommends executing the wildlings, Osha comes very close to death. If she had died, then Bran and Rickon lack an able-bodied adult to help them hide when Winterfell is taken by the Greyjoys, which might mean their "escape" is foiled, leading to their genuine death. Even assuming that they make it out of Winterfell, we now have the problem that there's no one to look after Rickon when Bran, Hodor, and the Reeds (Westeros's number-one rock band north of the Wall) split off, heading for the Wall – which, let's face it, is kind of par for the course with Rickon.

What if Bran dies? Robb dying at this point is extremely unlikely, given how handily he cuts through the wildlings. But Bran comes quite close to death three times in this chapter: first, the leg wound that could have easily opened up a major artery; second, the wildling who puts a knife to this throat; and third, Theon's extremely risky bow-shot. Now, the direction of the Bran storyline is the most opaque at the moment – George Martin hasn't really written much of Bran's stories in comparison to other plotlines, and the metaphysical nature of his particular story-arc shrouds much of what's to come in mystical vagueness. However, there are some concrete things we can point to: first, with Bran dead, he's not around to give the fatal order that left Winterfell defenseless, which means Winterfell perhaps doesn't fall, which, in turn, perhaps forestalls the Red Wedding. Second, Bran doesn't awaken Jon Snow's warging abilities, which might mean that Jon doesn't make it back from his brush with death.

What if Theon kills Bran? I doubt Robb would kill Theon for an accidental death, but there's no way in hell Theon's getting leave to go to Balon with his offer of alliance. In turn, this potentially means that Balon is forestalled from invading the north lest his son pay for it with his life, which, in turn, might obviate the Red Wedding and allow Robb to be reinforced by the 17,000 or so northmen left unmobilized when he departed south. So, a potentially very different War of the Five Kings results from this rather gruesome hypothetical.

<u>Book vs. Show</u>

The main difference here is that we don't get the direwolves acting so dramatically to protect their Stark charges. I understand from the showrunners that the animal actors in season one were incredibly difficult to work with, doubling shooting times and causing great expense, but some of the thematics of the direwolves is lost.

What people often forget about the direwolves is that they're not sweet and cuddly, and they're definitely not safe. They're terrifying and dangerous, and we see that in this chapter both in their attack on the wildlings and the genuine fear that peasants and guardsmen alike feel when they see them. The direwolves will kill people – sometimes real threats (Joffrey, the assassin, various Freys that Nymeria is busy killing), and sometimes people who are no danger at all (Shaggydog attacks Winterfell guards pretty indiscriminately, the various attacks on Tyrion). Like all magic in *A Song of Ice and Fire*, the direwolves are a "blade without a hilt," performing acts of a quasi-supernatural nature (Ghost finding the wight corpses; Grey Wind finding the goat path; Nymeria pulling Catelyn's body out of the river, where it can be found by Beric Dondarrion; etc.), but not in a way that's predictable or consistent.

The old gods are not fuzzy New Age conceptions of paganism with the edges sanded off. The First Men used to string up corpses in the godswood as a human sacrifice; the Faith of the Seven believed in exterminating other religions in war. For all that the fandom often looks askance at Rh'llorism, it's not that unusual for a religion in *Song of Ice and Fire*.

TYRION V

If only he had shut his mouth...

Synopsis

Tyrion is being starved and tortured in his cell by Mord the jailer. While he contemplates the awfulness of his surroundings, he recalls his first hearing in front of Lysa and Robert Arryn, where he unwisely antagonizes his hosts/captors after being accused of murdering Jon Arryn. After tricking Mord with an offer of gold and a confession, Tyrion confronts his accusers in open court and demands his right to trial by combat. With Jaime far away in the riverlands, Tyrion is lucky that Bronn steps forward to be his champion.

Political Analysis

In many ways, "Tyrion V" is the archetypal Tyrion chapter in *A Game of Thrones*, where you can really see George R.R. Martin getting fully to grips with Tyrion's personality and psyche, thanks to the use of the sky cell as a narrative event to isolate his protagonist for most of the chapter and the heavy use of flashbacks to bookend the real events of the chapter with Tyrion's perspective. The portrait of Tyrion Lannister that emerges is of a man who is prouder and angrier than he's often remembered as, someone who, for all his boasts to Jon Snow, is deeply wounded by the limitations of his body and what society makes of them, and who can't help himself from retaliating with vicious wit. At the same time, Tyrion is more self-critical than self-congratulatory, and spends much of the chapter recriminating with himself for letting his "dangerous big mouth" get the better of him when he knows that "submission and silence would have been his best defenses."

The hearings - the chief political events of the chapter take the form of two judicial hearings in the court of the Eyrie. In the first, Lysa threatens to lose the plot completely, when she shifts her story from blaming Cersei for the death of Jon Arryn to claiming that, "Tyrion the Imp, of House Lannister... murdered your father... slew the Hand of the King." To the extent that Lysa is thinking rationally at all, she was probably thinking of the need to maintain the anti-Lannister feeling in the Vale (part of the Littlefinger Conspiracy to eventually turn against the Lannisters?) and to discredit anything Tyrion might say that might cast doubt on the story that the Lannister Conspiracy is the sole perpetrator of these murders. However, this potentially could have unraveled most of Littlefinger's work, had Catelyn's news about the truth of the dragonbone dagger, Littlefinger's veracity, and Lysa's unreliability made it to Eddard Stark. Perhaps feeling fresh doubts about the whole affair, Catelyn forestalls the move to have Tyrion summarily executed via the Moon Door by calling to what passes for due process in Westeros: "this man is my prisoner – I will not have him harmed."

Lysa's decision to have him thrown into a sky cell is an interesting move. For all that Tyrion surmises that "Lysa Arryn... would send for him again, and soon. If not her, then Catelyn Stark would want to question him," the reality of Mord's beatings, the withholding of food, and the nature of the sky cells itself (more on this in a bit) suggest that perhaps Lysa thought that "he was growing weaker every day, and it was only a matter of time until Mord's kicks and blows did him serious harm... a few more nights of cold and hunger, and the blue would start calling to him, too." After all, a dead Tyrion could not challenge Lysa's story about the murder of Jon Arryn and would certainly have led to immediate all-out war between the Lannisters and Starks.

The second hearing throws an entirely different light on the matter. Lysa takes his offer of confession at face value, proof of the efficacy of the sky cells as an instrument of torture – "The sky cells always break them. The gods can see them there, and there is no darkness to hide in." Tyrion's POV offers graphic evidence of their ability to break the human mind and body: in addition to the exposure (it must be freezing that far up the mountain), withdrawal of food, and beatings, we can add indirect sleep deprivation and the psychological torment of sloped floors that make it impossible to rest without risking falling off the fourth wall. Given what we know about the nature of solitary confinement, it's surprising that Tyrion was able to keep his wits about him.

Tyrion's confession is startling proof of the inefficacy of torture – his confession, far from playing into Lysa's preferred narrative, is actually a satirical challenge to the Eyrie's version of Westerosi justice:

> "I am a vile little man, I confess it. My crimes and sins are beyond counting, my lords and ladies. I have lain with whores, not once but hundreds of times. I have wished my own lord father dead, and my sister, our gracious queen, as well..."

> "You are accused of sending a hired knife to slay my son, Bran, in his bed, and of conspiring to murder Lord Jon Arryn..."

> "Those crimes, I cannot confess – I know nothing of any murders... is this how justice is done in the Vale? [...] Does honor stop at the Bloody Gate? You accuse me of crimes, I deny them, so you throw me into an open cell to freeze and starve... where is the King's justice? Is the Eyrie not part of the Seven Kingdoms? I stand accused, you say. Very well. I demand a trial!"

While Tyrion's anger is quite genuine, there's a calculating side to all of this: he knows that the Arryns have a proverbial inflated sense of honor ("as high as honor," remember) that bars them from just killing him and dumping his body down the mountain. Tyrion's larger critique of Westerosi justice, that it basically boils down to a Hob's choice between a trial in front of a biased judge ("how could a trial threaten her, when her weakling son was the lord judge?") and a profoundly unequal contest of arms, is also a mix of genuine and self-interest. After all, Tyrion isn't appealing to any universal ethos of justice or fairness, but to the privileges of his class; "he was highborn, the son of the most powerful lord in the realm, the brother of the queen. He could not be denied a trial." Had Tyrion been born a peasant, he would have learned to fly.

Westerosi judicial customs stand out like a sore thumb, an odd early Medieval relic in a land that in technological and social development much more resembles the late Middle Ages/early Modern period (finance and commerce, for example, are highly advanced). Lords have the "right of pit and gallows," the authority to throw people into dungeons and hang them, which suggests that they hold exclusive judicial authority up to the point of capital punishment. As we see in *The Sworn Sword* and later in *Game of Thrones*, liege lords adjudicate in conflicts between minor houses, forming a judicial hierarchy with minor lords at the bottom, Lords Paramount acting as a court of appeals for their vassals, and the king as the Westerosi equivalent of the Supreme Court. On the other hand, this system is incredibly weak, given the lack of royal judges distributed throughout the Seven Kingdoms, and Tyrion's appeal to King's Landing doesn't go very far.

Instead, the strongest legal custom is the right to trial by combat, which shows the strength of the warrior ethos in Westeros, and the corresponding lack of influence of the Faith of the Seven (in comparison to the Catholic Church in Medieval Europe) and the kings of Westeros (as will be discussed in the historical section below). Indeed, Aerys II's downfall ultimately came when he violated the norms of trial by combat, turning a private feud between House Targaryen and Houses Stark and Baratheon into a general fear that no lord was now safe from the predations of the mad king.

Tyrion's political analysis – in addition to participating in these judicial hearings, Tyrion also has the opportunity this chapter to act as a political analyst, now that he has some free time to sit and think. The results are quite interesting:

> Lord Tywin would surely have sent out riders when the word reached him. Jaime might be leading a host through the Mountains of the Moon... did anyone outside the Vale even suspect where Catelyn Stark had taken him? He wondered what Cersei would do when she heard. The king could order him freed, but would Robert listen to his queen or his Hand? Tyrion had no illusions about the king's love for his sister... she would see the insult in this, not the opportunity.

This monologue is fascinating in terms of the different layers it shows about Tyrion and his understanding of the world around him: on one level, we see Tyrion as a keen observer of character, predicting that his father will respond military, that Robert will ultimately choose Ned over Cersei, and that Jaime and Cersei are too headstrong to see the political advantages of a position of supposed weakness. By taking the position of the accused, Tyrion potentially can force Eddard into open trial before the lords of Westeros, and politically damage him by the sheer thinness of the Starks' evidence – the incorruptible turned tyrant in the eyes of the world. Ultimately, the real danger of this option is to Littlefinger, who Ned would call to testify and would be exposed for his deceptions, which suggests that Littlefinger's arranging of Ned's attack was designed to prevent this from happening by shifting attention from the legal to the military sphere, and that Littlefinger got very lucky that his lie to Catelyn was never exposed.

We also see that Tyrion is a remarkably cynical observer, quite easily contemplating that Jaime or Cersei might have conspired at the murder of a child for all that he loves the former. The last tantalizing layer of his analysis is the way in which Tyrion immediately susses out that "if the old Hand had been murdered, it was deftly and subtly done... in contrast, sending some oaf with a stolen knife after Brandon Stark struck him as unbelievably clumsy." What has completely eluded the Starks all along, that the two murders bear no similar signature, is immediately apparent to him. Indeed, for a second, Tyrion almost realizes that there's a third party at work: "perhaps the direwolf and the lion were not the only beasts in the woods, and if that were true, someone was using him as a catspaw. Tyrion Lannister hated being used." To date, Tyrion is the only POV character in the book who has even come close to unmasking the Littlefinger Conspiracy, and it would have been fascinating had Tyrion had the time to investigate the murder of Jon Arryn when he, in turn, became Hand of the King; certainly, given **his** bent for justice, I think he would have pursued such an investigation with vigor.

Historical Analysis

Trial by combat and lordly justice were both ubiquitous elements of early Medieval law, but it's quite interesting that they've survived this long in Westerosi society, given the well-established historical trend of monarchs cementing their authority by expanding royal authority over the judicial system. Trial by combat is actually one of the more specific traditions in legal history, emerging out of the Germanic tribes who managed to resist the imposition of Roman rule and the Roman legal codes that went with it; it's not found in the Anglo-Saxon tradition, or in biblical legal traditions, or in the oldest legal system of them all, the code of Hammurabi. With the fall of Rome, the tradition spread with the expansion of Gothic, Frankish, and Burgundian tribes into the former Roman provinces we know now as France, the Lowlands, and northern Italy, and the Normans carried it into England after 1066.

While there is an inherent injustice in such trials, in that they favor the strong and the militarily trained – and, thus, privilege members of the warrior caste over peasants – George Martin tends to portray them in a more ambivalent fashion. Dunk, Glendon Ball, and Bronn all triumph on behalf of causes that Martin unambiguously portrays as righteous and innocent of wrongdoing, although the result is never without cost. The duel between the Mountain and Oberyn Martell is a more ambiguous result, given that both participants die (eventually), whereas Tyrion is clearly innocent of the murder of his nephew, Joffrey; on the other hand, Oberyn's use of poisons (and the possibility that he was partly responsible for the murder of Tywin Lannister) and the Mountain's confession suggest that both men were in some way guilty and judged accordingly. Sandor is victorious despite being clearly guilty of the execution of Micah the butcher's boy, but his duel could also be classified as a kind of painful penance for his sins, leading to a spiritual rebirth.

The reputation of lordly justice is far worse. As you might expect, given the extreme decentralization of power in the pre-modern era, it made a certain amount of sense for the strongest man in an area to act as judge in disputes, to prevent blood feuds by symbolically promising to take the side of the injured party in any subsequent violence. On the other hand, nothing in the career of a thinly-legitimized armed robber prepares you to deal justly with complex civil and criminal cases, and when a case is in the hands of a single, totally-unaccountable man with a personal stake in many cases, it's a recipe for corruption and bias. Hesiod, the Greek poet and contemporary of Homer, dedicated much of his poem *Works and Days* to this problem:

> ...o not let that Strife who delights in mischief hold your heart back from work, while you peep and peer and listen to the wrangles of the court-house. Little concern has he with quarrels

and courts who has not a year's victuals laid up betimes... you can raise disputes and strive to get another's goods. But you shall have no second chance to deal so again: nay, let us settle our dispute here with true judgement divided our inheritance, but **you seized the greater share and carried it off, greatly swelling the glory of our bribe-swallowing lords who love to judge such a cause as this. Fools! They know not how much more the half is than the whole...**

(ll. 170-201) Thereafter, would that I were not among the men of the fifth generation, but either had died before or been born afterwards. For now truly is a race of iron, and men never rest from labor and sorrow by day, and from perishing by night; and the gods shall lay sore trouble upon them... **There will be no favor for the man who keeps his oath or for the just or for the good, but, rather, men will praise the evil-doer and his violent dealing. Strength will be right and reverence will cease to be, and the wicked will hurt the worthy man, speaking false words against him, and will swear an oath upon them.**

Even the prosperous cannot easily bear its burden, but is weighed down under it when he has fallen into delusion. The better path is to go by on the other side towards justice, for Justice beats Outrage when she comes at length to the end of the race. But only when he has suffered does the fool learn this. For Oath keeps pace with wrong judgements. **There is a noise when Justice is being dragged in the way where those who devour bribes and give sentence with crooked judgements take her. And she, wrapped in mist, follows to the city and haunts of the people, weeping, and bringing mischief to men, even to such as have driven her forth in that they did not deal straightly with her.**

(ll. 225-237) **But they who give straight judgements to strangers and to the men of the land, and go not aside from what is just, their city flourishes, and the people prosper in it: peace, the nurse of children, is abroad in their land, and all-seeing Zeus never decrees cruel war against them. Neither famine nor disaster ever haunt men who do true justice, but light-heartedly they tend the fields which are all their care.**

The injustice and corruption of lordly courts offered a historic opening for medieval kings to extend their authority by offering a professionalized justice system, complete with royal statutes, judges, and lawyers that could offer some kind of consistent standard of legal due process. In contrast to local lords, kings were considered sufficiently removed from disputes to act as a truly neutral arbitrator, and the common folk and lesser nobility flocked into these courts, creating a new basis of direct political connection between king and subject apart from the feudal hierarchy. The ur-example of this process comes from the Norman kings of England: Henry I (1100-1135) created the first royal circuit courts to provide justice to the shires; Henry II (1154-1189) extended these circuit courts to all of the counties of England, and enacted the Assize of Clarendon, creating the first grand juries, separating felonies from misdemeanors, and creating the first legal handbooks that would be the foundations of English Common Law – and so on and so forth down through Edward I's expansion of royal warrants, Edward III endowing royal justices with the authority to try as well as investigate cases, Henry VII's founding of the Star Chamber Court and the expansion of the Justices of the Peace, etc.

One major exception to this expansion of royal authority – and the source of repeated conflicts between the Church and the crown from the reign of Henry II through Henry VIII - was the "benefit of clergy" to stand outside of royal law, to be tried by the church, with their own judges, juries, and statutes. By 1351, any man who could read the Bible had the right to have his case transferred into the more lenient clerical courts for all but the most serious of cases. This privilege afforded to the literate comes closest to Tyrion's class-based right to due process.

What If?

The high stakes of Tyrion's judicial hearings automatically create a rich foundation for hypothetical scenarios:

What if Tyrion is thrown through the Moon Door/dies in his cell? In the hands of a rather insane woman with total power, Tyrion comes very close to death here, and it's quite possible that had Catelyn not stepped forward, or had Tyrion overbalanced a few inches the wrong way in his cell, he would die then and there. This would change a lot of the plot: for one thing, Tyrion's not coming home to defend King's Landing, which means the city falls, and all hail King Stannis. For another, it means that Jaime doesn't get freed by Catelyn, since the pseudo-offer is never made in the first place. Finally, and most consequentially, it means that the Vale is forced out of neutrality right at the beginning of the war, as Tywin will not forgive someone killing a Lannister. (Also, I imagine this would hurt the Stark cause in terms of public relations, having murdered someone without due process.)

What if Bronn doesn't step forward? This is the trickier possibility; for all that Lysa says the trial by combat has to happen today, the reality is that, under the law, Tyrion has the right to a champion, and without a champion, the trial can't start. On the other hand, Jaime is currently a quasi-fugitive racing to Casterly Rock. So it may well be that Tyrion remains a prisoner at the Eyrie (and only the seven gods know if he can survive that) just in time for Littlefinger to arrive there. Unpleasant.

What if Lysa loses it more visibly? Part of this has to do with my continued frustration that Littlefinger's Conspiracy gets completely dropped by every other character than Sansa (and Varys, but we don't really see that happening), but I'd be really interested to see what would have happened had Lysa started saying too much about the murder of Jon Arryn; not as much as her confession in *A Storm of Swords*, but enough for Tyrion and Catelyn to fully realize that there's a third party working to set the Starks and Lannisters against each other.

Book vs. Show

This is one scene where you can really see the stellar job that Benioff and Weiss can do in adapting *A Song of Ice and Fire* for HBO - there's good material in this chapter, but the extensive use of flashbacks and interior monologue make it completely impossible to translate directly onto the screen. At the same time, you can see how they've changed the character of Tyrion to accommodate Peter Dinklage's force of personality. If we compare the actor to the book character, I think it's fair to say that Dinklage has a level of confidence and self-acceptance that Tyrion tries to project and wants to have but, ultimately, is just a bit too influenced by his childhood trauma to quite attain.

Hence the innovation of Tyrion's filthy, comic confession that goes far beyond the book's far tamer version. Dinklage had become a fan favorite since his introduction in the very first episode, but this monologue is where he became the breakout performance of season one and won his well-deserved Emmy. Just goes to show that adding new material into the show can be a huge plus, contrary to the expectations of book purists.

EDDARD X

"Someone has to rule this damnable kingdom. Put on the badge, Ned. It suits you. And if you ever throw it in my face again, I swear to you, I'll pin the damned thing on Jaime Lannister."

Synopsis

After a strange dream, Eddard wakes up to find Robert and Cersei at his door. The three of them have an unhappy conversation, Eddard gets his badge and gun back, and Robert leaves on a hunting trip during which nothing bad will happen.

Political Analysis

This is a short chapter, and likely to be a short recap. However, I expect next week's coverage of Tyrion's trial by combat to be a more in-depth analysis.

Tower of Joy – ah, the Tower of Joy. Friends turned against each other, doomed love, epic swordfights with some of the best warriors in living memory – it's got it all. A fan-favorite flashback and probably the most lamented omission from season one (as the House of the Undying was in season two), it's one of the few mysteries linked to Eddard Stark that remains relevant to the current plot.
But what are the political ramifications of this incident?

1. Assuming R+L=J, which is, frankly, the only theory that bears any dramatic weight to it, the fact that Ned Stark wins the skirmish and climbs the Tower of Joy means that Jon Snow is not raised as a Targaryen pretender. This avoids the problem of too many Targaryen pretenders for the Varys/Illyrio Conspiracy, because, honestly, they were having issues already with Aegon/"Aegon" and Viserys and Daenerys.

2. Lyanna's death in childbirth means the Lannister match happens. Now, it's quite possible that Lyanna would have died anyway, given the dangers of childbirth in a pre-modern environment. However, high stress is bad during pregnancy, so the thought that your brother

might die might have been enough to raise her blood pressure just enough at the wrong time. Potentially, had Lyanna survived the birth, she might have gone on to marry Robert, leaving the Lannisters as a potentially dangerous third-party, hated and distrusted by both the victorious rebels and the Targaryen loyalists.

3. A small conspiracy is formed to hide Jon Snow's birth from the world, and it's remarkably successful. As far as we know, none of the top players of the game of thrones (Varys, Illyrio, Littlefinger, the Queen of Thorns, Doran Martell, etc.) have any idea of who Jon Snow really is. This suggests that the conspiracy was limited to a few incredibly loyal people – Ned Stark and Howland Reed are obviously two of the participants, but way back in "Eddard I," he refers to "they had found him still holding her body, shaking with grief." So there must be at least one other person than Howland Reed who is likely to have known the truth of Jon Snow's birth – Wylla, the wetnurse of House Dayne, may well have been brought by Ser Arthur Dayne to look after the child, and is probably the best bet for the third party.

4. Three of the most famous members of the Kingsguard are not present at the Battle of the Trident because, instead, they were guarding Lyanna and the future heir to the Iron Throne. Had they been there and guarding Rhaegar, two things might have happened differently: one, it's possible Robert might have lost his duel with Rhaegar, which would have blunted the force of the Rebellion, if not broken it completely. Second, it's possible that Robert might have won and captured the three men, which probably would have meant they would have been pardoned and retained on the Kingsguard, which would have severely limited the opportunities to fill vacancies in the future.

The last and most personal impact is that Eddard, an honorable man and Robert Baratheon's closest friend, carries a secret with him for the rest of his life that mandates he maintain a distance between himself and Robert. With the exception of the Greyjoy Rebellion, Ned does not see Robert again after their reconciliation at King's Landing until the death of Jon Arryn, which, notably, means that his seat on the small council as Warden of the North remains vacant, aiding the process of Lannister infiltration that much more.

Ned's injury – the second thing we learn is that Eddard's injury has put him out of action for a critical seven days, which means that Robert is gone hunting when Eddard finally pieces it together that Joffrey is the illegitimate son of Jaime and Cersei, which means that Arya and Sansa's ship from King's Landing is delayed, which means Ned doesn't have the opportunity to make sure a message gets through to Dragonstone or Winterfell or anywhere else about the truth, and which, ultimately, means that Ned doesn't really have time to reach out to anyone else to plan out how to prevent Joffrey's ascension to the throne until it's too late.

As I've said before, Ned has to be literally hobbled in order for the War of the Five Kings to happen. If Catelyn's tragedy is like something out of Greek tragedy, where a woman devoted to family is made to suffer the loss of her (she thinks) entire family, Ned's tragedy is more reminiscent of tragedies like *Romeo and Juliet* or *King Lear*, in which timing (especially the crucial delay of news or a warning until just too late) is crucial.

Truth, justice, and the Westerosi way – when Eddard wakes up and is confronted by Robert and Cersei, he's faced with a series of confrontations that, ultimately, revolve around truth and justice: first, he's challenged implicitly by Robert as to what level of responsibility he has for "what Catelyn has done"; Ned, being the man himself, takes on all responsibility, but does so as "the Hand of the King... charged by your own lord husband to keep the king's peace and enforce the king's justice," which is impressive political maneuvering for a man doped up on painkillers.

Likewise, for as much as he's criticized for relying on Robert, it's notable that Robert trusts his word over Cersei when she again tries and fails to rewrite history, laughably claiming that "Lord Stark was returning drunk from a brothel. His men attacked Jaime and his guards." At the same time, Eddard's trust is damaged when he is denied the right to bring the Kingslayer to justice for his assault. Robert may not be the best king, but he does have the common sense to maintain a middle position between the Starks and the Lannisters in this conflict, charging Eddard to "command [Catelyn] to release the dwarf at once, and you will make your peace with Jaime."

Ultimately, it comes down to a question of whether the crown will favor the law or the older laws of blood, which is clearly the only laws that Cersei considers binding: "Jaime and Tyrion and your own brothers, by all the laws of marriage and the bonds we share. The Starks have driven off the one and seized the other," therefore the king should treat the Starks as the latter.

For the moment, King Robert chooses to honor the law, and, by re-appointing Ned as Hand of the King, implicitly agrees with Eddard's revision of history, that the seizure of Tyrion Lannister was a lawful arrest and not a private act of war against the king's peace.

Returned to service, Ned tries to tell his old friend the truth, but is too weak to reach Robert before Robert goes off "to the kingswood to hunt." Yet further proof that no one in *A Song of Ice and Fire* should ever wait to finish a conversation.

The Lannister Conspiracy: A question of timing – unbeknownst to the reader, as Robert leaves for the kingswood, the Lannisters hatch a second assassination attempt against him, this time banking on fortified wine laced with milk of the poppy to dull his reactions during the hunt.

As I've suggested before, there is a common signature to the Lannister Conspiracy: a slapdash, jerry-rigged style with a heavy emphasis on setting up "accidents" that may or may not pan out. As much as Varys might darkly speculate, the reality is that there's no guarantee that Robert Baratheon would actually be killed in the melee. Melees are chaotic environments, equally likely to see the would-be assassin or assassins blindsided by another opponent in a critical moment, or to be downed by the king himself, or simply never able to get to the king in the opening fray, where an assassination attempt might be hidden. Likewise, there's a high chance that Lancel's strongwine would not do the job – either because Robert doesn't encounter the boar randomly in the forest, or if he's just a bit luckier with his spear, or if the wound wasn't as bad. More on this later.

What's interesting is the timing of all of this. Cersei must have decided to do this the moment she left the room, since Robert is leaving for his hunt and she doesn't have much time to get to Lancel and get the strongwine set up. Which, in turn, means that either Eddard's mention of seeing Robert's bastard was enough for Cersei to realize that the jig was about to be up, and she needed to get Joffrey on the Iron Throne as soon as possible, or the fact that Robert chose Eddard over her in this conflict was proof enough that Eddard would have the Handship and the crown on his side in the coming Stark/Lannister war that she had to get Robert out of the way and claim the political high ground.

Historical Analysis

I don't really have much in the way of historical material for this rather personal episode. Sorry! More should be coming with "Catelyn VII" and "Jon V."

What If?

There aren't a huge number of hypotheticals for this chapter – I tend to focus on hypotheticals consistent with people's characters, and there really wasn't any chance that Robert was going to have Eddard arrested or, worse, for brawling in the street with a man Robert despises or for having Tyrion arrested, not for Cersei's sake.

What if Robert doesn't go hunting? One thing that I do see consistent with Robert's character is that he might decide to delay his hunting trip a day or two, if something comes along to distract him (a shiny rock, or maybe some yarn?) at a convenient moment. This has the potential to change many, many things:

1. It means that Robert is sitting in judgment when the riverlords come to seek royal justice. For all that Robert doesn't like getting in the middle of fights (as we saw with his judgment in "Eddard III"), open violence is one of the things that Robert understands and takes seriously. He'd definitely send more than 120 men out to capture the Mountain, and might even decide to go himself to get a chance to hit someone while upholding "the King's Peace." This changes the calculus for Tywin rather dramatically – capturing Eddard and forcing an exchange of hostages that keeps face is one thing, but open rebellion against the king is another.

2. It means that Eddard has the opportunity to get his kids out of the city as planned – which, in turn, means that Arya and Sansa probably get home safe. This means that, when open war breaks out, Robb doesn't have his sisters as a war aim and Catelyn has no motive to free Jaime Lannister. This gives Robb a great deal of strategic flexibility following the Battles of the Whispering Wood and the Camps: he could declare victory and go home, he could offer his sisters' hands in marriage to Houses Tyrell, Martell, Greyjoy, possibly Arryn, etc. to expand his coalition, etc. It also means that Theon taking Winterfell becomes potentially even more dire for the Starks if the sisters aren't married off by that point.

3. It means that Eddard has a chance to tell Robert about the truth. If this is the case, Jaime's an outlaw with a death sentence on his head, Cersei and her children are probably dead or in exile, at best, Robert remarries to Margaery Tyrell, and Tywin's screwed. Hence we see why Robert has to die, and why Cersei gets lucky.

Book vs. Show

This scene in the HBO show was pretty close to the book, with the significant loss of the Tower of Joy. While I would be the last person to get up in arms about the loss of every little flashback from the show, and I understand why some fan-favorites like this and the House of the Undying had to be cut, I do worry that David Benioff and Dan Weiss are setting themselves up for a big problem down the road.

Jon Snow's parentage is a major meta-mystery in the book series, but it really hasn't been mentioned for a season-and-a-half now, and we don't really have much of an opportunity to bring it back in to the plot. What I'm worried about is that the fandom isn't going to be that invested by season seven or eight when the truth that Jon Snow is the son of

Lyanna Stark and Rhaegar Targaryen comes out, and how that explains so much of what happened earlier.

My one caveat here is that the Reeds are a vehicle for re-introducing this plotline via the stories about the Tourney at Harrenhal, and the potential for Bran's greendreams being used as a loophole to get around the "no flashbacks" rule and the fact that Bran's storyline is the one where the showrunners are most in danger of burning through the back catalogue George R.R. Martin's built up.

CATELYN VII

"Enough, Ser Vardis!" Lady Lysa called down. "Finish him now – my baby is growing tired."

Synopsis

After learning of Edmure's military preparations for the coming Lannister assault on the riverlands, Catelyn observes the judicial duel between Ser Vardis Egen and Bronn the sellsword. Bronn defeats the older knight, and Tyrion Lannister is set free on the high road.

Political Analysis

In political terms, three interesting things happen in this chapter: first, we get an update on the beginning of the War of the Five Kings; second, we get a confrontation between Catelyn and Lysa and Catelyn's political assessment of the Vale; and third, we get the judicial duel between Ser Vardis Egen and Bronn.

The War of the Five Kings, part I – Catelyn belatedly receives a letter which explains that the War of the Five Kings is about to start, as "the Kingslayer is massing a host at Casterly Rock," and Edmure Tully has "sent riders to the Rock, demanding that Lord Tywin proclaim his intent." Right away, we get a major clue that the riverlands are in deep trouble, as Edmure shows precisely zero military sense, starting with the ridiculous notion that wars only start with a formal declaration and getting even worse when we learn that "Edmure has commanded Lord Vance and Lord Piper to guard the pass below the Golden Tooth. He vows to you that he will yield no foot of Tully land without first watering it with Lannister blood."

This is a terrible, terrible strategy.

To begin with, we know that Lord Vance and Lord Piper have only 4,000 men; Jaime Lannister's force numbers 15,000, and Tywin Lannister also has an army of 20,000 in the vicinity. You'd need a Thermopylae to even begin to offset the numerical disadvantage, and it's clear that no such defensive feature exists (given how handily Jaime defeats this army), and, even if it did, nothing stops the Lannisters from taking the

Gold Road to the south and completely bypassing these defenders (as Tywin Lannister will do shortly). To the extent that any defensive feature exists, it's the castle of Golden Tooth – which is a Lannister stronghold.

The bigger problem is that Edmure is defending a region that lacks genuine defensive barriers other than the rivers against a numerically superior foe – concentrating what forces you have in a single defensive line at the edge of your territory is a great way to lose your army. Rather, the riverlands are perfect terrain for a defense in depth; if Edmure had instead used Vance and Piper to delay the Lannisters while he raised his forces*, and had made his stand on the east bank of the Red Fork to use the river as a defensive force multiplier, he would have, in all likelihood, stopped Jaime's army cold (as he does with Tywin facing the other direction in the Battle of the Fords). At the same time, by making Jaime advance, he would have extended the Lannisters' supply lines while creating the possibility of using the Red Fork or the Tumblestone to land forces in Jaime's rear. Finally, by sticking close to the Red Fork, he creates the possibility of shipping his forces down the Red Fork to Pinkmaiden, where they can more easily march to block Tywin's army.

> * Which I estimate to be around 14,000, given that Robb's force almost reaches 40,000 when the northern army of 18,000 men plus the 4,000 Freys are momentarily united with the riverlords prior to Edmure releasing them.

Unfortunately, as we'll find out, Edmure approaches war with his heart, not his head.

Catelyn and Lysa – Catelyn's receipt of the letter prompts a confrontation and contrast with her sister, Lysa. As Catelyn correctly assesses, Lysa is no fit ruler of the Vale and a source of political disorder: "Lysa's policies varied with her moods, and her moods changed hourly... a woman who was by turns proud, fearful, cruel, dreamy, reckless, timid, stubborn, and, above all, inconsistent." Cat points out that, by allowing Tyrion to make a public confession as opposed to "hav[ing] the dwarf brought to them privately," Lysa has lost control of the process, allowing him to make a public claim of his innocence in the deaths of Jon Arryn and Bran. This is especially strange behavior, given that Lysa knows Tyrion didn't murder Jon Arryn, since she did, which makes his public statement all the more dangerous to her (unless she's sufficiently lost touch with reality that she's suppressed her own guilt or sufficiently confident of the sky cell's ability to break minds), and a private denial could have easily allowed her to return him to the sky cells without risking discovery.

Lysa's erratic nature is especially dangerous when it comes to her son. Robert is "utterly without discipline. He will never be strong enough to rule," because she can't deny him anything since, in her mind, he is the perfect child who is the reward for all her years of suffering, the stillbirths and miscarriages and the abortion. She will keep him as a child forever if she could, not that differently from Cersei and Tommen, but motivated rather by trauma and fear of loss, rather than thwarted ambition. As people keep saying, something is rotten in the state of the Vale, and like a fish, rot sets in head first.

Given this instability, we see from this chapter that Lysa is absolutely crucial to the success of the Littlefinger Conspiracy - above and beyond murdering Jon Arryn and luring Eddard Stark to King's Landing. In part by withholding information from Catelyn and, more critically, by preventing the Blackfish from taking "a thousand seasoned men and rid[ing] for Riverrun with all haste," Lysa keeps the Vale out of the War of the Five Kings. In order for the civil war to last long enough for Littlefinger to rise by acting as the only mediator with the Vale, the Vale can't enter on the side of the Starks, which it would otherwise do: with the Vale on his side, Robb would go from being outnumbered by the Lannisters nearly 2-1 (18,000 to 35,000 at this point in time) to outnumbering the Lannisters by 50% (18,000 + 35,000 = 53,000 vs. 35,000), threatening Tywin's eastern flank and rear as Robb descends the Neck, and providing Robb with a strong naval presence on the east coast of Westeros. Even a thousand seasoned men plus the Blackfish in command could have completely changed the outcome of the Battle of Riverrun to at least an evenly-matched siege (rather than a desperate last stand), which, in turn, would have freed up Robb Stark to go after Tywin's army head-on with a slight numerical advantage.

Yet another thing that has to go just wrong for Robb Stark to lose the War of the Five Kings - keep an eye on these, as there's going to be a bunch more.

By contrast, Catelyn in this chapter is a very sharp political observer and actor. To begin with, she responds to her sister's isolationism by recruiting her uncle, the Blackfish, who is one of the finest generals in Westeros (given Jaime's esteem, his experience in the War of the Ninepenny Kings, and his actions in the War of the Five Kings, he is definitely one of the better field commanders, and at least on par with Randyll Tarly). Second, Catelyn understands that "Alive, the Imp has value. Dead, he is only food for crows... what will we gain by the dwarf's death? Do you imagine that Jaime will care a fig that we gave his brother a trial before we flung him off a mountain?" For all that she takes the blame for losing Tyrion once she's kidnapped him, it's important to note that the trial wasn't her idea, and certainly she had no part in releasing him.

Indeed, her read of her sister is so astute that Catelyn almost cracks the mystery right then and there: "Lysa had named Cersei in the letter she had sent to Winterfell, but now she seemed certain that Tyrion was the killer... perhaps because the dwarf was here, while the queen was safe"; she can see her sister's story doesn't add up, but can't quite bring herself to believe that the letter might have been a deliberate lie intended to bring Eddard to King's Landing. Similarly, when Catelyn hears that Jon Arryn was planning to have Robert fostered at Dragonstone while knowing that the Lannisters were going to have him fostered at Casterly Rock, she nearly hits on Lysa's motive for killing Jon Arryn.

The duel – when the duel begins, Lysa Arryn mismanages it completely: starting with the fact that she chooses Ser Vardis when "the sellsword stood half a hand taller than his foe, with a longer reach... and Bronn was 15 years younger," and making Ser Vardis fight with a blade he's not familiar with (and which will fail him in a critical moment). She seems completely unaware that Bronn is winning when she orders Ser Vardis back on the attack, so sure is she of victory. When, instead, Bronn kills Ser Vardis, she at least has the presence of mind to order Tyrion and Bronn sent home via the high road, where there's an excellent chance for him to be slain by the hill tribes (honestly, the fact that Tyrion actually survived his brush with them, let alone recruited them to fight for the Lannisters, is quite incredible).

At the same time, the more interesting thing we learn is the facts behind Petyr Baelish's duel with Brandon Stark – Baelish seems to have tried a similar tactic to Bronn in choosing mobility over armor, but faced an opponent intelligent enough to match his opponent rather than give any advantage, however slim; we see the intensity of Baelish's desire for Catelyn, begging her for a favor, refusing to give in until he's virtually on the point of death, and even calling out her name when he thinks he was dying. Most importantly, we see the origins of a deep enmity – forbidden Catelyn's presence, Baelish refuses Edmure's friendship as "her brother had acted as Brandon's squire at the duel, and Littlefinger would not forgive that," and following that, "Lord Hoster Tully sent Petyr Baelish away in a closed litter" back home, which would have been a torturous experience for someone half-healed from such a wound. When we combine this knowledge with the fact that this must have coincided with Hoster Tully forcing Lysa to abort Petyr's child, then we can see the roots of an obsessive hatred of Houses Stark and Tully that has led to the virtual extinction of both houses as a result of Petyr's actions.

Historical Analysis

For someone so well versed in the historical literature, this chapter contains one of George R.R. Martin's few mistakes – namely, that he makes use of the old cliché that plate armor was so heavy that it heavily restricted knights in battle. This is a really old trope in historical fiction and fantasy, going back to early and inaccurate stories about the Hundred Years War in which, for example, knights at the Battle of Agincourt were said to have died because they fell off their horses and couldn't get back up to their fight. This percolated into *Dungeons & Dragons*, which decided that plate armor should be heavier and more restrictive in movement than chain mail (despite the opposite being true), and, from there, into the genre as a whole.

The reality is that full plate armor is, in fact, some of the easiest armor to move in, far less encumbering than chainmail. Plate armor is designed to distribute the weight evenly across the body, as opposed to hanging straight down off the shoulders like chainmail does, and is, thus, much, much easier to move about in and less tiring than the ringmail Bronn's wearing. That's one of the reasons why it was incredibly expensive.

We've discovered that you can move about quite easily in plate armor, doing jumping jacks, pull-ups, etc. You can find video evidence here. Simply put, Ser Vardis shouldn't have tired out faster than Bronn on account of his armor - the difference in their ages and the massive shield might have had something to do with it, but not the armor. However, the size and weight of his shield is also really out of whack: the kite shield Ser Vardis is using was used in the early Middle Ages prior to the invention of plate armor and would have weighed about six to 12 pounds, which isn't great, but it's not that heavy; by the time that full plate came around, knights were using the smaller and lighter heater shields (in part because the invention of full plate meant that you didn't need to rely on your shield as much and could instead use a smaller shield to deflect swords rather than to absorb blows), which weighed four to seven pounds, or bucklers, which weighed between one and three pounds.

Ultimately, I think Martin is simply going with the inaccurate picture of armor because it works better thematically, contrasting the pomp and pride of the nobles of the Eyrie with the crude practicality of Bronn the sellsword.

<u>What If?</u>

There a couple possibilities suggested in this chapter for hypothetical scenarios, often offered by the characters themselves, which, I have to say, I appreciate, as it makes my job much easier.

What if Bronn loses? Despite his cunning and mobility, there's a moment in the duel where Bronn almost loses his life to Ser Vardis Egen. Had this happened, Tyrion Lannister would have been found guilty and executed. This almost certainly would have escalated the war faster than OTL, but it's unclear whether anyone would have found out before

Ned's arrest and execution, so it might not have changed much until the siege of King's Landing, which would have resulted in Stannis's victory and a political catastrophe for House Lannister. So, all hail King Stannis. On the other hand, if the Vale takes the formal legal position that a Lannister murdered Jon Arryn and executes Tyrion, they definitely enter the war on the Starks' side, which means that Tywin will face a dangerous situation after the Battle of the Green Fork. Under the command of a canny commander like the Blackfish, there's no way the knights of the Vale don't come pouring out of the Bloody Gate and beat Tywin to Lord Harroway's Town and/or Harrenhal, trapping his army between themselves and Robb Stark's foot under Roose Bolton, which might lead to the total destruction of Tywin's army.

What if the Blackfish had gotten military support from the Vale? To an extent, this one is similar to the previous scenario, but had the Blackfish gotten 1,000 men or more from the Vale (certainly, quite a few of the lords of the Vale would have joined him on their own initiative, especially the Royces), as I said above, it's quite possible that Jaime's army is stopped at the Red Fork and doesn't succeed in smashing Edmure's army. This changes the strategic situation immensely; as I've said, it frees Robb up to hit Tywin directly, but it also means that the riverlords don't suffer a nigh-total defeat, which, in turn, requires regathering the Tully army and then the issue with allowing the riverlords to splinter in defense of their homes. It could well mean that Tywin acts more cautiously and Robb is free to march all the way down the kingsroad and join up with his uncle and grand-uncle, backed by the full might of the riverlands and the north.

What if Littlefinger had died in the duel? I've speculated on similar scenarios before, but the reality is that, if Littlefinger had died over 15 years ago, most of the plot of *A Game of Thrones* doesn't happen: Jon Arryn isn't murdered, Eddard isn't made Hand of the King, Bran isn't thrown out of a tower, etc. Instead, Jon Arryn and Stannis expose Cersei, she and Jaime and the children are likely executed, Robert remarries Margaery Tyrell, and Tywin faces a united Stark/Baratheon/Tully/Tyrell/Arryn force that he can't possibly beat.

Book vs. Show

The duel between Ser Vardis and Bronn is actually substantially different in the show, even leaving aside the more flamboyant elements of the Moon Door in the floor, etc. In the book, after Ser Vardis takes a beating from Bronn on his helm and arm, Ser Vardis hits Bronn in the face with his shield, knocking him off balance and nearly off his feet, which would have led to his death, and, again, a second later, when Ser Vardis goes for a two-hand cut to Bronn's exposed chest as Bronn's leaning on the statue for support.

In the show, this is reduced to one moment where Ser Vardis momentarily backs Bronn up to the lip of the Moon Door, but otherwise Bronn is far more in control of the duel. I find this a bit surprising, in that the showrunners missed out on the opportunity to raise the dramatic stakes somewhat.

JON V

"The collar is supposed to remind a maester of the realm he serves... a chain needs all sorts of metals, and a lands needs all sorts of people... the Night's Watch needs all sorts, too. Why else have rangers and stewards and builders?"

Synopsis

Jon Snow graduates into the Night's Watch, but Sam is left behind. Jon speaks to Maester Aemon privately to change his mind, stressing Sam's literacy and skill with animals.

Political Analysis

While nothing much of note happens in "Jon V," we do get a further glimpse into the structure and culture of the Night's Watch that further adds to our understanding of this institution in decline. (If you haven't read Stefan's essay about the decline of the Night's Watch, you should do so now.)

The state of the Watch – the first thing we learn is that Ser Alliser is graduating eight out of the 20 recruits, because "Gueren is marching five new boys up the kingsroad," and he needs "to make room for them." We know that Jon arrived at Castle Black as part of a group of three recruits, and that Yoren's extensive swing through the Seven Kingdoms was supposed to yield about 30 men for the Night's Watch, which gives us 55 recruits who arrive (or were supposed to arrive) at the Wall in 298 AL. If Ser Alliser maintains a steady "class size" of 20 trainees, and this timeline is correct in that Jon's been training for about four-and-a-half months, then we can calculate that about 33 men join the Night's Watch each year out of a pool of 55.

When we consider that our three crows from the "Prologue," Benjen's half-dozen, and the five who die from the other wight brought back to Castle Black are either MIA or KIA within the same timespan, we're looking at a growth rate of 1.8%... until we consider mortality rates from natural causes. From a cursory reading of the historical literature on medieval adult death rates of men, it's not unexpected that 14-50 men out of 1,000 (call it 32/1,000 to be safe) would die in a given year from disease, accident, or other natural causes.* It's not surprising, then, that the Night's Watch is in a state of gradual decline – they're losing a net of 17 men a year, or 1.7% of their total population, which doesn't seem like much until you consider that it means that only 60 years ago, the Night's Watch was double its current strength.

> * Georges Duby, *Rural Economy and Country Life in the Medieval West*, p.124; M.M. Postan, *Essays on Medieval Agriculture and General Problems of the Medieval Economy*, p. 182; Ole Jorgen Benedictow, *The Black Death: A Complete History*, p. 326.

An obvious source of the Night's Watch's problems is the training bottleneck – if Castle Black had two competent trainers instead of relying on the unsuited Ser Alliser, they could graduate enough men to train the entire pool of recruits each year, which would arrest the decline and put the Night's Watch on a shallow .5% rate of increase, which would take 2,000 years to get back to the Night's Watch's intended strength of 10,000 men. The number of recruiters could also be increased: besides Yoren, we only hear of one other recruiter, and no one who really does Yoren's roundtrip to King's Landing (which probably couldn't be repeated too often, given there's a limit to incarceration rates).

The Night's Watch's manpower problems are exacerbated by the way in which the divisions of the Night's Watch replicate its class divisions. As George R.R. Martin writes:

> *Every man who wore the black walked the Wall, and every man was expected to take up steel in its defense, but the rangers were the true heart of the Night's Watch. It was they who dared ride beyond the Wall... fighting wildlings and giants and monstrous snow bears...*
>
> *The order of builders provided the masons and carpenters to repair keeps and towers, the miners to dig tunnels and crush stone for roads and footpaths, the woodsmen to clear away new growth wherever the forest pressed too close to the wall...*
>
> *"The order of stewards keeps the Watch alive. We hunt and farm, tend the horses, milk the cows, gather firewood, cook the meals. Who do you think makes your clothing? Who brings up supplies from the south? The stewards."*

Despite the Night's Watch's egalitarian mythology, it's clear from the text that there is a hierarchy, with the rangers seen as "the true heart of the Night's Watch," romantic figures who symbolize military virtues of a military order. Sam envisions Jon inheriting the position of

First Ranger as a family fiefdom, Grenn and "everyone else" hopes to be chosen as a ranger, only Halder speaks up for the virtues of the builders, and no one wants to be a steward. This division – originally intended to combat the Night's Watch's smaller numbers by specialization – has become a source of weakness, as no more than a third of the Night's Watch can be brought to bear on any one task. As we'll see later, the Night's Watch can only muster 300 men for Jeor Mormont's Great Ranging, and one defeat at the Fist of the First Men is enough to almost shatter their effectiveness as a fighting force.

Likewise, with only 300 men to tend to 300 miles of Wall, the builders are no longer able to improve their defensive fortifications: "once... they had quarried immense blocks of ice from frozen lakes deep in the haunted forest... so that the Wall might be raised ever higher. Those days were centuries gone... now, it was all they could do to ride the Wall from Eastwatch to the Shadow Tower... making what repairs they could." Specialization is beginning to work against the interests of the institution: 600 men temporarily shifted to the builders could actually allow this order to reconstruct buildings, if not entire castles, and actually make improvements rather than trying to sustain the status quo. Likewise, as we'll see, the stewards of the Night's Watch can only provide supplies for the Night's Watch itself in the coming winter, which will prove insufficient when Stannis's army and the wildings arrive.

It's enough to make one a bit suspicious of Jon's easy argument for diversity in the Night's Watch in support of his friend, Sam. As we'll see later, that position is harder to maintain when the order of stewards isn't something that just happens to other people.

Jon's choices – one quieter moment in this chapter is Jon's decision on whether or not to take the black. As he points out, "he had come here freely, and he might leave freely... until he said the words. He need only ride on, and he could leave it all behind." It's not accidental that Jon rejects this option when he considers that "there was no place for him in Winterfell, no place in King's Landing," in part due to "Lady Stark's" rejection. If Jon Snow can't be a Stark of Winterfell, he'll take the exact opposite route to construct a family of outcasts, ignoring the reality that a bastard could easily become a maester, a septon, or a knight and build a more prosaic life for himself thereby.

Notably, although I think it's fair to say that Catelyn showed Jon Snow little welcome, it's not accurate to say that she's the sole reason Jon joined the Night's Watch. Rather, Jon's decision stems from a deeper complex about his mother, one that Ned Stark is at least partly responsible for, as he didn't explain that she hadn't been "a whore, or an adulteress... something dark and dishonorable, or else why was Lord Eddard too ashamed to speak of her?"

Interestingly, as Jon Snow chooses the Night's Watch, he goes about it in a very politically savvy way, using backdoor channels to

Maester Aemon to protect Sam from Ser Alliser, making an impassioned speech about why it's stupid to reduce the options open to a novice to either being made a man of or being killed, tailoring that speech precisely to appeal to a maester's sensibilities, and rebutting Chett's arguments with a precise counterattack that showcases Sam's erudition.

Historical Analysis

I've written quite frequently about the various historical parallels of the Night's Watch, and part of the reason it's tricky to stick with just one is that each facet of the Night's Watch revealed throws any one set of similarities out of whack. In this chapter, for example, we see that the Night's Watch is marked with a high degree of specialization and, in modern military jargon, has a low "tooth-to-tail" ratio of front-line soldiers to support staff.

Needless to say, this is incredibly unusual for medieval armies, which generally lacked this form of specialization and support staff. Systems of supply and provision were incredibly crude, basically little more than plunder; military engineers and artillerymen were not a part of the regular army but, rather, rare experts brought in for specific sieges. It's not really until the Napoleonic Era that we see specialized permanent military outfits devoted to administration, supplies and logistics, engineering, sapping, and mining.

More than the permanent specializations, it's the ratios that make the Night's Watch so unusual compared to its real-world medieval counterparts – 33% "tooth" to 66% "tail." For comparison, John J. McGrath in *The Other End of the Spear* describes that the US Army in WWI was 78% combat troops and 21.6% support staff. By WWII, as modern militaries became more mechanized, this ratio slipped to 68% to 32% (almost the reverse of the Night's Watch). Not until Vietnam do we see a US military where combat troops made up 35% (with administration at 30% and logistics and medical staff at a combined 35%).

In other words, what we have with the Night's Watch is a 20th-century army in the 15th century.

What If?

There's not a lot of scope for hypotheticals, given the rather low-key nature of this chapter, but I do see two possibilities:

Aemon had said no? I don't rate this as highly likely, given Aemon's desperate need for literate people who could possibly replace him as maester of Castle Black and his extreme senescence. However, if, for whatever reason, Aemon hadn't, a lot changes: chances are, without

Jon's help, Sam "dies in a training accident." And for all that some people find Sam's character a bit... one-note, it's impressive as to what the consequences of this would be: no ravens are sent when the Fist of the First Men is attacked, which means Bowen Marsh doesn't send the letter that Davos finds, which motivates Stannis to go north; the Night's Watch doesn't find out about the properties of dragonglass; Gilly and her child likely die, which means there's no child to swap for Mance's son; Jon Snow isn't made lord commander, which means the wildlings are screwed; Daeron doesn't forsake his vows in Braavos and doesn't get killed by Arya; Aemon maaaaybe is still alive; and Marwyn doesn't head off to Dany.

Jon had chosen not to take the vows? This is another big one. Jon has a lot more choices than he realizes; there's nothing that stops him from riding south and becoming a sellsword or a hedge knight, and, as I've said before, there's plenty of northern houses that would be happy to have someone with Eddard Stark's blood who's also good with a sword become a sworn sword and maybe marry into the family. This would also change a lot: Ygritte dies in the Frostfangs and Orell possibly survives (which might mean that the ranging party doesn't get tracked by the eagle), Quorin probably dies in a lonely last stand somewhere in the mountains, Castle Black isn't warned about the advance party of Thenn raiders (although, probably, the assault on Castle Black ends the same way), and the Night's Watch might have broken during Mance's assault. And so on, and so on...

<u>Book vs. Show</u>

This scene was completely left out from the show, and it's not a huge loss save for completists. Check back next week!

TYRION VI

"I'm no man's toady."

"Nor any man's friend."

Synopsis

Tyrion and Bronn, on their way on the high road, encounter Shagga, son of Dolf of the Stone Crows. Despite initial hostilities, Tyrion manages to convince the mountain clansmen to fight for him in exchange for superior arms and armor.

Political Analysis

"Tyrion VI" is a brief chapter, largely centered around Tyrion Lannister's deft handling of the threat of the Mountain Clans, but it's an interesting chapter because it gives us a sense of Tyrion's style as a political actor as opposed to a political observer or analyst.

Tyrion's alliance with Bronn – the first example of Tyrion's style comes as he cements a lasting alliance with Bronn the sellsword. This moment is far less comedic than in the show (here's your *Book vs. Show* difference): Bronn is suspicious, casually insults the other party with the dismissive label "dwarf"; Tyrion is superior and insulting right back, calling Bronn "scum"; and the two fundamentally disagree over how to deal with the mountain clans. So, instead of trying to charm Bronn, Tyrion approaches him on pragmatic grounds: "it was your blade I needed... not your love," he says, and quickly pivots to what he knows Bronn is interested in:

> "Duty, honor, friendship – what's that to you? [...] Lady Stark had no more need for you... but I did, and the one thing the Lannisters have never lacked for is gold. When the moment came to toss the dice, I was counting on your being smart enough to know where your best interest lay. Happily for me, you did."

The result is a literal spark being struck between the two men and the beginning of a relationship that will last for about two books' length. And, yet, it's a relationship that, like Tyrion's relationship with Shae, is founded on a presupposition of betrayal: "I've no doubt you'd betray me as quick as you did Lady Stark, if you saw a profit in it. If the day ever comes when you're tempted to sell me out, remember this, Bronn – I'll match their price, whatever it is. I *like* living." It speaks to the particular scars on Tyrion's psyche that the relationships he sets out to create are built with this same expectation.

Tyrion and Tysha – which brings us to the story of Tyrion and Tysha, which he brings up at the first opportunity, a strange choice for someone who otherwise is quite cautious in his dealings with strangers. It speaks to his feelings of desolation and tiredness that Tyrion immediately tells this story to this man he knows virtually nothing about (maybe because he knows nothing about him?). The way that Tyrion tells the story is also rather interesting – he spends very little time talking about himself, and focuses a lot on Jaime (who clearly plays the role of the hero here, and Tyrion noticeably thinks that the septon narced on him before Jaime) and Tysha herself – who occupies an ambiguous position here. On the one hand, her face "breaks his heart," and he can't forget her singing, but, on the other hand, he believes that "the girl was a whore." But the central figure more than anyone else is Tywin:

> "...to drive home the lesson, Lord Tywin brought my wife in and gave her to his guards... a silver for each man – how many whores command that high a price? He sat me down in the corner of the barracks and bade me watch, and at the end she had so many silvers, the coins were slipping through her fingers... Lord Tywin made me go last... and he gave me a gold coin to pay her, because I was a Lannister, and worth more."

The blocking of the scene isn't incidental – it's not just that Tyrion is watching this scene that, at the time, he doesn't think of as a rape, but Tywin is watching, too. He doesn't give orders from afar – he's on hand to stage-manage the whole affair, and he physically prompts Tyrion. There's something about that last part, that not just does Tywin create this gang-rape, but that he makes his son be complicit in it and watches his son as he does it, that unsettles in the way that the tragedies of the Houses of Atreus, Cadmus, Minos, and Erechtheus do, that dark nexus of violence, family, and sex that echoes through generations. And it speaks to the rottenness in the House of Lannister. Presentism often leads us to believe that Lannister victory in the War of the Five Kings was pre-ordained, but the truth is that history is always contingent. House Lannister got very lucky – we'll see how, specifically, as these recaps continue - but one major way is that the rampant dysfunction didn't spill out into public view until after the main battles were won.

Tyrion's telling also speaks to the fact that revenge is a key theme of Tyrion's character from the start. When Bronn says that "I would have killed the man who did that to me," Tyrion responds by saying "you may get that chance one day. Remember what I told you. A Lannister always pays his debts." He immediately begins to dream of murdering his father, and doing so by putting Tywin in Tyrion's place - just as will happen two books later. That's some impressive foreshadowing on George R.R. Martin's part.

Finally, there's an important political significance of Tyrion's wedding to Tysha - if Tysha is alive, or if she had children (which the Dwarf's Penny theory suggests), Tyrion wasn't free to marry Sansa Stark, and that marriage was invalid. This, likewise, invalidates any Lannister claim to the north (although, realistically, that claim was lost when Tyrion was attainted by his conviction as a regicide).

Tyrion's plan for revenge - while Tyrion's appeal to Bronn was precisely pitched at the sellsword's pragmatism, Tyrion switches to a very different register when he encounters Shagga, son of Dolf and the rest of the mountain men. Tyrion carefully alternates between appeals to greed - throwing around promises of silver and gold - to humor, to carefully-pitched insult when he brings up the "Stone Crows... shiver[ing] with fear as the knights of the Vale ride by." And it works, even though the mountain men clearly should laugh off this outlander who promises something so ludicrous as the Vale, because Tyrion has hit them deep in their fear and insecurity and sense of grievance.

It's also significant that Tyrion's first political action upon being freed from captivity is revenge on a huge scale - Tyrion really is Tywin's son in that regard. His hope is that, by arming the mountain clans and removing the edge that superior equipment gives the knights of the Vale, he may bring down the Arryns (or, at the very least, seriously inconvenience them). Whether this will have the long-term effect on the Vale that he promises is less clear - while we learn later that the mountain clans return to the Vale (sans Shagga, son of Dolf's Stone Crows, who prefer to stay in the Kingswood) with arms and military training and become increasingly dangerous, whether that's going to be enough to unseat the noble houses of the Vale is less clear. The mountain clans have low numbers (since mountains can't support as many people as the valleys), they don't have equipment or training in siege warfare and the knights of the Vale are all about castles, and they have very little cavalry.

But if they can't take the castles themselves, they probably can cut off the mountain roads between the Bloody Gate and the Eyrie, or between the Eyrie and Strongsong, increase the cost of punitive expeditions to the forces of House Arryn, and probably seize control of the mountainous areas where large cavalry armies are constrained by the terrain.

However, if Littlefinger succeeds in rallying the knights of the Vale around a campaign to retake the north in the name of Sansa Stark, he may find his plans to rise to the very heights of power undone by his old nemesis, albeit completely by accident. If the knights of the Vale leave, the mountain clans will definitely pour into the power gap in the same way that the ironborn took advantage of Robb Stark's absence from the north.

One thing that I do find irritating in the extreme is that while Tyrion plans to "ask some questions about that dagger," he completely drops the ball on this when he gets to King's Landing. Now, on one level, while I understand that Tyrion has more pressing concerns, like preventing Stannis from sacking the city and preventing his sister and double-nephew from burning it down beforehand, it really annoys me that not only does Tyrion not act against Littlefinger, he doesn't even bother with accumulating evidence that Littlefinger basically set the Starks against the Lannisters (an act of treason/disloyalty that you'd think even Tywin would be interested in).

Historical Analysis

As I've said before, I'm a huge partisan of peasant rebellions against the medieval nobility, in no small part because one of my ancestors, one Adam Attewell, a butcher of London, was a member of John Ball's "Great Society" and took to the high roads of Essex when the Great Peasant's Revolt of 1381 began, calling on the peasants to rise up against their masters because London was with them. However, the sad truth of history is that most peasant rebellions ended in defeat – and for the sake of the mountain clans dreaming of retaking their lands from the knights of the Vale, we should ask why this was the case.

The Franco-Flemish war is probably the best case for the peasants: initially, the French were able to seize control over Flanders by defeating the count of Flanders's traditional armies and exploiting the political divisions between the counts and the cities, who remained neutral during the initial invasion due to ongoing conflicts over taxation. When the new French governors disappointed hopes for better government, political division was replaced by ethnic unity as the urban guilds allied with anti-French noblemen and massacred the French garrisons and population of Bruges. As I've mentioned before, bad terrain and disciplined infantry allowed the Flemish to defeat French knights at the Golden Spurs in 1302 and then to hold them off at Arques the following year, when the French failed to break the disciplined ranks of Flemish infantry. In the end, the French had to ally with the Dutch to gain naval superiority and get the Flemish to sign the Treaty of Athis-sur-

Orge, where the French were able to take Lille, Douai, and Bethune and force the Flemish to pay huge penalties to the king of France, while still maintaining their independence.

If a bloody stalemate is the best case, how else could a peasant rebellion end up? In the case of the French Jacquerie – where the peasants of northern France rose up in opposition to the imposition of a military draft, high taxes, and the inability of the nobility to stop the English burning large parts of France – the lack of organization of the peasants, combined with the capture and brutal execution of their leader, Guillaume Cale, when he went to the king's tent to negotiate, destroyed peasant morale and allowed the French knights to punch through their center at the Battle of Mello, leading to the deaths of some 20,000 peasants both on the battlefield and in a reign of terror that swept through northern France.

The English Peasant's Revolt of 1381 followed a similar trajectory, where after the rebels, under the command of radical preacher John Ball and former soldier Wat Tyler, seized London, the king invited Wat Tyler to negotiate with him at Smithfield, only for a royal soldier to murder him when Wat rode over from his army to negotiate with the king. Following the death of Wat Tyler, royal armies were mobilized to hack down the disorganized rebels, with more than 2,000 losing their lives.

Finally, in the case of the German *Bauernkrieg* of 1524-5, the peasants were able to use defensive fortifications to their advantage, but lacked any cavalry or artillery, and, thus, weren't able to effectively fight the disciplined formations of Landsknecht mercenaries, and were extremely vulnerable to cavalry charges when not behind fortifications. The scale of casualties are quite astonishing, with over 300,000 peasants fighting against their feudal overlords, and fully 100,000 perishing in the fighting.

So while arms and armor might help the mountain clans in the short term, the odds are not good on them actually succeeding in their rebellion. But good luck, Team Smallfolk!

What If?

I feel we've covered the main hypotheticals of Tyrion either dying or being captive such that he's not present in King's Landing for the siege, so I won't waste time repeating them here, but there is one interesting change to the "Tyrion is held captive" hypothetical, which is that, if Tyrion is present in the Vale when Petyr leaves King's Landing, he might have a chance to wreak some revenge on Littlefinger.

Book vs. Show

The show doesn't really change the text very much, besides splitting Tyrion's story about Tysha from the scene with the tribesmen in episode eight and moving it to episode nine, which potentially changes the Tyrion/Shae relationship quite dramatically, in that Shae walks into the relationship knowing Tyrion's past precisely.

The main thing that changes is the tone of the relationship between Tyrion and Bronn, which initially is quite prickly and standoffish at the beginning, into something more recognizable as an odd couple-style buddy comedy.

EDDARD XI

"It is all the king's justice... north, south, east, or west, all we do is in Robert's name."

Synopsis

Eddard Stark sits in judgement on the Iron Throne in Robert's absence and learns of Ser Gregor Clegane's attack on three villages in the riverlands. Unable to ride out himself, Eddard decrees a sentence of attainder and death on Clegane, and tasks Lord Beric Dondarrion to carry out the royal decree, rather than Ser Loras Tyrell.

Political Analysis

Ah, "Eddard XI." For someone studying the internal politics and history of Westeros, this chapter is hands-down one of my absolute favorite in the book, because it's a rare glimpse into the Hand of the King acting as the Hand of the King, sitting in judgement on the Iron Throne and speaking with his liege's voice. And while I think I'll get some pushback on this this, this chapter is "Exhibit A" for my case as to why Eddard Stark should not be dismissed as a mere fool who was destined to lose the "game of thrones," because his decision in this chapter to declare Gregor Clegane an outlaw is actually a clever political move, and it's not an accident that it's one of the very few times where he actually uses the powers of his office.

Gregor as Tywin's pawn, the three knights as Hoster's pawns - the chapter opens in media res as Eddard finishes hearing testimony from the survivors of Gregor Clegane's attack on the towns of Sherrer, Wendish Town, and the Mummer's Ford, villages that likely belong to House Piper, given their proximity to Pinkmaiden. This point is important because the legal action here is being brought by Ser Raymun Darry, Ser Karl Vance, and Ser Marq Piper on the orders of Hoster Tully - the peasants here are witnesses and exhibits of a wrong done by one lord to another. As George R.R. Martin writes, "the villagers... had thought they were being dragged here to name Lord Tywin a red-handed butcher before a king who was his son by marriage. He wondered if the knights had given them a choice." If the game of thrones can be likened to chess, these three villages aren't even pawns but mere squares on the board, denied agency even by those who are sworn to defend them and who claim to speak for them.

Political imperatives impinge on the law almost immediately as Pycelle springs to Tywin's defense, arguing lamely that "you cannot know that this outlaw was Ser Gregor" because "there are many large men," even though Ser Gregor is nearly eight-foot tall and almost impossible to mistake, then arguing that Ser Gregor has no need to raid villages because "he holds a stout keep and lands of his own," retreating to the fact that "Lord Tywin Lannister is the father of our own gracious queen," then trying to get the case moved to Lord Tywin's court or to delay judgment until Robert arrives. The naked partisanship coming from a man sworn to be completely neutral in political conflicts is so blatant that Eddard is even moved to crack jokes about it. For all that Eddard has been labelled the worst politician in Westeros, given that even as inexperienced a schemer as Eddard Stark can see right through Pycelle, I really think Pycelle deserves the title.

Indeed, Eddard is quite canny about the political and military strategy behind Ser Gregor's seemingly senseless violence. At first glance, he realizes that Tywin's random attacks were intended to "bleed off strength from Riverrun, goad [Edmure] into scattering his swords," and accurately gauges both Edmure's gallant idiocy and Tywin's pragmatic cunning. On a strategic level, Tywin's feint has drawn Edmure's counter-attack out of line, leaving him vulnerable to the true attack. However, Eddard can also see Hoster Tully's political thinking at work: since Tywin has attacked "in the guise of a common brigand," an aggressive response would allow Tywin political cover with King Robert (although, given that we know Tywin also intends to draw out Eddard Stark and capture him, it's not clear how hard Tywin's trying to hide his hand here). Receiving a royal judgment that places Tywin in the wrong reverses the political situation, placing the Tullys as the loyal king's men and Tywin as the violator of the king's peace.

Eddard's political/military strategy - which is just what Eddard does. Brushing aside Pycelle's appeal to the decentralized nature of Westerosi justice, he asserts a claim to universal monarchical authority to dispense "the king's justice" to anyone who breaks "the king's peace," even if that means breaking the protocols of sub-infeudation. Acting as Hand of the King, Eddard tasks 120 men to:

> "Ride to the riverlands in all haste, to cross the Red Fork under the king's flag, and there bring the king's justice to the false knight Gregor Clegane, and all who shared in his crimes. I denounce him, and attaint him, and strip him off all rank and

titles, of all lands and incomes and holdings, and do sentence him to death."

The details of Eddard's orders are important: even though 120 men are not enough to deal with Tywin's army, the important thing here is that they are riding under the king's flag and in the king's name, and empowered to deal not just with "Gregor Clegane," but also "all who shared in his crimes." In other words, Lord Beric Dondarrion and his men have the authority to not merely execute Gregor Clegane but, also, legal authority to deal with anyone who protects him – and anyone who interferes with them is committing treason against the king. And as we'll see in the next Eddard chapter, he sets this up very deliberately. Just as Tywin Lannister is trying to lure out Eddard Stark, Eddard Stark is trying to lure out Tywin Lannister to where he can have the lord of Casterly Rock attainted and can therefore attack him with the Seven Kingdoms (or, at least, the north, the riverlands, and the stormlands) behind him.

And it works. For all that we think of Eddard as a political naif and Tywin as a Machiavellian genius, the outcome is that Eddard Stark isn't captured by Tywin, but, rather, Tywin attacks men under the king's banner and lets them get away. Eddard bests him almost completely. If Robert had not died precisely when he did (which points to how important Martin's timing is to the construction of his story), Tywin Lannister would have been declared a rebel, traitor, and outlaw – deeply damaging his political legitimacy and likely costing him the military support of the crownlands. As I've said from the beginning, when Eddard Stark uses the powers of his office, he wins; he ultimately loses because he fails to make full use of his authority.

The Loras conundrum – after Eddard's decree, Lord Varys comments that he should have allowed Ser Loras to join the expedition, since "a man who has the Lannisters for his enemies would do well to make the Tyrells his friends." This is a sound bit of advice... in a world in which Robert Baratheon lives. After all, Ser Loras has nothing more than a personal grudge against a Lannister bannerman, and while the Tyrells are tight with Renly Baratheon, they're unlikely to pony up substantial numbers of troops against Tywin Lannister without a stronger motive. Mace Tyrell *likes* sitting on the sidelines of a fight; that's how he's survived and prospered for some time, and he's not going to stop now... unless his son was attacked by Tywin Lannister.

On the other hand, as much as I hate to disagree with the master of whisperers, I'm not sure Eddard made a huge mistake here. Loras doesn't have enough swords at King's Landing to win the future Battle of the Mummer's Ford, and Robert is going to die. Once Robert dies, a civil war is going to happen, and the Tyrells enter the war against the Lannisters, anyway. So what would have changed? Well, just wait for the *What If* section...

Historical Analysis

Despite Pycelle's undoubtedly unbiased belief in decentralized judicial authority, the historical reality is that it was very important for kings to interfere in violent clashes between their vassals, lest the feuding between noble houses escalate into a wider conflict.

One of the best examples of this process was the famous – or infamous – feud between the Percys of Northumberland (an incredibly powerful noble house of whom it was said that "Northumberland knew no prince but a Percy") and the Nevilles of Westmorland (the dynasty that would give rise to Richard Neville, Earl of Warwick and "Kingmaker" of the Wars of the Roses), who were the Wardens of the Western and Eastern Marches, respectively. By the 15th century, the two greatest noble houses of the north of England had been rivals for over a hundred years and had begun to take opposite sides in national politics as a matter of course: the Percys, under Henry "Hotspur" Percy, had rebelled against King Henry IV in 1403, whereas Ralph Neville had married Henry IV's half-sister and held the north for the king during the rebellion.

Tension rose in 1452-53 when the bishopric of Carslile, which controlled some 1,400 miles of territory right on the borders of Westmoreland and Northumberland, was given to a Percy despite having traditionally been occupied by younger sons of the Nevilles, and when the ancient manor house of Wressle (one of the original holdings of the Percy family before their ill-fated rebellion) passed to Sir Thomas Neville as part of a marriage settlement. The Percys, under Lord Egremont (the younger son of the earl of Northumberland), began raising troops and ignored royal commands (which happened to be carried out by Nevilles) to disband their forces; Sir John Neville (the younger son of Richard Neville, the Earl of Salisbury, who was the younger brother of Ralph Neville, the Earl of Westmorland... and you thought Westerosi noble households got complicated) raised up men to personally arrest Lord Egremont, and the two fought a series of pitched skirmishes across northern England, raiding and destroying estates.

Violence against property spread to violence against persons: when the Percy manor of Topcliffe refused to give up the location of Lord Egremont, Sir John Neville threatened to hang the entire household; Egremont retaliated by ambushing a Neville wedding procession. The two houses began mustering armies in the tens of thousands, and at Stamfort Bridge in 1454, the two houses met in open warfare with hundreds dead and Egremont captured by Sir John. Rather than ending the conflict, this prompted both sides to look for allies – the Nevilles allied with the House of York and the Percys with the House of Lancaster, and they became the chief lieutenants on both sides. At the First Battle of St. Albans in 1455, Richard, Duke of York and Richard Neville defeated the Lancastrian army, but the death of Henry Percy, Earl of

Northumberland turned the Percy-Neville feud into a blood vendetta. After the Battle of Wakefield in 1460, Richard, Duke of York; Richard Neville, Earl of Salisbury; and Sir Thomas Neville (who had unluckily inherited the house of Wressle) died at the hands of a Lancastrian army made up largely of Percys.

And on and on it went. The lesson here: early intervention is always better than trying to fight fires in full blaze.

What If?

I generally see four major hypotheticals here (there's no way that, if Eddard is sitting on the Iron Throne, he's going to let Tywin get away with ordering hundreds of civilians murdered, so I discount "Eddard does nothing" out of hand). They are:

What if Eddard goes personally (assuming a lesser injury)? We know that Tywin wanted to capture Eddard, hence trying to draw him out of King's Landing, and trade him for Tyrion, thus saving face for the Lannisters while humiliating the Starks. That's one possibility of the ambush at the Mummer's Ford. On the other hand, Tywin didn't have everything his own way at that battle: Beric manages to make a fighting retreat before Gregor's contingent hits his army in the rear, and the core of Beric's companions survive and make their escape. Which brings up the possibility that it might be Eddard Stark rather than Beric Dondarrion who is granted the Rh'llorite last rights and comes back from the dead, or that he simply survives the battle. This changes things dramatically – for one thing, Stark strategy changes dramatically if they hear that Eddard Stark is alive and in the field in the riverlands, since there's more of a possibility of at least a truce between the two houses; if Eddard Stark can make it back to his son's armies, Ned would assume command as Lord of Winterfell and Hand of the King. In turn, this means that the Starks ally with Stannis Baratheon from the very beginning of the war, which, in turn, might mean a Stark drive for King's Landing following hard on the heels of Robb's victory at Riverrun, which would probably take the capital long before Renly could get there. Indeed, the political positions of the two Baratheon brothers would be greatly changed: with Eddard Stark corroborating Stannis's letter and proclaiming him king, Stannis seems like a much more viable candidate from the beginning, and Renly's political support is greatly undercut.

What if Loras had gone? As I said, given that the Tyrells enter the war against the Lannisters anyway, it's tricky to figure out how much actually changes. One thing that does come to mind is that the Tyrells might be more inclined to view the Starks as allies, which might mean that Renly signs an alliance with Robb Stark on the spot when Catelyn meets him, and/or that the Tyrells reach out to Robb Stark rather than Tywin Lannister following Renly's death. After all, the Starks are a powerful house in control of two of the seven kingdoms, and Mace has sons and daughters and nieces and nephews who could marry into the Starks, so it's not a bad idea from Mace's perspective. It would immediately change the war: even if his western offensive had been cut short as in OTL, Robb would have enough men to assault King's Landing and wipe out the Lannisters, regardless of whether Tywin-minus-the-Tyrells was enough to save the capital from Stannis. On the other hand, if Loras got captured at the Mummer's Ford, the Tyrells might seek a Lannister alliance even more readily than in OTL. On a hypothetical third hand, if he dies at the Mummer's Ford, there's no deal to be made at Tumbler's Wells, and Tywin would have to save the capital on his own and, even if he had succeeded, would have had to face the Starks and the Tyrells together or separately – a much more difficult task. However, in that scenario, there'd be a decent chance that Mace Tyrell would blame Lord Stark for getting his son killed, scotching any hope at an alliance.

What if Eddard had time to react to the Battle of Mummer's Ford? By the time that word arrives of Tywin Lannister's ambush at the Mummer's Ford, Eddard was four days in the dungeons and Robert was dead. But had Robert managed to delay his appointment with destiny by a few days, things change dramatically.   Firstly, as I've already suggested, Eddard would probably take the opportunity to declare Tywin a rebel and traitor, and use his authority as Hand to call the banners of the Vale, the stormlands, Dorne, the Reach, etc. to suppress the fighting. Secondly, he'd probably start raising forces in the capital (probably by turning to Renly and his allies, but not yet with Renly's coup proposal souring the deal) – and may have simply taken over the gold cloaks outright as a military matter. This would have put Eddard at a much better position when Robert died.

What if Robert had been sitting in judgment? Here's one that I'm really unsure about. While it's definitely true that Robert has little patience for judicial matters, generally wants to avoid confrontations in favor of saying "you deal with this" (as in the case with his trial over the direwolves), and wants this Stark-Lannister conflict ended, as Eddard Stark will say later, he feels very differently about lords who break his peace. A brawl in the streets could be hushed up with a command to return Tyrion, but the burning of villages and outright warfare between Houses Lannister and Tully goes further than that. I think there's a decent chance that Robert would ride out himself or have accepted Eddard's plan to have Gregor Clegane punished (since he knows that Gregor's a violent maniac). This changes a lot: Tywin can't confront the king openly and may have to back down once Eddard is forced to return his son; if Cersei accelerates her assassination campaign such that Robert dies while out in the field, there may not be even the small army in King's Landing that was the case in OTL. Again, the damage to Lannister legitimacy might have been huge.

Book vs. Show

In the show, Eddard is even more politically astute. In addition to his original command, he has Tywin Lannister summoned to court "to answer for the crimes of his bannermen," and requires him to arrive within the fortnight or "be branded an enemy of the crown and a traitor to the realm." With this action, Eddard places the Handship and, thus, the crown firmly on the side of the Starks and the Tullys – if Tywin does not submit to royal justice, then he'll be publicly condemned as a rebel; if Tywin does submit, he'll have to leave his army behind, lest he appear to be making war on the king and, in any case, couldn't possibly lead an ambush on Beric Dondarrion at the Mummer's Ford. More importantly, it commits Robert to this course personally, preventing him from trying to stay out of the conflict since the crown has now been directly invoked.

Again, if Robert had lived even a few days longer than in OTL, this masterstroke would have changed the opening of the War of the Five Kings dramatically. If Tywin had refused to come, then it's quite likely that the military forces of the crownlands and the capital would have been mobilized against him and out in the field when Robert dies, such that Cersei has no military forces to launch a coup or to prevent Stannis from taking King's Landing. If he had come, then it's highly unlikely that the cautious Kevan Lannister would have assaulted Beric Dondarrion's forces at the Mummer's Ford, at the least delaying the sweep through the southern riverlands and the fall of Harrenhal.

SANSA III

"Life is not a song, sweetling. You may learn that one day to your sorrow."

Synopsis

Sansa talks with Jeyne Poole about her father's actions last chapter, gets creeped on by Littlefinger, gets into a fight with Arya, argues with her father about being sent back to Winterfell, and helps uncover the last piece in the puzzle of Jon Arryn's investigations.

Political Analysis

"Sansa III" is going to be a bit of a short recap, because much of the chapter is a recap of Sansa's perspective during "Eddard XI," so that not that much new happens. However, George R.R. Martin does further develop a number of interesting themes.

First, the theme of romanticism, which I've discussed at length in the previous two Sansa chapters. At this point in her life, Sansa thinks that Loras should be the one sent out after Ser Gregor because he "even *looked* a true hero, so slim and beautiful," that men aged 22 are too old to be heroes, and it's wrong for someone as "old and smelly" as Yoren to be a member of the Night's Watch (even though, as we'll see, Yoren is one of the most selfless, and characteristically unseen, heroes of the series). What's new here is a sense of agency in this romanticism - Sansa is not merely recapitulating the lessons she's learned, but rather actively trying to re-write reality to fit the stories she prefers, in this case inventing a dream in which Joffrey hunts the white hart. However, as we'll see, reality always creeps in at the edges of Sansa's romanticism, as, by this point, Sansa is darkly aware that "Joffrey liked hunting, especially the killing part," although she remains in denial about his more *homo*cidal tendencies.

I think this is why we have this moment where Lord Baelish suddenly appears, almost like the serpent in Eden, to creep on her while offering some of the benefits of adulthood (the right to question her elders) and some of the harsher lessons - that "life is not a song, sweetling. You may learn that one day to your sorrow." This meeting is even more disturbing in retrospect, given that Baelish is actively working to destroy her family, attempted to get Sansa's hand in marriage, and is currently grooming her in many unpleasant ways. In his own way, Littlefinger is a dark satire of Sansa's outlook, someone whose obsession with Catelyn Stark both as a romantic conquest to be recreated in Sansa's person and as one of the architects of the destruction of his own romantic story and, therefore, someone whose families he intends to destroy lies just underneath his pretense at cool, cynical rationality.

I also think this approach to reality explains something of the conflict between Arya and Sansa in this chapter. Arya doesn't really fit into Sansa's model; she's a highborn lady who doesn't look or act like a highborn lady, and, for Sansa, this gets rolled up into a role as someone who "tries to spoil everything... she can't stand for anything to be beautiful or nice or splendid," in part because her appearance is a reminder of the rudeness of real life, ratty clothes and skinned knees and all, and because she keeps insisting on unpleasant truths about the world – and about Joffrey – that don't fit into Sansa's stories.

Secondly, the ongoing story of Eddard's investigation comes to a climax. We get the moment at which Eddard figures out the truth of Joffrey's birth, thanks to Sansa's insistence that "he's not the least bit like that old drunken king," and the moment when Sansa decides to inform on her father to Cersei. Realizing that Joffrey is not Robert's son, Eddard seeks to do exactly what Jon Arryn sought to do when he reached the same point in his investigation, only for both men to be undone from within. We see in this chapter Sansa's motivations for running to Cersei (probably Sansa's most significant action in the book), to prevent the loss of her romantic dream of the life she wants to lead, but the question of the impact of her decision to do so remains one of the more hotly-contested issues in the fandom.

So what did Sansa's actions result in?

Eddard's defeat by Cersei? No. Cersei is informed of Eddard's intentions by Eddard, and it was Littlefinger who provided the muscle for her coup (or counter-coup). Sansa probably gave her advance notice of Eddard's intention to act, but it was notice she was going to get in any case, and Cersei's main plan to murder Robert and install her son on the Iron Throne was basically underway.

Sansa's capture and Arya's escape? Probably. After all, Sansa didn't know and couldn't have told Cersei that Eddard had realized the truth of Cersei's incestuous adultery (she finds that out from Eddard), his dealings with Littlefinger and Renly hadn't happened yet, and, thus, the details of Eddard's planned coup couldn't have been given away. However, what could have been given away is that Eddard was planning to get Sansa and Arya away – thus, when the coup is underway, Lannister soldiers are on hand just as the Stark household is planning to leave, with agents in place at the Tower of the Hand and at the docks, where the *Wind Witch* was waiting to take them to White Harbor. If this hadn't happened, it's quite possible that Sansa, Arya, and the rest of the Stark household would have been out of the city when Eddard was captured.

Eddard's death? No. It's pretty damn clear that this came out of Joffrey's own cracked brains, and Sansa shouldn't be held accountable for it. Sansa was responsible for the offer of clemency being offered, which got Eddard out of the dungeons long enough to "confess," but given Littlefinger's likely role in persuading Joffrey to execute her father, it's quite likely that, had Eddard remained schtum in Sansa's absence, Littlefinger would have probably had him murdered in his cell in order to prevent an exchange of hostages from ending the hostilities between Stark and Lannister (however momentarily – once Eddard's released, he's going to go to war on behalf of Stannis).

On a side note, it's interesting that Sansa has a kind of waking wolf dream about Lady at this point. Honestly, I find the warging subplot one of the more opaque and less interesting in the series, and I don't think that Sansa's turnaround is going to be related to her warging abilities, but it's an open question that people should feel free to talk about in the comments.

Historical Analysis

The white hart (a hart is an archaic term for a stag) has a deep background in mythology and folklore – Quintus Sertorius, the great Roman general-turned-rebel, famously owned a white deer that he claimed to be a gift from the goddess Diana, who would utter prophecies to him; the Celts believed that the white hart was a messenger from the "otherworld" that would appear when taboos were about to be violated, as a symbol of purity; in Hungarian mythology, the white stag leads the brothers Hugor and Magor to Scythia, founding the Hunnic and Magyar peoples. The early Christians latched on to this iconography like they did so many symbols, such that Saint Eustace (a martyred Roman general) sees a crucifix between the antlers of a white stag and converts.

Medieval storytellers of Arthurian legends mixed all of these pagan and Christian traditions together into something more recognizable from Sansa's stories – the white hart appears in the forests around Camelot, inducing Arthur's knights to chase after it, but the beast is incredibly difficult to hunt down and instead leads the knights to some other objective. Sir Percival chases a white hart into the domain of the wounded Fisher King so that the land can be healed (although, in another book, he kills a white hart); Sir Gawaine chases another white hart that appears at the marriage of Arthur and Guinevere, but ends up dishonoring himself when he kills a lady in the hunt.

Given the historical allusions to innocence, and the eventual fate of the white hart (to be discussed later) in this book, I wonder if its appearance at this point of the narrative is meant to suggest the innocence of the realm that's about to be lost in the ensuing War of the Five Kings.

What If?

There's really only one hypothetical question here: **what if Sansa doesn't go to Cersei?** As I've discussed above, this alternate timeline does not mean that Eddard's attempted coup is going to succeed, but it probably means that Sansa and Arya get away from the city. This has some very interesting consequences:

1. Without Sansa in captivity, Eddard doesn't make a confession. This doesn't mean that he's going to have a dramatic scene where he gets to publicly reveal everything he knows to the people of King's Landing - Cersei isn't that stupid and isn't going to have Eddard in public without assurances that he's going to keep his mouth shut about the truth - or that that denunciation would have been believed and acted upon. But it would mean that his death would be delayed, and the timing of his death is important, because a week later comes Robb Stark's victory at Riverrun and Jaime's capture. In that scenario, Cersei is going to be extremely careful about keeping Eddard alive and well to trade for Jaime - a trade that might actually work.
I don't think it happens - Littlefinger needs Eddard dead in order to keep the war going, so Eddard probably dies in his cell - but that does change things. Instead of Eddard dying at Joffrey's hands, he instead dies mysteriously. That's not going to change how Robb and Catelyn are going to view the situation, but it would change how the Lannisters view the event. Instead of being a regrettable failure that nonetheless has to be publicly endorsed since it's the king who did it, it's now a reason to look inwards for who was responsible for their hostage's death. And that could have all manner of consequences.

2. Sansa and Arya probably make it to White Harbor. Now, it's an open question about whether Eddard sends a letter with them detailing the truth of his investigations, but let's say he does. Firstly, this changes the politics of the Stark war effort; if they know about Eddard's wishes regarding the true king, the Starks aren't going to go for the King in the North, which is helpful in terms of making alliances, but, at the same time, they're probably committed to Stannis. Stannis probably has a much easier time getting support from the stormlands, etc. if he's got a substantial northern army backing him, and his letter is more likely to be believed if Eddard's letter corroborates his arguments,

which weakens Joffrey's and Renly's standing as claimants to the Iron Throne. Incidentally, this also means that Robb doesn't approach Balon with his proposal for an alliance, since he wouldn't be thinking in terms of secession, although whether that stops an invasion or just the capture of Winterfell is up for debate.

The biggest change here is probably to Sansa and Arya's trajectories, and a bit less so to Catelyn's. Both Sansa and Arya are spared a huge amount of trauma (seeing their father executed, being viciously abused by Joffrey, being hunted and seeing the worst of the war in the riverlands, etc.), but their character development becomes an open question. Sansa will be slower to abandon romantic tropes, and Arya's turn to the dark side gets short-circuited if she never goes to Harrenhal and she remains under Syrio Forel's tutelage. The hypothetical plotline of Sansa's betrothal to Willas Tyrell might well become a reality, especially after Renly's death, when Robb is greatly in need of allies; Arya might be engaged, although, in hand, she's probably too valuable to be wasted on a Frey. What is likely is that Catelyn is much more likely to remain in the north since all four of her younger children are up there - in all likelihood, this greatly improves the north's response to the ironborn attack (assuming this happens), but it also possibly butterflies away Catelyn's negotiations with Walder Frey, her journey to Bitterbridge and Storm's End, and much of Brienne's storyline - and Jaime's, for that matter.

Book vs. Show

The show excises a lot of this material, which makes sense since a lot of it is inside Sansa's head, and cuts directly to Eddard telling Sansa and Arya they're about to leave. It also adds a scene where Joffrey brings Sansa a present to make up for his anger towards her (albeit on his mother's instructions), which I actually think works rather well to remind the audience of what she sees in Joffrey and why she might turn to Cersei in desperation.

On the other hand, we don't get as much the idea of Sansa's romanticism, in general - as opposed to how it narrowly applies to Joffrey and her future with him - and we lose the interaction between her and Littlefinger, the latter of which especially would have been useful for future character development.

EDDARD XII

"When you play the game of thrones, you win or you die. There is no middle ground."

Synopsis

Now that he's solved the mystery of Jon Arryn's murder, Eddard speaks briefly with Pycelle and Littlefinger, and then has a meeting with Cersei Lannister. The two speak frankly, but fail to reach common ground.

Political Analysis

To continue my rollercoaster analogy, "Eddard XII" is where you hit top speed and you're zooming down the incline, and you can see that something's not quite right (loose screws, a supporting strut that's not quite in the right position), but you're going way too fast to stop.

Eddard's investigation completed – for all that we tend to focus on the end of the chapter, the beginning of the chapter belies Eddard's reputation as a political naïf. As we discussed last time, his gambit of sending out Beric Dondarrion as a royal representative is basically working: "Lord Tywin is greatly wroth about the men you sent after Ser Gregor Clegane," Pycelle informs Ned, but as Eddard points out, "Lord Beric rides beneath the king's own banner. If Lord Tywin attempts to interfere with the king's justice, he will have Robert to answer to. The only thing his Grace enjoys more than hunting is making war on lords who defy him." Given Robert's actions at Summerhall and the Greyjoy Rebellion, Eddard is likely right about the king's reaction to any attack on his banner. And, at the end of the day, Tywin does, in fact, attack the king's banner, so that Eddard's trap is sprung. How many people in *A Song of Ice and Fire* can claim they actually politically outmaneuvered an opponent?

Secondly, as we can see, Eddard is hardly fooled when it comes to the machinations of the royal court: he can see plainly that Pycelle is the queen's spy, "bound straight for the royal apartments, to whisper at the queen," and as for Littlefinger, "the man was too clever by half...

there was scarcely a man in this city he trusted." Likewise, he puts little trust in Varys, who "for all his protestations of loyalty... knew too much and did too little." Eddard's downfall has many causes, but that he blindly trusted is not one of them – it is far more accurate to say that he gambled on which way Littlefinger would jump and guessed wrong, but more on that later.

Thirdly, Eddard has now succeeded in his initial task, to solve the mystery of "the sword that killed Jon Arryn." He knows that every time the Lannisters and Baratheons have inter-married (and it's quite frequent, with two marriages inside 30 years, which is otherwise unusual in Westeros), "always he found the gold yielding before the coal." And Eddard is fully aware of how dangerous this knowledge is: "he asked himself what Jon Arryn might have done, had he lived long enough to act on what he'd learned. Or perhaps he had acted, and died for it." Ned Stark knows that this knowledge might be his death – and Robert's.

The white hart and the recall – one of the interesting things that one notices on a careful re-read is the critical importance of timing when it comes to how long King Robert will be hunting, and Joffrey's return back to court. In the first place, we learn that "they found the white hart... or, rather, what remained of it. Some wolves found it first, and left His Grace scarcely more than a hoof and a horn. Robert was in a fury, until he heard talk of some monstrous boar deeper in the forest." On the level of dramatic timing, this turn of events is crucial – Robert has to be kept away long enough that Eddard cannot have an opportunity to tell him the truth about Joffrey's true parentage, but not so long that Eddard has an opportunity to send Cersei away before Robert's death can allow her to put Joffrey on the Iron Throne and seize power through him. As I have said many times, attention must be paid to how intricately Martin times this – a matter of a day or even a few hours one way or the other, and Eddard's story might not have been a tragic one.

Likewise, Joffrey's return is highly significant. Regardless of whether she learns about Eddard's knowledge and his actions, Cersei has clearly acted by this point to bring about her husband's death and seize the monarchy itself. In order for her mission to succeed, she must have the crown prince on hand to enthrone.

On a symbolic level, it is highly significant that, just as at the beginning of this story, the sigil of House Stark was found having caused the death of the sigil of House Baratheon and vice versa, here we see that wolves have devoured the symbol of the king. In omens, repetitions and reversals are always significant, indicating a pattern being weaved by the fates that sends ahead of the event ripples through time – and so, here, Starks and Baratheons are found brought together by death. And just as Eddard thinks that his actions will prove to be "Robert's death" (in the sense that they will mortally wound his pride, his trust in others, and the tranquility of his country), he is preparing to act in a fashion that Varys will argue brings about his best friend's death.

At the same time, there is also an interesting contrast between the white hart and the boar. As I've discussed before, the white hart symbolized purity and innocence, especially in the context of medieval Europe; the boar, on the other hand, represented wild anger, uncontrollable rage, virility (hence the unfortunate singer's link between the king's supposed emasculation and his defeat at the hands of the boar), and suicide (as wild boars were known and feared for their ability to – even when stabbed with a spear – pull themselves up the spear and kill the hunter). In this chapter, King Robert goes in search of innocence and instead finds violent death as both he and the boar seek to kill even while dying; it's possible to see this hunt as a kind of symbolic suicide as Robert slays his drive for living.

Ned's biggest mistake? – finally, we get to the crux of Ned Stark's storyline in *Game of Thrones*, which is worth quoting extensively:

> *"I know the truth Jon Arryn died for," he told her.*
>
> *"Do you?" The queen watched his face, wary as a cat. "Is that why you called me here, Lord Stark? To pose me riddles? Or is it your intent to seize me, as your wife seized my brother?"*
>
> *"If you truly believed that, you never would have come."*
>
> *"My brother, Jaime, is worth a hundred of your friend."*
>
> *"Your brother?" Ned said. "Or your lover?"*
>
> *"Both." She did not flinch from the truth...*
>
> *"My son, Bran..."*
>
> *To her credit, Cersei did not look away. "He saw us."*
>
> *"How is it that you have had no children by the king?"*
>
> *She lifted her head, defiant. "Your Robert got me with child once... my brother found a woman to cleanse me."*
>
> *"You know what I must do."*
>
> *"Must!" She put her hand on his good leg. "A true man does what he will, not what he must." Her fingers brushed lightly against his thigh, the gentlest of promises. "The realm needs a*

strong Hand. Joff will not come of age for years. No one wants war again, least of all me... if friends can turn to enemies, enemies can become friends."

"I shall say this only once. When the king returns from his hunt, I intend to lay the truth before him. You must be gone by then. You and your children, all three, and not to Casterly Rock... no matter where you flee, Robert's wrath will follow you..."

"And what of my wrath, Lord Stark?"

This moment is often seen as Ned Stark's biggest mistake, a blundering error committed by a man with more honor than sense. And, yet, if you look at the context of the conversation, there's a lot more going on here. To begin with, one has to point out that if Ned Stark lets his honor get the best of him, Cersei Lannister is almost equally inept at intrigue. Ned Stark has proof that Cersei has committed adultery, but no proof that she committed incest – and yet Cersei volunteers this fact, and claims responsibility for the first attempt on his son's life when she could have very well made something up. It's not surprising that the Lannister Conspiracy was known to virtually everyone at court. It might be argued that Cersei's admissions here should be offset by the fact that her plan to kill Robert Baratheon and install her son as king was already underway, so that telling the truth to Eddard Stark was ultimately harmless.

However, that wasn't true at the time, and Cersei knew it – while she had already dispatched the order to get Robert drunk, that was no guarantee that he actually would die in the hunt. Likewise, Cersei did not yet have military hegemony within the capital – at this point in time, she "has a dozen knights and a hundred men at arms," but that's not nearly enough, especially given the number of enemies Cersei has collected in King's Landing. Even minus the 20 men he sends with Beric Dondarrion, Eddard Stark has 30 Winterfell men, Renly has access to over a hundred, there are a substantial-but-unknown number of Robert's own soldiers who accompanied him up to Winterfell, and the gold cloaks answer to the Hand and the master of laws (and have yet to be bought by either side). Even more so, it's fully within Eddard's powers as Hand or in his own private capacity to hire a hundred or so mercenaries to bulk up his forces. Cersei's offer of both sex and a political alliance that would leave Eddard in power as Hand of the King is the best proof that the political situation was still fluid at the time, and that Cersei herself was in a substantial amount of danger.

However, it's absolutely the case that Eddard had a number of ways of dealing with the situation that he does not avail himself of: there's no reason why Eddard couldn't have had multiple witnesses present, or have sent out letters to be opened in the event of his death (after all, he has about two weeks before the dying Robert returns, which gives him plenty of time), in order to prevent himself from being silenced; likewise, there's no reason why Eddard couldn't have seized the opportunity to forcibly-but-non-violently deport the queen and her children on the next ship heading to Essos before Robert's return; he could have used the time to hire mercenaries and canvass the support of Renly, Robert's personal bannermen, the crownlands houses, and so on.

Historical Analysis

It's been a while since I did a proper historical parallel about a main character, but starting with this chapter, I intend to do a multi-part series on Eddard Stark's historical parallel – Richard Plantagenet, Duke of York, the first major leader of the Yorkist cause during the Wars of the Roses.

In later segments, I'll go into some of the particular events in Richard Plantagenet's life that makes me see a parallel, but here I'll start with the broad outlines. Like Eddard Stark, Richard was a powerful nobleman with huge landholdings in the north of his country, in this case much of Yorkshire, Lincolnshire, Northamptonshire, Wiltshire, and Gloustershire. He also had a father who died at the hands of a king – Richard, the 3rd Earl of Cambridge, executed by Henry V for attempting to depose him, which means that Richard Plantagenet would start his career serving the son of the man who killed his father. Also like Eddard Stark, he married the daughter of a great house who would become pivotal players in the Wars of the Roses, Cecily Neville of the Nevilles of Westmorland, Salisbury, Northumberland, and Warwick.

Richard, Duke of York was also a career soldier during the final stages of the Hundred Years' War in France, put in command of the defense of Normandy, recapturing territory in northern France that had been lost to the resurgent French, then in defense of Gascony, and so on. It was in France that Richard began to dissent against royal policies that he blamed for English losses in the war, especially the preferment of the Beaufort dukes of Somerset, the first two of whom proved to be inept military leaders. Richard's later interest in becoming Lord Protector of the Realm while the king was incapacitated, and his conflict with the Queen Margaret d'Anjou (who supported the Beauforts and was alleged to have cuckolded the king with Edmund Beaufort, 2nd Duke of Somerset), found their foundation in his accusations of incompetence and corruption within the royal court.

So, here, we have a great northern nobleman, son of an executed father, with a sound military reputation, who comes into conflict with a powerful queen over questions of corruption within the royal court.

Next time: it's not easy being a Protector of the Realm.

What If?

In a chapter that ultimately comes down to a single decision, there's a lot of room for coin-flip hypotheticals. I will probably miss some, but look forward to debating any in the comments.

What if Eddard doesn't talk to Cersei? To many, this is the most obvious change; if Eddard does the smart thing and keeps his mouth shut, he'll defeat the evil queen and her usurping son, prevent the war, etc. However – and I realize this might be controversial – I'm not sure how much this changes. Leaving aside the question of how much Cersei knows about Eddard's investigation (she's probably been spying on him, but how much intel she got is unclear), she is already committed to installing Joffrey on the Iron Throne the moment her husband is dead, and the queen regency for her is an existential life goal.

So Cersei was probably intending to make some moves that would make Eddard her enemy even more so than status quo, although (depending on how genuine her offers are in this chapter) she may have originally intended to have Eddard front for her and double down on the Joffrey-Sansa wedding as a way to neutralize the Starks in the coming civil war – even though that's complicated, in turn, by the fact that her father is in the process of attacking his brother-in-law. Her finding out that he knows Joffrey is illegitimate and isn't going to stand for his enthronement probably pushed her in the direction of getting rid of the Lord Protector, but she was probably intending to do so, anyway. Perhaps the most information Cersei got out of the affair is that Eddard isn't going to move on her person but is going to oppose her plans, which gives her a sense of how much room she has to maneuver, but is that all that much in the grand scheme of things?

However, the big question here is to what extent Cersei's plans for what goes down in the Throne Room in OTL were predicated on the need to deal with Lord Eddard (i.e., was she actively looking to make deals to pick up more soldiers when Littlefinger came along, or was buying the gold cloaks enough of an obvious play that she would have done it regardless?). It's possible that, if Cersei didn't know what Eddard was planning, she might not have enough men on hand to, for example, grab Eddard's daughters and close off the gates and have the docks watched, and it's possible (although unlikely, given what happens between Ned and Littlefinger) that she might have missed the opportunity to buy them altogether. One interesting possibility – assuming that Cersei's fear is that she's isolated in King's Landing, which is expressed in this chapter – is that Cersei does a runner down the gold road to get the royal family into Lannister territory, leaving the capital in Ned's possession.

What if Eddard exiles Cersei before Robert comes back? To me, this would be the most significant diversion from the OTL; Eddard could have come to the conclusion that the only way to avoid the bloodshed-on-the-floors scenario he so loathes (more on this in the next Eddard chapter) is to forcibly remove the queen from King's Landing, rationalizing that, however unpleasant it is to arrest the queen and her children, it's better than having Robert kill all of them (and Eddard was willing to have them arrested when it came down to it, in OTL). It's quite possible that Eddard pulls this off – Renly would probably see this as second-best to arresting them, but that's less crucial when Robert is still alive and the Renly/Tyrell Conspiracy is still his go-to move; Littlefinger might feel differently about Eddard not being down with Joffrey's regent if Stannis on the throne isn't part of the deal.

This creates an interesting variation on some of my previous "Eddard's counter-coup works" scenarios. If Cersei and Joffrey are gone when Robert returns mortally wounded, then Stannis is drafted into the will, and we get a Stark/Baratheon/Tully/possibly-Tyrell alliance against the Lannisters. However, unlike previous iterations, instead of the Baratheon/Lannister claimants being dead, they're still alive and active in Essos. This could make things rather complicated – while Tywin would probably face a difficult situation on the mainland (his 45,000 against the 55-140,000 the alliance could bring together), he could probably pull back to a defensive position of defending the two mountain passes into the westerlands while sending money to his daughter and the "rightful heirs" in Essos to hire mercenary armies for an eastern invasion. Then everything turns to a question of allies: Tywin's going to reach out to the Greyjoys and offer them carte blanche in return for them attacking the north and the riverlands, and trying to pry the Tyrells (and maybe Renly) away from Stannis and Eddard, since there's not the prospect of a royal wedding for Margaery. Whether the Tyrells jump is iffy – Renly has good prospects as potentially Stannis's heir, so they might decide to make their OTL alliance and hope/encourage Stannis to die in battle after he takes out the Lannisters, but it's 50/50 between that and Joffrey's hand. The Martells settle back with some popcorn to watch their hated enemies kill each other; Lysa Arryn will stay out as long as Littlefinger tells her to, but it will be harder for her to do so with a king on the Iron Throne with a sensible marriage.

What if Eddard has witnesses? Here's where George Martin's inattention to public opinion (save for the isolated incidents of the riot and the Antler Men) makes alternate history difficult. Cersei potentially made a huge mistake by admitting everything to Eddard; if Eddard had thought to bring, say, the High Septon and several influential lords within earshot of their conversation, he might have been able to rally public opinion to his side after Robert's death by publicly outing the queen as an incestuous adulterer and murderer. Here, teasing out the impact is difficult to do: we only get one riot in King's Landing, but had multiple riots broken out as a result of the diminished legitimacy of the royal family, that would be an interesting complicating factor – can a relatively small ersatz army of police offers simultaneously defend a city from siege when the city is at war from within? Alternatively, we might also see Stannis's open letter being taken more seriously across the Seven Kingdoms if Eddard's name is attached to the allegation and it's proceeded by widespread rumors that the queen killed the Hand because he spoke the truth.

What if Cersei doesn't say anything? While Eddard gets most of the opprobrium for being honest in this scene, we should also keep in mind that Cersei says a lot more than she needed to. Admitting adultery when your interrogator has the family trees to prove it is one thing, but I've always been nonplussed by the way in which Eddard and Stannis both leap to the (correct) conclusion that Cersei is schtupping her brother and, say, not any other blond man in the entire city. (Possibly this is just Martin cutting a bit of a corner for the sake of narrative convenience.) Likewise, I really feel that Cersei would have had a much better chance of managing Eddard Stark had she not, for example, immediately preceded her seduction attempt or her offer of an alliance by admitting that she tried to kill his son (yes, I know Jaime carried it out, but she implicitly admits culpability in this chapter).

Book vs. Show

Benioff and Weiss made the intelligent decision to play this scene pretty much straight from the book (with the exception of the "I worshiped him" bit, but they have to retcon a bit since they made the change regarding Robert and Cersei having a child), given how amazing the dialogue is in the source material. However, they made the decision to omit Cersei's offer to sleep with Eddard.

This is kind of a big change for the character, emphasizing more Cersei's confident schemer side and downplaying her use of her sexuality, and it's one that's been carried forward in the series with the removal of the Kettleblacks from the series. I'm not entirely sure how I feel about this – on the one hand, *Game of Thrones* has enough problems with gender without making Cersei both a Jezebel-type as well as an Evil Queen type. On the other, I am somewhat worried about the knock-on effects for seasons four and later. For example, how are they going to handle the breach between Jaime and Cersei (unless they throw everything onto Lancel)? Or Cersei's plan to destroy Margaery via the Kettleblacks, and her own fall from grace?

While her outreach to Eddard is somewhat disposable in the final analysis, it's absolutely crucial for both major political plots and the character development for Cersei, Jaime, Lancel, Margaery, the Sparrow High Septon, etc.

DAENERYS V

"He was no dragon... fire cannot kill a dragon."

Synopsis

Dany passes through the Dothraki's hazing ceremony and receives a prophecy of her child's future, which pleases the *khal*. Viserys is less pleased, until Khal Drogo gives him a golden crown – at which point, he doesn't feel much of anything anymore.

Political Analysis

It's a bit strange even to me, but it kind of feels good to be back in Essos in "Daenerys V," after 10 chapters of densely-plotted Westerosi political machinations. In this chapter, we get a further helping of Dothraki culture and assess the life and (gruesome) death of Viserys Targaryen, the King Who Never Was.

Dothraki culture gets complicated – as I've mentioned before, the Dothraki culture presented in *A Game of Thrones* is far more complicated than what we got on the HBO series's first season, when it comes to their role in Essosi commerce, their ability to move back and forth between different material cultures, and the way in which the *khalasar* itself creates certain cultural values and ideals often invisible to Westerosi observers.

In this chapter, the reader – along with Daenerys – gets exposed to more (and more complicated) aspects of Dothraki culture, beginning with the tricky question of gender. First, we learn that the women of the *dosh khaleen* wield an enormous amount of cultural, religious, and political power across the whole of the Dothraki people: "When their lord husbands died... they were sent here, to reign over the vast Dothraki nation. Even the mightiest of *khal*s bowed to the wisdom and authority of the *dosh khaleen*." Given their role as the center of religious and mystical power within the culture, and the fact that the *dosh khaleen* are really the only trans-*khalasar* institution in Dothraki life, one might conclude that the Dothraki are a matriarchal society, akin to Native

American tribes where only men could be chiefs, but where the women of the tribe alone elected who the chief would be.

At the same time, we learn that "if the mother... choked on the blood or retched up the flesh... the child might be stillborn, or come forth weak, deformed, or female." Equating female sex with deformity, weakness, and death doesn't exactly suggest gender equality, let alone matriarchal values. Likewise, the fact that the Dothraki creation myth omits women altogether (the first man and the first horse being born at once in an act of *parthenogenesis,* without the involvement of any female force) points to a misogyny equal to, if not more so than in, Westerosi culture.

So which is it – matriarchy or misogyny? Well, it could either, could well be both, with a form of separate spheres in which some women (notably, only the wives of the *khal*s gain power, not rank-and-file Dothraki women) are given power within specifically-female areas of life, while excluded from military and economic power. Unfortunately, we're unlikely to get much more data, unless Dany takes a trip back to Vaes Dothrak and we get to see more of the *dosh khaleen*. The larger point here is that cultures are incredibly complex, and readers should be very careful about getting all of the data in before we, as outsiders to that culture, make judgments.

On a different cultural topic, we can also see more of the Dothraki's cultural imperialism and sense of manifest destiny. We've already seen a bit of this with the Dothraki custom of dragging the statues of foreign gods back to Vaes Dothrak as tribute to the superior virtues of the Great Stallion, but here we get a much fuller explanation of how the Dothraki see themselves in the world: "As swift as the wind he rides, and behind him his *khalasar* covers the Earth, men without number... his enemies will tremble before him, and their wives will weep tears of blood... the milk men in the stone tents will fear his name... the prince is riding, and he shall be the stallion who mounts the world." Dany's son is prophesied to be the Dothraki messiah, the "*khal* of *khal*s" who "will unite the Dothraki into a single *khalasar*, and ride to the ends of the Earth... all the people of the world will be his herd." In other words, a key part of Dothraki self-identity and religious purpose is a sense of imperialist Manifest Destiny.

Which gets to something that I've noticed in discussions of *A Song of Ice and Fire* online and the critique of Daenerys's storyline, especially in *A Storm of Swords* and *A Dance with Dragons,* as a colonialist one in which a white woman (practically an albino) saves the benighted eastern masses of people of color by striking down their Orientalist despot masters and establishing an enlightened government. I've written elsewhere why I think this analysis is exporting post-colonialist theory that emerged out of our Earth's historical experiences, especially in the 18th to 20th century, and why it misses some of the subtleties of the specific historical and anthropological experiences of this different world, and that our colonialist readings (while absolutely valid and a necessary part of the discourse) shouldn't overwhelm an anti-slavery reading of the plot. However, the reason I bring this up here is to note that Dany isn't the only one with imperialist or colonialist ideology in the world of *Ice and Fire*, that the Dothraki have it, as well.

Indeed, within the context of the series, to the sense that "Manifest Destiny" thinking appears, it mostly comes out of Essos: the Valyrian Freehold's imperial ambitions continue to structure the culture and politics of the continent, much of the Ghiscari culture is a re-invention of an older imperialist tradition, the Volantine belief that they are the rightful heirs of Old Valyria and their attempts to reclaim that empire by force, the conflicts between the Free Cities over the Disputed Lands, Aegon the Conqueror's belief in "one land, one king," and now the Dothraki belief that they were meant by the gods to rule the world. The same attitudes don't really appear among the Westerosi, who notably stay out of Essosi politics save when it involves rival claimants to the Iron Throne (as in the case of the War of the Ninepenny Kings), save perhaps among the ironborn, who believe that they have the right to reave and to rule. The larger point here: just because we have an analogue for Medieval England, and an analogue for Renaissance Continental Europe and points east, we can't assume that West = colonialist and East = colonized. We need to look beyond geography and analyze the historical dynamics of the world in question before we begin to compare them to our own.

What Viserys was – and now the death of Viserys Targaryen, third-ish of his name. George R.R. Martin has given us many deaths of villains – from Joffrey choking to death to Tywin's will being overcome by the rudeness of biology – but I don't know whether he's ever given us a more pathetic villain, brought to his death a complete failure reduced to helpless, babbling pleas for mercy.

So what was Viserys, in the end? At one point, Dany points to their shared past, that "he is my brother... and my true king... he was the only one left... he is all I have." In the past, Viserys was once the hope of his house, a figure of childhood memories of judgment and protection who loomed over Daenerys, a role that Dany still gives him – witness her willingness to hand over the dragon eggs. At the same time, this moment is one in which that image of Viserys is destroyed before his death; note that the moment Viserys puts his sword to her belly, Dany refers to him as "this man who had once been her brother." Jorah points the way to the truth, that Dany now has a husband, a child-to-be, and a destiny that has nothing to do with him anymore.

To Varys and Illyrio, Viserys's place is uncertain. Given their hold over Young Griff/Aegon VI and the intense level of secrecy they wove around him and the focus on his education and training, compared to the extensive neglect of Viserys (who was allowed to wander as the

Beggar Prince for around five to six years before Illyrio gave him a place to live), Viserys seems like a pawn used as a distraction to keep Robert Baratheon's eyes away from the true prince they meant to place on the Iron Throne. At the same time, the fact that Viserys's name was used on the marriage contract with the Martells, whose support is vital for a successful landing in Westeros, suggests that, at least at one point, he was considered important to their plans (unless they were sufficiently ruthless enough to gamble that Doran Martell wouldn't really care which Targaryen prince his daughter would be betrothed to).

To Khal Drogo, Viserys seems to have been something of an appendix from the beginning – after all, if you've got a son who's supposed to be the stallion who mounts the world, why bother giving the "Iron Chair" to his whiny uncle? One thing that's absolutely clear is that Viserys's lack of understanding of Dothraki culture killed any possible working relationship between the two of them; a *khal* isn't going to respect a Cart King, a Sorefoot King, which is probably one of the reasons Illyrio wanted to keep Viserys away from the *khalasar*.

Ultimately, it's his lack of understanding – "she knew what a drawn sword meant here, even if her brother did not" – his failure to adapt to this new culture he's living among, that brings Viserys to his death by cultural snobbery.

There is one other important thing to note about Viserys and the manner of his death. While it's true that Martin is willing to kill any character when it suits his story, it's absolutely not true that anyone dies randomly in *Song of Ice and Fire* (he's far too intricate in his plotting for that). Here, we have the first on-screen death of a major character (depending on how major one considers Jory Cassel), and it's the death of a king in the act of being crowned. In *Ice and Fire*, prophecy always comes with its own heralds and forerunners, echoes of the future rippling backwards in time. Here, the message is clear – kings are going to die, and the crowning of kings is going to bring horror rather than joy. Anyone wondering what's going to happen to Robert and Joffrey just needs to pay attention.

Historical Analysis

Another sign that George Martin never acts randomly is that he doesn't choose just any form of death for Viserys, but a historically-famously form of murder, death by pouring of molten gold. The Consul Manius Aquillius was despised by the people of Anatolia for levying crippling taxation upon them to fill his own purse (Aquillius had previously managed to skate from a charge of maladministration as governor of Sicily based on his war record), and so when Mithridates of Pontus defeated him at Protostachium, he was paraded through the streets of Anatolia's capital on the back of a donkey, where Mithridates the Great had molten gold poured down his throat to the cheers of the crowd.

When Marcus Licinius Crassus, the richest man in Rome and so infamously avaricious that he was called "Crassus rich as Croeseus" (the inventor of coinage), invaded the lands of the Parthian emperors to plunder the riches of the East, and was routed at Carrhae, the victorious Parthians meted out the same fate to him (having heard of and clearly been impressed by Mithridates's punishment). According to Plutarch, his head was then used as a prop in a staging of *The Bacchae* at a Parthian royal wedding.

In some tellings of his death, the Emperor Valerian (the only Roman emperor ever to be captured on the battlefield, again by the Persians) was forced to swallow molten gold as the crowning of ritual humiliations (that began with being used as a human footstool for the Emperor Shapur the Great), possibly as a way to mock the emperor's offers of lavish ransoms if he was freed. Following this death, the emperor was skinned and the skin stuffed so that it could be kept as a trophy of the greatness of the Persian emperors. If you think George R.R. Martin has a sick mind, all I can say is look at this historical example and realize that, if anything, Martin is rather tame compared to the kings and emperors of history.

It's not accidental that Viserys's death in this fashion comes after he attempts to steal Daenerys's wedding gift and use to it to further his royal ambitions - Martin is symbolically punishing the prince for his vanity, his pride, and his greed. At the same time, it's not an accident that all of these historical deaths involved the triumph of an eastern monarch over a western one; Martin's playing with some Orientalist tropes here, but instead of this death being seen as an outrage that must be avenged, as they were historically, instead it's shown as a righteous judgment for a coward and a bully, and one that clears the way for a queen who combines East and West to rise.

What If?

There's really only one hypothetical that matters here (yes, there's also the possibility of "what if Viserys had actually managed to kill Dany's baby?" but given that the baby dies anyway, it doesn't really change anything; Viserys might have gotten away with stealing the eggs if the timing had been different, but I think the rule of Chekov's Dragon Eggs holds): **what if Viserys had avoided his brutal death here?** It's not likely, given his raging ego and need to be recognized as the most important person wherever he goes, but it's possible Viserys gets so drunk that he passes out and sleeps it off without ever making it to the feast, so maybe he survives.

On one level, Viserys's story is kind of done, so it seems a bit unfair to keep dragging things out. However, on a petty and personally-satisfying level, it would be kind of hilarious to see his sister birth the three dragons that his family has been trying and failing to achieve since the time of Aegon III. On a plot level, it might actually change things a bit - the Martell marriage doesn't need to be changed, so Quentyn probably isn't sent to Meereen, which means he probably isn't burninated to death by Rhaegal in the attempt to tame... Viserion. In turn, this may well mean that a forthcoming alliance between the Martells and Aegon VI (Blackfyre?) is forming, which seems likely to happen in *The Winds of Winter*.

Book vs. Show

The major thing we gain from the transition from book to show is the addition of the scene between Jorah Mormont and Viserys, where the knight prevents the prince from stealing his sister's dragon eggs. It's a great scene, because it makes Viserys's actions less insane and provides a strong throughline when it comes to his motives, that his betrayal of Dany ultimately comes from his insecurity and thwarted desire for love and admiration and, ultimately, his realization that he is not the dragon he desperately feels he must be. It's also a good scene because it rounds out Jorah Mormont's feelings towards Daenerys, by putting his loyalty to her and his desire for her in conflict.

EDDARD XIII

"Joffrey is not your son," he wanted to say, but the words would not come... So Ned bent his head and wrote, but where the king had said 'my son, Joffrey,' he scrawled 'my heir' instead. The deceit made him feel soiled. The lies we tell for love."

Synopsis

Ned Stark is awoken to find that Robert Baratheon, first of his name, is dying. In his last act for his oldest friend, Ned writes down his last will and testament more in the spirit than the letter of Robert's intent. Now regent of the Seven Kingdoms of Westeros, Ned sends a letter to Stannis Baratheon naming him the new king. He then has two meetings, one of which he thinks goes better than the other.

Political Analysis

In a way, my analysis of Eddard Stark as a political actor throughout *A Game of Thrones* has all been leading to this point – the moment where Eddard Stark makes his most important and penultimate political decision, refusing to take up Renly or Littlefinger's offers, then trusting Littlefinger to buy the gold cloaks or him. There's a lot to get into, so be prepared for a long post.

A side note on Ned and mental health – before I begin, I want to talk about a question I've been pondering for some time. In this chapter, Ned suffers a rather horrendous nightmare where he's in the tombs of his ancestors with living statues and his sister weeping blood. Then, once he wakes up, his initial reaction to seeing three knights of the Kingsguard is to have a flashback to the Tower of Joy. This is not the first time that Ned's had episodes that could be construed as traumatic nightmares or waking flashbacks: he has a moment in "Eddard XII" where he "thought of pale blue roses, and for a moment... wanted to weep"; in "Eddard X," there's his fever dream of the Tower of Joy; in "Eddard IX," "riding through the rainy night, Ned saw Jon Snow's face in front of him"; as far back as "Eddard I," we learn that "he could hear [Lyanna] still at times," and we see him hearing "promise me, Ned," in "Eddard II," as well.

This has led some to consider whether Eddard Stark has, from the very beginning of *Game of Thrones*, been suffering from Post-Traumatic Stress Disorder. Certainly, he does seem to fit some of the criteria set out in the *DSM IV*: "exposure to a traumatic event" (Ned suffered the loss of his sister, brother, and father in quick succession, and then spent two years fighting in a war in which he saw heavy combat, suffered significant wounds, and was witness to the massacre at King's Landing), "persistent re-experiencing" (Ned has both flashbacks and nightmares that revolve around what he's seen in the past, and spends a lot of time thinking about what happened at the Tower of Joy and the Sack of King's Landing), "persistent avoidance and emotional numbing" (perhaps his intense gloominess and rigid self-control?), "persistent symptoms of increased arousal" (not so much, which is where this theory shows its weakness), and so on.

If Ned has PTSD, and it's not a lock that he does, I think this throws his decision-making in the later chapters of *Game of Thrones* into a different light: instead of seeing Ned as driven totally by honor into making stupid decisions, it instead suggests that what we have here is a veteran who suffered huge losses in the Rebellion for whom taking on the job of Hand has meant re-exposure to triggering events of violence (the two attempts on Bran's life; the fracas between Arya, Sansa, Joffrey, and how the queen handled it; the death of Ser Hugh; the murder of his guards; his own injury), and who is, perhaps, subconsciously trying to avoid a breakdown of his mental stability by choosing options that preclude further violence.

The will - Robert Baratheon's will, and Ned's part in crafting and implementing it, is one of the most frequently-debated topics in *A Game of Thrones*. On the one hand, this event is held up as a rare example of Ned finally bestirring himself to do something underhanded in the pursuit of a greater good, and finally acting in a political way. On the other, it's also seen as Ned's greatest error (although some would put his conversation with Cersei in first place), where an honorable fool puts his trust in untrustworthy men and his faith in a piece of paper.

After all, it's argued, what use is paper when swords determine who wins the game of thrones? Well, as Varys puts it:

> "In a room sit three great men: a king, a priest, and a rich man with his gold. Between them stands a sellsword, a little man of common birth and no great mind. Each of the great ones bids him slay the other two. 'Do it,' says the king, 'for I am your lawful ruler.'

> "'Do it,' says the priest, 'for I command you in the names of the gods.'
>
> "'Do it,' says the rich man, 'and all this gold shall be yours.'
>
> "So tell me – who lives and who dies?"
>
> "Power is a curious thing, my lord... Power resides where men believe it resides."
>
> *A Clash of Kings*

In other words, paper can matter a great deal – because what we're talking about here is legitimacy. Cersei may pretend that swords are the only things that matter, but, at the end of the day, her first move was to put Joffrey on the Iron Throne and proclaim him king, not to launch an armed coup without justification. Littlefinger may be something of a nihilist and a sociopath, but he understands the value of titles and old names. So legitimacy still matters, and wills can be powerful sources of legitimacy – after all, Stephen may have usurped the crown from the Empress Maude (or Aegon II from Rhaenyra if you're being picky), but Henry I's will (or Viserys I's) was still important enough to pull half the kingdom behind the challenger to the throne and fuel a civil war that lasted for years. A will was enough to make Richard III Lord Protector of England, and that was enough to make him king. Octavian Caesar was a rather unimpressive youngster competing against a decorated and beloved military commander in Marc Antony, but, at the end of the day, Caesar's will naming him his son and heir was vital to his becoming Augustus.

If anything, Eddard's real mistake here was that he didn't rely enough on the will, failing to publicize it widely – instead, Eddard sleeps on the matter, intending to announce his regency in the morning. Had he acted more like Stannis did with his open letter, and had it proclaimed throughout the capital that very night that Eddard Stark was "Lord Regent and Protector of the Realm," he could have parlayed the legitimacy of Robert's will into real political power among the smallfolk of King's Landing, the noble houses of the crownlands (to say nothing of the Vale, those stormlands houses that went with neither Stannis nor Renly, and the Dornish), the other non-Lannister nobles present in the capital, and, possibly, even among the rank-and-file of the gold cloaks. Certainly, Eddard was thinking in those terms when he had Pycelle and Renly witness the sealing of the will (and it may be that Pycelle's eagerness to slip Robert some milk of the poppy ASAP was aimed at forestalling Robert from making an official will), and summoned the small council to have it read out the next morning.

It would also be interesting to see what would have happened had Eddard Stark more widely publicized his declaration that Stannis Baratheon was the rightful heir to the Iron Throne. Remember, the cover story that Eddard eventually agrees to before Baelor is that "I plotted to depose and murder his son and seize the throne for myself." As I've argued before, if it had become public knowledge that Eddard Stark had claimed that Joffrey was a bastard and Stannis was the rightful heir, this would have changed the political and military situation at the start of the War of the Five Kings – if Stannis starts the war with it known that two of the Seven Kingdoms are going to back him, then I think he gets much more support among the stormlords and has a better shot with the lords of the Vale; Renly would still get the bulk of the stormlands and the Reach, but important houses like the Florents would be swayed both by the practical politics and the legitimacy of the regent's decree.

At the end of the day, it's not 100% one way or the other. It's not that military power didn't matter during the coup and counter-coup that's about to ensue, but the nature of its importance isn't quite what many people think. Eddard didn't need military hegemony within King's Landing to succeed – only military parity long enough to allow him to get the word out, prevent Cersei from capturing himself and his family, and hold out for Stannis, who, with 5,000 men on Dragonstone, could easily take the capital at this point in time. Had he simply prevented Cersei from gaining local hegemony the day Robert dies, this would be a very different story.

The military balance of power – and, indeed, the military balance of power was finely balanced at this precise moment: Cersei has "a dozen knights and a hundred men at arms," and she has a lot she needs to do (hold the seat of government, defeat opposing forces, secure the gates and the port, maintain public order). Ned Stark came south with 50 men, loses three when Jaime Lannister attacks him, and then gives 20 to Beric Dondarrion, so he now has a total of 27 men. At this point, it's too late to reinforce or recruit, which, as I've argued, was a major mistake, but those aren't the only men in the city. We know that Renly has access to 100 men, and we also know that there are anywhere between 100 and 200 "king's men" (either crownlanders or Baratheon bannermen) who came up to Winterfell and back to King's Landing.

Moreover, we're talking about a situation where physical control of the throne itself and a very few people is enough to seize political power. When it all goes down in the throne room, Cersei only has 26 men of her own on the spot and relies heavily on the treachery of the gold cloaks to win the day. A better timing of Ned's coup or, even, a moderate shift in the balance of forces in the limited space in the room, and there's a sword at Joffrey and/or Cersei's throat and the coup goes the other way – it's ultimately about having the most men at the precise point where you need them.

So, by any count, there's potentially an anti-Lannister military superiority in the capital, as long as the Stark and Baratheon forces can unite, *if the gold cloaks stay out of it*. Of course, the moment the gold cloaks get into it, victory goes to whoever controls them – but only if the conflict is decisive. As I've said above, if Ned had succeeded in getting the word out to Stannis and avoided capture, quite possibly it's Stannis's 5,000 who would be decisive.

The two offers – on to the heart of the chapter: Renly and Littlefinger's offers and Ned's objection to them.

In the first case, Renly offers Ned "a hundred swords in your hand" and proposes to:

> "Strike! Now, while the castle sleeps... get Joffrey away from his mother and take him in hand. Protector or no, the man who holds the king holds the kingdom. We should seize Myrcella and Tommen, as well. Once we have her children, Cersei will not dare oppose us. The council will confirm you as Lord Protector and make Joffrey your ward."

On a pragmatic level, Renly's offer makes a lot of sense – it would be possible for Ned and Renly together to establish local superiority of force, gain control over the person of the heirs, and, thus, take control of King's Landing. And Renly is quite correct that seizing the moment in the face of Lannister ruthlessness is key. To this extent, then, those who criticize Ned for rejecting him are justified.

At the same time, there's more going on here than just Ned's honor. I'll get to my criticism of Renly's plan as an alternative to civil war later, but first I'd point out that Renly's political skills fail him a bit here. In the first place, Renly fails utterly to gauge the man he's dealing with and frame his plan *as a means to avoid bloodshed*, even though he knows that Eddard was the kind of man who would resign the Handship rather than accede to the assassination of a young girl. Second, Renly doesn't offer much in the way of a political alternative to the status quo (notably, he doesn't put himself forward for the throne, a difference from the show that really wrong-footed me [more on which later]) – keeping Joffrey as one's "ward" is a really short-term plan with no solution for what happens when a young man whose family has been held prisoner gains his majority and becomes king. Third, as I'll point out later, Renly doesn't account for some critical factors that would have led to civil war despite his coup.

At the same time, I think Ned deserves some opprobrium here – but not about being honorable. Most importantly, Ned says nothing to Renly about Joffrey's legitimacy and his plan to make Stannis king; even more so than Renly, he completely fails to offer a political alternative to Lannister dominance. While Renly might not have liked the idea of

Stannis as king that much, he may well have responded to the argument that Stannis's 5,000 men were necessary for survival. Almost as importantly, Ned doesn't make an actual request for Renly's swords for any plan, despite knowing that "he might well have need of Renly's hundred swords." It's a massive mistake apart from the question of honor.

In the second case, Littlefinger is told of Ned's plan to make Stannis the king, and argues that "Stannis cannot take the throne without your help. If you're wise, you'll make certain Joffrey succeeds." In a speech that is so perfectly pitched to run counter to everything Eddard Stark is that I'm fairly certain Littlefinger had no intention of ever carrying out this plot, he argues that:

> "Stannis is no friend of yours, nor of mine... He'll give us a new Hand and a new council, for a certainty... And his ascent will mean war. Stannis cannot rest easy on the throne until Cersei and her bastards are dead. Do you think Lord Tywin will sit idly... Casterly Rock will rise...
>
> "Joffrey is but a boy of 12, and Robert gave you the regency, my lord. You are the Hand of the King and Protector of the Realm. The power is yours, Lord Stark. All you need do is reach out and take it. Make your peace with the Lannisters... it will be four years before Joffrey comes of age... Long enough to dispose of Lord Stannis. Then, should Joffrey prove troublesome, we can reveal his little secret and put Lord Renly on the throne."

I will explain why this plan is insane in a moment, but I want to be clear: being too honorable to take up Littlefinger's offer, and ultimately then honorable enough to trust that Littlefinger will follow him despite turning him down, is not the reason Ned Stark fell from power. *The reason Ned Stark falls from power is his inability to understand institutional power.* Instead of understanding the fiscal powers of the state as an institution that exists outside of the man who occupies the office, he sees Littlefinger as "the man who pays" and thinks that he has to use Littlefinger. In reality, Ned is Hand of the King and Lord Protector of the Realm – he doesn't need Littlefinger to take command of the City Watch.

I've discussed before that Ned Stark has every authority to simply replace Janos Slynt and his leading officers and take command of the gold cloaks, but even if we accept for the sake of argument that he's left it too late to do that, Ned could simply seize the royal treasury and buy their support himself. His 27 men isn't enough to take on Cersei, but it's more soldiers than Littlefinger has, so he could simply open up the vaults and use the gold to buy Slynt and every mercenary in the city. Indeed, as Hand of the King and Lord Protector, this wouldn't even be illegal;

he's got full authority to make use of royal funds as he sees fit, and he's ultimately responsible for making sure the guard gets paid.

Why these plans are insane – Ned Stark is frequently criticized for turning down these offers, to the point where sometimes it's argued that, to the smallfolk, Eddard is just as much a villain as the Lannisters because his stubbornness and attachment to personal honor caused the War of the Five Kings, whereas if he'd taken up either offer, war would have been averted.

However, both plans ignore several key factors that, by this point, made war inevitable and which render these plans unfit for purpose:

1. Stannis already knows about the incest and is going to war. Ever since his time investigating with Jon Arryn, Stannis has believed that Cersei's children are abominations born of incest and that he is the true heir to the Iron Throne – hence why he's been gathering 5,000 men to protect himself from the Lannisters and seize the throne from the usurpers (or the usurper's usurpers, if you're a Targaryen loyalist). Regardless of whether Ned takes up the offer of either Renly or Littlefinger, there's going to be a civil war between those who uphold Joffrey's right to the throne and those who hold for a legitimate Baratheon. If he takes up Renly's offer and has Joffrey seized, Ned is going to be in the impossible situation of having to defend his "ward" from Stannis while his "ward's" family fights him at the same time.

While Renly says that Cersei won't fight them while they hold her children, what he ignores is that Tywin's not the kind of man who rolls over when someone kidnaps his blood relations – he's already making war on the riverlands for Tyrion's sake, and he's not going to do less for his daughter and her son who Tywin sees as the foundation of a Lannister dynasty. Thus, Ned will have to defend the capital with insufficient forces from Stannis, who'll have a free hand to raise the stormlands against the Lannisters (since Renly will be stuck in King's Landing and unable to rally his bannermen), while the main Stark forces are up in the north with Tywin's army between them and the capital.

If, on the other hand, Ned takes up Littlefinger's offer, even assuming Tywin's interested in making peace with the Starks, Littlefinger offers no evidence why Renly would back Joffrey and the Lannisters over Stannis when we know that Renly views the Lannisters as a threat to his lie. It's much more likely that Renly would react to a Stark/Lannister alliance by rallying the stormlands and the Reach (possibly even allying with Stannis to further bolster his numbers), which means there's going to be a grueling civil war, not an easy pushover like Littlefinger predicts.

2. Renly is already trying to seize the throne. We've seen already how Renly was scheming with the Tyrells to shove Margaery into

Robert's bed, and we will see that Renly will later marry Margaery to give himself the military might to seize the throne. As I've said, if Eddard takes up Littlefinger's plan, Renly's going to decamp to Highgarden and rally the south against the Lannisters, which means there's going to be a drawn-out civil war, as I've said.

This also acts as a major problem for Renly's plan – at some point, he's going to need Joffrey out of the way, which means that Eddard is going to be in the awful position as guardian to a lad likely to be murdered, and allied to a man who wants to overthrow him and take the throne. All of this is going to be going on as Littlefinger and Varys work to destabilize King's Landing from within (because they both want the civil war to continue), and while Eddard is likely having to fight both Tywin and Stannis.

3. Both plans don't reckon on Balon Greyjoy. While Robb Stark gets a lot of criticism for letting Theon back, people don't really think about how long it takes to pull a navy together and plan an invasion of a territory as big as the north. Balon Greyjoy must have been planning this for months, if not years, waiting for any vacuum of power (just as he did when Robert was on the throne, smf just as his grandfather, Dagon, did during the Great Spring Sickness) to attack.

So, regardless of which offer Ned takes up, he's going to be in a difficult situation in which either he calls in the army of the north to defend his position in the south or can't get any reinforcements at King's Landing because Robb Stark is fending off the Greyjoys. It's hugely problematic for Renly's plan – what happens if the Greyjoys prevent Eddard from bringing Stark troops to bear when Stannis attacks the city, regardless of which way the Lannisters go? It's also hugely problematic for Littlefinger – a Stark/Lannister alliance becomes much less invincible against the Baratheons (or the Baratheon/Tyrells) if Balon attacks *either* the Starks or the Lannisters.

4. Both plans don't reckon on a Targaryen invasion. As we know, Varys and Illyrio are plotting to grab themselves a Dothraki army and the Golden Company, and both or either force is going to land on Westeros soon – indeed, despite Varys getting thrown off schedule by Stannis's assault on King's Landing and the sudden reversal with Dany's dragons, in OTL Aegon lands in the stormlands about two years from now. Neither plan is well-suited to deal with this – Littlefinger assumes that the Targaryen loyalists wouldn't rise against a Stark/Lannister alliance, but doesn't really have a plan about how to keep both the Dornish and the Reach from doing so with or without the arrival of a significant professional army and a Targaryen candidate for the Iron Throne. Likewise, Renly doesn't seem to have a good grasp on Dornish politics – possibly because of his connection to the Tyrells – and assumes they'll be down with the Tyrells backing a Lannister on the Iron Throne.

Ultimately, both plans ignore powerful factions that will become engaged in the War of the Five Kings (although, to be fair, neither could have predicted the last factor, and it would have been a stretch to assume the next-to-last factor), and assume that political actors will act in a completely uncharacteristic fashion.

Ned's mistake isn't that he doesn't take up either plan, but, rather, that his own plan – seize the throne and hold it for Stannis – is hobbled by Ned's inability to make use of institutional power (and not acting quickly enough).

Historical Analysis

Last time, I began my argument that Richard, Duke of York was the historical counterpart to Eddard Stark in general terms. In this installment, I'm going to show how their political careers paralleled each other in many ways, as both men strove to right a tottering monarchy and clashed with a powerful queen and her allies.

First, some background: much of the Wars of the Roses grew out of political conflicts that broke out after the death of Henry V in the Hundred Years' War. In 1425, English power was at its height in France, thanks to Henry V's victory at Agincourt and in the conquest of Normandy that followed: Brittany, Normandy, Gascony, Aquitaine, Poiters, Champaigne, Maine, Anjou, and Paris were all under direct English rule, and the powerful duchy of Burgundy was a major English ally. Following Henry V's death, political power was divided nominally between Jon of Lancaster, Henry V's brother and the duke of Bedford, who was made governor of Normandy and regent of France, and his younger brother, Humphrey, Duke of Gloucester, who was made Protector of England.

However, English public policy was paralyzed by clashes between Bedford and Gloucester over who was really in charge, and a second division between Gloucester and Henry Beaufort, the Bishop of Winchester (and, later, Cardinal), the former of whom favored war with France and the latter, peace. Despite Gloucester being named Protector, Beaufort was much better at influencing the Privy Council and controlled much of the regency government between 1422-1437. He was especially good at advancing the careers of his Beaufort relatives, especially the earls and dukes of Somerset, and in making an alliance with the powerful de la Pole family, especially William de la Pole, the Earl and, later, Duke of Suffolk, who he groomed as his political heir.

All this is important, because when, in 1435, Richard, Duke of York went to France to replace the aging duke of Bedford, he began to clash with Suffolk, Somerset, and Beaufort when the war began to turn against England. Paris had been lost in 1436, and York, along with the renowned soldier John Talbot, had barely held off a French invasion of Normandy in 1437. In 1439, as Beaufort attempted once more to make peace, he sent Somerset to France as lieutenant governor, an act York viewed as deliberately undercutting his position as regent and as retaliation for York supporting Gloucester in his criticisms of Beaufort's policy of offering concessions for peace. In 1443, France unexpectedly invaded Gascony, and Somerset botched the defense of the province, losing it completely, while York had to hold Normandy without reinforcements (Somerset would die in 1444, with some historians suggesting that he may have killed himself in shame, and was replaced as earl by his brother, Edmund). York developed a lifelong hatred for Somerset and the Beauforts, who he believed were deliberately undermining him and promoting military incompetents.

In 1444, Bishop (now Cardinal) Beaufort and the earl of Suffolk proposed a truce with France accompanied by the marriage of Henry VI to Princess Margaret of Anjou, despite a secret provision of the truce that required England to give up the provinces of Maine and Anjou, despite Margaret's lack of a dowry. Suffolk was the main negotiator for the English and stood in for Henry VI at their engagement, which fueled rumors of an affair between the two, which would dog the queen and her bannerman for years (similar to Cersei). The following year, York returned to England to be replaced by the brother of the Somerset who lost Gascony, while Suffolk took Beaufort's place as the leading figure in domestic government, just as the news that Maine and Anjou were to be handed over was leaked. York joined Gloucester in his criticisms of the Beaufort pro-peace contingent, and when Gloucester was arrested by Suffolk for treason and died suddenly while under arrest in 1447, York took up his banner (shades of Jon Arryn). He was exiled to Ireland for his pains.

Just like Ned Stark, York had a strong reputation as an honest administrator who opposed the corruption and maladministration of the Beauforts, but lacked political support among the great nobles. When an impatient Charles VII of France seized Maine in 1448 and invaded Normandy in 1449, Somerset proved to be completely unable to stop him, and Normandy was lost, as well. At the same time, the queen succeeded in getting Somerset and Suffolk made dukes, and protected both men from charges of treason, which, in turn, fueled rumors that the queen was also sleeping with Somerset.

In 1450, Richard, Duke of York landed in England, raised an army, and marched on London, where, in an act reminiscent of Ned Stark, he knocked on the king's door and simply asked him to reform the government. Admitted to the Privy Council, York pushed the Commons to pass an Act of Resumption to restore the king's finances (reminiscent of Eddard and the tourney) and to have Somerset impeached. Thanks to Margaret's lobbying, Somerset was promptly released from prison, and Henry VI refused to remove him from office, despite the House of Commons 1451 petition to do just that. In 1452, York lost patience with trying to go the legal route (given the queen's interference) and formed an army to march on London. His forces met up with a royal army at Blackheath, but rather than go to arms, York agreed to disband if Henry VI would have Somerset arrested. The king agreed, but, thanks to the queen's lobbying, went back on his word, and York narrowly avoided arrest.

In 1453, the political landscape underwent an earthquake when Henry VI had a nervous breakdown and went catatonic for a year, just as the queen gave birth to a son many claimed was a bastard. Somerset and the queen attempted and failed to form a regency under themselves, but Richard was named Lord Protector and regent during the king's incapacity. Promptly arresting Somerset, York proved an effective regent, quelling public disorder, and restoring royal finances... only to have all his work undone in early 1455, when the king recovered from his breakdown, dismissed York, freed Somerset, and returned to his free-spending ways.

This cycle would repeat itself over and over again: later that year, York took to the battlefield again when the queen and Somerset maneuvered for his arrest, crushing a royal army at St. Albans, where Somerset died and the king was captured. Once again, York was regent, the king went mad, and the royal finances were restored... only for Henry to recover in 1456, sack York, and the cycle to begin again.

So... rumors of royal adultery, an unwilling politician trying to right a government paralyzed by debt and corruption, and growing conflict between the regent and the queen.

Next time: Richard and Ned mount a failed coup.

What If?

Oh, there's so much great material for hypotheticals here:

What if Ned proclaims himself that night? One legitimate criticism that has nothing to do with Ned's honor is that he simply failed to act fast enough, presuming things would wait for the next day. Even with his reluctance to commit bloodshed at this point (he'll get a lot less unwilling next chapter), he might have been willing to publicize that he had been named Lord Protector and regent. As I've discussed earlier regarding publicizing his support for Stannis, the outcome of this change is hard to forecast: given the political tumult, I doubt public legitimacy would have swayed the gold cloaks, but like the London mob, if the smallfolk and merchants of King's Landing had known and believed that Eddard Stark was the rightful regent, they could have proved a formidable force to destabilize Cersei if they'd begun to riot when Eddard was arrested. While it wouldn't have prevented his death, it would likely have accelerated the pace of public discontent in the capital, greatly complicating efforts to hold the capital as Stannis draws near, especially...

What if Ned's letter/kids get through? I've kind of done this hypothetical to death, but I want to point out Martin's intricate plotting in the fact that Eddard writes a letter to Stannis proclaiming him king, but waits until the evening tide of the next day to send it (along with his two kids). Twenty-four hours' difference and the letter gets into Stannis's hands, with dramatic consequences for Stannis and Robb's relations during the War of the Five Kings.

What if Ned asks Renly for his aid? Eddard never tells Renly that Joffrey isn't legitimate (although Renly probably knows), and he certainly never asks Renly for his support in holding the throne for Stannis. I honestly don't know whether Renly would pick the long game of supporting Stannis in the hopes of replacing him later or becoming his heir, but it would set up a fascinating situation. Let's say Renly and Eddard manage to hold the capital with their hundred and twenty-odd men – the ensuing race for King's Landing as the armies of Houses Lannister, Stark, Baratheon, and Tyrell rush to defend their precariously-isolated respective family members and seize power would be something to see.

Book vs. Show

HBO does this chapter very, very differently from the book, and not necessarily in a better-versus-worse way. Instead of leaving Renly's intentions opaque, as happens in the book, here Renly straight-out tells Eddard he wants to be king and Eddard should support him, and that Stannis can't rule. It's a powerful scene, so effective that I genuinely forgot that Renly doesn't declare for himself and had to be reminded of this fact. It makes Renly out to be a better man than he is in the books. It also changes Ned's refusal somewhat – instead of rejecting Renly out of fear of bloodshed, Ned's refusal is more principled (Renly has no right to rule at all) rather than squeamish.

JON VI

"I never asked for this," he said stubbornly.

"None of us are here for asking."

Synopsis

Jon Snow takes his vows as a member of the Night's Watch, alongside Samwell Tarly, despite being initially less than enthused about being sorted into ~~Hufflepuff~~ the stewards.

Political Analysis

"Jon VI" gives us a nice breather from the heavy intrigue in King's Landing, but it also gives a further glimpse into the institutional politics of the Night's Watch, both the good and the bad of it.

Center-stage here is the lord commander, Jeor Mormont, who gives the longest explication of his personal vision of what the Night's Watch is and what it should stand for that he puts forth in the entire series:

> *"You came to us outlaws... poachers, rapers, debtors, killers, and thieves. You came to us children. You came to us alone, in chains, with neither friends nor honor. You came to us rich, and you came to us poor. Some of you bear the names of proud houses, or no names at all. It makes no matter. All that is past now. On the Wall, we are all one house.*
>
> *"...A man of the Night's Watch lives his life for the* realm. *Not for a king, nor a lord, nor the honor of this house or that house, neither for gold nor glory nor a woman's love, but for the* realm *and all the people in it."*

In the context of Westerosi society, Mormont's vision is both sweepingly radical and subtly conservative. The Watch is seen as a formally egalitarian institution that erases pervasive class distinctions – although it's noticeable that, in addition to your genuine criminals (rapers, killers, and thieves), you also have people forced into the Watch by economic necessity (poachers and debtors). Given the powerful attachment to house in a feudal society that distinguishes sharply between smallfolk, knights, and landed houses great and small, to argue that "we are all one house" is a powerful statement of equality that could appeal to many. Likewise, for formal criminals, the promise of a clean slate is quite an incentive.

At the same time, it's a demanding ascetic worldview that insists on a total separation from the human family – "our wife is duty, our mistress is honor" – in favor of the makeshift brotherhood of the order, which is a lot to ask of anyone. In Medieval Europe, monastic orders had a hegemonic religious worldview at hand to use to backstop the strictness of their rule; the Night's Watch does not have that luxury. The Watch does make use of religion – the lord commander is making this speech in front of the altar in a sept of the Seven, after all. However, his rhetoric is entirely secular, to the point of cosmopolitanism (hence both the old gods and the new).

Rather, Mormont posits a nationalistic foundation to shore up allegiance to the Night's Watch's strict rule. The realm is held up as a universal entity, where all the divisions of class and region are erased; especially in the lord commander's idea that "all the people" are due protection as members of the realm, it approaches the early modern idea of the Commonwealth that marked much of Tudor politics. It's an incredibly high-minded ideal, but a rather abstract one, especially given the historical context. Westeros has only been a polity for three hundred years, and, even then, a highly federalized one built on top of Seven Kingdoms and three peoples; it has a common language, but not a common religion, culture, or ethnic heritage. Without the experience of an extended military conflict with a different people to provide the impulse to unite and define oneself in opposition to the Other, nationalism is far too weak a reed to rely on in a crisis.

It's also a rather traditionalist view of the Night's Watch, as we can see from the Night's Watch oath:

> "Night gathers, and now my watch begins. It shall not end until my death. I shall take no wife, hold no lands, father no children. I shall wear no crowns and win no glory. I shall live and die at my post. I am the sword in the darkness. I am the watcher on the walls. I am the shield that guards the realms of men. I pledge my life and honor to the Night's Watch, for this night and all the nights to come."

So, here, we have in an eight-thousand-year-old oath the concept of allegiance to the "realm," although here it's pluralized, reflecting the lack of continent-wide identity prior to the Targaryens. However, there is a species-based identity that speaks to the fact that the Night's Watch was formed at a time when humanity's unity was enforced by a very real threat from a hostile Other. And it's an identity that must have been quite powerful, given that the Night's Watch predated the Andal invasion yet seems to have been one of the few institutions that was maintained for thousands of years thereafter.

However, if we look beyond Jeor Mormont's idealism and commitment to tradition to look at Jon Snow's lived experience, it all begins to break down. Jon Snow's reaction to being sorted into the stewards shows that, in spite of the rhetoric of equality, there are stark gradations of status between rangers, builders, and stewards that mirror the class divisions between the nobility and the smallfolk. Even someone with Ned Stark's benevolent paternalism, who himself made the argument just the previous day that the Night's Watch has need for all three groups, cannot maintain the polite fiction that all Night's Watchmen are equal when his own privilege is affected. As his friends point out to him, "the stewards are fine for the likes of you and me... but not for Lord Snow." At the end of the day, Jon Snow's concept of fairness is based on a self-identity as a warrior bound up in his highborn upbringing.

Likewise, Jon Snow's humbling assignment turns out to be an example of class hierarchy and nepotism in action. As Sam describes, "you'll also take his letters, attend him at meetings, squire for him in battle... you'll know everything, be a part of everything, and the lord steward said Mormont asked for you himself... he wants to groom you for command!" Rather than selecting an experienced officer to promote from within, Mormont is looking to groom a 14-year-old from one of the Great Houses to succeed him, and the bastard son of his former liege lord, at that. Jon Snow simply fits the model of elite leadership – a well-educated warrior from an illustrious family and an accustomed habit of leadership over smallfolk – better than a Cotter Pyke ever could. The problem is that pushing highborn newcomers up the chain of promotions is an unstable model of succession; not only is the quality of the successor in question (especially if the lord commander unexpectedly dies before he can give his steward more than a year of training), but it leads to discontent within the officer corps from people like Alliser Thorne, Bowen Marsh, and so forth, who feel their experience has been overlooked.

Historical Analysis

Class influencing military command isn't anything new, of course, as one might expect given the historical presence of military castes and classes. During the Medieval era, it was axiomatic that the nobility would lead on the battlefield and that commoners were inconsequential – which caused problems at Crécy and other battles where the nobleman's desire for glory overcame his common sense. This began to change in the early modern period, as a number of factors (the creation of standing armies, a vast increase in army size, the increased importance of infantry, the more elaborate forms of drill needed to move large blocks of infantry around a battlefield in an organized fashion, etc.) made a professional officer corps (less likely to be noblemen taking a temporary leave of absence from their landed estates) more important for success in arms.

This didn't end class hierarchy within the army so much as make the officer corps a locus of contention between commoner professionals and the old nobility. During the English Civil War, for example, the quality of noble leadership was so uneven on the Parliamentary side that the creation of the New Model Army went hand-in-hand with the Self-Denying Ordinance that banned members of Parliament (the Commons, as well, but crucially the Lords) from serving as officers, thus ensuring that the leadership of the army would be made up of professional soldiers promoted on merit (with the notable exception of Oliver Cromwell, who possessed both a seat in Parliament and undeniable military skill). Among the many reforms that were rolled back during the Restoration of Charles II was the New Model Army and the dangerous idea of a professional officer corps (professional officers had shown a nasty tendency to harbor the idea that, as men of merit, they and not kings should rule).

And given that standing armies were now seen as dangerous to English liberty, Parliament was unwilling to grant Charles II enough money to have one of those. Charles's solution was to sell military commissions to the highest bidder, which turned out to be a win-win for him: since officers were now expected to supply the regiments they had purchased, it didn't cost him as much money to fight wars, and it made sure that the officer ranks would be made up almost exclusively of the rich, who were unlikely to be approve of further revolutions. Although the practice remained controversial for several years, by 1719 there were official price lists established by the government setting out how much a lieutenantship went for, how much a captaincy, and so on all the way up to colonel.

It's pretty clear that there's a basic problem of quality control with this kind of system – once you move past a social order in which the wealthiest members of society spend their entire lives from childhood on training for war, there's no guarantee that someone who purchased their commission knew what they were doing. Yes, the purchase-of-commission system gave Britain Wellington, but it also gave them some of the worst military bumblers of history.

For a devastating portrait of the purchase of commissions leading to utter military disaster, the 1968 production of the Charge of the Light Brigade really can't be beat.

What If?

I don't really have much in the way of hypotheticals for this chapter, since Jon refusing to take the oath doesn't really seem to be in the cards.

Book vs. Show

The show plays this chapter pretty close to the text, so I don't have much for this chapter.

Apologies for the brevity, but the next chapter should give me more to work with.

EDDARD XIV

"Those were the king's words," Ser Barristan said, shocked.

"We have a new king now," Cersei Lannister replied.

Synopsis

Eddard Stark wakes up, finds out his best friend is dead, has the will read out, attempts to set things right, and is betrayed and captured. Not his best day.

Political Analysis

Although "Eddard XIV" isn't the last Eddard chapter in *A Game of Thrones*, it is essentially the end of his political career; after this chapter, Lord Stark will be many things – a bargaining chip, a political symbol, a historical figure – but not a political actor.

As I discussed in the previous Eddard chapter, Eddard does make one smart move in summoning the small council immediately on the death of King Robert to install himself as regent, notably ensuring that Ser Barristan Selmy (a pillar of legitimacy in the public's eyes, as even Tywin agrees) was on hand to read the will and lend his authority to Eddard's regency. Indeed, Eddard is actually playing the game of thrones here: "The need for deceit was a bitter taste in his mouth, but Ned knew he must tread softly here, must keep his counsel and play the game until he was firmly established as regent." Eddard even thinks to himself that he intends to delay revealing the truth of the succession until "Arya and Sansa were safely back in Winterfell, and Lord Stannis had retuned to King's Landing with all his power." Unfortunately for him, what Eddard has neglected here is the crucial importance of timing – Littlefinger has already made his deal with Cersei (the precise terms of which we'll get into later), Sansa has informed Cersei of Eddard's timing and his intent to get his children out (and only that), and Renly has fled in the night.

Faced with a choice between the long play and a swift strike, Eddard has chosen... poorly.

Littlefinger's Nessun Dorma – Littlefinger's actions here are crucial – by making Eddard sure that the gold cloaks are on his side, Littlefinger ensures that Eddard reacts to news about Renly fleeing the city with all his 100 swords with equanimity, and even the news of Joffrey being installed on the throne: "Ned had expected Cersei to strike quickly; the summons came as no surprise." While it's clear that Eddard has made a crucial mistake of timing – failing to see that the crucial moment to get his children to safety and himself publicly proclaimed as the rightful regent was the previous night rather than this morning – it also underlines how crucial his belief that he has the gold cloaks is to Littlefinger's plans, because, without that, Eddard would likely have copied Renly in booking it out of King's Landing (or, at least, attempting to).

However, Baelish's actions are rather ambiguous and unclear on a different level. It's clear that, at some point, Littlefinger must have struck a bargain with Cersei for his support, given that he survives the cabinet reshuffle despite Cersei hating him. On the other hand, we know that Cersei turned down Littlefinger's bid for Sansa's hand in marriage (shudder), and that Harrenhal and the title of Lord Paramount of the Riverlands was Littlefinger's deal with Tywin as his quid-pro-quo for sealing the Tyrell alliance. So, what did Littlefinger ask for at his moment of greatest influence over Cersei Lannister?

At the same time, we can learn a lot about Littlefinger's style as a conspirator from his actions here. As reckless as Littlefinger can be, he's quite cautious at this moment – after all, there's no practical limitation that prevents him from kidnapping Eddard Stark, Cersei, and Joffrey and trying to use them to bring both the Starks and Lannisters to their knees and declare himself king, or to sell them to Renly or anyone else who's willing to buy a slightly-used kingdom. So, even though I'm quite convinced he's a sociopath, he's at least intelligent enough to recognize that there are limits to his power at this moment in time.

However, there's also a very personal, sadistic side to his actions, as well; there's no need for Littlefinger to personally slip the knife under Eddard Stark's chin with the dagger that was used in the attempt on Bran's life. The only reason is to ensure that Eddard Stark knows that it's he, Littlefinger, who's responsible for his downfall, because this is very much personal. Littlefinger is acting here to revenge himself on the man who married the woman he loves (and who, in his head, loves him in return) and to prove himself to be the man's intellectual superior.

It is this latter quality that makes me look askance at those who see Littlefinger as a peerless mastermind who will triumph over all in the end. The man's Achilles Heel – his Gatsby-like desire to turn back time while revenging himself on the families who injured him as a young man, and his insecure need to show himself to be the smartest man in the room – is so well-established by George R.R. Martin that I can't see his downfall *not* happening.

The failed coup and the question of paper – it's worth noting that, at the crucial moment, Eddard Stark was willing to breach the rules of honor and law to seize the state itself:

> *"Your son has no claim to the throne he sits. Lord Stannis is Robert's true heir."*

> *"Ser Barristan, seize this traitor."*

> *The Lord Commander of the Kingsguard hesitated. In the blink of an eye he was surrounded by Stark guardsmen, bare steel in their mailed fists... the Hound drew his longsword. The knights of the Kingsguard and 20 Lannister guardsmen in crimson cloaks moved to support him...*

> *"You leave me no choice... Commander, take the queen and her children into custody. Do them no harm, but escort them back to the royal apartments and keep them there, under guard."*

When it comes right down to it, despite being fooled by Littlefinger, Ned Stark comes within inches of actually pulling off a coup d'etat. And because, in medieval polities, the symbol and the reality of power are more directly linked than in our times, Cersei is terrifyingly vulnerable to such a coup – in order to push Ned Stark out of the regency, Cersei has to put Joffrey on the Iron Throne and keep him there to give him the aura of a king rather than a pretender, and, in such situations, the military doctrine of "power to a point" means that if a few soldiers can get to within a sword's length of either Eddard or Cersei and Joffrey, that side wins even if it's outnumbered.

And the sides are more evenly matched than appears in hindsight. The throne room constricts the total number of soldiers that can be in the room – Eddard has eight, Cersei has 20, and the gold cloaks have 100, and that's about as many men as can fit into the room. Obviously, in OTL the 100 gold cloaks are decisive, but potentially, had Eddard brought all of his 20 men and just rushed the throne, he might have had a fighting chance of capturing either Cersei or Joffrey and ending the fight with speed of maneuver. Indeed, if Eddard had actually reached out to Renly and requested his military support, their 120 men would have probably been enough in that confined space to carry the day, with a little luck.

And this gets me to why I think the fandom is wrong when it accepts on face Cersei's arguments that "power is power" and that paper shields are useless – legitimacy matters a great deal in politics, which is why Cersei's placed her son on the throne instead of holing up in a more defensive position, and why she waits until Eddard has both openly spoken and acted against Joffrey in front of the small council to spring her trap. Military hegemony does decide whether Eddard's words count as treason in the throne room, but military hegemony in the other direction, with the shift of a hundred men, could have meant that Cersei tearing up the king's will would have been seen as open treason – and in situations in which the military positions are evenly matched (if Renly's men had also been in the room), paper can be the all-important factor.

Notably, legitimacy has a public dimension. Here and now, Cersei has claimed legitimate authority in the capital with a private show of force and the astute use of monarchist symbolism. But look at how quickly she loses it, first to Tyrion when he arrives with a piece of paper declaring him Hand of the King, next when the Flea Bottom mob rises up against the "brotherfucker" in the name of "King Bread," and then disastrously against the High Septon and his mob of sparrows.* There are limits to the "power of power."

> * Likewise, Eddard ignoring the public dimensions of legitimacy is crucial. Only in the small council room and the throne room is it known that Eddard Stark has been named regent of the Seven Kingdoms; only in the throne room does Eddard declare Stannis to be the true heir to the Iron Throne. If Eddard's status and intentions had been a matter of public knowledge, Cersei's counter-coup and Eddard's public execution would have been instantly politically contentious in ways that they just weren't in OTL.

Historical Analysis

In our last Eddard chapter, I discussed how Richard, Duke of York spent the years 1450-1456 in a state of extreme frustration with the state of national policy, trying to right the fiscal ship of state and get Somerset and Suffolk behind bars, being made regent when Henry VI lost his mind only to be sacked when Henry recovered, taking up arms against the queen, becoming regent again when Henry relapses only to be sacked again, and on and on.

After the first battle of St. Albans, an extremely uneasy peace reigned for about four years; Queen Margaret worked to oust Yorkist supporters from royal office and extend her influence through the ranks of the kingdom's sheriffs while York rose in popular esteem by defeating the Scottish king (a secret ally of Margaret, and an alliance that would cause real political problems for the Lancastrians in the future) and Warwick by a successful naval campaign against French, Spanish, and British pirates (while indulging in a little piracy against France, Spain, and the Hanseatic League, because hypocrisy is a game everyone can play). The spirit of the times was best exemplified by the famous "Love-Day" ceremony on the 24th of March, 1458, when Henry VI and the archbishop of Canterbury sought to end the growing feud by having the Houses of Plantagent (York) and Neville (Warwick) parade to St. Paul's Cathedral hand-in-hand with the Lancastrian Houses of Beaufort (Somerset), Percy (Northumberland), and Clifford, with the duke of York escorting the queen herself, where the two sides pledged peace and put up huge monetary pledges against any resumption of violence.

The eternal peace lasted about a year – by summer 1458, the queen moved against Warwick, accusing him of piracy and ordering him to appear before the Privy Council. Warwick arrived with 600 armed men, and denounced the Council's actions as a show-trial; the city of London, who loved the charismatic, fantastically-wealthy pirate hunter (who sold them a lot of pirated goods on the cheap), promptly rioted, forcing the investigation to be shelved. In the fall, Warwick was either accidentally almost skewered or narrowly avoided assassination by a roasting spit while passing through the royal kitchens at Westminster; the resulting scuffle turned into a fight between Warwick's men and the royal guard that led to Warwick fleeing to Yorkshire with a royal warrant for his arrest.

Both sides armed themselves for war in early 1459, as York and Warwick renewed their accusation that the prince of Wales was a bastard and the queen was a tyrant, while the queen denounced Yorkist armament as treason. Warwick moved quickly to take London without firing a shot and marched to Ludlow to be united with York's army; his brother, the earl of Salisbury, fought his way past a royal army twice his size at Blore Heath to unite with the Yorkist army.

Finally, the two sides came head to head, 25,000 Yorkists staring down 30,000 Lancastrians – and something amazing happened: Richard, Duke of York refused to fight the king in person and ordered a retreat to Worcester. The king's army followed the Yorkist army to Ludlow, where Yorkist moral plummeted. Andrew Trollope, Warwick's right-hand man at Calais, defected with his entire forces, swelling the royal army to between 40-60,000 men. Outnumbered and desperately low in morale, York, Salisbury, and Warwick fled in the night for Calais, and the Yorkist army scattered.

For three months, "the queen and those of her affinity ruled the realm as her [sic] liked, gathering riches innumerable."* At the so-called "Parliament of Devils," York, Salisbury, Warwick, and all the Yorkist lords were attainted for high treason and stripped of their lands, with York's wife forced to bear witness.

* Davies's Chronicle cited in Weir, Alison, *The Wars of the Roses*.

By late June 1460, the Yorkists had readied themselves for an invasion of England. Warwick, Salisbury, and York's son, the earl of March, landed at Sandwich with 2,000 men. The southeast of England, which had shared London's fondness for Warwick, rose up for the Yorkists, and by July 2, Warwick entered the city with 40,000 men, stating that his cause was to undo the queen's misrule in the name of the innocent and the deceived King Henry. As the Yorkist army marched north to link up with York's presumed landing in the west, they ran into the royal army at Northhampton. In the driving rain, Warwick advanced on the Lancastrians from three directions, claiming that he would speak with the king or die trying – and as he reached the earth-and-wooden-stake defenses, the Lancastrian flank under the command of Lord Grey promptly dropped their weapons and helped the Yorkists over the fortifications. Within a half hour, the battle was over, with the Lancastrian soldiers in panicked flight and the king arrested by a common archer; hearing the news, Queen Margaret fled to Scotland.

With total victory in his grasp, York landed in North Wales and marched to reclaim his wife, his children, and his lands. From there, he marched to London, timing it perfectly to coincide with Parliament's first sitting. By this point, Richard, Duke of York was done with regencies and Lord Protectorships – he was descended from the second son of Edward III (the line of the Mortimers of the earldom of March), whereas Henry VI was descended from the usurping Henry Bolingbrooke, son of the third son of Edward III, John of Gaunt. By law and right, in Richard's mind, he was the rightful heir to the throne; compared to his lunatic cousin, Richard was the superior soldier and administrator. All England should welcome the return of good government.

Richard entered the city bearing the royal arms of England and carrying the sword of state before him. He dismounted his horse at Westminster Hall and entered the hall with his sword still in his hands. He marched up to the throne and placed his hands on the throne, laying claim to the kingdom. Instead of cheers of acclamation, Richard was met with total silence.

He had completely misjudged the political sentiment of the Parliament – incensed as they were with royal misgovernment, they were not ready to unseat an anointed monarch.

What If?

Any time when you have that many swords being swung in a confined space, a lot of different things can happen. Some entertaining possibilities include:

What if Ned succeeds? Let's say, by some really lucky chance, that one of the Stark guards gets within sword range of either Joffrey or

Cersei, and this forces the Lannisters in the throne room to surrender. This sets off a chaotic situation in which Eddard is besieged inside the throne room by the 100 or so Lannisters outside, outnumbered but with the ultimate bargaining chip. Littlefinger, thus, has the opportunity to switch sides once again if he wants, because no gold cloak is going to attack the Starks if that might lead to the death of a royal. Meanwhile, this changes the military situation immediately: Tywin can no longer afford to focus on the riverlands and desperately needs to get his hands on some Starks important enough to force a trade (which was his intention from the beginning), but he also needs to get to King's Landing before Stannis can arrive, establish local military superiority, and grab the Iron Throne before Renly. What happens then, I have no idea.

What if Ned dies? A sword or spear goes awry and, all of the sudden, Lord Stark is dead on the throne room floor. Cersei, no doubt, would push the story that he died committing treason, but the very isolation that made her preemptive coup work would probably work against it here, with conspiracy theories immediately springing up. Notably, Cersei loses the opportunity to either do a trade with Robb once the Battle of the Whispering Woods happens or to use Eddard's public confession to bolster her political position. The Starks, meanwhile, most likely go from rescue mode to total war as Robb rides into battle knowing his father has been murdered by the Lannisters. Most likely, Jaime loses his head on the spot – thus butterflying away his later release, the defection of the Karstarks, and any hope of peace with the Lannisters.

What if Cersei dies? Depending on who's in charge once the fighting stops, things probably go badly very quickly. If it's Ned, then one more ton of guilt lands on his shoulders, but he's now the undisputed power in the capital and probably can hold it together long enough for Stannis to show up. However, now Tywin's out for blood, and I highly doubt any retreat to Harrenhal happens. The war in the west gets very ugly very quickly, but the politics of the south gets very complicated, with Stannis on the throne with the allegiance of the north, and Renly in Highgarden weighing his options. If it's the Lannisters, then Joffrey's got no one holding him back: Ned's dead, so's Sansa, and there's no responsible adult in charge. The capital collapses into chaos while Tywin and Robb seek to revenge themselves on the other; Joffrey's probably torn to pieces by the starving mob, and Stannis arrives and gets ready for another siege.

What if Joffrey dies? This one actually works out well for both sides, in that neither of them now have to deal with a giggling psychopath on the Iron Throne. If it's Ned, then, again, the thing with the guilt and now Sansa's really upset, but at least Tommen won't be a problem while he waits out the siege; Cersei, on the other hand, is at

Medea-levels of vengeance-madness. If it's Cersei, well, it's an open question whether love of her brother or love of her son takes precedence.

What if everyone dies? Fighting men can get carried away, and now there's a huge damn mess on the floor of the throne room and no one's clear about who's in charge. Littlefinger does the awkward-collar-pull gesture, Stannis praises R'hllor, both Robb and Tywin are furious (but don't really have many options at this point), and the war goes on.

Book vs. Show

The show played this one pretty straight, so nothing to discuss here. Better luck next time!

ARYA IV

"The first sword of Braavos does not run."

Synopsis

Ser Meryn Trant and five Lannister guardsmen attempt to capture Arya Stark during the attack on the Tower of the Hand. Thanks to Syrio Forel's sacrifice, Arya manages to escape to the stables, where she recovers Needle and kills a stableboy who attempts to turn her in for a reward. She vanishes into the depths under the Red Keep.

Political Analysis

"Arya IV" contains one of my favorite set-pieces in all of *A Game of Thrones* – Syrio's duel with the Lannister guardsmen and Ser Meryn Trant – and it's clearly one of George R.R. Martin's favorites, since the episode he penned for season one included this scene and not, say, Ned's beheading. However, it's one that I don't think the fandom has really grasped correctly, for reasons I'll get into later.

Syrio's death – before we discuss the fight scene, we have to discuss Syrio's fable. Naturally for a figure who might as well have a handwritten sign by Joseph Campbell spelling out "THE MENTOR" hanging around his neck, Syrio's last lesson to Arya is to import to her that the "heart of it," the quality that makes one a true swordsman, is "the true seeing," the ability to distinguish between our romantic expectations that a great lord should own a "fabulous beast" and the mundane reality we live in. Given the way in which magic and storytelling are so linked throughout folk culture, the ability to tell the difference between the story and the reality is the ultimate power (it's not an accident that Campbell emphasizes self-knowledge over and over again).

And the critical importance of "true-seeing" is demonstrated immediately: Arya is immediately confronted with a situation in which she's presented with the appearance of authority (Lannister guardsman and a "Sworn Brother of the Kingsguard") and has to divine the truth – that Lord Stark wouldn't send Lannister guardsmen in place of Stark men, and that wearing a white cloak doesn't make you a good guy (these hints are getting a bit anvilicious on the fifth re-read). It is this skill that will guide Arya throughout her deconstruction of the Hero's Journey - Arya alone sees Jaqen H'gar for who he is and of what use he can be made, Arya can look through the illusions of the House of Black and White, and so on and so on. This lesson, more so than the actual art of swordsmanship, is Arya's secret weapon.

Which gets me to the death of Syrio Forel - because Syrio Forel is dead, and has to be dead, and would probably be offended if someone tried to bring him back to life. In a dramatic sense, Syrio has to die because he's the Mentor - and the Mentor always dies in the hero's journey to raise the stakes (since the hero is now alone and unprotected), but also to allow the hero to begin her process of maturity and becoming independent (since the hero now has to stand on her own two feet without hints). Think Obi-Wan Kenobi, or Yoda, or Pa Kent, or Gandalf, or Dumbeldore, or Merlin. More importantly, think Eddard Stark, Yoren of the Night's Watch, and Jaqen H'gar (at least, symbolically), all fathers or substitute fathers whose deaths mark the evolution of Arya's story and her character.

Moreover, Syrio's death perfectly fits with Martin's dramatic sensibilities - the entire fight is symbolically a clash between the outnumbered and outgunned plucky underdog and the big bully, between the elegance and beauty of the art of the sword and the crude reality of steel swords and plate armor, between doing the right thing and taking the consequences and doing the wrong thing for base profit. In a more pandering work, Syrio would win because most people have been on the underdog's side for the most part in their lives and want to see the wealthy and the powerful get their comeuppance (hence pretty much every sports movie or slobs-vs.-snobs movie ever made). But Martin is something of an existentialist when it comes to drama - what matters is that Syrio stands up for the right and defies evil, even when that means facing a knight of the Kingsguard with a broken practice sword, not that Syrio succeeds. (Look at a lot of Martin's set-pieces: what matters is that Tyrion chooses to go out and fight for King's Landing, not whether he actually succeeds; what matters is that Jaime chooses to dive into the bear pit, not whether he slays the bear; and so on.)

Which brings me to why Syrio would want to be dead - because in this moment, this former First Sword of Braavos-turned-dancing master, far from his home, is offered a beautiful death (in Greek, *akalos thanatos*). He gets to be the champion of right and the beauty of his craft, and to save a child from imprisonment and possible death. He gets to go down swinging against impossible odds, with the chance to humiliate one of the Kingsguard. He gets to become, in the mind of one girl and any man who comes out of that room alive, a legend. Survival means that, one day, Syrio Forel's feet will lose their nimbleness, his sword arm will forget its strength, and he will likely die of old age, alone and unremembered. Why would anyone want to take it from him?

The attack on the Tower of the Hand – a second key thing that happens in this chapter is that the Tower of the Hand is attacked – we know that five men are sent to capture Arya, and we see that an unknown number were dispatched to deal with the remaining 12 Stark guardsmen protecting the Hand's daughter, with one casualty. Which I think helps to complicate the picture of the coup – rather than being able to concentrate her forces in the throne room, Cersei had to divide them, some to the throne room, some to the Tower of the Hand, some to the city gates, and some to the docks.

In that context, we can see how genuinely narrow Cersei's manpower advantage was. Had the gold cloaks simply stayed out, it's quite possible that Eddard and Renly could have overpowered the Lannisters by concentrating their forces and aiming them straight at Cersei and Joffrey. It also explains how Arya is able to escape in the chaos of the attack.

Speaking of which – this chapter marks the first time that Arya kills someone, and it's noteworthy that she kills not a Lannister soldier but a commoner boy whose death is as sudden, pitiful, unnecessary, and traumatic as it can get, complete with "accusing eyes." This is important to note, because who Arya kills and why is going to become a crucial measuring device for how her story is not going to follow the classical hero's journey.

Historical Analysis

In previous chapters, I've compared Arya to famous women warriors to get some basic questions about gender and violence out of the way before we get into the heart of Arya's storyline. However, at this point, a decidedly non-militant comparison arises: Anastasia, or, to be more precise, the Grand Duchess Anastasiya Nikolayevna Romanova. Like the historical Anastasia, Arya is going to disappear and become an instant mystery, with both Starks and Lannisters and Brienne of Tarth all trying to figure out where she went to, complete with impostors trying to fill the hole she left.

What's interesting about the Anastasia thing, apart from the way in which romanticism went hand-in-hand with a particular revisionist history of pre-Bolshevik Russia, is how old this phenomenon is, dating back to an earlier era when the person of the monarch was more important, when ideas about divine right had more prevalence, and when the lack of ubiquitous photography made it easier for people to believe that some con artist might actually be the long-long whoever. After Richard II was executed, Henry IV faced more than one rebellion in which a figure purported to be Richard II was used as a symbolic figure to inspire loyalists; during the reign of Henry VII, a number of impostors popped up, including a Lambert Simnel who claimed to be, at various times, Richard III or the son of George of Clarence, a Perkin Warbeck who claimed to be Richard, Duke of York (the younger prince in the tower) and who attempted two separate rebellions before being unmasked as Flemish, and so on and so forth.

The reason why any of this is more than an amusing historical footnote is that it points to the way in which the image of a king, the name itself, can be a thing of power. In *Henry IV, Part 1*, the Welsh wizard and rebel Owen Glendower boasts to Harry Hotspur that he can "call spirits from the vasty deep"; the skeptical Hotspur, fighting over how to divide the kingdom should their rebellion succeed and worried about their forces for the coming battle, replies, "Why, so can I, or so can any man, but will they come when you do call for them?" Some names work better than others, and it really should come as no surprise that men will rise in the north at the name of "the Ned" and his daughter.

What If?

I really only see one hypothetical in this chapter (aside from the inevitable and unpleasant question of death):

What if Arya had been captured instead of escaping? One of the major tensions in *A Song of Ice and Fire* following this chapter is how Arya's disappearance prevents the possibility of peace, first by preventing Tyrion from genuinely following through on any offer to trade the Stark daughters for Jaime Lannister, and, second, by ultimately undermining the possibility of some kind of reconciliation between the Stark north and the Lannister south through some legitimate dynastic marriage. Arya being captured would make that more likely, but not necessarily probable – as I'll point out later, the children-for-Jaime trade was doomed from the start.

Book vs. Show

There's not much to say here, because this scene is beautifully shot and written by George Martin himself. So let's just enjoy the moment.

SANSA IV

It was not supposed to happen this way. She had to wed Joffrey... she had even dreamed about it. It wasn't fair to take him away from her on account of whatever her father might have done.

Synopsis

Sansa is summoned before the queen and the small council and informed of her father's treason. She is then browbeaten into sending a series of letters to her family to tell them to come to King's Landing if they want to be seen as loyal.

Political Analysis

If "Sansa I" through "Sansa III" are a deconstruction of romantic medievalism, then "Sansa IV" is right at the boundary between the romantic illusion and the awakening to the horrific realities behind the fairy-tale world of brave knights, beautiful maidens, and just kings and queens. And, yet, Sansa hesitates at the threshold of enlightenment throughout the chapter, even when one would think that the evidence of dead bodies piling up around her would require her to keep moving, which is a big part of why some people reading the books get so annoyed with Sansa (outside of those whose dislike is driven by misogyny).

However, as I've argued, Sansa is something of a stand-in for the reader as the subject of critique – just as Martin was implicitly saying that fantasy fans are like Sansa in that they prefer to believe in a make-believe world that ignores the inherent exploitation and inhumanity of the feudal system that's part and parcel of the medieval world, I think Sansa's actions here are, at least in part, critiquing people's heroic fantasy of how they'd deal with crisis, and the subconscious fear that the reader would act like Sansa has a good deal to do with why some readers react so negatively to this part of her story.

Whether we're talking about any number of historic atrocities or something as recent as the spree-shooter scenario, people want to believe that they'd be cool under fire, that they'd take down the shooter or stand up against tyranny, when the reality is... that people differ. In a crisis, some people act heroically (with no guarantee of success), some people act cowardly, some just freeze – and your chance of survival has much more to do with luck than any part of your character. And as we've seen over and over again, the reality is that people living in the midst of horror can and do delude themselves and buy into absurd fantasies rather than to confront the reality of their own helplessness.

But so intently do people need to believe that the human spirit always triumphs over adversity that it's become a completely cliche element of origin stories. In some ways, both Arya and Sansa are critiques of this cliche – Arya gets the classic hero's journey tropes (the sword, the mentor, the magic coin, etc.) but none of it gives her the self-knowledge that brings about agency and control over one's environment; Sansa suffers the realistic scenario of victimization and passive survival.

We can see the slow arrival of reality in Sansa's world throughout this chapter. The description of the battle for the Tower of the Hand focuses on the question of realism with laser-like precision: "Somehow, knowing that the fighting was real made all the difference in the world. She heard it as she had never heard it before, and there were other sounds, as well, grunts of pain, angry curses, shouts for help, and the moans of wounded and dying men. In the stories, the knights never screamed nor begged for mercy." And, yet, the Sansa that hears all of this still believes that Jeyne's father is fine and that the queen will fix all of this, and sees Jeyne as a child for not understanding how the rules work. Likewise, after the second day of complete silence, Sansa still dreams of marrying King Joffrey. Finally, when her father's situation is revealed to her, Sansa believes that her marriage to her "gallant prince" is the way things are supposed to happen and that everything can be fixed.

Sansa's decision to agree to Cersei's demands are ultimately motivated as much by her desire to keep believing in a world in which things happen the way they're supposed to as they are by her desire to help her father, and the humanness of that choice is something that's hard to accept.

Two days of silence – one curious thing that happens in "Sansa IV" is that there's a strange period of two days when "the silence of the grave had settled over the Red Keep," which is broken by the tolling of the bells for the death of King Robert – to the surprise of Sansa. This is somewhat puzzling; yes, Eddard hid the news about Robert's death from his kids, but was it really a secret from the rest of King's Landing?

In either case, why hide the evidence of Robert's death – given that Cersei's entire narrative of her counter-coup is that Eddard attempted to "steal Prince Joffrey's rightful throne… the moment the king was dead." Ned's coup and Cersei's counter-coup were hardly secret – if Sansa could hear the dying, pretty much everyone in the castle could do the same, and it's not unlikely that parts of the city could hear, as well. Likewise, it's completely impossible that someone out of the hundreds of servants and gold cloaks and Lannister guardsmen who witnessed the events didn't spread the word about what happened, even in the form of unreliable gossip.

Moreover, I don't understand what the utility of this decision was – the start date of reigns was historically vital, and kings were very particular about these things. Henry VII, for example, officially dated his reign from the day before the death of King Richard III at Bosworth Field in order to place everyone who had sided with the then-reigning monarch as traitors in law, allowing him power to fine and imprison them at his pleasure, thus aiding his drive to place the nobility of England under the heel of the monarch. I just don't see how advancing the date of Robert's death helps Cersei and Joffrey.

Or maybe I'm just over-analyzing an unimportant detail.

The interview – what's much more important is Sansa's interview with the queen and the heart of the small council (Littlefinger, Pycelle, Varys), the real meat of the chapter. It's an interesting scene in part because it's the first time that we see Cersei interacting with the core of the small council (Martin pointedly describes Littlefinger as sitting at Cersei's left hand, Pycelle kept at the end of the table, and Varys hovering above), a political dynamic that will essentially dominate *A Song of Ice and Fire* until Cersei's being deposed in *A Feast for Crows*, and how the major conspirators are going to interact in "public" outside of Eddard Stark's presence.

Littlefinger be creeping – Littlefinger's presence here really defies the stereotype of the immaculate mastermind. To begin with, Littlefinger is openly creeping on Sansa, to the point where "she could feel Littlefinger staring. Something about the way the small man looked at her made Sansa feel as though she had no clothes on." Even Cersei notices how weird he's acting when he openly states that "she reminds me of the mother, not the father... Look at her. The hair, the eyes. She is the very image of Cat at the same age." He might as well be carrying a cue-card around with him that says, "I am obsessed with getting back teenage Catelyn Tully because I am not dealing well with teenage drama, and I am motivated by an intense desire to revenge myself against those who wronged me." Hence his ludicrous comment that Eddard Stark's sons don't matter, but "Lady Catelyn and the Tullys" should be feared – yet more evidence that Littlefinger is not acting rationally here.

The second important thing he does is to take possession of Jeyne Poole, and the coolness with which Cersei basically sells a child into sex slavery as long as it's not done "in the city" is quite disturbing. However, the fact that Littlefinger asks for Jeyne Poole at this point is significant – he's beginning to set up his plan for a fake Arya that will be put into effect in *A Feast for Crows*, over a year later. I honestly doubt that Littlefinger was planning to have the fake Arya married to the Boltons in order to expose her once he got Sansa married to Harry the Heir; rather, he was just thinking that a fake Arya would be useful in many different future scenarios (a potential peace offering to the Starks that would work long enough to get Jaime out of custody? A source of intelligence on Winterfell itself? A bargaining chip to win the support of a powerful, unmarried lord to be named later?), especially if Arya was dead, and realized that he could manufacture Jeyne into something useful.

Finally, there's an interesting little moment where he gets snippy with Cersei when she tells him to keep his sex-slaving out of the city, which brings up an interesting question: was this around the time that Littlefinger had asked for Sansa's hand in marriage? We know from Cersei's chapters in *A Dance with Dragons* that Littlefinger asks around the time that Ned Stark is alive and in prison, but that Cersei turns him down because "he was much too lowborn." Given that Littlefinger likely turns against Cersei at this point by influencing Joffrey into having Eddard Stark executed, it may well have been the case that what Littlefinger wanted in return for the gold cloaks was Sansa's hand in marriage (which, in combination with the later Harrenhal deal, would have allowed him to rise in the ranks of the nobility and protect himself if the Starks ended up on top). Cersei turns him down, which prompts Littlefinger to go to Plan B (have Ned executed, exacerbate the civil war, prevent Sansa from being traded away by Cersei).

(Addendum: interestingly, Littlefinger stays out of the discussion about the letters altogether.)

Pycelle, the bad cop – as someone who's one of the worst conspirators in King's Landing and generally out-of-the-loop, Pycelle takes a very prominent role as Cersei's bad cop – providing false testimony of Eddard's treason, arguing against the marriage to Joffrey on the grounds that "a child born of traitor's seed will find that betrayal comes naturally to her," backing up Cersei on Sansa's letters, and, in general, being an unctuous presence. And unlike Littlefinger and Varys, he's largely unaware of the larger meta-conspiracies at work (outside of his suppositions about Cersei's children and Jon Arryn).

What makes Pycelle's presence here especially irritating is the sheer hypocrisy of his tirade against treason. After all, this is a maester who routinely breaks his vows of chastity, a doctor who violated the precept of "first, do no harm" by stopping an effective regimen and allowing Jon Arryn to die of neglect under his care, and a member of the small council who repeatedly betrayed his vows of loyalty to the Iron Throne, first to King Aerys, then to Jon Arryn and Ned Stark.

Varys playing the long game – as is his wont, Varys holds back for the most part - he's the first one to declare Ned Stark a traitor, a clear sign that he's accepted the new regime at least publicly, but unlike Cersei and Pycelle, he doesn't verbally work over Sansa to get her to agree. He shows some sympathy to Sansa, but from a position of "helpless distress," and doesn't get in the way of Cersei's objective here.

Interestingly, we know that Varys has got his hands on Eddard Stark's seal – which is something that hasn't really come up much, but could be potentially quite valuable down the road. Given Varys's skills at mummery and forgery (back when he was "returning" people's letters in Pentos), he could easily produce a carefully edited version of Ned Stark's "last testament" backing up Tommen's bastardy as a way to discredit the Lannister/Baratheon claim on King's Landing just as Aegon VI brings his army to bear.

Cersei's gambit – what's curious about Cersei's gambit here is how much effort she's putting in to browbeating a child into sending these letters – after all, if the larger point (as Catelyn will describe it later) is to remind Robb and Catelyn that she's got Sansa and Eddard under her thumb in order to cow them into quiescence, she could easily send that letter herself without the need for this playacting.

Indeed, her whole strategy here is a bit odd – to give Cersei credit, she's at least suggesting the outline of a modus vivendi (that they'll let Ned go and marry Sansa to Joffrey if the Starks play nice), rather than attempting all-out war against both the Baratheons and the Starks. However, her modus vivendi couldn't possibly stick.

To begin with, as Cersei well knows from her father, a great house simply cannot allow their members to be treated like this – to allow the Lannisters to assault their head of house, arrest him, and then to hold their children captive, is to announce to the world that House Stark is weak and can be attacked without retaliation. Moreover, there's the fact that Tywin and Jaime have attacked the riverlands – the extended family of the Starks has spilled blood and lost lands, treasure, and men to the Lannisters, and that's equally hard to ignore. And there's also the fact that Arya is still missing and Cersei can't give her back, which is rather crucial.

At the same time, Cersei knows that Stannis is out there and Renly's escaped to Highgarden – if Eddard lives and heads for the Night's Watch, the word is going to get back to Robb and Catelyn about the whole incest thing. Given what Cersei's done to their family, they're going to believe the worst about him, especially if Ned's willing to bend his honor enough to confirm when they hear from Stannis. So, at the most, Cersei's bought herself a few months.

However, the call to come to King's Landing and bend the knee in person doesn't quite fit the model of Cersei the peacemaker. Given what Aerys did to Rickard Stark, and now what's happened to Eddard Stark, the whole of the north is going to see that command as essentially an order of execution. Either Cersei knows that this is how Robb and Catelyn will see it and doesn't care – either because she's underestimating the power of the Starks and thinks they're too cowed to react like a Lannister would in the same scenario, or because she wants to somehow get them to fight a limited war because she's got hostages – or she's really badly misjudged the political situation.

And the saddest thing of all is that this is the height of Cersei's political control over the situation – the Starks, Baratheons, Tyrells, and Tullys are still largely hypothetical enemies, her enemies in the capital are in chains, and her family is too far away to take her power away from her. It's all down-hill from here.

Historical Analysis

So, in the grand game of historical parallels, I've previously rather briefly suggested that Anne Neville is a good fit for Sansa. Given the situation that Sansa finds herself in, I thought I'd explore this parallel a bit more. The thumbnail sketch is that both women were daughters of powerful northern lords who became the center of a rebellion against a powerful queen whose son the lords claimed was a bastard and lacking in royal blood, and that both women found themselves divided between the two sides of the war (Anne married both Lancastrian and Yorkist princes, Sansa is engaged to Joffrey and then married to Tyrion, who, in many ways, resembles Richard III).

However, the point I want to emphasize is that both women were at one and the same time a symbol of power, desired as heiresses to the north when the male line was extinguished in war, and very much at the mercy of the powerful feudal powers around them. Richard Neville was not known as the Kingmaker for nothing, and very much positioned himself as the pivot of English politics, using his family as bargaining chips – at least according to some sources, Anne was engaged or was intended to be engaged to Richard, Duke of Gloucester (the future Richard III) when her father wanted to unite the Houses of York; when he changed sides and allied himself to Margaret D'Anjou and the Lancastrian cause, Anne was married to a stranger, Prince Edward of Lancaster. A year-and-a-half later, she was married to Richard of Gloucester, although here it seems Anne had some agency in the matter and wanted the match.

Likewise, Sansa's marriage to Joffrey, however much initially desired on romantic grounds, is ultimately decided by questions of dynastic alliances in the crypts of Winterfell. Following the death of her father, when she very much would like to be rid of Joffrey, she doesn't have much of a choice. Her marriage to Tyrion is the very definition of unwilling, and it's unlikely that her wedding to Harry the Heir will be much better.

Hopefully, Sansa will end more happily than Anne, but it'll take some luck and some smarts... as we'll see down the road.

What If?

Given that not a lot happens in this chapter, there's only scope for a few hypothetical scenarios I see here.

What if Sansa had dug in her heels? Let's say that, for whatever reason, Sansa decides not to send the letters and sticks to it. On the one hand, this isn't going to change much with Robb and Catelyn; Robb's going to march for King's Landing no matter what letters Cersei sends. On the other, it might change some things with Sansa and Cersei. After all, Cersei's paying a lot of attention here to how pliable Sansa's going to be (because if Sansa actually becomes a hostage-bride, she needs to make sure that her son isn't going to get assassinated on his wedding night), so a bad response might mean that Sansa comes in for more strict captivity to break her spirit – ironically, saving her from Joffrey's tender mercies.

What if Cersei had agreed to Littlefinger's request? This is extremely unlikely, but let's say Littlefinger was more forceful in his negotiations with Cersei, and Cersei, caught in between a rock and a hard place, sells off Sansa. To begin with, this now means that Littlefinger is either a potential lord of Winterfell, replacing the hypothetical Tyrion, or protected from the wrath of a vengeful King Robb if the Starks are victorious – a nice win-win for Littlefinger. If he can scoop up Harrenhal as per OTL, then arrange for Lysa's death, then become Robert Arryn's guardian as his "good-uncle," then he's really getting close to being the pivot point in the War of the Five Kings. However, it also means that Littlefinger will have to head up north to claim his territory there, and that's not going to be easy for a man who doesn't have the military training of a Bolton.

However, it also means that Catelyn's behavior might be altered – if she realizes how much Littlefinger betrayed her (unlike in the show, Catelyn doesn't really confront this fact in the books), she might be the only person in Westeros who could figure out Littlefinger's behind the whole war. Likewise, if it's known that Sansa is essentially lost to her, she probably doesn't make her disastrous call at the end of *A Clash of Kings*, which might mean that the Starks might avoid the Red Wedding by trading Jaime back to Tywin.

What if Jeyne Poole hadn't been given to Littlefinger? One really has to step back and admire George R.R. Martin's intricate plotting when you realize that he set up, in a seemingly inconsequential line in the very first book, the fake-Arya plotline that will be so pivotal to the main plot of his fifth book – because Jeyne Poole is really the only possible candidate for a fake Arya. And without a fake Arya, things become very interesting, indeed. Once Sansa disappears and Tyrion's attainted, there really isn't a fig leaf of continuity that Tywin can throw over the Bolton takeover. While this does mean that "Ned's girl" isn't quite the rallying cry she is in OTL (which, in turn, might spur Manderly to be more proactive in getting Rickon off of Skagos), it also means that Roose Bolton loses much of the legitimacy that allowed him to bring the Dustins, Ryswells, Lockes, Stouts, and half the Umbers into his mistrustful coalition. Thus, when Stannis makes his move, Roose is likely down to little more than his own house and the Frey expeditionary force.

However, in an impressive display of the butterfly effect, this changes events at the Wall much more profoundly – without Jon Snow's "sister" in harm's way, there's little need to have Mance Rayder saved and then sent to Winterfell. In turn, this means that much of the information in the "Pink Letter" remains valid, which, in turn, may rob the conspiracy against Jon of its justification/catalyst for a coup d'etat, given that Jon Snow would have much, much less reason to openly betray his vows and march south.

Book vs. Show

This scene in the show, while well-acted, really does suffer from the lack of internal monologue, given that much of the meta-plot in this chapter is about how Sansa's viewpoint is or isn't changing after the attack on the Tower of the Hand. Likewise, some of the machinations are changed here – Littlefinger argues that "she's an innocent – she should be given a chance," which indicates his interest in Sansa but didn't happen in the book; Varys is much more silent than he is in the chapter; and so forth.

The major change is that, rather than have the emphasis for Sansa's motivation to write Cersei's letters be her desire to maintain the world in which she's still going to marry Joffrey, there's much more of an emphasis on Sansa trying to save her father, which makes her actions more understandable and sympathetic than in the text.

However, given that Martin himself wrote this episode, maybe he's trying to make a point to the fanbase.

JON VII

Let it burn... gods, please, please let it burn.

Synopsis

The bodies of two of Benjen Stark's ranging party are found and brought back to Castle Black in clear defiance of the collective subconscious and genre awareness. Jon learns of his father's imprisonment and the death of the king, and attempts to frag Alliser Thorne. While under house arrest, Ghost warns him of the approach of evil, and Jon ventures forth to do battle with a wight with poor understanding of personal space and hygiene, saving a nude Jeor Mormont in the process.

Political Analysis

I somewhat hesitate to describe this section as "political," since it doesn't particularly describe this chapter particularly well, but since the Night's Watch is a public institution and this chapter does bear somewhat on how the Night's Watch deals with its most ancient enemy, I suppose it fits (besides, it's too late to change the format now).

The Benjen mystery – the first major thread of the chapter picks up right where the last Jon chapter ended, with the discovery of the two dead men from Benjen Stark's ranging. The discovery of Othor and Jafer Flowers constitutes one of the few pieces of evidence of the extended missing-persons case that is this storyline in *A Song of Ice and Fire*, so we should examine this closely. Here's what we learn in this chapter:

1. **Benjen Stark's group of rangers separated at one point.** We don't know under what circumstances – they could have been attacked, and Othor and Jafer were captured/turned into wights, but the rest escaped; they could have all been turned, but only these two are sent back (see the *Book vs. Show* section for more on this); they might have been sent back as messengers or fled as deserters and were intercepted; etc. But this fact seems important to me: it suggests something more than the whole ranging party being wiped out (which would be a bit

repetitious, given what happens to the other rangings). Benjen et al. encountered something that required two parties of rangers important enough to warrant the danger of dividing an already-small group.

2. **Whatever killed these two rangers happened far away.** As the lord commander notes, one of the two men had a signal horn on him that wasn't heard to blow. Now it's possible that "no horn was blown," but from context it seems more likely that George R.R. Martin put this in here to give a hint about distance. A human voice from a good elevation can be heard for about a mile, and using a hunting horn will amplify that distance to two miles. Between this and *CSI*-Sam noticing that there's no blood on the ground, these men were not attacked within a day's ride from the Wall. Given that Mormont's Tommy Lee Jones in the *Fugitive*-style search doesn't turn up anything, we know it wasn't within 34 miles of the Wall, either. While we can't trust Craster's word further than we can throw him, it's clear they got killed somewhere north of Whitetree – my guess is that they were attacked somewhere between the Fist of the First Men and that abandoned village.

3. **These men were not directly killed by White Walkers, but were clearly turned.** We've seen White Walkers in combat way back in the "Prologue," and they use ice swords, not recognizable axes. This chapter suggests one of two possibilities – that they were set on by wildlings (or, possibly, turned wildlings) or that Othor was turned and then killed Jafer Flowers. Both are quite plausible – we know from the "Prologue" and, later, from Jon's time with Mance Rayder that wildling camps have been attacked and turned, but the nightmare scenario of a zombie outbreak-like iterative turning process, where first one ranger and then another succumbs and then turns on his fellows, is quite compelling. What's interesting is that it makes a break in the pattern of White Walker behavior – in the "Prologue," while wights are used to lure in Night's Watchmen, the White Walkers themselves emerge to "play" with their victims. Here, they seem to be acting in a more standoffish fashion – as happens again with the Fist of the First Men. I don't know why their behavior changed, but it does make me curious.

4. **It's possible there are survivors other than Benjen.** Especially in Martin's series, one has to abide by the rule that "no body, no murder." If Martin had wanted to make it clear that the entire group was dead, he could have very easily added more wights – as the TV show does. However, within the book canon, I think it's quite possible that some of the four rangers who went with Benjen may show up in a forthcoming Bran chapter to let us know what happened here.

It's not very much to go on – but it's all we get until Jon gets to the Fist of the First Men, so we'll have to be content with the evidence as it stands.

The Others – the second major thread in this chapter concerns the Others, because, aside from Sam's storyline in *A Storm of Swords*, this is one of the few times we get to see the Others in action up close and personal and learn what the Night's Watch actually knows about their primordial enemy… which turns out to be not much.

Certainly, there is no conscious recognition that these corpses are something other than natural, despite the ample physical evidence that something is deeply wrong with bodies that don't bleed or smell and that their eye colors have changed. However, the Night's Watch does seem to have preserved a collective unconscious memory of the great enemy: "'Burn them,' someone whispered. One of the rangers – Jon could not have said who. 'Yes, burn them,' a second voice urged." Given the way in which Jon is about to step forward as a heroic figure at the end of this chapter, it's telling that it's the unnamed and unknown common soldier, the ranger who's seen things out beyond the wall, who remembers. Deep down somewhere in their DNA, the Watch still clings to their original mission.

The Watch does learn some things about the wights when they encounter them: their blood clots and dries, they don't smell like corpses (at least during the day*… more on this in a minute), they don't rot (which is a major advantage compared to your standard *Walking Dead* zombies, which have a limited shelf life before their muscle tissue degrades to the point when they can no longer move), their eye color changes to blue (which, given blue eyes aren't rare at all, is likely to be an inconsistent indicator in Westeros), and they absolutely freak out even well-trained hunting dogs and horses. This last is quite significant – both in that the wights potentially eliminate the Night's Watch's advantage in disciplined cavalry, and that the Night's Watch can use animals as an early detection system or weights.

> * One genuine uncertainty is the question of whether the wights are or can be active during the day. On the one hand, the wights are clearly inactive when the Night's Watch first encounters them and then come alive at night, but this raises the question of how much rationality they (or, potentially, their White Walker "handlers," if the Others can exercise that neat a degree of control) have. Are they capable of "playing dead" in order to get brought behind the Wall they can't cross, or did the White Walkers control them with that level of cunning? Certainly, the fact that the wight went for the Lord Commander's Tower suggests some remaining level of rationality remaining inside the former ranger, and Coldhands is clearly sentient (although that

may be due to the intervention of the children of the forest). However, once again, we can't rule out the hypothesis that a White Walker is "directing" Othor to take out the lord commander.

As the budding hero about to slay his first monster, Jon Snow is gifted with a special source of knowledge – Old Nan's folklore, which, in Martin's universe, is a mainline to the true oral history that has preserved the old ways in the face of the maesters' tunnel vision. And what Jon remembers from Old Nan is that "in that darkness, the Others came riding... Cold and dead they were, and they hated iron and fire and the touch of the sun, and every living creature with blood in its veins. Holdfasts and cities and kingdoms of men fell before them, as they moved south on pale, dead horses, leading hosts of the slain. They fed their dead servants on the flesh of human children." Assuming for the moment that Old Nan's stories can mostly be taken at face value – feeding the dead on the flesh of human children seems like an embellishment, given what we've seen of the wights in action – we learn some really interesting details. First, that the Others/White Walkers are sentient and motive-driven, albeit motivated by an omnicidal desire to extinguish all human life. Second, the Others dislike "iron and fire and the touch of the sun," indicating potential weaknesses. We know that iron will break on their ice armor, but we actually haven't seen what happens when an iron blade makes contact with a White Walker's flesh; we know that they avoid fire (hence the nightfires) even if it's not the instant kill that it is with wights; and there's a suggestion that the Others might be nocturnal, which, as I discussed above, could be a huge advantage for the Night's Watch if they can make use of their daylight hours.

At the same time, though, Jon Snow still believes that "the Others are only a story, a tale to make children shiver." Truly, he knows nothing.

He learns quickly when night falls and the wight, Othor, attacks the Lord Commander's Tower. One question I've always had is why Othor killed the guard on Jon's door, allowing Jon and Ghost to get free and save Mormont. It seems a bit *deus ex machina*, a way to get Jon Snow to the right place at the right time to start his hero's journey with a magic sword. The only explanation I've ever been able to think of that doesn't go that route is that the wight started from the bottom of the tower and killed anything standing between it and Mormont.

However, in what is one of the underrated fight sequences in *A Song of Ice and Fire* for sheer horror and a genuine feeling of danger, we learn a lot about the wights. To begin with, the "active" wight gives off a "queer and cold" smell strong enough to make people near them wretch – this suggests strongly that the wights aren't constantly active, which suggests some kind of active/inactive cycle (probably tied to the sun). In part, this helps to explain why the undead horde hasn't hit the Wall yet despite being present at the Fist of the First Men at the beginning of *A Storm of Swords* – if your undead army can only trudge during the night, it limits how fast you can move.

Next, we learn that wights, for all their clumsiness, have an impressive durability even for zombies. Ignoring severed limbs and torn-open stomachs isn't anything new, but limbs remaining animated after being severed is a significant advantage over the standard zombie. Likewise, although evidence is a bit sketchy, it doesn't seem that decapitation particularly works against them, eliminating a standard trump card of the genre. Seemingly, fire is the only thing that works on wights – and, as we see later, fire isn't the most reliable weapon.

Finally, we learn that wights aren't particularly interested in eating people, given the ample opportunity Othor has with the guard and with Jon himself. So we have zombies that don't hunger for brains, which is highly unusual for the genre, which is a great way to make them more threatening to jaded fans. No way to distract the wights – if they're coming for you, they're going to focus on you specifically. One of the few positive notes: no zombie infection prior to death; if you can survive a wight, you don't turn, which is one of the few things that might keep the Night's Watch alive.

Historical Analysis

Surprisingly, zombies not being real means there's a dearth of historical parallels to analyze. Next chapter, however, we're going to get deep into feudal politics.

What If?

As with earlier combats, any time one draws steel with the intent to kill, the timeline can go haywire:

What if Mormont had died? Let's say Jon never leaves his cell, or the guard escapes being killed and won't let Jon out, and Mormont is killed by the wight, Othor. In addition to destabilizing the Night's Watch leadership, this would dramatically reshape the course of future events. To begin with, Mormont's ranging never happens – which means 250+ Night's Watchmen never die, including the core of experienced rangers like Quorin Halfhand, Jon never meets Ygritte and never goes on rumspringa with Mance Rayder. On the downside, the cache of dragonglass is never found and Sam never finds out what kills White Walkers, leaving the Night's Watch with much less information. The

Night's Watch warnings now come with added force; it's not just tales of walking dead, but the lord commander himself murdered by a wight. I also think the Night's Watch would view the wights as more of a threat, whereas, in OTL, there's something of a split between the veterans of the ranging and those who stayed behind. Things just spiral from there – assuming the Night's Watch survives Mance's siege, Jon's not going to be the lord commander, Bran and the Reeds aren't going to get through the Black Gate of the Nightfort, and with a thousand men, the Night's Watch isn't going to give Stannis anything near as much, and so on and so on.

What if Jon had died? This one gets really nuts. Quorin Halfhand's expedition vanishes without a trace, Ygritte dies, the sneak attack on Castle Black may or may not succeed, the Night's Watch potentially falls apart during the siege, it's possible no one can get a majority as lord commander, the wildlings are left to die behind the Wall, Stannis likely seizes most of the Gift and the waycastles outright and then quite possibly is defeated at the Dreadfort thanks to lack of information about the north and Bolton treachery, Mance Rayder is never sent to Winterfell, which means poor Theon never escapes, there's no Pink Letter and no coup, Asha Greyjoy probably isn't captured at Deepwood Motte, and, quite possibly, the world is doomed.

What if there were a zombie outbreak at Castle Black? This is my favorite. Assuming recursive wights, let's say either/or of the above happens, but also Jon/Mormont rises as wights and begin killing. With most of Castle Black asleep behind closed doors, the night-time assault is unrelenting. Let's say a few survivors manage to get the story out – sure, the other waycastles are going to mobilize, but how quickly can they get there? The emptiness of much of the Gift will slow the wights down in terms of snowballing, but it doesn't look good. The really interesting thing is what happens to Robb and Bran here – if the dead have risen, the north doesn't march the wrong way, and the mobilized army will, in all likelihood, rush to the Wall's defense; Mance probably thinks twice about assaulting the Wall, but who knows how the politics will shake out. I doubt the south will initially stop its civil war just because the dead are rising – the riverlands fall to Tywin, and without Robb Stark costing him manpower and time, Tywin can (and needs to) move quickly against Renly and Highgarden, although he's still out-numbered by more than two-to-one. This may mean that Tywin attacks Renly before Stannis does, which would make things very interesting if then Renly dies and Stannis steps in as in OTL. With Tywin as an open foe (remember, he doesn't offer to help people up before he's beaten them down), Highgarden may have no choice but to turn to Stannis for a claimant to the Iron Throne. This sets up the full-on Stannis vs. Tywin war we never really got to see in OTL. If the northern army stays in the north, Balon's invasion is likely redirected, likely to Lannisport (and, maybe, the Reach, as well, but Lannisport has the weaker navy), and now there are no Lannister forces left in the westerlands – does Casterly Rock fall to the wily ironborn?

In short, *chaos reigns.*

Book vs. Show

This is one scene that I felt wasn't done very well in the show – the lack of the dead guard outside his door meant that the horror element didn't really sink in until the fight. Likewise, I felt the blocking of the fight itself (especially the bit where Jon breaks out of the first chokehold), the loss of the animated hand and the fingers in the mouth, and the overall abruptness of the end made Othor's undead presence less otherworldly and frightening and Jon seemed in less danger than in the book.

Certainly, I think the wight special effects got much better by the end of season two/the beginning of season three (although I'm still smarting at the loss of the Battle at the Fist of the First Men), and they have plenty of time to get better at it, given how long it's going to be until we see the wights again. Still, improvement is needed.

Also, the show tacks on an attack at Eastwatch that didn't happen in the book, which may suggest the potential survivors are not important and/or zombies.

BRAN VI

"My lord father taught me that it was death to bare steel against your liege lord... but, doubtless, you only meant to cut my meat."

Synopsis

The Karstarks arrive at Winterfell, joining the Boltons, Cerwyns, Hornwoods, Mormonts, Glovers, Tallharts, and Umbers as the forces of the north prepare for war. Bran and Rickon aren't dealing well with the situation, with Bran uncomfortable with the attention paid to his disability and Rickon falling further into feral child syndrome, with a healthy helping of abandonment issues. Osha gives Bran a warning that Robb's army is marching the wrong way, but it's too late. The Young Wolf is entering the War of the Five Kings.

Political Analysis

"Bran VI" is a rare interesting Bran chapter (to me, at least), in no small part because it focuses not on mythic hero's journeys, dream sequences, or folk tales as per usual, but really gets into the meat of Westerosi politics – and what's especially rare, the politics of the north. Because if it's one thing I want to demonstrate in this chapter analysis, it's that the north has its own game of thrones, equally complex as that in the south.

Robb Stark's crash course in feudal politics – after Robb Stark calls the banners, he rapidly has to deal with the consequences of doing so, consequences that should rapidly disabuse anyone's notion of the north as a land of tough, honorable people who don't hold with sneaky southern ways.

Because the lords of the north haven't just come because of their deep sense of honor – they've come because they want stuff:

> Roose Bolton and Robett Glover both demanded the honor of battle command... Maege Mormont told Robb... she had a granddaughter she would be willing to have him marry. Soft-

> spoken Lord Cerwyn had actually brought his daughter with him... Jovial Lord Hornwood... asked [for] a certain holdfast taken from his grandfather, and hunting rights north of a certain ridge, and leave to dam the White Knife.

As I'll discuss in the *Historical Analysis* section, this is pretty typical of feudal politics, and the waters here are deeper than they first appear. To begin with, you'll notice how often the subject of Robb's hand in marriage comes up; in a kingdom where power is divided between one great house and many lesser houses and in which political relationships are inherently mixed with personal relationships, the standard pre-Southron Ambitions Conspiracy practice of the lords of Winterfell marrying their vassals is a key part of how power is modulated. For the great house, a family member eligible for marriage (especially an heir of the house) allows the lord to make his vassals compete for his favor, keeping them loyal. For the lesser houses, getting one of their own married into the great house means a leg up in internal disputes that the Lord Paramount arbitrates in – and a whole bunch of houses think they can get their hooks into Robb.

We see quite a few examples of what kinds of disputes I'm talking about right there – the holdfast Lord Hornwood wants belongs to someone else, as do the hunting rights. Damming the White Knife would majorly weaken House Manderly, which relies on that river to dominate northern commerce. In a feudal society where power comes from the exchange of land for military service, everything belongs to someone, so the distribution of lands and resource rights is the very coinage of influence but, paradoxically, also the source of conflict (as we'll see when Lord Hornwood dies, leaving his lands up for grabs).

At the same time, "Bran VI" also shows us that the same feuds and divisions we see in the southern kingdoms (the Brackens vs. the Blackwoods, the Florents vs. the Tyrells, the Yronwoods vs. the Martells) also exist in the north in an equally dangerous format. Even before the war begins, "one of Lord Bolton's men knifed one of Lord Cerwyn's," setting up a conflict that will carry forward into the conflict over the Hornwood lands, the Battles of the Green Fork, the Sack of Winterfell, the Ruby Ford, and the coming Battle of Ice. Likewise, "Roose Bolton and Robett Glover both demanded the honor of battle command," and we'll see down the line that Robb's choice between the two men has long-running consequences: Glover supports the eventually-successful strategy of relieving Riverrun and takes Harrenhal by subterfuge, Bolton orders him to his intended death at Duskendale, and Glover will return the favor by allying House Glover with Stannis against the Boltons.

You really have to admire George R.R. Martin's intricate plotting; minor details that seem like mere window dressing in book one set up major, world-altering political events in book three and are still shaping events in book five.

Finally, we can also see that the north has a unique version of the game of thrones, one which none of the major schemers are prepared for. Unlike in the south or, even, in the Vale, the lords of the north don't respect bloodlines above all else; they require personal authority to back it up. Hence the Greatjon Umber testing Robb's strength by "threatening to take his forces home if he was placed behind the Hornwoods or the Cerwyns in the order of march," not because the Umbers have a feud against the Hornwoods or Cerwyns (as we'll see later in *A Dance with Dragons*, the Umbers are happy to work with them), but to see if Robb Stark is really "so green he must piss grass." This is the Reynes and the Tarbecks in microcosm: the authority of the lord has been challenged from below, and all of his vassals are looking to see whether Robb can save face.

One of the reasons why "Bran VI" interests me is that we get a rare glimpse of SmartRobb (as opposed to his evil twin, StupidRobb) in how the acting Lord of Winterfell deals with all of these pushy lords. To begin with, in the face of all of these demands and requests, Robb "answered each of them with cool courtesy, much as Father would have done, and somehow he bent them to his will," without giving them what they want. Robb doesn't choose a battle commander, or marry, or give lands away, which is an impressive political feat for a neophyte. Likewise, when Greatjon Umber openly challenges him, rather than getting angry or drawing his sword, Robb calmly lays out the consequences for the Greatjon's actions in a way that re-emphasizes the lord-vassal relationship, and then unleashes Grey Wind against him – the symbol of House Stark itself, and a potent indicator that House Stark has been chosen by the old gods themselves to be the unquestioned leaders of the north. The result is that Robb instantly quashes Umber's insubordination in front of all his lords.

It's an impressive performance, even compared to the mighty Tywin at the same age; Tywin destroyed two houses and turned their castles into ruins, strengthening himself but weakening the westerlands. Robb converted his upstart vassal into his strongest supporter.

The War of the Five Kings, early stages – we get a little bit of detail about how the War of the Five Kings begins in the north – in almost total ignorance. "Lord Eddard was a thousand leagues away, a captive in some dungeon, a hunted fugitive running for his life, or, even, dead. No one seemed to know for certain; every traveler told a different tale." And, yet, there are some kernels of truth in these stories: King Robert is dead, Eddard's guardsmen were slain, the Baratheons are planning to besiege King's Landing, and Renly did flee south.

When Sansa's letter arrives, the Starks get a little bit more information – that Robert is dead, Joffrey is on the Iron Throne, and that his father and Sansa are prisoners. And, yet, if Cersei thought this would cow the Starks, it has the opposite effect. The Starks remember that "Lady... had gone south, and only her bones had returned. Their grandfather, old Lord Rickard, had gone, as well, with his son, Brandon, who was Father's brother, and two hundred of his best men. None had ever returned." There is no trust between Winterfell and the south, and so Robb "meant to go. Not to King's Landing and not to swear fealty, but to Riverrun, with a sword in his hand."

That last part is critical – Robb is already beginning to form his strategy in the War of the Five Kings. At the moment, the Lannisters are beginning to push into the riverlands, although the Battle of the Golden Tooth and the first Battle of Riverrun haven't happened yet. If Robb Stark wants to rescue Lord Eddard and the two Stark girls, his best bet is to merge his forces with those of House Tully. I estimate that the Tullys have somewhere around 10-16,000 men currently under arms (given what Edmure is able to pull together for the Battle of the Fords later, minus the Freys), although most of them are still in the process of mustering and mobilization. If Robb can muster the 18,000 men he can mobilize in time and join them to the Tullys before the Lannisters can eliminate them as a military threat, then their combined forces would just about equal the 35,000 men Tywin has mustered. From a position of equality, and with the Lannisters needing to deal with larger threats to the south, Robb might be able to force a handover of his family members.

And if it hadn't been for factors completely out of his control, Robb might have succeeded in his limited war aims.

Bran the Cassandra – the other major theme of this chapter is the idea of a failed intersection between the world of the political and the world of the metaphysical. Early in the chapter, Bran notes that he "had always liked the godswood, even before, but of late, he found himself drawn to it even more. Even the heart tree no longer scared him the way it used to. The deep red eyes carved into the pale trunk still watched him, yet somehow he took comfort from that now. The gods were looking over him." One might consider this nothing more than Bran becoming more religious after a major crisis if it wasn't for the fact that, in the same paragraph, Bran thinks he's been "dreaming, and talking with the gods," and once he's done remembering the events of the past day, Osha shows up and explains to him that the old gods are actually speaking to him, that "your lord brother will get no help from them, not where he's going. The old gods have no powers in the south... how can they watch your brother when they have no eyes?"

On one level, this is an alternative Mentor, teaching Bran the secret knowledge that the skeptical, empirical Lewin has denied. However, Osha goes on to emphasize that this information has a purpose – "the cold winds are rising... wights, with blue hands and cold, black hands... [Robb]'s bound on marching the wrong way. It's north he should be taking his swords. North, not south." Unfortunately for Bran, he never gets a chance to warn Robb, because, in tragedies, the prophets are always ignored.

Even if he'd gotten a chance, it's quite probable that no one would have listened, as "Bran VI" shows us the first time that ableism really kicks in for the otherwise-privileged Stark. Repeatedly throughout the chapter, Bran's disability is the source of frustration (when he can't climb and run where he wants to), shame (when he's seen being carried in Hodor's arms), difficulty (getting knocked in the head when Hodor runs through doors), and mockery. Despite Bran's brave attempts to ignore their mockery in a Tyrion-like way, Bran is laughed at by Karstark lancers, the "lords bannermen gave him queer, hard stares... as if they wondered by what right a green boy should be placed above them, and him a cripple, too," and the two Karstark sons openly (if quietly) talk about how it's better to be dead than crippled and that Bran is likely broken in mind as well as body.

Historical Analysis

George R.R. Martin's passion for medieval history really stands out in this chapter, as the depiction of the assembling of a feudal army departs significantly from the de-politicized portrait in most works of fantasy, where honor and duty are unchallenged and traditional obligations between kings and their subjects are seen as sacrosanct – complete with the requisite notions of True Kings, Noble Knights, and other lies that Sansa believed.

Historically, vassals tended to be just as likely to view their liege lord's call to arms in much the same way as rich people today view an ominous letter from the IRS as they would to see it as an honor, unless there was a good chance at plunder. After all, fighting was expensive – the whole point of a feudal contract exchanging land for military service was that the vassal didn't need to be paid or supplied while out on campaign because the land would give them the resources to do that themselves – and it took up valuable time that a knight could be using to kill and rob people on his own time, when he could retain 100% of the loot. Thus, feudal contracts were written in such a way that spelled out exactly how many days service the vassal owed.

For example, in the last writ of summons to a feudal levy in England in 1385, King Richard II summoned 13,734 men to go fight the Scots. These men, consisting of 1/3 men-at-arms (i.e., knights) to 2/3 archers, signed on for a term of between 20-40 days. And by this point in English history, the traditional methods of feudal obligation had already begin to break down – England had abandoned an exclusive reliance on the general feudal levy in 1327, and monarchs increasingly resorted to charging their vassals a scutage tax in lieu of service and hiring professional soldiers. These last levies required payment to induce them to fight, and the 40 days of campaign scheduled cost the modern equivalent of £10.5 million.

If they didn't get paid, or if their time ran out, soldiers would (and did quite frequently) turn around and go back home. All of which means that, in addition to being slow to muster, feudal armies had to be monitored and held together continuously or they could easily disintegrate. This meant that the feudal army was a political entity, because the commanders of the largest units were the biggest lords with the most land, and once one got to a certain level of land and military power, lords began to treat the king less as an overlord and more as a *primus inter pares*. If they didn't get treated with the necessary respect, or if the king turned them down once too often when they asked for some nice bit of conquered land or some looted treasure, they'd not just desert, but might rebel against their lord.

All this is to say, when we talk about the War of the Five Kings, we have to be very, very careful about applying modern military thinking to how we analyze events. As Catelyn Stark reflects later: "this host her son had assembled was not a standing army such as the Free Cities were accustomed to maintain, nor a force of guardsmen paid in coin. Most of them were smallfolk... when their lords called, they came... but not forever." Greatjon Umber's threat here was quite significant – if he goes home, anywhere between 2-3,000 men go home with him. It may well be the case that refusing Roose Bolton a command means that his 4,000 men stay home, or that the Hornwoods will leave after doing the bare minimum if they don't get their holdfast and their hunting rights; at the same time, Robb has to exercise his authority at some point, lest by giving way every time, he abandons all control over his subordinates. Robb has to develop a fine-tuned sense of which demands are drop-dead red lines and which are not, which requires a fine-tuned understanding of the personality, character, and interests of each lord.

Thus, none of the leaders in the war, be it Robb or Renly or Stannis or, yes, even Tywin, can treat their sub-commanders and their soldiers as professional soldiers who follow orders or get thrown out of the army and who earn their paycheck year-in, year-out. This is really significant when we think about the degree of command and control any of these leaders have over their armies during the War of the Five Kings.

Keep this thought fixed firmly in the front of your mind – we'll be coming back to it again and again.

What If?

Speaking of which, many of the hypotheticals in this chapter revolve around some of these difficult feudal negotiations:

What if Robb chose Robett Glover over Roose Bolton? While I've often seen people pose the hypothetical of Roose vs. the Greatjon, I find this comparison to be far more interesting. In the OTL, Robbett Glover is a not particularly prominent minor character who nonetheless is one of the more competent of Robb's generals – he made the right call when it came to relieving Riverrun versus taking Tywin head-on; as best as we can tell, he did well at the Battle of the Green Fork, commanding the center and keeping his forces together during the retreat (avoiding capture, unlike so many northern lords); he successfully captures Harrenhal, one of the greatest fortresses in Westeros; and while he was defeated at Duskendale, there's a limit to what you can do when you're outnumbered and set up for death by your commanding officer. By contrast, Roose Bolton is an outright traitor (although we'll talk later about why and when he changes sides) who, even before murdering his king, seems to have tried to kill as many of the other northerners as he could.

If Robett becomes commander of the northern foot, a huge cascade of changes occurs. The Battle of the Green Fork could change completely, given that the strategic mission was to delay the Lannisters; it's quite possible that, rather than march all the way down to the Ruby Ford (which is near the crossroads) as in OTL, Robett chooses instead to wait for Tywin up the river (and fight a defensive battle, which is a better move when leading an all-foot army against an army with substantial cavalry), meaning that Tywin is further away from the crossroads and potentially can't make it across back to Harrenhal. Barring that, one thing that's definitely butterflied is the pointless loss of 3,000 men at Duskendale and 2,000 men at the Ruby Ford. With 5,000 more men under his command, Robb Stark would have been in a much better position to keep on fighting or to retake the north after the Freys defect. Most importantly, the Red Wedding might be butterflied away altogether; to begin with, Robett might not have heeded Edmure's command to withdraw the 400 Stark men from the Twins, but it might also be the case that neither Lord Walder nor Lord Roose decide to pull the trigger when they'd still be outnumbered 8,000 to 14,000.

What if Robb got married at Winterfell? This one's a bit out there, but if Robb had somehow done poorly in his negotiations with the northern lords (or just decided to for teenager/not-wanting-to-die-before reasons), he might have gotten married to Jonella Cerwyn or Dacey, Alysane, Lyra, or Jorelle Mormont. While this wouldn't have been politically useful, it certainly would have been less damaging than the Westerling marriage – and would have completely butterflied it away, and, with it, possibly the Red Wedding. Worst case scenario at the Crag, Robb has the expected wartime affair and feels like a heel about it and maybe damages his marriage. The more interesting consequence is what happens at the Twins. In negotiations, it's sometimes quite useful to have an external limit placed on you so that you can point to it and say "sorry, I can't agree to that"; Catelyn couldn't have agreed to give away Robb's hand in marriage and Walder probably would have had to ask for something else (probably Edmure) in exchange for his support. However, I would caution people not to assume that Walder put the Red Wedding into action out of spite alone; Lord Frey is a cautious cat, and after the Lannister/Tyrell merger, he was probably looking desperately for any rationale to pull out of the Stark/Tully alliance. However, it does mean that Robb's army doesn't diminish after the Crag: instead of being whittled down by 4,000 men, Robb potentially can bring together an army of 38,000 men when he gets back to Riverrun. While being outnumbered 2 to 1 by the Lannister/Tyrell alliance isn't ideal, it certainly is enough men that a few victories against parts of their forces could bring the two sides down to a rough equality of forces, and enough men to mount a successful defense, especially if he can use the Trident and fortifications like Harrenhal to reduce the enemy's relative strength further below the recommended 3:1 ratio for attackers.

What if Robb marches north? See the previous Jon chapter; the only way this could happen is if there's a zombie outbreak at the Wall. This would totally butterfly away the north's involvement in the War of the Five Kings.

<u>Book vs. Show</u>

This scene is foreshortened considerably in the show, which is probably a positive when it comes to the difference between interesting reading and good TV, but it does mean that you don't get the same sense of these feudal relationships being worked out, and it seems more a personal thing between the grizzled veteran and the youngster. (Also, as far as I'm aware, the Umbers don't have a rivalry with the Glovers in the books; rather, the Greatjon's beef is with being placed behind the Hornwoods and Cerwyns, who seem like lesser houses than the Umbers).

However, it's an excellently-done scene. Richard Madden is an older, more confident Robb Stark and comfortable with pushing back at a vassal who's questioning him; the wolf-work here is really good (although I'd have preferred having the sword come out of the sheath more; it's less clear that the Greatjon actually pulls steel here). Most of all, Clive Mantle is excellent as Greatjon Umber, managing to project seven-feet tall in personality despite being not quite as tall in real life (although 6'6" is pretty good in acting circles). His presence was much missed in seasons two and three of the show, and I really hope the showrunners bring him back for Stannis's storyline in the north in the future.

DAENERYS VI

"The stallion who mounts the world has no need of iron chairs."

"To Rhaego, son of Drogo, the stallion who will mount the world... to him I will give this iron chair his mother's father sat in."

Synopsis

Despite Dany's entreating, Drogo refuses to march west and invade the Seven Kingdoms. Dany visits the Western Market, where she suffers mild peril from a hapless amateur assassin before being saved by Jorah. Drogo changes his mind and gives a stirring *WWF Smackdown* promo.

Political Analysis

Drogo and the Varys/Illyrio Conspiracy - "Daenerys VI" is a slightly unusual chapter for *A Game of Thrones* in that it largely centers around the political side of her story - especially how events in Essos are intersecting with the King's Landing plotline. To begin with, it's interesting that the chapter begins with Dany failing to persuade Khal Drogo of the virtue of crossing "the black salt sea" with "wooden horses with a thousand legs" in order to regain an "iron chair," despite the conversation taking place just after Drogo takes "pleasure" in her. It's a sign, however oblique, that Dany isn't going to fit into the role of a political wife who acts through her husband (in the same way that, say, Margaery excels in), that her skills and her story are otherwise.

This failure is also significant in that Drogo's flat refusal to envision crossing the narrow sea calls into question his part in the Varys/Illyrio Conspiracy: namely, did Drogo ever intend to lead an army to Westeros in the name of his wife and her family? If not, what was the unseen negotiation between Illyrio and Drogo about, even if it wasn't understood as a bargain of a bride for an army? Illyrio's involvement in the exchange is somewhat inexplicable if that last bit wasn't part of the point, given his investment in a Targaryen restoration. On the other hand, while Jorah seems confident that Drogo will change his mind eventually, as "the Dothraki do things in their own time for their own reasons," Drogo's refusal seems quite emphatic.

Given that both Varys and Illyrio are intelligent men, and how far back Varys informed King Robert of the wedding (the best *Game of Thrones* timeline I've seen estimates Varys's information as being passed on six months after the wedding, and it is now six months since that happened), it may well have been the case that Varys and Illyrio had always planned to use a failed assassination attempt against Dany to force Drogo's hand, and that the only difference that the attempts on Bran's life made were to accelerate the timeline somewhat. It would very much fit Varys's style as a conspirator – hands-off to an extreme, using the resources of others to do his work for him while remaining out of sight, and a high degree of precision and delicacy (after all, the attempt has to be both credible but not successful, which is difficult to gauge from a continent away). More on this below where I talk about the assassination.

The egg and the blood of dragons – it's not just a thematic signposting that Dany fails to act as a political wife – it's also a subtly important plot point. It is Dany's sense of frustration and despair that causes her to breathe new life into "the fading memory of a red door" and to once again think of herself as "blood of the dragon... the last, the very last... the seed of kings and conquerors," who cannot ultimately be at home among the Dothraki (again, back to our old theme of assimilation). Daenerys could be content to just be the mother of the stallion who mounts the world, but the dragon cannot be. And it's this feeling that drives Dany to react to an attempt on her life by putting dragon eggs in a charcoal brazier.

It's also telling that, right around when she makes the decision to do this, Dany feels a moment of disassociation, literally "hear[ing] her own voice saying, 'Ser Jorah, light the brazier,'" as if from outside her body and wonders later whether "was it madness that seized her then, born of fear? Or some strange wisdom buried in her blood?" Someone more versed in the darker side of Targaryen history might have answered both, since the Targaryens have shared a common obsession with awakening dragon eggs since the time of Aegon III. Aegon III summoned nine eastern mages to hatch the remaining eggs; his son, Baelor, sought the intercession of the Seven through prayer to no avail; Aegon IV attempted to create mechanical dragons; Aerion Brightflame sought to drink wildfire to become a dragon, and Aerys II may have sought to do the same on a larger scale with his collaboration with the Alchemists' Guild (given Hallyne's comments). Even a "good" Targaryen like Aegon V ultimately destroyed himself and much of his family in the attempt to waken dragons at Summerhall.

Why and how Dany succeeded where they failed is something I'll discuss in the future, but I did find it interesting (given Melisandre's prophecies about Azor Ahai) that Dany thinks that "a dragon was air and fire... not dead stone," which suggests that the stone dragon breathing shadowflame is somehow a perversion of the natural order.

Vaes Dothrak – to set the stage for the major event of this chapter, we are treated to a more in-depth look at Vaes Dothrak as the place where east and west meet: "the caravans made their way to Vaes Dothrak not so much to sell with the Dothraki as to trade with each other." As England was once the workshop of the world, Vaes Dothrak is the world's marketplace. Notably, it's also where commercial culture intersects with gift culture, with neither truly dominating; while Dany believes that the Dothraki may "not truly comprehend this business of buying and selling," it's telling that the Dothraki manage to get themselves paid in salt and silver (two universal commodities of the ancient world) without having to incur any of the normal risks of long-distance trade.

At the same time, we also get something of a portrait of intercontinental commerce. The west (which, in a show of trans-cultural relativism, here includes the Free Cities of Essos's western coast) brings garlic and pepper (spices historically being one of the most profit-intensive-by-volume commodities of the premodern era); Lysene perfumes, Pentoshi dyes, Myrish lace and textiles (the Free Cities' predominance in luxury manufactured goods suggests their advanced economies relative to Westeros, much in the way that the Benelux region outpaced much of the rest of Europe in the early Modern period); Lannisport goldworks (whose relatively advanced manufacturing might explain why Lannisport is a thriving port despite being on the wrong side of Westeros for commercial purposes); and, of course, wine.

In exchange, the East brings exotic animals (manticores, elephants, and the zorses of the Jogos Nhai, who seem to be a semi-nomadic people that live north of Yi Ti); wine, safrron, and jade from Yi Ti; amber and dragonglass from Asshai; spices from Qarth (one of the few products made by a city otherwise built on export-import); and the gods alone know from the exotic cities of Bayasbhad, Shamyriana, and Kayakayanaya. We also get a sense of a truly rich diversity of ethnicities and cultures: the Jogos Nhai are plains-dwelling zorsemen whose moon-singing religion somehow is the largest denomination in Braavos; the people of Asshai are "dark and solemn" but, noticeably, not the same as the Shadow Men who wear tattoos and masks (which corrects the common misconception that Quaithe is of Asshai); the pale people of Qarth, who we'll get to know more of later (their pale skin may be a sign of Valyrian ethnic heritage or not, but it does point to the fact that Essos is incredibly racially diverse, but not predominantly of color as far as we know – a point that will be important when we come to Dany's campaign against the slavers later); the people of Yi Ti, whose queues, jade, and poetry suggest an analogue to China under the Manchu; and Bayasbhad,

Shamyriana, and Kayakaynaya, who seem to have a strong tradition of women mercenaries and body-piercing.

The reason I take the time to describe all of these different cultures is to point out that people who take George R.R. Martin to task for creating a "savage and brutish monolith" in Essos really haven't paid close attention to his writing. While Martin certainly does exoticize the east to an extent (in part, I would surmise because of his love of older historical fiction and fantasy works that borrowed liberally from Orientalist traditions in Western literature), he clearly has paid attention to how his world works and made these cultures far more than caricatures. Essos is a place of staggering diversity, but it's also a continent whose history, geography, culture, and economy are actually logically connected – think of the interactions between Valyrian and Ghiscari cultures and their influence hundreds of years later, or how the Dothraki play such a critical role in creating and maintaining inter-continental trade routes. It's also a place, not to put too fine a point on it, that is materially, economically, and culturally far more advanced than Westeros, and always has been – which means that, as readers, we have to be very, very careful about making assumptions about racial privilege and colonial mentality in a world whose history is not our own.

The assassination attempt – and now to the main event, the assassination "attempt" by the hapless wineseller. I use scare quotes there because of how clearly staged this seems in retrospect: Dany is lured to the market where an assassination attempt is about to take place because Jorah informs her of a caravan of 400 horses under the command of a merchant captain from Pentos has arrived, bearing letters from Illyrio. The moment Jorah gets his letter from Illyrio in private, he knows what's going to happen – pegging this one wine merchant out of a huge crowd as the specific threat to Dany. While Jorah says, "I did not know... until the man refused to drink, but once I read Magister Illyrio's letter," I highly doubt the letter only warned of King Robert's offer. I think the letter quite explicitly named the assassin so that Jorah would save her, thus ingratiating himself with Daenerys and Drogo as Varys and Illyrio's controller on the inside of the *khalasar*. Further evidence of the set-up is seen in the fact that, when merchant Captain Byan Votyris arrives on the scene, "he seemed to know what had happened without a word being spoken."

Another detail that points to the fakery of this attack is how completely incompetent the assassin is – he seems not to recognize Daenerys until she is named right in front of him, he makes a clumsy switch between wine casks, he hesitates and stalls when challenged, he's a terrible liar with a bad case of the flopsweats, and so on and so forth. It all screams patsy.

And keep in mind, this is an assassination attempt by Varys. As we see from *A Dance with Dragons* (and, as I will argue with regards to

Tywin, *A Storm of Swords*, as well), when Varys wants someone dead, he attacks with precision, thoroughness, and utmost stealth. When you see him being this sloppy, you know it's on purpose. And lo and behold, the outcome of this attack is to accomplish precisely what he wanted back in "Arya III" – Drogo changes his policy on a dime and will now invade Westeros.

And what I like about Drogo's oath is that it already sets up the idea that we're not going to get a sanitized, heroic "rightful heir overthrowing heroic usurper" narrative – Drogo comes to give his son the Iron Throne not out of any sense of justice, but because of a personal vendetta; he comes not to liberate Westeros, but to bring destruction, mass rape, slavery, and cultural destruction to its people. And Dany bears full culpability for this.

Historical Analysis

In the past, I briefly compared Vaes Dothrak to Genghis Khan's capital city of Karakoroum. In this section, I'm going to briefly discuss the Silk Road, before focusing more specifically on the history of silver and salt as trade goods.

Historically, the Silk Road is the closest equivalent we have of the way in which Vaes Dothrak unites two continents. First linked up around 130 BC, when the Han Dynasty defeated the nomadic Xiongnu and linked China to the Hellenized Bactrian kingdoms in modern-day Afghanistan (and, thus, to Persia and points west), the Silk Road stretched for 4,000 miles from Turkey to China and lasted as a major trade route for around 1,500 years.

While silk might be quite exotic, the histories of two more mundane commodities – silver and salt – help to explain why the Dothraki take their tribute in these forms (the seed, I'll leave up to your imagination).

In no small part due to its abundance, silver was the practical currency of both the Roman Empire and the Chinese Empire (Rome also used gold, but it tended to be for higher denominations, while the humble silver denarius became so ubiquitous that it serves as the origins of the Spanish dinero, the Arabic dinar, and the d used for British pennies up until 1971). Silver was just rare (and pretty) enough to be widely considered valuable and common enough to serve as a basis for currency (in the second century AD, Rome circulated more silver than all of Europe and the Abbasid Caliphate combined five times over in the 9th century AD). It also posed some of the first problems of trade imbalances in world history – the strong Roman demand for Chinese silks (there's the Silk Road again!) caused a significant drain of silver eastward that frequently destabilized Roman currency values. The Chinese insistence on silver in exchange for tea, silk, and porcelain in the 19th century caused a similar currency drain from Western Europe, which led to the adoption of opium from India as a product that generated its own demand, and then the Opium Wars.

Salt seems a far more humble commodity, but no less influential on world history. Prior to the modern age, with our mass-production systems and easy access to refrigeration, salting was one of the few technologies available to preserve food – which led to it being considered universally valuable. As a result, many fortunes were founded on salt: Rome itself was founded on top of an ancient salt road, which helped the settlement grow from a tiny hillfort community into the master of Italy. The "Old Salt Route" between Lübeck and Lüneburg produced so much "white gold" that it helped to provide the foundation for the Hanseatic League and massively undermined the economic strength of 16th-century Poland, whose prosperity had relied heavily on salt exports. Genoa and Venice fought wars over control of the salt trade; the salt tax (known as the gabelle) was so despised in 18th-century France that it was a leading complaint during the French Revolution. The British East India Company levied a high tax on Indian salt in 1835 to force India to import salt from Britain (where there was a center of salt production in Cheshire), and, thus, the salt tax was one of Mohatma Ghandi's major targets in his noncooperation campaigns of the 1930s.

Needless to say, the Dothraki seem to have a pretty sweet (or is that salty?) deal worked out for them in Vaes Dothrak.

What If?

I only see two conceivable hypothetical alternatives to the events (really, just the event) of this chapter:

What if the attempt had succeeded? In the highly unlikely event that Varys hadn't completely scripted out the wineseller's failure, let's say Dany and Drogo drink the wine as Dany had intended. With both of them dead, the geopolitics of Essos change dramatically. Slaver's Bay is never destabilized with the conquest of Astapor, Yunkai, and Meereen; Varys and Illyrio have to move on their Aegon/Golden Company plan much, much sooner (possibly by maneuvering to try to bring Pentos and/or Tyrosh in on their side, in a recapitulation of the War of the Ninepenny Kings); Volantis doesn't shift towards the tigers; and Euron Crowseye has to come up with a different plan, which potentially makes the ironborn far more dangerous than they are to Westeros in OTL. The metaphysics are more uncertain but more momentous – the dragons are never reborn, which may mean that magic doesn't regain its strength (it's not entirely clear whether they're cause or consequence of magic's revival), which might tip the balance of the Battle of Blackwater Bay, and it may well be that the entire world is doomed.

What if Drogo never decides to go to Westeros? The wineseller somehow kills himself out of pure stupidity, or never sees Dany in the market. Potentially, history changes once again – with a strong enough butterfly effect, Drogo never takes his wound and never encounters Mirri Maz Dur, so he may very well survive – as well might Dany's son. At some point, but much later, the War of the Five Kings gets much, much worse when a Dothraki army lands in Westeros. Many of the same geopolitical forces change, but it may well be that the rebirth of the dragons still happens; after all, blood magic and dragon lore isn't unknown in Westeros.

Book vs. Show

The show did this one pretty much on the nose, with the added wrinkle of showing us Jorah meeting a non-mute little bird (which, WTF?) to make it very clear to show-watchers what's going on with the assassination attempt.

CATELYN VIII

"You have no choice... our best hope, our only true hope, is that you can defeat the foe in the field."

Synopsis

Catelyn Stark and Brynden Tully arrive at Moat Cailin accompanied by the forces of House Manderly, where Catelyn is reunited with her son, Robb, now in command of the northern army. The two of them have a difficult conversation, but come to an understanding about which path the Starks will take.

Political Analysis

"Catelyn VIII" is a crossroads for Robb and Catelyn Stark's relationship, as Robb Stark completes his transformation from a 14-year-old boy to the commander-in-chief of the northern forces in the War of the Five Kings, and Catelyn Stark has to come to terms with that relationship. And in light of how significant parts of the fandom view these characters through polarized lenses (a trend that existed before the HBO show, but increasingly more so after seasons two and three), I think it's important to take a moment to step back and analyze these two characters and their relationship before we plunge headlong (and we're going to plunge deep) into the War of the Five Kings.

It's important because I think the contending Robb and Catelyn partisans have often resorted to caricature in debate, and I don't think it's helpful or necessary to characterize Robb as a bland cookie-cutter fantasy protagonist without an intelligent thought in his head (who should have listened to his mother at every turn) or Catelyn as an eternally-depressed killjoy single-handedly responsible for the destruction of her house. Rather, I would argue that both characters are interesting, complex, and flawed people, but whose strengths and flaws are so often mutually connected, paralleled, and reinforcing, that it doesn't make sense to choose one over the other.

Robb Stark, playing the man's part - I have to admit that in my first few reads through this chapter, I found the portrayal of Robb Stark here to be an annoying reversion to the StupidRobb of old, especially in his display of childish indecision (especially when compared to his self-confidence and directionality seen in "Bran VI"). However, when I came back to the chapter with fresh eyes for this essay, I realized that I had misunderstood what Robb was actually thinking and how that was affecting his behavior in this chapter.

To begin with, I had misunderstood that Rob's uncertainty isn't actually about the war (although things are not going well, and he has reasons for concern, as I'll discuss later), but, rather, about his family: "I brought this whole army together... but I don't... I'm not certain... if we march... even if we win... the Lannisters hold Sansa and Father. They'll kill them, won't they?" When it comes to his military strategy, Robb knows what he wants to do – which I'll discuss in a bit. However, the political side of this, and the key question about what will happen to the Starks that are held prisoner, is completely out of his control and is, thus, the source of his dilemma.

Likewise, Robb is not politically ignorant. To begin with, he understands the meaning of Sansa's letter, and he notes the absence of any mention of Arya. More significantly, he's thinking in geostrategic terms: his immediate aim is to link the Starks and the Tullys together, and one of his first comments to his mother about the political situation is that "I wrote to Aunt Lysa, asking for help. Has she called Lord Arryn's banners, do you know? Will the knights of the Vale come join us?" In other words, Robb's immediate political objective is a quite sound one: to re-assemble the power bloc of the Stark/Tully/Arryn alliance that was the key to victory in Robert's Rebellion. (On a side note: it's quite simply impossible for anyone to have predicted that Lysa Arryn would decisively block the lords of the Vale from going to war against the Lannisters, as they wanted, which is one of the two most influential of Littlefinger's moves in the entirety of the War of the Five Kings to date.)

Most importantly, Robb is clearly thinking about a way to end the war by "a trade of hostages," Tyrion for Eddard and Sansa. Again, it's impossible for Robb to have predicted that his mother (or, more accurately, his aunt) would have let Tyrion escape right when the outbreak of war made him the most valuable. Indeed, it's probable that Robb chooses to attack Jaime at Riverrun (and, especially, to plan out the Whispering Woods) in order to capture Jaime for an exchange of prisoners. In the case of both Tyrion and Jaime, outside forces (aka George R.R. Martin's sense of dramatic timing) interfere at just the right moment in ways that are outside the norms of feudal warfare to prevent any exchange of prisoners.

Catelyn Stark, mirroring indecision – I also changed my mind about Catelyn this re-read. I can certainly see how this chapter would polarize both supporters and detractors of Catelyn, in that she seems to be, on the one hand, running rings around her son intellectually (which makes it understandable why people would find her more interesting than her son in this moment), but also relentlessly undermining him (which makes it understandable why other people might find her an unpleasant point of view to read).

However, in her own way, Catelyn is being as indecisive as her son, in that she both wants Robb Stark to be a man and can't quite bring herself to accept it. From the first moment that she first sees her son for the first time in months, "Catelyn wanted to run to him... and hold him so tightly that he would never come to harm... but here, in front of his lords, she dared not. He was playing a man's part now, and she would not take that away from him." And, yet, the first moment she gets Robb alone, she immediately emphasizes his youth and why he shouldn't be leading the army, saying, "You are 15 now. Fifteen and leading a host to battle," and when Robb replies that there was no one else who could lead the army, she retorts that "who were those men I saw here a moment ago... you might have given the command to any of them... they are men, Robb, seasoned in battle. You were fighting with wooden swords less than a year past."

When Catelyn sees how she's damaging her son's self-confidence with this particular line of argument, she backtracks: "You ought never have left. Yet I dare not, not now. You have come too far. Someday, these lords will look to you as their liege. If I pack you off now, like a child being sent to bed... they will remember, and laugh about it in their cups. The day will come when you need them to respect you, even fear you a little. Laughter is poisonous to you, much as I might wish to keep you safe." And, yet, she seems to have trouble remembering that the same general principle applies not just to Robb and his bannermen, but also between Robb and herself, such that comments such as, "You are my firstborn, Robb. I have only to look at you to remember the day you came into the world, red-faced and squalling," keep undercutting the confidence she tries to install just a moment later.

Likewise, in trying to bolster Robb's confidence by reminding him that, "You cannot afford to seem indecisive in front of men like Roose Bolton and Rickard Karstark. Make no mistake, Robb – these are your bannermen, not your friends. You named yourself battle commander. Command," it doesn't help Catelyn to bring back the earlier topic of his immaturity and youth by saying, "Be certain... or go home and take up that wooden sword again," but she can't seem to help herself.

Weighing the two – ultimately, I think both Robb and Catelyn have points to make. Robb is quite young and is definitely placing himself in danger; as we see with the Red Wedding, the Stark cause is lost if he should fall. And there are some signs that he's letting himself get pushed a bit by his bannermen – as we can see from the way he references Galbart Glover or Bolton or the Karstarks – but, at the same time, this can be over-emphasized. Robb has shown himself capable of ruling his bannermen, as we saw from "Bran VI," and it may well be that his gesturing in their direction is a consequence of Catelyn's appeal to adult experience.

At the same time, though, I think Catelyn is wrong about the major question of their exchange – whether Robb had to lead the army himself. As we saw from "Bran VI," and as Catelyn Stark herself recognizes, these lords are incredibly fractious even in the presence of a Stark who outranks them – putting Roose Bolton, Rickard Kastark, the Glover brothers, Greatjon, or Helman Tallhart, let alone Theon, in charge would alienate and offend the other northern lords, and it's questionable at best whether the lords would be willing to defer to an equal so far away from the eyes of their liege lord. Likewise, the same logic that leads Catelyn to recognize that Robb has to ensure that his men hold him in respect when it comes to the question of whether he should return home or retreat to Winterfell also applies to the question of whether he should have taken command. Despite his age, Robb Stark is the Stark in Winterfell (and, in less than a week's time, he's going to be the lord of Winterfell), and unfair as it might be, he would have always been looked down upon as a coward and a weakling had he sent another man to command in his stead.

The larger point here is that you don't need StupidRobb to have SmartCatelyn and vice-versa. RobbStark is an inexperienced young man trying his best, and Catelyn Stark is a woman with political experience and keen wits who can nonetheless make mistakes of her own (her offer to "take Lord Robert [Arryn] with her, to foster him at Winterfell for a few years," for example, permanently alienates her already-unstable sister, and although we can't hold this against her, either, appointing Rodrik Cassel castellan of Winterfell was ultimately devastating to the Stark cause). Neither of them is perfect or worthless.

The War of the Five Kings: the Lannisters' opening move – you have to hand it to George Martin – he knows how to stack the deck against his protagonists to raise the stakes, and this is no exception. The Starks enter the War of the Five Kings in the worst possible situation: their traditional allies are either incommunicado (the Arryns), politically divided and thousands of miles away (the Baratheons), or almost completely wiped out right at the beginning of the war.

In their opening campaign of the War of the Five Kings, the Lannisters have engineered a nigh-total defeat of the Tullys with just three battles. I slightly differ from BryndenBfish (and Westeros.org) in that I think Tywin split the Lannister forces before Golden Tooth and took the Gold Road through the pass at Deep Den before crossing the hills to hit the Mummer's Ford from the south. My reasoning for this is as follows: to begin with, given how little information the Lannisters could have had about the Tully military situation, a two-pronged assault could have allowed Tywin to respond to a successful riverlands defense at the

Golden Tooth by marching west into their rear, trapping them between the two Lannister armies and attacking from a completely unexpected direction. The alternative would open the Lannisters up to the danger of being bottled up in the pass, where their superior numbers could less easily be brought to bear, giving the Tullys the time and opportunity to mobilize their forces and for the Starks to make it down the kingsroad. Secondly, I think this minor change better fits the text: to begin with, the Battle of Golden Tooth* is emphasized as happening at "the pass" that Vance and Piper are attempting to hold, which would make it difficult, if not impossible, for two armies to have divided just prior; likewise, the description of the battle describes only the "Kingslayer" on the field as opposed to the Kingslayer and Tywin, whereas Tywin is described as "bringing a second Lannister army around from the south" at the same time that "they were battling in the pass," which suggests that he wasn't present.

> * Side point: again, a slight disagreement with BrynedBFish. Not that I disagree that speed and mobility were useful, but the Battle of Golden Tooth pitted 4,000 riverlanders against 15,000 Lannister bannermen. Given this disparity in forces, I think Jaime just attacked frontally and overran them with his superior numbers. Indeed, given how Jaime reflects back on his earlier career in *A Feast for Crows*, I think Jaime's first two battles were simple affairs in which he was able to use superior numbers and then surprise to overwhelm an inexperienced foe, leading him to be overly-confident when facing the Starks.

Instead, Tywin "fell upon" Beric Dondarrion as Beric was crossing the Red Fork, and the element of surprise suggested in that word choice and confirmed later further convinces me that Tywin was not advancing on the Red Fork from the front (and, thus, likely to be seen by Beric Dondarrion's force as they crossed the ford), but, rather, attacked from an unexpected southern flank. Saved from formal attainder by a matter of days, Tywin is then able to bring his army against the southern riverlands, taking Raventree Hall, Pinkmaiden, Stone Hedge, and Harrenhal and keeping them from reinforcing the main Tully force at Riverrun just as Jaime's assault on Riverrun prevents the forces there from moving into Tywin's rear as he marches.

It's an impressive piece of soldiering: in three battles, Tywin has essentially taken out the riverlands as a military threat (with the exception of Houses Mallister and Frey), although Robb won't learn about that for another chapter, and placed himself at a strategic crossroads that allows him to advance north up the kingsroad to block the Starks, southeast down the kingsroad to reinforce the capital should the Baratheons attack, or west on the river road to reinforce Jaime at Riverrun.

The War of the Five Kings: Robb's choice – this defeat complicates Robb's initial strategy to link up with the Tullys, bring himself up to numerical parity with the Lannisters, and then force a battle in which he could seize enough prisoners to make an exchange of prisoners possible. Instead, he's faced with a difficult choice: either "take the battle to Lord Tywin and surprise him" (as the Umbers argue for) or to "go around his army and join up with Uncle Ser Edmure against the Kingslayer" (as the Glovers and Karstarks recommend).

While presentism might make this seem like a very straightforward choice, the reality is that both carried huge risks. "If we try to swing around Lord Tywin's host, we take the risk of being caught between him and the Kingslayer," while being outnumbered by two-to-one and without hope of reinforcements from the Tullys. Likewise, "if we attack him... he has more men than I do, and a lot more armored horse." Eighteen thousand men versus 20,000 men is a narrow enough margin to call it an even fight, but it's just as risky – given the difficulty of destroying an army in the field, the danger is that even if Robb succeeds, Riverrun falls and Jaime is freed up to advance and link up with his father.

It is at this moment that we see the beginnings of Robb Stark as a military prodigy. At this moment, Robb Stark characteristically sees a third option that none of his bannermen have seen – "split our host in two," prevent the two Lannister forces from uniting by putting the Green Fork "between Jaime and Lord Tywin" (given that there's no ford on the Green Fork between the Ruby Ford and the heavily-fortified Twins, if Tywin takes his army over the bridge over the Trident, he either has to go all the way up or all the way back), and then march "down the west bank to Riverrun," which allows him to reinforce on the way to attacking Jaime's army. If this attack succeeds, Robb could double back east on the river road and take Lord Harroway's Town, trapping Tywin between Moat Cailin, the Green Fork, and the bridge over the Trident, potentially knocking out the Lannisters in one campaign.

At the same time, Robb perfectly reads his opponent, realizing that "when Lord Tywin gets word that we've come south, he'll march north to engage our main host," putting more distance between his force and Jaime's. Indeed, when it comes to military strategy, Robb will consistently predict Lord Tywin's actions throughout the war in such a way that Robb can dictate Tywin's responses to his actions, whereas Tywin repeatedly misreads his opponent and has to find a political solution.

Ironically, it may have been Robb's decision (prompted by Catelyn, so they both share responsibility) to choose Roose Bolton that prevented his initial riverlands campaign from ending with the total destruction on the east bank of the Green Fork... more on this in "Tyrion VII."

Historical Analysis

It's at this point that we should discuss the historical analogue to Robb Stark, one Edward of York, later known to history as Edward IV (although, as we'll see in *A Storm of Swords*, Robb's also got strong parallels to William Douglas, the 6th Earl of Douglas, that unhappy lord of the Black Douglases). Edward took command of the Yorkist cause in the worst of all possible circumstances: the Yorkist army had been crushed at Wakefield (more on this in "Eddard XV"), with his father, Richard, Duke of York; his brother, Edmund, the Earl of Rutland; Richard Neville, the Earl of Salisbury (the father of the "Kingmaker," Richard Neville of Warwick... see where Martin gets his repeating names from?); and 2,500 Yorkist men dead on the field, with the rest scattered to the winds.

Edward heard about the defeat while celebrating Christmas at Shrewsbury. Nineteen at the time, Edward IV was now the earl of March, Chester, Cambridge, and Ulster and the duke of York, the largest landholder in England and a wanted fugitive. Safely in the midst of his Marcher territories, York raised an army at Ludlow to meet Margaret D'Anjou as she marched south into England at the head of a Scottish army to meet her Welsh supporters, who were marching east to link up with her and catch the Yorkist upstart before he could link up with Warwick at London.

Acting with instinctive speed and decision, Edward turned his army to meet the Welshmen head-on on his own home ground. On the morning of Candlemas (February 2nd) 1461, his army arrived in Mortimer's Cross, where, in the sky above the Yorkist army, a parhelion of three suns appeared in the sky. As his soldiers stood in bewilderment at this ominous sign, the young lord rode out among his men, persuading them that the astrological marvel indicated a special blessing from the Holy Trinity and a prophecy that the three sons of York (himself; George, Duke of Clarence; and Richard, Duke of Gloucester) were favored by God.

Believing they were fighting for the Lord, his army marched out to meet a Welsh force that outnumbered them and routed them, driving Owen and Jasper Tudor and their forces across seventeen miles, leaving 4,000 of their men dead on the field.

The legend of Edward IV, the "Sun in Splendor," began that day.

What If?

"Catelyn VIII" gives us some interesting hypotheticals, mostly regarding the military situation:

What if Robb had chosen Greatjon Umber or Robbett Glover instead of Roose? As I suggested back in "Bran VI," Robett Glover is an interesting potential candidate for command who seems to have fallen under the radar in this chapter despite being put on par with Roose the previous chapter. It's hard to tell why this happens, but I think Robett would have done much better than Roose (what with the whole rampant disloyalty thing... more on this in a bit). Now, Greatjon Umber might have fallen for Tywin's planned rout of his vanguard, but, as I'll discuss more in the next Tyrion chapter, I think he might have succeeded beyond where Bolton did just by not engaging in a failed night march. Again, keep this in the back of your mind when considering the next chapter.

What if Robb goes straight at Tywin? Assuming for the moment that Robb was able to grab the 4,000 Freys at the Twins as in OTL, that would have put his army at 22,000 to Tywin's 20,000. Moreover, Robb being an unusually perceptive commander, it's unlikely that he would have fallen for Tywin's trap, and it's especially likely that he would have picked a more advantageous place for the battle to take place – probably right next to the Twins, using the sight of his army crossing the bridge to lure Tywin into an attack (intended to prevent Robb crossing and attacking Jaime), and then using the Twins themselves as an anvil against which to pound Tywin Lannister's head. While Riverrun may have fallen in the meantime (unlikely, given how long it holds out in worse circumstances later in the War of the Five Kings), taking out Tywin effectively ends the war for the Lannisters and the Starks. On the other hand, Robb might have been badly beaten and forced up the causeway as Jaime reinforces his father from the south.

What if Catelyn goes to Winterfell/Rodrik Cassel doesn't become castellan? On the one hand, I can see why George Martin wanted Catelyn to stay in the main theater of the war so that he could continue to use her as a main POV in *A Clash of Kings* and *A Storm of Swords*; however, at the same time, Catelyn doesn't really get to accomplish much at Riverrun. Her family is either incoherent or remains at odds with her, her diplomatic mission to Bitterbridge fails due to author fiat/the will of R'hllor, and then she dies. However, had she gone north to Winterfell, she probably would have been a better organizer of the north's defenses against the ironborn than an eight-year-old child, which probably would have butterflied away the fall of Winterfell and, thus, in all likelihood, the Red Wedding. Alternatively, had anyone more cautious than Rodrik Cassel been chosen by Catelyn Stark as castellan of Winterfell, she could have had it both ways.

Book vs. Show

This scene is substantially different in "The Pointy End," George R.R. Martin's episode for the first season of the HBO show. The Robb Stark of the show is more mature and more confident, but still in need of emotional reassurance. Catelyn Stark still argued against Robb leading the army, but Robb pushes back from a more equal position. The two of them discuss both politics and war on level terms, but Catelyn remains a formidable political wife, rather than a pushover. Martin is able to take the heart of this chapter and make it work despite the change in age, and Michelle Fairley and Richard Madden turn what was in the books a rather unequal exchange between a 14-year-old boy and his somewhat overbearing mother into a strong working relationship.

My larger point here is that I think an older, smarter Robb could have worked in the show without diminishing Catelyn Stark's role in the ways that disappointed many of her fans. I would argue the problem really doesn't start until season two, and can still be fixed with some judicious fan-editing, but more on that later.

TYRION VII

"Tyrion, have you forgotten your courtesies? Kindly acquaint us with our... honored guests."

Synopsis

Tyrion arrives at his father's camp with Shagga, son of Dolf, Timett, son of Timett, and Chella, daughter of Cheyk and the rest of the mountain men. After getting an update from his father about the course of the war, Tyrion watches his father reach an agreement for the mountain men's military service, and embark on a risky course of action.

Political Analysis

In "Tyrion VII," we are finally introduced to the biggest off-screen political actor in Westeros to date (at least, until Doran Martell becomes more prominent), the one and only Tywin Lannister. In addition to seeing the ice-cold relationship he has with his younger son in person for the first time, we also get a small sample of his political sensibilities, especially when he handles the unexpected arrival of the mountain men with *sprezzatura*.

Before the mountain men arrive, we learn two things about the lord of Casterly Rock: first, that "Lord Tywin did not believe in half-measures," which applies to everything. Even with no one around, he sets up formidable defenses; rather than simple tents, he builds elaborate pavilions; rather than simply punishing the Tullys, Tywin sacks the Inn at the Crossroads, a historic site that has lasted since the reign of Jaehaerys I, as if to erase any trace that a Lannister was once humiliated there. The style is deliberately over-the-top, calculated ostentation to lend Tywin the image of a larger-than-life figure whose wealth and wrath is beyond counting. Second, that – above all else – "no man sheds Lannister blood with impunity." As further elaborated in the show, Tywin holds to an almost Confucian conception of family as the ultimate source of all value, such that he's casually, almost gleefully willing to abrogate every value of his society (loyalty to his king, the protection of the innocent, helpless life, the laws of guest right, the social contract in a broader sense) in order to advance his family.

At the same time, though, I think the HBO show slightly misreads Tywin's philosophy somewhat – this is someone who cares deeply what other people think about him, and always has. Hence the shaving of the head the moment he goes bald, hence putting people who make jokes about him in an oubliette, hence the war. This is a man whose entire life has been driven by the desire to silence the laughter aimed at his father; glory counts for everything.

And then we get to Tywin handling the mountain men. It's an impressive display, especially because someone who, in all other respects, is the most snobbish man in Westeros (who even looks down on other great houses) doesn't so much as bat an eyelash when he's unexpectedly thrust into a dangerous negotiation with a bunch of volatile barbarians. It's a sign that, as much as Tywin believes in status and hierarchy, he values his personal dignity and self-image more than the social niceties. In part, I think it explains how Tywin is able to deal with people like Gregor Clegane.

What's more interesting is how little Tywin's method of operation follows the stereotype of Lannisters buying their way through life – the clansmen are both incredibly paranoid about being bamboozled in any deal-making ("lowlands lords have lied to the clans before," they remind Tyrion even before this meeting begins), and very insistent that Tyrion's "promise of silk and steel" is the price for him not dying, and that they're not willing to throw in "fighting for the Lannisters" as a freebie. Instead, Tywin uses a combination of insincere flattery ("even in the west, we know the prowess of the warrior clans of the Mountains of the Moon") and reverse psychology to appeal to the warrior pride of these men and women. They won't march for steel or gold, but mention that "the men of the winterlands are made of iron and ice, and even my boldest knights fear to face them," and the mountain clans trip over themselves to sign up.

This ability to read other people in political situations is all the more surprising given how little Tywin displays this empathic understanding in war, as we'll see later.

Tyrion's reflection on the Mountain Men – while only a minor detail in the chapter, I did find it interesting that the democratic spirit of the mountain men who believe that "we are free men, and free men by rights sit on all war councils" is seen by Tyrion as a sign of their backwardness and lack of civilization. It's a moment where the true "otherness" of historical perspective really hits you in the face; we're used to the 21st-century assumption that democratic government and freedom of speech are universal human rights, but the historical reality is that, well into the 19th century, "conventional wisdom" viewed democracy as a dangerous and unstable system of government, at best suitable only for small, homogeneous city-states, and at worst doomed to slide into anarchy as Aristotle and Thucydides argued, as the *kyklos* of political transformation (from monarchy to tyranny to aristocracy to oligarchy to democracy to anarchy, although the precise sequence differs based on which Greek political theoretician one's talking about) requires.

The idea that the franchise ought to include the entirety of the male population only really took hold in Europe after World War I, where mass mobilization for total war required the participation of the whole of the population; women's suffrage followed on the heels of a war ostensibly fought to "make the world safe for democracy" in the US, UK, and Germany, but France and Italy didn't adopt truly universal suffrage until 1944 and 1946, respectively.

At the same time, the readers of *A Game of Thrones* have been generally used to seeing Tyrion as a sympathetic point of view, in no small part because his views are closer to our modern sensibilities in other regards – his embrace of literacy and intellectualism, his sympathy for social outcasts, his struggles against ableism, and his cynical attitude to feudal mores. It's, therefore, that much more shocking that *this* character feels that "this was the trouble with the clans; they had an absurd notion that every man's voice should be heard in council, so they argued about everything, endlessly. Even their women were allowed to speak. Small wonder it had been hundreds of years since they last threatened the Vale." At the end of the day, Tyrion is still a feudal aristocrat living in a medieval era, with all of the prejudices of his class and time. In Tyrion's view, endless talking sessions are inefficient compared to the unquestioned command of a single leader who can provide unity of purpose and make quick decisions (which is ironic, given how much he chafes under his father's command).

Indeed, his comment that "Tyrion meant to change that" may suggest that, rather than simply intending to arm the mountain men, Tyrion may have planned to set up one of the Mountain Men (most likely Shagga, son of Dolf or Timmett, son of Timmett) as a client king of the Lannisters and then use the king to enforce lowlander military discipline and training. After all, while steel weapons and armor would allow the mountain men to face the knights of the Vale on equal terms man-to-man, they're still going to be outfought when guerrilla attacks give away to set-piece battles, and they're going to have to learn siege warfare if they're going to take the Vale. So rather than an altruistic proposal to allow the original inhabitants of the Vale to reclaim their lands from their oppressors, Tyrion's objective here is to raise the classic colonial army of native subalterns armed and trained in European styles to wreak his personal vengeance on Lysa Arryn.

This isn't to suggest that Tyrion's necessarily a bad person by the standards of his society, but it does suggest that he's more like his father than either of them would like to admit.

The War of the Five Kings: the Lannister campaign – in "Tyrion VII," we also get an update on the progress of the War of the Five Kings, our first from a Lannister perspective. At the moment, it's mostly good news from their perspective. Jaime has routed Edmure's army at Riverrun, taken the heir of House Tully captive (although, one wonders what would have happened had Jaime taken the precaution of sending his prisoner off to the Golden Tooth or Casterly Rock rather than keeping him at his camp... more on this later), and is putting the capital of the riverlands under siege. With the exception of House Mallister of Seagard and House Frey of the Twins, both of which have the Trident between them and the Lannisters, the riverlands are no longer a military threat to the Lannisters.

However, as I've argued before, the Lannisters' success is largely due to Edmure's lack of military sense. Throughout this campaign, Edmure made the classic mistake of trying to maintain a perimeter defense instead of conducting a defense in depth, thus allowing Lannister spearheads to break through his overly-extended lines and rampage deep into the heart of the riverlands (which is rather reminiscent of France's initial error in its 1940 campaign). Given his need to gather his forces and drill his levies (to say nothing of giving the Starks time to come to his aid), Edmure would have been much better off if he had accepted that Tully lands between the Golden Tooth and the Red Fork would be lost and fallen back instead on the riverland's natural defenses. Given how the Mallisters and the Freys are able to hold out in the face of the Lannister onslaught, I am even more convinced that a successful use of the rivers as barriers to movement, defensive force multipliers, and interior lines (much in the same way that Frederick the Great used interior lines to defeat the numerically superior French/Austrian/Russian alliance in the Seven Years' War) are the key to a defense of the riverlands.

At the same time, as we learn in this chapter, the flip-side of the Lannisters' rapid advance is that they've massively extended their supply lines (by five hundred miles or more), which leaves their rear vulnerable. Hence "Marq Piper and Karyl Vance... loose in our rear, raiding our lands across the Red Fork," and "Beric Dondarrion [and] that fat jape of a priest... making a nuisance of themselves by harassing my foraging parties." For the moment, this isn't a problem for Tywin because he can ~~live off the land~~ get first ravage on the riverlands, and he's numerically superior to the guerrilla forces raiding his supply lines and rearguard. However, as we'll see later, it'll become much more problematic if an army of equal size can get between him and his base of supply and reinforcements in the riverlands. In this fashion, the rapid advance resembles trying to ride a runaway boulder; you've got to keep the momentum up or you'll dash to pieces.

If we're in the business of assessing Tywin Lannister as a military commander, what can we say about this point? In his favor, we can say that Tywin is an excellent coordinator of logistics (in that he's able to put an army of 35,000 into the field much faster than his opponents);

he's a competent tactician (wins the Mummer's Ford with some style, pulls off an excellent flanking/encircling maneuver through the Gold Road, executes a flawless *chevauchée* through the southern riverlands, etc.), although it should be noted that this is exclusively against numerically-inferior troops and inferior opposing generals; and he's at least a decent strategist (in that every move he's made so far is directed at the overall goal of knocking out his nearest enemy and getting his army in a position to defend King's Landing). However, as BryndenBFish points out, he makes a critical error of generalship in underestimating Robb Stark: "The Stark boy is a child. No doubt he likes the sound of warhorns well enough... but, in the end, it comes down to butcher's work. I doubt he has the stomach for it." As far as ability to read your opponent goes, a critical higher-order skill for military commanders, Tywin shows little ability.

Likewise, even if he held Robb Stark in "slight esteem" and believed he could easily defeat him in the field, it's a major mistake for Tywin Lannister to march from his position here at the Inn at the Crossroads, which is not only well-fortified and would allow him to easily crush an overly-hasty assault from the Starks, but is also positioned at a strategically-vital crossroads that allows him to easily move west along the river road to reinforce Jaime, east on the high road to block the Arryns (should they sally forth from the Bloody Gate), or south to protect King's Landing. His decision to march north makes it impossible for him to come to Jaime's defense unless he either marches back to the Ruby Ford with a hostile army at his back or forces a crossing over the heavily-fortified Twins, and puts him in real danger of being trapped between the Green Fork, the Trident, and the mountains.

The only logic that explains his actions is that "the boy may hang back or lose his courage when he sees our numbers... the sooner the Starks are broken, the sooner I shall be free to deal with Stannis Baratheon." Given how often this sentiment is expressed in the next couple of chapters, I'm really curious as to why Stannis didn't attack more quickly, before Cersei was able to expand the City Watch and fortify the city or Tyrion was able to arrive; most likely, he was worried about his ability to hold the city against siege with less than 5,000 men, but I can't help but think that his letters demanding allegiance would have gotten a better reception had he been sitting the Iron Throne at the time.

The mystery of Bolton's march – which brings me to the question: why did Tywin Lannister not fall into that trap? Because Roose Bolton forced the Battle of the Green Fork at a time and place that does not make military sense. Considering that Robb's orders are simply to "continue the march south, to confront the huge Lannister army," Roose's decision to force a night-march down the kingsroad to fight a battle near the Ruby Ford still doesn't make sense:

1. Given that Robb's strategic plan (which Roose is clearly aware of) is to attack Jaime's army at Riverrun, the farther Roose allows Tywin to march up the kingsroad puts Tywin that much further away from the Ruby Ford and any ability to reinforce his son. So, why prevent Tywin from marching north and increase the risk that he might work out Robb's plan and shift his army over the Green Fork?

2. Given that, if Robb wins at Riverrun and relieves the forces inside, he creates the strategic possibility to swing east via the Red Fork and the river road to get behind Tywin and between him and the crossing over the Trident, trapping him between two armies that now both roughly equal Tywin's in size, potentially ending the war in a single stroke. However, that possibility only exists if Tywin has advanced far enough up the kingsroad that he can't scramble back to the southern bank of the Trident – so why prevent him from marching?

In a related note, Roose's casualties, plus his retreat practically back to Moat Cailin, means that when Tywin realizes he's been strategically outmaneuvered and has to retreat, Roose isn't in position to harry him from behind and on the flanks as he marches – the moment of maximum vulnerability for Tywin's army.

3. Given that he's outnumbered by Tywin's men 20,000 to 16,000 and has few cavalry, an attack is supremely risky. Military doctrine normally suggests that a three-to-one advantage is required to make an attack likely to succeed; that ratio makes it more favorable for Roose to "confront Lord Tywin" on the defensive, where he can make the most of his smaller numbers and weaken Tywin's advantage. Likewise, the imbalance in cavalry means that Roose Bolton is vulnerable to being flanked and then overrun; a defensive posture would reduce those risks, and would, moreover, allow Roose to more easily choose a battlefield where he could protect his flanks or find broken/high ground that would allow an infantry army to triumph over a cavalry-heavy force (as was the situation at Crecy, Poitiers, and Agincourt).

In fact, the explanation that seems most likely to me is that Roose, knowing that his battle was merely a delaying action, decided to use the opportunity to begin putting his plan to weaken his northern rivals into action. One of the easiest ways to do that without making it obvious what he was doing is to put his army through an unnecessary night march and then attack a larger opponent, making sure to put his own house's forces in a position of safety while placing his rivals in the position of maximum danger. Night marches are exhausting affairs at the best of times, especially a night march that must have stretched close to 500 miles (from the Twins to the Ruby Ford). Roose's army would have arrived exhausted and hungry, compared to the well-rested and -fed Lannisters. Especially in pre-modern war, one can never underestimate the effect that sleep and food can have on an army. Hand-to-hand combat in armor is very tiring (hence why the Roman legions learned to rotate their lines rapidly, to give their men time to catch their breath, grab a drink or some food, and keep up their stamina); walking into a battle without a good night's rest and a good meal has historically been the cause of many a defeat. Indeed, it might well explain why the north's right flank unexpectedly crumples.

It's not that Roose wouldn't have taken a victory if he could have gotten one, but given his failure to adequately screen his advance (compared to the consistent success of northern scouts throughout the War of the Five Kings), it does suggest that victory wasn't his chief objective at the Green Fork. A successful night march could have allowed the north to defeat an unprepared Lannister force, but the way in which Roose's decision seems to go against every other military consideration is suggestive that his self-serving objectives were already in play in this opening battle.

Historical Analysis

On to historical parallels. In previous segments, I've realized that I have neglected to fill in my picks for the Lannisters, so I might as well quickly sketch them out here before filling them in with more detail in later chapters. As you can pick up from my historical discussions in the various Eddard chapters, I see a strong similarity between Cersei Lannister and Margaret D'Anjou, the leader of the Lancastrian cause and Richard, Duke of York's nemesis. Unfortunately, while that works quite well in describing her relationship vis-a-vis Ned and Joffrey, it doesn't hold as well for the rest of her family, as Margaret was conspicuously without male family at her side during the Wars of the Roses. What works a bit better is a parallel to Lucrezia Borgia, both as a woman rumored to have an incestuous affair with her brother and a woman who ruled in place of her father. Likewise, Jaime Lannister works rather well as Cesare Borgia, a skilled soldier with no scruples whatsoever and hostile intentions to his brothers-in-law.

For Tywin himself, he does resemble Rodrigo Borgia to an extent, as a political heavyweight who used his immense wealth to its utmost, who sought to build a political dynasty that would live forever (which came crashing down immediately after his death), and who was intimately well-versed in treachery and under-handed dealings. On the other hand, Tywin has zero interest in religion, and most of his power has come through war – which suggests a different Renaissance figure, one Cosimo de Medici. The founder of the Medici dynasty, Cosimo used his vast wealth to control Florentine politics without holding public office, and spent much of his career fighting in the Lombardy wars between

Milan, Venice, and Florence for dominance over Northern Italy. Not a bad parallel for the lord of Lannister.

At the same time, I also want to talk a bit about the democratic philosophy of the mountain men and why it is that George R.R. Martin puts his most democratic principles in the mouths of barbarians (the mountain men, the wildlings, etc.). I have a sneaking suspicion that Martin is a fan of the great French historian Fernand Braudel, who, in his masterwork *The Mediterranean in the Age of Phillip the II*, argued that:

> *If social archaism (the vendetta among others) persisted, it was above all for the simple reason that mountains are mountains: that is, primarily an obstacle, and therefore a refuge, a land of the free. For there, men can live out of reach of the pressures and tyrannies of civilization... here, there was no landed nobility with strong and powerful routes... here, there was no rich, well-fed clergy to be envied and mocked... there was no tight urban network, so no administration, no towns in the proper sense of the word... the hills were the refuge of liberty, democracy, and peasant "republics."*

To Braudel, the pioneer of the longue durée (the idea that the true drivers of history are long-term forces, rather than short-term crises or episodic events, especially changes in the environment over geological time), the idea that the "steepest places have been, at all times, the asylum of liberty" was a geological truth, cutting across centuries and cultures, that explained the relationship between all central authorities and outlying regions, be they the Kurds and Druses or the Balkans, Greeks, and Albanians resisting the Ottoman imperial state, or the Abruzzi of the Appenine mountains resisting the power of Rome from the empire through to the papacy.

At the same time, Braudel was very clear that this liberty meant something more than un-reflective slogans about "live free or die" – the liberty of the mountains isn't simply freedom from taxes and central authority, it means severing oneself from civilization, society, and time itself. There is a cost as well as a value to it; the freedom of the mountains brings with it the freedom to enjoy poverty and the grinding struggle for existence in the rocky soil of the high places, the freedom to engage in never-ending vendetta in a world in which there is no law that the weak can apply to against the strong, the freedom to engage in banditry, stealing the property of others and suffering the penalties thereof.

All of this applies to both the mountain men and the wildlings – their freedom does not mean what we think it means.

What If?

"Tyrion VII" only offers a few opportunities for hypotheticals, so let's dive in:

What if Tywin doesn't march? Here, we can see how Tywin might have screwed himself, because had he remained at the Crossroads, he might have gotten warning of the Battle of the Whispering Woods in enough time to move at least part of his army back to Riverrun in time to attack Robb's army when it attacked Jaime's main force, potentially ending this theater of the war in one fell swoop, and saving half the Lannister forces for the fight against the Baratheons and Tyrells. Likewise, he might have been able to inflict much heavier casualties from his prepared defensive position than he did in the OTL Battle of the Green Fork. Certainly, he would have been much safer in the event that the two battles go the same way they did in OTL in terms of being able to make it to Harrenhal.

What if Tyrion gets his dad to sign off on his plan for the Vale? Granted, Tywin's immediate concern is the Starks and then the Baratheons, not the Arryns, but the Vale is still a major player that (unless Littlefinger is being very forthcoming) Tywin has no reason to believe won't be hostile to his family. Distracting them with a guerrilla insurgency would likely take the Arryns out of the war for some time, and in the worst-case scenario, he succeeds in having his son killed as per spec. The interesting thing from Tyrion's side is that it means he's not around for the Battle of the Green Fork, where he easily could have died, and not around to become acting Hand of the King (which probably means that King's Landing falls and/or is burned to the ground), but gets to wreak utter havoc in the Vale, possibly taking out the Eyrie itself. Although he doesn't yet know it, this would massively screw with Littlefinger's plans, which would suit Tyrion just fine.

What if Tyrion gets sent to fight the brotherhood without banners? This is mostly the same as the one above, with the added wrinkle that perhaps Tyrion gets captured by the brotherhood and comes face-to-face with the metaphysical plot of *A Song of Ice and Fire*, which he has resolutely avoided to date.

Book vs. Show

This scene is played pretty straight in the show – not much to report here.

SANSA V

"...as you love me, you do me this kindness, my prince."

Synopsis

Joffrey and Cersei hold court for the first time and announce some turnover in personnel: Ser Barristan is out, and the Hound and Janos Slynt are in. Sansa makes a plea for her father's life that Cersei really should have paid more attention to.

Political Analysis

"Sansa V" is the last moment of Sansa's innocence, so we should probably savor it before George R.R. Martin destroys it in front of her eyes. But, first, let's take a look at the Dynamic Duo of Westerosi politics, Joffrey and Cersei, as they embark on their first day on the job.

Joffrey and Cersei in (mis)government – and what a first day it is. Joffrey and Cersei begin by "read[ing] a long list of names, commanding each in the name of king and council to present themselves and swear their fealty to Joffrey... [or] be adjudged traitors, their lands and titles forfeit to the throne." On the face of it, this isn't a terrible idea – it's good to make clear who your friends are and your enemies are (although making people choose sometimes moves neutrals over into the enemy camp) and to get the law and legitimacy on your side. However, historical precedent has rather tainted this as a political tactic; the last time a king summoned lords to King's Landing on pain of attainder, he ended up having everyone who arrived executed without due process of law. Hence, Cersei is immediately inviting comparisons to Mad King Aerys, especially when she includes all of the children of the houses summoned.

The list itself is rather interesting: in addition to the usual suspects (Stannis [although it's notable he hasn't actually done anything that could be construed as treasonous yet], Renly, the Tullys, the Starks, all of their associated bannermen, and Beric and Thoros), which is all well and good except for the fact that you can't really enforce any of this when your enemies have their armies in the field, Cersei goes a bit crazy with naming almost every prominent neutral house in Westeros: the entirety of the Tyrells ("brothers, uncles, sons"), Doran Martell "and all of his sons," and the Arryns and their bannermen (although this one falls halfway between the former and latter categories). Given the historical precedent and the reputation of the Lannisters, this action runs the extreme risk of pushing two more of the eight great houses into open rebellion. Indeed, the Tyrells will shortly declare themselves for Renly (which was probably going to happen anyway, but Cersei's actions don't help).

After Item 1 on the agenda is complete, Cersei moves on to a bit of a cabinet reshuffle: Eddard Stark is out and Tywin Lannister is Hand of the King, and Stannis is out and replaced with Cersei as queen regent. In many ways, this is the best political move Cersei makes, consolidating her family's position in King's Landing and achieving her life's ambition of having explicit political authority in her own right, with only "a soft murmuring from the lords around her... quickly stilled." However, it is amazing how short-lived her authority is – by giving Tywin the Handship, she covers his recent treason with the blanket of back-dated legitimacy, but ultimately loses control over her own camp by creating a rival authority within the Baratheon-Lannister court, as we'll see in *A Storm of Swords*. At the same time, it's incredibly obvious that, despite her lifelong ambitions to achieve a position running the small council, Cersei really doesn't have any ideas for what comes next if things don't go according to plan.

Moreover, while consolidating one's position is all very well, it's also true that one critical lesson about feudal politics that Cersei has never gotten is that, in a feudal system, political influence comes from spreading power around, not concentrating it in one's immediate family. The downside of having so many Lannisters on the small council is that you have less bargaining chips with which to expand one's political coalition (which, as I've pointed out in "Bran VI," is also your military coalition). Cersei's actions here risk alienating potential allies by denying them patronage and constructing an outsider group that's larger than the insider group.

This is only further confirmed when Cersei has Janos Slynt made a small councilor and the lord of Harrenhal. Immediately, "the muttering was louder and angrier," as the lords of the court bitterly resent a commoner being raised to the top of the lesser houses as a blatant act of quid pro quo. Moreover, since Slynt is a Lannister creation without any outside power base, it's another example of the Lannisters keeping all the goodies for themselves. And as Tywin will point out later, this is a major case of Cersei overpaying for a one-time service; she'd have been better off replacing Janos Slynt with some crownlands lord and keeping Harrenhal open for future political negotiations.

And then there's the removal of Ser Barristan Selmy – the acme of knighthood, a symbol of honor and virtue, and a signifier of continuity between the two dynasties – and replacing him with Jaime Lannister as the lord commander and Sandor Clegane on the Kingsguard. Again and again, Cersei is packing the court with Lannister loyalists, and destroying every element of precedent and stability. While it's Joffrey's idea to have him arrested for calling him "boy" and mentioning Stannis (the first sign of Joffrey's rampant paranoia), the idea of placing him in a glorified cell "north of Lannisport" isn't much better.

On their own, some of these political moves make sense, and others don't. But rolling them out all at once sends entirely the wrong message: instead of continuity, we have sudden breaks with precedent; instead of favors being widely doled out in return for loyalty, they're being hoarded for the Lannister family. And, unlike in the show, Cersei really can't claim that Joffrey's at fault – this is her plan.

Sansa's plan to free her father – as if to spit in the eye of those who believe that Sansa is a purely passive character, it's at this point that Sansa steps forward to try to save her father by asking for "mercy" while acknowledging that "he must be punished." Sansa makes a very clever argument: she relies heavily on Eddard's relationship with Robert (gesturing in the direction of the old king's memory and the ideal of continuity), she throws Renly and Stannis under the bus (which, given that Joffrey is paranoid about them and has just attainted them, is a good idea), and wraps it up with appealing to the conventional wisdom that "milk of the poppy fills your head with clouds." And under any other circumstance in Westerosi politics, her argument would work – it is simply insane to execute sitting lords of great houses, as seen by the fact that the only person who's ever done it was Aerys II.

On the other side of the ledger, however, we have to note that Sansa's belief in the chances of her plan do show that the transition from innocence to wisdom is coming along rather slowly – as she puts it, "it will all come out well, Joff loves me and the queen does, too, she said so." Obviously, by this point with her father imprisoned and her sister vanished and her entire family attained down to the Rickon level, Sansa should probably not accept everything Cersei tells her on its face. At the same time, we have to consider how a 12-year-old child who's led an extremely sheltered life and has been held prisoner would respond under these conditions.

However, we have to note that her appeal at least initially works. Varys finally starts making some moves – notably, he makes the worst possible pitch to get Ser Barristan to accept his forcible "retirement" by stressing material comforts (an insult to a man who's observed a lifelong vow of poverty), downplays Ser Barristan's ostensibly-pro-Stannis comments (which is unusual for a man whose trade is in ferreting out treason, but, as we learn later, was motivated by his desire to win over Ser Barristan for the Targaryens), and argues that "they say wisdom oft comes from the mouths of babes." I'll discuss why Varys wants Ned saved more in the last Eddard chapter, but I did want to note the irony that the man who stoked Aerys II's paranoia and who offered loyal advice to the king right up to the sack of King's Landing is arguing for leniency, whereas Pycelle (who seems to have lost his ability to detect his own hypocrisy some time ago) is holding the hard line against treason when he himself betrayed King Aerys in Tywin's name.

Joffrey seems nonplussed and a little bored – he's willing to defer to his mother's wishes as long as Eddard takes it back and everyone admits that he's the king. He doesn't seem to care that much (I don't think Littlefinger's quite got to him yet – more on this in "Eddard XV"). Cersei seems somewhat nonplussed by all of this, which is perhaps the best sign of how sloppy and short-sighted she really is as a political actor. Eddard Stark is the best possible hostage she could have in this situation – even before Jaime is taken captive and the Stark/Tully army is about two-and-a-half week's ride away from King's Landing, it would be incredibly advantageous for her to swap Eddard for the Starks pulling out of the war and remaining loyal, while keeping Sansa to ensure they keep their promises, so that House Lannister can bring the entirety of its power to bear on the Baratheons. Right now, the Starks have been repeatedly offended and abused by the Lannisters, but it hasn't gone beyond the point of no return yet.

And yet... as I'll discuss in the next Sansa chapter, Cersei completely drops the ball on this. For some reason, as I'll discuss next chapter, she outsources the work to Varys and Littlefinger rather than handling it herself. The eventual plan doesn't make a whole lot of sense; having Ned Stark take the black after "confessing" his crimes preserves her cover story... except for the fact that Stannis already knows. It does give her a total victory over Ned, permanently taking him out of the game of thrones, but, in the larger scheme, that's not actually in her long-term interests. Eddard is a mature ruler who's already shown his preference for a peaceful solution, whereas his son has shown that he's more interested in vengeance, given that he's already marched his armies south while she held both his father and sister; having Eddard take the black keeps him out of power and makes Robb lord of Winterfell. Does she really think he's going to turn around once his father's out of harm's way without a formal agreement? And even if Robb were willing to make a formal peace treaty or, even, a truce, taking Eddard's return to his family off the table to begin with is a poor place to start. It's a very strange mix of over-ambitious and half-assed.

Historical Analysis

I intend to get into the last days of Richard, Duke of York, in the next (and last) Eddard chapter, and Joffrey's historical parallels in the next Sansa chapters, and I already discussed the "Parliament of Devils" in a previous Eddard chapter, so I don't have anything left for this section. Next chapter, however...

What If?

I can really only think of one major hypothetical here:

What if Joffrey/Cersei says no? Ironically for all concerned, things might have worked out better for everyone if Sansa had gotten turned down here. After all, there's no particular hurry with Ned, as they have him quite securely locked up in the dungeon. And even a slight delay changes things dramatically... in about a week, Renly will crown himself in Highgarden; in about two weeks, Robb will have won his first two battles and Jaime will be his prisoner. In that situation, Eddard is far too important an asset to be sent off to the Night's Watch or blithely executed. A small delay, and Eddard Stark might actually survive. Sansa probably still remains a captive, however.

Book vs. Show

The show played this one almost word-for-word, so nothing to report here.

EDDARD XV

"...the queen would not have waited long in any case. Robert was becoming unruly, and she needed to be rid of him to free her hands to deal with his brothers. They are quite a pair, Stannis and Renly. The iron gauntlet and the silk glove."

Synopsis

Ned Stark gets a prison visit from Varys, and the two have a civilized discourse on the nature of honor, honesty, and mercy as they contemplate an offer of clemency.

Political Analysis

"Eddard XV" may well be the best argument that Ned Stark's plotline in *A Game of Thrones* is essentially one long noir detective story. Here, our fearless detective hits the end of the road: he's got a bad wound that's not going to heal (if this was '30s noir, he would be gut-shot at this point), he's cracked the case, but is at the mercy of his enemies – and he's going to be forced into an impossible, morally-compromised choice by a seemingly omnipotent conspiracy between exposing the treason and corruption at the heart of the power structure and saving his family. As he puts it himself: "he damned them all: Littlefinger, Janos Slynt and his gold cloaks, the queen, the Kingslayer, Pycelle and Varys and Ser Barristan, even Lord Renly... yet, in the end, he blamed himself."

A discourse on honor, truth, and mercy – and, thus, it's entirely fitting that so much of "Eddard XV" revolves around a dialogue on honor, truth, and mercy – both before and after Varys arrives, Eddard is contemplating the decision he's going to have to make, as if he somehow knows it's coming. And what's interesting about this dialogue is how complicated the situation is from the standard "honor is stupid" narrative that much of the fandom seems to have bought into. While Robert's ghost does mockingly ask "Can you eat pride, Stark? Will honor shield your children?" the fact that Robert's face turns into Littlefinger suggests that this statement shouldn't be read straightforwardly, especially when, as Ned points out, his major mistake with Robert wasn't that he was too honorable but, rather, that "I lied to you, hid the truth."

This is why Ned's discussion with Varys has a quality like two ships passing in the night: on the one hand, Eddard says that "the madness of mercy" led him to "tell the queen that you had learned the truth of Joffrey's birth," with Varys arguing that, "It was not wine that killed the king – it was your mercy..." (which he's doing for his own reasons, as I'll discuss a bit later). On the other hand, Varys also tells Ned that, "You are an honest and honorable man... Oftimes, I forget that. I have met so few of them in my life... when I see what honesty and honor have won you, I understand why." The fundamental tension in his life, the reason why Ned's in this dungeon, is that, ultimately, he is torn between the dictates of honor and the dictates of humanity in ways that can't be easily resolved in favor of either side.

After all, it could be argued that, had Ned been as straightforwardly, unbendingly just and righteous as Stannis is described, Ned would be safe but Cersei and her children would be dead. Instead, his humane desire to protect both his friend's feelings and the life of three innocent children impels him to break his own code of conduct. Likewise, I think the fact that Ned chooses this chapter to go into full-blown flashback mode about the Tourney of Harrenhal, especially focusing on the crown of winter roses that symbolizes the promise he made to Lyanna, is no accident. The other major defining moment in his life when Ned has been forced to choose between his honor and mercy, he chose the latter and paid for it with permanent damage done to his reputation, his marriage, and his nephew's happiness. So when it comes to his decision in this chapter, the outcome is almost pre-ordained.

Which brings me back around to noir and, especially, the existential nature of the genre – namely, that for the detective, the search for truth is ultimately not about outcomes or consequences or about bringing the bad guy to justice. Think about the end of *Chinatown*, where Jake Gittes watches Noah Cross get away with murder, rape, fraud, and theft across the whole of the San Fernando Valley, and has to walk away. What matters is that the detective chooses to find the truth.

An interview with the Spider – "Eddard XV" also gives us the most extensive (and putatively honest dialogue) by Varys, the Master of Whisperers this side of the "Epilogue" to *A Dance with Dragons*, and it's not an accident that, in both cases, Varys is unburdening himself to a dead man. The Spider is extremely cautious. At the same time, though, as much as I think we learn about Varys, he's not being totally frank here, and I think some of the confusion people have about this character is that they're taking him at his word in this scene.

George R.R. Martin foregrounds this fact by having Varys announce at the outset "each man has a role to play, in life as in mummery. So it is at court. The King's Justice must be fearsome, the master of coin must be frugal, the lord commander of the Kingsguard must be valiant… and the master of whisperers must be sly and obsequious and without scruple." His dramatic purpose, in other words, is to be untrustworthy. At the same time, when Eddard presses him on "who do you truly serve?" and "Your own ends. What ends are those, Lord Varys?" there is a level of consistency between his answers here and his dialogue with Kevan Lannister that suggests he's not lying outright or trying to get Eddard to trust him (as we'll see later).

Instead, as I have argued in the past, I think Varys genuinely believes that he "serve[s] the realm, and the realm needs peace," but the peace he has in mind is more akin to Thomas Hobbes's conception of the peace that is the purpose of a sovereign power with complete power to prevent a war of all against all, so something of a lie by omission. Consider that Varys came to Westeros as the 20 years of peace and prosperity of Tywin Lannister's first term were starting to curdle into the paranoid reign of a king who used wildfire to burn suspected traitors, and has since lived through a civil war marked with betrayal and the bloody Sack of King's Landing, and Jon Arryn's 15-year truce marked by corruption, intrigue, and murder. His objective is not a "thin" peace, but a lasting and profound peace enforced by his enlightened absolute monarch, Aegon VI (more on this in *Hollow Crowns, Deadly Thrones, Part V*). And in order to achieve this peace, as the arch-utilitarian he is, Varys is willing to wade through oceans of blood – as in the case of his actions with Tyrion and Tywin in *A Storm of Swords* (can't wait for this chapter!), or his assassination of half the small council to plunge King's Landing into chaos.

However, there's an extremely precise timing at work, because Varys declines to destabilize the monarchy by helping Eddard escape here, and suggests that, "If there was one soul in King's Landing who was truly desperate to keep King Robert alive, it was me." This might be dismissed as self-serving double-talk – after all, Varys informed Ned of the assassination attempts against King Robert after the fact, and we haven't seen him actively preventing them – except for the fact that, as we saw in "Arya III," Varys really did view Robert's death and the conflict between the Starks and Lannisters as complicating his schedule for a Targaryen restoration. So, clearly, Varys is telling the truth in so far that he didn't want Robert to die while the Targaryen restoration wasn't ready.

So, how does Eddard Stark's confession or escape fit in the plans of the Varys/Illyrio Conspiracy? I think our first clue comes with Varys's description of Stannis as a terrifying force of justice, the "iron hand" to Renly's "silk glove." Varys's primary intention at this point must be to prevent Stannis from taking the Iron Throne, since he'd be too formidable as a general to guarantee Aegon's victory, whereas the Lannisters could be easily pushed off the Iron Throne by a strategic revelation of Cersei's misdeeds (once Tywin's out of the way...). Hence his alliance with Tyrion in *A Clash of Kings* and his actions in *A Storm of Swords*. Given what he's learned of Eddard's intentions, Varys knows that freeing Ned Stark would lead to the Starks supporting Stannis, which he doesn't want. By contrast, having Ned Stark take the black keeps the truth about Cersei's children hidden for the meantime while the Lannisters deal with Stannis, and gives Varys leverage with House Stark.

Indeed, one could say that, overall, Varys consistently acts to remove any political figure of the generation of the Rebellion who would presumably be adamant against the return of the Targaryens – he does nothing when Jon Arryn's death is plotted, allows Ned Stark to fall from grace, works to keep Renly and Stannis off the throne, then pivots to eliminate Tywin Lannister – all of which works to reduce any resistance to a Targaryen restoration. After all, Ned Stark might be adamantly opposed to a Targaryen returning to the throne, given what happened to his brother and father, but Robb would be far less so, especially if the Targaryens promised him revenge against the Lannisters.

Varys on Cersei – in "Eddard XV," we also get Varys's cogent analysis of Cersei's political actions, which makes them somewhat more understandable. What I had completely forgotten here is that Varys emphasizes the role of fear in her motivations, that:

> *"Cersei is frightened of you, my lord... but she has other enemies she fears even more. Her beloved Jaime is fighting the river lords even now. Lysa Arryn sits in the Eyrie, ringed in stone and steel... in Dorne, the Martells still brood on the murder of Princess Elia... and now your son marches down the Neck with a northern host at his back."*

> *"...the king's brothers are the ones giving Cersei sleepless nights... Lord Stannis in particular. His claim is the true one, he is known for his prowess as a battle commander, and he is utterly without mercy. There is no creature on Earth half so terrifying as a truly just man... so here is Cersei's nightmare: while her father and brother spend their power battling Starks and Tullys, Lord Stannis will land, proclaim himself king, and lop off her son's curly blond head... and her own in the bargain."*

This begins to make more sense – Cersei definitely saw Eddard Stark as the primary threat, given his position as Hand of the King, but the reason she hasn't done anything about Eddard since she deposed him, and the reason why both with Sansa's letter and this offer she is (however ineffectually) trying to push the Starks into momentary quiescence, is that her attention is focused on Stannis and Renly and she wants to free up her father and brother to come save her. This would fit with her actions later in *A Game of Thrones* and in *A Clash of Kings*, when she attempts to summon her father to defend King's Landing despite the strategic danger this would offer in allowing Robb free reign in the westerlands and the possibility that all of the Lannisters' enemies could converge on King's Landing, surrounding Tywin and the capital. And it would also explain why she's choosing now to act – Renly's gotten away, Stannis is marshaling his forces, but Tywin and Jaime have been drawn west and north away from King's Landing, just as she'd feared.

At the same time, Cersei's actions don't look particularly good even in this light. Given the importance of Ned Stark at this moment, the fact that she's left him in the black cells, where he could easily die of infection, gone for him taking the black (which would potentially scotch a trade, since Robb wouldn't really consider his father being exiled to the Wall a fair exchange for Jaime being returned to Cersei), and outsourced it to Varys and Littlefinger, suggests a level of inattention and lack of forethought that's really inexcusable.

Varys on Littlefinger – which brings us to this tantalizing little morsel: in "Cersei II" in *A Feast for Crows*, we learn that "Joff was supposed to spare his life and send him to the Wall. Stark's eldest son would have followed him as lord of Winterfell, but Sansa would have stayed at court, a hostage. Varys and Littlefinger had worked out the terms." This rarest of all collaborations, between the two greatest conspirators and manipulators in all of Westeros, is a tantalizing little detail, especially since we don't see Littlefinger's hand here.

In fact, when Eddard questions whether Varys and Littlefinger are working together, the master of whisperers responds that, "I would sooner wed the Black Goat of Qohor [than be in league with Baelish. Littlefinger is the second most devious man in the Seven Kingdoms. Oh, I feed him choice whispers, sufficient so that he thinks I am his." To me, this points to a few critically important things: firstly, one important way in that Varys has had the upper hand on Littlefinger for a loooong time is that he's been a major source of Littlefinger's intelligence and that he's gotten Littlefinger not to trust him, but to underestimate him, which is even better. Secondly, it suggests that Varys is more aware of Littlefinger's skills than vice-versa, especially given Baelish's comments about the eunuch. Thirdly, that both men had a deep interest in the outcome of this situation.

Varys, I think, genuinely wanted Ned to go to the Night's Watch, as I've suggested. And Littlefinger may well have, too, at first – after all, it's a lot easier to get Catelyn and/or Sansa to marry you if they're not grieving over the death of an immediate loved one that you have caused, and so much more satisfying to force Ned to spend the rest of his life knowing Littlefinger has either/both of them in his clutches and there's nothing he can do about it. However (and this is where I think I need to revise my statement from "Sansa IV"), Cersei also tells us in the same paragraph that she had planned to break the engagement between Sansa and Joffrey, but that "I would have made Sansa a good marriage. A Lannister marriage. Petyr Baelish had offered to wed the girl himself, she recalled, but, of course, that was impossible; he was much too lowborn." It may well have been during these negotiations that Baelish decided to persuade Joffrey to execute Ned Stark instead, which would fit with his improvisational, impulse style (consider that it would mean he got literally nothing out of the deal, and, even if he had succeeded in his marriage plans, he still would have been a long way from inheriting Winterfell), an impulse that dramatically reshaped Westerosi history.

Varys's offer: honor vs. family - finally, we come to the crux of the chapter: Varys tells Ned that, "I want you to serve the realm... tell the queen you will confess your vile treason, command your son to lay down his sword, and proclaim Joffrey the true heir. Offer to denounce Stannis and Renly as faithless usurpers... if you will give her the peace she needs and the time to deal with Stannis, and pledge to carry her secret to the grave, I believe she will allow you to take the black." And in order to get Eddard to agree, Varys appeals to his sense of self-preservation and then to his sense of proto-nationalism, both of which fail.

Ultimately, Eddard insists on placing his personal values of truth and honor above the "greater good," as all good noir detectives must do. And, indeed, it's what he should do - because what Varys is offering is a terrible deal. He's just been informed that Cersei is in a terrible situation and wants to make a deal, and that House Stark is beginning to bring resources into the field that can only improve his current position. Taking this deal gives the Lannisters everything they want, while giving Stark himself only the merest semblance of life, and leaving his daughter in harm's way. It's the definition of a one-sided exchange.

The best possible advice would be for Eddard to hang back and wait, see if the Stark army can't improve his negotiating position. And I think both Eddard and Varys realize that Varys is peddling bad advice here, because Varys sidesteps to a completely different tack to break his resistance: "And your daughter's life, my lord? How precious is that? [...] The next visitor who calls on you... could bring you Sansa's head." What I think much of the fandom doesn't realize is that Varys is lying here: Eddard himself and Sansa are far too important as hostages to be killed now, in complete opposition to what Varys tells him. It's especially the case that having Sansa killed at this point could only harm the Lannisters, not help them; killing Sansa isn't going to stop Robb if having his father imprisoned didn't. Only Joffrey's complete lack of sense and Cersei's inability to react quickly changes that fact.

On a symbolic level, Eddard is choosing family over honor. On a practical level, he's being lied to, coerced, and rushed into making the last mistake of his life.

Historical Analysis

When we last left Richard, Duke of York, he had put his hand on the throne of England and claimed it as his by right, only to be met by stunned silence. A few days later, on October 16th, York went to the House of Lords and formally presented his demanded to be recognized as the rightful king of England, presenting them with a document detailing the succession of the kings of England, and specifically how, as the descendant (on his mother's side) of Edward III's second son, Lionel, Duke of Clarence (in addition to being the direct descendant of Edward III's fourth son, Edmund, Duke of York), his claim to the throne trumped that of Henry VI, whose grandfather had usurped the throne from Richard II, despite being the son of the third son of Edward III. If you've ever wondered why Martin spent so much of *A Game of Thrones* describing lines of descent, it's because this stuff really mattered, and people died in their thousands because of it.

However, unlike the Great Council of 233, which was willing to act to decide a contested line of succession, the House of Lords responded with a (polite) campaign of resistance through delay: first, they inquired as to why he hadn't put forward this claim before but instead claimed to be acting only in the cause of good government. Richard's response: "Thought right for a time rest and be put for silence, yet it rotteth not, nor shall it perish."* Second, they went to King Henry VI to ask for his opinion; after that, they canvassed judicial experts. Finally, they engaged in a lengthy debate over whether, even if Richard was the rightful king by law, they could abrogate the oath of loyalty to Henry VI and his son (which Richard also sworn, a further embarrassment). York left Westminster with a declaration that he would be heir apparent to Henry VI, and the sentence of attainder on himself and his followers revoked, but without the declaration he had wanted, and with his political reputation in tatters.

* Weir, Alison. *Wars of the Roses*, loc. 4650.

Meanwhile, Queen Margaret d'Anjou was marching on York with an army of Lancastrian loyalists and Scottish allies, some 20,000 strong. Knowing that he had to meet this threat or lose everything, York and his ally, Salisbury, marched north with an army of 9,000 men that swelled to 12,000 on the march, fortifying himself at Sandal Castle, where he awaited the arrival of reinforcements from his son, Edward of March, and

Salisbury's son, the earl of Warwick, as the Lancastrian host descended upon him.

On Dec 30th, falsely believing himself to be reinforced by Lancastrian soldiers under Andrew Trollope that were masquerading as Yorkist men (shades of Janos Slynt and the gold claoks), York marched out of Sandal Castle to meet the center of the Lancastrian army. When the two hosts clashed, the hidden Lancastrian right and left (which, together with the center, amounted to an army twice the size of his own) emerged from the woods to smash into both of his flanks (and here we see the inspiration for the Battle of the Whispering Woods) at the same time. This disastrous decision, which gave rise to the mnemonic "Richard of York Gave Battle in Vain" for the colors of the visible spectrum, ended the Yorkist army there and then. Richard, Duke of York, died on the field of battle, his army either fleeing in panic or surrounded and being chopped to pieces, with 2,500 men dead on the field. His 17-year-old son was murdered after his surrender by Lord Clifford, who cried "by God's blood, thy father killed mine. So will I slay the accursed blood of York."

After his death, York's body was propped up on an ant-hill by Lancastrian soldiers, who crowned him with a paper crown, hailing him as the "king without a kingdom." When Clifford escorted Queen Margaret to view the heads of York, his son, Rutland, and his ally, Salisbury (who also was executed following the battle), she ordered that the heads be placed on pikes on Micklegate Bar atop the walls of York so that "York shall overlook the town of York."

In William Shakespeare's version (a highlight of *Henry VI, Part 3*), the horror of Wakefield is magnified by flipping the order of events: Rutland is murdered before the duke of York, who is, in turn, denied the dignity of death in battle so that he and his nemesis, Queen Margaret, can have one final confrontation.

It is a scene of grotesque indignity, the unnatural inversion of the ceremony of installing a new king (complete with paper crown, a mole-hill for a throne, and blood to anoint him), the cruelty of a mother waving the death of her enemy's son in his face, a great warrior forced to weep and dance before his tormentors like a bear being baited. It's not an accident that it's this image of a northern lord brought down by a vengeful, bloody queen that inspired Ned Stark and Cersei Lannister, or, for that matter, Lewis Carroll's Queen of Hearts ("off with his head, off with his head!").

In history, Richard, Duke of York's death, however horrific it might seem, ended nothing and solved nothing. As discussed earlier, Richard's death at Wakefield made his son, Edward, the largest landholder in England and the Yorkist claimant to the throne; the simultaneous death of Salisbury made his son, Warwick, the wealthiest man in England. The two men would unite their forces at London, and the war would continue.

What If?

What if Varys had smuggled out Eddard? This counterfactual goes a long way towards revealing Varys's motives at this moment. If Eddard is released, then not only does Robb Stark gain a major advantage (no need to bargain over Jaime and a much clearer exit strategy), but also the Stark forces learn of the truth of Joffrey's parentage before they irrevocably decide for independence. This most likely means not only that House Stark sides with Stannis, but also that Stannis's public letter is corroborated by the Hand of the King. This could well have a cascading effect on Westerosi politics: the lords of the stormlands would, at the least, split rather than only side with Renly; the Vale might be pulled into the war against Lysa's wishes due to Stark/Royce influence and the cover of King Robert's Hand's command. While at that point a two-stage war, first Stannis and the Stark/Tully army against the Lannisters and then the Stannis/Starks/Tullys against Renly and the Tyrells (a great Motown band name, by the way), is most likely, it's possible that the War of the Five Kings might have been forestalled then and there in favor of a recapitulation of Robert's Rebellion with Tywin playing the role of Rhaegar.

On the other hand, it's possible that Varys could have secured Eddard's support for a restoration of the Targaryens... if only he had known that Eddard was protecting another Targaryen claimant to the Iron Throne. Although perhaps he did know, and he was worried about a potential rival to Aegon... /tinfoil.

What if Eddard said no? Ironically, if Eddard has just thought a little bit longer about the offer and played for time, things would have worked out better for almost everyone: if Eddard is alive when news of the Whispering Woods arrives in King's Landing, there's no way that Cersei jeopardizes her precious Jaime with a public confession. A straightforward trade of Eddard for Jaime is worked out, which is great for Eddard, Cersei, Jaime, Robb, Tywin, and maybe even Varys (who could ensure Stannis's defeat and the Starks owing him a favor). I doubt that this ends the Stark/Lannister conflict; the Lannisters have repeatedly attacked both the Starks and the Tullys and would still be holding Sansa and Arya (putatively) hostage, and Eddard would probably be pushing for a declaration in favor of Stannis. However, it would probably be the best possible chance for a peace on that side of the conflict for a time, in that the Lannisters have more important crises to deal with and the Starks have their primary war aim accomplished.

Book vs. Show

With the significant exception of the omission of the hallucinations/flashbacks, this scene is otherwise played pretty straight in the TV show (with the exception of playing up Eddard's willingness to die as a soldier, which is omitted in the text in favor of a sharper focus on the question of truth and honor). On the other hand, I do worry that the initial decision to avoid flashbacks and prophecies (fools, too, come to think of it) will cause problems later on – how are the showrunners going to get to R+L=J and still have the same impact if the idea hasn't been planted in the audience's head?

Their only go-to at the moment, as far as I can tell, is Meera's story about the crannogman and the Knight of the Laughing Tree, but that's a hard one to go on without context.

CATELYN IX

"The Freys have held the crossing for six hundred years, and for six hundred years they have never failed to exact their toll."

Synopsis

Robb Stark's host arrives at the Twins to find that Walder Frey has holed up in his castle with 4,000 men rather than marching south to fight with Edmure Tully, who, they discover, has been roundly thrashed at Riverrun. Given the urgency of the situation, Catelyn Stark is sent to negotiate with the lord of the Crossing. Robb agrees to pay his price in order to put his larger stratagem in motion.

Political Analysis

"Catelyn IX" is a very rich source of material for this section, in that the events of the chapter revolve around a political negotiation between Catelyn Stark and Walder Frey, and the theme of the chapter revolves around the question of what kind of political learning Robb Stark has acquired and what use he'll make of it. It's also a chapter that I've been looking forward to for a long time, because this bargain is a subject that I think much of the fandom is simply wrong about... more on this a bit later.

Robb's political learning – one of the few maxims of presidential politics that I've found to be generally accurate is that one of the best qualities a leader can have is the capacity for growth. It's a good sign, therefore, that when Catelyn checks in on Robb's development as a leader in this chapter, he shows a capacity for political learning. First, we learn that Robb "would ask one of his lords to join him... each day... so that they might confer as they marched; he honored every man in turn, showing no favorites, listening as his lord father had listened, weighing the words of one against the other. *He has learned so much from Ned*, she thought... *but has he learned enough?*" We've seen Ned doing this from Arya's perspective, and it's nice to be reminded that, in his own sphere, Ned engaged in good political practice and that Robb has learned this from him. As Richard Neudstadt wrote in *Presidential Power*:

> *A president['s] first essential need is information... to help himself, he must reach out as widely as he can for every scrap of fact, opinion, gossip bearing on his interests and relationships as president. He must become his own director of his own central intelligence. For that directorship, two rules of conduct can be drawn from the case studies in this book. On the one hand, he can never assume that anyone or any system will supply the bits and pieces he needs most; on the other, he must assume that much of what he needs will not be volunteered by his official advisers.*

By listening widely to his bannermen and comparing their advice and information, Robb is giving himself both the widest possible lens of information but also gaining a perspective from which he can judge his advisers. It's a good start.

More importantly for the question of political learning, when it comes time for Robb to choose between his personal happiness and the war effort, he shows his willingness to sacrifice the former for the latter, consenting to the betrothal in order to cross the river. Unlike Renly or Stannis, who get frequently distracted from the task at hand when an issue of their reputation is raised, Robb prioritizes victory over the Lannisters and his father's rescue over everything else – another good sign.

Let's make a deal (with Walder Frey) – as I mentioned above, the major political event of the chapter is that Catelyn trades Robb's (and Arya's) hand in marriage for the support of House Frey.* This betrothal, and Robb breaking it, is seen by many of the fans as *the* cause of Robb's downfall, which, in turn, places the blame for House Stark's defeat in the War of the Five Kings squarely on Robb's shoulders. However, as I will demonstrate in succeeding chapters from here to the Red Wedding, it is not the case that Robb breaking his marriage pact was the cause of his defeat.

> * Side note: while Catelyn does accomplish her immediate objective of getting the bridge crossing and the 4,000 men of House Frey, the fact that she has to give up both Robb and Catelyn to the Freys suggests that she might not have worked out the best deal possible. One sign that there might have been a better deal on the table comes from Walder himself when he says, "Your family has always pissed on me, don't deny it... years ago, I went to your father and suggested a match between his son and my daughter... Lord Hoster would not hear of it. Sweet words he gave me, excuses, but what I wanted was to get rid of a daughter."

Between this and Walder's offer of a Red Wedding, I think getting Edmure married into the Freys was something that Walder wanted very dearly and might have considered a fair bargain for his support. Selling Edmure's hand in marriage would have, in turn, kept Robb's hand in marriage open for a dynastic alliance that would have been absolutely necessary in winning the War of the Five Kings and maintaining an independent north afterwards.

Indeed, there is a basic philosophical inconsistency between the widely-held position that Eddard's defeat was the result of his being too honorable and the position that Robb's defeat was caused when he lost his honor. One cannot take at face value that "in the game of thrones, you win or you die" and turn around and argue that one should never break one's vows; either Robb should have been willing to break any vow, any law, any custom of Westeros in order to win (as Tywin does), or the callous calculus that Cersei follows is completely wrong.

More importantly, the question of whether Robb should have kept his word to Walder seems to rest on the mistaken assumption that Walder Frey was primarily reacting to the insult. Throughout "Catelyn IX," it is repeatedly remarked on that Walder Frey is a disloyal man who will not uphold his vows and who cannot be trusted in the slightest. As Catelyn points out the moment she sees his host drawn up at the Twins, "It was the Trident all over, damn the man. Her brother, Edmure, had called the banners; by rights, Lord Frey should have gone to join the Tully host at Riverrun, yet here he sat." Walder Frey's protestations that he meant to send his swords are patently false, given that every other riverlands house made it to Riverrun to fight in the battle. The fact that Ser Jared Frey, the liar, swears "on his honor" that Walder's intent was good only confirms this. Likewise, his protestation that "I swore oaths to the crown, too" are, ultimately, hollow (and, ultimately, more directed as setting up a bidding war for his loyalty) - Edmure's call to fight went out almost a month before King Robert died, and the declaration that the Tullys and their bannermen would have to come to King's Landing or be attainted couldn't have reached him until after the battles of Golden Tooth and Riverrun, which ought to have made him a traitor by association. In other words, Walder Frey is blackmailing the Starks over something he is, by rights, obligated to do, anyway.

At the same time, Catelyn has a pretty good read on Walder Frey's character: "Some men take their oaths more seriously than others... he has an old man's caution and a young man's ambition, and has never lacked for cunning... this bore Walder Frey's seal beyond a doubt... hold back, wait, and take no risk unless forced to it." This kind of a man doesn't act solely out of a grudge; while, clearly, Walder Frey is a bitter man who treasures his grievances, he didn't get to where he is today by letting his grievances overpower his sense of self-preservation. In that light, Robb marrying Jeyne Westerling is less the cause of Walder Frey's betrayal than the excuse.

So... given that he's dealing with a patently bad actor, who is blackmailing them over something he's obliged to do anyway, and who won't hesitate to betray them, it makes no sense to hold that Robb should have kept his word to Walder Frey at all costs. As Machiavelli says in his chapter on "How Princes Ought to Keep Faith" (one of his most controversial chapters in *The Prince* and what might have gotten his book banned by the church):

> *Everyone understands how praiseworthy it is in a prince to keep faith, and to live uprightly and not craftily. Nevertheless, we see from what has taken place in our own days that princes who have set little store by their word, but have known how to overreach men by their cunning, have accomplished great things, and, in the end, got the better of those who trusted to honest dealing. Be it known, then, that there are two ways of contending, one in accordance with the laws, the other by force; the first of which is proper to men, the second to beasts. But since the first method is often ineffectual, it becomes necessary to resort to the second. A prince should, therefore, understand how to use well both the man and the beast... but since a prince should know how to use the beast's nature wisely, he ought of beasts to choose both the lion and the fox; for the lion cannot guard himself from the toils, nor the fox from wolves. He must therefore be a fox to discern toils, and a lion to drive off wolves.*
>
> *To rely wholly on the lion is unwise, and, for this reason, a prudent prince neither can nor ought to keep his word when to keep it is hurtful to him and the causes which led him to pledge it are removed. If all men were good, this would not be good advice, but since they are dishonest and do not keep faith with you, you in return need not keep faith with them, and no prince was ever at a loss for plausible reasons to cloak a breach of faith. Of this, numberless recent instances could be given, and it might be shown how many solemn treaties and engagements have been rendered inoperative and idle through want of faith in princes, and that he who was best known to play the fox has had the best success.*

I would argue that Robb's major mistake was that he didn't break his vow in a more calculated manner. As Catelyn points out, "boys might play with swords, but it took a lord to make a marriage pact, knowing what it meant." Robb Stark is the heir to Winterfell, and will shortly be the lord of Winterfell, and, then, King in the North; in the middle of a civil war, he needs to be marrying much higher than the Freys and their 4,000 men. Asha Greyjoy could bring several hundred ships and 10,000 men; Arianne Martell could bring 25,000 spears and has a burning hatred of the Lannisters; the Tyrells have the largest army in Westeros, are already inclined to oppose the Lannisters, and have more than four unmarried female relations. Catelyn essentially admits as much, when she thinks, "If you had to fall into a woman's arms, my son, why couldn't they have been Margaery Tyrell's? The wealth and power of Highgarden could have made all the difference in the fighting to come."

Indeed, Robb should have been willing to break his oath to the Freys the moment it would have advanced the interests of his house, and used hostages and his 400 men at the Twins to force House Frey to remain in the field in defense of their liege lord.

Update on the War of the Five Kings – also in this chapter, we get a major update on the War of the Five Kings. Now, we've already seen from the Lannister perspective what the First Battle of Riverrun did for them, in that it basically eliminated the riverlands as a military threat to the Lannisters. At the same time, it massively screws the Starks by taking out 20,000 allies that they badly needed in order to bring themselves up to the Lannisters' level (once again, George R.R. Martin raising the stakes on our protagonists). The description of the battle given in this chapter raises new questions: namely, how exactly did it take place such that "the Kingslayer has destroyed Edmure's host and sent the lords of the Trident reeling in flight" to such an extent that "the Kingslayer went through him like an axe through ripe cheese?" What is the total military strength of the riverlands?

It's historically unlikely for an army to be so utterly destroyed in the field, especially since Jaime had 15,000 men and Edmure probably had somewhere between 16-20,000 men (his army is described as the "massed power" of the Tullys, Edmure raises 11,000 men at the Battle of the Fords after the losses of the first Battle of Riverrun, and Vance and Piper's 4,000 were not present), putting them fairly even in numbers. If I had to guess, I would say that surprise is responsible, given the shock and the lopsided result; Edmure had sent Vance and Piper to block the river road pass and most likely didn't have scouts or pickets out to warn him of the sudden result. Especially given the fact that the riverlords mobilized for war after the Lannisters, I think Edmure was drilling his new recruits and organizing his forces as the different lords came in when he was attacked – and, as history has shown, green troops do not respond well to surprise attacks.

However, this also raises the question of what the massed forces of the riverlands are. Elio estimates that the riverlands have anywhere between 20,000 and 45,000 men, which is a very wide range that he admits is based on the disjuncture between what one would assume the riverlands could support, given its size, the fertility of the region, the importance of rivers for trade and logistics, etc., and what Martin has written about their forces. Now, given that they lost somewhere in the region of 3,500 men at the Golden Tooth, that the Freys withheld their 4,000 men, and that the riverlords got back up to a force of almost 20,000 right after the Battle of the Camps and then again to 11,000 (minus the Freys) at the Battle of the Fords (which suggests that most of the army broke and ran rather than was cut down), I think the riverlands must support at least 30-35,000 soldiers normally. Add 4,000 men of Vance and Piper, plus 4,000 Freys, plus around 20,000 at Riverrun, and it gives you 28,000 men. This probably doesn't include much of the southern riverlands (or the "lower Trident"), which took significant casualties from Tywin's march to Harrenhal and Gregor's chevauchée after the Green Fork, which probably makes up between 7-10,000 men.

All of this has huge military implications for Robb's campaign. As we will see later, the military strength of the various contenders in the War of the Five Kings is constantly fluctuating and can do so very quickly – so that a good commander has to be a good politician, always monitoring the health of his coalition and looking to expand it so that his effective fighting force keeps growing rather than shrinking. With one deal with the Freys, Robb goes from being outnumbered compared to Tywin by 2,000 men to outnumbering his opponent by the same margin. Likewise, given the size and importance of House Mallister of Seagard (and that the Mallisters are one of the few forces to retreat in good order from Riverrun), I think Robb arrived at the Whispering Woods with at least 2,000 men more than he departed the Twins with, contrary to A Wiki of Ice and Fire's estimates.

At the same time, however, Robb was heavily relying on both surprise to maximize his offensive multiplier and the geography of Riverrun to divide his enemy into sections that he could outnumber locally and, thus, defeat in detail, thus allowing him to split his army into 16,000 foot to 6,000 horse and taking the smaller force into battle. Here I agree with BryndenBfish, who concludes that Robb took a good calculated risk in this part of the campaign, although I would stress more the extent to which Robb's decision to make this gamble was informed by his and his uncle's understanding of the geography of Riverrun. If Jaime had been able to have all 15,000 men united as one force, I think Robb's actions would have more resembled his actions in the show... more on that later.

Historical Analysis

So while we're talking about Walder Frey, I might as well take this opportunity to discuss the topic of treachery in the Wars of the Roses. While the war has often been seen as a bitter, entrenched struggle between families bent on victory and revenge, which it was, it was also a conflict in which individual lords and entire families betrayed their liege lords repeatedly, switching sides over and order again – one major reason why all of the kings who succeeded Henry VI all focused on reducing and then eliminating the "affinities" (paid soldiers wearing the livery of a nobleman) of the noble families of England.

Some of the more impressive scoundrels of the Wars of the Roses include:

"Perfidious" Lord Stanley, the Earl of Derby (a good pick for historical parallels to Walder Frey), who came from a staunch Lancastrian house, but was married into the Yorkists through the earl of Warwick. At the Battle of Blore Heath, one of the opening battles of the war, Stanley raised 2,000 men at his king's command but then withheld them just a few miles away as a Lancastrian army was defeated by a smaller Yorkist force. When Edward IV took up the Yorkist cause, Stanley defected and fought alongside the new king; when Warwick defected from Edward IV, Stanley fought to restore Henry VI for the last time. Remarkably, he managed to get appointed to Edward IV's royal council even after his betrayal. He then married Margaret Beaufort, the mother of Henry Tudor, while helping Richard III fight the Scots. Famously, Stanley held back his forces at Bosworth Field despite Richard III holding his son hostage, and then charged Richard's rear once the king was fully committed, personally crowning Henry VII to make sure he ended up on the right side.

Andrew Trollope, a career soldier, was one of Warwick's closest lieutenants from his service at Warwick's side in Calais. After sailing to England with Warwick's fleet, Trollope defected to the Lancastrians with his entire force at Ludlow. His tactical genius proved invaluable to Margaret D'Anjou, as he devised the stratagems of sending false reinforcements to York wearing looted surcoats to lure him out of Sandal Castle, and in hiding the two wings of the Lancastrian forces in the woods to destroy the Yorkist army at Wakefield, and was knighted at the Lancastrian triumph of the Second Battle of St. Albans. Less skilled at "re-ratting" than Lord Stanley, Andrew Trollope died on the field at Towton.

Lord Grey, a veteran of the wars in Acquitaine, served the Lancastrian cause consistently... right up until the Battle of Northhampton, when he ordered his men to lay down their arms as Warwick's forces neared the fortifications of the Lancastrian left flank, after which Warwick rolled up the line, sent the Lancastrian army into a panicked rout, and captured King Henry VI. For his pains, Lord Grey was awarded a disputed manor, the position of Lord Treasurer, and, with the hand of Joan Woodville, the title of earl of Kent. Apparently, the wages of treason are real estate.

William Neville, the uncle of the Kingmaker and Baron of Fauconberg, fought by Richard, Duke of York's side in France for 17 years. After being ransomed by the king and then paid a thousand pounds in restitution, Neville fought for the Lancastrians at the First Battle of St. Albans, but then managed to get appointed to the Royal Council during Richard's reign as Lord Protector; when the wars started up again, Neville defected to the Lancastians again with perfect timing, right before the disastrous Battle of Wakefield. When Edward IV came along, Neville fought for the new king, and got made Lieutenant of the North, Lord Admiral, and the earl of Kent (Lord Grey would take the title after his death in 1463).

And that's just the early Wars of the Roses; I haven't even gotten into the Edwardian or Ricardian phases yet. So if you think that George R.R. Martin lays it on thick with the Florents and the Tyrells, the Brackens and the Blackwoods, the Boltons and Freys, etc., if anything he's slightly understating how thoroughly "each for his own" became the way to survive in our own timeline.

<u>What If?</u>

Given the momentous decisions involved in "Catelyn IX," this chapter gives rise to a number of hypothetical scenarios:

What if Robb had brought some wood? One of the hypothetical scenarios I've always wondered about is what would have happened if Robb (or Brynden the Blackfish) had brought a load of lumber to the Twins, for example from White Harbor, to use in rafting or pontooning across the Green Fork. Martin somewhat exaggerates the time it takes to cross a river in order to force Robb into making this particular choice, but, historically, the earl of Warwick was able to rebuild the bridge at Ferrybridge the day before Towton in far less than a day (given that he had to slowly force a crossing under fire, and then had time at the end of the day to set up camp as well as to repair the bridge), and Edward IV then had to repeat the feat the next day when a surprise Lancastrian attack forced a retreat and a torching of the repaired bridge, and then went on to fight the Battle of Towton. If Robb had had the opportunity to build a pontoon bridge or raft across the Green Fork, Catelyn would have been able to negotiate a much better deal with the Freys, given that the Freys' most potent bargaining chip would have been neutralized, and in the case of a pontoon bridge, gives the Starks a bargaining chip to throw to the Freys.

What if Catelyn had negotiated a different deal? So, let's say either that Catelyn had that to work with or that Walder would have been interested enough in the possibility of getting Edmure's hand in marriage. If Robb can get across the Twins without offering his hand in marriage, then the politics of the later War of the Five Kings change dramatically. For example, let's say Robb's offer to the Greyjoys had more meat on the bone than the offer to make Balon king of the Iron Islands – if, instead, he had offered a marriage alliance between their two houses? While Balon would likely have reacted with hostility, Asha Greyjoy, with her mind on pinecones and seashells, might have reacted differently. A Stark-Greyjoy alliance garners Robb 10,000 ironborn and their fleet, frees up 17,000 northmen to come down south and reinforce him, and potentially allows Robb to take Lannisport from the sea and enough troops to keep Casterly Rock under siege, while putting his total forces in the riverlands up to 55,000, which would be enough to take on a Lannister-Tyrell alliance and get to equal footing or better with one or two victories in the field. Likewise, if Catelyn Stark had had the presence of mind at Bitterbridge, she might have been able to nip in before Littlefinger and create a Stark-Tyrell alliance strong enough to win the War of the Five Kings for the Starks outright, even with the temporary loss of the north (and, hey, both groups hate the Lannisters and the Greyjoys!).

What if there was no deal? Let's say Walder is just too cautious on a given day to cross Lord Tywin, and no deal is reached. So Plan A is off the table, and Robb has to go with Plan B – go straight at Tywin and gamble on a sudden victory. With Brynden Tully in charge of his scouts, there's no way the night march is detected. If 18,000 northmen hit Tywin's army completely unexpectedly, it's quite possible that the War of the Five Kings goes mirror-image, with Tywin (and, maybe, Tyrion) in Jaime's place and Jaime now seeing the Starks between him and King's Landing. This would be very interesting, indeed, especially with a Jaime who's still in his over-confident and reckless phase, but especially in political terms – Tywin hasn't heard word one about the Stark perspective on the war, and he and Tyrion might be smart enough to put two-and-two together about who's really responsible for the war. At the same time, it's really unclear what happens politically once Tywin's a prisoner – Jaime is aggressive and reckless, but would he risk his father's life? Would Cersei? Granted, it would probably be too late to save Ned's life, but with Tywin in chains, Cersei might actually have to give in to Robb Stark's demands.

Book vs. Show

One of the plotlines that has been the most changed in the transition from book to show is the War of the Five Kings, and as I'll point out going forward, this has often been for the worse. However, one change that I found intriguing is Robb sending only 2,000 men vs. 16,000 down to confront Tywin while he crosses the Twins. Despite the callousness of sending 2,000 men to their deaths, this probably would save many lives overall, given 2,000 casualties versus the 4,000 to 6,000 that BookRoose seems to have suffered at the Green Fork (more on this in the next Tyrion chapter). It also gives Robb Stark many more men on the west side of the Green Fork to use for his invasion of the westerlands, which, if Benioff and Weiss had thought carefully about this part of the plot, definitely makes the "take Casterly Rock" plan more sensible (and one wonders why it didn't happen earlier, between seasons two and three).

Historically speaking, it's perfectly possible for a force of 2,000 men to masquerade as a larger force - it happened repeatedly during the American Civil War, for example, so the change isn't necessarily a bad one from a historical or military perspective.

It's what comes after where things get screwed up.

JON VIII

"The sword, the sword, the sword!"

Synopsis

Jon Snow gets a sword and has a series of conversations with Jeor Mormont and Aemon Targaryen that he doesn't really understand the point of.

Political Analysis

Zombie talk – in "Jon VIII," we check in with the aftermath of the wights' attack on Castle Black. Whereas the previous chapter focused specifically on the assassination attempt on Lord Commander Mormont, here we learn that:

> *"It would seem that there were only the two of... of those creatures, whatever they were – I will not call them men... the other wight, the one-handed thing that had once been a ranger named Jafer Flowers, had also been destroyed, cut near to pieces by a dozen swords... but not before it had slain Ser Jaremy Rykker and four other men. Ser Jaremy had finished the job of hacking its head off, yet had died all the same when the headless corpse pulled his own dagger from its sheath and buried it in his bowels."*

This is why I said in the previous chapter that the evidence is ambiguous about whether decapitation kills wights – "finished the job" suggests a certain finality, but the corpse can still use tools and kill what's within reach, but that could easily be a case of "death throes" killing the killer. We do get confirmation that normal steel can, in fact, kill wights, but they take a hell of a lot of killing, requiring being "cut near to pieces." This is a good thing for the Night's Watch, given the difficulty of using fire in combat, but it's definitely a silver lining on a very dark cloud.

At the same time, this information raises an interesting question: if two wights could kill at least six men, why didn't the Others send more wights (as the lord commander notes)? We know that they have at least two more wights – Waymar Royce and Will – who are black brothers who conceivably would be brought to the other side of the Wall for burial to be re-activated. One possibility is that the Others considered that having two separate parties of dead rangers might make the Night's Watch too suspicious about the corpses to bring them back (it was a near thing, in any case) – which itself tells us that the Others have quite a bit of rationality, more so than we often assume.

Death and succession – the fact that Rykker specifically dies suggests that the grim fates (aka George R.R. Martin) are clearing the way for Jon Snow to rule, well over two books before the election takes place. Rykker is a highborn knight with both military experience (he fought for King Aerys at the Sack of King's Landing) and 15 years of service with the Watch. With that background and as Acting First Ranger, Rykker would have been a leading candidate as lord commander – the kind of person with the right class background to appeal to Ser Denys Mallister and the experience required to pass muster with Cotter Pyke. His death, along with Thoren Smallwood at the Fist of the First Men and Donal Noye during the Siege of Castle Black, eliminates most leaders of any standing from Castle Black, leaving Jon Snow.

It's also in this chapter that we see the first sign that Jeor Mormont really is grooming Jon Snow to succeed him as lord commander of the Night's Watch. And I have to say, while it seems more Standard Fantasy Protagonist/Hero's Journey/Freudian Symbolism on first read, once you've read *The Sworn Sword*, this action seems far more consequential because it's grounded in history. As we saw from the case of Daemon Blackfyre, giving a Valyrian sword to a bastard can be a politically potent symbol of succession, potent enough to cause a civil war. And in this case, Jon Snow is getting not just any Valyrian sword, he's getting the family sword of House Mormont. This is a statement that everybody in Castle Black understands: Jon Snow is now Jeor Mormont's adopted son and heir in all but name. And, yet, even this can't stop Jon Snow's daddy issues.

Institutional memory and the Night's Watch – following up on the last Jon chapter, we have the central question of why the Night's Watch has forgotten the enemy they were created to fight: "We ought to have known. We ought to have remembered. The Long Night has come before. Oh, eight thousand years is a good while, to be sure… yet if the Night's Watch does not remember, who will?" Certainly, forgetting that the living dead and their masters are real and not legends trotted out to impress guests is a massive failing. At the same time, it's not surprising that the Night's Watch's records are as patchy as Sam will find them later.

Consider, if you will, what eight thousand years means. The Abusir Papyri is perhaps the oldest document not written on stone or clay, and it's 4,300-plus-years-old; the oldest document period is the Kish tablet (written on clay tablet) that is some 5,500-plus-years-old, and that document is considered to have been written at the transition from proto-writing to writing itself. Eight thousand years from our current time predates writing itself, the use of bronze, and the invention of the wheel.

There is no human institution that has lasted eight thousand years. The Katoch dynasty in India dates back 6,300 years, and that was back when Katoch rulers were claiming to have fought the god Rama, but that's a family that came in and out of power. The Catholic Church claims to be the oldest continually-operating institution at some 1,900-odd years, but even then, there are popes for which we have almost no documentation of.

So, it's already beyond human experience that a single institution could exist for eight thousand years. But even if an institution lasted that long, it's beyond human experience that they'd have written records dating that far back; even if they did, they'd probably be unreadable. Languages go extinct all the time, but even living languages change enormously. Consider this, the oldest surviving text in Old English:

> *nu scylun hergan hefaenricaes uard*
> *metudæs maecti end his modgidanc*
> *uerc uuldurfadur swe he uundra gihwaes*
> *eci dryctin or astelidæ*
> *he aerist scop aelda barnum*
> *heben til hrofe haleg scepen.*
> *tha middungeard moncynnæs uard*
> *eci dryctin æfter tiadæ*
> *firum foldu frea allmectig*

Can you read that? Unless you've taken special classes in Old English, you can't, and that document ("Caedmon's Hymn") is only 1,263-years-old. Honestly, I'm surprised that folk tales about the White Walkers have survived this long.

Aemon's theory of the Night's Watch – along with the revelation that Maester Aemon is a Targaryen, "Jon VIII" also gives us a good helping of Aemon's political theory. This, in turn, is critically important for understanding why Jon thinks and does the way he does as lord commander in *A Dance with Dragons,* as Aemon is the most significant influence on his political thinking, if we can judge by the number of mentions in internal dialogue.

The first and most significant element of Aemon's theory of the Night's Watch (and politics) is a sort of proto-internationalism. More so than Varys, whose conception of the realm is a kind of proto-nationalism, Aemon sees the Night's Watch and the realm it protects as beyond even the concept of the nation: "They pledged as well that the Night's Watch would take no part in the battles of the realms... when the Andals crossed the narrow sea and swept away the kingdoms of the First Men, the sons of the fallen kings held true to their vows... When Aegon slew Black Harren and claimed his kingdom, Harren's brother was lord commander on the Wall... he did not march." (Incidentally, this detail suggests that, contrary to current ironborn thought of a strict separation between the islands and the "greenlands," the Iron Islands were part of the larger culture and polity of Westeros.) If the realm is greater than the nation both in terms of the state and in the sense of a people with a common language, history, culture, ethnicity, and identity, then it becomes something closer to a kind of cosmopolitan humanism that we see later when Jon Snow justifies his alliance with the wildlings on the grounds that the Night's Watch swears to protect the "realms of men" (note the significant plural). Indeed, I think it can be argued that without Aemon's teaching here, Jon Snow might not have managed to make his mission with the wildlings into more than just espionage.

At the same time, we learn quite a bit about the history of Westeros through its oldest institutions. For one thing, we learn that the current Seven Kingdoms were once "a hundred quarrelsome kingdoms," which suggests that, even prior to the Targaryen conquest, Westeros was undergoing a process of political centralization as regional powers established large-scale, long-term polities – and that, perhaps, the Seven Kingdoms might have been united without Aegon. On the other hand, we also learn that "in the days when the Seven Kingdoms were seven kingdoms, not a generation passed that three or four of them were not at war." In this sense, we get an idea of how impressive the Targaryen accomplishment was, and why the dynasty inspired such loyalty; like the Tudors, they demanded supremacy but offered peace. One interesting question is why, during these eight thousand years, the Starks didn't seek to conquer or assimilate a force of some 10,000 men (even if those 10,000 men had no permanent fortifications against them) – perhaps the answer is that the Starks used the Night's Watch as a place to put surplus male relations as a consolation prize, preventing civil wars.

The second major element of Aemon's theory is his idea that "love is the death of duty, the bane of honor," which ties into his later advice that Jon Snow (and Aegon) should "kill the boy and let the man be born." With all due respect to Maester Aemon, I think this is a major flaw in his thinking, and one that's caused an enormous amount of damage to the Night's Watch. As we've seen, vows of celibacy damage its capacity to recruit to the point where the Night's Watch has to look the other way when it comes to Mole's Town. In a larger sense, without a positive spirit of camaraderie within the Night's Watch such that individual soldiers build up a loyalty to one another as well as the institution, the strict discipline of the Night's Watch becomes brittle - as we see at Craster's Keep and again with Jon's assassination. Likewise, I think the fact that Eddard is held up as the paragon of honor in this chapter just as he's preparing to break his honor to protect his family is something of an internal critique from Martin about the weakness.

Indeed, historically and philosophically, love has often been seen as the exact opposite, a spur to military discipline. As Plato writes in the *Symposium*:

> ...if there were only some way of contriving that a state or an army should be made up of lovers and their beloved, they would be the very best governors of their own city, abstaining from all dishonor, and emulating one another in honor - and when fighting at each other's side, although a mere handful, they would overcome the world. For what lover would not choose rather to be seen by all mankind than by his beloved, either when abandoning his post or throwing away his arms? He would be ready to die a thousand deaths rather than endure this. Or who would desert his beloved or fail him in the hour of danger?"

This model was actually put into practice with the Sacred Band of Thebes. The Sacred Band was the elite fighting force of the Greek city-state of Thebes, composed of 150 pairs of male lovers precisely on the assumption that love would strengthen their sense of solidarity. The Sacred Band had an astonishing track record: in the Boetian War of 378 BC, their first engagement, the Sacred Band at the core of a force of 18,700 turned back a Spartan force of nearly 30,000 largely due to the Sacred Band's dogged defense of their fortifications and discipline in the face of the Spartan hoplites. At the Battle of Tegyra in 375 BC, the Sacred Band was challenged by a Spartan force of 1,000-1,8000 hoplites and broke the Spartan line, causing the Spartans to rout - the first time in recorded history that the Spartans were defeated by an inferior force. At the Battle of Leuctra, the Sacred Band permanently destroyed Spartan hegemony by cutting down 4,000 hoplites on the field, a loss the Spartan slave society could not replenish. Their end came at Chaeronea in 338 BC when, up against Phillip II and his son, Alexander of Macedon, the rest of the Theban army broke and ran, but the Sacred Band stood their ground and fought virtually to the last man, impressing the Macedonians so much that they permitted the Thebans to build a stone lion memorial to the fallen dead.

Love is a powerful force.

Historical Analysis

I've sort of already done the historical analysis above. More next chapter!

What If?

The only major *What If?* here is Rykker's death. If he lives, and survives the Fist of the First Men, it's quite possible Jon never becomes lord commander of the Night's Watch, and survives *A Dance with Dragons*. I have no idea how Rykker would have dealt with either Stannis or the Wildlings, given that we know so little of his character.

Book vs. Show

The show played this one pretty straight. The one criticism I have is that they allowed the severed wight hand to completely fall out of the narrative in season two, along with Alliser Thorne himself (although he's reappearing in season four). Not a huge problem, but I feel that the hand offers a more concrete connection between the Wall and the King's Landing plots than just reading a message via raven.

DAENERYS VII

"Princess... you have a gentle heart, but you do not understand. This is how it has always been."

Synopsis

Khal Drogo and his *khalasar* sack a Lhazarene village in the process of being sacked by a different *khalasar* to raid slaves for their trip across the ocean, and Khal Drogo slays Khal Ogo and Khal Fogo to do it. Dany insists that his wound be treated by Mirri Maz Duur.

Political Analysis

It's interesting that so many fans of *A Song of Ice and Fire* were frustrated by Daenerys's plotline in *A Dance with Dragons*, given how much of it seems to be prefigured in this chapter. The return of the rightful heir to the throne, a fantasy trope older than Ivanhoe and Tolkien and so often made out to be a relatively bloodless affair in which the evil usurper and some presumably-evil guards die, here brings about the slaughter of innocent Lhazarene and raiding Dothraki alike.

And for those who argue that Dany is not responsible for what's happening here, it is explicitly stated by Daenerys herself that "this is the price of the Iron Throne." It is not even the case that the Lhazarene are "collateral damage" in an otherwise-justified war for the throne. The Lhazarene are paying for the ships that will take Dany's army across the sea: "I've told the *khal* he ought to make for Meereen... they'll pay a better price than he'd get from a slaving caravan. Illyrio writes that they had a plague last year, so the brothels are paying double for healthy young girls, and triple for boys under 10. If enough children survive the journey, the gold will buy us all the ships we need, and hire men to sail them."

While I would argue that George R.R. Martin's pacifist critique of war is tempered by his understanding of both the romantic allure of warfare and the realities of geopolitics, there is little ambiguity in this moment: "This is the way of war. These women are our slaves now, to do with as we please." This is not simply war as we have seen it at the Green Fork or, even, in the riverlands; this is systematized war on a defenseless people to produce slaves for the Essosi economy that Jorah, Drogo, Illyrio, and Dany intend to make use of. Pay attention to the description of the Unsullied Daenerys liberated in Astapor, or the slaves freed at Yunkai or Meereen – there are Lhazarene faces in those crowds, and Dothraki put them there. The next time you see a gif on Tumblr that seeks to equate Dany with an imperialist ignorant of Ghiscari culture, remember that *the Lhazarenes aren't part of that culture.*

Moreover, this is slavery explicitly justified by Dothraki racism: "They were herders of sheep and eaters of vegetables, and Khal Drogo said they belonged south of the river bend. The grass of the Dothraki sea was not meant for sheep… The Lamb Men lay with sheep – it is known… does the horse breed with the sheep?" If you recall from earlier, the Dothraki believe they have a manifest destiny to rule over the lesser peoples of Essos; here, we see this manifest destiny in action, and it's just as ugly as any imperialist conception from our own history. And as I'll discuss later, this attitude has more than a few historic parallels.

Dany's reaction to this organized human misery is quite instructive; she "hardened her heart" against murder and slavery, but when she is faced with the reality of the sexual slavery of children, something that comes far too close to her own situation sans-Stockholm Syndrome, she can't help herself: "Make them stop… I want no rape." Her moral reaction, however driven by selfish motives, nevertheless serves to move Dany away from her position as an assimilated Dothraki to becoming, once again, Rhaegar's sister. And yet, what often gets overlooked is that Daenerys's actions immediately lead to violence because she has broken with Dothraki custom: "Johqo's arakh flashed, and the man went tumbling from his shoulders. Laugher turned to curses as the horsemen reached for weapons… the readers looked at her with cold, black eyes." The seeds of Mago and Jhaqo's defection, which will undo all of Dany's humanitarian hopes, are sewn here. All of this happens because Dany cannot see the impossibility of the romantic vision that "if your warriors would mount these women, let them take them gently and keep them for wives." For her own sanity, Dany has willingly forgotten that she herself was a slave and that the Dothraki are not figures out of a romance novel.

It's not an accident that her attempt to sanitize Dothraki culture is immediately followed up by one of her most fateful decisions in *A Game of Thrones*: to have her husband healed by Mirri Maz Duur. Dany knows that this goes against taboo, that, to the Dothraki, "a maegi was a woman who lay with demons and practiced the blackest of sorceries, a vile thing, evil and soulless, who came to men in the dark of night and sucked life and strength from their bodies." It was bad enough when Dany was suggesting that Dothraki and Lamb Men were symbolically equals, but this decision will completely undo her position and kill her husband.

On that topic, it's really quite clear that Mirri Maz Duur plans to take revenge from the outset: "The Great Shepherd sent me to Earth to heal his lambs," she says, and immediately Qotho denies her statement of spiritual equality with a slap and the statement that, "We are no sheep." The next time that she says "the Great Shepherd guards the flock," she's not referring to Khal Drogo. To be clear, Mirri Maz Duur had motive, means, and opportunity to kill Khal Drogo and Rhaego.

Historical Analysis

The relationship between the Dothraki and the Lhazarene echoes a persistent trend in Eurasian history and pre-history in which nomadic horse-riding peoples warred against and (mostly) conquered settled agricultural peoples. The ancient Scythians, who conquered a territory from the Black Sea to the Caucuses and beyond into Central Asia from the 7th century BC into the 2nd century AD (when they were largely defeated by the Goths), successfully held off the Persian Emperor Darius the Great through a series of guerrilla campaigns, fought a series of (unsuccessful) wars against Phillip II and Alexander of Macedon, and warred against Mithridates the Great for control of the Crimea.

Their wealth ultimately came from their control of the slave trade that stretched from the basins of the Danube and the Don south down to the Black Sea to Greek ports, and it's for this reason that Scythians are often depicted as carrying both bows (given the natural combination of horse cavalry and archery) and whips – much like the Dothraki. In his history, Herodotus describes the Scythians triumphing over a slave revolt as follows:

> ...by fighting against them, we deplete both our forces and the number of our slaves. Let us drop our spears and bows and take up whips. Seeing those weapons in hand, they imagined that they were our equals... but when they see us with whips instead of weapons, they will understand that they are only our slaves, and will not be able to resist us.

A similar antagonism between horse nomads and settled farmers equally describes the relationship between the Mongols and the Slavic peoples from the invasion of 1223, which brought down Kievan Rus', through to the rise of Moscow through a complicated series of wars and diplomatic alliances against the various khanates in the 13th and 14th centuries, to the victories of Ivan III and Ivan the Terrible in the 15th century that broke the power of the khanates. While the legend of the "Tartar yoke" owes more to tsarist propaganda than historical evidence, the Mongol invasion of 1223 reduced the Russian population by 500,000 (or 6.6% of the total).

Likewise, much of the history of China could be described as a series of wars between the various empires of the river basins and various horse-riding nomadic tribes: the Xirong (the Chinese name for these people, which literally means "western warlike peoples"), who bedeviled the Zhou Dynasty in the 10th through 8th century BCE and many of the warring states before being defeated by the Qin in the 4th century; the Xiong-nu, who warred with the Han in the 2nd century BCE and whose defeat allowed for the completion of the Silk Road; the Wu Hu, who brought on "the throwing of China into disorder by the five barbarian tribes" in the 4th century; the Mongols, who conquered China in the 13th century CE; and the Manchu, who built the Qing dynasty that ruled China for almost three hundred years before being overthrown.

In general, if you're thinking that Martin is being particularly brutal, he's probably cribbing from history.

What If?

What if Drogo gets healed by the eunuch men? Granted, there's still a possibility that Drogo still would have died of infection, but Dany would probably still have turned to Mirri Maz Duur to save her "sun-and-stars," which leads us back to the OTL. But let's say a simple cauterization and stitching works, and Drogo heals from his wounds. In this scenario, Dany visits Slaver's Bay not as a conqueror and a liberator, but as a buyer and seller. Given the approximately 500 miles from the Lhazarene village to Slaver's Bay, she'd arrive in Meereen around the time that Drogo dies in OTL, some 19 days from now. Given a week for the selling of people and the buying and provisioning of a fleet, and the distance between Meereen and Westeros on a mostly-coastal route taking one safely around Valyria, Dany might have arrived in Westeros as early as Tyrion's arrival in King's Landing as Hand of the King. Most likely landing in Dorne, what would have happened there is unclear. Forty thousand Dothraki are a mighty force, but not enough to take on the roughly 400,000 soldiers of Westeros and succeed... but enough to bloody all participants sufficiently that, when Aegon and the Golden Company arrive and defeat the foreign invader, no one's left to dispute his claim to the Iron Throne.

Book vs. Show

The major difference between the book and the show is that Qotho outright challenges Drogo over the issue, leading to an epic duel between the two. This scene, invented at the behest of Jason Momoa, is one of those great examples of the difference between media: in the book, we can read easily about how great a warrior Khal Drogo was without ever having to see it on the page, because our imaginations are used to filling in the details. In a visual medium like television, however, the audience expects to be shown rather than told about these kind of things, and it gives a great sendoff for a character who, let's face it, doesn't really accomplish much despite being quite important for Dany's development as a character.

TYRION VIII

"Lord Cerwyn, Ser Wylis Manderly, Harrion Karstark, four Freys. Lord Hornwood is dead, and I fear Roose Bolton escaped us. The Stark boy was not with them, my lord. They say he crossed at the Twins with the great part of his horse, riding hard for Riverrun."

Synopsis

Tyrion arrives at the Lannister campsite to find out he's been assigned to the vanguard come the battle. After spending a night with Shae, he is rudely awakened to find that the Stark host is marching on them. The Battle of the Green Fork is fought, with the Starks being driven off with substantial casualties. However, Robb Stark isn't there...

Political Analysis

"Tyrion VIII" contains two events of note: the Battle of the Green Fork and Tyrion meeting Shae. I'll discuss the two in reverse order, since I have a lot more to say about the Greek Fork and don't want to jump back and forth.

Shae – needless to say, the difference between BookShae and ShowShae is staggering. The book version is introduced in a way that is meant to remind the reader and reflect on Tyrion's relationship with Tysha (and women in general). She's described as "slim, dark-haired, no more than 18 by the look of her," whereas Tysha is described as "dark-haired, slender, with a face that would break your heart... lowborn, half-starved, unwashed... yet lovely," and was around 14-years-old when Tyrion met her. After they first have sex, "a song filled his head... a song I learned as a boy," the song he associates with Tysha. And with hindsight from how their relationship will end, you can see how important this connection to Tysha is to get Tyrion to the place where, driven by trauma and rage, he murders her and his father.

Likewise, the relationship that Tyrion wants isn't just the "girlfriend experience" he asks for in the show – it's explicitly described that Tyrion's relationship with Shae is based on his disability: "'Be certain that you tell her who I am, and warn her of what I am.' [...] There was a look the girls got in their eyes sometimes when they first beheld the lordling they'd been hired to pleasure... a look that Tyrion Lannister did not ever care to see again." Indeed, Tyrion tests this with his wordplay about her former paramour and reacts to her nickname of "my giant of Lannister" with pleasure, remarking that "for a time, she almost made him believe it." This is why Shae's perjured testimony about Tyrion's treason hurts far less than the revelations about his sexual practices and, especially, that nick-name.

The War of the Five Kings: the Battle of the Green Fork - on to the battle - and what a battle this is. Re-reading this chapter has been a fascinating experience, because this battle made absolutely no sense to me the first time I read it. Indeed, for the longest time, I was under the misunderstanding that this battle was a contested east-west crossing of the Green Fork, even though the battle takes place on a north-south orientation (such was my confusion!). Now that I have re-read the chapter, I understand it much more clearly, and I think the confusion is intentional for several reasons. I have to thank BryndenBFish for his excellent work on the battle itself and the question of Roose's treason, which helped to crystallize some of my inchoate thoughts. I hope my analysis adds to his work, as, for once, I don't have a contrary opinion.

To begin with, I am only further convinced of my theory that Roose Bolton deliberately botched this battle. Re-reading the chapter's description of the pre-battle operations, we learn two things: first, Brynden Tully's mission to ensure that "Addam Marbrand... will not know when we split" was absolutely successful, as the Lannisters learn from "Ser Addam's outriders [that] the Stark host has moved south from the Twins... Lord Frey's levies have joined them. They are likely no more than a day's march north of us." In other words, Stark scouting operations on the right bank of the Green Flank don't seem to have failed. This is confirmed by the second fact, which is that it's not the case that Marbrand detected Roose on his night march. Rather, when "the horns called through the night, wild and urgent, a cry that said hurry, hurry, hurry," the Lannister host was *surprised* by the movement and only discovered Bolton's forces when they saw "his host... less than a mile north of here, forming up in battle array." This last point is crucial.

The entire point of a night march is to move at full speed to get into contact with an unexpected enemy as quickly as possible. You don't stop a mile away to draw up in formation and offer a set-piece battle and give your larger opponent a chance to mobilize; you slam into your enemy as quickly as you can, using the disorganization and shock of the attack to carry the day. This is born out in a number of historical examples:

The **Battle of Lincoln** in 1141 CE (one of the major turning points in "the Anarchy") - Earl Robert of Gloucester "cunningly concealed his purpose all the way from Gloucester to Lincoln, keeping the whole army in uncertainty, except for a very few, by taking an indirect route... he resolved to risk a battle at once, and swam across the racing current of the river mentioned above with all his men." No pause to form up into battle array; Gloucester piled straight into battle straight across a contested river crossing and crushed King Stephen's army between his army and the garrison of Lincoln castle.

The **Battle of Falkirk** in 1298 CE – in which Edward I triumphed over William Wallace. The battle began with a night march in which the left battalion of the English forces slammed straight into the enemy's knights and archers, requiring King Edward's personal intervention to reorder his disorganized cavalry, which had broken their peers but failed to break the Scottish infantry's schiltron formation; that task would devolve to the English archers, who massacred the tightly-packed Scottish pikemen.

The **Battle of Sekigahara** in 1600 CE – began with a night march of Tokugawa's Eastern Army literally stumbling into Ishida Mitsunari's army due to a dense fog that had masked the positions of the two armies.

The **Battle of Culloden** in 1746 CE – started with a night march in which two-thirds of the Jacobite army mounted a night attack despite orders to the contrary because the messenger carrying those orders missed them in the dark.

Bolton's actions here have no explanation, given his experience as a commander and competence later displayed when fighting for his own house. His pause almost a mile away to form up into battle gave the Lannisters crucial time to mobilize their forces; had he simply kept marching, the Starks would have fallen on a sleeping army with no opportunity to get themselves into line and under chain of command, and, thus, unable to carry out their plan. However, this is only **Exhibit A** in my case against Roose Bolton.

Tywin's bloodless (and bloody) plan – it's interesting that Tyrion somewhat misunderstands Tywin's plan in this chapter (a sign of his inexperience, given how quickly Tyrion will learn). While Tyrion assumes that the decision to place his mountain men in the vanguard is intended to "rid himself of his embarrassing get for good," Tywin's actual objective here is to leverage the "lack [of] discipline" of Tyrion's men, with Tyrion's possible death a mere bonus: "I put the least disciplined men on the left, yes. I anticipated that they would break. Robb Stark is a green boy, more like to be brave than wise. I'd hoped that if he saw our left collapse, he might plunge into the gap, eager for a rout. Once he was fully committed, Ser Kevan's pikes would wheel and take him in the flank, driving him into the river while I brought up the reserve." Now, I don't think that Tywin ranks among the great generals of Westeros – most of his early victories seem to have taken place against enemies he vastly outnumbered, and he's beaten by Edmure Tully despite Edmure's general lack of skill – but this chapter shows that he's a skilled commander, who understands how to make use of his particular forces

George R.R. Martin's intricate detailing of the Lannister line of battle (that BryndenBFish does a great job on) is not matched with any level of detail on the northern troops – a sign that Martin is up to something. We learn that Tyrion's "uncle would lead the center... the foot archers arrayed themselves into three long lines, to east and west of the road, and stood calmly stringing their bows. Between them, pikemen formed squares; behind were rank on rank of men-at-arms with spear and sword and axe. Three hundred heavy horse surrounded Ser Kevan, and the lords bannermen Lefford, Lydden, and Serrett with all their sworn retainers." The right flank "was all cavalry, some four thousand men, heavy with the weight of their armor. More than three quarters of the knights were there, massed together like a great steel fist." The reserve is unusually large, "a huge force, half mounted and half foot, five thousand strong," meaning that the 16,000 northmen are going to slam into a front line of 15,000 before Tywin plunges that reserve in like a dagger.

The left flank is put up against the riverbank, "the left of the left. To turn their flank, the Starks would need horses that could run on water... this wing, too, was all cavalry, but where the right was a mailed fist of knights and heavy lancers, the vanguard was made up of the sweepings of the west," lighter cavalry and a deliberately easy target. Indeed, I would argue it's something of an obvious trap – the vanguard of a medieval army is the leading force and tasked with the toughest fighting, and in an army the size of Tywin's, one would expect it to be much larger than a mere 5% of the total army.

The plan is quite simple: the right holds against the Stark left, the center gets ready to contain the Stark breakthrough, and the reserve is placed to drive Stark's army against the river. A pity it doesn't actually happen that way.

The battle and Bolton's (lack of a) strategy – part of the reason that it doesn't happen that way is that Roose's actions on the battlefield makes little military sense. To begin with, we have **Exhibit B** in my case: the question of why in the hell Roose is attacking a force that contains at least 7,500 heavy cavalry (Marbrand's 4,000 are three-quarters of the total knights, plus the 300 around Kevan, plus the 2,500 in the reserve) and 1,000 light cavalry on the left flank when he has around 600 cavalry – and why he's attacking at all. The northern attack on the Lannister left flank is described as "boiling over the tops of the hills, "and Kevan's assault is described as having "pushed the northerners against the hills." Given the enormous defensive advantage given to disciplined infantry fighting from the high ground, especially when fighting heavy cavalry, Bolton had the perfect opportunity to eke out an unlikely victory by retaining the high ground and forcing the Lannisters to attack, an opportunity he squanders without cause or benefit. Moreover, Roose's main action – the attack on the Lannister left – involves only infantry, "advancing with measured tread behind a wall of shields and pikes," rather than sending in his limited cavalry to open up a gap that his infantry could exploit against the Lannister center.

We can see the inappropriateness of this tactic almost immediately: the Stark attack never lands, because the Lannister left is fast enough to counter-charge first, forcing the Karstark infantry into a slapdash schiltron. This shield wall is easily broken by the Mountain and the mountain men (great band name, by the way), and then the Stark right is forced into a chaotic retreat that's made all the worse once the Lannister center and reserve is brought in to finish the job.

In other words, Roose Bolton is doing the exact opposite of what the Saxon army of Harold Godwinson did to try to win the battle of Hastings – take the high ground, which can be easily held by a disciplined shield wall of infantry against heavy cavalry trying to charge up-hill and avoid charging into feigned retreats, where the superior mobility of cavalry can be used against slower infantry. No experienced infantry commander would make this mistake, especially once he laid eyes on his enemy's dispositions.

Exhibit C is the mysterious absence of much of the northern army. As BryndenBFish has noted, the Flayed Man of House Bolton isn't seen on the field, despite the fact that it makes up a full quarter of their numbers. I would point to additional absences that make little sense: the first is the absence of the northern cavalry in the fight, given how crucial they would have been to making the attack on the left actually succeed. The second is the absence of the northern archers; the northern infantry is described, without exception, as being composed of spearmen operating in shield walls when it should have quite a few archers, given that it's the whole of the Stark foot. The third is the total absence of any description of the north's left flank engaging in the battle at all (and the relative absence of the north's center, which we only hear about later in the battle, when Kevan pushes forward), which, you would think, would have come more into play when the Lannisters commit their entire reserves to their left (which would be on the Stark's right). This last part is quite mysterious: given the geography of the battlefield, the Starks should be trying to get around the Lannister's *right*, not the left, so that it can roll up the flank in the direction of the river, trying to push their enemies downhill, instead of trying to fight up the gradient the entire way. And, yet, we never see or hear of any action other than the Stark right on the Lannister right.

Given that the northern host is only 16,000 strong, the absence of the Boltons (4,000 men) and the northern cavalry (600) and the northern left (approximately 5,300 men) suggests that, perhaps, only 6,100 of the northern host – the unlucky northern right – were fully engaged in the battle. This failure to commit the bulk of the northern forces to the fight suggests that, just as is later the case at Duskendale and the Ruby Ford, Bolton is deliberately throwing a third of his army into the meat grinder.

Exhibit D comes with the mysterious beginning of the battle, which opens with the *Lannister* archers firing first: "A vast flight of infantry arched up from his right [i.e., from the center, where Kevan commands]... the northerners broke into a run, shouting as they came, but the Lannister arrows fell on them like hail." This also fails a very basic test of military skill: in medieval warfare, you send out your archers first, to clear away the enemy's archers, so that your infantry is no longer threatened and your archers can safely concentrate on disrupting your enemy's infantry formation. Given how ineffective Norman archers were at penetrating an in-place shield wall on the high ground at Hastings, the Lannisters' initial volleys should have been an ineffective tactic, and, yet, it's successful in disrupting spearmen trying to charge on foot – and it's not answered. Only later do we see massed missile fire that could conceivably be from the Starks, and then it's directed at the one place on the battlefield where the Stark infantry could be hit by friendly fire (as BryndenBFish points out).

Again, this makes no sense: given the impossible task of attacking a largely cavalry force, the northern commander should have used his archers from the outset to engage the Lannister archers from the high ground, while the Lannisters ineffectually fire up-hill. This factor is normally dominant: at the Battle of Towton, for example, a strong opposing wind was enough to make the Lancastrian archers fire short, allowing the Yorkist archers to advance without being threatened, pluck up the Lancastrian arrows feathering the ground, and use them to decimate their opposing numbers with the wind adding to their range. Likewise, at Hastings, firing up-hill was enough to render the Norman archers completely useless. Bolton should then have had the archers screening his infantry advance to allow them to keep their shield walls intact and to disrupt the enemy's formation.

One of these errors on their own would suggest incompetence most uncharacteristic to the carefully-planned victor of Harrenhal and Moat Cailin. All four together point to malice. This is compounded by the politics of the situation.

The politics of the War of the Five Kings – as Brynden has noted, Roose Bolton makes very sure that all casualties come out of other houses, chiefly Karstarks, Hornwoods, Cerwyns, Glovers, Manderlys, and Freys. We can see this especially from the list of important bannermen killed or captured in the battle: Lord Halys Hornwood, Lord Medger Cerwyn, Harrion Karstark, and Ser Wylis Manderly. The first thing that's obvious is that Roose Bolton is eliminating his regional rivals – House Hornwood is immediately to his south, House Cerwyn is to his southwest, House Karstark is to his north, and House Manderly is the other major power of the north's eastern coast (House Glover represents more of a personal rival, in that Robett Glover vied with Roose for a command). By putting their forces in the front lines, Roose Bolton ensures that their houses are weakened while the 4,000 men of House Bolton remain intact, a strategy he will return to at Duskendale and the Ruby Ford.

However, there is also a political edge to his actions that goes beyond basic geopolitics. Each of these houses has a significance to Roose Bolton: Halys Hornwood (as we saw earlier) is an expansionist lord, vying to dam the White Knife, gain hunting privileges north of a ridge, and regain a certain holdfast taken from his grandfather – and while the White Knife primarily affects House Manderly, geography suggests that the latter two items are Bolton lands. Eliminating Lord Hornwood nips that threat in the bud. On the positive side, killing the lord of Hornwood, thanks to his son's simultaneous death at the Whispering Woods, opens up the whole of the Hornwood lands to Bolton expansion – a topic I'll get into in greater detail in *A Clash of Kings*. The Manderlys are a major power player in northern politics, as White Harbor dominates northern trade and the White Knife gives the Manderlys a swift route to the interior. As we'll see in *Clash*, the death of the Hornwoods immediately places the Manderlys and Boltons in conflict, one that carries through to *A Dance with Dragons*. The Karstarks are a more long-term threat – if House Bolton is attempting to expand south, House Karstark sits at his rear, with close to his number of soldiers. Moreover, in a political sense, the Karstark's blood ties to House Stark would always give them an edge over the little-liked Boltons in vying for the support of the other lesser houses in picking a new great house for the north.

I concur with Brynden that it's not possible to tell in *A Game of Thrones* what Bolton's plans were at this moment, whether he was planning from the outset to betray Robb Stark. However, what we can say is that Bolton not only botched the battle, but did so in such a way as to weaken his nearest rivals, and put himself closest to the north should Robb Stark fall in battle. Most definitely something to keep an eye on in the future.

Historical Analysis

The Green Fork is a bit of a mishmash in terms of historical parallels. As I've already suggested, the geography of the battle resembles nothing so much as a bizarro Battle of Hastings where the

Saxons don't even bother to hold the high ground and just charge straight down into the Normans to be hacked into pieces. In the historical Battle of Hastings (1066 CE, as you probably already know if you come from the UK), the forces of King Harold Godwinson executed a grueling 200-mile march from Stamford Bridge, where he had trounced the Norwegian king, Harald Hardrada, down to Hastings on the southern coast. Unlike Bolton, Harold's intent wasn't to surprise the Normans as much as it was to stop them marching from the coast towards London, but the result was the same: an exhausted army of Saxons going up against well-rested Normans.

However, unlike Bolton, Harold Godwinson wasn't acting the fool. He put his men on top of a tall ridge with swampy ground below it, and rivers anchoring his flanks – the perfect location for infantry to fight cavalry. I've stood on that ridge at Battle Abbey, and it's a steep slope that I would hate to have to run up knowing there was a Saxon longaxe coming for my face.

Harold got his men into a strong shield wall and kept them there as long as he could (probably as long as he was alive, but accounts differ about how and when Harold died); this shield wall completely defeated the Norman archers who fired up the hill, and easily stood off repeated up-hill assaults by Norman infantry and then knights from about nine in the morning until the mid-afternoon. At some point, possibly when Harold died to a freak arrow shot, the Saxon's discipline began to falter when the Normans engaged in a series of feigned retreats and the Saxons broke the shield wall to pursue them, only to be cut down when the Norman cavalry wheeled around and charged them on level ground. When the rumor circulated that Duke William of Normandy was dead, the Saxons charged down the hill en masse, where they got caught between the Normans at the bottom of the hill and a cavalry contingent that had circled around behind them. At this point, the Norman archers could now fire with full effect – and at this point, Harold seems to have died, either from an arrow to the eye or a sword to the head, and the Saxons broke and were ridden down.

Politically, however, the Battle of the Green Fork resembles nothing so much as the 2nd Battle of St. Albans. If you will recall from last time, at the Battle of St. Mortimer's Cross, Edward of York had made his triumphant entry into the Wars of the Roses by destroying a Welsh army led by Jasper Tudor that was marching to link up with Margaret D'Anjou's main Lancastrian force that was marching from Wakefield to London. It was Richard Neville, Duke of Warwick, known as the Kingmaker, who attempted to bar her passage even as Edward marched east.

Warwick tried a hell of a lot harder than Bolton to win his battle. Known for his immense wealth, Warwick had splashed out for Burgundian mercenaries armed with flaming arrows and crude handguns, crossbowmen with pavise shields, and a fearsome array of cannons to try to make up for the fact that he was outnumbered 10,000 to 15,000. His archers, placed in high windows in the city itself, held back the Lancastrians for several hours, long enough to enable Warwick to establish a new defensive line, complete with artillery, caltraps, and his Burgundian mercenaries. Unfortunately for Warwick, 2nd St. Albans was fought in the driving snow, which dampened his gunpowder, rendering his artillery ineffective. Just when it looked like his defensive line might hold, Warwick's close lieutenant, Sir Harry Lovelace, who had taken a £4,000 bribe to switch sides, deserted in the middle of the battle, opening a gap in the Yorkist line that the Lancastrian mounted knights poured through.

With his army broken or defecting, Warwick pulled his 4,000 remaining men away from the battle, leaving 2-4,000 men dead on the field and, crucially, leaving the captured King Henry VI on the field to be recaptured by the Lancastrians. Only the onset of night allowed him to avoid total defeat. Warwick would go on to link up with Edward of York, get their combined army safely to London, and have the duke of York crowned Edward IV, King of England.

Like the Battle of the Green Fork, 2nd St. Albans was a tactical success in the east immediately overshadowed by Edward IV's military prodigy in the west.

What If?

As usual, a battle offers some interesting scope for hypothetical scenarios. Two major scenarios suggest themselves:

What if Tyrion is captured or killed? During the battle, Tyrion is getting beaten around by a northern horseman who knows who he is and is trying to capture him. Almost by accident, Tyrion manages to gore his horse with a foot-long spike on his helmet (which is ridiculous), but doesn't get killed when the horse falls on top of him. Granted, if Tyrion had been captured, it's mostly likely he would have been recaptured during the Lannister advance, but if he hadn't... well, with an extra Lannister, Robb might well have been willing to trade Tyrion for Sansa, given that he'd still have Jaime in reserve. This gives Tyrion some very valuable time to compare notes with Jaime about what the business is with the dagger and Bran, and possibly springs Sansa from King's Landing. If that doesn't happen, or if Tyrion dies, then he's not around to be acting Hand. Which means the duty falls to Kevan, who's not going to be nearly inspired enough to counter Cersei or construct the boom chain. In all likelihood, King's Landing falls, giving Robb the perfect opportunity to crush Tywin Lannister once and for all.

What if Tywin's plan succeeds? Other than just raising the body count on both sides, the only way this might change the larger macro plot is if somehow Roose Bolton is removed from command, either by Robb Stark (more on why this doesn't happen in OTL later) or by being captured or killed on the field. While unlikely, this potentially could help the northern war effort by preventing the disasters of Duskendale and Ruby Ford, and potentially the Red Wedding, as well, if cautious Lord Frey isn't willing to take on the whole of the north by himself.

Book vs. Show

The show massively diverges from the book at this point, eschewing the battle in favor of having Tyrion be knocked out by one of his own men and waking up after the battle. While on one level, I understand that budgetary pressures make battles very difficult, and this isn't the most important of the battles (since it's been downgraded to a mere 2,000 men diversion against the Lannisters), but it verges on being demeaning to have Tyrion's first moment where he realizes that he actually shares some of Jaime's skill and love of battle be reduced to a punchline. Moreover, we lose the entirety of this political intrigue.

CATELYN X

Grey Wind threw back his head and howled... it was a terrible sound, a frightening sound, yet there was music in it, too. For a second, she felt something like pity for the Lannisters below. So this is what death sounds like.

Synopsis

Catelyn Stark watches and waits as her son, Robb, rides off to face Ser Jaime Lannister at the Whispering Woods. The result is a total rout for the Lannisters, the capture of the Kingslayer, and an open road to Riverrun.

Political Analysis

"Catelyn X" catches George R.R. Martin at his most lyrical, in his description of the Battle of the Whispering Woods. You can really see why he wanted to use (and keep using) Catelyn Stark as a POV, so that (in contrast to "Tyrion VIII," which emphasized the chaos and confusion of being in the thick of battle) he could overlook the battle from such a majestic aerial position, while still using the limitations of first-person narration to keep up the tension until the final reveal.* It's not an accident that Martin chooses the moment when Robb rides off with all the hopes of House Stark on his shoulders to tell us that "no one was safe. No life was certain." The basic rule of thumb that goes all the way to the Red Wedding and beyond is right there in the first book.

> * Having Catelyn be the POV also allows for a really impressive discussion of the way in which gender roles have restricted her life into one of the dutiful daughter, fiancée, wife, and mother. I don't really have a lot to say about this that hasn't already been said much better elsewhere, but I am genuinely impressed how much George Martin puts into to three paragraphs.

The War of the Five Kings: the Battle of the Whispering Wood – the Battle of the Whispering Wood is an interesting contrast with the Green Fork, in that it's also a trap being sprung – but unlike Tywin's trap, which was based on a fundamental misconception of his opponent's psychology, here Brynden Tully and Robb Stark perfectly read "the gilded knight who men said had never learned to wait at all... restless, and quick to anger" and totally lacking in "patience." As a result, whereas Tywin's trap fails to spring and Bolton pulls back most of his army, here Jaime's force is wiped out.

The Battle and, indeed, Robb's entire riverlands campaign is a great example of the use of force concentration to achieve local superiority of numbers: the Lannisters have "twelve thousand foot, scattered around the castle in three separate camps... [and] two or three thousand horse," whereas the Starks have six thousand horse, but the Stark force is all in one place, allowing it to outnumber the Lannisters at each separate point. While surprise is important, and Brynden's work in screening the Stark force is vital, there's more than surprise going on here (as opposed to at Oxcross, where it's the only important factor) - the geography of Riverrun nullifies the numerical superiority of the Lannisters, prevents them from concentrating their forces, and opens them up to being defeated in detail. Indeed, it's quite probable that Riverrun's placement was intended in part to create just such a situation.

At the same time, the degree to which the odds are uneven here seems to be exaggerated. Either Martin has made a math mistake (not unlikely - it's not his strong suit) or Galbart Glover is unusually wrong in screwing up his count. The Starks are not outnumbered "three to one" (i.e., 6,000 to 15,000) - indeed, it's quite likely that they're not even outnumbered two to one. After all, "Lord Jason Mallister had brought his power out from Seagard to join them," along with "hedge knights and small lords and masterless men-at-arms who had fled south when her brother, Edmure's, army was shattered beneath the walls of Riverrun" (another detail that suggests a surprise attack).

Now, we don't know precisely how many men House Mallister has, but we can extrapolate from some details in the text. First, House Mallister is one of the larger houses in the riverlands, commanding a major castle in a strategically-vital location guarding against the ironborn; as a result, it's one of the few lesser houses we know that has its own navy. Second, it commands both a sea-port and the headwaters of the Blue Fork of the Trident, making it a natural conduit for trade - and, thus, increasing its financial resources. Third, the Mallisters held off a major assault by the ironborn by themselves - as the ironborn have around 15,000 men, assuming a defensive advantage of three-to-one, a figure of around 5,000 makes sense. Fourth, at the Battle of the Fords, the Mallisters are put in charge of defending four fords, which suggests they have enough men to keep a viable force at each ford.

Putting all of these factors together, I can't see the Mallisters having less than 4,000 men. Which would mean that Robb's total forces here are at least 10,000 men - and given the hedge knights, small lords, and men-at-arms mentioned, it's probably closer to 11,000. It's still an overall disadvantage against the full Lannister force, but much less so, and one that explains why Jaime's force of 2-3,000 horse is so completely wiped out here: Robb had enough men present to completely encircle Jaime's force with a force larger than Jaime's at each flank.

Jaime makes it much easier for them by responding perfectly to their bait by chasing a small party of Tully outriders led by Brynden Tully into a trap (as they knew he would, having observed him "rid[ing] out with his knights thrice already" for no good reason, out of boredom), and critically ignoring the loss of his outriders when entering a heavily-wooded valley with sharply-slanted ridges on either side. As he rushes up the valley, the Mormonts, Umbers, and Mallisters charge in from the east (likely circling around the Lannister rear, given their signal that "the last of Jaime's riders had entered the trap"), while Robb and the Freys charge from the west, and the Karstarks hit the Lannisters from the front, all the while archers shower the Lannisters from the heights.

Thus, Robb achieves that rarest of all military prizes, the encirclement in full, which has been the sine qua non of military strategy since Cannae. And it's notable that it's very much a collaboration between Robb and Brynden – Brynden brings the local knowledge about how the rivers would divide the enemy and the intelligence on Jaime and he screens Robb's forces, but it's Robb who "had studied the map his uncle had drawn him. Ned had taught him to read maps," and designs the stratagem for Brynden to "raid him here... a hundred men, no more... when he comes after you, we will be waiting here," ready to surround the Lannister force. Rather than an old soldier using an inexperienced boy as a figurehead, this is much closer to an experienced coach developing a prodigy.

I'll get to Jaime's capture in a second, but consider the implications of the total destruction of the Lannister host (at the cost of around 300 men) for the Battle of the Camps. Now, the follow-up battle is 11,000 northmen and riverlanders against three forces of 4,000 westerlanders that entirely consist of foot, allowing Robb to replicate his strategy of force concentration to achieve another total victory. One battle sets up the next, with the objective being to, in one stroke, eliminate Jaime's army, liberate the riverlands to add them to his own forces, and put Tywin in a bad position where Robb can extract the necessary concessions to accomplish his primary war aims or potentially destroy Tywin's army outright.* Only Joffrey's bloodlust (aided and abetted by Littlefinger's desire for maximal chaos) prevents this campaign from achieving nigh-perfect success.

> * This is another case where George Martin's tight plotting shows itself: if Roose doesn't force-march or fights a smarter Battle of the Green Fork that gives him a chance to harry Tywin's army as it marches south rather than choosing to retreat up to Moat

Cailin (which would put him closest to Winterfell if Robb falls...), Tywin might not have gotten across the river in time and might have been trapped against Moat Cailin to the north, the Green Fork to the west, the Mountains of the Moon to the east, and the Trident to the south.

Which brings us to the political consequences of Jaime's capture. As Robb notes straight off, "he's more use alive than dead." Jaime is a sufficiently-important-enough prisoner to exchange for his father and his sisters, especially since he's got three additional Lannisters to add to the pot. Where the north goes from there is unclear: even if Tywin's immediate impulse is to fight the Baratheons first, there's the reality that he can't allow a hostile riverlands to stand in between the westerlands and the crownlands over the long run, or allow the north to openly defy the throne. But, potentially, Jaime is a big enough deal to end the war then and there, something I'll discuss much more when I get into *A Clash of Kings* and the impact that Catelyn's decision there has on Robb's decision-making in *A Storm of Swords*. At the same time, Jaime as a prisoner isn't a total blessing. It raises major political problems from the jump: "Lord Karstark will want his head on a pike" because the Kingslayer killed his sons, which will make the Karstarks a barrier to any peace settlement short of the complete destruction of House Lannister, and Rickard Karstark's grief will make him impossible to control by the normal political means open to Robb (even as Robb shows little difficulty keeping the other northern lords with him happy). It also sets up the Karstarks to be double-agents of the Boltons in *A Dance with Dragons*, when they might well not have been had the Karstark lads survived. At the same time, the death of Daryn Hornwood (at Jaime's hand) combined with his father's death at the Green Fork sets up the Hornwood crisis of *Clash*. More on that later.

Robb's bodyguard – the other political detail that I find interesting is the creation of Robb's quasi-Kingsguard: "Many of their sons had clamored for the honor of riding with the Young Wolf... Torrhen Karstark and his brother, Eddard, were among his 30, and Patrek Mallister, Smalljon Umber, Daryn Hornwood, Theon Greyjoy, no less than five of Walder Frey's vast brood, along with older men like Ser Wendel Manderly and Robin Flint. One of his companions was even a woman: Dacey Mormont." In addition to ensuring Robb's survival when Ser Jaime makes his last-ditch charge, the creation of these bodyguards (which never get a collective name, but I like the term "the Wolfguard") has some interesting political implications. Like the custom of fostering, this builds close relationships between Robb and many of the heirs of his bannermen (Houses Karstark, Umber, Mormont, Hornwood, Manderly, and Flint are a good coalition to have) and sets up Robb to have a much easier time of reigning over the north when these young men come into their inheritances. It's also notable that we're already seeing signs of political ties forming between the north and the riverlands with the presence of the Mallisters and the Freys.

It's a custom that seems to have some precedent in the north: Brandon Stark rode with Ethan Glover, Kyle Royce, Elbert Arryn, and Jeffory Mallister, a selection that's quite reminiscent of his father, Rickard's, plan to unite the north, the Vale, and the riverlands into a political coalition. When Eddard rides to the Tower of Joy, he does so again with Ethan Glover (who, no doubt, felt a special responsibility to deal with the Lyanna situation, given his involvement with Brandon), Howland Reed, William Dustin, Martyn Cassel, Theo Wull, and Mark Ryswell. Again, look at the selection: the Wulls are from the mountain clans at the far north of the Starks' territory, the Reeds from the far south, the Dustins and the Ryswells from the western shore, and House Cassel from the center.

I would guess that this custom goes back to the Kings of Winter – having a lordly bodyguard is both carrot and stick, holding out the hope of close relationships (and, thus, political influence) with the ruler, while requiring the various lesser houses to give up a hostage in the event of rebellion. It's just strange they don't have a formal title or iconography in the same way that the Kingsguard does.

Historical Analysis

Militarily, the Whispering Wood is something of a mishmash: the outriders drawing out an outnumbered force and the use of the woods to hide a devastating two-flank assault resembles nothing so much as a reverse Wakefield, with Ser Jaime playing the part of "Richard of York Sally[ing] Forth in Vain." The Kingslayer's desperate, last-minute charge to cut down the opposing leader and destroy the political hopes of the opposing dynasty is clearly taken from the Battle of Bosworth Field, when King Richard III, seeing himself outnumbered and betrayed, led 1,000 knights on a desperate charge into Henry Tudor's command group. No mean fighter, King Richard personally cut down two of Henry's standard-bearers, but was unable to break through Henry's bodyguards. At which point the perfidious Stanleys chose this moment to change sides and attack the Yorkist rear.

But in its political impact, the Whispering Woods and the Battle of the Camps, taken together, had the same impact as the bloody field of Towton. When we last left Edward IV, he had just been crowned in London after triumphing at St. Mortimer's Cross. However, Queen Margaret D'Anjou was marching south and now had her husband by her side. If Edward was to prove himself king of England in more than name, he'd have to do something that his father had struggled so often to pull off – attack and defeat a sitting king of England on the field.

For this battle, Edward would pull out all the stops – sending men to muster men in his and Warwick's lands throughout the Midlands, and collecting more men along the way until he had a host to match the Lancastrian army (sources differ on how many men exactly fought at Towton, but estimates range from around 60,000 [with the Lancastrians outnumbering the Yorkists by 5-10,000] to 100,000. While these numbers don't seem that big to veterans of George Martin's novels, consider that they represented 2% of the entire population of England, and far more of its military-age male population.

Towton started, as I've discussed earlier, with Edward IV and Warwick forcing a crossing over the River Aire in the face of stubborn opposition from Lord Clifford (who had murdered Edward IV's brother, Edmund of Rutland). So important was this crossing that Warwick killed his horse in front of the whole vanguard to show that he would "die with his men than yield another inch," and that Edward IV personally led his vanguard to force the crossing; Lord Clifford fought to the very end of his strength, but unexpectedly died when he loosened his gorget to catch his breath and caught a stray arrow (likely Martin's inspiration for Quentyn "Fire" Ball).

With Edward refusing a Palm Sunday truce, the two armies proper met on a plateau with each side claiming one of two facing ridges – both sides with a river to their back that could prove fatal to an army that attempted to retreat. As I mentioned earlier, a blizzard and driving wind hampered the Lancastrian archers while giving both fresh arrows and added impetus to the Yorkists under Lord Fauconberg that wreaked havoc on the Lancastrian ranks. This deadly barrage forced the Lancastrians off their high ground and into a charge on the Yorkists, who eagerly moved forward to meet him.

The Yorkist left was unexpectedly charged by a force of Lancastrian cavalry hidden in a woods on their flank and had to be personally reinforced by Edward of York while Warwick held the center. The battle collapsed into a grueling pushing match as both sides contended for the meadow, with the Lancastrians slowly pushed back to the west. At this point, reinforcements from the duke of Norfolk arrived and drove into the Lancastrian left flank, breaking it. The Lancastrian army turned and ran – at which point the Yorkists mounted their horses and rode them down, shouting, "Spare the commons! Kill the lords!" (The first time those enlightened words had been said on an English battlefield.)

In their flight, the Lancastrians ran straight into the freezing waters of the Cock Beck River, overloading the single makeshift bridge, which collapsed. In the chaos, York and Warwick's orders were ignored completely such that no quarter was given as men were hacked down on the run, drowned in the river, or simply trampled underfoot by their own comrades in their haste to get away. The affair had lasted 10 hours, and the result was that one percent of the population of England, anywhere from a third to a half of those fighting, lay dead, tossed into a mass grave. It remains to his day the bloodiest battle in English history, with casualties outstripping those of the Battle of the Somme in World War I when considered proportionally.

But, politically, the battle was "Edward's bloody coronation." The Lancastrians were broken, losing Clifford, Northumberland, Scrope, Dacre, and the turncoat Andrew Trollope. The Lancastrian army was nonexistent, and Margaret and King Henry VI were forced into headlong flight. Virtually every Lancastrian lord remaining (the Percys, the Rivers, etc.) bent the knee then and there, no doubt prompted by the executions of some 42 knights Edward deemed too obstinate to be trusted. John Neville was raised to the rank of Lord Montague; Fauconberg the archer was made earl of Kent; and Warwick gained much lands from the Cliffords and the Percys of Northumberland, making him the king's lieutenant in the north in fact as well as in title.

Not until Edward's break with Warwick would the Yorkist hold on England be shaken.

What If?

As I have said, battles always give rise to many hypotheticals, but the Whispering Woods more than most, given the nature and object of Jaime's charge:

What if Robb dies? If Jaime kills Robb, it doesn't stop his army from being crushed on the field and then again at Riverrun as the north seeks to avenge their fallen leader. However, it almost certainly means that the Starks pull out of the war once Riverrun is retaken, probably with Jaime being traded for Sansa and peace by Catelyn – which probably means that the Greyjoy invasion is butterflied away and that the north declares for Brandon Stark, King in the North, with its whole army mustered above the Neck. The riverlands would be placed in a difficult situation but probably left alone by the Lannisters until the Baratheons were dealt with – the tricky thing being how Tywin gets Ser Stafford's 10,000 around the riverlands to reinforce his men. With the Lannisters focusing on the east, Renly's strategy of slow-rolling his way to the Iron Throne likely has to go by the wayside in favor of a direct assault on Tywin's army and King's Landing at the same time (since he easily has the numbers to do both). Quite possibly, Renly wins and then mysteriously dies, leading to Stannis being enthroned.

What if Jaime dies? If Jaime takes an arrow or a spear or a sword in his desperate charge, this has some interesting long-term impacts. First, it means that the Karstarks don't ever rebel, which leaves Robb in a much better political situation in *A Storm of Swords*.

Second, it means that the Starks don't bother with negotiations with the Lannisters, which frees up their attention to focus on the Vale, the Reach, and Stannis, and butterflies away Tyrion's escape attempt and the dispatch of Ned Stark's corpse. Third, it may well mean that Cersei loses it completely and becomes a much more unstable entity in *A Clash of Kings*, possibly leading to Sansa's death and a much more difficult time for Tyrion in trying to hold the city against his sister and Stannis both. Fourth, it means that no one's left to take control of the riverlands, ensuring that they remain much more of a bleeding ulcer for the Lannisters to deal with after Tywin's death.

What if Theon dies? As I'll discuss in the opening chapters of *Clash of Kings*, it's entirely unclear that Theon remaining with the Starks would have prevented the invasion. However, if Theon dies, a couple things change – first, the Starks no longer hope for Balon Greyjoy's assistance and might prepare better for an attack from the sea. Second, Winterfell doesn't fall, ensuring that there is a central rallying point for the Starks in mobilizing the 17,000 men of the north to repel the ironborn invaders. Which as I'll discuss in *Clash* was pretty much bound to happen – the ironborn don't have enough troops to hold the north, and the north just doesn't have enough inland rivers on the west coast to allow for easy penetration into the interior. Even with Victarion taking Moat Cailin, eventually enough troops will be rallied to retake it from the ironborn. Which changes things dramatically from Robb's perspective in *Storm of Swords* – with Moat Cailin re-cleared and the ironborn repelled, he's got much less incentive to drop everything in the south and rush back to the north. Which, in turn, means he doesn't need the Freys nearly as much, especially when he can bring some of his 17,000 men south to reinforce his army; let's say he leaves 7,000 on the western shore to guard against the ironborn – that brings Robb back up to as many as 37,000 men, with a solid defensive position on the Trident. Even with the Tyrells added to the Lannisters, that's enough men that a few victories could even the odds. Finally, if Winterfell is intact and Moat Cailin is retaken, Roose Bolton might think twice about betraying Robb, potentially butterflying away the Red Wedding.

What if Karstarks don't die? I've sort of covered this with Jaime dying, but this butterflies away Rickard Karstark's rebellion and execution, and the loss of the Karstark forces. In the longer term, this potentially changes the northern campaign in *A Dance with Dragons* – with the Karstarks a going concern and Arnolf Karstark no longer in a position to stir up trouble, the Karstarks might well decide to take on the Boltons themselves rather than allying with the Boltons and forcibly being allied to Stannis. After all, they've got Stark blood and, as far as they know, the Starks are all dead – they would be the natural heirs to Winterfell.

What if Denys Hornwood doesn't die? With a Hornwood heir, we don't get political chaos in the north on the eve of an ironborn invasion. This means that the eastern houses, especially the Manderlys and Boltons, can be much more easily mobilized to repel the ironborn, with consequences as suggested above. More on this in *A Clash of Kings*.

<u>Book vs. Show</u>

This is where the show and the book really start to diverge and, in my opinion, is where Benioff and Weiss lose the plot when it comes to the war effort, despite doing a rather good job explaining the military and spatial logic of the opening act of the War of the Five Kings in the first season.

Now, I don't blame them for how they shot this scene: having Catelyn waiting on a hill to find out what happens is taken straight out of the book, and I think Robb's return and the scene with Jaime works quite well. I am a bit annoyed that all of the strategy behind the battle is stripped out when all it would have taken was a few quick lines from Ser Rodrick Cassel and some DVR'ed horn blowing to get enough in to mollify the fans. I don't think much of Robb's anti-inspirational speech, given that it's parroting Catelyn's pessimistic outlook rather than Robb's own thoughts at the time, but it's not a huge issue.

What I really mind is completely dropping the ball on Riverrun and failing to explain the political ramifications of the battle, as I've hinted at earlier. It would have been incredibly easy for the showrunners to tease Edmure and Brynden Tully without having to cast them or scout locations for Riverrun: all they'd have to do is replace Robb's downer speech with Catelyn's speech from the chapter about "you have lopped the head off the snake, but three quarters of the body is still coiled around my father's castle at Riverrun. If we want to rescue your father..." and have Robb say, "We'll need Riverrun and the riverlords. Don't worry, Mother – I have a plan for the Lannister army there," and have him ride off again. Then, in the King in the North scene in the next episode, have one of the extras say "Lord Edmure Tully thanks you for his rescue and pledges his sword and those of the riverlords to you" early on.

Then, in season two, you use the same repeated mentioning of an off-screen presence that they pulled with Stannis in the first season: have Robb mention in his first scene that Brynden has sent word that there's a new Lannister army threatening Riverrun from the west, or have Bolton or Karstark complain that Edmure let the riverlords go and how they could have used those troops, and then, at the end of the season, some extra comes in and says, "Lord Edmure reports that Tywin is marching west from Harrenhal!" Catelyn responds with a worried look, but Robb smiles and says, "Just as I planned. Tell Lord Edmure to hold Riverrun."

And that sets up the reveal at the beginning of season three at Riverrun without any need for the transposition of Tywin and the Mountain or the weirdness with Harrenhal that completely butchered the logic of the northern war effort.

DAENERYS VIII

"This must not be!"

"This will be."

Synopsis

Drogo, on the verge of death, falls off his horse and a *"khal who cannot ride is no khal."* Desperate to keep Drogo alive, Dany agrees to Mirri Maz Duur's blood magic. This violation of Dothraki taboo unleashes total chaos within the *khalasar*. At this point, Dany goes into labor, but the only option for OB/GYN care is inside the tent, where Mirri Maz Duur is communing with the shades of unquiet spirits, so Jorah carries her in. And you thought your health care system was messed up…

Political Analysis

The main event of this chapter is Drogo's death-in-all-but-name and the political fallout that results. And it's significant that this crucial turning point balances on the importance of culture. Dany's rise to power all through this book has come from her ability to assimilate into Dothraki culture – but no convert ever has a perfect grasp on the finer points of their adopted culture, and here she hits the wall and loses everything when she fails to see how her personal desires conflict with the Dothraki way.

The first way that Daenerys undermines herself is in failing to understand the different ways in which Dothraki and Westerosi understand leadership. Perhaps because Khal Drogo was the *khalakka* of Khal Bharbo, Dany assumes that the same traditions of blood inheritance dominates Dothraki culture in the same way that it shapes virtually everything about Westerosi society. However, in the moment, she forgets that "a *khal* who could not ride could not rule." The consequences of Drogo's fall from power and Dany's failure to understand it shape the entire chapter: the moment Drogo falls, Qotho immediately slips out from the chain of command, and Dany's ability to command the *khalasar* in the name of her husband is weakened, as "it is not for a woman to bid us halt... not even a *khaleesi*." While Dany is temporarily able to cow him, she quickly finds that "a man and his bloodriders share one life, and Qotho sees it ending. A dead man is beyond fear." Qotho will form the nucleus of a xenophobic faction that will split the *khalasar*, as we see on his return.

Next, believing in error that her son can rule in Drogo's place and keep the army under her command, Dany fails to understand that "the Dothraki will not follow a suckling babe. Drogo's strength was what they bowed to, and only that. When he is gone, Jhaqo and Pono and the other *ko*s will fight for his place, and this *khalasar* will devour itself. The winner will want no more rivals. The boy will be taken from your breast the moment he is born. They will give him to the dogs." As a result of her misjudgment, Daenerys misses out on her chance to escape and places both her life and that of her unborn child in danger.

Finally, Dany willfully ignores how abhorrent Mirri Maz Duur's blood magic is to the Dothraki and what this means for her insisting that the maegi see to Drogo's wound. For all that Dany insists that "this is the same. The same," to the Dothraki, "blood magic is forbidden," and for those who practice it, "kicks are too merciful... we will stake her to the Earth, to be the mount of every passing man. And when they are done with her, the dogs will use her, as well. Weasels will tear out her entrails and carrion crows feast upon her eyes." Daenerys's public insistence in carrying out this ritual alienates virtually the whole of the *khalasar* and, in the eyes of many, makes Daenerys equally culpable in Drogo's death by evil magic.

This decision destroys the unity of the *khalasar*. Qotho and Haggo and Cohollo (the older men of the bloodriders) arriv, bringing the traditional Dothraki healers and symbolically taking up the position of the defenders of tradition. Dany tries to stop him bodily, and the immediate result is the death of Quaro, Mormont's wounding, the death of Haggo and Cohollo, and almost her own death. Within moments, the *khalasar* is broken: "She saw the crowd dispersing, the Dothraki stealing silently back to their tents... some were saddling horses and riding off... fires burned throughout the *khalasar*." Crucially, Dany's flouting of tradition means that when her baby comes unexpectedly, the "birthing women... will not come. They say she is accursed."

For the sake of a cut, Dany loses *khal*, *khalasar*, baby, and everything...

The second way that Daenerys defeats herself her is failing to understand the cultural meanings embedded in Mirri Maz Duur's blood magic. I've already argued that Mirri Maz Duur had means, motive, and opportunity to poison Khal Drogo (more evidence on that in the next Dany chapter), but here we see how this poisoning works out to her advantage. Within a week, the *khalasar* that destroyed her village is murdering itself, the man who led the effort is the helpless subject of her necromancy, and Dany gives her consent (a critical factor in a lot of folklore) to give her free reign. And none of this would happen if Drogo didn't fall from his horse. She succeeds because Dany deceives herself as to which death "may pay for life," even though Mirri Maz Duur points out "this is not a matter of horses," and in no small part because of her ability to read Dany and understand that the *khaleesi* would violate any taboo.

Historical Analysis

What happens to Drogo's *khalasar* in "Dany VIII" has many historical parallels – after Atilla was defeated at Châlons in 451 CE by Flavius Aetius, he was eventually forced to withdraw from Italy, but, in the meantime, the Eastern Roman Empire invaded across the Danube and defeated the Huns in their home provinces. Preparing to mount a campaign against them, Atilla died of a severe nosebleed while blackout drunk at a wedding feast (although some scholars argue that the Emperor Marcian had him assassinated via his new bride). Immediately, his sons Ellac, Dengizich, and Ernakh fell to fighting over who would inherit, and his army broke into three feuding portions who were destroyed on the banks of the Danube in 454 CE by the Ostrogoths, destroying the Hunnic empire forever.

The case of the great Genghis Khan works less well – while his death was an enormous setback, the Mongol Empire regrouped under Ogedei Khan and continued to expand, conquering the Manchu, completing the conquest of China, and completing the subjugation of the Persians. Indeed, it wasn't until 60 years later that the Mongol Empire began to break down into civil wars between rival khans, but, even then, many of the successor khanates lasted for several centuries.

However, the process by which *ko*s fight to become the new *khal* and the former *khalakka*s are killed, unless they are strong enough to stake their claim to the succession by force of arms, is reminiscent of many patterns of fratricidal warfare seen in kingdoms with either non-primogeniture inheritance (which creates an incentive for brothers to turn against one another when the land is divided between them) or in systems where polygamy created many sons with potentially-equal claims to the throne. Fratricide or fratricidal wars were fairly common in Pharaonic Egypt and the Ottomans essentially institutionalized the practice of the oldest son having his brothers executed from the time of Mehmed II (1444-1481) through to Ahmed I (1603-1617).

Something to keep your eye on when we see what happens when primogeniture breaks down in *A Clash of Kings*. The results can be messy...

What If?

There's really only one hypothetical I can see coming out of this chapter:

What if Dany runs away with Jorah? The interesting thing with Dany departing the OTL at this point is that Dany actually has, at this point, everything she needs to wake the dragons – she knows the basics of blood magic now ("only a death can pay for life"), she's got the eggs, and she's got to take drastic measures to regain her path now that she's lost her *khalasar*. So this particular Chekov's device is still up on the mantle ready to go to save the world. However, Dany running away has some interesting offshoots: does this draw her back into the direct control of Varys and Illyrio, who've been handling her rather on the long finger ever since Pentos? Will Jorah keep playing the role of her controller (incidentally, I've never understood why Jorah didn't tell her that Varys and Illyrio are working together, so that technically he was spying on her on behalf of her supporters), or is he so far gone into his romantic/territorial phase that he'll try to break free of their grasp and manipulate her? (While this is more of a question for *Clash of Kings*, I've always wondered whether Varys/Illyrio foresaw that eventuality and sent Ser Barristan to her specifically so they could nip him in the bud.)

Jorah's intended destination of Asshai is quite interesting, as well: its remoteness compared to Pentos suggests that Jorah isn't exactly a loyal spy any more, and it's an extremely magical place, so it's quite possible Dany could wake not just three dragons, but an army of them, given that Asshai is where "dragons stir beneath the sunrise." Indeed, it seems like Asshai may be a foregone pleasure if we're to get Dany back to Westeros ever, given that it would essentially double the length of her trip back to Westeros – unless she goes for the whole circumnavigation thing and lands on the west coast, but that seems unlikely.

Book vs. Show

While I thought this scene in the show was generally well-acted and -shot – and I liked the fight scene with Ser Jorah and Qotho – this is where budgetary restraints really started to bite. It was always a problem that Drogo's 40,000 screamers could never be seen on screen (would it have really cost that much to have a few establishing CGI'd shots of the whole *khalasar*?), but it really bit here in that the fight involves two people rather than a total breakdown of the *khalasar*.

ARYA V

"My mother bids me let Lord Eddard take the black, and Lady Sansa has begged mercy for her father... but they have the soft hearts of women."

Synopsis

Arya Stark, hiding out in Flea Bottom, narrowly avoids a Lannister trap at the riverfront wharf and becomes a witness to the confession and execution of her father, only to be saved by Yoren.

Political Analysis

"Arya V" is primarily concerned with a single act of madness, but before we get to that, I want to spend a bit of time discussing some of the interesting detail in this chapter that sets up a lot for Arya's plotline through the next two books.

Arya on the streets – the first thematic element we see is Arya beginning to discover poverty, which sets up her role in *A Clash of Kings* and *A Storm of Swords* as a lens into the impact of the War of the Five Kings on Team Smallfolk. The picture isn't very pretty:

> The lives of the residents of Flea Bottom revolve around a daily struggle to appease hunger by any means necessary, with crime being a common survival strategy: "Her lord father had taught her never to steal, but it was growing hard to remember why... the silver bracelet she had hoped to sell had been stolen her first night out of the castle, along with her bundle of good clothes, snatched while she slept... all they left her was the cloak she had been huddled in, the leathers on her back, her wooden practice sword, and Needle." Here, George R.R. Martin is deconstructing the Hero's Journey – normally, the hero at the outset of her quest gains talismans or artifacts from his guardian to aid him on his way, in a way that often saps the "point of no return moment" of its dramatic power (how often does Luke Skywalker actually mention the traumatic loss of his aunt and

uncle the moment after it happens?). Here, Arya is immediately robbed and thrown into destitution, barely able to survive. Rather than gaining competence or having competence suddenly imbued on her in the form of magical talismans, Arya is helpless until she encounters Yoren – because, in real life, children make for lousy Chosen Ones.

The poor of King's Landing experience poor food and sanitation: "In the Bottom, there were pot-shops along the alleys where huge tubs of stew had been simmering for years... mostly, she tried not to think about the meat... she feared so much pigeon was making her sick." One of the "realist" elements often left out of high fantasy is the reality of an agricultural society with high investment in livestock and working animals, no understanding of the germ theory of disease or public health, and a society with high levels of inequality, to boot (the wealth of kings doesn't come from working for a living, after all). It's a running problem I have with fantasy in which the messy and unpleasant factors of pre-industrial society have been buried underneath J.R.R Tolkien's reflexive anti-modernism. It's nice to have Martin putting it back in.

Exploitation and abuse are a constant danger: "Arya could feel them watching. Some of them stared at their boots or their cloak, and she knew what they were thinking. With others, she could almost feel their eyes crawling under her leathers; she didn't know what they were thinking, and that scared her even more." Now, this gets us into an area where people have genuinely mixed feelings about the world of A Song of Ice and Fire – some view the ubiquity of sexual threat in Westeros to be a mark against the series and, potentially, a mark of misogyny on the author's part; others that it's a feminist statement that sexual violence is a genuine threat in the world, and Martin clearly represents it as an evil to be fought. I'm not sure where I stand on this specific instance, but it is clearly working here as a piece with starvation, crime, and malnutrition as part of a world of danger that class inequality makes women of different castes experience difficulty.

There isn't instant solidarity between the oppressed: "She had tried talking to the children she saw in the street, hoping to make a friend... but she must have talked wrong or something. The little ones only looked at her with quick, wary eyes and ran away if she came too close. Their big brothers and sisters asked questions Arya couldn't answer, called her names, and tried to steal from her." If the common folk are actually depicted in mainstream fantasy, they are overwhelmingly depicted as either the **Happy Peasants** who love their rightful king and their heroic knights (which, if the same phenomenon was shifted in setting from Medieval Europe to the Antebellum South, would be called out as problematic a lot more often) or the kind of **noble, suffering poor united in resistance** against their oppressors. Neither depiction really gives the poor agency and human diversity of character that Team Smallfolk deserves. It's good to see Martin taking a leaf from Terry Pratchett in pointing out that, "The common people... they're nothing special. They're no different from the rich and powerful except they've got no money or power. But the law should be there to balance things up a bit. So I suppose I've got to be on their side."

The overall thrust of this narrative, as we'll see going forward, is to drum into our heads a realist message: suffering isn't ennobling – it's just suffering. The hunger and physical danger that Arya will experience in *Clash of Kings* and *Storm of Swords* doesn't make her stronger, or build character, or make her "closer to the earth" in some New Agey way – it's trauma that no one should experience, let alone romanticize.

The power of rumor

> *Open your ears; for which of you will stop*
> *The vent of hearing when loud Rumour speaks?*
> *I, from the orient to the drooping west,*
> *Making the wind my post-horse, still unfold*
> *The acts commenced on this ball of earth:*
> *Upon my tongues continual slanders ride,*
> *The which in every language I pronounce,*
> *Stuffing the ears of men with false reports.*
> *I speak of peace, while covert enmity*
> *Under the smile of safety wounds the world.*
>
> Prologue, *Henry IV, Part II*

The second theme introduced in this chapter is the role that rumor plays in structuring what we could call the popular politics of the streets – a power that can help stir a city into riot, turn a king into a legend, or sway great houses one way or another in a civil war. Rumor can be surprisingly accurate ("The talk in Flea Bottom was that the gold cloaks had thrown in with the Lannisters, their commander raised to a lord, with lands on the Trident and a seat on the king's council" is almost word-for-word what Sansa saw earlier), completely wrong ("Some said her father had murdered King Robert and been slain in turn by Lord Renly. Others insisted that Renly had killed the king in a drunken quarrel between brothers"), or fanciful and allegorical ("One story said the king... died eating a boar, stuffing himself so full he'd ruptured at the table").

What all of these rumors have in common is that they sort the confusing, dimly-perceived world of elite politics into simple narratives that fit into tropes ordinary people can make sense of the world with. Lord Stark must be a traitor because being executed is what happens to traitors, and to think otherwise transforms the highest institutions of power – endorsed and maintained by tradition, custom, and religion – into terrifying monoliths hurling down death at random. Rumor transforms existential uncertainty into rational cause and effect – as all narrative does.

Thus, in the rumors of Flea Bottom, we can get a glimpse of the construction of popular political ideology. The great anthropologist Clifford Geertz famously turned his "thick description" method to Balinese cockfights to tease out the symbols of status, power, masculinity, and crime that ordinary people used to construct "webs of significance" that explained the world around them. In "Ideology as a Cultural System," he turned the same method in a political direction, explaining ideology as more than a collection of blind, irrational prejudices – instead, ideology is a kind of symbolic framework that allows people to "formulate, think about, and react to political problems," especially in a time of chaos, when people are trying to react and understand dizzying changes in the political world around them.

This may seem a bit hi-falutin' and, perhaps, farfetched, but I promise you, when we see Team Smallfolk chanting "King Bread" even as they raise up cobblestones against royal swords, ideology is at work. For those of you familiar with *The Princess and the Queen*, it takes something more than self-interest to explain why the poor and starving of King's Landing would take the awe-inspiring step of fighting dragons with their bare hands.

"True seeing" on the docks – the third element we see is the way in which Syrio Forel's teachings have influenced Arya, which we'll come back to as his mantra becomes a core part of her character development, as she sees through the Lannisters' disguise:

> *When she saw the guardsmen on the third pier, in grey woolen cloaks trimmed with white satin, her heart almost stopped in her chest. The sight of Winterfell's colors brought tears to her eyes... the* Wind Witch *was the ship father had hired to take her home... still waiting! She'd imagined it had sailed ages ago...*
>
> *Ashamed to let them see her crying like a baby, she stopped to rub at her eyes. Her eyes, her eyes, her eyes, why did...*

> Look with your eyes, *she heard Syrio whisper.*
>
> *Arya looked. She knew all of her father's men. The three in the grey cloaks were strangers.*

This gets to John from the comments's point about the extent to which George Martin is deconstructing standard fantasy tropes; I disagree somewhat in that deconstruction, properly done, isn't an attempt to discredit a trope outright but to subject it to critique so that it can be reconstructed better. Here, Martin is using realism to critique the compartmentalized threat facing the lone hero that evinces itself into a single incident (think Luke at the bar of the Mos Eisley cantina) and then never again. He's also doing it to raise the stakes for Arya so that when Syrio's voice pops up in her head like Obi-Wan Kenobi, it feels more earned. He's also doing it to evoke some interesting parallels – with Yoren as the substitute rescue that emphasizes essence over appearance (because Yoren doesn't look like rescue in the slightest) – the "true seeing" vindicated once again.

Another detail we learn is how careful Cersei is being here – "The guards let no one out. Those who were allowed to leave left by the King's Gate or the Iron Gate, but Lannister men-at-arms in crimson cloaks and lion-crested helms manned the guard posts there... searching wagons and carriages, forcing riders to open their saddlebags, and questioning everyone who tried to pass on foot." Cersei is desperately trying to ensure that Eddard Stark did not get word out other than by Fat Tom and is doing everything right when it comes to making sure that Arya Stark can't flee the city on her own. The comprehensive degree of care she evinces here only makes what comes next all the more damning.

The execution of Ned Stark – and so we come to the main event – an event carefully stage-managed to prevent the truth of Ned Stark's investigation from coming to light, to discredit him specifically if he ever decides to tell anyone, and to establish in the public's mind that "Joffrey Baratheon is the one true heir" to the Iron Throne. The staging is well-done: Eddard Stark has been "dressed in a rich grey velvet doublet with a white wolf sewn on the front" (to hide the fact that he's been imprisoned by the Lannisters and, thus, might be a subject of pity rather than a figure of hatred), Cersei is in full mourning gear (I love that she can't bring herself to wear full black and has to sneak some triumphant Lannister red), and the small council is there to give political legitimacy and the High Septon to lend religious legitimacy to the spectacle. The only tell that this is all choreographed is that "Sansa... looked so happy" at the confession of her father.

There's an interesting parallel in this moment, as Eddard Stark goes to her perjured death: it's Arya who witnesses the death of her father's integrity as "Sansa had hidden her face in her hands," but it's

Arya who has her face covered by Yoren as Sansa witnesses his physical death (and, indeed, will be the witness to the reality of his death in her next chapter). It's something of an interesting inversion of how their character arcs work – Sansa is the one who witnesses symbolic destruction (think Ser Barristan in "Sansa V"), whereas Arya's going to become very, very familiar with the physical reality of death. I'm not entirely sure why George Martin chooses to go this way (this blog focuses on history and politics over literary analysis for a reason...), but it's an interesting choice, and I look forward to discussing it in the comment thread below.

However, the choreography falls apart the moment Joffrey calls out, "Ser Ilyn, bring me his head!" The symbolism of the moment is bizarre. The king is rejecting not just his intended bride (who he takes a second to smile at, in a purely sociopathic move), and not just the queen regent (who has the actual political power at this moment), but the High Septon on the doorsteps of the holiest place in the Seven Kingdoms; it's rather surprising that Martin has the crowd react with wild approval, given the way that the desecration comes up later (perhaps too much gilding on the lily ahead of the whole "demon monkey" twist in *A Clash of Kings*?). Overall, it's not a great introduction to the boy king.

Speaking of choreography, we learn a great deal about who's behind this sudden u-turn from how the different actors on stage react: "The High Septon clutched at the king's cape, and Varys came rushing over waving his arms, and even the queen was saying something to him, but Joffrey shook his head."

The **High Septon** we can eliminate from our inquiry – he's clearly a well-meaning, if corrupt, functionary who'll be dead in a few months. He's clearly ineffectual in that one would think the High Septon could physically intercede here on religious grounds and forbid the killing on the steps of the Great Sept, if only to allow a cooling-off period where calmer heads could prevail, but at least he's trying to save Ned Stark.

Varys is clearly not the culprit and seems genuinely moved to act in public in a way he really doesn't ever again. However, I do want to stress one thing that I've seen floating around r/asoiaf and other message boards: to the extent that this event represents a defeat for Varys, it's an extremely minor one. Clearly, Ned Stark's survival is not a major objective for him – if it were, he could have smuggled Ned out of the dungeons easily days earlier. Nor is it the case that Varys doesn't want a civil war or wants it to happen later – go back to "Arya III," and you'll see he's clearly the one acting to *accelerate* the Targaryen invasion because he doesn't think the civil war can or should be delayed. What Varys wants, for the moment, is to prop up the Lannisters until Stannis Baratheon, who he views as the greater threat to his success (Stannis being a follower of magic, an uncompromising enemy of Varys, a good battle commander, and, as a Baratheon, a stalwart of the new regime against a restoration), is beaten, and he wants the truth about Cersei kept hidden until he's ready (which is why everyone should keep their eyes on Tyrek Lannister – more on this later). The death of Ned Stark weakens the Lannister cause, but Robb Stark was unlikely to retreat, anyway, and Varys is able to work with Tyrion to accomplish his anti-Stannis move quite handily and without Ned's story leaking. If it's a defeat, it's one that touches none of his core objectives.

Cersei is clearly not behind this – not only does she speak to Joffrey to get him to stop, but everything we know about her strategic position says this is the last thing she wants: it gains the Lannisters nothing, since Ned Stark is already a beaten man politically, it ensures the Starks are in the war to stay and, thus, will continue to tie up her father, and, as we'll see shortly, it puts Jaime in mortal danger. However, this moment also shows Cersei's profound limitations as a conspirator; in addition to being generally slapdash and reactive, she doesn't think well on her feet. Contrary to what many have argued, I think there are ways around Joffrey's snafu: she could physically intercede, she could point to the religious defilement issue, she could assert her own authority as queen regent, etc. However, in the moment, she tries to talk Joffrey out of it and then does nothing – which is awfully reminiscent of how she panicked in "Bran II" and then tried to cover her ass later on.

Littlefinger, however, does nothing. He is there, however: "The short man with the silvery cape and pointed beard [who] might be the one who had once fought a duel for Mother." I had forgotten this detail up until this re-read, in part because of the way he drops out of the narrative the moment things start to happen, in part because Arya's paying attention to movement and action and not the reverse. And I think this absolutely matches his MO: firstly, it's focused entirely on his past relationships – it makes Catelyn a widow and free to wed, while punishing the man who "took her from him." Secondly, it's done through several layers of plausible deniability – Joffrey takes responsibility, and I doubt he remembers whatever catty comment from Littlefinger that prompted him to go off-script. Thirdly, it directly harms Cersei, who just turned him down for Sansa's hand in marriage. Fourthly, it ensures that the civil war he wants will not have a swift resolution.

So qui bono, indeed.

Historical Analysis

I've covered the death of Richard, Duke of York previously, and I want to talk more about the distaff side of the Yorkist cause in "Sansa VI," so see you next chapter!

What If?

What if Eddard takes the black? If Cersei's crazy plan actually works, the big question is whether Eddard would keep his word. On the one hand, he's sworn to secrecy, Ned Stark is an honorable man, and there's the added issue of Sansa's safety. On the other hand, Ned's oath is quite specific - he swears to "the High Septon and Baelor the Beloved and the Seven," all elements of a foreign religion he does not belong to. This might signify that Eddard is planning to revenge himself against Cersei and the Lannisters - while Eddard Stark doesn't have a fanbase in King's Landing, an open letter proclaiming Stannis to be the true king and Cersei Lannister as a traitor, adulterer, and murderess would certainly reshape the War of the Five Kings. Bringing over the Starks and the Tullys to Stannis's side at this exact political moment would bump him up from merely 5,000 men to having ~45,000 men and the support of two great houses.

While Stannis isn't a popular figure, I do think these facts would lend more weight to his own letter, making it more likely that the stormlords more evenly divide between the brothers, and I do think that the lords of the Vale would begin to act independently of Lysa, given such a public justification. This likely moves forward the attack on King's Landing - which means Tywin would himself have to realign his forces towards the capital. At the same time, Renly and the Tyrells would also have to speed up their march to prevent a power bloc from seizing the capital before they could. So we might be looking at a Battle-of-Five-Armies pileup, as every single contestant for the Iron Throne races to the finish line.

However, if Eddard doesn't say anything, I don't think the plot of the War of the Five Kings changes that much; with both of his sisters imprisoned (as far as he knows), Robb Stark isn't about to go back home - nor can he accept the insult to House Stark's reputation without weakening his family's position (especially with House Bolton poised to take advantage), which rather makes Cersei's plan pointless. However, it would dramatically reshape some other plots: Eddard Stark is travelling with the same Night's Watch group that Arya escapes with, which would be rather heartwarming, in retrospect, which might well mean that Arya and her father go on the run in the riverlands with a much better chance of Arya getting to her family faster. If Eddard makes it to Castle Black, he'd probably arrive roughly at the same time that Jon leaves for the Great Ranging – which makes him a natural choice for commander of the Wall when Mance Rayder attacks, and for lord commander thereafter. And, hopefully, at some point, Jon Snow finds out the truth about his parentage.

What if Eddard speaks the truth? If Eddard had come to similar conclusions as I had in his last chapter and decided that he and his daughter are too valuable to be executed (a rational expectation in an irrational universe) and to use the mass audience to speak his mind – it's unclear how much this changes things. He'll die, certainly, as he did in OTL, but Robb's army probably keeps Sansa alive for the nonce. However, the political impact of his statement is hard to gauge: the mob's not going to turn on Joffrey right away, especially when they see the Lord Hand's head come off. But as we see in *Clash of Kings*, the narrative of royal bastardy and incest fits into the allegorical narratives the poor like and is enough to stir them into violent action, especially when hunger puts an edge to discontent. So when Stannis's letter arrives in King's Landing, it will probably find a more receptive audience – meaning not just one riot, but many, which potentially could keep enough of the gold cloaks busy or sufficiently demoralize them to cause the city to fall. The larger question is whether the story gets out of the city – Cersei's certainly trying to control egress from the King's Landing, but there just isn't a way to keep rumor penned in like that. Now, a rumor that Ned Stark was executed for upholding Stannis's right to the Iron Throne isn't as valuable as an open letter stating the same, but it couldn't hurt.

What if Arya is captured? Arya comes very close to being captured on the steps of the sept of Baelor, had Yoren not taken the time to grab her. I don't think it's possible that she could have prevented Eddard's death or killed Joffrey – there's just too many men with swords between her and her target – but it could potentially change things down the road. Ultimately, Tyrion's negotiations with the Starks in *Clash* are hamstrung by the fact that he doesn't have an Arya to trade, and if it's politically unfeasible to trade Jaime for both girls, it's even more unfeasible when the Lannisters don't have both bargaining chips in hand. If Tyrion did have both girls, while it's not likely, it is possible that the trade between him and Catelyn could have gone through without being horribly botched – which, potentially, opens up the Stark/Tyrell mid-war alliance that I'll talk about more later. If the Blackwater goes down the same way at OTL, we might even see a Sansa/Willas proposal thrown out there as a Tyrell move to triangulate vis-a-vis the Lannisters. Indeed, I would argue there's an outside possibility that, post-the Sack of Winterfell, Robb Stark himself might have been willing to eke out a truce on a Jaime-for-sisters basis (if done right).

Book vs. Show

In this chapter, George R.R. Martin does something really interesting – rather than have Eddard's death scene be told through his own POV, which at 20.8% of the text is the most dominant perspective of the novel, he chooses instead to have the event take place through the eyes of his children, and takes pains to focus on the *impact* of Eddard Stark's death on both of his daughters, as if to further jam it into our heads that our expectations about conventional fantasy tropes about main character plot armor should be thrown out the window. (He even has the "camera" turn away to further enhance our confusion and disbelief about what's going on.) It's a brave, unconventional, and shocking way to stick this most vital of landings...

And the show goes 180 degrees the other way. While we get Arya and Sansa's perspectives communicated quite clearly, with Arya's scramble up to the statue and Sansa's hopeful, smiling face, the show goes right into Eddard Stark's head in the final moment, complete with the heavy breathing echoing in our ears as a man goes to his death. And yet... it works. The death of Eddard Stark still hits the audience like a ton of bricks, and the critical impact on Arya and Sansa is told through acting, which is really the only way it could be in this medium.

At the same time, the show makes a significant change that's actually quite effecting and helps to push back on the "DumbNed" attitude all-too-often present in both the book and show fandoms – rather than delivering Eddard Stark a complete and total abnegation of his life and what it stood for, the same kind that poor Richard of York suffered at Wakefield, the showrunners add a grace note. A single word.

Baelor.

Amidst the wreckage of an entire life, Benioff and Weiss give Eddard Stark a tiny moral victory – he gets to spot his daughter on the statue of Baelor the blessed and direct Yoren's attention, and the last thing he sees before he dies is her absence on the statue, so that he dies knowing that she's safe. It doesn't undermine or change his character arc in the slightest – Eddard Stark still chooses family over honor, he still dies horribly and unjustly before the eyes of his children – but it gives a degree of mercy.

Is it less avant-garde? Yes. Less uncompromising in its refusal to give the audience a happy ending? Yes.

I couldn't care less. Well done, Benioff and Weiss. It doesn't get you off the hook for sins of commission or omission past, present, or future, but if anyone thinks the showrunners don't get the material at all – I offer this as Exhibit A in rebuttal.

BRAN VII

"You must put these dreams aside – they will only break your heart."

Synopsis

Bran has a dream of **his father** in the crypts of Winterfell, so Maester Luwin takes him down there to find... an increasingly feral Rickon (someone please call CPS!). Then it's story time, until a messenger comes with bad news...

Political Analysis

Okay, I'm going to make this a short one, because, honestly, I don't really care for this chapter and feel that "Bran VI" makes a better wrapping-up point for his storyline in *A Game of Thrones*. However, there are a few topics worth discussing.

The manpower of the north – in this chapter, Bran witnesses Ser Rodrick training replacement guards, who are described as "the oldest were men grown, 17 and 18 years from the day of their naming. One was past 20. Most were younger – 16 or less." Likewise, Maester Luwin argues that "your lord father took the cream of his guard to King's Landing, and your brother took the rest, along with all the likely lads for leagues around." Some have argued that this is evidence that the north is badly undermanned and that Robb's 18,000 represented the whole of their troops.

I disagree – rather, I think it's evidence of uneven levels of mobilization throughout the north. When Robb Stark was mobilizing his forces, he must have recruited heavily from those closest to Winterfell, as those would be the soonest to arrive (witness the 3,000 fighting men of the hill clans not being mobilized until *A Dance with Dragons*). The reference to "leagues around" suggests a concentric circle around Winterfell, describing those areas of House Stark's own demesne, where people can most easily walk to the castle itself. Thus, I think my estimate of 17,000 men left unmobilized in the north still stands.

Bran's dream – this is something where I forgot the details beyond the obvious plot device of signaling Eddard Stark's death. In the book version, "the crow... the one with three eyes... flew into my bedchamber and told me to come with him, so I did. We went down to the crypts. Father was there, and we talked. He was sad... something to do about Jon, I think." It's always been a bit puzzling why the Three-Eyed Crow would care that Eddard Stark is dead besides George R.R. Martin setting up Bran's greenseer nature one more time ahead of the reveal in *A Clash of Kings*. However, the mention of Jon is quite interesting. I've never thought of Bran as the vehicle for the revelation of R+L=J before, but I can see how they could make it work for that plot without getting Howland Reed up to the Wall to meet Jon Snow.

What I'm not sure of is why the Three-Eyed Crow chooses to intervene in the political side of things, given that he acts to ensure that Bran doesn't remember what he saw in the tower until we've reached a point in the narrative where we're rapidly running out of characters who he could tell who would care. One solution to this is that Bloodraven, being up on the Targaryen prophecy about the "song of ice and fire," believes that it's somehow important to the metaphysical side of things that Jon Snow know his parentage. I don't know why it would matter for that plot, and why, in that case, Bloodraven didn't reach out to also-a-warg Jon Snow.

Thoughts?

The Kings of Winter and the statues – one detail I really like in this chapter (and which I'd definitely keep if this chapter had to be scratched) is the descriptions of the Kings of Winter, in part because it confirms my theory that Eddard was an outlier in his family, and his personality and values come more from his time as Jon Arryn's ward than from being Rickard Stark's son. Consider the descriptions of the Kings in the North: "Grim folk... shaggy men fierce as the wolves at their feet. Others were shaved clean, their features gaunt and sharp-edged... hard men for a hard time." This speaks more to the wildness of the "wolf blood" than a family devotion to honor.

Consider the character of the Starks we learn about. They're militaristic and expansionist to a fault: Jon Stark drove out sea raiders and built castles to protect his east coast, Rickard Stark conquers the Neck, Theon Stark (btw, how weird is it that Theon is named after a Stark? Or is it the case that it's just a common northern name that the ironborn kept?) was called "the Hungry Wolf, because he was always at war," Rodrick Stark "won Bear Island in a wrestling match" (which I think is actually a metaphor for a contested struggle with the ironborn), and Cregan Stark was one of the best swordsmen of all time . As we learn in *A Dance with Dragons*, the Starks spent the better part of a thousand years fighting the Arryns over the Three Sisters in no small part because of the sea raid on the north's east coast. They also have intense emotions –

Brandon the Shipwright was so in love with the sea that he attempted an impossible voyage, Brandon the Burner reacts by putting an entire navy to the torch, Brandon "the Wild Wolf" had one hell of a temper, Lyanna was headstrong and independent to a fault, and even "stern" and political Lord Rickard chose to go out with "harness on his back."

While I think we need more evidence to be absolutely sure – here's hoping for *The She-Wolves of Winterfell* coming out soon to give us plenty of data to work from – all the signs point to the family characteristic of the Starks being a violent temper, with the "wolf" in "wolf blood" signifying a predatory and aggressive attitude, although it's possible that grimness and dourness is a part of the Stark heritage Ned did inherit. It's possible that this may be some kind of inherited bipolar disorder, as manic episodes can be associated with irritation and aggression as well as euphoria and impulsivity (which would fit Brandon and Lyanna pretty well), with Ned falling more on the depressive end of things. On the other hand, I'm not sure whether medicalizing and pathologizing these family traits is a good idea (although the Targaryens' mental health is pretty hard to discuss without it).

And here's where I think this is important: Ned Stark was fostered at the Eyrie at the age of eight; at the time that he became lord of Winterfell, he'd lived in the Vale longer than he'd lived in the north and, arguably, lived his most formative years there. Consider how the same process made Theon Greyjoy more of a "greenlander" than an ironborn, and then think about how many qualities Ned Stark shares with Jon Arryn – a focus on honor and honesty, trust in his peers, placing his duty over personal safety, etc. It makes you wonder if Ned Stark had had more of the "wolf blood" than he did, whether Littlefinger would have bled to death outside a brothel and Cersei would have been taken prisoner in a godswood.

On a final issue: I've read the theory that the extra statues in the crypt are there to hide Rhaegar's silver harp. I don't really think that's right, because I think the salience of the harp has declined too far. If we were still in *A Game of Thrones*, there would be enough people of Ned Stark's generation who would remember Rhaegar's silver harp enough to make that specific silver harp (as opposed to a silver harp that could be made at any time) identifiable. But at this point... how many people would remember and care?

Other things to note

1. Maester Luwin has a cache of dragonglass arrowheads – which possibly suggests that there's a supply of the things left in Winterfell even after the fire, and perhaps even more under the castle. More evidence for my theory that the Final Battle against the Others will take place at Winterfell after the Wall has fallen.

2. We get a huge info dump on the children of the forest and the Andals – I think I'll push this forwards to another chapter, where I can actually bring some of this historical information to bear on actual plot.

Historical Analysis

I'm planning on doing something on comparing the Andal invasion to the historical Anglo-Saxon invasions of Britain, but I think I'll push it to later in the series, as well, to where it bears more on plot.

What If?

There aren't really any major choices made at this time, so nothing to report here. Tune in next time, because "Sansa VI" has plenty of stuff to work with.

Book vs. Show

The show trims this chapter down substantially, leaving out a lot of the world-building and backstory (that, to be honest, wouldn't work very well in a visual medium). However, one of the things we lose is how severe Rickon's decline into ferality has become – he's attacking people, living in the crypts, and basically becoming less and less verbal over time. A minor detail, but something that's stuck in my mind when I think about Davos encountering Rickon on Skagos.

SANSA VI

"How long must I look?"

Synopsis

Sansa wakes up to the nightmare that is now her life, gets beaten by Ser Meryn Tranton under Joffrey's orders, watches Joffrey dispense justice, and is then brought to see her father's head on a spiker and considers "whether 'tis nobler in the mind to suffer the slings and arrows of outrageous fortune, or to take arms against a sea of troubles, and by opposing end them."

Political Analysis

"Sansa VI" is a brilliant conclusion of George R.R. Martin's deconstruction of romantic fantasy, and it strikes me as strange that so many people don't see the deconstruction, especially after this point, because so much of the chapter revolves around imagery of waking up from dreams to see a nightmarish reality around them.

And as she wakes up, Sansa suddenly can see everything clearly: "Sansa stared at him, seeing him for the first time… She wondered how she could ever have thought him handsome. His lips were as soft and red as the worms you found after a rain, and his eyes were vain and cruel." And what's important is that from this moment on, Sansa refuses to give in – she openly states "I don't want to marry you," tells Joffrey to his face that "I hate you," and, when faced with her father's head on a spike, taunts Joffrey with the idea that "maybe my brother will give me your head." Even when she takes the Hound's advice – which I'll discuss in just a second – she resists inside by refusing to give Joffrey the reaction he wants, insistent that, "He can make me look at the heads, but he can't make me see them."

Indeed, in this chapter, Sansa moves from being a romantic idealist to an outright cynic, turning on her own illusions: "There are no heroes, and she remembered what Lord Petyr had said to her, here in this very hall. 'Life is not a song, sweetling,' he'd told her. 'You may learn that one day your sorrow.' In life, the monsters win." And the context of this shift is crucial – it comes right in the midst of Joffrey's judgments as Sansa muses on justice, "wishing she could hurt [Lord Slynt], wishing that some hero would throw him down and cut off his head." This desire for cosmic and absolute justice, "to right the unrightable wrong," to be delivered by some external paragon of virtue, has been right at the heart of romantic medievalism from long before the time of Cervantes. If George R.R. Martin's deconstruction in the Sansa chapters has a thesis, I think it could be summed up as "there is no justice – there's just us." Indeed, I would argue that one could interpret the character arc of many female protagonists of *A Song of Ice and Fire* as a transition from desiring justice to come from above to enacting it themselves – whether we're talking about Catelyn becoming Lady Stoneheart, Brienne slaying the very symbol of the devastation of the riverlands, or Arya's Batman-origin saga. And I'm willing to lay money on the same happening with Sansa's arc in *The Winds of Winter*.

At the same time, Sansa doesn't and can't wholly reject the tropes of chivalric romance – as the Hound (her fellow critic of the gap between the knightly ideal and reality) reminds her, they can also be a means of survival when you're dealing with a psychopath who thinks in fairy-tale logic. "Save yourself some pain, girl, and give him what he wants... he wants you to smile and smell sweet and be his lady love... he wants to hear you recite all your pretty little words the way the septa taught you." By working within the genre, Sansa can eke out survival – and if she survives long enough, she may yet learn to prosper. Although the difficulty is that Joffrey is only half inside the logic of fairy tales, and the other half is madness. "He wants you to love him... and fear him" makes sense in Machiavellian politics, but not in a marriage.

In the court of the crimson king – at the same time, the revelation of Joffrey's evil goes deeper than the surface level – the moment he gets in power, with no one willing to check him, his psychopathy comes to the fore. And it's a truly terrifying blend of sadistic cruelty and an eerie parallel of Sansa's immature romanticism. On the one hand, Joffrey states with a straight face and an odd spirit of wounded righteousness that "if he hadn't been your father, I would have had him torn or flayed, but I gave him a clean death"; who has his knights beat his intended wife; who only shows interest in "what it pleased him to call justice" when it means he can order a thief's hand chopped off, a minstrel's tongue ripped out, or a woman to be imprisoned for the sake of love; who casually speaks of having Sansa executed for bearing "stupid babies"; and who has the godsworn executed.

On the other hand, there's something terrifyingly childish about Joffrey's sadism. When he comes to Sansa, Joffrey speaks of, "Mother says I'm still to marry you... my mother tells me it isn't fitting that a king should strike his wife"; when he's walking Sansa to see her father's head, he inquires about his birthday present as if he hadn't executed her father only a few days earlier; and when he learns that his uncle has been defeated by Robb Stark, when he has Sansa beaten it's because she's not acting as a "true wife," in a deliberate echo of Sansa's belief in a "true knight," and his plan to "raise a host and kill your brother myself" while Renly and Stannis menace King's Landing is exactly the kind of romantic delusion that Sansa once believed, only reflected over gender lines.

It's this combination that makes Joffrey so dangerous, in that it makes him a tyrant who's only interested in violence rather than power: "Nine cases out of ten seemed to bore him; those he allowed his council to handle, squirming restlessly... when he did choose to make a ruling, though, not even his queen mother could stay him." To Joffrey, being a king means that he gets to impose a boy's cruelty on others – thieves should have their hands chopped off, people who love traitors "must be a traitor, too," and technical disputes over property rights should be settled in duels to the death. If it were Cersei in charge all the time or if Joffrey were a power-hungry despot who actually ruled with an iron fist, there would be a certain predictability to it. Instead, all there is total uncertainty about who's actually in charge at any point in time and the cruel farce where the same king who still does what his mommy tells him and sneaks around her back using childish loopholes can also order grown men to their deaths.

On a side note – while I intend to go further into depth with this in part five of *Hollow Crowns*, there is an interesting question about where Joffrey is getting these ideas. On the one hand, the idea that all traitors must be punished, all thieves maimed, all fights must be to the death, probably doesn't come from Robert, who – whatever else he might have been –was a man who generally forgave his enemies if they weren't blood Targaryens, and was never interested in punishment. More likely, although it's not precisely clear from the text, is that the same woman who demanded bloody satisfaction for a dog bite impressed on her son that royal justice ought to be severe – but failed to foresee how her son might interpret her lesson.

Speaking of one of the distinctive elements of the new king's madness, I think Joffrey's clear misogyny has roots in both parents. We can clearly see an inheritance from Robert in his belief that a "true wife does not mock her lord" (with Cersei's independence as proof in Robert's eyes that she's not a proper wife), that violence is the way to correct one's wife (even though doing so oneself is "unkingly"), and that the only thing that matters about a wife is whether she can bear children. At the same time, Joffrey clearly gets instruction on gender issues from his mother: "You truly are a stupid girl... my mother says so... she worries about our children, whether they'll be stupid like you." Cersei's massive internalized misogyny is a topic I plan to get into in *A Feast for Crows*, but the comment from Joffrey that "women are all weak, even her, though she pretends she isn't," reminds me a lot of Cersei's exceptionalist identity.

Historical Analysis

Anne Neville lived most of her life as a bargaining chip for the House of Warwick, as was the case for many women of her caste and time. Born in 1456 in the very castle of Warwick that served as the heart of her father, the duke of Warwick's empire in the north of England, Anne was, in a sense, a participant in the Wars of the Roses by birth - her father was the Kingmaker and the richest man in England, her mother was a de Beauchamp and the heiress of Warwick, and her maternal great-aunt was the wife of Richard, Duke of York and the mother of the "three suns" of York. Indeed, she spent much of her childhood at Middleham Castle, where Richard, Duke of Gloucester and George, Duke of Clarence were fostered and, thus, grew up with some of the major political and military actors.

While there isn't much direct evidence, it was widely rumored that the Nevilles and the Yorkist Plantagenets would strengthen their blood ties by marrying Anne to Richard and George to her older sister, Isabelle. However, within eight years of Edward IV's triumph of Towton, both of the Neville girls became collateral damage in the feud between king and Kingmaker - Edward blocked the engagement of his brothers to the two girls after their father objected to his own marriage to Elizabeth Woodville. Isabel was married to George two weeks before her new husband and her father fought her brother-in-law at Edgecote Moor. When Warwick's rebellion fell apart politically, Anne's hand was the price of a Lancastrian and French alliance necessary for an invasion of England in 1470.

Anne the former Yorkist was, thus, married to Edward of Lancaster (although the marriage wasn't consummated in case a later change of plans would be politically advantageous to both sides), the heir of her family's long-time enemy, placing her on both sides of the Wars of the Roses. When Edward of Lancaster was killed at the Battle of Tewksbury, Anne had lost both father and husband in a period of about two weeks. The next year, she married Richard of Gloucester, who had fought on the opposing side at both Barnet (where her father had died) and Tewksbury.

These twists and turns of fate have given way to two fundamentally incompatible myths. In the Ricardian story, Anne and Richard were a pair of star-crossed lovers who were meant to be together, unluckily divided by civil war and Anne's marriage to a psychopathic prince (one of many inspirations for Joffrey), and finally reunited at last when the Good Guys triumph. In the Lancastrian story, brought to life most vividly by Shakespeare's *Richard III* (Act I, Scene II), Anne is a dupe who is seduced by her husband's murderer through appeals to her vanity, only to be cast aside when the monstrous tyrant decides to throw her over for his own niece. What historical evidence exists leans somewhat to the Ricardian side - Anne Neville went to some lengths to get married to Richard of Gloucester, although it's hard to know whether this was due to True Love or her desire to get out of the custody of her brother-in-law, George of Clarence, whom she clearly hated.

This part of Sansa's story clearly takes from the Ricardian portrait of Edward of Lancaster as a sadistic little bastard (literally, in the eyes of the Yorkists). More on this when we get to Sansa's interactions with Tyrion.

What If?

This chapter gives us only a few hypothetical scenarios, but they're doozies:

What if Sansa pushes Joffrey? For a moment in this chapter, Sansa has the opportunity to kill Joffrey – although almost certainly at the cost of her own life – but chooses not to. If she had, some really interesting things happen: in the short term, Tyrion's management of King's Landing gets much easier, since Tommen is a tractable child and not prone to murdering starving peasants, and Cersei will have something other than himself to focus on. (On the other hand, as we've seen from *The Princess and the Queen*, bad PR that involves tragic deaths of noblewomen can have explosive consequences.) It's quite possible that the Tyrell marriage alliance still happens – although a young child under his mother's regency is less appealing a prospect than a crowned king on the verge of his majority (and it's not clear whether the sunk-cost issue played into the second marriage). The Purple Wedding, however, is completely butterflied away, which means Sansa (assuming she isn't murdered on the spot) isn't vanished, Tyrion isn't accused of treason (and doesn't marry Sansa, come to think of it), Oberyn Martell never fights the Mountain, and Tywin isn't killed by his own son. Now, it's possible that some of these same events happen differently – the Tyrells aren't the only ones who know how to use poison, and Oberyn is clearly looking to kill everyone involved in his sister's death one way or another – but it wouldn't be the same. At the same time, with Sansa dead, Jaime Lannister isn't freed by Catelyn, and it may well be that the Starks pull out of the war using Jaime as the lever, since the person responsible for Ned Stark's death is dead.

What if Joffrey marches on Robb? This hypothetical is absolutely hilarious. It would require Cersei being more incompetent than usual to allow this, but I could see a scenario in which Joffrey marches out of King's Landing at the head of six thousand gold cloaks, and Stannis takes the undefended city in a cakewalk and crowns himself king on the Iron Throne before Renly can get to it. This sets up a strange retread of the Siege of Storm's End, except, this time, Stannis has a huge symbol of political legitimacy on his side and a huge navy to keep the food flowing into the capital. While Renly's army is too big for Stannis to defeat on the field, his political coalition could well begin unraveling if the Reacher lords begin to worry about what happens if Stannis survives. Now, the larger question is whether Tywin intercepts Joffrey before Robb's army utterly destroys his green forces somewhere in the riverlands – if he does, then Tywin's army is a bit bigger, and Robb has less incentive to march west and every incentive to put the head of House Lannister and their claim to the Iron Throne under siege at Harrenhal. If he doesn't, it's quite likely that Joffrey dies on the banks of the Trident, dealing the Lannisters a devastating blow to their political legitimacy and inflating Robb Stark's military legend even more. Tywin is reduced to a rebel lord with 20,000 men cut off from their home territory, facing enemy kings to both sides.

Book vs. Show

The show played this pretty straight, with the exception of the somewhat older Joffrey being less childlike and more sadistic in his particular kind of insanity. It's not a huge change, however.

DAENERYS IX

"Look to your khal *and see what life is worth, when all the rest is gone."*

Synopsis

Daenerys wakes up from the ordeal of childbirth to find that her child is a stillborn monstrosity, her husband a living corpse, and the *khalasar* she needs to retake the Seven Kingdoms with is scattered. And yet Daenerys does not break – already her mind has turned to the occult legacy of House Targaryen. She says goodbye to Drogo.

Political Analysis

"Daenerys IX," despite being a penultimate chapter to the fiery climax of Daenerys's story arc, is actually a much more interesting chapter in retrospective than it is on a first read. It becomes even more so since the under-appreciated final Daenerys chapter of *A Dance with Dragons*, which demonstrates that when you think George R.R. Martin's plots have jumped the rails, there is always a plan.

The case against Mirri Maz Duur – before I get into the thematic heart of this chapter, I do want to back up my earlier arguments regarding Mirri Maz Duur's complicity in the murder of Drogo. The godswife appears in the chapter in a way she never has before – "Dany understood in that moment that the maegi was stronger, and crueler, and infinitely more vicious." Right off the bat, she announces that Rhaego "was scaled like a lizard, blind, with the stub of a tail and small leather wings like the wings of a bat. When I touched him, the flesh sloughed off the bone, and inside he was full of graveworms and the stink of corruption. He had been done for years." Magic has slain Daenerys's child in the womb.

Now, some have argued that this was caused by Jorah bringing Daenerys into the tent during Mirri Maz Duur's spell when he wasn't supposed to. However, the maegi's comment just a bit later complicates this. While she sets forth that the tent was dangerous, she also denies that the spell was supposed to be the exchange of the life of Drogo's horse for Drogo's extended life: "No, that was a lie you told yourself. You knew the price." In other words, the plan always had been for Mirri Maz Duur's spell to kill Rhaego and transmute Drogo into a mindless husk – and in order to do that, Drogo had to be brought to the point where he was on death's door so that Dany would agree to make the exchange. The death of Drogo was necessary for the whole of her plan to be successful, and she had the means, motive, and opportunity to poison Khal Drogo to the point where she could gain the consent to kill Dany and his child and violate his body against Dothraki taboo.

Indeed, she almost says as much when Dany accuses her of "murder[ing] my child within me." The maegi replies: "It was wrong of them to burn my temple... that angered the Great Shepard... the stallion who mounts the world will burn no cities now. His *khalasar* shall trample no nations into dust." In other words, we have a confession in all but name to the murder of Dany's child – but the mention of the burning of her temple, the destruction of the village of her people, and her own rape have nothing to do with Dany's unborn child. Those events happened because the *khalasar* of Khal Drogo came to her village – and, thus, her motive points directly to Khal Drogo as much as it does to a preemptive defense against the stallion who mounts the world. In addition, we should pay attention to her claim that the Great Shepherd was responsible for this – as we saw in "Dany VII," Mirri Maz Duur clearly sees herself as the hand of god ("the Great Shepherd sent me to Earth to heal his lambs") and said from the outset that "the Great Shepherd guards the flock" at a time when Khal Drogo posed a clear and present danger to the other villages of the Lhazarene.

Once again, I say: means, motive, opportunity.

Waking the dragon – in the very beginning of this chapter, Daenerys has a vision which stretches from her childhood through to her marriage, the death of her brother, including meeting her son: "Her son was tall and proud, with Drogo's copper skin and her own silver-gold hair... when he opened his mouth, the fire poured out. She saw his heart burning through his chest, and in an instant he was gone... she wept for her child... but her tears turned to steam as they touched her skin." It's a rather startling move for Martin to frame the death of Dany's son as a moment where she is choosing to sacrifice her son's life in favor of her own, choosing to become the dragon rather than birth him as Daenerys spiritually replaces her brother, Rhaegar, as a dragon in fact as well as in sigil. Note how the recurring phrase shifts from Viserys's threatening "you don't want to wake the dragon, do you?" to the negative "don't want to wake the dragon" to the affirmative "want to wake the dragon" to the imperative "wake the dragon."

It's in this moment, wrapped in a prophetic dream that comes as much from her Targaryen blood heritage as it does from Mirri Maz Duur's blood magic, that Dany arrives at the plan to hatch her eggs, thus why "they found her on the carpet, crawling toward her dragon egg." Well before she's reminded that "only death can pay for life," Daenerys already knows that she can bring them to life at the cost of someone else's. Which lends itself to an interesting question about blood magic: how much do you need to know what you're doing? Clearly, Mirri Maz Duur has had some training, and so, too, have the three R'hllorite priests (Thoros, Melisandre, and Moqorro), and presumably the follower of the old gods that Bran witnessed through the treenet did, as well, but Dany didn't, nor did Beric Dondarrion, and it worked for them. So it's possible that all that blood magic requires is willpower and death – which leads to an interesting question: would the Mad King's exit plan actually have worked, birthing a dragon from nothing?

Speaking of Targaryen madness, one of the things that *The Princess and the Queen* has revealed is that deformed dragon-babies run in the family – which reduces Mirri Maz Duur's involvement to the graveworms thing, although it could be argued that the spell brought out latent tendencies already existing in the blood, as it were. Which makes a lot more sense to me than the idea that the Targaryens could engage in that steady a practice of very-close incest (brother-sister rather than cousin-cousin) and not have to deal with nasty recessive alleles popping up. As I've discussed before, royal incest in history tended to go hand-in-hand with infanticide – given the importance of the "Targaryen look" as a sign of semi-religious awe and legitimacy, I would imagine this would be doubly true for the ruling house of Westeros.

The wages of taboo – on an entirely different track, "Dany IX" also shows the consequences of Dany's desperate attempt to save her husband. Where once Drogo's *khalasar* was an entire world unto itself and a geopolitical force to be reckoned with, now "a count might show a hundred people, no more. Where the other forty thousand had made their camp, only the wind and dust lived now." Unlike the people of Westeros, for whom the land structures their identity and lives, to the Dothraki the nation is the people.

For a micro-second, Dany tried to use the memory of Drogo to hold back the tide of Dothraki culture – the commandment that "it is the right of the strong to take from the weak." It failed completely, and the old pattern reasserted itself quickly, as "Ko Pono left first, naming himself Khal Pono, and many followed him. Jhaqo was not long to do the same... there are a dozen new *khalasar*s on the Dothraki sea, where once there was only Drogo's." And for all that Martin has been criticized for making the Dothraki a supposedly one-dimensional picture, there is a deep cultural logic at work: a nomadic society where property is only what one can carry doesn't think about succession in the same way that a settled agricultural society does; the division and multiplication of *khalasar*s ensures that population pressures don't over-tax the Dothraki sea beyond the capacity of *khal*s to keep their people fed; the interplay of *ko*s, *kha*s, and *khal* offers incentives for loyalty to keep the chain of command intact and the hope of advancement to keep *khalasar*s from breaking off all the time instead of at punctuated, culturally-mediated occasions; and, at the same time, the fear of a *khalasar*'s destruction and the reality of inter-*khalasar* warfare is mediated by the religious promise of Vaes Dothrak, that come the time of prophecy, the Dothraki will all be one.

Likewise, the revenge of Mago and Jhaqo is an assertion of Dothraki culture and tradition against a foreign interloper – Mago symbolically reasserts both his own position and the proper order of Dothraki gendered hierarchy by brutalizing the child the *khal*'s foreign wife "stole" from him. Likewise, Jhaqo strengthens his position as a newly-forged *khal* by offering "restitution" to his man who he could not protect when he was Ko Jhaqo (which must have hurt his standing within the *khalasar*) – and, in return, gains a loyal bloodrider.

Moreover, George Martin clearly invests more importance in this incident than people had thought for a long time, because of all the *khalasar*s that Daenerys finds herself among in her misunderstood final chapters of *A Dance with Dragons*, it is the same *khalasar* that she promised "by the Mother of the Mountains and the Womb of the World" that "before I am done with them, Mago and Ko Jhaqo will plead for the mercy they showed Eroeh." At this very moment, Dany coins her mantra "if I look back, I am lost" – and, yet, she has "gone back to go forwards."

The prophecy – now we come to Mirri Maz Duur's prophecy – one of the few prophecies that made it from the book to the show, by the way, and one of the most frequently misunderstood. The "object" of the prophecy isn't the return of Dany's fertility, or the birth of her child – those are signs of the prophecy's fulfillment. The object is the return of Drogo "as he was."

Now, I agree with those who argue that there are clear signs that the prophecy is being fulfilled: the Martells have risen up in the west while Quentyn Martell died in Meereen, the Dothraki sea is drying out, and the great pyramids of Meereen have been "blowing in the wind" of Dany's dragons' breath. Likewise, I think that *part* of the prophecy has come true with regards to Dany – I think she underwent a miscarriage on the Dothraki sea at the end of *A Dance with Dragons*, and is now capable of bearing a child. However, the prophecy requires that "your womb quickens again, and you bear a living child" – and Dany hasn't yet given birth to a living child.

As to what it means for Drogo to come back, I'm not sure. I doubt it refers to his literal resurrection; his body is clearly burnt to ashes, and I don't think the *khal*'s actual return would have much dramatic purpose at this point. It could refer to Drogo returning as her "sun and stars" – so, perhaps, the prophecy suggests that Dany's next child would be the reincarnation of Drogo or be named after Drogo in the same way that Drogon was. A third option is that the prophecy might be referring to Daenerys's death – that Drogo will return to her in the sense that the two of them are united in the afterlife (certainly, the show's version of Dany's visions in the House of the Undying points in this direction).

Historical Analysis

One of the strange things about modern social and cultural politics is how often people assume that birth control and family planning came into existence around 1960, whether they think of them as a liberating force or the source of cultural and moral decline. However, one of the things one learns as a historian is that human beings are startlingly similar over huge gaps in time, in terms of the things they worry about, the things they strive for, and the difficulties they struggle with. As far as family planning goes, it's one of the closest things to a historical constant I've ever seen, with the major differences being what kinds of technologies are available, and how the physical and cultural environment creates relatively stable patterns of incentives.

Pretty much at any time and place one can name, humans have sought to modulate their fertility for various reasons – and, quite often, they've turned to infanticide to do so, regardless of cultural and religious taboos around death and childbirth. By comparing both the spacing between births and, especially, patterns of gender wherever records of childbirth can be found, demographic historians have uncovered an entire world of human activity that's almost never written about directly.

In Medieval and Early Modern England, for example, trends shifted from roughly equal births of men and women in the 13th century to a dramatic shift to male births around the time of the Black Death until well into the 15th century – suggesting that families were responding to shortages in the labor market and trying to make sure that they had enough male children to work the farm and inherit the estate. In the 17th century, infanticide was common among young female servants who lacked the capacity to start a family and whose labor was necessary in weaving, dairy production, and other agricultural labor markets, and the practice of women being secluded from men but accompanied by other women during "lying-in" sometimes resulted in communal verdicts of "stillbirths" and, other times, in prosecutions for murder, depending on a number of different factors.

As a number of historians have found, Medieval and Early Modern Europe practiced infanticide regularly, despite the Catholic Church placing enormous social taboos against it starting at the end of the 4th century CE – with some historians describing it as halfway between a discretely-sanctioned social practice and a crime. For example, in Medieval and Early Modern Belgium, infanticide was legally considered not merely murder but witchcraft, and punished by burning, legal torture, or being drowned in a river. However, in the Early Modern period, the courts shifted to treating many cases as accidental deaths and ordering lesser punishments. Likewise, in England, various legal loopholes were created in the 17th century to modulate verdicts against single women (especially those who might otherwise become a drain on the poor relief system).

This practice was not confined to Europe. In Han China, for example, we have scattered evidence that infant abandonment was considered illegal – but exceptions were made in law for children born with deformities, and trends in law went back and forth between those who saw abandonment as murder and those who saw it as an unpleasant necessity for families who could not support another child. In Early Modern Japan, there's strong evidence that peasant families deliberately limited family size in order to better reap the benefits of economic growth and rising incomes; keeping family size under control allowed for more income per capita within the household and prevented either dowries or inheritances from over-taxing the family's estate, both of which were powerful economic motives. In the period between 1600 and 1870, Japan managed to drop its population eight million people below previous historical trends, and the results were a marked improvement in standards of living. However, as historians have noted, it wasn't just about economics – in Japan, married couples seem to have selected for gender balance within the family, but only after the second baby.

The larger point to all of this is – if you ever think that a social or cultural custom is brand-new, it probably is a very old custom being experienced in a different way due to a change in technology or environment or institutions.

What If?

While I try to consider most hypothetical scenarios, I try to keep them within the bounds of consistent character motivations and personalities – and I don't see any way that Dany doesn't make the decision to euthanize Drogo and have Mirri Maz Duur burnt to death. Everything in her story up to this point – everything in her personality, all of her motivations – is leading her to this point.

Some things may well be destined to happen.

Book vs. Show

The show played this one pretty straight, so I don't have much to say. My only complaint is that I felt the lack of a visibly-huge *khalasar* earlier in season one did make the reveal of their disappearance a bit disappointing, as you couldn't see the difference that much.

TYRION IX

Tyrion... hurled his empty cup to the floor, where it shattered into a thousand pieces. "There's your peace, Ser Harys... you'll have an easier time drinking wine from that cup than you will convincing Robb Stark to make peace now."

Synopsis

Tywin's army reaches the Inn at the Crossroads after a long forced march, only to find that Robb Stark has smashed Jaime's army and relieved the siege of Riverrun. After a dispirited war council, Tywin decides to march for Harrenhal and burn the southern riverlands. For his display of political and military sense during the council, Tyrion is made acting Hand of the King and sent to secure the Lannister position at King's Landing.

Political Analysis

"Tyrion IX" is a somewhat understated chapter, especially in comparison to the political drama of "Catelyn XI" or the metaphysical drama of "Daenerys X." However, it's actually packed with a lot of information about the military and political side of the War of the Five Kings. So strap in - this is going to be a long one.

The War of the Five Kings: aftermath of the Battle of the Green Fork - the chapter opens in media res, but does quite a bit of backtracking (in terms of Tyrion's memory, other people describing past events, etc.). The Lannisters have succeeded in force-marching down the kingsroad and reaching their old position at the crossroads, without being harried by Roose Bolton, "the remnants of his host" being "north of us" in the area of the "Twins and Moat Cailin" - one more consequence of his decision to throw the battle of the Green Fork.

At the same time, even not being harassed by northmen, the Lannisters took losses: "His father had set a grueling pace, and it had taken its toll. Men wounded in the battle kept up as best they could or were abandoned to fend for themselves. Every morning, they left a few more by the roadside, men who went to sleep never to wake. Every afternoon, a few more collapsed along the way. And every evening, a few more deserted." However, these casualties don't seem to show up later in the narrative where Tywin's army comes up – although I'll keep an eye out for this in *A Clash of Kings* and *A Storm of Swords* to see if my memory has diverged from the text.

And, yet, these casualties are unlikely to be minor; Tywin's army force-marched over three hundred miles immediately after a battle, and, historically, force-marches can be killer. For example, during the Mexican-American War, Santa Anna engaged in two epic 240-mile force-marches (the first to attack General Taylor's force at Buena Vista, and the second retreating from said battle) and lost 25% of his force each time. Given Santa Anna's poor logistics and the added physical difficulty of marching through the desert, that's probably a high proportion (Tywin wasn't dealing with extreme hot or cold, had adequate supplies, etc.), but it's not unlikely that 1-2,000 men (or 5-10%) were either left behind, went AWOL, or died of their wounds from the battle while on the march (at a rate of about 50-100 a day). Add onto that the fact that, even with Roose Bolton's best efforts to throw the Battle of the Green Fork, the Lannisters took 500 casualties in the vanguard alone, it seems unlikely that Tywin Lannister's army remained at 20,000 men. In fact, I think it's more likely to say that Tywin's down to about 17,000 men when he holes up in Harrenhal.

The reason for this counting exercise is that I think this might explain why Tyrion wasn't able to call on the military forces of the crownlands and had to rely on the gold cloaks instead. After all, the crownlands are a relatively small kingdom that fields around 10,000 men, and the island houses were backing Stannis – so perhaps 5,000 men were available, period, and then you have to account for the fact that the crownlands houses fought for the Targaryens in Robert's Rebellion. If I had to explain both their non-appearance and the fact that Tywin's army bounced back from these losses, I'd say that what probably happened is that Tywin grabbed about 3,000 men to recoup his losses at the cost of King's Landing's defenses.

Interestingly, this cost was paid in order to reach Riverrun itself and the Lannister army there ("It had all been for nothing. The rush south, the endless forced marches, the bodies left beside the road... Robb Stark had reached Riverrun") – rather than either to rescue Jaime himself or to get to safety – which makes a kind of cold-blooded sense, given that Tywin's army isn't immediately being threatened, and that linking up with the 12,000 Lannister men at Riverrun could potentially have allowed Tywin to overwhelm Robb Stark's smaller force and regain the upper hand in the War of the Five Kings.

The War of the Five Kings: the Battle of the Camps – what made this sacrifice pointless is Robb Stark using his superior mobility to cover the 300 miles between the Twins and Riverrun far faster than

Tywin could cover roughly the same distance from the battlefield of the Green Fork to the crossroads (let alone the 250 miles from the crossroads to Riverrun). Clearly, Tywin must have been hoping that Jaime's army could hold out just long enough for him to arrive and catch Robb between the two forces, as he did more successfully with the Battle of the Blackwater. In any case, he had an overriding need to get to the crossroads quickly, lest Robb Stark steal a march on him and take the southern side of the crossing, trapping Tywin's army between him and Roose Bolton.

Superior mobility and the use of surprise is clearly a key element of Robb Stark's style as a commander – but the Battle of the Camps involved more than just that.

A large part of the strategy revolved around the unique geography of Riverrun: "The castle is situated at the end of the point of land where the Tumblestone flows into the Red Fork of the Trident. The rivers form two sides of the triangle, and when danger threatens, the Tullys open their sluice gates upstream to create a wide moat on the third side... to cut off all the approaches, a besieger must needs place one camp north of the Tumblestone, one south of the Red Fork, and a third between the rivers, west of the moat." As I've discussed earlier, this feature of the Tully defenses allowed Robb Stark to achieve local superiority of numbers and more cohesive command-and-control against a larger force; each camp is only 4,000 men and can't easily reinforce the others or coordinate between them. Given his upbringing in Riverrun, the Blackfish was likely the originator of this part of the strategy (in addition to his "vanishing" of the Lannister outriders), as his successful screening operation at the Whispering Woods had impressed Robb to the point of giving him an independent command (a promotion from commanding outriders).

Other elements of the battle, however, resemble Robb's strategy from the Whispering Woods – for example, Robb could have kept his entire 11,000-strong force together and attacked each camp separately, using his numbers to overrun each unit in detail. However, as with his overall riverlands campaign and in the Whispering Woods, Robb Stark has a preference for dividing his army to achieve a strategic effect – in this case, preventing the camps from reinforcing one another and maximizing casualties by ensuring that two-thirds of the Lannister army can't retreat in good order. In this case, Robb likely split his army into one chunk of 5,000 and another chunk of 6,000, still maintaining numerical superiority on both sides. The result is that the Lannisters suffer 8,000 casualties – for a total of 11,000 between his two battles.

In addition, Robb Stark seems to have a preference for staggered attacks – both here and at the Whispering Woods, Robb Stark frequently has one division of his army attack before the other, in order to direct his enemy's attention and fix their formations in place, so that his second division can land with greater effect. In a sense, we can think of this as

Robb Stark generalizing the "refuse" – a cavalry tactic in which a squadron separates into two lines, the first of which collides with the enemy line and disrupts their formation so that the second line can scatter them definitively – from the squadron level to the battlefield level, a sign of his training as a heavy cavalryman.

This is a riskier strategy – as we see on the western camp, Robb's larger force of Stark, Mallister, and Umber men didn't quite have the ability to overwhelm the western camp once it had gotten a shield wall together, which was an easier task for the Lannisters there because, unlike on the north bank, they could anchor their flanks against both the Tumblestones and the Red Fork. But, as we've seen before and since, part of Robb Stark's style as a commander is to put himself in the thick of the action and, thus, build a legend for himself among his men and his enemies. And while BryndenBFish correctly notes the advantage of a battlefield commander staying back to retain command-and-control, what I think he fails to mention is that it is also a truism of medieval warfare that personal charisma matters – just as only Edward IV in person could have guaranteed the critical seizure of a crossing of the River Aire or kept the center of his army solid under pressure on Towton field, Robb Stark's presence inspires his men to improbable feats and demoralizes his enemies in a unique way, creating victories which otherwise wouldn't exist. After all, how many other generals have a direwolf at their side?

Taken together with the Whispering Woods and the Green Fork, I have argued that Robb Stark's actions as a whole represent a nearly-flawless strategic campaign: in three battles, Robb Stark has moved from a strategic position of being isolated from his main ally to being united with his ally; from facing two armies, one of which can move against him while the other is free to act, to now having two armies operating against Tywin's one; from being isolated at the Neck to placing himself in the heart of the riverlands; and in reducing the Lannisters' forces from 35,000 under arms to around 18,000 in the field (a 31.4% reduction in effective fighting strength), and 4,000 bottled up in the Golden Tooth, with 10,000 raw recruits in the westerlands who can be called up in time. The Starks and Tullys together now outnumber Tywin Lannister by about two to one.

Robb Stark now has Jaime Lannister, a numerical and positional advantage over Tywin Lannister, the forces of the riverlands by his side – and victory under his original war aims under his grasp. Unfortunately, thanks to Joffrey Lannister and some other unforeseeable forces, things won't work out that easily – but for his debut campaign, I think Robb Stark deserves more credit than he gets.

The War of the Five Kings: the Lannisters' strategic situation – to understand Tywin Lannister's thinking in this moment, I cannot recommend BryndenBFish's analysis highly enough. Here, I intend merely to add on to his work. As the Lannister council of war gathers at the Inn at the Crossroads, the situation cannot be bleaker. As Ser Kevan helpfully sums up for us:

> "Jaime has left us in a bad way. Roose Bolton... [is] north of us. Our enemies hold the Twins and Moat Cailin. Robb Stark sits to the west, so we cannot retreat to Lannisport and the Rock unless we choose to give battle. Jaime is taken, and his army, for all purposes, has ceased to exist. Thoros of Myr and Beric Dondarrion continue to plague our foraging parties. To our east, we have the Arryns, Stannis Baratheons sits on Dragonstone, and, in the south, Highgarden and Storm's End are calling their banners... Robb Stark will have Edmure Tully and the lords of the Trident with him now. Their combined power may exceed our own. And with Roose Bolton behind us... Tywin, if we remain here, I fear we might be caught between three armies."

This situation presents Tywin with a number of problems. Geographically, Tywin is surrounded from north, east, west, and, potentially, to the south and is in genuine danger of being encircled – even if he breaks out of his current location, he's still in danger of losing the west, facing a battle while outnumbered, or losing King's Landing. Moreover, the shock of sudden and overwhelming defeat (on top of a grueling series of maneuvers) after an unbroken series of victories has divided his bannermen between those like Ser Harys Swyft, who arguee that "we must sue for peace," and Ser Addam Marbrand, who recommends "we should march on them at once."

Neither man is offering good advice, but both have a kernel of a point. Swyft points to the genuine long-term problems facing the Lannisters in their present position: "The Starks and the Tullys sit squarely across our line of supply. We are cut off from the west! They can march on Casterly Rock if they so choose, and what's to stop them?" Previously, commenters have pointed out that medieval and early modern armies lacked the logistical capacity to maintain supply lines for any great distance, let alone the 890 miles between Lannisport and the Inn at the Crossroads. Supply lines require quite a bit of organization – on the dispatch side, you need someone to requisition, warehouse, and send out the right amount and composition of supplies, you need to organize convoys with military escorts, food for the teamsters, guards, and animals, spare draft animals and axles and wheels, you need someone really good at organization on the receiving end to make sure goods are properly stored and distributed and that good records are kept so that you know what you need and where and when you need it. Now, part of this is George R.R. Martin's numbers problem kicking in again – Westeros is just too big for a medieval setting.

However, at a certain point, you have to let this kind of caviling aside and accept that, in this world that Martin has created, supply lines are a major concern for the Lannister army. After all, given that they've been burning a large swath of it and intend to accelerate that program, there's a limit to how long 18,000 men can feed themselves off the southern half of the riverlands, and there's not much help they can get from the crownlands, which have to help feed a capital city of 500,000 people. If the War of the Five Kings had more resembled the siege-intensive warfare of the early Middle Ages rather than the battle-intensive late Middle Ages Wars of the Roses, it's quite possible that Tywin Lannister could have been penned in to Harrenhal until he starved to death.

However, the flip side of this is political (and, here, I think I have something to add) – Tywin's army at the crossroads is not a modern professional military; they are a feudal army that serves a liege lord for a certain space of time, and does so through a bilateral system of exchange of political influence ultimately depending on the ability of the lord to protect his vassals. As Robb Stark will learn to his sorrow in *A Storm of Swords*, "How can I call myself 'king' if I can't hold my own castle?" As I've argued elsewhere, the same applies to Tywin. If their holdfasts are threatened and Tywin can't protect them, then the lesser houses of the westerlands have no reason to stick around; if Tywin can't protect himself, then the political regime he built on the fear generated by the "Rains of Castamere" will collapse, and his army will dissolve.

On the other hand, Addam Marbrand has a point – two battles aren't a war, and the Lannisters have strategic resources they can count on – even if his initial advice to rush headlong at Robb Stark's larger army with Roose Bolton in a position to cut off the Lannisters from behind is deeply stupid. As even Ser Swyft notes, the Lannisters have reserves: "Surely, our friends at court could be prevailed upon to join us with fresh troops... and someone might return to Casterly Rock to raise a new host." While it's a bit odd that Ser Forley Prester marched west to the Golden Tooth (which must have involved crossing the Red Fork) as opposed to east to Harrenhal (which wouldn't), the reality is that the Lannisters can usually hold the mountain passes and can raise another 10,000 men, which balances the numerical odds and puts the Starks in a nasty position with Lannister armies to both their west and eastern flanks.

The War of the Five Kings: the political situation – the political situation isn't much better than the military one – at a fundamental level, the Lannisters in the field and the Lannisters in King's Landing are not working as a cohesive unit. Joffrey "broke [peace] when he decided to ornament the Red Keep with Lord Eddard's head," which means they can't "forge a peace with Winterfell and Riverrun, a peace that would have given us the time we need to deal with Robert's brothers." (It's interesting to note that Tywin was willing to deal on the terms that Robb Stark hoped to achieve by capturing Jaime, which was far more than even Cersei was contemplating.) At the same time, the Lannisters face an existential threat from the south: "Renly Baratheon wed Margaery Tyrell at Highgarden... and, now, he has claimed the crown." What's interesting is that, while Tywin clearly sees this as dangerous, he doesn't react to it as such – he doesn't march for King's Landing, and insists that "we must finish our business with young Lord Stark before Renly Baratheon can march from Highgarden," suggesting that Tywin isn't shifting his thinking as much as he ought to.

Interestingly, Stannis plays an ambivalent role in Tywin's political calculations. On the one hand, Tywin states that "I have felt from the beginning that Stannis was a greater danger than all the others combined." On the other, he notes that "yet he does nothing. Oh, Varys hears his whispers... what does it mean, is any of it is true?" In the end, Stannis is essentially shrugged off. In hindsight, this suggests that Stannis might have missed his window of opportunity – had he declared himself as king two weeks before now and sailed immediately, he'd have had a two-and-a-half-to-one advantage, hit King's Landing before siege preparations were completed, and undercut his brother politically. Then again, Tywin's dismissal turns out to be incorrect later when Stannis picks up 20,000 men at Storm's End.

Meanwhile, neither Cersei nor Joffrey is thinking straight down in King's Landing and threatens to collapse their northern front in order to shore up their southern. Tywin's political diagnosis is scathing: "I blame those jackanapes on the small council – our friend, Petyr, the venerable grand maester, and that cockless wonder, Lord Varys. What sort of counsel are they giving Joffrey... whose notion was it to make this Janos Slynt a lord? [...] Dismissing Selmy – where was the sense in that?"

So, overall, it's a mixed picture – Tywin accurately pinpoints their political problems in King's Landing but seems to have fallen into a bit of a sunk-cost fallacy when it comes to his Stark-first strategy.

The War of the Five Kings: Tywin's new plan – Tywin reacts to his setback in a decisive fashion – "I have no intention of remaining here... on the morrow, we make for Harrenhal... I want Ser Addam's outriders to screen our movements... unleash Ser Gregor and send him before us with his reavers.... each is to have three hundred horse. Tell them I want to see the riverlands afire from the Gods Eye to the Red Fork." It's a defensive move, but it's quite clever – Tywin can hold Harrenhal until the westerlands raise a fresh army, and as BryndenBFish notes, chevauchées in the riverlands and separate Lannister armies worked quite well for him in the past, and they make sense now. Burning the southern riverlands unleashes the same political threat against Robb Stark that a march on the west poses to himself – Houses Darry, Blackwood, Bracken, Smallwood, Lychester, and the other lords of the hills cannot afford to let their holdfasts burn. Ten thousand men in the westerlands can link up with 4,000 men at the Golden Tooth, and House Lannister is back to fighting weight.

It doesn't quite work out, but it's a decent plan. However, and I want to point this out to some people who've fallen for Tywin's self-serving justifications for the Red Wedding, it's also a military strategy predicated on premeditated war crimes. Tywin sits in council listening to Ser Gregor Clegane's talk about motivating outriders by cutting out people's eyes in an escalating cumulative fashion (someone went to the duke of Cornwall school of human resources management), and decides he's going to give this psychopath 300 men and a mandate to murder civilians and destroy everything in his path – and just to add put a fine point on it, he throws in the maimer Hoat and professional baby-stabber Ser Amory Lorch and gives them 300 men each.

And then he gives Tyrion a mandate to rule in King's Landing – more on that in *A Clash of Kings*!

Historical Analysis

As we've seen before, one of the reasons why the Wars of the Roses lasted for more than 30 years is that very rarely did anyone ever get completely defeated. More likely, the nobles would scatter, flee the country, regroup with a new army, and try again – which is probably why people shifted from taking prisoners and asking for ransoms to killing nobles on sight, because allowing that chivalrous tradition to continue meant war without end.

After Edward IV's crushing victory at Towton, Margaret D'Anjou didn't give in for a minute. Rather, she packed herself and the royal family and 6,000 Lancastrian soldiers up to Scotland, which meant that Edward IV had to contend with a crowned king in exile complete with a male heir to the throne, and a queen who had built an alliance with James III, King of Scotland – even if that meant ceding English territory in the north and Prince Edward's hand in marriage to James's sister, Mary Stewart. In June 1461, the same month of Edward IV's formal coronation in London, Margaret invaded England and laid siege to Carlisle, but was driven back by the Yorkist lord Montague (Warwick's brother); having failed there, she pressed on south for Durham, where Warwick, now the Warden of the East and West Marches, stopped them from crossing the River Tyne and held the north for York. In 1464, the north rose again for Lancaster under the duke of Somerset, who was then defeated by Montague at Hedgeley Moor and Hexham. A year later, Henry VI was recaptured by Warwick, and Edward IV reached a treaty with James of Scotland that forced Margaret to flee for France.

However, by 1468, when the last Lancastrian holdout in Wales had finally been defeated, Warwick had broken with Edward IV, and the whole damn thing would start over again.

What If?

There really isn't a hypothetical I can see here – there's no way Tywin's army marches faster than Robb can ride, and I really can't see Tywin blundering west or south.
Check back next chapter!

Book vs. Show

The show did this scene rather well, although my same complaints about the collapse of any kind of geographic sense in season two holds for the Lannisters as much as it does for the Starks. While the first season leaves us with a clear scenario – Tywin's marching to Harrenhal, the Mountain is burning stuff – there's no explanation of the army gathering in the westerlands that would give Robb's victory in episode 204 some geographic and strategic meaning.

Another big change from the book to the show is how Tyrion reacts when Tywin makes him acting Hand of the King and tells him he was chosen because "you are my son." In the show, this is a moment of profound importance for Tyrion, where he's finally been given some respect by his father, and he's notably moved by it. In the book, Tyrion is instantly outraged, believing that Tywin has given up on Jaime and turned to Tyrion only when he had no options left.

I think both versions work.

JON IX

"My place is here... where is yours, boy?"

Synopsis

Jon Snow tries to run away from the Night's Watch, and his friends bring him back. He talks with Commander Mormont about priorities and makes a choice about whether he's going to ride south or north.

Political Analysis

"Jon IX" is a bit of an odd chapter to end on – and it throws up a lot of questions about to what extent George R.R. Martin is engaged in a process of critical deconstruction. On one level, Jon Snow is one of the most obviously traditional protagonist figures in the series – he's a Hidden Backup Prince with a Legendary Weapon and a Magic Pet - and in this chapter, he Refuses the Call so blatantly and emo-ishly that, somewhere long, long ago and far, far away, Luke Skywalker is wincing.

On the other hand, I wonder if that's part of the point – hewing closely to the path well-traveled in order to both critique the immaturity and problematic nature of the Refusal of the Call, but also to set up expectations for the quest that the lord commander presents him with... that Jon Snow will promptly abandon in *A Clash of Kings* in favor of a morally-ambiguous special forces mission with Qorin Halfhand.

Jon's choice – part of the reason that I don't particularly like this chapter, and prefer Jon's plotline in *Clash of Kings* or *A Storm of Swords* to *A Game of Thrones* (which is not the case on the show – more on that in future podcasts), is that Jon Snow is acting particularly childish. He knows full well that "a stranger wearing black was viewed with cold suspicion in every village and holdfast north of the Neck" (note not killed on sight, but definitely noticed and pointed out to pursuers), and that "once Maester Aemon's ravens took flight, Jon knew he would find no safe haven. Not even at Winterfell. Bran might want to let him in, but Maester Luwin had better sense. He would bar the gates and send Jon away." Practically, escape is improbable – a return to home is impossible.

Even when he imagines (in fine teenage romantic outcast fashion) that "he would be condemned to be an outsider, the silent man standing in the shadows... wherever he might go through the Seven Kingdoms, he would need to live a lie... He tried to imagine the look on Robb's face when he revealed himself. His brother would shake his head and smile... he could not see the smile. Hard as he tried, he could not see it." There's an entire social structure of symbolism, taboo, and obligation that has been built up in the north over 8,000 years to keep the Night's Watch a functional institution. The only way Jon Snow's escape would end is with him forcing his family to execute him for being an oathbreaker – thus, coming full circle back to "Bran I."

If there is a redemption for all of this mawkish self-pity, it comes from the fact that Jon's comrades come to bring him back by appealing to his sense of family ("we're your brothers now") and the positive motivating force of camaraderie by pointing out that "here are your choices. Kill me, or come back with me." Although there's cracks in the walls and the roofs are crumbling down, the foundations of the Night's Watch as a social institution that can motivate people through a sense of common belonging, purpose, and meaning are still functional.

Likewise, the fact that "I ordered a watch kept over you. You were seen leaving... if we beheaded every boy who rode to Mole's Town in the night, only ghosts would guard the Wall" shows that both at the top and bottom of the Night's Watch, there is both an understanding of the psychology of individual members and people as a group and an understanding that the Night's Watch needs organizational flexibility to hew to the spirit rather than the letter of their vows (a lesson Bowen Marsh clearly failed to learn).

Mole's Town – speaking of institutional flexibility – let's talk Mole's Town, and how the economics of this works. On a basic level, it's not surprising that the Night's Watch has a sexual outlet for its men: there's a long and often ignoble tradition of homosocial institutions of men "bowing to the inevitable," whether we're talking the classical to Napoleonic "camp follower" or "army wife," or the dark history of World War II "comfort women," or the more humane practice of conjugal visits in prison. I also wouldn't find it surprising that there's a blind eye turned to same-sex relationships within the Night's Watch, as well, just to keep the organization functioning.

But especially for an order of men who take vows to "take no wife... father no children," a brothel offers a handy loophole that keeps desertion down and morale at acceptable levels. After all, the veil of uncertainty hanging over any birth in Mole's Town would prevent any family tie interfering with one's loyalty of the Night's Watch. In fact, I'm a bit surprised we don't hear of same existing at Eastwatch or the Shadow Tower – but that feeds into the overall issue of how many people actually live in the Gift. In order to support about a thousand people at the Wall, there must be between 1,800 to 9,000 smallfolk producing for the Night's Watch (the Stewards are not nearly large enough in numbers to feed and supply themselves plus 600 men) – which, while still a very small population, given the size of the Gift (a fully-populated Gift could easily support 1.3 million people), it seems a bit more substantial than the one horse farmer Jon meets plus Mole's Town.

The question is how Mole's Town's workers get paid, buy supplies, and so forth. One possibility is that they get paid in-kind. After all, the Stewards have their hands on meat, timber, cloth, metal wares, etc. most of their lives, and given that the Night's Watch engages with seafaring traders, they must also get their hands on trade-goods on a regular basis. On the other hand, this kind of organized, widespread theft would be deleterious to the proper functioning of the Night's Watch's resource-management system. Another possibility is that they get paid with coin. While the Night's Watch doesn't pay wages, the institution has stores of coin for trade, to pay for the travel of their recruiters, etc. I wouldn't be surprised if the Night's Watch has a system of cash bonuses for extra work or unpleasant or difficult jobs – it's not an uncommon system in prisons, for example – and the men of the Night's Watch pay for sex with that money.

A third possibility is that there's an institutional arrangement – after all, the Mole's Town brothel is located on Night's Watch land, so they're technically tenants of the order. However, you can't eat free rent, so it may be the case that the Night's Watch supplies the brothel in-kind, which makes it a lot more like the organized military brothels of the 20th century. However, the text doesn't seem to support this reading.

So which is it?

Mormont's thesis: a critique of fantasy? – if there is a central idea to this chapter, something that makes it a worthy conclusion to Jon Snow's story in this book, it's Lord Commander Mormont's argument – and I would argue, by extension, Martin's argument – about what's important in the world of Westeros. Despite being literal witness to the return of mankind's ancient enemy, Jon Snow has attempted to desert from that fight, to privilege his family over the broader family of humanity. And, yet, Mormont starts his argument with an appeal to practical realities: "Your brother is in the field with all of the power of the north behind him. Any one of his lords bannerman commands more swords than you'll find in all the Night's Watch. Why do you imagine they need your help? Are you such a mighty warrior, or do you carry a grumkin in your pocket to magic up your sword?"

I don't think it's an accident that George Martin frames this speech as a critique of the cult of heroic individualism in the fantasy genre – one lone man (and it's almost always a man), wielding a magic sword, saving the world by his own actions, is pretty ubiquitous. And, yet, for all that Martin makes Jon Snow the closest thing to a traditional fantasy protagonist, he undercuts that almost immediately: from this point through to *A Dance with Dragons*, Jon Snow will kill exactly two people whose names we learn, but neither will shape the world as much as Jon does by refusing to kill, by speaking to and learning from – and, ultimately, mobilizing – people into new ways of behavior. Whether it's the brothers of the Night's Watch or the wildlings or Stannis himself, Jon's heroism is that of a community organizer, not a one-man-army.

At the same time, I think Martin is engaged in a critique, not a denunciation. As important as the political side of *A Song of Ice and Fire* is – and as someone writing a blog devoted to that side of the story, believe me, I care about it – there is no way of escaping the fact that George R.R. Martin presents the metaphysical threat to Westeros as being more important: "The cold winds are rising, Snow. Beyond the Wall, the shadows lengthen. Cotter Pyke writes of vast herds of elk, streaming south and east toward the sea, and mammoths, as well... Rangers from the Shadow Tower have found whole villages abandoned, and, at night, Ser Denys says they see fires in the mountains, huge blazes that burn from dusk till dawn. Quorin Haldfhand took a captive in the depths of the gorge, and the man swears that Mance Rayder is massing all his people in some new, secret stronghold he's found... when dead men come hunting in the night, do you think it matters who sits the Iron Throne?"

And yet, and yet... the fact that Martin went to such lengths to give us a political storyline, one that arguably takes up the overwhelming majority of the text, gives this a different feel. In many fantasy works, the only threat is the metaphysical threat, and the source of evil is Evil, and the mundane is portrayed as something to be tossed aside or transcended. I've never been that comfortable with this tendency; it devalues ordinary human lives, and it teaches the wrong lessons about where injustice comes from and what it looks like. But by layering the one on top of the other, Martin makes both seem more intense and vivid – the Mountain is as real a threat to the ordinary riverlander as the White Walker is to the ordinary wildling. There is a danger in fixating on the mundane to the exclusion of all else – that way lies the War of the Five Kings. Then again, there is a danger in fixating on the metaphysical to the exclusion of all else – that way lies Summerhall and Robert's Rebellion.

In the words of Lester Freamon, all the pieces matter. And what Westeros desperately needs is a hero who pays attention to the big ones and the small ones.

Historical Analysis

There's not much to discuss this chapter that I haven't discussed above. But come back next time for an extensive look at the history of regional independences!

What If?

Not a whole lot happens in "Jon IX," but I can see a couple of possibilities:

What if Jon kept riding? In part, Jon Snow's potential future has already been outlined by George R.R. Martin. But it's done so only up until the current point in time. Certainly cetibus paribus, Jon Snow's foolish actions would earn him a death sentence – but Jon Snow's desertion is about to coincide with an ironborn invasion of the north. Who better to lead a guerrilla insurgency against the foreign occupiers than Ned Stark's grown-up warrior son, complete with direwolf? I doubt the hill clans would be checking ID any time soon, and the Night's Watch is about to be kept busy by Mormont's Great Ranging. It's possible, but not exactly guaranteed, that Jon Snow could foil Theon's attack on Winterfell – which has huge ripple effects when it comes to Robb Stark's strategy, the Red Wedding, Ramsay Bolton's rise to power, and the political position of the north vis-a-vis Stannis Baratheon. If he doesn't, he's still the natural focus point for a loyalist resistance to the Boltons and Stannis's go-to pick for new lord of Winterfell.

What if Mormont doesn't march? Another possibility that comes to mind is that Mormont decides against taking one-third of the Night's Watch's fighting strength up into beyond-the-Wall. This changes things in a number of ways – to begin with, it means the Night's Watch isn't going to come face-to-face with the White Walkers (yet), and that Jon Snow never breaks his vows. It also means that Mance Rayder's army is going to face a stronger foe, both in terms of raw numbers and leadership quality. (I'll go into this more in *A Clash of Kings* and *A Storm of Swords*, but I've never quite understood how Mance's army on its way to the Wall missed the White Walker force that had attacked the Fist of the First Men.) Quorin Halfhand isn't going to fall for the Weeper's tricks, so the Battle of the Bridge of Skulls is nowhere near as bloody for the Night's Watch. With patrols up by a third, it's questionable whether the Thenn's raiding party makes it over the Wall or, at least, unnoticed. Beyond the battle, Stannis isn't going to have nearly as strong a hand against a Night's Watch that's almost as strong as his army, with experienced leaders at its helm. But is the Night's Watch flexible enough to bend to meet the true threat?

Book vs. Show

The show played this straight from the text, so I don't have anything to say – other than that the rousing montage of the Night's Watch setting out, which I quite like, seems to have set up a weird trend of dramatic montages that then get undercut by what follows. For example, Jorah's montage in season one is oddly undercut (in retrospect) by the fact that the Night's Watch's battle on the Fist of the First Men happens entirely off-camera; likewise, Asha/Yara's preparation montage from the end of the third season is going to feel strange in retrospect when she doesn't find her brother until she gets captured by Stannis.

It's an odd tic, as it seems to set up the audience for disappointment.

CATELYN XI

Catelyn watched them rise and draw their blades, bending their knees and shouting the old words that had not been heard in the realm for more than three hundred years...

"The King in the North!"

"The King in the North!"

"THE KING IN THE NORTH!"

Synopsis

Catelyn Stark is reunited with her father, Hoster Tully, for the first time in 15 years. Afterwards, she joins her son, Robb, for a contentious council of war and peace, before the Greatjon provides a solution.

Political Analysis

Oh... how I have been waiting for this chapter, savoring it like a treat you keep for a special occasion and save the leftovers of to enjoy later. It's one of my absolute favorites in the books, and possibly *the* political turning point of *A Song of Ice and Fire*. It's also a tremendously complicated chapter that is frequently misunderstood. So let's get into it.

(Note: I had planned to discuss Catelyn and guilt, Hoster Tully's illness, and the way in which family shapes the rise and fall of House Tully, but this essay is already running overtime, and I might as well save that discussion for later Catelyn chapters.)

The War of the Five Kings: phase two – if, for House Lannister, the end of the first phase of the War of the Five Kings saw them surrounded by enemies and with few good options, House Stark is faced with a bewildering array of options of contenders to ally with or locations to attack – but it can only choose once, it has a limited amount of resources to distribute between fronts, and the stakes of all of its choices are incredibly high. And, yet, people who argue the Starks were doomed from the start (or that there was a clear, easy option to win the war) are dead wrong, and using the worst kind of presentist, over-determined logic.

One thing that is frequently forgotten, and which I have gone to pains to emphasize, is the delicate balance of feudal politics. As Catelyn observes of the council of war, "each lord had a right to speak, and speak they did... and bargain... and threaten... and walk out." Robb Stark does not have an absolute claim on the loyalties of his subordinates; even when he becomes King in the North, his subjects' duty to him is embedded in a reciprocal system of obligations that requires him to look after the interests of his followers, lest they cease to follow him. His victory at the Whispering Woods and the camps have ironically increased the difficulty of this endeavor by adding the riverlords into the mix: "Edmure sat in the high seat of the Tullys... word of the victory at Riverrun had spread to the fugitive lords of the Trident, drawing them back... Karl Vance came in, a lord now... Ser Marq Piper was with them, and they brought a Darry... Lord Jonos Bracken arrived from the ruins of Stone Hedge... and took a seat as far away from Tytos Blackwood." For Robb just to keep his army functioning at around 40,000 men, he must balance their interests with the interests of the "northern lords [who] sat opposite... the Greatjon sat at Robb's left hand... Galbart Glover and Lady Mormont were to the right of Catelyn... Lord Rickard Karstark... took his seat like a man in a nightmare." And on both political and military tracks, these lords have profoundly different interests at stake and ideas about how to accomplish their aims.

The War of the Five Kings: the Starks' political options – it's appropriate that the beginning of the political conversation starts with the news that "Renly Baratheon has claimed his brother's crown," because of how thoroughly this scrambles the larger question. On the one hand, the Starks cannot bend the knee to Joffrey because of his murder of Eddard, but "that makes him evil... I do not know that makes Renly king. Joffrey is still Robert's eldest trueborn son, so the throne is rightfully his by all the laws of the realm. Were he to die, and I mean to see that he does, he has a younger brother... but if Joffrey is the lawful king and we fight against him, we will be traitors." Without the truth Eddard died for, the Starks are rebels without a candidate to place on the Iron Throne, and in order to make a political settlement that allows them to stop being rebels, as was the case during Robert's Rebellion, they have to have one.

The difficulty is that Renly "is crowned... Highgarden and Storm's End support his claim... if Winterfell and Riverrun add their strength to his, he will have five of the seven great houses behind him." The short-term political logic (advocated for by Lord Bracken and Ser Marq Piper – take note) points to Renly over Joffrey – but the long-term logic of

Renly's crowning is deeply destabilizing, as Lady Mormont implicitly notes. As Robb notes, "If their one is king, still, how could it be Lord Renly? He's Robert's younger brother. Bran can't be lord of Winterfell before me, and Renly can't be king before Stannis." As I have argued in longer form over at Tower of the Hand, Renly's attack on the principle of primogeniture is deeply destabilizing – he has the most troops now, but there's no guarantee that his son, or his grandson, or his great-grandson would, turning every single turnover of the crown into a civil war since, under Renly, armed strength would be the only legitimating force. And as Robb's example of Winterfell shows (and, indeed, as we see born out among the Freys later on), the same principle holds true for all lesser lordships – if a younger son can preempt an older son, then every lordship in Westeros is under the same threat.

Moreover, the existence of Stannis again complicates the situation. He's got "the better claim," and, thus, doesn't threaten to destabilize the entire sociopolitical structure of Westeros, but "the right" has no bannermen to answer its call. At the same time, declaring for Renly makes an enemy of Stannis as well as Joffrey, and the size of Stannis's army could change quickly; declaring for Stannis means making an enemy of Renly – there's no single candidate for a coalition to form around as there was in Robert's Rebellion.

Even the seemingly safe path offered by Ser Stevron Frey has its dangers: "Wait – let these two kings play their game of thrones. When they are done fighting, we can bend our knees to the victor, or oppose him as we choose." The downside of this is that not all these options are equal, and peace and a political settlement is still not guaranteed: Joffrey has declared all of the people at this table to be traitors and rebels, and if he wins, they may not get a chance to bend the knee. Renly might allow for a political settlement after the fact, or he could choose to steamroll over them so that the Tyrells could expand their lands to the north. If Stannis wins, he's unlikely to let bygones be bygones... and any winner, while certainly weakened by fighting for the Iron Throne, would, by virtue of being king, have most of the Seven Kingdoms to call on to subdue the rebels while the Starks and Tullys stand isolated.

Above all, the problem is uncertainty – no one knows who's going to be on top at the end of the war, and picking the winner can be the difference between prosperity and destruction for a noble house.

The War of the Five Kings: the Starks' Military Options – the Starks' military position is equally as complicated as their political situation – as you can see below, the Starks have local superiority of numbers (but just barely), their forces are divided by rivers, and they face enemies to their southwest and southeast (and, for the sake of clarity, I'm leaving out the ironborn for the moment). Despite Robb Stark's manifest successes in his riverlands campaign, he faces an eerily similar situation to how he started: two Stark/Tully armies facing two Lannister armies in two different places. And now he has the added wrinkle of the immense defensive multiplier provided by the fortress of Harrenhal.

The council of war is split between mutually-exclusive courses of action. "Many of the lords bannermen wanted to march on Harrenhal at once, to meet Lord Tywin and end Lannister power for all time. Young, hot-tempered Marq Piper urged a strike west at Casterly Rock. Still others counseled patience. Riverrun sat athwart the Lannister supply lines... let them bide their time, denying Lord Tywin fresh levies and provisions while they strengthened their defenses and rested their weary troops... [or] march to Harrenhal and bring Roose Bolton's army down, as well... [or] move south to join their might to [Renly]." All of these options have their advantages and disadvantages:

Harrenhal – the advantage of attacking Harrenhal is that it takes out the largest enemy army facing them and fully liberates the riverlands, whereas other strategies will leave the southern riverlands at the mercy of Lord Tywin (I would guess that the "many of the lords bannermen" in favor, in addition to Tytos Blackwood, are heavily weighted in the southern riverlands). Moreover, with Tywin taken out, the political unity of House Lannister collapses for generations, and King's Landing will likely fall without the Starks having to intervene. At the same time, attacking Harrenhal with only a two-to-one advantage is an extremely risky option that's quite likely to end in failure... and if the initial assault fails, they run the risk of a new Lannister army of 14,000 descending on their undefended rear and catching them against the walls.

Casterly Rock – ultimately the choice that Robb Stark goes with, attacking the westerlands has a number of advantages. It removes the threat of a 14,000-man army appearing on the Stark/Tully western flank at the same time that Tywin menaces their eastern flank, keeping their most dangerous enemy at a one-to-two disadvantage. Moreover, as we'll see, threatening the west is the only thing other than moving on King's Landing itself (interestingly, an option no one mentions; I could easily imagine Robb swinging down between Tywin and King's Landing) that would actually lure out Tywin from the defenses of Harrenhal. And with the Casterly Rock army gone, rather than having King's Landing at their back, now Tywin is the one surrounded by his enemies.

Wait – Jason Mallister, a lord of the northern riverlands whose lands are protected by all three forks of the Trident, urges waiting and building up their own forces, while (implicitly) holding Harrenhal in a loose siege to prevent it from reinforcing or resupplying itself. This isn't a bad idea – taking estimates from the Roman legions, an army of 18-

20,000 men eats 40 tons of food a month, so it's quite possible to starve out an army of that size over time. Indeed, the difficulty of feeding so many men in one place is one of the reasons why medieval castle garrisons tended to range from 30-40 men to around 200 (which is yet another reason why Harren the Black's great architectural achievement is a white elephant). On the other hand, this leaves the southern riverlands exposed to Tywin's raiders and runs the risk that a new Lannister army of 14,000 will be raised and trained.

South – realistically, this is more of a political strategy than a military one. Moving Robb Stark's army down to Highgarden or Bitterbridge (even leaving Roose Bolton's 10-12,000 in place to keep watch on the riverlands) leaves the riverlands completely open. While a Stark/Tyrell/Baratheon host of 120-130,000 would no doubt crush everything in its wake, the amount of damage Tywin could do in the meantime is terrifying to think of. More on this in the *What If?* section.

The question of peace – at this point, Catelyn Stark stands up and makes an eloquent plea for peace:

> *"Why not a peace? [...] [Ned] is gone, and Daryn Hornwood, and Lord Karstark's valiant son, and many other good men besides, and none of them will return to us. Must we have more deaths still? [...] I understand futility. We went to war when Lannister armies were ravaging the riverlands, and Ned was a prisoner... we fought to defend ourselves, and to win my lord's freedom. Well, the one is done, and the other forever beyond our reach... I want my daughters back... if I must trade our four Lannisters for their two Starks, I will call that a bargain and thank the gods."*

For many fans of Catelyn Stark, this is a crucial moment, where a woman takes a clear-sighted stand against war in the face of short-sighted, misogynistic, macho militarism, and also a moment in which George R.R. Martin's anti-war sentiments are made plain. Unfortunately, it's also seen as a moment where StupidRobb dooms himself, his family, and the north with his hot-headed pursuit of vengeance – and I think that misses the point.

Instead, I think this is a case in which Martin has constructed an unavoidable tragedy in which, however good in principle and hindsight peace might be, it was entirely impossible in the moment. And we can see this in some of the shortcomings of Catelyn Stark's arguments. In her speech, Catelyn Stark defines the terms of war and peace in such personal terms – the liberation of Ned Stark and the return of her daughters – that her appeal doesn't reach very far outside her family. After all, the riverlands did not fight to free Ned Stark and don't care if Catelyn's daughters are ransomed, and, contrary to her argument that "the one is done," the riverlands are still being ravaged by Tywin Lannister's marauders, and there are 20,000 Lannister men entrenched in Harrenhal, the historical seat of power.

If peace is going to come, it's going to take a far greater settlement than the return of the two Stark daughters and a truce of uncertain duration. As Brynden Tully points out, "peace is sweet... but on what terms? It is no good hammering your sword into a plowshare if you must forge it again on the morrow." While Catelyn can "go home... and weep for my husband," while watching "Robb, ruling at Winterfell from your father's seat... live your life, to kiss a girl and wed a woman and father a son," the riverlands cannot. At the end of the day, they're still sitting between the westerlands and the crownlands, and with nothing but Tywin Lannister's word to protect them should the Starks accept a truce and march home. As Jonos Bracken points out, "Gregor Clegane laid waste to my fields, slaughtered my smallfolk, and left Stone Hedge a smoking ruin. Am I now to bend the knee to the ones who sent him?"

Moreover, the same political uncertainties that have bedeviled this council of war also hold in peace. As Tytos Blackwood correctly points out, "if we do make peace with King Joffrey, are we not then traitors to King Renly? What if the stag should prevail against the lion – where would that leave us?" While we know from hindsight that Renly is going to be murdered and Stannis defeated, the lords of the north and the riverlands don't have that knowledge, and, at the time, it was much more likely that either Renly or Stannis would triumph over the Lannisters than the opposite. Even making peace could threaten war, with the riverlands once again bearing the brunt of the fallout from House Stark's political choices.

Ultimately, I think there is right on both sides: in the argument that further slaughter when the north's initial war aims were concluded would be pointless, but also the argument that, from this position, there really wasn't a way to go backwards without concluding that the sons of the north and the riverlands had died for nothing. And if there is one thing that Catelyn Stark's fellow grieving parents demand, the one war aim that unites Brackens and Karstarks, it's that the deaths of their sons have some meaning, so that some order is retrieved from chaos. It is absolutely an irrational desire, but also an inescapably human one.

The question of independence – amid all of this fractious debate, it's ironically the Greatjon who comes up with a political solution to their common dilemma:

> "Renly Baratheon is nothing to me, nor Stannis, neither. Why should they rule over me and mine, from some flowery seat in Highgarden or Dorne? What do they know of the Wall or the wolfswood or the barrows of the First Men? Even their gods are

wrong. *The Others take the Lannisters, too... why shouldn't we rule ourselves again?"*

However, it should be noted that this is entirely an argument about northern independence, based on northern historical, cultural, and religious differences from the south (after all, outside the Blackwoods, "their gods" applies to the riverlords as much as it does to the Baratheons or the Lannisters). And it's made possible by northern geographic distance from the rest of Westeros. And, notably, it's the northern lords who rise to second Greatjon Umber's motion and make their pledge of fealty to King Robb, First of His Name. This is a political objective that has deep historical roots that northern houses can respect, that gives Lord Karstark and all the other grievers out there a larger meaning to their loss.

And once it's done, the riverlords have little choice in the matter. Half of the army just declared independence, and unless they swear fealty to Robb Stark and become his vassals with a claim to his protection, then they're going to be left to fend for themselves, still living next-door to the "red castle and [the] iron chair." Without allies, eventually the riverlands will fall to either the Lannisters or the Baratheons or the Tyrells or the Greyjoys, as they did before the arrival of Aegon the Conqueror.

Robb cannot refuse this offer. I want to emphasize this, because I feel far too many of his critics fail to recognize it. As the liege lord of the north, he owes protection to his vassals – as they have just made themselves rebels to every claimant in the field, turning them down flat is tantamount to saying that he views them as rebels and won't protect them from whichever king is king, which would forfeit their military support for him in the field. Likewise, turning down the freely-offered fealty of the riverlords means turning down the 11-20,000 men they command in the field, which means trying to fight a war for independence against the rest of Westeros with only the north's manpower.

Moreover, and this is the point that I think gets overlooked far too often: *assuming that independence will fail is completely presentist.* Save for the last three hundred years out of a history 8,000 years long, the north has been an independent kingdom; even after the arrival of the dragons, Dorne maintained its independence against an otherwise-united Westeros for a hundred and fifty years. Given the political divisions of the War of the Five Kings preventing the united power of Westeros being sent against them, the north had a good shot at establishing its independence, and, as I'll explain in my discussion on *A Clash of Kings* and *A Storm of Swords*, it took a very specific set of dominos falling for Robb Stark to be defeated. Even then, the north is rising up against their Lannister-allied overlords and has a good chance of overthrowing the Iron Throne for a second time.

Moreover, it's also historically common for an independent Westerosi kingdom to hold the riverlands in addition to its home territory: the stormlands held the region for three hundred years before losing them to the ironborn (which probably, in turn, helps to explain how the stormlands avoided being conquered by the reach), who, in turn, held them for three generations as part of the Kingdom of the Isles and Rivers. As much as the southern riverlands (or the Hills, as they might also be described) represent a potential quagmire, holding the Trident offers a number of potential advantages: it controls the kingsroad approach to the north, preventing any approach on Moat Cailin; it's much more fertile than the north, so there's a possibility for a productive grain-for-wool trade; the 20,000 men of the riverlands (and the riverlands, potentially, could raise more, if it were better governed) would be invaluable in keeping an independent kingdom at fighting weight against the Lannisters; and having a base near King's Landing is strategically important in terms of forestalling any attempt to reunite the Seven Kingdoms.

Historical Analysis

A good example of the possibilities of an independent kingdom in the north comes from the history of Scottish independence. While in its orientation to the Wall and the wildlings and House Stark's similarities to the House of York, the north resembles the North of England, with its great capital city of York standing in for Winterfell, in its history of self-rule the north bears a strong political resemblance to medieval Scotland, which managed to keep itself independent of a much larger and richer neighbor for several hundreds of years.

To begin with, we have to recognize that the history of Scottish independence is far more nuanced than the stark romantic and nationalist lines that are drawn in the public memory. To begin with, there's the complicated reality that many medieval Scottish lords held lands in both England and Scotland and married back and forth: Robert the Bruce was the lord of Annandale and the earl of Carrick, but his family also had land in both Yorkshire and Normandy and could trace its lineage back to Henry I of England; the Stewarts who would succeed from the Bruces were originally Bretons; and from 1113 on, the kings of Scotland also held the English title of earl of Huntington, and frequently claimed the earldom of Northumbria (and, if they could get their hands on it, as was attempted by King David I during "the anarchy," Westmorland and Cumberland, as well). Just as holding the title of duke of Normandy made the kings of England both technically vassals and realistically independent monarchs, the kings of Scotland in the 12th and 13th centuries occupied both positions vis-a-vis their English landholdings.

Moreover, the Wars of Independence that lasted from 1296 to 1357 were a dizzyingly complex affair that could equally be described as a civil war between two rival claimants, the Bruces and the Balliols, both of whom were, at various times, either allies or enemies of the English and who both held lands in England and Scotland. King John Balliol usually gets labelled as a quisling of King Edward I of England (the so-called "Hammer of the Scots") in large part because he had the bad luck to be in charge when Edward I invaded Scotland (with the Bruces' support), but he was also the originator of the "Auld Alliance" with France that gave Scotland a continental European ally and became a mainstay of Scottish politics from 1295 to 1560 (more on this topic later). Likewise, while Robert the Bruce is seen as a nationalist hero striving against lapdogs of the English, he flipped sides repeatedly, especially between 1302 and 1306, and many of his enemies were the clans Comyn and MacDougall, who fought Robert the Bruce because he'd murdered Jon Comyn, the lord of Badenoch and Lochabe and a potential rival for the throne, or the Balliols, whose throne the Bruce had usurped.

However, the point has to be granted that, despite coming up against some of the strongest warrior-kings of England (both Edward I, the Hammer of the Scots, and Edward III of Crécy and Poitiers), Scotland proved itself impossible to govern from England. Despite the failure of the Bruces' dynasty and ongoing challenges from the Balliols, the Stewart dynasty of Scotland ruled an independent nation from 1371 through to 1603. Even after the "Union of the Crown," with the accession of James of Scotland to the throne of England, Scotland remained an independent and frequently-decisive force in British politics throughout the "Wars of the Three Kingdoms" of the 17th century through to the Act of Union in 1707.

At least from the historical evidence, northern independence over the long term is absolutely possible.

What If?

This chapter is absolutely chock-full with hypothetical scenarios, so let's dive straight into them:

What if Robb declares for Stannis? Let's say Robb declares for Stannis, then gets the letter, and Catelyn and he connect the dots about Bran and Eddard and Jon Arryn. Well, this gives the north and the riverlands (and, potentially, the Vale) a pretty good cause to fight for – Eddard Stark and Jon Arryn were murdered trying to defend the lawful succession to the Iron Throne. Militarily, Stannis probably sets sail for Saltpans or Lord Harroway's Town to link up with the Starks and Lannisters. With a combined total of 45,000, they could either take out Harrenhal right there before marching on King's Landing, or split the army 20,000 to 25,000 to keep Harrenhal under siege while they march on King's Landing, while Stannis's navy blockades the bay. Approaching from the north completely obviates the wildfire strategy, and the city likely falls. And then things get complicated as Renly finally shows up with an army at least twice their size, and two of the Seven Kingdoms stares down another two (unless Melisandre has Renly killed, anyway).

What if Robb announces for Renly? This is why the "Robb should have declared for Renly" theory has problems. Let's say Robb announces for Renly: on a political level, Robb gets some political favors, but not much – he's got two kingdoms behind him, but Renly already has two that bring far more troops to the table. And then Renly dies... so where does Robb go from there? He can't go back to the Lannisters, which means he probably has to side with a grudge-keeping Stannis, and is now locked into the wrong side of a 60,000-versus-80,000 match-up. Robb Stark probably could protect Stannis's flank and rear long enough for King's Landing to fall, but not without heavy casualties and for an uncertain reward. He might be able to ally with the Tyrells himself if he breaks his word with the Freys, but it's unlikely, as a Lord Paramount can't offer the same long-term political status that a royal marriage can, and even then (as I'll discuss more in *Clash of Kings*), it's not as much of a slam-dunk as it appears.

What if Robb sues for peace? Here's where the hidden costs, as it were, of Catelyn's proposal kick in: let's say Robb Stark sues for peace to get his sisters back... and then finds out the Lannisters lost Arya. Either peace gets derailed, and we're back to square one, or he makes the trade and his political position among his own men gets badly weakened. Now, it's possible that Robb can return north before the ironborn invasion starts – I highly doubt he can get back in time to forestall it – but now he's facing an invasion with a divided base of supporters who've lost respect for his leadership. The Hornwood conflict is going to kick off while Robb's busy fighting ironborn, minus the 11-20,000 riverlanders, and now Roose Bolton might very well repeat his ancestors' rebellion, with support from the Karstarks taking the place of the Greystarks. And then he's going to have to deal with the huge disruption of the wildlings and the threat beyond... all the while as Tywin prepares for an eventual invasion (remember, he only makes peace after he's beaten people to their knees).

The bigger problem is the riverlands, which have now been thoroughly ravaged by the Lannisters and left out to dry by the Starks; while the Starks can, at least for the moment, forestall a Lannister invasion by fortifying Moat Cailin, the riverlands have no such protection, with the westerlands to their west and the crownlands to their east, and only the word of Tywin Lannister that they aren't going to be ground into the mud. Catelyn's father, brother, and uncle will pay the price for their loyalty to their kin.

What if Robb waits? On a surface level, Ser Stevron's recommendation looks like good realpolitik: wait out the fighting and deal with whoever's left when they're tired out from fighting. The problem is that there's no guarantee that fighting necessarily saps the strength of your enemies: if everything apart from the riverlands stayed the same as in OTL, then Renly would die and Stannis would be beaten at the Blackwater, and Robb Stark would now face a combined Tyrell/Lannister host of as much as 134,000, on top of a likely Greyjoy rebellion. Except that, in this scenario, Robb, the north, and the riverlands have no political out – because he's conceded that he is, by rights, the vassal of whoever the king on the Iron Throne is.

Book vs. Show

This is one scene where I feel like the show got the heart right but the head wrong – in *Game of Thrones*, this sets up the audience to believe in Robb Stark as the symbol of justice for the Starks (which is absolutely necessary for the Red Wedding to have the impact it needs to), it foregrounds Robb and Theon's relationship in order to set up Theon's betrayal, and it gives a nice, rousing wrap-up to the Stark storyline for season one.

However, I think it makes two major errors of omission. Firstly, it completely leaves out the riverlords, with the exception of a virtually-unrecognizable (and unnamed) Jonos Bracken – which, as I've pointed out, completely obscures the political context for the rest of the War of the Five Kings, in that Robb Stark is now politically committed to the defense of the riverlands and that half of his army is now made up of riverlanders. While I understand that Edmure and Brynden Tully hadn't been cast yet, there's no reason they couldn't have used a few of the extras in that scene, mentioned who they were, and stated that, in thanks for their liberation, the riverlands pledge their fealty to Robb Stark. It renders a major part of Robb Stark's plotline for the next two seasons geographically and politically unintelligible.

The second and equally serious omission is that they leave out Catelyn Stark's plea for peace. The first warning sign that the show was starting to mishandle her character, this speech is vital for setting out that Catelyn and Robb have different interests and that Catelyn is more than a side character in her son's story, setting up her freeing Jaime Lannister at the end of season two and their contentious relationship in season three. It's so unnecessary – the speech would take up less than a minute, it doesn't distract from building up Robb Stark as he has to be built up, and the audience is absolutely capable of dealing with this level of nuance.

Unfortunately, it's (mostly, but not all) downhill from here as far as the show goes.

DAENERYS X

"As Daenerys Targaryen rose to her feet, her black hissed, pale smoke venting from its mouth and nostrils. The other two pulled away from her breasts and added their voices to the call, translucent wings unfolding and stirring the air, and for the first time in hundreds of years, the night came alive with the music of dragons."

Synopsis

Daenerys Targaryen attempts amateur blood magic... and succeeds.

Political Analysis

Well, here we are at last, at the end of *A Game of Thrones*, and at the end of the world Westeros and Essos have lived in for 150 years and which once lasted for 3,000 years before Valyria existed – a world without dragons.

Blood magic – the starring event in "Dany X" is the waking of the dragon eggs, and yet the ceremony itself – and what it tells us (or doesn't) about how blood magic works - is incredibly opaque and contradictory. To begin with, we have the testimony of Mirri Maz Duur that "it is not enough to kill a horse... by itself, the blood is nothing. You do not have the words to make a spell, nor the wisdom to find them... loose me from these bonds, and I will help you." Accepting this at face value is problematic – to begin with, since Daenerys clearly succeeds in awakening fossilized dragon eggs, it's not the case that the right spell is necessary (unless we assume that, for some reason, Mirri Maz Duur used her song while being burned to death to wake the dragons, which I strongly doubt). Second, we have to consider that the maegi is confused about Dany's objective here – when she says "it is not enough to kill a horse," this suggests that she thinks Daenerys is trying for round two with Drogo; the same rules may not apply to waking dragon eggs that apply to raising humans from the dead. Third, her plea (and offer) to Dany suggests that she's lying to try to convince her not to go through with the ritual and, thus, save her own life.

If we assume for the moment that Mirri Maz Duur is lying here, then the blood itself is important on its own, more so than any magical incantations – which is supported by Daenerys's actions here and Beric Dondarrion's actions later. Alternatively, as suggested above, it may be that a ritual to wake dragon eggs has different rules than one to bring the dead back to life. Then again, it may also be the case that, just as living dragons are foci that enhance magic around them, that dragon eggs act as a focus or a catalyst for magic, and this explains why Dany was able to cast the spell without training. This would explain why mages might answer Aegon III's call for help, or why a Myrish wizard would be interested in waking Euron's dragon egg, or what went wrong at Summerhall, or why dragon eggs might be sold in Asshai.

However, we also get a second statement on blood magic when Dany has Mirri Maz Duur bound to the pyre: "'It is not your screams I want – only your life. I remember what you told me. Only death can pay for life.' [...] as she stepped away, Dany saw that the contempt was gone from the maegi's flat black eyes; in its place was something that might have been fear." This change in Mirri's attitude further suggests that the words aren't necessary for magic to work – perhaps spells work to refine and focus magic, whereas Dany here relies on the magic equivalent of brute force. But, clearly, lifeforce itself is powerful – which makes me somewhat skeptical of S. Alexander's underlying assumption in the otherwise-intriguing "Grand Unified Theory of Magic in Westeros." If only a death can pay for life, I don't think Drogo on the pyre or Dany's child in the womb count – both are already dead before Dany's ritual starts, and we have to be careful to separate the requirements and effects of Duur's ritual (which clearly used up Rhaego's life essence) from the later ritual.

Finally, we have the question of blood and fire – as Dany thinks to herself as she walks into the fire, "she was the blood of the dragon, and the fire was in her. She had sensed the truth of it long ago... but the brazier had not been hot enough." It's possible that what was missing from earlier Targaryen attempts to wake dragons is the combination of fire with blood magic; we know that Summerhall involved "sorcery, fire," but there's no mention of blood sacrifices (as opposed to people being murdered ordinarily), Aegon III tried magic but not fire, and Aerion fire but not magic. We also have to consider that there literally is magic in Daenerys's blood – prophecy and the ability to bond with a dragon, although, clearly, fire immunity is not included (as opposed to a high degree of tolerance for heat). It's perhaps the case that a Targaryen trying to do blood magic untutored can succeed where others would fail.

There is also the question of whether what we're seeing in this chapter is one ritual or two. As we've learned from *The Princess and the Queen*, the process of bonding a dragon is a difficult and highly-risky one, and no one ever is able to bond with more than one dragon. And, yet, Daenerys has managed to bond with three dragons (although it's not clear she could ride Viserion and/or Rhaegal). Given that the chapter combines imagery of birth and marriage repeatedly, it's possible that what we have here is two rituals – one to waken the eggs and another to bind them to her.

I don't have much proof for this besides the fact that, contrary to what I had remembered, the dragons awoke before Dany had fully entered the fire: "She heard a crack, the sound of shattering stone. The platform of wood and brush began to shift and collapse in upon itself... and something else came crashing down, bouncing and rolling, to land at her feet; a chunk of curved rock, pale and veined with gold, broken and smoking. The roaring filled the world, yet dimly through the firefall Dany heard women shriek and children cry out in wonder. Only death can pay for life." Daenerys "stepped forward into the firestorm, calling to her children," after the first two eggs had cracked, suggesting that the ritual had already worked and that the eggs had hatched and the dragons were alive. This "calling" seems to have both protected Daenerys from the fire and literally bonded them to her as her children, as they appear to make an exception to their cooked-meat-only diet to drink in her mother's milk – from the source, as it were.

Ultimately, I think this chapter leaves us with more questions than answers – but, luckily, we get more data in *A Clash of Kings* and *A Storm of Swords*.

The last temptation of Daenerys Targaryen – given that this chapter literally involves the death and rebirth of a messianic figure (especially given how she's received by the slave population in Essos in *Storm of Swords* and *A Dance with Dragons*), it's appropriate that, in this chapter, we see Jorah repeatedly offer Daenerys options to abandon her destiny and live a normal life instead: "I have nothing to offer you but exile, but I beg you, hear me. Let Khal Drogo go... I promise you, no man shall take you to Vaes Dothrak unless you wish to go... Come east with me. Yi Ti, Qarth, the Jade Sea, Asshai by the Shadow. We will see all the wonders yet unseen, and drink what wines the gods see fit to serve us... Drogo will have no use for dragon's eggs in the night lands. Better to sell them in Asshai. Sell one, and we can buy a ship to take us back to the Free Cities. Sell all three and you will be a wealthy woman all your days." What's interesting is that Jorah is offering two highly contrasting scenarios – one in which Jorah is appealing to Dany's interest in exploring the far east of Essos, and another in which Jorah offers comfort and safety in the Free Cities, the equivalent of her red door (more on this in the *What If?* section later).

Moreover, Dany's offer to the three warriors of her *khas* and their threefold rejection has a ceremonial quality that reminds me of Peter's threefold denial in the New Testament: in each case, she says, "To you I give... that was my bride gift, and ask your oath, that you will live and die as blood of my blood, riding at my side to keep me safe from harm," and, in each case, she is refused in terms that reinforce that Daenerys is once again violating taboo. Jhogo states that, "This is not done. It would shame me to be bloodrider to a woman"; Aggo refuses, saying, "I cannot say these words. Only a man can lead a *khalasar*"; and even Rakharo offers only to make her a *dosh khaleen*.

Because what Daenerys proposes here is a total inversion and transformation of Dothraki society on every level. To begin with, she proposes that a slave society eliminate all distinctions of bondage – "I see the faces of slaves. I free you. Take off your collars. Go if you wish – no one shall harm you. If you stay, it will be as brothers and sisters, husbands and wives." It is this last that is the most radical – Daenerys is not merely manumitting her slaves, but states outright that slaves and freeborn Dothraki will now be equal in her new *khalasar*, striking at the heart of the Dothraki economy and social hierarchy. At the same time, she also proposes a revolution in gender, with her proposals stating that there will be a female *khal*, that brave warriors will serve as bloodriders to a woman, that a woman might have the right to name *ko*s, and that *khaleesi*s will have agency over their life course after the death of their *khal*s.

Dany rejects all three offers she receives and stays true to her destiny. Her three warriors will become the first bloodriders of a new *khalasar*, and Jorah shall receive instead a Valyrian steel sword from the breath of her dragons (which might well be the missing ingredient) and a place in her Queensguard. As a true messianic figure does, Daenerys Targaryen does not adopt the roles of the old world, but creates a new one.

Historical Analysis

Generally speaking, it's a bit hard to find historical parallels to mystical events of this kind – so we'll have to look to folklore and myth instead. The iconography of Dany's rebirth resembles nothing so much as a reverse mirror-image of the birth of Venus from the sea foam on the shores of Cyprus. In the legends, Venus was born in a similarly violent and disruptive event: the god of time and prosperity, Cronus, castrating his father, Uranus (the sky), at the behest of his mother, Rhea (the Earth). This Freudian inversion of father and son is a moment of mystical generation: from the blood of Uranus came the nymphs of the ash-tree, who would give birth to mankind; the race of giants who would war against the gods themselves; and the Furies, those ancient forces of vengeance and punishment. But from the white sea-foam that rose up from where the testicles fell into the sea came forth Aphrodite, the positive force of love, fertility, and luck.

In both that case and this one, we have this interesting combination of the elemental (fire and water) and the primal (murder and castration), producing both beauty and terror in the same act. It's not surprising, therefore, that Daenerys's birthing of the dragons has produced religious upheaval in Essos, beginning first among the members of her *khalasar* who now have no objections to being led by a female *khal*.

In real-world terms, however, we don't have an example of an event that changed our world in the same way that Daenerys's ritual has changed her world, until July 16, 1945 with the Trinity nuclear test in New Mexico. Robert J. Oppenheimer, the head of the Manhattan Project, was a bit of a poetic soul and chose the name of the Trinity test from John Dunne's poetry. Before Trinity, a small-but-respected fraction of the scientific community speculated that an atomic chain reaction could ignite the atmosphere, as a "new force [was] loosed on the Earth." After the Trinity test, we lived in the Atomic Age, in which war was transformed from an activity that produced death on a mass scale but in a contained region, to something that could wipe out all life on Earth, even without the very skies being set on fire.

What If?

I genuinely don't think there actually are hypotheticals here; everything in Daenerys's life has been leading her up to this moment. However, for the sake of argument, let's ask what happens if Dany had taken up these options with or without dragons:

What if she goes east with Jorah? This gets us to the knotty question of Jorah's loyalty (or lack thereof) to Varys and Illyrio – Jorah's first offer here seems to go absolutely against the interests of his supposed patrons, who repeatedly attempt to get Dany to come west, where they can exert influence over them (more on this later). If Dany goes to "Yi Ti, Qarth, the Jade Sea, Asshai by the Shadow," it may well be that she learns blood magic and is able to wake the dragon eggs, after all, but her advent in the west would be delayed by the distance of several thousand miles. Moreover, Westeros would be dealing with a Witch Queen who had never led a crusade to end slavery nor learned some harsh lessons in the difficulties of rulership.

What if she goes west with Jorah? In this version, where Jorah remains loyal to Varys and Illyrio, the conspiratorial duo hit the ultimate in fluke-draws with the sudden emergence of dragons. My guess is that Illyrio introduces her to her "nephew" then and there, and makes damn sure that the marriage goes through early on, before Dany's mature dragons raise her beyond influence. When the dragons are of size, the Golden Company lands in the stormlands as in OTL, except this time with a king and queen and three dragons. And all of Westeros will tremble.

What if she goes to Vaes Dothrak? This is the least likely of some least-likely scenarios, but... if Dany arrives in Vaes Dothrak with dragons, the one thing the Dothraki historically feared, all bets are off. Maybe all three get strangled to death, or maybe she becomes the Great Khaleesi of the Dothraki, and a horde of hundreds of thousands begins burning its way across Essos to construct an empire the likes of which even Valyria had never seen.

Book vs. Show

I have almost no complaints about how this was done in episode 110 of *Game of Thrones*. The showrunners, the actors, and the visual-effects artists produced something we really had never seen on television before and proved that this could be more than a medieval-setting soap opera – a genuinely-believable fantasy show on television.

My one complaint is that, by leaving out Eroeh and Jhaqo and Mago, the show has kind of dropped the Dothraki as a major plot element that seems to be a major part of Daenerys's story in *The Winds of Winter*. But we'll have to wait and see where George R.R. Martin goes with that.

ABOUT THE AUTHOR

Steven Attewell is the author of Race for the Iron Throne, a blog that examines the history and politics of the *Song of Ice and Fire* series and HBO's *Game of Thrones*. He has a PhD in History from the University of California, Santa Barbara, where he studied the history of public policy and was a political and union activist. In addition to Race for the Iron Throne, Steven is also a co-podcaster on *Game of Thrones* at the Lawyers, Guns, and Money podcast, writes about public policy at the Realignment Project, and is a co-author of the *Tower of the Hand: A Hymn for Spring* anthology book.

Printed in Great Britain
by Amazon